Encyclopedia of American Indian Costume

Encyclopedia of American Indian Costume

Josephine Paterek

ABC-CLIO
Denver, Colorado
Santa Barbara, California
Oxford, England

Library of Congress Cataloging-in-Publication Data

Paterek, Josephine.
Encyclopedia of American Indian costume / Josephine Paterek.
p. cm.
Includes bibliographical references and index.
1. Indians of North America—Costume—Encyclopedias. I. Title.
E98.C8P37 1993 391'.0089'97—dc20 93-39337

ISBN 0-87436-685-2

00 99 98 97 96 95 10 9 8 7 6 5 4 3

ABC-CLIO, Inc.
130 Cremona Drive, P.O. Box 1911
Santa Barbara, California 93116-1911

This book is printed on acid-free paper ♾.
Manufactured in the United States of America

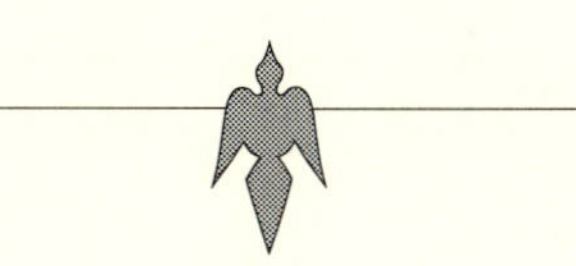

To My Family—

My Husband, Pat
Our Son, Bill
Our Daughter, Susan
Our Son, Tim

Contents

Acknowledgments . . . . *ix*
Introduction . . . . *xi*

American Indian Costume

Chapter One 5
Southeast

Chapter Two 41
Northeast

Chapter Three 83
Plains

Chapter Four 147
Southwest

Chapter Five 189
Great Basin

Chapter Six 209
Plateau

Chapter Seven 243
California

Chapter Eight 293
Northwest Coast

Chapter Nine 345
Subarctic

Chapter Ten 383
Arctic

Appendix One 431
Clothing Arts of the American Indians

Appendix Two 461
Glossary

Bibliography 473
Illustration Credits 487
Index 493

Acknowledgments

No book is the product of one mind, especially an encyclopedia based on the work of many persons.

I want to thank my colleagues at the University of Wisconsin at River Falls for their help and encouragement:

To the late Dr. Terry King of the History Department, for whose course on American Indian art I wrote a paper on the dress of American Indians and first discovered the possibility of a book on the subject.

To Dr. James Weil of the Anthropology Department, who helped me develop the chapter on the Southwest and who helped shape my understanding of anthropology.

To Professor Walt Nottingham, inspired and inspiring teacher of fibers, who worked with me on Appendix One, "Clothing Arts of the American Indians."

To Dr. Susan Beck of the English Department, who set me on the right track by telling me I should consult a reference publisher rather than the university presses I had been contacting.

To Dr. Nicholas Karolides, assistant to the dean, who said, "Why not try my publisher—ABC-CLIO in Denver?"

To Jane Pierce of the Chalmer Davee Library, always encouraging, always helpful.

I owe special thanks to Richard Conn, former curator of the Denver Art Museum, who graciously read and commented on the chapter on the Northwest.

I would like to thank my friends who have listened to me patiently; during the course of many conversations, I developed new insights, new approaches to problems, and new ideas for organization. Their words of encouragement helped me greatly when my confidence ebbed. So, many thanks to Professor Mary Barratt; Professor Robert Beck; Edna Bishop; Bill Clocker; Dr. John Buschen; Professor Jerald Carstens; Flo Duran; Jerry Fineberg; Dagmar Frye; Ida Mae Gravelle; Ethel Johnston; Dr. Beverly T. Mead; the Paukners, Owen, Elaine, and David; Ruth, Ed, and Peggy Walker; Dr. Don Washburn; Paul and Thelma Willink; Dr. Walker T. Wyman and Helen Wyman. Thank you all.

Thanks also to friends who loaned me books and journals: Cathy Caleva, Rosemarie Dakota, Ruth Mead, Mary Pickford, and Ed Walker.

Thanks to Bill Paterek for his continuing interest and his help in doing research on tattooing.

Special thanks to Brian Rosenthal, computer charmer, who straightened me out on many things and took care of the computer when it became confused.

Special thanks also to Jens Gunelson, expert photographer, who helped unfailingly with a multitude of photography problems.

And thanks to Ruth Washburn, who expertly and laboriously proofread endless pages of typescript.

Deepest appreciation to Sue Burch, who built up a magnificent library for me and made it possible for me to visit many museums with their collections of Indian art and costumes. Deepest appreciation, too, to Tim Paterek for coercing me into entering the Computer Age, for setting up the word processor and printer for me, and for fishing me out when I inadvertently entered into an alien mode.

And finally, greatest appreciation to my husband Pat for vacuuming, doing dishes and household chores and, in many ways, making it possible for me to work on The Book.

Again, no book is the product of one mind, but, of necessity, a tremendous amount of material must be channeled through one mind—in this case mine. Any errors in this book are solely my fault. *Mea culpa!*

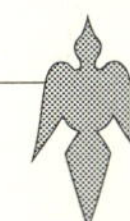

Introduction

The young Navajo man stands and looks down at the glass case before me in which rests a pair of fiber sandals. They are well made of shredded sagebrush bark and are partially burned. A small label says that they are about 9,000 years old, one of the earliest extant articles of dress from the North American continent. The young man looks at the sandals, then turns away. He is wearing a plaid flannel shirt and faded blue jeans. His long hair is pulled to the back and fastened with a rubber band.

The dress of North American Indians north of Mexico was exceedingly varied. It ranged from fiber skirts to buffalo robes, from brilliantly feathered warbonnets to simple headbands, from elaborately beaded vests to fur parkas. It encompassed the flora and fauna of the entire continent. Some of the elements of dress were based on tribal usage, on styles and designs that had been handed down from generation to generation, their origins lost in the shifting mists of time. Other elements were chosen by the individual, either as a simple matter of choice or as determined through visions or dreams. These highly diversified elements came together to create a unique, complex, and extraordinarily beautiful costume.

The first problem in researching and writing this book was to impose some sort of organization on the mountain of unrelated information. Organization on the basis of language was not feasible because adjacent groups may have worn similar garments yet may have spoken entirely different languages. Furthermore, peoples speaking closely related languages may have lived half a continent apart and may have worn completely unlike clothes. A cultural organization, based first on generally accepted culture areas, and then on traditional tribal groupings, seemed more useful, allied as it is to the environmental and cultural factors that seem most directly to influence dress.

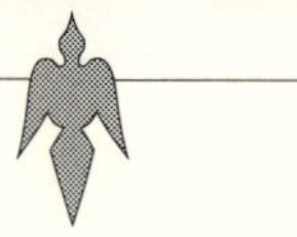

The large question of chronology arose. The dress of American Indians evolved through the millennia following the original settlement of the continent, and then was suddenly and fundamentally influenced by the coming of the Europeans; at what point in time does one describe the costume of a particular group? Before or after European contact? If the latter, at what time during the postcontact era?

Part of the question is answered by default: because of the poor preservation of clothing and the limits of archaeological research, so little is known of prehistoric dress that a useful survey of the continent is impossible. In addition, the historical records following contact vary widely in reliability and completeness. The early postcontact dress of some tribes is known from detailed historical paintings, photographs, extensive ethnographic descriptions, and the sheer persistence of traditional costume into modern times. For other groups there is virtually no useful information, sometimes because early European chroniclers were not interested in costume, or because records were lost, or because some native groups were destroyed by warfare and disease before records could be made.

The availability of information on early Indian costume is also greatly influenced by the artists who portrayed certain groups at specific times. The works of John White, Karl Bodmer, and George Catlin, for example, tend to narrow our conceptions into the time span in which each of these artists worked. Furthermore, some tribes were prominent during one part of the postcontact era but not at others. For example, the Iroquois were a matter of great concern to European chroniclers during the eighteenth century, when the Iroquois confederacy was a key power broker in the Northeast, but as their political and military influence waned following the American Revolution so did interest in their affairs and their material culture. As Indian-white warfare moved onto the Plains more was recorded about the Sioux and the Comanche. Relatively little was recorded about the Kwakiutl of the Northwest Coast until the late nineteenth century, but research at that time, led by researchers trained in the new science of anthropology, resulted in a wealth of systematic information about Kwakiutl costume.

Another great factor is that of mobility. Studying Indian costume is like turning abruptly into a crowded and chaotic thoroughfare where people are hurrying to and fro, some chasing, others being chased, some moving continuously, others settling down, some buying, some selling, others simply borrowing. Individuals and entire nations moved across the American landscape, some forced slowly by continual white encroachment, some relocating by choice, and others moved systematically through the "removal" policies of the federal government. Does one describe the costume of the Cherokee when they lived mostly in the Southeast or what they wore after they were forcibly evicted from traditional lands and removed to Oklahoma? Does one deal with the costume of the Cree of the Northeastern Woodlands? Or the Swampy Cree of Hudson Bay? Or the Cree of the high northern Plains? Time and space would not permit describing the dress of every group in every situation, even if the historical record were tolerably complete.

The result here is a compromise. In general, the focus of this work is traditional (non-European) dress and the early transition to European materials and actual elements of European costume. For some groups the relevant time period is the sixteenth century; for others, the late nineteenth and early twentieth centuries.

Inevitably a book of this type must resort to generalized statements, and yet it is imperative to remember that there was much local and individual interpretation of tribal traditions. When, for example, a statement is made to the effect that the Blackfeet tended to wear black moccasins beaded with certain designs, the reader should understand that individuals could choose to wear other styles and could well be influenced in such decisions by contacts with other groups, contacts usually more common among men than women.

Like other peoples, American Indians in the early postcontact era wore clothes for a variety of reasons, the most obvious being protection against the elements or adaptation to the environment. The local and regional environment largely determined not only the materials available for the making of clothes, but the requirements of protection that the clothing had to meet. The Eskimo could not survive the harsh Arctic winter without their superbly tailored fur garments. Men in early California and the Northwest Coast went naked most of the time, but

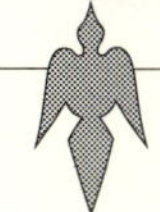

when the rains came, they donned capes and hats of shredded cedar bark or other fibers that effectively shed the downpour. Higher altitudes mean cooler temperatures and when the people of a valley went into the mountains to hunt they added warmer garments. Terrain also affects clothing worn. Desert people wore hard-soled moccasins to protect their feet from thorns, cactus spines, and rocks. The Indians of the Southeast wore swamp moccasins as they sloshed through lowland marshes. Woodland Indians wore garments with short fringes that would not catch in the underbrush, but the Plains warriors gloried in their long, fluttering fringes. Most Indians traveling in snow country wore snowshoes. The Indians of the Pacific Northwest went barefoot because they spent so much of their lives in canoes or on sandy beaches.

The environment demanded—and it gave the materials. The tall tule grass of California provided skirts and crude sandals. The people of the Northwest Coast used the inner bark of the cedar tree for garments, while the peoples of the Southeast found the inner bark of the mulberry equally useful. Deer were common across most of the continent, except in the far north where caribou were more common, so deerskin was the most widely used hide. Buffalo on the Plains furnished warm robes. Where large animals were not abundant, smaller animals such as rabbits, squirrels, and marmots were made into warm outer wear. Even bird skins could be used for clothing as well as adornment.

There were other functions of clothing, and a highly significant one was to establish tribal identity, often shown by the type of moccasin worn and the style of beadwork used to embellish those moccasins, by a certain cut of garment, or by a characteristic type of headdress.

Within the group the individual could indicate by clothing and accessories such things as membership in certain societies, military exploits, and socioeconomic status. Military raiment was an essential element both for membership in the societies and for protection in battle, as the warriors donned body armor, helmets, and shields. In addition, feathers worn indicated, by particular clipping or manner of wearing, special exploits achieved by a man in war. The many ceremonials, a fundamental part of social and cultural life, gave the participants an opportunity to display their status. The Tlingit chief's hat had cylinders atop it, each cylinder representing a potlatch or feast that he had given to substantiate his claims to prestige. In some areas, men and women of high status could embellish their garments with certain forms of ornamentation denied to members of the lower classes, and the poor slaves found in some tribes were denied any form of clothing decoration. The spirituality of garments was assured by their basis in dreams or visions, so that a certain cut or form of decoration might have had a special or secret meaning to the wearer. The medicine men or shamans wore certain garments and accessories efficacious in curing the sick. There was an element of spirituality or magic in much of ceremonial dress—it meant that the garment or mask turned the wearer into another being.

It has been suggested that modesty in dress was not a part of native life until the concept was introduced by missionaries. However, although men of California and the Northwest Coast went naked much of the time, no woman in these cultures would consider appearing in public without a skirt or at least an apron. Nudity was almost nonexistent among the women of all Indian tribes. A costume could function in certain ways to show many things about an individual. It could show age, for example; many tribes had ceremonies marking the attainment of puberty and, in many cases, special costume elements were worn. The Hopi maiden wore the spectacular "butterfly" hair arrangement, which was changed for a matronly hairdo when she married. Sex was also indicated by costume. The tunic or shirt of the male was often lengthened for the female. Women often wore knee-length leggings, almost never the thigh-length leggings of the men. The berdache, or homosexual male, showed his sexual preference and social status by adopting female clothing. Costume was a form of self-expression, reflecting the desires, emotions, and artistic abilities of the wearer. Some garments showed that the wearer was ready for marriage and adulthood. Some displayed deep sorrow, as the loss of a loved one was mourned, not only by the cutting of the hair (a widespread custom in North America), but also by the donning of specific items, such as the mourning belt of the Shasta of California, woven from the hair of the deceased. In their artistic expressions, the makers and decorators of garments were concerned with such elements as balance

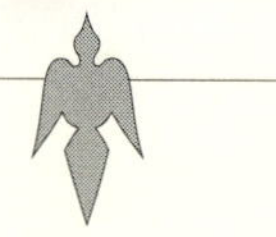

(usually symmetrical), harmony, color (with its many symbolic references differing from tribe to tribe), sound (the addition of deer hooves and tin tinklers to garments was common in some areas), and even scent, for sweet grass, with its enduring perfume, was added to many articles.

The costume of the Indians shifted constantly, for there was a far-reaching trade network on the continent; materials, ideas, and fashions were traded and adopted, changed, and traded further. But there was seldom a departure from the basic garments worn by most North American Indians: shirts, leggings, breechclouts, dresses, moccasins, and robes.

Within the chapters, after a brief description of the area, there is information on the general costume of the region, followed by descriptions of the dress of specific tribes. The table at the beginning of each chapter indicates which groups are treated in detail in the chapter by indicating the page number on which the specific discussion begins. The groups are arranged within chapters in alphabetical order. The following categories of dress are discussed for each group (with some variation): Men's Basic Dress; Women's Basic Dress; Footwear; Outer Wear; Hair Styles; Headgear; Accessories; Jewelry; Armor; Special Costumes; Garment Decoration; Face and Body Embellishment; Masks; and Transitional Dress. Each section is completed by a list of key sources of information.

Appendix One, "Clothing Arts of the American Indians," surveys materials and techniques, such as tanning, spinning, weaving, and quillwork. Appendix Two is a glossary of terms referring to articles of clothing, accessories, and ornaments.

The bibliography is arranged by topic, with subsections for general works on Indian costume, general works on Indian art, works on historical artists and photographers of native North Americans, and for the costume of each of the ten culture areas.

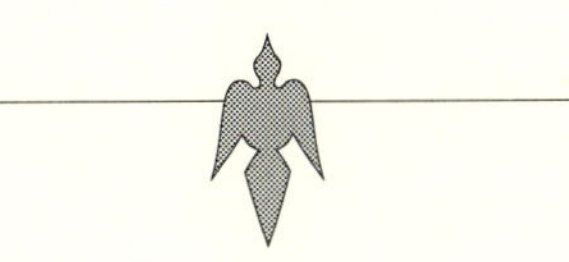

Encyclopedia of American Indian Costume

YOHOLO-MICCO.

A CREEK CHIEF.

Chapter One

Costume of the Southeast

Above: A Cherokee man wears a turban and full shirt, styles also popular among whites in the 1830s.

Above: The women of a Florida Seminole family wear the long dresses of the Victorian era.

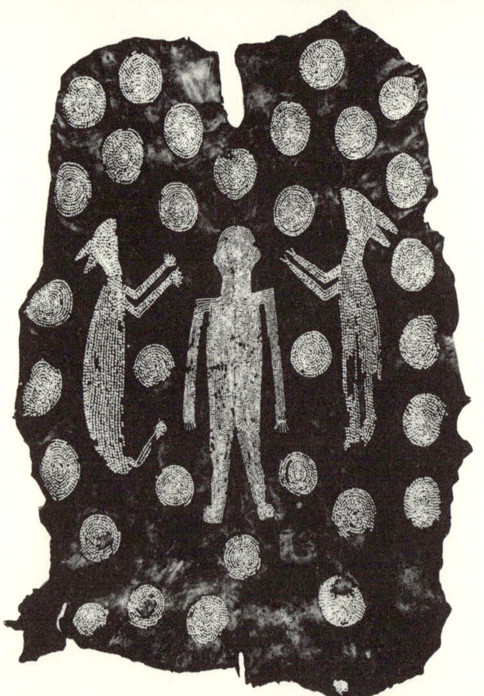

Above, right: A beaded Cherokee bag made in the style of a European cartridge pouch.
Left: A mantle of deer hide with beadwork decoration, thought to have belonged to Powhatan, chief of the Powhatan Confederacy, who died in 1618.

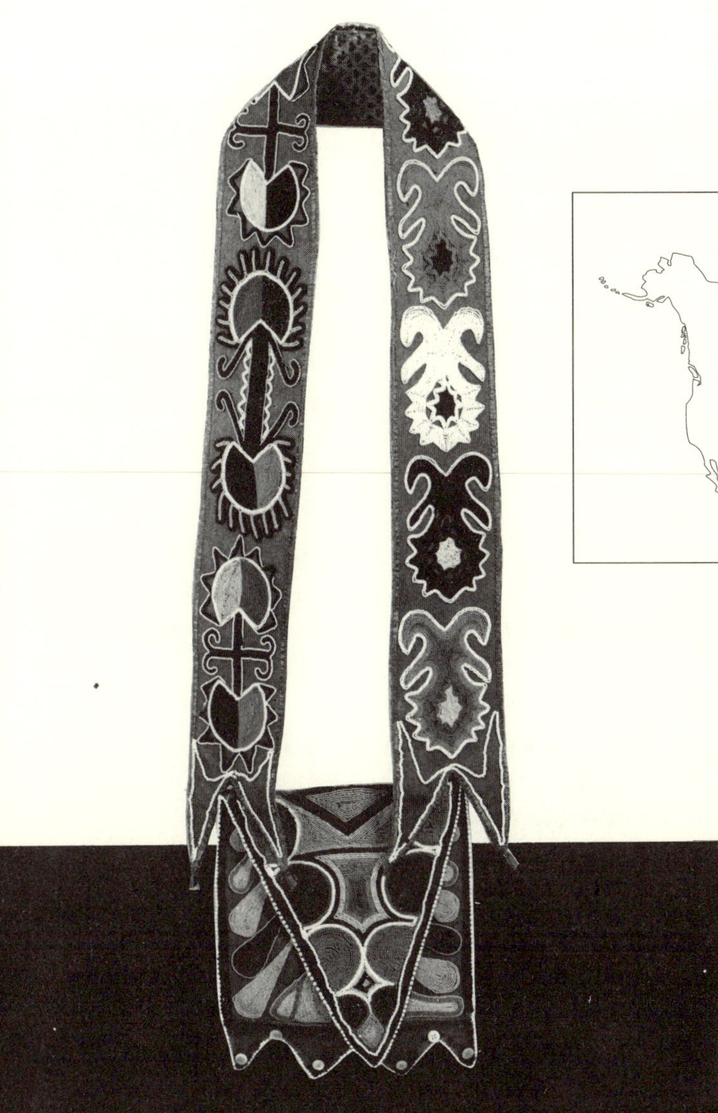

Southeast

It was in the Southeastern Woodlands that Europeans first came in contact with American Indians north of Mexico. Many of these early travelers and explorers recorded their observations, and their surviving letters and journals have provided much information on the dress of the region's original inhabitants.

The land is everywhere cut by watercourses: streams tumble down the mountains, churn through the rapids of the "fall line," and meander sluggishly through the coastal plain. The inhabitants lived in settlements along the rivers, particularly near flood plains, which provided fertile soil for crops. The climate is mild with long growing seasons and abundant moisture. This woodlands region is dominated by oak, pine, and, in the tropical swamps of the south, cypress. Along the coast are numerous bays and inlets offering an abundance of fish and shellfish.

The region was occupied at least as far back as the end of the last ice age, around 10,000 B.C. The earliest settlers of the region, known today as Paleo-Indians, may have come from the Plains and their subsistence is thought to have been based largely on the hunting of large, Pleistocene mammals. With the warming climate and the decline of the Pleistocene fauna, the people adopted an increasingly sedentary way of life based on more diversified hunting and gathering; this era is known today as the Archaic period. The Archaic merged into the Woodland period, marked by the development of agriculture, about 3,000 years ago.

The Mississippian culture arose about A.D. 700, and was characterized by larger settlements, the establishment of complex chiefdoms, and the building of ceremonial centers with the characteristic flat-topped pyramids. The culture reached its peak before the arrival of the Spaniards and collapsed soon after their coming. The early Spanish explorers in the sixteenth century, searching for gold, were

Peoples of the Southeast

Alabama, p. 8
Apalachee
Atakapa
Biloxi
Caddo, p. 9
Calusa, p. 10
Catawba, p. 33
Cheraw, p. 33
Cherokee, p.11
Chickahominy
Chickasaw, p. 15
Chitimacha
Choctaw, p. 16
Creek, p. 18
Cusabo
Guale
Houma
Koasati
Mattaponi
Mobile
Monacan
Muskogee
Natchez, p. 20
Nottaway
Pamunkey
Pomeioc
Potomac
Powhatan, p. 22
Rappahannock
Saponi, p. 33
Secotan, p. 26
Seminole, p. 28
Siouan, p. 33
Taensa
Tekesta
Timucua, p. 34
Tunica
Tuscarora, p. 33
Tuskogee-Creek
Tutelo, p. 33
Yuchi, p. 35

aggressively cruel to the native inhabitants, who retaliated relentlessly. James Adair and William Bartram in the eighteenth century traveled throughout the region, leaving excellent records. John White, A. De Batz, and Simon Du Pratz left pictorial information. Swanton has been the authoritative writer in this century on the historical culture of the Southeastern Indians.

There was great diversity in the languages spoken: Muskhogean, Algonquian, Caddoan, Iroquoian, and Siouan languages were all represented. However, these peoples showed considerable similarity in culture, especially in their clothing and accessories. Some authorities see a Mexican influence in their dress and customs.

By the mid-nineteenth century, many of the Southeastern tribes had been destroyed or dispersed by European colonization. Others had been removed, usually forcibly, to the Indian Territory, which later became Oklahoma. It was a tragic era, epitomized by the Cherokee "Trail of Tears." Uprooted from their traditional lands, the people took on new ways in their new homes. With the many tribes that came into the new territory, there was a fusing of cultures, and tribal identities in customs and dress were soon lost.

A few groups remained. Among the best known today are the Cherokee of the North Carolina mountains and the Choctaw in Mississippi; other groups are the Catawba of South Carolina, the Houma and Chitimacha of Louisiana, a few communities of Creeks, and the Alabama-Coushatta in Texas. Some remnants of tribal costume are retained for tribal functions or tourism, although many have adopted parts of stereotypical Plains dress. The Lumbee are perhaps the largest group in the Southeast today, and claim some descent from the colonists of the "lost colony" of Roanoke; however, they have kept little of their original language or culture. The USET, the United Southeastern Tribes of American Indians, is an effective, ongoing alliance of Cherokees, Choctaws, Mikosukis, and Seminoles.

General Dress

Men's Basic Dress

The men wore the fitted breechclout, usually of deerskin tanned to an incredible softness, and they wore it continuously, even when stripped "naked" for war or games. In the southern areas, breechclouts were made of woven vegetable fiber strands. By the mid-1800s they were wearing breechcloths, often of strouding, with flaps in front and in back. Most of the men wore thigh-length leggings, particularly when traveling, that were gartered below the knees with a woven band or fringe. Because of the warm climate and by choice, little else was worn, except for a long sash sometimes wrapped about the waist with the long tasseled ends falling at the sides. At times these sashes were worn over one shoulder and tied at the side.

Women's Basic Dress

The women usually wore skirts of skin or of fiber in a wraparound style, an apron, or a draped form, extending from the waist to the knees. Another garment that was often used was a shawl or cape draped under one arm and fastened on the other shoulder. These garments were of deerskin, twined mulberry bark, woven buffalo hair, or the softened skin of buffalo calves, and were usually deeply fringed. Women's leggings, when worn, were knee-length and gartered. By Adair's time (1775), skirts were of strouding in the wraparound style, held in place by a leather belt.

Footwear

Both sexes normally went barefoot, but when they went into the swamps or forest they wore the ankle-high "swamp moccasin," which was a one-piece affair of skin or hide laced up the back and at the toes with thongs. The back laces were left long so they could be tied about the ankles for security. Beverley, an early traveler, said that at times an extra piece was sewn on the bottom to make a heavier sole.

Outer Wear

In the winter the men wore a garment of skin, somewhat like what we would call a "poncho" or a mantle, but which they called a "matchcoat," an English derivation from an Algonquian word. These garments were of a variety of skins: deer, marten, and cats of different kinds. For warmer robes, bear, elk, and raccoon furs were used in the northern sections, while in the western areas buffalo robes were popular. Robes were made of other materials, such as the woven inner bark of the mulberry tree, or feathers,

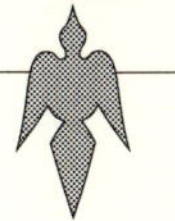

especially turkey, attached to a base of fiber netting. The women donned the same types of robes as the men, but they did not wear the feather mantles.

Hair Styles

Men commonly wore their hair in a roach, the head being shaved at the sides through the use of clamshell tweezers, and an upstanding fringe left at the top with a scalplock left at the back. At times the hair was shaved only on one side and sometimes the scalplock was worn at the sides, twisted in various ways and decorated with feathers, pieces of fur, swansdown, or small stones tied into the hair. When at war the different Indian nations wore the hair in varying styles to distinguish friend from enemy. Women wore the hair long and loose, as a rule, although it was usually cut short in times of mourning. They, too, wore their hair in different styles, often braiding it, twisting it, or rolling it in pleasing ways. For decoration they used flowers in the hair, or shells or stones fastened in place; women rarely wore feathers, either in the hair or attached to garments.

Headgear

The Southeastern Indians normally went bareheaded. Feathered headdresses were worn on ceremonial occasions by men of higher status and a few tribes wore caps or hats.

Accessories

Accessories were few. Superbly woven sashes, made of the inner bark of the mulberry tree and created by means of a finger-weaving technique, were popular items; often these sashes had beads worked into the complex designs. Belts of snakeskin were prized by the men. Some early pouches were made in a peculiar pointed shape and hung from the belt; these carried such items as tobacco, a pipe, and fire-making materials. Some bags or pouches were made from a deer's paunch or bladder.

Jewelry

A variety of jewelry was worn. Instead of the ear spools of ancient times, the men slit the ear along the edge, binding the lobe with thongs until it was healed; a piece of lead was then fastened to it to lengthen the opening. Afterwards it was bound round with copper wire, and often the white plumes of egrets were fastened into the opening. Women also pierced the earlobes, but not as extensively as the men, and they wore earrings of strings of pearls in clusters, bird claws, buttons, or plugs. Necklaces and bracelets were made of pearls or beads of copper; strands of these beads or pearls were also worn around the ankle or just below the knee. Women filled tortoiseshells with pebbles and fastened them to the legs when they danced. Rarely is mention made of nose ornaments and then only as a man's decoration. Labrets, or lip plugs, made of pieces of cane or carved wood, were found among the peoples of the Gulf Coast. Large shells with holes bored for hanging around the neck, called gorgets, were often delicately incised with designs.

Armor

References to body armor are scanty. Some observers mention rawhide breastplates or headpieces, and there are a few records of armor made of pieces of cane tied together with thongs; but armor seems not to have been important to these tribes. Instead of a breechclout, a warrior frequently wore a fringe of shredded mulberry bark suspended from his snakeskin belt.

Special Costumes

The garb of shamans or medicine men seems to have been highly individualistic; sometimes they wore feather cloaks; otherwise they went naked except for the skins of small animals or birds, especially owls, stuffed and hung about the waist. They generally wore the hair in a roach, erect like a cock's comb, the rest of the hair being shaved in asymmetrical patterns. In many places a white circle on the forehead was the distinguishing mark of a shaman. Various amulets, bones, feathers, bear claws, and strips of fur were hung about the body to complete the costume.

Garment Decoration

The tanned skins used in clothing were often dyed various colors, including red, yellow, green, blue, and black. The finger-woven belts or sashes featured geometric designs in the eastern areas, V's and W's especially; in the western areas circular motifs were popular, such as double scrolls, circles alternating with crosses, or circles inside diamond shapes. These forms continued to be used in nineteenth-century beadwork.

Face and Body Embellishment

Personal adornment took many forms. The hair was often anointed with bear grease and red ocher to make it appear glossy and black; also, the grease was said to check the heat in summer and to make the body feel warmer in winter. Body paint was popular, especially for war and games, so it was essentially a masculine adornment; red was most commonly used, then black, yellow, and russet, with white being reserved to mark the end of a festival. Tattooing was usually blue, although other colors are mentioned, including red from cinnabar. Designs took the form of scrolls, flowers, stars, animals, crescents, and other symbols. Both sexes seem to have favored tattooing as a form of ornamentation, but the males were more extensively tattooed. This decoration in most cases was based on status, and when the tattooed man was not entitled to it, he was forced to remove the marks, a rare and painful process. Head deformation by skull flattening was practiced by some tribes, using a bag of sand or a block of wood wrapped in buckskin to apply pressure to the infant's skull. Some believed it would not only improve the appearance, but also the eyesight.

Masks

Masks were used in a variety of ceremonies. They were usually carved of wood (especially buckeye) in animal or human forms.

Transitional Dress

The Southeastern Indians made the change to European garb comparatively early, due to their contacts with the Spanish, French, and English explorers and traders beginning in the sixteenth century. Breechcloths for both sexes were made from blue stroud cloth obtained from the traders. The Charles Bird King paintings, which were done in Washington, D.C., in the 1830s, show how some men had converted to European styles, at least for purposes of visiting the nation's capital. They wore the typical cloth coats of the time with the dropped shoulder seams, white shirts with high collars, and black cravats. Large silver bands encircled the head, surmounted by one or more ostrich plumes. Or they wore cloth turbans, wrapped in the contemporary European fashion, again with plumes. One or more silver gorgets hung on the breast. Silver armbands, beaded woven sashes, and embroidered or beaded shoulder bags added to their elegance. They wore moccasins or skin boots. Some of them displayed tattooed designs on the face. This was the last of what might be referred to as a distinctive Southeastern costume. The women also changed over to European fashions, especially with the use of plain or colored cotton cloth, calico, or gingham. They wore the long, flounced, full skirts of the period, the blouses with long, full sleeves and large collars, the latter often ornamented with rows of silver brooches. They continued to wear their hair in braids well into the twentieth century. Colorful ribbons hung from the back of the head, a style that has continued in favor even to the present. When they had their photographs taken, they displayed multiple strings of beads around the neck and many earrings. But moccasins were abandoned in favor of "store-bought" shoes.

Alabama

The Alabama were members of the Creek Confederacy who lived in southern Alabama along the Alabama River and belonged to the Muskhogean language family. The name, also spelled "Alibamu," meant "medicine gatherers" or "thicket clearers." The first European contact was with Hernando de Soto's expedition in 1541.

Men's Basic Dress

Men wore the skin breechclout; when in the woods or traveling, they wore skin leggings. Some garments were of woven fibers.

Women's Basic Dress

Women wore the apron skirt woven of bark or nettle fiber; a shawl or cape covered one breast only, usually the left, and was fastened on the shoulder, leaving the right arm free. For cooler weather or traveling they wore knee-high leggings, which were gartered. By Adair's time (1775) they were wearing wraparound skirts of stroud cloth, held in place with a leather belt. About that time they were also wearing a short waistcoat or blouse made of calico, linen, or other cloth, with lace or bead decoration.

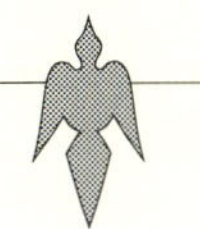

Footwear
Usually these people went barefoot; however, when more protection was needed they wore the typical Southeastern swamp moccasin.

Outer Wear
Both sexes wore the matchcoat or mantle of deerskin. For ceremonial wear and as a symbol of high status, feather robes were donned by the males.

Hair Styles
Typically men wore the hair in a roach or in four braids, two in front, two in back. Women usually wore the hair parted in the center and with the two parts gathered into a large "bun" or bundle in the back, fastened with a large bone hairpin and tied with a cord or woven band. By the mid-1700s, some women had adopted the practice of braiding the hair.

Headgear
Both sexes wore headbands of netting or skin thongs. Men sometimes wore a bison horn headdress in times of war. When silver became available, men in positions of importance wore headbands of that metal, often with short points resembling a crown. Later, too, handkerchief headbands were popular.

Accessories
Aside from a few bags or pouches of deerskin or woven fibers, few accessories were carried by the Alabama.

Jewelry
A ring of copper, later of silver, was worn in the nose into the nineteenth century. Copper or shell gorgets, sometimes several at once, covered the chest. Copper bracelets and rings encircled the wrists and fingers. Necklaces made of strings of beads or pearls were hung around the neck or gathered in clusters on the shoulders.

Garment Decoration
Using the inner bark of the mulberry tree or nettles for fibers, some weaving was done by these people. Occasionally, skin garments were painted.

Face and Body Embellishment
Red, black, and yellow were the most common colors of body paint used. Alabama women, in early times, were said to have blackened their upper lips with charcoal, and even into modern times they put small spots of red, sometimes of yellow, on the cheeks. Tattooing was practiced by both sexes, but to a limited extent. Some skull deformation took place.

Transitional Dress
Women adopted a short blouse or "waistcoat" of cloth, worn over a cotton skirt. Earrings were fashioned from silver coins. Silver rings were made, sometimes with a shield welded onto them. By the mid-nineteenth century, the Alabama had changed over to European garments almost completely.

Key Sources
Swanton, John R. *The Indians of the Southeastern United States.* New York: Greenwood, 1969.

Caddo

The Caddo, a loose confederacy of about 25 small tribes, lived on the Red River in the northeastern section of Louisiana and into Texas. They spoke a Caddoan language, found among scattered groups from Texas to Nebraska and North Dakota. Primarily villagers and farmers, the Caddo also hunted buffalo and were marginal to the Plains culture area. Buffalo robes were important trade items. The Caddo also exported salt and osage wood for making bows. Their first European contact was with Hernando de Soto's expedition in 1541. In the seventeenth century they established a lasting trade relationship with the French fur traders. The name *Caddo* comes from their word for "true chief."

Men's Basic Dress
Men wore the skin breechclout, usually an apron type, at all times. They added leggings when necessary for protection in rough terrain.

Women's Basic Dress
A skirt was commonly worn, made of deerskin or a material woven from the inner bast of the mulberry tree. With this, instead of wearing the usual upper garment fastened on the shoulder, Caddo women wore a deerskin poncho. Young girls, even when infants, wore an apron or breechclout of grass fibers.

Footwear
Both sexes normally went barefoot, but when entering swamp or forest or in winter they wore the swamp moccasin.

Outer Wear
The poncho-like buffalo robes, with a hole in the center for the head, were worn in cold weather; at other times a deerskin mantle in the same style sufficed. Some mantles were decorated with colorful feathers.

Hair Styles
Most of the men seem to have had the hair cut off except for some locks that they rolled around a piece of wood and wore at the side of the head. Some did not cut the hair, but all men had a scalplock at the back. Many men followed the northern fashion of greasing the hair and adding reddened swansdown or duck down for ceremonial occasions. Women simply wore their hair parted in the middle and fastened carefully at the back in a bun style.

Headgear
Headbands, when worn, were of woven buffalo hair.

Accessories
Belts, garters, and pouches were made of woven buffalo hair.

Jewelry
Caddoan men were noted for the nose rings they wore; they also lengthened the earlobes, into which feathers and other ornaments were fastened. The women wore multiple necklaces of beads. They also did fine ornamentation on the shell gorgets generally worn by the men. The hair tie, a leather ornament in a bow shape, usually beaded and with ribbons attached, was used to hold the hair in place at the back.

Garment Decoration
Finger-weaving was done with buffalo hair, worked in simple geometric designs. Buffalo hides were occasionally painted in the Plains fashion. After contact, they used ribbons and some ribbonwork, especially for hair ornaments, and a limited amount of beading on garments.

Face and Body Embellishment
Both sexes tattooed their faces and bodies. Some men had figures of birds and animals tattooed on their bodies while others had zigzag lines for ornament. Women had breasts tattooed, also lines from the forehead to the chin, triangles at the eyes, and tattooed lips. Body paint was considerably used by the women, especially red, black, and yellow. Some of the Caddo practiced skull deformation, but it was a custom that seems to have died out by the time the Spaniards and French arrived.

Transitional Dress
Little mention of Caddo costume is made after contact. With their wide trade contacts, they seem to have converted to European dress by 1800.

Key Sources
Parsons, Elsie C. “Notes on the Caddo.” American Anthropological Association *Memoirs* 57.

Swanton, John R. “Source Material on the History and Ethnology of the Caddo Indians.” Bureau of American Ethnology *Bulletin* 132: 140–148.

Calusa
This large tribal confederacy was located on the west coast of Florida down to the Keys and through much of the interior of southern Florida. They were Muskhogean speakers. Known for their hostility to the Spanish incursion (they killed Ponce de Leon in 1521), they were famous for their piracy, for the golden wealth they acquired from Spanish wrecks, and for the vast quantity of pearls they wore. They had close ties with native peoples of the Caribbean, trading with them with fish, amber, and skins, the skins obtained in trade from the north. They were not primarily farmers or hunters, for deer were few, but they fished and collected shellfish and wild vegetable foods. Frank Hamilton Cushing added much to our knowledge of the aboriginal Calusa through his research at Key Marco.

Men's Basic Dress
Men went nearly naked, wearing only a breechclout of braided palm leaves. Because of the scarcity of deer, the Calusa were one of the few Southeastern tribes that did not use deer hide for garments.

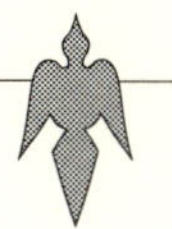

Women's Basic Dress

Women also went nearly naked, wearing simply a fringe of palm fronds or an apron of Spanish moss. They seem to have used some sort of cordage as a fringe, for Cushing found remains of fringes and elaborate tassels made from finely spun cords of cottonwood tree down; these were dyed, some green, some yellow, all indicating a high degree of craftsmanship in the making of such cords.

Footwear

Both sexes went barefoot at all times.

Outer Wear

In this tropical climate, there was little need for outer garments. Occasionally, feather mantles were donned by chiefs. Some Calusa men wore a robe of "lion" (panther) skin, representing a deed of great bravery.

Hair Styles

Women wore the hair long and flowing, often with flowers as ornament. Men wore the typical Florida hair arrangement: the hair gathered into a topknot, with a fringe below, and with feathers or pelts of small animals cascading from the topknot.

Headgear

Cushing found remains at Key Marco of what he regarded as bark headdresses, similar to those of Northwest Coast Indians. The Calusa were also reported to have worn pieces of gold on their heads. Some mention is made of occasional use of a palm-leaf hat.

Accessories

Belts were worn with the palmetto skirts and breechclouts; these were also of palmetto or other plant fibers.

Jewelry

Cushing found at Key Marco many fine articles of adornment, such as ear buttons decorated with shell, earplugs for common wear, superbly crafted brooches of wood inlaid with shell, bunches of long, delicate, translucent fish spines, probably used as necklaces or wristlets, large labrets, and delicate plates of pinna or tortoiseshell, pierced to facilitate attachment to a dress or for use as gorgets. Some shells were beautifully painted, others inlaid; some seem to have been used as pendants to decorate breechclouts. San Miguel describes a Calusa or Tekesta chief coming to meet his party with his body adorned with strings of beads hung in clusters about his neck, biceps, wrists, above and on his ankles, and below his knees.

Garment Decoration

The only evidence of garment decoration seems to have been the use of finely corded fringes and tassels made of palmetto leaves and other fibers.

Face and Body Embellishment

The Calusa men used red, black, yellow, and russet paint on their bodies in time of war. No mention is made of either skull flattening or tattooing.

Masks

Cushing found what he believed to be ceremonial masks, with holes at the sides for strings to hold the mask in place; some had eyes of inlaid conch shells.

Key Sources

Cushing, Frank Hamilton. "Exploration of Ancient Key Dwellers' Remains on the Gulf Coast of Florida." American Philosophical Society *Proceedings* 35: 329–432.

Fairbanks, Charles H. *Ethnohistorical Report on the Florida Indians.* New York: Garland, 1974.

Fontaneda, Hernando de Escalante. "Memoria de las cosas y costa y Indios de la Florida." In *Coleccion de varios documentos para la historia de la Florida y tierras adyacentes.* Buckingham Smith, ed. Vol. 1. London.

Cherokee

The Cherokee were the largest and most powerful tribe of the Southeast. Hodge says their name meant "cave people," indicative of the many caves found in that part of the country. Inhabiting the mountainous regions of the southern Appalachians, they were divided into the Upper, Lower, and Middle Cherokee, depending on location and, especially, the dialect spoken. Neighbors of the Creek, they were like them in many ways, although they differed in their physical appearance and in their language, which was Iroquoian. Bartram stated that they were the largest people he had ever seen, both the men and the women being unusually tall. Timberlake said they were very gentle to those who were their friends, but implacable in their enmities. In 1820, the Cherokee adopted a government based on the U.S. Constitution. About that time Sequoyah invented his "syllabary," an alphabet based on sounds, the only example of an indigenous creation of a system of writing without European intervention in North America north of Mexico. Despite widespread acculturation, the Cherokee were forcibly evicted from their ancestral lands in the late 1830s in the tragic "Trail of Tears" and relocated to the Indian Territory.

Tuch-ee, a Cherokee chief, wears a large cloth turban with plumes, characteristic of the 1830s. His shirt has a large fringed collar.

The Cherokee were painted by Charles Bird King in Washington, D.C., in the 1820s and by George Catlin in the 1830s.

Men's Basic Dress

Skin breechclouts of the apron type were worn at all times by the men. For protection in the forest, knee-length leggings were donned. A light skin poncho was added for cooler weather as well as for protection. By the mid-1700s the men were wearing cloth shirts of European make.

Women's Basic Dress

Cherokee women wore a wraparound skirt of skin, held in place with a belt, and a poncho or cape over the torso. The skirt might also be made of material woven from the inner bark of the mulberry tree. They, too, wore knee-length leggings in the forest.

Footwear

Both sexes went barefoot as a rule, but added buckskin moccasins, which were said to have been decorated with porcupine quills, for travel and special occasions. Quillwork may originally have been obtained in trade, for the Cherokee and others of the Southeast did not traditionally do this type of work. The swamp moccasin was also worn at times, with its lacings up the front and back and wound around the ankle.

Outer Wear

Timberlake said in 1762 that the Cherokee wore large mantles or matchcoats, but that older people informed him that formerly they had worn buffalo-skin mantles for winter and lighter ones of feathers in the summer. It is unlikely that feather robes were generally worn, however; such elegant garments were typically reserved for headmen on important ceremonial occasions. Plaid blankets, commercially made, were popular with both sexes by the early 1800s. By the middle of the century the men were displaying expertly tailored coats of European style, caped and beautifully embellished with floral embroidery.

Hair Styles

Men shaved their heads leaving a roach from front to back along the top of the head, often with a fringe

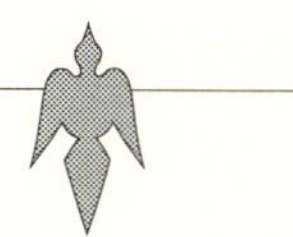

of hair along the forehead; this roach was often augmented with deer hair or opossum hair dyed yellow or red. The women wore the hair long and flowing, or "clubbed" in the back and tied in place with a thong; for special occasions they added ribbons at the back.

Headgear

The Cherokee went bareheaded most of the time. In cold weather they might add a hood of fur. Headdresses for ceremonies featured brightly colored plumage from various birds.

Accessories

Belts of leather or woven garters and sashes were common accessories. Many men had pouches with pointed ends hanging from the belt for carrying necessary articles, such as paint and tobacco.

Jewelry

Bracelets and armbands of copper were popular. The ears were slit and stretched to an enormous size, such a painful process that only one at a time was treated in this way. When healed, they were wound with copper wire, and from this hung pendants and rings. Besides wearing copper rings in their noses, Cherokee men tied into the nose the coarse diamonds found in that area. Timberlake mentions a "collar of wampum," which may have been necklaces.

Garment Decoration

Timberlake said some quillwork was done by the Cherokee women, but it was rare. After the introduction of glass beads, some floral beadwork was done on pouches and shoulder bags, especially using circular motifs. Silk thread from the traders was used to embroider floral designs on ceremonial coats. Braid was also used as decoration, as well as short fringes. Spinning wheels and looms were introduced in the late eighteenth century; woolen cloth was produced, and is still profitably made today for the tourist trade.

Face and Body Embellishment

Tattooing was highly important to the Cherokee. At an early age, a boy was tattooed with symbols on the arms, trunk, and thighs, such designs as flowers, animals, stars, and the sun, with many later additions being made. Warriors of the tribe were not only

A beaded Cherokee bag is made in the style of a European cartridge pouch.

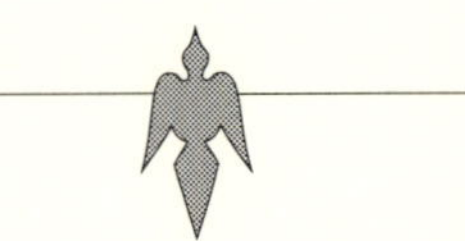

extensively tattooed, but were painted in addition, using red paint for success, blue for defeat or trouble, black for death, and white for peace and happiness. Women were almost never painted. There is no evidence of the practice of skull flattening in infants.

Masks

The Cherokee used masks during ceremonies, including preparation for hunting. Some men used masks topped with a rattlesnake skin to indicate fearlessness.

Transitional Dress

In 1762 three Cherokee chiefs went to London as ambassadors, and the portraits and drawings made by English artists, including Sir Joshua Reynolds, show the intermingling of European and Indian dress. They wore full-sleeved cotton shirts with turn-down collars. Instead of the earlier shell pendants, they wore gorgets of silver crescents. Most of their hair was shaved to create a roach and a scalplock. They wore robes of cloth edged with braid and leggings attached to moccasins. Feathers, knives, and silver armbands added to their dramatic dress. Women adopted the European styles fairly early; they wore the cotton dresses with full flounced skirts, the fitted bodice, and long sleeves. John Mix Stanley painted a council meeting at Tahlequah, the new Cherokee capital in Indian Territory, in 1843;

Three Cherokees of the Savannah River region of Georgia and South Carolina visited London in 1762. The Indians, whose faces are tattooed, wear cloth shirts, legging-moccasins, and cloth robes with braided edges. Silver gorgets, gifts from the English, hang around their necks.

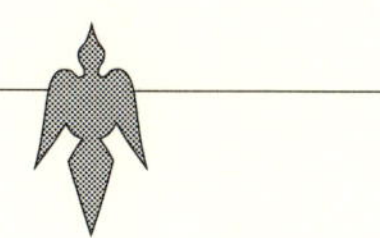

some are shown wearing turbans with plumes, some are bare-chested, and others wear shirts, blanket coats, and leggings. By mid-century they had shifted almost totally to European dress. It is said that in 1911 the feather bonnet of the Lakota Sioux was introduced to the Cherokee, and they adopted it for some public ceremonies, especially those performed for the benefit of tourists.

Key Sources

Bartram, William. "Observations on the Creek and Cherokee Indians." American Ethnological Society *Bulletin* 3(1): 1–81.

Malone, H. T. *Cherokees of the Old South.* Athens: University of Georgia Press, 1956.

Speck, Frank G. and Leonard Broom. *Cherokee Dance and Drama.* Berkeley: University of California Press, 1951.

Timberlake, Henry. *The Memoirs of Lieut. Henry Timberlake.* London, 1765.

Woodward, Grace Steele. *The Cherokees.* Norman: University of Oklahoma Press, 1963.

Chickasaw

The Chickasaw, a Muskhogean-speaking tribe, lived on the headwaters of the Tombigbee and Yazoo rivers in northeastern Mississippi and resembled the Choctaw in many aspects of material culture, language, and customs, although they were often at war with them. Like the Choctaw and the Creek, they seem to have been descendants of the people of the Mississippian culture. Adair visited them in 1775 and recorded much about their customs and social life. Bernard Romans painted them that year, along with other Southeastern Indians.

Men's Basic Dress

Men wore the deerskin breechclout for daily wear, with a poncho-like upper garment for visiting and travel. Winter garments were long and shaggy, made of the skins of bears, panthers, beavers, or otters; the fur and hair were retained but softened "like velvet cloth."

Women's Basic Dress

Women wore a skirt of woven mulberry bark or of deerskin. To this was added, when necessary, an upper garment like the men's poncho. Swanton says the women wore beaded strings of buffalo hair around the legs in place of leggings; these were considered not only ornamental but also preservatives against miscarriages, hard labor, and other evils.

Footwear

Adair said that these people made their moccasins for common use out of the skins of bear and elk, well dressed and smoked to prevent hardening. Moccasins of deerskin were worn for more social occasions. Usually, however, both sexes went barefoot.

Outer Wear

In the northern part of Chickasaw territory, bear hides were utilized in making heavy winter robes. Also in cold weather the women wrapped themselves in the softened skins of buffalo calves, with the shaggy skins outward. Some beaver-skin garments seem to have been worn. Adair said that the Chickasaw women made turkey-feather robes from the long neck and breast feathers, twisting the inner ends of the feathers into a netting made of the strong, durable fibers of hemp or of the inner bark of the mulberry tree.

Hair Styles

The men wore the roach along the top of the head, sometimes with a fringe across the forehead; to this they fastened tufts of beautiful feathers, the skin of a hawk, the wing of a red bird, or attractive native stones. To the scalplock at the crown of the head they attached a large conch-shell bead. Women sometimes rolled the hair into a bunch on the top of the head, or they braided it and bound it with strings of beads.

Headgear

The Chickasaws, like most other Southeastern tribes, went bareheaded, but occasionally wore a headband fastened to a netting to form a sort of cap. Another form of headgear was made by winding a thick skein of threads around the head, with the ends hanging down at the side as tassels.

Accessories

The usual leather belts, woven sashes, and woven garters were added to Chickasaw costumes. Bags and pouches, fiber-woven or of tanned leather, contained necessary items.

Jewelry
Shell gorgets hung around the necks, especially those of the high priests. Adair (1775) mentions that both sexes wore strings of beads around the wrists. Men followed the usual custom of lengthening the lobes of the ears and binding them with wire in order to hang hoops, pendants, or dangling strings of beads from the aperture. Adair notes that the custom was going out of fashion in his time. Nose ornaments were worn by the men.

Special Costumes
Swanton gives a long description of a costume worn by a shaman or priest; briefly, he wore a white waistcoat, a consecrated skin over his shoulders, special white moccasins painted with the sacred color red, a white conch-shell gorget, and a wreath of swan's feathers as a crown.

Garment Decoration
The woven cloth, made from the inner bark of the mulberry tree, was adorned with animal figures, probably painted. Finger-weaving techniques were also used for garters, belts, and sashes featuring simple geometric designs such as chevrons and arrows. Netting of mulberry fibers formed the bases for the feather mantles.

Face and Body Embellishment
Body painting apparently had social significance. Red, yellow, and white colors of earth for the paint were found on the bluffs along the Mississippi River. War captains and other men of distinction were tattooed, often with figures of serpents or other animals; these figures were esteemed not only as ornament but were calculated to frighten enemies. A warrior who gave himself tattoos to which he was not entitled was made to remove the marks in public, a painful process of rubbing green corn juice into the scraped tattoos. The Chickasaw are reported to have practiced skull deformation.

Transitional Dress
Closely allied to the Creek and Choctaw, the Chickasaw joined them in adopting European garb in the early nineteenth century. They, too, were forcibly removed to Indian Territory in the infamous "Trail of Tears," where they joined others of the Five Civilized Tribes, and where tribal distinction in dress was eventually lost.

Key Sources
Cushman, H. B. *History of the Choctaw, Chickasaw, and Natchez Indians.* Greenville, TX, 1899.
Gibson, Arrell M. *The Chickasaws.* Norman: University of Oklahoma Press, 1971.
Speck, Frank G. "Notes on Chickasaw Ethnology and Folk-lore." *Journal of American Folklore* 20: 50–58.

Choctaw

The Choctaw, Muskhogean speakers living in middle and southern Mississippi, were the largest of the Southeastern tribes next to the Cherokee. The name *Choctaw* may be a corruption of the Spanish word *chato,* which means "flat" or "flattened," and may refer to their practice of skull deformation. In early times the men let their hair grow so long that the tribe was called "Long Hairs" both by themselves and others. The traders called them "Flats" or "Flatheads." First European contact was the de Soto expedition in 1540. John White painted the Choctaw in the early 1600s, De Batz did sketches of them about 1735, and Catlin in 1834 painted the men playing chunkey, a ball game.

Men's Basic Dress
Men wore the simple fitted breechcloth with a flap front and rear. When playing chunkey, their breechcloth was small, fitted without flaps, and attached to a wide leather belt. Leggings are not mentioned in records; perhaps they were unnecessary because these people lived along the rivers and on the broad, open savannahs.

Women's Basic Dress
Simple wraparound skirts of the kilt type were worn by the women, reaching from the waist to the middle of the leg; this was made of skin or of a material woven from spun bison hair or a kind of grass. They also made the usual cloth out of the inner bark of the mulberry tree, dyeing it yellow with sassafras root; with further dyeing, it became red. The torso was bare, with the addition of a short cape or

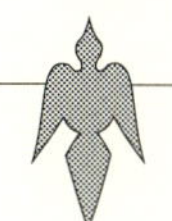

poncho of skin for warmth. Children went naked until old enough to walk.

Footwear

Deerskin moccasins were worn by both sexes for dress occasions or traveling; otherwise they went barefoot. They were able to tan leather to a fine softness, and they decorated moccasins with beads, feathers, and such.

Outer Wear

The women made beautiful turkey-feather mantles using especially the long feathers of the neck and breast, fastening them into a cord netting made of hemp or mulberry-tree bark. This type of robe was not only very warm but pleasing to the eye. Little mention is made of outer garments of fur or skin.

Hair Styles

The Choctaw were famous for their long hair, but shortly after European contact the men began to wear the roach, with the upright fringe on top, widening at the back to cover the lower part of the head and the back of the neck. The hair was then decorated with various ornaments, including colorful feathers. Women wore the hair long and loose, formed into two braids, or bound into a queue in back wrapped with bison hair.

Headgear

Like most of the American Indians of the Southeast, the Choctaw went bareheaded most of the time. For ceremonial wear they created headdresses of feathers in a wide variety of styles.

Accessories

Belts, sashes, pouches, and garters were finger-woven of buffalo hair or mulberry-bark fibers. A small pouch for powder and shot was made of a gourd upon which the skin of a raccoon, otter, or mink had been shrunk and afterward hardened. Another type of pouch was made by sewing one of these skins over a horn. Men carried feather fans, which were symbols of social status as well as a form of adornment.

Jewelry

Little mention is made of jewelry among the Choctaw. Aboriginally they made beads of wood, some as large as acorns, as well as chinquapin nuts dyed in various colors, and the red seeds of the haw.

Special Costumes

Catlin, in his paintings of Choctaw men playing chunkey, showed the many players wearing small breechclouts attached to a wide belt and fringed collars, or a "mane," which may have been of dyed egret feathers. Some players wore long, fringed "tails" of white horsehair or quills. Some of the men painted their bodies in swirling designs of swastikas, suns, serpents, and other symbols. The members of one team painted the bodies white: an effective method of identifying the sides. We also have a sketch by Catlin of the Choctaw Eagle Dance showing the dancers, their bodies painted white, carrying eagle tail feathers in their hands, wearing feathers over their breechclouts, and with one tall eagle feather in their hair.

Garment Decoration

Women wove belts with a peculiar running-scroll design; although these belts, as well as woven sashes, were created with beadwork in the early nineteenth

A tattooed Choctaw athlete wears a fitted breechclout, a horsehair cape, and a beaded belt. The horsehair tail shows his status as an accomplished chunkey player.

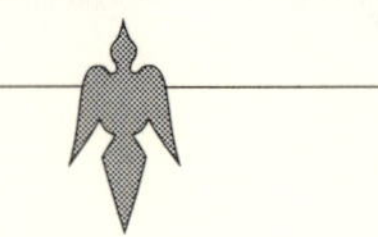

century, the design was indigenous to the area and may be found on the pottery of the Mississippians. Sashes, belts, and garters were made from spun bison wool and dyed or adorned with beaded designs. Sassafras root made a yellow dye; with further immersion, a red hue was obtained. Shoulder bags and moccasins were also beaded. Some leather belts were decorated with designs created with metal studs. Boots were ornamented with lace and silver bells.

Face and Body Embellishment

There is no particular description of tattooing among the Choctaw, and the only reference to body painting is in connection with the game of chunkey and the Eagle Dance. But they were widely known for their practice of skull flattening, effected by means of bags of sand or a hinged piece of wood applied to the heads of infant boys; although almost all males were treated in this way, the custom does not seem to have been widely applied to females.

Transitional Dress

Cloth came into use with the advent of trade with whites. The men favored breechcloths of blue strouding in the fitted style, the ends falling down to the knees in front and back, and ornamented with beads, tinsels, lace, or other decoration. From the paintings of Catlin and Charles Bird King we see that the men, particularly for special occasions, wore European-style clothes: cotton shirts with wide collars, jackets with dropped shoulder seams, wide belts decorated with metal studs in various designs, and trousers. Medals or silver crescent gorgets were suspended by ribbons on the neck. Women also adopted European styles: long, full skirts, often flounced at the bottom; long sleeves, usually gathered into cuffs; and wool shawls, often plaid. Like the others of the Five Civilized Tribes, the Choctaw retained little of their traditional dress after the removal to Indian Territory.

Key Sources

Bushnell, David I., Jr. "The Choctaw of Bayou Lacomb, St. Tammany Parish, Louisiana." Bureau of American Ethnology *Bulletin* 48.

———. "Drawings of A. de Batz in Louisiana. 1732–1735." Smithsonian Institution *Miscellaneous Collections* 80(5).

Cushman, H. B. *History of the Choctaw, Chickasaw, and Natchez Indians.* Greenville, TX, 1899.

Edwards, John. "The Choctaw Indians in the Middle of the Nineteenth Century." *Chronicles of Oklahoma* 10(3): 392–425.

Swanton, John R. "An Early Account of the Choctaw Indians." American Anthropological Association *Memoirs* 5(2).

———. "Source Material for the Social and Ceremonial Life of the Choctaw Indians." Bureau of American Ethnology *Bulletin* 10(3).

Creek

The Creek-Muskhogee confederation formed the largest division of the Muskhogean language group, including such tribes as the Creek, Coosa, Cofitachiqui, Alabama, and Kasehta. The Creek were the largest group in this loose confederation. The name was given to them because of the creeks flowing through their territory, which covered most of Georgia and some of Alabama.

Differentiation was made between the Upper Creek, who lived along the Coosa and Tallapoosa rivers, and the Lower Creek, who lived for the most part along the Georgia-Alabama border. According to Creek accounts they migrated from the southwest and many authorities believe they may have arisen from the ruins of the Natchez; their culture was similar, with its rigidly structured social organization and sumptuary laws in matters of dress.

The Creek were painted by Verelst in 1734, sketched by Trumbull in 1790, and painted by King in the 1820s and by Catlin in the 1830s.

Men's Basic Dress

Men wore a fitted breechclout hanging down before and behind. Creek men seem to have worn leggings more than neighboring tribes; these were of leather dyed black, laced with white thongs, and bordered with fringes of colored leather. Boys went naked until they reached the age of puberty.

Women's Basic Dress

Women wore a calf-length skirt wrapped around the waist and tied in place with a thong; this was of a single piece of buckskin, or of several small skins sewn together. They also used a textile woven from fibers of mulberry-tree bark; along the Georgia coast

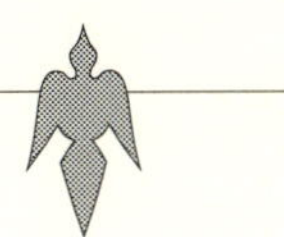

tree moss was used instead. It is difficult to tell if these women wore leggings; authorities mention "boots about their legs" or "moccasins extending to the calf of the leg." Girls were invested with skirt and moccasins from the time they began to walk.

Footwear
Moccasins were made from both bison and deer hide, using a single piece of leather. They were "ornamented according to fancy." However, both sexes went barefoot most of the time.

Outer Wear
The Lower Creek women were said to have worn white mantles made of thread from the bark of the mulberry tree, thread as fine as "the best thread from Portugal" but stronger. These were worn with the ends fastened on one shoulder. Some mantles were made with thread spun from slippery-elm bark, others with thread from a plant like a daffodil. Women also wore short cloaks or shawls of flamingo feathers or the colorful plumage of other birds; this was unusual, for seldom did the Southeastern women wear feather garments. Muskrat-fur cloaks and ankle-length feather robes were reserved for the chiefs. Mantles were also created of deerskin, painted with bright designs, as well as sable and wildcat skins, but the latter were said to give out a strong smell.

Hair Styles
Men often cut the hair in a roach, but it was on the front of the head, with a braid on each side and a scalplock in the back pulled through a hair tube hanging behind. Others wore the roach widened at the back, covering the nape of the neck. Some men preferred a tonsure like a monk, a single fringe of hair all around the head. Women never cut the hair but braided it and fastened the braids into a topknot, skewered with a bone or shell hairpin. Both sexes treated the hair with bear grease, to give it luster, and a paste or powder made of the red berries of the sumac.

Headgear
A swan-feather bonnet was worn at festivals—by men who rated such an honor. Another form of headdress was a diadem or band, about four inches wide, decorated with stones or beads, encircling the head, embellished at the front with a high, waving plume of crane, heron, or flamingo feathers. Some headbands were decorated with porcupine quillwork, obtained in trade.

Accessories
Turkey-feather fans were carried about at dances by the men, not only as a sign of leadership but also to protect the eyes from the smoke of the fire. Garters, sashes or belts, and pouches were made of material woven from thread spun from mulberry or bass bark fibers; finer stuff came from a silk-grass fiber. Shoulder bags or bandeliers were popular items. These articles were painted with symbolic designs.

Jewelry
The Creek made extensive use of jewelry and other forms of decoration. Men thrust a ring through the septum of the nose. They also lengthened the ear lobes, wound them with copper wire, and hung pendants and clusters of beads from the aperture, or they inserted brightly hued feathers or soft white-heron plumes. Women wore smaller earrings. Pearl bracelets were popular. The only ornament resembling an anklet was the use of terrapin shells containing pebbles fastened about the ankle to add rhythmic sounds while the women were dancing. Shell gorgets, one or more, were suspended at the neck. Pearls, obtained from river mussels or from bivalves along the Atlantic coast, were made into necklaces and worn in profusion. Beads were also made from a berry called a "wild cherry." Members of the nobility often wore ornaments decorated with porcupine quills (from the north) or wampum (not adopted until after white contact); the lower classes were carefully restricted in their use of ornamentation.

Armor
Found in a temple were breastplates like corselets, headpieces made of rawhide, and round and oval shields.

Special Costumes
A shaman usually wore clothing of white buckskin, consecrated skins were draped on his body, and he wore white moccasins decorated with a few streaks of red. A shell gorget on the chest and a wreath of swan

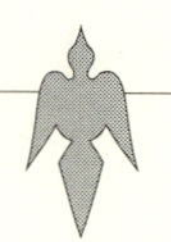

feathers completed his outfit. During the summer festival called the "busk" or the Green Corn Rite, spectators and participants alike were dressed in white. The village chief wore a duck-skin headdress surmounted by white feathers. The faces and torsos of the honored warriors were painted red.

Garment Decoration

Devoted to decoration, the Creek used many forms of it. From spun vegetable fibers the women wove bands for garters, belts, sashes, headbands, and shoulder bags. These were woven in simple geometric designs with V's, W's, and diamonds predominating, and were finished off with fringes and tassels. Any porcupine quillwork was probably imported. Skins and the woven fabrics were dyed, particular in reds and blues. Brass or silver bells from the traders further adorned garments and boots.

Face and Body Embellishment

Tattooing was especially practiced by the Creek warriors using scrolls, flowers, animals, stars, crescents, serpents, and sun designs, the latter usually placed in the center of the chest. The body was often divided into "zones," which were then filled in with such symbols and representations. All of these were conceived to be visible marks of achievement and exploits. In addition, the men might paint the head, neck, and breast with vermilion designs. Among the women, only prostitutes painted themselves. There is no historical evidence of skull deformation among the Creek.

Transitional Dress

After European contact, women wore a short cotton "waistcoat" decorated with lace or beads. Ribbons obtained in trade were hung abundantly from the head and the shoulders, a custom that continues to the present for special occasions. Early in the ninteenth century they adopted the long, full skirts and full-sleeved blouses of the whites, adding plaid or plain wool shawls for warmth, and from then on they generally followed European fashions. By the late eighteenth century the men, too, had adopted European styles: full-skirted coats, cotton or linen shirts, cravats, knee breeches, and such. The only evidence of native costume in the paintings of that period and the next century were the occasional nose rings, earrings, silver gorgets, beaded sashes, tattooed faces, and use of feathers. The Creek were removed from their lands by the federal government in the "Trail of Tears" to join the other Five Civilized Tribes in Oklahoma, and tribal identification by costume was lost.

Key Sources

Bartram, William. "Observations on the Creek and Cherokee Indians." American Ethnological Society *Bulletin* 3(1): 1–81. Facsimile reprint of 1853 edition.

Hodgson, William B. "The Creek Confederacy." Georgia Historical Society *Collections* 3(1).

Speck, Frank G. "The Creek Indians of Taskigi Town." American Anthropological Association *Memoirs* 2(2).

Swanton, John R. "Early History of the Creek Indians and Their Neighbors." Bureau of American Ethnology *Bulletin* 73.

Natchez

Sedentary agriculturists living along the lower Mississippi River, the Natchez spoke a Muskhogean language of the Hokan-Siouan language family. Their name, from a French word of uncertain origin, is usually pronounced "Natch-is." There were two branches: the Taensa and the Natchez. They seem to have represented a lingering into historic times of the Mississippian culture and many anthropologists see Mexican influences in their lifeways and architecture. The Natchez had a strong hereditary class system. The chief—the "Great Sun"—was the object of tremendous veneration, but he was answerable to a council of nobles. Below the nobles were the "honored people" and below them in status was a large lower class. This class system, however, was not completely rigid and allowed for some social mobility. De Soto, marching through the Natchez territory, claimed to be the Sun's younger brother, but was unable to dry up the Mississippi, so they harassed him until he left. Other Spanish travelers and explorers, as well as the French and English, visited the Natchez, but the tribe's decline had already begun, and the Natchez were virtually destroyed by the eighteenth century. A. de Batz, a French artist, made drawings of them during a

visit in 1732, and Le Page du Pratz sketched the Natchez during the 1750s.

Men's Basic Dress

The simple apron-style skin breechclout, held in place by a thong, was indicative of rank, for only the chiefs were permitted to wear black; others wore white. Some breechclouts were painted with designs, such as red, yellow, or black lines and figures, and some breechclouts featured a tail in back. With colder weather men donned a poncho made of two deerskins and thigh-length fitted leggings, gartered at the knees and tucked into the moccasins.

Women's Basic Dress

When the Natchez girl was about ten years of age she began wearing a kind of fringed apron made of thread spun from mulberry inner bark. After puberty she replaced it with the woman's knee-length wraparound skirt, either of the mulberry fibers or of deerskin. In colder weather a poncho-like upper garment, usually of skin, was worn.

Footwear

Although the Natchez normally went barefoot, occasionally they wore deerskin moccasins; de Batz gives us a description of this footwear, explaining how they were sewn like a sock, going all the way around the foot, and joined in front by means of bearskin thongs. Eight or nine inches high, they had no soles or heels.

Outer Wear

Mantles were made of deerskin or the woven mulberry fibers. Swan or duck mantles were worn by a favored few, women as well as men of the honored class, while turkey feathers were reserved for more common people. We have a drawing by de Batz of a Natchez man wearing a buffalo robe with the tail left on and with the inner side painted with geometric patterns. Robes were also made of beaver pelts, six being required for one mantle.

Hair Styles

The Natchez men had a hair style reminiscent of monks—the hair cut short and the top shaved to form a tonsure; one lock was left at the top, to which feathers or other ornaments could be fastened. Other hair styles were followed; the hair might be shaved on one side only and the hair on the other arranged in various bizarre fashions, or the entire head might be shaved except for a roach. Women wore their hair long and flowing, in several braids, or in a queue in the back, into which beads or porcupine quills were interlaced. Men plucked out their beard hairs with clamshells or copper tweezers.

Headgear

As was true of so much of Natchez costume, adornment was indicative of rank, and only high personages were permitted to wear the feather headdresses, while swan feathers were reserved for the Great Sun and his immediate circle.

Accessories

Few accessories were worn except for belts and occasional pouches that hung from the belt. Feather fans were for the honored few. Bison wool was finger-woven into garters.

Jewelry

Both men and women pierced the ears and distended the lobes to accommodate earrings of shell, stone, copper, or feathers. Shell gorgets and bead necklaces were worn, but only noble children below the age of ten were permitted to wear pearls.

Armor

No indication was found of garments worn specifically as armor by the Natchez, but they probably wore the protective garments of cane and bison leather typical of the Southeast. Warriors were extensively tattooed, their skin amounting to a scoreboard, for each tattoo represented a deed of valor. Important warriors had a war club tattooed on the right shoulder.

Special Costumes

Sumptuary laws were rigidly enforced among the Natchez. Du Pratz has left us a description of the special feathered headband of the Great Sun—a netted cap that supported a diadem of red and white seeds or beads, into which were placed swan feathers eight inches long arranged in a curved line, each topped by a tuft of hair and a little hairy tassel dyed a brilliant red.

Garment Decoration
Various fibers—bison wool, mulberry bark, and opossum hair—were finger-woven into belts, sashes, and garters, featuring simple geometric designs; these were finished off with fringes and tassels. Skins were dyed black, red, or white and painted with geometric patterns. Imported porcupine quills were obtained to create the rare pieces of quillwork.

Face and Body Embellishment
Tattooing began at an early age; both boys and girls had small tattoos on the noses, which were added to bit by bit according to rank or valorous deeds. Designs were in the form of suns, serpents, war clubs, or such and might cover the entire bodies of noted warriors and wives of the nobility. The tattooing was done by pricking designs into the skin with a bone awl or a garfish bone and rubbing charcoal into the perforations. Skull deformation was practiced by means of a contrivance of board and clay pads applied to the heads of infants. Most of the Natchez women blackened their teeth daily with a mixture of wood ashes and tobacco. Painting of the face and body was also performed with mineral pigments, ochers, and clays, which were mixed with animal fat. The colors and designs used were based on personal fancy, certain ritual rules, or significant dreams.

Transitional Dress
The Natchez were destroyed so soon after white contact that there was almost no adoption of European dress.

Key Sources
Charlevoix, Pierre F. X. de. *Journal of a Voyage to North America.* 2 vols. London, 1761.
Cushman, H. B. *History of the Choctaw, Chickasaw, and Natchez Indians.* Greenville, TX, 1899.

Powhatan

Powhatan was a confederation of tribes in the tidewater country of Virginia brought under one control by Chief Powhatan in the late sixteenth and early seventeenth centuries. Algonquian speakers, they were members of the Potomac, Rappahannock, Pamunkey, Chickahominy, Chesapeake, and Powhatan tribes. The confederation existed only from Powhatan's unification to the death of his son in 1644, but the constituent tribes probably existed long before the confederacy did. The name, meaning "falls in a current of water," refers to the area from the tidewater to the "fall line" of the interior. The people lived in villages and practiced agriculture, but subsistence also depended on fishing, hunting, and gathering. They dressed more like the Southeastern peoples than their Algonquian cousins to the north, a fact that may be attributed to the climate. First

A sixteenth-century Powhatan wears a modified roach by leaving his hair long at the back and knotting it at his right ear. His apron, made from an animal skin that includes the tail, is fringed at the top and bottom.

European contact was in the late sixteenth century. We are indebted to Captain John Smith's 1624 account for much information on the lifeways of these tribes, an account that includes some drawings by an unknown artist. Beverley in 1705 and Strachey in 1849 wrote extensively on the Powhatan. Strachey describes their physical appearance, saying that the men had long, thick black hair and no beards, and were generally tall and straight.

Men's Basic Dress

Men wore an unusual type of breechclout; made of deerskin, it was draped, tied in the back (which was left bare), and was characteristically fringed. At times there seems to have been a folded-over section, also draped and fringed. Some seem to have worn a tail behind. Instead of this draped breechclout, some men wore a lightweight garment of skin, also draped and fringed, and fastened on one shoulder. When hunting or during severe weather, men wore gartered leggings. The very poor covered themselves with grass or leaves fastened to their belts.

Women's Basic Dress

Women wore the fringed, draped, apron-like garment, but usually with a back apron as well. They, too, wore the draped skin piece fastened on one shoulder; these were sometimes folded over at the top resulting in a double fringe. Adolescent girls wore a cord through the crotch to which moss was fastened to cover the pubic area. It is questionable whether women wore leggings; they may not have needed them since the apron affairs were knee-length or longer.

Footwear

Normally the Powhatan people went barefoot, but when they wore moccasins, they were the typical swamp moccasin, the pouch-like article laced at the toe and the back, and with the laces tied around the ankle; some had a piece of leather sewn to the bottom to thicken the sole.

Outer Wear

Winter robes, called "matchcoats," were not sleeved, but were simply a flat piece of skin, usually tied on the shoulder; sometimes belted, they were made of various skins such as raccoon, weasel, beaver, otter, or rabbit, but commonly of deerskin. The finest robes, worn winter and summer, were those of feathers, particularly turkey. One was mentioned as being made of mallard heads, which must have displayed a lustrous iridescent sheen. There is a surviving garment, "Powhatan's Mantle," that gives us an idea of those worn. It is of deerskin with small disks of shells, similar to wampum, sewn to the mantle in spirals and in animal and human shapes.

"A cheiff Ladye of Pomeiooc" has her right arm in a sling of pearls, copper beads, or smooth bones and wears a draped apron fringed at the top and bottom.

Hair Styles

Almost all men of the Southeastern Woodlands removed the facial hair, but we do find a few examples in this area of men keeping their beards. A common hair style was to shave the right side of the head, so it did not interfere with drawing the bowstring, leaving a roach on top and the left side full-length. The long hair was anointed with walnut oil to make it sleek and shiny, dyed red with puccoon root, and was then tied up in various fashions, with ornaments affixed. Girls shaved the front and sides of the head and wore the remaining strands in braids. Married women cut their hair below the ears. Most women left a "fringe" of bangs across the forehead. They, too, tied ornaments into the hair.

A young girl, age 7 or 8, wears a bead necklace, and a thong to which is fastened moss to cover her groin

Headgear

Headbands, not common in the Southeast, were found often in this tidewater country. Some women wore wreaths of twisted cord while others preferred flowers in season. Feathered headgear was reserved for the men, particularly for shamans or priests. A stuffed hawk and vulture wings were used as embellishment for headdresses.

Accessories

Bags, belts, and garters were woven of buffalo hair, opossum fur, or "silk grass." These fibers were finger-woven in geometric chevron and diamond patterns. Some belts were of leather.

Jewelry

Pearls were often used as ornamentation, worn as necklaces or dangling in loops from the ears. Copper beads were also popular, both preferable to the shell beads found in use by neighboring tribes. There is some reference to wampum, which was acquired in trade from the north. Ear decoration was extensive, for the ears were pierced in several places to allow for not only pearls and copper beads, but also legs and claws of some birds and other animals. Occasionally we hear of a warrior wearing strings of beads or pearls as a fringe on a band around the calf of the leg. Nose ornaments were rare.

Special Costumes

Strachey tells us of a priest or shaman's costume. Besides the typical feather cloak, his headdress consisted of 12 or more snake or weasel skins stuffed with moss and hanging all around the head; above these was a circlet of feathers. The face was painted, and the shaman carried a rattle as a symbol of his profession.

Garment Decoration

Garments woven of mulberry bark and native hemp were dyed in such hues as black, yellow, and,

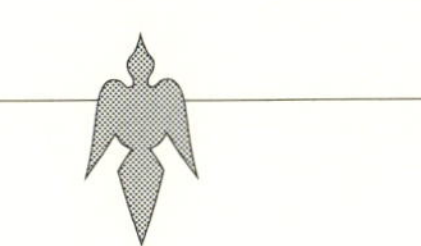

This animal skin cloak decorated with shells is thought to have belonged to Powhatan, leader of the Powhatan Confederacy in eastern Virginia at the time of the English colony at Jamestown. Powhatan, father of Pocahontas, died in 1618.

especially, red; they were often fringed. Shells were sewn on garments, as in the case of Powhatan's Mantle, in disks and figures of men and animals. Wampum was sewn on as decoration, but glass beads seem not to have been used until much later; by that time tribal distinctions of dress were lost.

Face and Body Embellishment

Body paint was worn by males, especially yellow and black. Women seem not to have favored this custom, probably because they were more extensively tattooed than the men, and may not have wanted paint covering their tattooed designs, for the tattoos were a matter of great pride with them. This tattooing was done in a manner rarely found among Indian tribes—through branding. They took iron, cut in various shapes and symbols, rubbed in coloring matter, heated it over the fire, then seared the flesh with it, leaving a permanent imprint. Men, as shown by the artist John White, often had distinguishing marks tattooed on their backs. The use of iron does not necessarily imply white contact, for iron was a valued trade item, whether of native or meteoric origin. There is no reference to skull flattening among these people.

Transitional Dress

Powhatan and his people were quick to adopt European styles of dress, particularly such cloth garments as wool mantles and red or blue breechcloths. But the population was devastated rapidly with the measles and smallpox brought by the Europeans and was nearly wiped out, leaving but few to carry on their traditions or become assimilated into the colonial culture. We do have a portrait of Powhatan's daughter, the famous Pocahontas, painted in 1616 after she married John Rolfe and went to England; she is dressed like any English lady of the early seventeenth century.

Key Sources

Beverley, Robert. *The History and Present State of Virginia in Four Parts—By a Native Inhabitant of the Place.* London, 1705.

Harriot, Thomas. *A Briefe and True Report of the New Found Land of Virginia.* New York: Dover, 1972. Reprint of the 1590 Theodore de Bry edition.

Hulton, Paul H. and David B. Quinn. *The American Drawings of John White, 1577–1590.* 2 vols. Chapel Hill: University of North Carolina Press, 1964.

Jefferson, Thomas. *Notes on the State of Virginia* [1787]. Thomas P. Abernethy, ed. New York: Harper and Row, 1964.

Pollard, J. G. "The Pamunkey Indians of Virginia." Bureau of American Ethnology *Bulletin* 17.

Rountree, Helen C. *Pocahontas' People: The Powhatan Indians of Virginia through Four Centuries.* Norman: University of Oklahoma Press.

———. *The Powhatan Indians of Virginia: Their Traditional Culture.* Norman: University of Oklahoma Press.

Smith, John. *Works, 1608–1631.* Edward Arber, ed. Birmingham, England: English Scholar's Library, 1884.

Southwell, Sir Robert. "The Method the Indians in Virginia and Carolina Use To Dress Buck and Doeskins." Royal Society of London *Philosophical Transactions* 17: 532–533.

Speck, Frank G. "Chapters on the Ethnology of the Powhatan Tribes of Virginia." Museum of the American Indian *Indian Notes and Monographs* 1(5).

———. "The Rappahannock Indians of Virginia." Museum of the American Indian *Indian Notes and Monographs* 5(3).

Stern, Theodore. "Chickahominy: The Changing Culture of a Virginia Indian Community." American Philosophical Society *Proceedings* 96(2): 157–225.

Strachey, William. "The Historie of Travaile into Virginia Britannia, Expressing the Cosmographie and Commodities of the Country, Together with the Manners and Customs of the People," *Hakluyt Society Publications* 6. London, England.

Secotan

The tribes of North Carolina represent the southernmost extension of the Algonquian language. Included were the Roanoke, the Secotan, Pamlico, Pomeioc, and others. The Secotan have been selected here because of the fine watercolors done by John White in 1590, later reproduced as engravings by

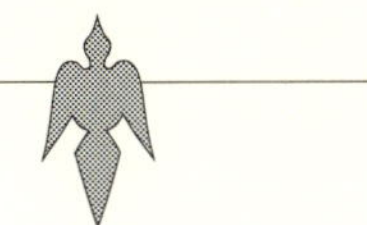

Theodore de Bry, with commentary by Thomas Harriot. It is a notable example of Indian costumes and lifeways recorded before the changes wrought by European influence. The first contact seems to have been the arrival of the English ships in 1585 to establish the ill-fated Roanoke colony; both White and Harriot were of this group, but they had sailed back to England for supplies and when they returned, the colony had disappeared.

Men's Basic Dress

The men wore the draped apron-shape breechclout of deerskin, often with an extra part folded over; both sections were fringed and often decorated with beads. A tail, probably buffalo, hung down behind; in some cases, an animal pelt was hung in front from a belt-thong. Breechclouts were also made of grass or feathers. Over this was sometimes worn a fringed skin garment fastened on the shoulder, too short to be termed a mantle. Leggings do not seem to be mentioned in the sources, but garters are, so one could perhaps assume leggings.

Women's Basic Dress

Women wore the same draped, folded-over, fringed breechclout as the men, but often with the addition of a similar garment on the back. Their breasts were bare, unless they added a fringed skin piece fastened on one shoulder. Along the coast some skirts were fashioned of Spanish moss. Little girls wore a thong through the crotch to which was fastened moss or milkweed bark as a form of covering.

Footwear

The Secotan normally went barefoot, although John White does indicate an occasional use of a sock-like moccasin, and Lawson says they wore "shoes" of deerskin or bearskin, which had no heel but fit the foot snugly.

Outer Wear

Since rabbits were abundant in the area, some cloaks were made of rabbit skins. Lawson mentions "matchcoats" made of raccoon, beaver, or squirrel skins. Lighter weight mantles were of tanned deerskin. Turkey feathers and the heads of mallards were also formed into outer garments. Most of these were fastened on one shoulder.

Hair Styles

The roach was commonly worn by the men, either with a knot at the nape of the neck or with a forehead crest; some men wore a feather or feathers in the hair. The women wore the hair fringed or "banged" in front and either knotted at the nape or hanging loose at shoulder length. There is some evidence of the use of bear grease and red hair dye to dress the hair.

Headgear

Some women wore a headband of a twisted cord; some headbands are described as "wreaths of fur."

Accessories

Apart from the garters mentioned above, the only accessories seem to have been shoulder bags, fringed at the bottom, used to carry personal items.

Jewelry

Ear ornaments consisted of clusters of pearls, bird claws, or pendants of bone or shell. Bracelets and necklaces were also of pearls and copper beads. No mention is made of nose ornaments. Harriot shows one woman of Roanoke wearing a copper gorget.

Armor

Some armor was made of wicker or cane, fastened together with sinew; with this was worn a wooden breastplate and a leather wristguard. Bark shields were carried.

Special Costumes

White painted a shaman wearing a mantle of rabbit skins, his hair shaved in two crests across the head from ear to ear. He also painted a "conjurer," wearing nothing but a pelt hanging from a belt-thong in front; in addition, a bag featuring a very long fringe hangs from the belt. A small stuffed black bird is fastened above the right ear as a sign of office.

Garment Decoration

Almost the only form of decoration was the use of fringes made of Spanish moss or basswood fibers.

Face and Body Embellishment

Women were tattooed to a limited extent on the arms, legs, cheeks, and calves of the legs. Men were

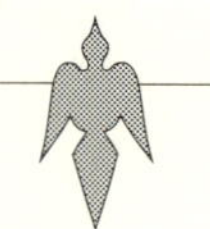

not tattooed as much, except for certain marks on the back to indicate rank and relationship. Bodies were painted for ceremonial dances, using plant and mineral pigments mixed with fats. There was no indication given of skull deformation practices.

Transitional Dress

The remaining Indians of North Carolina quickly adopted the Englishman's cloth, using red and blue "baize" or stroud cloth for breechcloths or shirts, held in place with belts. Women also adopted short petticoats of wool and both sexes wore woolen mantles.

Key Sources

Ashe, Samuel A'Court. *History of North Carolina.* 2 vols. Greensboro, NC: Van Noppen, 1908–1925.

Catesby, Mark. *The Natural History of Carolina, Florida, and Bahama Islands.* 2 vols. London, England, 1731–1743.

Dillard, Richard. "Indian Tribes of Eastern Carolina." *North Carolina Booklet* 6(1).

Harriot, Thomas. *A Briefe and True Report of the New Found Land of Virginia.* New York: Dover, 1972. Reprint of the 1590 edition of Theodor de Bry.

Hulton, Paul H. and David B. Quinn. *The American Drawings of John White, 1577–1590.* 2 vols. Chapel Hill: University of North Carolina Press, 1964.

Lawson, John. *History of Carolina, Containing the Exact Description and Natural History of That Country.* Richmond, VA, 1937.

Milling, Chapman J. *Red Carolinians.* Chapel Hill: University of North Carolina Press, 1940.

Rights, Douglas L. *The American Indian in North Carolina.* Winston-Salem, NC: John F. Blair, 1957.

South, S. A. *Indians of North Carolina.* Raleigh: North Carolina Division of Natural Resources, 1976.

Seminole

When first visited by Bartram in 1791, the Seminole were a small tribe, and they had almost become extinct by 1800. After the Creek Wars of 1813–1814, refugee Creeks fled to the Florida swamps, joining the Seminole in their almost impregnable natural fortress; here they continued the fight with the United States in the First Seminole War of 1817–1818 and the Second Seminole War of 1832–1842. They were joined by a few Calusas, some runaway slaves, and a few fugitives from other tribes. The name *Seminole* itself, applied to the earlier group, was a Muskhogean word adapted from the Spanish *cimarron,* meaning something originally domestic that has turned feral, with shades of *frontiersman* rather than *runaway;* the Creeks of Florida adopted the name. After the Second Seminole War, in which their great leader Osceola was killed by treachery, some Seminoles moved to Oklahoma; those who remained divided into two groups—the Muskogee or Cow Creek Indians and the Mikosuki or Big Cypress Indians. They remained unconquered by the United States.

Men's Basic Dress

Of all the Southeastern Indians, the Florida tribes were least supplied with deer hide and deer sinew. The men wore breechclouts of woven or braided palmetto leaves with three ends, two passing around the waist and one hanging down in front, each end terminating in a tassel of the palmetto. There is no certain reference to the wearing of leggings by these people.

Women's Basic Dress

Most women wore skirts of tree moss or palmetto fronds; a few seem to have worn wraparound skirts of deerskin. In colder weather, they added a short wrap or shawl of skin to cover the torso.

Footwear

The Seminoles went barefoot at almost all times; the men may have worn the swamp moccasin.

Outer Wear

Women wore mantles of woven palmetto leaves. As special wear, men wore feather cloaks, made from the abundant colorful plumage of local birds.

Hair Styles

The hair was worn in a variety of ways. Women let the hair grow long and wore it flowing, with flowers as decoration, or tied it into a clump at the back.

A Seminole identified as Old Tallahassee wears sashes across his long shirt. His woven garters tie at his knees over front-seam leggings; his moccasins are one piece with a seam at the front.

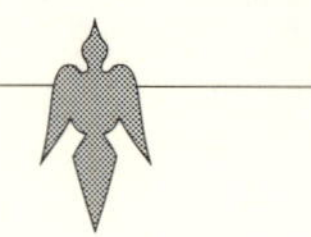

Men wore the roach, with the addition of a fringe across the front of the head, and a scalplock behind. At each temple a tuft of hair was allowed to hang to the bottom of the earlobe.

Headgear

According to Pareja, woven palm-leaf hats were worn. The most common headdress was a crown of feathers.

Accessories

Bags were woven of palmetto and other grasses.

Jewelry

Because little clothing was necessary, ornamentation was extensive. These Indians delighted in pearl and copper beads. Amber was found here in greater quantity than almost anywhere on the continent and was used for beads. Beads were also made from fish bones and animal bones. Gold and silver ornaments were treasured, not from native metals but as loot from Spanish ships bound from Panama through the Florida straits where they foundered. Many wore rather large bones as earrings. Shell gorgets were also popular.

Face and Body Embellishment

As was true of Florida Indians generally, the Seminole engaged in extensive tattooing of the body, especially chiefs and their wives. Most of the designs were geometric, with few curved lines; women's designs were different from the men's. There is no evidence of skull flattening.

Transitional Dress

The transitional costume of the Seminole may be divided into three periods: the time during and after the Seminole Wars, the late nineteenth century, and the modern period.

For information on dress during the first of these periods, we gain much knowledge from the great McKenney-Hall portfolio of Indian portraits. Ten of them are of Seminole leaders. These men wear the turban with feathers or plumes, so popular during the first half of the nineteenth century; some have a metal band around the bottom of the turban. Most of these men have a beaded strap over one shoulder that holds a pouch at the side; the straps are beaded in geometric designs featuring triangles and zigzags especially. They wear one or more crescent-shaped silver gorgets, chased with elegance, and most wear a peace medal on a thong or ribbon, presented to them by the U.S. government. They seem to have adopted the shirt as worn by their white contemporaries, either with the stand-up collar and cravat or the more casual "Lord Byron" style. The shirts are belted in with a bright-colored sash. Three of the ten men have mustaches.

Two of the portraits are full-length and show the rather unusual but typical male Seminole garment—the skirt, really a dress, which reaches to the knees and is quite full. It is difficult to tell where this style came from; probably it was a form of the white man's shirt belted in. The leggings of these two seem to have been developed from the swamp moccasin, but are higher, more fitted, and have buttons or similar ornaments up the front. The moccasins have the typical puckered toe.

There are few if any pictures of Seminole women of the early nineteenth century, but we know that they were wearing the printed-cotton dresses or blouses and full skirts of the white women, with a cloth shawl for warmth if necessary.

Concerning garment decoration, some beadwork was done in the early nineteenth century, probably a continuation of the Creek beading. This appeared in bands used for shoulder bags and belts; designs were often of symbolic creatures such as terrapins and diamondback rattlesnakes and finished off with fringes. Garters were braided in a finger-weaving technique, using especially diamond patterns, and beads worked in as the weaving progressed. Small fringes adorned leggings.

MacCauley, who visited the Seminole in 1880–1881 and again in 1887, provided excellent information on the costume of the late nineteenth century. The male attire consisted of the dress or tunic, from neck to knees, belted at the waist with a bright sash, a kerchief tied at the neck, a turban, a breechcloth, and, rarely, moccasins. The shirt had rather full sleeves, ruffled at the cuffs, and was often bound with wide (two-inch or three-inch) metal armbands. A sketch from MacCauley's work shows the shirt with a wide band of embroidery or braid at the bottom. It had a narrow rolled collar, buttoned or left unbuttoned. The belt was of leather, often red, and, because the garment was pocketless, articles were

A Seminole family poses for a photographer. The women wear long skirts and many necklaces of beads and coins. The man wears a vest, a long shirt, and a tall turban fashionable among the nineteenth-century Seminole. All are barefoot.

suspended from the belt—hunting knives, pouches containing bullets, powder, tobacco, or other items. The Seminole man used his neckerchief as a coin purse, knotting coins into the corner of the scarf. Sometimes more scarves or neckerchiefs were added, as many as seven or eight, all in bright red or yellow cotton prints. The turban was made of one or more shawls, often of a Scotch plaid, folded into strips diagonally and wound about the head, leaving the top open; several shawls were used for this so that the final turban was very large, as much as 20 inches in diameter. The folds of the turban were used as another pocket for tobacco, pipe, or other object. This was an elaborate headdress, usually donned only for visits to white settlements. In camp, the attire was simple—breechcloth, possibly moccasins, and occasionally leggings, which were often of red flannel decorated with braid strips, or the leggings might be of buckskin.

The Seminole woman of this period typically wore two garments: a short, full, wrist-length cape and a full skirt gathered to a waistband, sweeping the ground, and made of a printed cotton, such as calico or gingham. According to MacCauley, the women never wore moccasins or headgear. In cool weather a shawl was thrown over the shoulders. For decoration, the skirt was often banded with strips of braid purchased from the traders. This seems to have led to the later characteristic Seminole style in which clothing was made of tiny, bright-colored scraps of cloth pieced together into patterned strips that were then sewn together, a technique probably copied from the popular pieced quilts of the nineteenth century. The widespread use of the sewing machine among Seminole women was certainly a factor in the creation of this style of garment.

Beads were worn, sometimes in large quantity; MacCauley tells of one woman who wore as many as 200 strings of good-sized beads about the neck, hanging down the back and covering the neck up to the ears. Earrings were worn by both sexes; the women pierced the ears in many places along the rims, while the men enlarged the holes in their ears so they could thrust feathers through them. Silver, obtained from quarters and half-dollars, was made into ornaments and attached to belts, sashes, turbans, and dresses. Much beadwork was in evidence—strips of beading to decorate belts, pouches, pouch straps, dresses, and garters to bind the leggings occasionally worn.

The men wore the roach, with a fringe of hair across the forehead; at the sides one strip of hair was left to hang down in front of each ear. Later, they adopted white hair styles, but retained the lock before the ears. Women wore the hair in a knot, sometimes made into a cone at the back of the head, with ribbons tied into it, while the front was in "bangs."

The distinctive Seminole patchwork technique began in the mid-nineteenth century with the application of silk ribbons and braid sewn onto the full skirts of the period in bands of various widths. Probably in an effort to use all scraps of the expensive cloth, patchwork was resorted to, used with the braid and ribbons. By 1900, when hand-operated sewing machines became available to Seminole women, patchwork was used exclusively, and for entire garments. Today, predominantly for the tourist trade, garments are still made of patchwork, but prints or solid colors are used and often such fabrics as satin have come into use.

The Seminole Indians have preserved more of their costume heritage into the modern period (since 1930) than any other tribe of the Southeast. They have retained the typical garments made of strips of pieced cloth. The men wear shirts made in this manner, shirts with long full sleeves and a collar; this is all that is left of the warrior's dress. With the shirt they wear dark, nondescript trousers, often frayed at the bottom, and a straw hat or a turban made of a headscarf. The women wear the cape and skirt of pieced material, but a blouse is usually now worn under the cape or with the skirt alone. Only a few women wear the multitude of strands of beads; most are satisfied with one or two strings of "store" beads. However, the hair style is unique; the hair on the front of the head is combed forward, tied and fanned out over a cardboard frame and fastened in place, the frame tipped either to the right or the left. The back hair is covered with a net or cloth cap. Both sexes often go barefoot, although sometimes "store" shoes are worn.

Key Sources

Emerson, William Canfield. *The Seminoles.* New York: Exposition, 1954.

Fairbanks, Charles H. *Ethnohistorical Report on the Florida Indians.* New York: Garland, 1974.
Feder, Norman. "Seminole Patchwork." *American Indian Hobbyist* 6: 1–18.
MacCauley, Clay. "The Seminole Indians of Florida." Bureau of American Ethnology *Annual Reports* 5: 469–531.
McReynolds, Edwin C. *The Seminoles.* Norman: University of Oklahoma Press, 1957.
Sturtevant, William C. "Seminole Men's Clothing." In *Essays on the Verbal and Visual Arts.* Seattle: University of Washington Press, 1967.

Siouan

Siouan-speaking tribes dominated the coastal areas south of the coastal Algonquians, and were also in the Piedmont regions of the Carolinas and Virginia. Major groups were the Catawba, Cheraw, Saponi, and Tutelo. The Tuscarora, an Iroquoian group, were very similar in their dress.

Men's Basic Dress

Men wore the breechclout, said to be of a very soft deerskin, which they did not tan but rubbed hard between the hands and with fingernails that were grown long for that purpose. Leggings may have been worn for travel.

Women's Basic Dress

Women wore two garments: these were often fashioned of cloth made from Spanish moss, the inner bark of the mulberry tree, or the softened bark of the basswood tree. One garment was a wraparound skirt, the other a shawl fastened on one shoulder, leaving the right arm uncovered. Deerskin, when available, was worn by the wealthier people.

Footwear

The Siouan Indians of the Southeast usually went barefoot, but swamp moccasins were sometimes worn.

Outer Wear

Matchcoats, or mantles, were made of fur or feathers, and, when available, deerskin. The feather cloaks were made of turkey feathers or the green part of mallard heads, sewn together with deer sinew or strands of silk grass. Lawson mentions the use of panther skins for robes.

Hair Styles

The men rolled the hair up on each ear, or sometimes made a roll on the top of the head or at the temples. Another style was to cut the hair on one side of the head within an inch or two of the roots, leaving it standing upright. Women let their hair grow long and coiled it into a long roll at the back, which they tied with thongs or strings of beads. Both sexes used bear grease and red dye to enhance the hair; the red came from puccoon roots, brought from the mountains.

Headgear

The Southeastern Siouans generally did not wear headgear.

Accessories

Girdles were woven of opossum hair in a finger-weaving technique.

Jewelry

Copper ornaments were extremely popular. The Tuscarora made frequent western trips to obtain the metal; it was made into hair ornaments and earrings, and into beads that were strung into loops for adorning the wrists and upper arms.

Garment Decoration

To their garments woven of mulberry bark and their girdles of opossum hair, the Siouan women added fringes dyed red with puccoon root.

Face and Body Embellishment

Tattooing seems to have been ignored by the Siouans in favor of painting on the face, breasts, biceps and thighs. Commonly they would paint the face red, making a circle of black around one eye and a circle of white around the other. These colors came from lampblack, white clay, and cinnabar; the cinnabar was obtained from Cheraw territory. The Catawba, at one time the most powerful tribe in the Carolinas, were said to have flattened the heads of their infants, but this does not seem to have been common among the Siouans.

Transitional Dress

The Siouans were quick to adopt the trade cloth brought by the English, especially blue and red strouding, which was used to make fine breechcloths and skirts. Woolen mantles and shawls were also adopted. The men began to wear trousers, shirts, and coats, the women to wear the long, full, cotton dresses, and tribal distinctions in garments were quickly lost.

Key Sources

McGee, W. J. "The Siouan Indians: A Preliminary Sketch." Bureau of American Ethnology *Annual Reports* 15: 153–204.

Mooney, James. "The Siouan Tribes of the East." Bureau of American Ethnology *Bulletin* 99.

Speck, Frank G. "Siouan Tribes of the Carolinas as Known from Catawba, Tutelo, and Documentary Sources." *American Anthropologist* 37(2): 201–225.

Timucua

The Timucua, of the Muskhogean language stock, lived near the St. John River and present-day St. Augustine, Florida. They were a confederation of tribes forming one of the largest and most important groups in Florida encountered by the Spaniards. Ponce de Leon met them in 1513. In 1564 Jacques Le Moyne did many paintings of them; these were later made into engravings by Theodore de Bry for his 1590 history of America. Le Moyne was the earliest known European to paint the Indians of the continental United States. Hodge described the Timucuas as tall, well-made, almost entirely naked except for a breechclout, and spectacularly tattooed. They had entirely disappeared by 1736.

Men's Basic Dress

Men wore a characteristic breechclout of deerskin wrapped around the hips and passed through the crotch. This seems to be the southern edge of the use of deerskin in Florida. In some cases, a fringe of shells hung below the breechclout, and at times an animal pelt was suspended in the back as a tail.

Women's Basic Dress

Some women wore a wraparound skirt of painted deerskin, but the usual garment was of Spanish moss, draped around the hips, with the torso left bare. One painting by Le Moyne shows a woman wearing nothing but a fringe of moss or palmetto fronds fastened to a strip passing over one shoulder. One of the paintings shows women wearing only a girdle with shells suspended on cords to form a fringe, and with a purse-like affair hanging down in front to cover their genitals. Swanton mentions that Bishop Calderon was disturbed by such nudity and left them clothed in tree moss "from neck to feet."

Footwear

The Timucuas went barefoot at all times.

Outer Wear

There is much mention of feathers in connection with Florida Indians, but the Timucuas seem not to have used feather mantles to any extent. One painting by Le Moyne shows the chief Saturiba wearing a deerskin mantle so long that it requires a man to walk behind holding the mantle up so it will not drag on the ground; it is fastened with a knot on the shoulder.

Hair Styles

Men let the hair grow long and gathered it up into a topknot, into which feathers were fastened; during time of war, arrows were carried in this topknot. A fringe was left below it, all around the head. Out of the top was sometimes suspended an animal pelt or two. Women wore the hair long and loose or gathered at the back into a roll.

Headgear

Saturiba, chief of the Timucua, seems to have worn a crown of feathers. A headdress made of a stuffed eagle was a mark of honor indicating great war exploits. Some men wore a small stuffed animal as a hat. Pareja observed a palm-leaf hat worn by women.

Accessories

Belts are mentioned, some of leather painted red, some of leather with metal disks attached, probably of copper. Le Moyne says girdles were hung with little oval balls of gold, silver, or brass (presumably copper earlier), which made a tinkling sound. The only fans in the paintings seem to be large ones carried by men to cool the chief and his wives.

Jewelry

Since clothing was minimal, there was great emphasis placed on ornamentation. Women, especially, wore great quantities of pearls—in necklaces or in strings fastened around the wrists, ankles, or elbows; some wore strands of beads over one shoulder and under the opposite arm. Men also wore strands of beads below the knees, at the elbows, and around the wrists; another favorite ornament consisted of disks of shells or metal fastened onto leather strips and worn around ankles or knees. Men wore large gorgets (eight to ten inches in diameter) hung about the neck; some authorities think they may have been worn as armor as well as ornament. Earrings consisted of large balls, ear spools, or a bone or bird claw thrust through the ear. A unique ear ornament was a small fish bladder passed through the hole in a pierced ear; this bladder, when inflated, shone like a pearl and was often dyed red to appear like a ruby. No nose ornaments seem to have been worn by these people.

Armor

Besides the shell gorgets mentioned above as possibly being worn as protection for the chest, the Timucuas wore armor of some sort, probably sticks of cane fastened together with sinew, but the use of armor was quite rare in this area.

Garment Decoration

Some use of painted skins is mentioned although they were apparently rare and much treasured; a red leather belt is also recorded. Fringes seem to have been the only adornment, often with danglers (probably copper cones) or shells strung into the fringe. A mantle is mentioned as having been ornamented with "rushes of different colors."

Face and Body Embellishment

The Timucua were probably the most extensively tattooed of any tribe of American Indians, the chief men and their wives more so than others, so it was indicative of social status. Some chiefs had the entire body covered with tattoos from neck to ankles to wrists; these were in geometric patterns as well as suggestions of scrolls and flowers, but there were no representations of animals. Women's designs were different from the men's. Tattooing was accomplished by pricking the skin with a bone needle until the blood started flowing, then rubbing in certain substances for color. Swanton mentions indigo, which would give a pale blue, but the most common material for tattooing was lampblack.

Transitional Dress

The Spaniards were in control of Florida until it was ceded to Great Britain in 1763; the only influence in dress was the attempt on the part of the Spanish missionaries to make the natives cover their nakedness. However, there was little trading in cloth, such as by the English, so there was almost no change in Timucuan dress before the tribe died out.

Key Sources

Le Moyne, Jacques. *Narrative of Le Moyne, an Artist Who Accompanied the French Expedition to Florida under Laudonniere, 1564.* London, 1591.

Romans, Bernard. *A Concise Natural History of East and West Florida.* Vol. 1. New York, 1775.

Wenhold, Lucy L. "A 17th Century Letter of Gabriel Diaz Vara Calderon, Bishop of Cuba, Describing the Indians and Indian Missions of Florida." Smithsonian Institution *Miscellaneous Collections* 95.

Yuchi

The Yuchi or Ucheans (the name means "situated yonder") lived near the Chattahoochee and Savannah rivers in a loose confederacy with the Creeks; they did not mix with them but apparently adopted many of their customs. Although they were agriculturists, they were less sedentary than most of the neighboring tribes. De Soto heard of them in 1539 but the first white contact was in 1566. They seem to have disappeared from the records in the nineteenth century.

Men's Basic Dress

Men wore the fitted breechclout of deerskin, with the ends hanging down before and behind. Leggings of deerskin were worn in colder weather and when traveling.

Women's Basic Dress

Women wore the wraparound skirt, calf-length, made either of deerskin or of woven mulberry bark.

Footwear

Like most Southeastern Indians, the Yuchi went barefoot almost all of the time, but wore the typical swamp moccasin when traveling in the swamps and forests. These were of deer hide, although buffalo hide is also mentioned.

Outer Wear

Some mantles for both sexes were made of the material woven from the inner bark of the mulberry tree. Men wore deerskin cloaks or feather mantles; the latter were for important personages.

Hair Styles

Men wore the roach with a scalplock in the back and a fringe of hair along the forehead. Later they let it grow shoulder length and Speck mentions that it was cut by laying the tresses across a flat stone and sawing it off with a sharp-edged stone. Women wore their hair long and flowing or tied into a clump at the back.

Headgear

The Yuchi normally went bareheaded. Occasionally headbands were worn, created of finger-woven strips made of mulberry-bark fibers; feathers were often attached to these headbands, which were for ceremonial use and then worn only by men.

Accessories

The Yuchi were famous for their beautifully wrought belts, sashes, and garters, woven of mulberry-bark fibers or bison hair, and featuring designs of chevrons and zigzags. This fine craftsmanship was later shifted to beadwork and the use of woolen yarn. The Yuchi women also made shoulder pouches or bandolier bags worn by the men at the side. In these articles, representations of the sun, sky, or clouds were common; very often there was a realistic portrayal of a turtle, in imitation of a mythical being who used a turtle for a side pouch. Turkey-feather fans were carried and used by the older men and chiefs as a sign of leadership.

Jewelry

Woven neckbands were worn by the men, while the women tended more toward necklaces, especially of pearls. Hair ornaments were popular. Men lengthened the earlobes in order to insert pendants, clusters of beads, feathers, or such. The men wore shell gorgets, one or more, on the chest.

Garment Decoration

Beaded bands for shoulder bags, neckbands, leg bands, and hair ornaments worn by the men were made in a technique whereby the beads were strung on the weft during the process of weaving, producing the same design on both sides; woven sashes were also created in this manner. These featured realistic portrayals of moons, stars, crescents, and animals, especially turtles. In the twentieth century, women's garments were decorated with rows of silver brooches.

Face and Body Embellishment

Body paint, on the part of the men, was used to indicate status, to show whether one was a chief or belonged to the warrior society. The chief had both eyes surrounded with red, and there were horizontal bars of yellow and blue on the cheeks, as well as small spots of blue at the corners of the eyes. The warrior characteristically painted one-half of the face red, the other half black. Women sometimes used a spot of red paint on each cheek, said to indicate willingness to grant sexual favors. Tattooing seems to have been minimal, and no mention was made of skull deformation or of nose ornaments.

Transitional Dress

Swanton gives extensive information on the changeover of Yuchi dress to European costume. Men wore a bright-colored calico shirt and a long coat of deerskin, fringed and held in place with a colorful sash. The breechcloth was of stroud cloth, with flaps hanging in front and in the rear. Leggings, of deerskin or strouding, were attached to the hips and were gartered below the knees. Deerskin moccasins were worn. The men wore a ring similar to that of the Creek—of silver with a shield welded onto the ring proper. Turbans of wrapped cloth were held in place by a metal band; feathers were often attached to this headgear. Beadwork neck bands, beaded hair strips, earrings, bracelets, and armlets completed the costume, along with a beaded shoulder bag. Women wore printed or plain calico-cotton dresses, often embellished on the shoulders, breast, and lower part of the skirt with silver brooches. Short leggings, gartered at the knees and, at times, moccasins completed her garb. Earrings and bracelets of metal and beadwork were favored jewelry. Necklaces often featured large blue beads, said to have something to do with fertility. For festive occasions, a large, curved metal comb was worn in the hair, from which dangled many ribbons. Wide belts were decorated with beadwork.

Key Sources

Bauxar, J. Joseph. "Yuchi Ethnoarchaeology." *Ethnohistory* 4(3): 279–301; 4(4): 369–404.

Speck, Frank G. "Ethnology of the Yuchi Indians." University of Pennsylvania, University Museum *Anthropological Publications* 1(1).

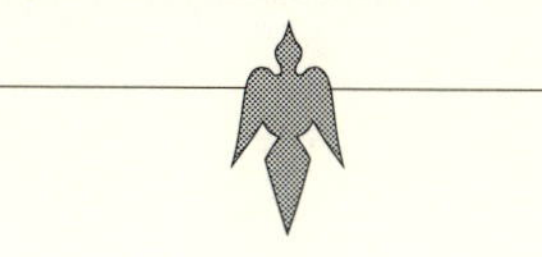

Chapter Two

Costume of the Northeast

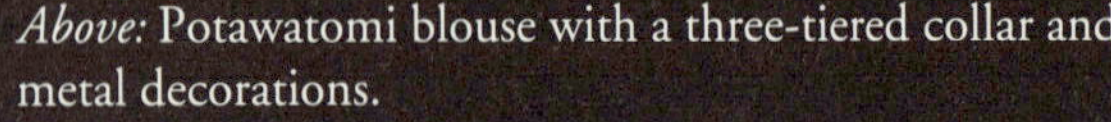

Above: Potawatomi blouse with a three-tiered collar and metal decorations.
Below, right: A Potawatomi man's cloth shirt with beaded panels.
Below: In this 1850s photograph, a Potawatomi boy poses shyly with his bow and arrows.

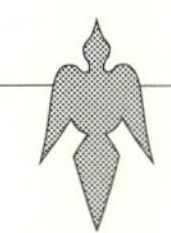

Above: A Delaware leather and cloth bag, above, with porcupine quillwork.
Left: The Potawatomi adapted traditional beading, quillwork, and other techniques to their nineteenth-century dress, with ribbonwork on their dresses.

Peoples of the Northeast

Abenaki (Western), p. 45
Cayuga
Chippewa, p. 47
Conestoga
Conoy
Delaware, p. 49
Erie
Esopus
Fox, p. 51
Huron, p. 53
Illinois
Iroquois, p. 55
Kahokia
Kaskaskia
Kickapoo
Mahican
Malecite
Mascouten
Massachusetts
Menomini, p. 58
Miami, p. 60
Michigami
Mohawk
Nanticoke
Narragansett
Neutral
Niantic
Nipmuck
Ojibwa (Southeast) p. 62
Oneida
Onondaga
Ottawa
Passamaquoddy
Penobscot, p. 65
Peoria
Pequot
Piankeshaw
Potawatomi, p. 67
Sauk, p. 70
Seneca
Shawnee, p. 75
Susquehannock
Tobacco (Petun)
Tuscarora
Wampanoag
Wappinger
Wenro
Wea
Winnebago

Northeast

The area encompassing the northeastern United States and southeastern Canada is a beautiful land with heavily forested rolling hills and rounded mountains, flat salt marshes of waving grass, surf-beaten beaches and rocky coves, tumbling brooks, broad rivers, calm lakes, and westward swelling prairies.

Paleo-Indians penetrated these woodlands around 10,000 B.C., their subsistence depending at least in part on the hunting of large Pleistocene mammals. The diversification of the Archaic period began about two millennia later, and was followed by the Woodland period, characterized by the development of agriculture and the adoption of pottery, beginning about 2000 B.C. and lasting to the time of European contact. Various regional cultures developed, such as the Adena and the Hopewell of the Ohio River valley.

European contact cannot be precisely dated. In the far Northeast there is evidence of the presence of Norsemen around A.D. 1000. There were many French and Basque fishermen working the rich waters of the Grand Banks off Newfoundland in the sixteenth century, but the extent to which they interacted with the native people is unclear. When the Europeans did come as colonists in the early seventeenth century, they generally took little interest in recording the Indian way of life; rather, they took what help they could get in colonizing, then pushed the "savages" westward. There are records made by Jesuit missionaries among the Iroquois, Algonquin, and other tribes in the seventeenth century, and we also have records from Cartier, Champlain, and La Salle in the sixteenth and seventeenth centuries. Some of the early colonists, such as Roger Williams, wrote fascinating accounts of the Indians; but by that time the native culture had been fundamentally changed by contact with the newcomers.

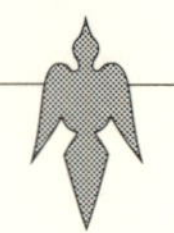

With European contact the Indians became accustomed to the use of European goods and they found themselves in the difficult position of having to engage in the fur trade in order to satisfy their needs and wants. With this reliance came the loss of their own tribal techniques of providing food, clothing, and shelter from the products of their own environment. The traders' use of whiskey in fur trading further corrupted the Indians' culture, and devastating epidemics disrupted the social fabric of Indian society. It was a situation that repeated itself, with variations, across the continent, but in the Northeast it happened early, quickly, and with incredible devastation.

The region divides into three general areas: (1) the Atlantic coast and New England with its Algonquian speakers; (2) the Lower Great Lakes (Ontario and Erie) dominated by the Iroquois-speaking tribes; (3) the Upper Great Lakes (Huron, Michigan, and Superior), also an Algonquian language area. Some Siouan languages were spoken in the west.

Deerskin predominated in the costume of the Northeastern Indians, for the white-tailed deer roamed freely through the forests and into the western prairies; moose were also fairly abundant, the hides made into heavier garments. This clothing was not tailored but made of simple pieces of skin, often created for convenience according to the shape of the hide itself and seamed where necessary. The short fringes along the seams and at the edges were characteristic of Woodland dress, for longer fringes would have caught in the underbrush.

In the Northeast today, many of the tribes have vanished, but a few remain and hold onto elements of their traditional culture. There are large contingents of Iroquois in New York State and Canada; Eastern Abenaki in Maine; and small groups in Pennsylvania, Maryland, and other states of the Eastern Seaboard; some groups are in Michigan and Wisconsin; and many have moved to Oklahoma.

General Dress

Men's Basic Dress

Men wore breechclouts of the fitted type with the flaps hanging down in front and in back. At times the kilt form was worn and sometimes the apron type with the front and back simply tied together, making a belt unnecessary. This breechclout was often decorated with quillwork or embroidery. Thigh-length leggings were snugly fitted; in summer knee-length leggings held in place by garters were common. These were not constructed in tubes but were flat pieces of skin tied at several points down the outside of the legs and usually ending in a fringe. For winter wear, leggings and moccasins were sometimes combined into one garment.

Women's Basic Dress

Women in early times wore a simple wraparound skirt, knee-length and held in place by a belt; it overlapped on the side, forming what Feder calls "the Algonkin split skirt." When the weather became cooler, a poncho-type upper garment was added, with a slit or hole for a neck opening. By the time of European contact the women were wearing a dress made from two skins that hung from the shoulders by means of straps and were seamed at the sides, the so-called "strap-and-sleeve dress"; to this was added, when needed or desired, separate sleeves that were fastened together at the back of the neck and caught together in front by a strip of buckskin that often continued around the waist. The sleeves were fastened at the wrists, but there were no underarm seams. These dresses were knee-length or longer depending on the size of the skin and the inclination of the wearer. Knee-length leggings were gartered and fitted to the ankles by means of ties or lacings.

Footwear

Moccasins (the word is from an Algonquian term) were of two general types. The first was a one-piece ankle-high style with a seam down the front of the foot and one up the back; a thong was attached so that the moccasin could be bound around the ankle for security, leaving the top up for warmth or turned down. The second was a three-piece style in which the moccasin sole was drawn up and puckered to fit an oval or U-shaped vamp over the instep; the third piece, a long rectangle, was either folded over to make a narrow tube through which a drawstring could be passed, then attached around the top of the moccasin, or the strip was left flat and used as a cuff. The oval insert and/or the cuffs could be embellished

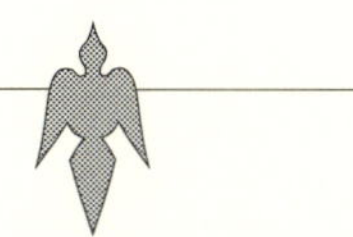

A Kickapoo man, photographed in 1907, wears a cloth shirt, leggings, and an elaborately beaded breechcloth. In addition to many strands of beads, he wears metal armbands and an otterskin turban. The metal plates across his chest are likely from the Southwest.

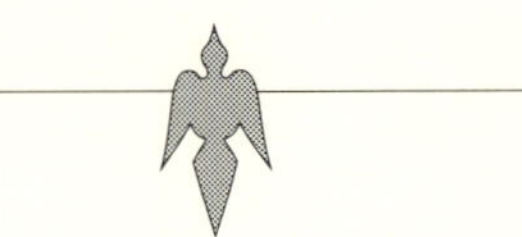

with quillwork or embroidery, or the moccasins could be left plain for everyday wear. A third form of footwear was the "hock boot," a clumsy affair made from a section of an animal's hind leg or hock, so there was a natural bend to the "boot." These were laced up the front and cattail fluff or deer hair was often stuffed into the boot for warmth. Snowshoes were necessary in winter to track the deer, moose, or caribou with speed and endurance. All were essentially the same—a frame of ash that was steamed and bent into shape and then laced with a webbing of rawhide strips.

Outer Wear

In the fall and spring deer-hide robes were worn; in the winter they were of beaver (the warmest), bearskin (the heaviest), or of many pelts of small animals sewn together. Rabbit-skin robes were usually made for the women and children.

Hair Styles

Women wore the hair long and flowing or in braids. For special occasions, the hair was "clubbed," that is, gathered into a large knot at the back resembling a beaver tail, then decorated with quillwork ornaments. Men sometimes wore two braids, but the most characteristic hair style, especially for warriors, was the "roach," often called a "Mohawk." To form a roach, the head was shaved except for a central ridge of hair cut short and left standing from the forehead to the nape; one long lock was left at the back—the scalplock—a prized possession, for one of the first things a warrior tried to do in battle was to cut off an enemy's scalplock. It was often tightly braided and decorated, it could hang loose, or it might be wrapped and made to stand upright, or it might be bound near the scalp and allowed to splay out over the top of the head like a small parasol. Artificial roaches were made of deer hair dyed red with the addition perhaps of the white hairs of a porcupine; this roach was held in place by a "roach spreader," usually of bone, which had a hole in it through which the scalplock could be drawn and the roach anchored securely in place. A single eagle feather was often worn at the rear, held in place by means of a swiveling socket, a part of the roach spreader. Both sexes dressed the hair daily with bear fat to keep it shining and smooth.

Headgear

Women wore nothing on their heads except for a fur cap or hood in bitter weather; however, in some areas we find both men and women wearing a woven headband to which feathers or other ornaments might be attached, although feathers were usually a male prerogative. Turkey, crane, and heron feathers were used as well as eagle. Sometimes the entire skin of a fox or an otter was tied around the head, the tail left flapping. Hunters wore animal skins on the body and antlers on the head in order to approach game more closely.

Accessories

Men, especially, wore pouches or bags that had one strap going over the shoulder; these were of deerskin decorated with quillwork or embroidery. Small bags made of basswood or other fibers often hung from the belt. Sashes in bright geometric patterns, an important item of trade, were woven of vegetal fibers mixed with moose and buffalo hair. Garters and tumplines were also woven.

Jewelry

A few beads were made of shell, rolled copper, bone, and wood, strung together into necklaces; other jewelry items were rings, bracelets, earrings, hair ornaments, gorgets (breast ornaments) of ground and polished slate, fossil crinoids, and, rarely, nose rings. Much wampum was used for ornamentation, a material highly characteristic of the Northeastern Indians; the word itself comes from "Wampanoag," a southern New England tribe. It was of two kinds:
(1) The white wampum came from the central column of whelks, quahogs, and other shells;
(2) The purple, much more valued, was obtained from quahog clams. The shell was laboriously formed into beads that were then woven into patterns to create belts, necklaces, bracelets, headbands, and caps. At first only chiefs were privileged to wear wampum, but slowly it evolved into different usages; belts, the most common form, were used as written records, as compensation for various crimes, as ransom for captives, as symbols for treaties, and as a form of accreditation for envoys of peace. It was not really money, as we use the term, until the fur trade boomed.

Armor

There is some evidence of rod armor having been used.

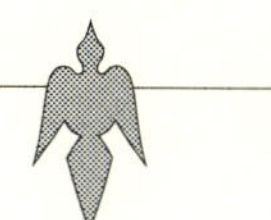

Special Costumes
Women cut the hair short for the mourning period and the flesh, especially on the arm, was often lacerated. Men painted the face black, but if in partial mourning, painted a black circle around each eye. A widow also painted the face black with charcoal, and was not to marry until the paint (mixed with resin and ashes) wore off.

Garment Decoration
Some finger-weaving was done with materials such as basswood and other bast fibers, nettle, buffalo wool, and opossum hair. Using a twining technique, these fibers were woven into bags, pouches, garters, sashes, and occcasionally kilts. The objects were decorated with porcupine quillwork and moose-hair embroidery. European glass beads were valued merchandise from the earliest postcontact times, especially blue and white ones. Floral beaded designs were characteristic, and were said to have originated from the embroidery of French nuns. Beading reached exuberant proportions by the end of the nineteenth century, when beadwork was almost solid on many items of dress.

Multihued silk ribbons brought by the traders were sewed onto garments in silk-applique style. The woman cut a mirror-image design from a ribbon of one color and sewed it onto a ribbon of a contrasting color; these strips were then applied to skirts, shawls, breechcloths, moccasins, and other cloth garments.

Face and Body Embellishment
Both sexes used fish oil and bear fat to keep the skin smooth and pleasant to the sight and touch. Both men and women used paint on the face and body, bright red often being applied to the forehead and cheeks.

Transitional Dress
Cloth, metal, and glass beads were European trade items that greatly influenced Indian costume in the Northeast. "Stroud cloth," which was widely traded, took its name from a small factory in England that specialized in making blankets; actually, the heavy cloth was used there as a blotter in soaking up the blanket dyes. The red, blue, or green fabric was made into breechcloths, dresses, lightweight blankets, and other articles of dress. Broadcloth and calico, both printed and plain, were sewn into dresses, skirts, blouses, leggings, and men's shirts. At first these garments were fashioned in the Indian style; later, European clothes were copied and finally the Indians purchased the ready-made clothes available.

Moccasins were the last items of native clothing to be abandoned, but by the end of the nineteenth century most Indians were wearing "store bought" shoes and the everyday clothes of the whites. The front-opening European coats were adopted, the military greatcoats being much sought after. Vests were worn, at first in a squarish style, later in the fitted European shape.

Metal was another popular item of trade. Women happily adopted the steel needles and scissors obtainable. Silver, in the form of coins, was made into brooches, often in the form of crucifixes and crosses after the French missionaries arrived. Round brooches, decorated and perforated with various designs, were used, often in great profusion, on women's blouses. Men wore silver armbands, head circlets, peace medals, and sometimes nose pendants.

Abenaki (Western)

The name *Abenaki* is a corruption of a Montagnais word meaning "dawn land people." The Eastern Abenaki lived in Maine along the coast and inland; the major tribe was the Penobscot (discussed later in this chapter). The Western Abenaki inhabited most of Vermont and New Hampshire and part of Quebec. Tribes were the Mississquoi, Winnepesaukee, Pennacook, Sokoki, Cowasuck, Winooski, and others. They were farmers, hunters, and fishermen. Because of their interior location, European contacts were few until the French missionaries arrived in the seventeenth century.

Men's Basic Dress
Men wore a breechclout with a long deerskin sash wrapped two or three times about the waist, knotted and tied with long fringed ends hanging down. A simple piece of lightweight buckskin was sometimes tied on one shoulder with the other arm exposed; separate sleeves, tied across the chest, could be added as needed. Thigh-length leggings were gartered below

the knees and featured short decorated strips or fringes at the bottom side seams; in winter the leggings were sometimes footed.

Women's Basic Dress
Women wore a wraparound skirt reaching below the knees with a tanned deerskin belt. Worn with these were knee-length leggings. In cooler weather, a simple piece of skin with a hole for the head was donned.

Footwear
Moccasins of tanned deerskin were the three-piece type, with one piece for the bottom and sides, another for a vamp over the instep, and a third for ankle flaps which could be worn up or down. Two characteristic styles were the "rabbitnose" and the "beavertail." Winter boots were made of the hock of the moose with the fur left on; inner moccasins or rabbit fur linings gave added warmth. Snowshoes were necessary for tracking animals in the deep snows of winter.

Outer Wear
A robe made of two panels of moosehide fastened at the shoulders was worn by both sexes in winter; these had sleeves to be added as needed. Winter robes, preferably of beaver pelts and often belted, were fastened in front with thongs so the arms could be left free.

Hair Styles
Both sexes usually wore the hair long and loose, sometimes secured by a headband with two feathers added at the back. Married men coiled the hair into a knot on the top of the head secured with thongs; women also sometimes braided the hair and coiled it on the crown.

Headgear
Usually the Abenaki went bareheaded, but the hunter might wear a conical hat of birchbark, useful for shedding rain, or a cap made of the skin of a buck's head with the antlers attached, enabling him to get closer to his prey. Another style of cap was that made from a moose's shoulder hump, the long hairs forming a natural crest; at the back might be worn a feather or two, but no more. Both sexes wore a skin or fur hood in winter, often with a feather at the point; men's hoods were longer, covering the upper shoulder.

Accessories
Customarily a knife in a sheaf was worn suspended about the neck. Pouches hung from the warrior's belt, including one made of two clamshells that contained smoldering punk for a fire. Garters, pouches, and belts were necessary items.

Jewelry
Pendants were made of polished slate and some were set with garnets found locally. Necklaces were made of beads of shell and small tubes of rolled copper. Slate gorgets had one or two holes for suspending about the neck; some were rectangular, some diamond-shaped, others circular. Hair ornaments of shell, slate, or copper were popular.

Garment Decoration
Garments and accessories were embellished with paint (ocher), porcupine quillwork, or moose-hair embroidery; early designs were geometric, later curvilinear in a modified floral style.

Face and Body Embellishment
There is no evidence that these Indians practiced skull deformation or decorated their bodies with tattooing. They were fond of red ocher, which was used particularly in their funeral rites, but do not seem to have used it to any extent for face and body painting.

Transitional Dress
Already by the eighteenth century these Indians had acquired European ways of dress; they used stroud cloth and commercial cloth for dresses and other garments, wool blankets in place of fur robes, and European-style shirts or tunics for the men. Garments of wool or cotton were much more comfortable than deerskin in the moist climate. However, even in the mid-eighteenth century, some of the older Abenaki dressed in the traditional style.

Key Sources
Calloway, Colin G. *The Western Abenakis of Vermont: 1600–1800.* Norman: University of Oklahoma Press.

Charland, Thomas M. *Histoire des Abenakis d'Odanak (1675–1937).* Montreal: Editions du Levrier, 1964.

Crockett, Walter H. *The Green Mountain State.* 4 vols. New York: Century History, 1921.

Daniels, Thomas E. *Vermont Indians.* Poultney, VT: Journal Press, 1963.

Day, Gordon M. "Western Abenaki." In *Handbook of North American Indians. Vol. 15: Northeast.* Pp. 148–159. Washington: Smithsonian Institution.

Haviland, William A. and Marjory W. Power. *The Original Vermonters: Native Inhabitants, Past and Present.* Hanover, NH: University Press of New England, 1981.

Mauralt, J. A. *Histoire des Abenakis depuis 1605 jusqu'a nos jours.* Quebec, 1866.

Chippewa

The Chippewa were, and are, one of the largest and most important Algonquian tribes of the upper Great Lakes. The name means "people of the puckered moccasin" or "to roast till puckered up," referring to the manner in which they made their moccasins; they were also called the Mississauga. *Chippewa* is *Ojibway* (Ojibwa) in the Indian language and there has been some confusion between the two terms; often used interchangeably, the term *Ojibway* is preferred in Canada and the term *Chippewa* in the United States. Living in small, scattered bands in northern Michigan and Wisconsin, they hunted, trapped (especially beavers), fished, and gathered (particularly wild rice). With their neighbors, the Ottawa and the Potawatomi, they formed a loose confederacy called "The Three Fires" by the whites. The Chippewa drove the Sioux from the Great Lakes area and fought vigorously with the Sauk/Fox. Their first contact with whites seems to have been in 1634, when they met Jean Nicollet at Sault Ste. Marie. They have been well described by painters. James Otto Lewis traveled among them in 1820, producing paintings for his portfolio of Indian portraits in 1835. Charles Bird King, during the 1830s, copied Lewis's work and painted those chiefs who traveled to Washington to see the Great White Father. In the mid-1830s George Catlin sketched and painted them and Johann Baptist Wengler did watercolors of them in 1851.

Men's Basic Dress

The Chippewa men wore the breechclout (the *auzeum)* with rather long flaps in front and back; some wore a kiltlike garment fringed at the bottom. Close-fitting leggings were worn to above the knees and gartered below the knees, or were thigh-length and tied with thongs or straps to a belt. In cooler weather a buckskin poncho was added.

Women's Basic Dress

Women wore the strap-and-sleeve dress, two pieces of skin fastened at the shoulders, with or without a belt; sleeves, when worn, were tied on at the back and across the chest. Under this was worn an underskirt in a tube form made of woven nettle fibers. Knee-length buckskin leggings were wider than those of the men.

Footwear

Early soft-soled Chippewa moccasins were well-fitted with a puckered seam running up the front and a plain seam in the back. Later, the moccasin with a vamp was adopted, with the skin puckered into the vamp and a seam from toe to vamp. Cuffs on both styles could be worn up and fastened around the ankle with thongs or folded down. Rabbit or muskrat fur was used to line the moccasins in winter. Men liked to attach a foxtail, which would be allowed to trail behind. Vamps and cuffs were decorated with quillwork or moose-hair embroidery in floral patterns. Snowshoes were made in the usual manner—a strip of ash steamed and bent into shape with a netting of deer- or moose-hide strips. Round or "bearpaw" snowshoes were for women and children; the tailed type worn by the men had a characteristic Chippewa flattened front instead of a curve.

Outer Wear

Some Plains influence could be seen in the use of buffalo robes with the hair and tail left on, often painted in geometric designs. Cloaks of deerskin or of fur were draped over both shoulders and fastened in front with ties.

Hair Styles

Catlin has given us a sketch of many variations in hair styles among the Chippewa. Men tended to wear the hair loose, in different lengths, occasionally braided in two large braids with a scalplock at the back, or in a small braid at each side along with loose hair, also with a scalplock at the back. Warriors liked to stiffen this lock with material so it stood up straight for several inches. Women wore the hair loose or in two braids to which were often added brightly dyed strips of deerskin or other ornamentation.

Headgear
Headgear had the flavor of the Woodlands as well as the Plains; occasionally the horned headdress of the Sioux warrior could be seen. The roach was reserved for battle attire. A headband of strap leather was decorated with feathers—eagle, woodpecker, quail, pheasant, or drake feathers. A man who had scalped an enemy could wear two feathers; one who had captured a wounded prisoner wore five.

Accessories
The medicine bags of the Midewiwin society were proudly displayed by the members of that society; usually made of an otter or beaver pelt, they were embellished with quillwork on the paws and tail and contained "medicine" articles sacred to the wearer. Weaving was done for garters, sashes, shoulder bags, and pouches. Belts were of leather or strips of fur. Leather mittens, often decorated with quillwork or embroidery, were necessary winter wear. Feather fans were carried by the men.

Jewelry
Ornaments were typical of Woodland culture. Gorgets were of polished slate or shell with two holes drilled for suspension by a thong. Beads for necklaces were made of thin pieces of copper rolled into small tubes, of shell, of sections of fossilized crinoids, or of bird claws. The ears were pierced and ear spools, often of copper, were fastened in place; some ears were decorated with hanging clusters of beads. Rarely, nose rings were attached through the septum. Fur anklets were proud items of adornment, as well as sashes of eagle feathers stylishly slung over one shoulder.

Armor
For warfare, the Chippewa had large rawhide shields and made some use of slatted wooden armor of the rod-and-slat type.

Special Costumes
When a person died, the body was washed and dressed in its finest clothing and ornaments; the hair was carefully braided and a brown spot with a red line through it was painted on each cheek. A widow selected a wardrobe from the deceased, made it up into a bundle, and carried it with her at all times, treating it with great respect as if it were her husband. After a mourning period of one year she was free to remarry.

Garment Decoration
Both sexes liked to wear dark garments, the tanned leather often dyed with black walnuts; decorative embellishments, such as quillwork or beadwork, were made in lighter colors. When cloth became available, the Chippewa still preferred the darker colors. Bags and sashes were finger-woven of twisted nettle fibers or buffalo hair in a twining technique.

Face and Body Embellishment
Face and body painting was popular among the Chippewa, but was usually reserved for warfare and special occasions; typical colors were red, black, green, and yellow. At times green spots were painted in an arc across the face.

Transitional Dress
Hudson's Bay blankets with their broad colored stripes on white became popular items of wear. Cloth dresses for women became common, usually with a skirt to the mid-calf in length; cloth leggings or pantaloons replaced the deerskin variety. "Tinklers," (small tin cones often made of snuff can covers), brass bells, and silver brooches were attached to dresses in rows. The women adopted shawls, usually heavily fringed. Men wore the coats, shirts, and trousers of the white men, adding such Indian wear as breechcloths, now in an apron form, front and rear, and heavily beaded; vests, at first square, later fitted, also heavily beaded; headbands with feathers; and beaded bandolier bags. Turbans were of cloth wound about the head or of fur, both types sporting feathers. A black neckerchief was frequently worn. Silver was used extensively for armbands, crescent-shaped gorgets, and headbands. Ribbonwork was used rarely by the Chippewa, and never developed into the rich art form of other Great Lakes tribes. But beadwork

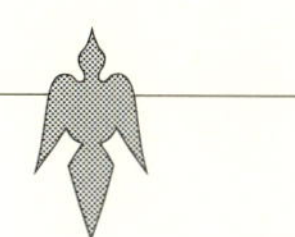

was adopted and used exuberantly by these people; diamond designs or stylized foliage shapes were the favored forms. The heavily beaded costumes, rich with feathers, are worn now at the powwows and other tourist attractions, as well as at native rites.

Key Sources

Brill, Charles. *Indian and Free: A Contemporary Portrait of Life on a Chippewa Reservation.* Minneapolis: University of Minnesota Press, 1971.

Coleman, Sister Bernard. *Decorative Designs of the Ojibwa.* Washington: Catholic University of America, 1947.

Copway, G. *The Traditional History and Characteristic Sketches of the Ojibway Nation.* Toronto: Coles Publishing Company, 1972. Originally published in London, England, in 1850.

Densmore, Frances. *Chippewa Customs.* St. Paul: Minnesota Historical Society Press, 1979. Reprint of 1911 edition.

Hickerson, Harold. *The Chippewa and Their Neighbors: A Study in Ethnohistory.* New York: Holt, Rinehart & Winston, 1970.

Hoffman, Walter J. "The Midewiwin or Grand Medicine Society of the Ojibwa." Bureau of American Ethnology *Annual Reports* 7: 143–300.

Kohl, Johann Georg. *Kitchi-Gami: Life among the Lake Superior Ojibwa.* St. Paul: Minnesota Historical Society Press, 1985.

Landes, Ruth. "The Ojibwa Woman." Columbia University *Contributions to Anthropology* 29.

Lyford, Carrie A. *Ojibwa Crafts.* Stevens Point, WI: Schneider, 1982. Reprint of 1943 edition.

Pohrt, Richard A. "19th Century Michigan Chippewa Costume." *American Indian Art Magazine* (Summer 1986): 44–53.

Ritzenthaler, Robert E. "Southwestern Chippewa." In *Handbook of North American Indians. Vol. 15: Northeast.* Pp. 743–759. Washington: Smithsonian Institution.

Tanner, Helen (Hornbeck)."The Chippewa of Eastern Lower Michigan [1965]." In *Chippewa Indians.* Pp. 347–374. New York: Garland, 1974.

Taylor, Lolita. *Ojibwa: The Wild Rice People.* Native American Contributions to Progress, Wisconsin. Indianhead, VT, 1976.

Delaware

The tribes of the mid-Atlantic coast were dominated by the Delaware, a close-knit federation of many Algonquian-speaking peoples, including the Munsee, Conoy, Esopus, Nanticoke, and other tribes, living along the length of the Delaware River and adjacent areas in New Jersey, New York, Delaware, and Pennsylvania. They referred to themselves as "Lenni Lenape," the "real men," but were called Delaware by the English because of the river. They signed a treaty with William Penn in 1682, a meeting immortalized in the famous painting by Benjamin West. Other painters, notably Gustav Hesselius, also portrayed them during the colonial period.

Men's Basic Dress

Men wore the tanned deerskin breechclout with the flaps hanging front and back. Thigh-length leggings, also of deerskin, were fastened at the sides with thongs and were gartered just below the knees.

Women's Basic Dress

Most of the time the women wore only a kilt-type skirt of skin, knee-length, wrapped around the hips and held in place by means of a belt; some skirts were made of cloth woven of Indian hemp. Knee-length leggings were added when the weather was cooler.

Footwear

Moccasins were simple one-piece affairs of tanned moose or deer hide with a seam at the back and up the front. Cuff flaps were large, almost brushing the ground. Temporary moccasins of cornhusks have been reported. In winter snowshoes were necessary for travel in the mountains.

Outer Wear

Tanned deerskin cloaks, called "matchcoats," were worn by both sexes; these were untailored pieces of skin fastened at the neck, leaving the arms free. Sometimes these mantles were draped over one shoulder and belted. Typical decoration consisted of concentric circles or spirals of shell beads. Winter robes were of bear, wildcat, beaver, wolf, raccoon, or other furs sewed together. Waterproof cloaks of turkey feathers were cherished, fashioned by tying the feathers into a netting made of hemp.

Hair Styles
Earlier, men had shaved the heads, leaving only a scalplock hanging behind; or they left standing a brush of stiff hair two to three inches long from the forehead to the nape, with a scalplock hanging from the crown. Later they wore two braids, along with the scalplock to which feathers were attached. At times the hair was worn loose with a wampum-decorated headband to confine it, or was gathered at the back like a ponytail. Women wore the hair in braids behind (some say four braids) or "clubbed" it into a bundle, which was then covered with a pouch also decorated with wampum or made elegant with hourglass-shaped ornaments beautified with quillwork. Both sexes smoothed the hair with applications of animal grease (such as bear or raccoon) or marrow.

Headgear
Headbands were strips of deerskin decorated with wampum, often with a feather or two attached at the back; headbands might also be of snakeskins. At times a square cap was worn, covered with patterned wampum. Chiefs might wear a crown of upstanding turkey feathers, dyed red. A young girl, after her menarche, wore a special headdress that partially covered her face, indicating to the tribe that she was now of marriageable age.

Accessories
Finger-woven belts, garters, sashes, and bags were important accessories. Belts of snakeskin were mentioned as being decorated with whale fins and whale bones. Knives were carried in a sheath suspended at the neck for quick availability. Pouches to carry tobacco and other needs were often made of the entire pelt of a small animal such as squirrel or rabbit.

Jewelry
For earrings the earlobe was often cut so a large loop was formed, into which were fastened feathers, copper ornaments, or strings of wampum. Even as late as 1859 nose rings or other ornaments were worn, but they were uncommon. Bird wings and claws, animal teeth, copper beads, wampum, and other shells were strung into necklaces and bracelets. Ruffs of down encircled the neck. A Conoy chief often wore a fish-shaped copper ornament on the forehead.

Armor
Warriors wore a wooden helmet for warfare, carried a wooden war club on a thong, and had large rectangular shields made of moose hide or of wood, covering the body to the shoulder.

A Delaware leather and cloth pouch made in the early 1800s, outlined with beads, combines traditional porcupine quillwork and tin tinklers.

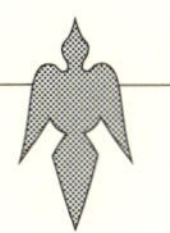

Special Costumes
Special attire was worn by warriors when going into battle—certain designs for face painting, headbands of snakeskin or red turkey feathers, and fox or wolf tails attached to the head so they stood upright.

Garment Decoration
Wampum designs adorned shoulder bags, belts, garters, and cross belts; if not decorated with wampum, they were enhanced with quillwork or moose-hair embroidery in floral symmetrical designs, stylized rather than realistic. Simple finger-weaving was done in diagonal or chevron designs. Finger-weaving also produced the netted bases for the feather cloaks.

Face and Body Embellishment
Tattooing of the face and body, especially of the men, continued even into the twentieth century; animal figures were favored. Face painting was common. Men preferred geometric or animal designs; women rouged the cheeks with red in a small circle, and reddened the ear rims and eyelids. Both sexes painted the part of the hair red for special occasions. Black paint was made from charcoal or graphite fragments, and red from earth ocher, bloodroot, or berry juices; white and yellow clays were also used. Relatives of the dead painted their own faces black at the time of interment.

Transitional Dress
Because European contact had come so early and in such numbers, the Delaware adopted European fashions beginning as early as 1650. As elsewhere, quillwork and the use of buckskin declined, replaced by beadwork and cloth. Men favored the cloth shirt, worn loose and hanging to the knees. Women wore wraparound skirts of stroud cloth, then began to adopt the full-skirted nineteenth-century fashions, made of trade cloth and featuring yokes, ruffles, buttoned-up fitted bodices, and fitted sleeves. German or coin silver brooches, headbands, armbands, and gorgets of a crescent shape were all popular. Little remained of the past except the braided hair and moccasins, and even the latter were slowly replaced by "store bought" shoes.

Key Sources

Feest, Christian F. "Nanticoke and Neighboring Tribes." *Handbook of North American Indians. Vol. 15: Northeast.* Pp. 240–252. Washington: Smithsonian Institution.

Goddard, Ives. "The Delaware." *Handbook of North American Indians. Vol. 15: Northeast.* Pp. 213–239. Washington: Smithsonian Institution.

Gowing, Clara. "Life among the Delaware Indians." Kansas State Historical Society *Collections* 12: 183–193.

Harrington, Mark R. "A Preliminary Sketch of Lenape Culture." *American Anthropologist* 15(2): 208–235.

Howard, James H. "Ceremonial Dress of the Delaware Man." Archaeological Society of New Jersey *Bulletin* 33.

Kinietz, W. Vernon. "Delaware Culture Chronology." Indiana Historical Society *Prehistory Research Series* 3(1): 1–143.

Myers, Albert C., ed. *William Penn: His Own Account of the Lenni Lenape or Delaware Indians, 1683.* Moylan, PA: A. C. Myers, 1937.

Newcomb, William W., Jr. "The Culture and Acculturation of the Delaware Indians." University of Michigan, Museum of Anthropology *Anthropological Papers* 10.

Speck, Frank G. "The Nanticoke Community of Delaware." Museum of the American Indian *Contributions* 2(4).

Stewart, Ty. "Oklahoma Delaware Women's Dance Clothing." *American Indian Crafts and Culture* 7(6): 4–22.

Weslager, C. A. *The Delaware Indians: A History.* New Brunswick, NJ: Rutgers University Press, 1972.

Fox

The Fox were usually treated with the Sauk as one tribe (especially by the United States government), although they spoke different dialects of the Algonquian language and were actually two separate groups. The two peoples seem to have had a common descent from the Chippewa and were united from about 1735 to 1804, at which time they split, then came together again from 1832 to 1852. The Fox called themselves the "red earth people," because of the kind of earth from which they believed themselves to have been created. They were sometimes referred to as the

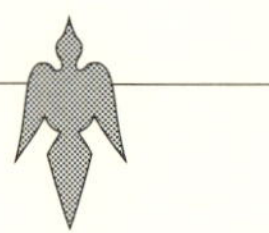

Musquakie, and Father Hennepin in 1680 referred to them as the Outagamis, a Chippewa word meaning "people of the other shore." They have retained much of their traditional culture into the twentieth century.

Originating around the Upper Great Lakes, they lived in Michigan, Wisconsin, then Illinois, where they began to adopt elements of the horse/buffalo Plains culture. They were involved in the fur trade, did some fishing, agriculture, and surface mining of lead ore. Several painters portrayed the Fox: James Otto Lewis at Prairie du Chien in 1825; George Catlin and Karl Bodmer in the 1830s; and Charles Bird King in Washington in 1837.

Men's Basic Dress

In the summer the men wore moccasins and a breechcloth, adding in winter thigh-length leggings and a shirt, all of tanned deer or elk skin. Leggings were fairly fitted, with fringes at the sides starting below the knees and with a large pointed flap in front almost obscuring the moccasins. Seamed up the front, these leggings were gartered (sometimes with fur bands), with flaps or thongs hanging from the garters.

Women's Basic Dress

Anciently, women wore a simple wraparound skirt of tanned deer or elk skin, secured with a belt or thongs. A poncho-type shirt might be added for warmth. Knee-length leggings were gartered just below the knees with woven strips. These items of clothing were of deer or elk skin.

Footwear

Moccasins were the one-piece soft-soled type with a seam up the front from toe to instep, often covered with a strip of quillwork. There were very large decorated flaps or cuffs on the moccasins (unless the legging flaps were large); women's moccasins had much smaller flaps.

Outer Wear

Lightweight robes were of deer or elk skin. Buffalo robes were donned in winter, the fur left on and the inner side tanned and painted in the Plains manner.

Hair Styles

Warriors flaunted the roach, shaving the head except for a tuft from front to back or side to side, leaving only the scalplock at the back. Later roaches were of deer hair dyed red and fastened to the scalplock by means of a bone roach spreader; often a single feather was attached to the roach. Some men shaved the head leaving merely a tuft at the crown; others left a long lock in front of each ear. According to Catlin, Pashapohaw, "the Stabber," wore long untrimmed locks "to indicate unsatisfied revenge." Women generally wore the hair long, gathered at the neck in back and adorned with a "hair binder" of a square or hourglass shape richly ornamented with quillwork. Sauk/Fox men were divided into two groups: (1) the Oshkosh or Braves, whose particular color was red and who customarily wore the roach; (2) the Kishquakis or the Long Hairs, whose color was blue and who wore the hair long.

Headgear

The most common headgear for men was the otter-fur turban made of a single pelt, with the tail extending out at the side or down the back, usually with a large circular ornament affixed to it. Some men wrapped a long sash around the head in a turban manner. Kishkekosh, a Fox chief, was painted in 1837 wearing a buffalo-horned headdress that he had taken from a Sioux warrior in battle.

Accessories

Long sashes were wrapped several times about the waist with the long fringed ends hanging at the side, or in a bandolier fashion over one shoulder. Other accessories were those common to Prairie tribes—the medicine bag of the Midewiwin society, fans of hawk or eagle feathers, and pouches enhanced with colorful quillwork.

Jewelry

Jewelry was a matter of prestige as well as ornamentation. Grizzly bear–claw necklaces were highly prized; often these had been taken off an adversary in battle and were passed down from one generation to the next. Both sexes pierced the ear lobes, which were then distended and adorned with rings, hoops, clusters of beads, tufts of down, and feathers. Rarely, nose rings were worn. Bracelets and necklaces were popular.

Special Costumes

Death was a highly ritualized event with a mourning period of six months to a year. The grieving person

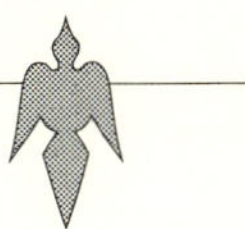

blackened the face with charcoal, abstained from the use of vermilion paint or dress ornaments, and was expected to show sorrow by exhibiting an unkempt appearance and shabby clothing; moccasins were required to be worn during the entire mourning period.

Garment Decoration

Women wove long sashes of buffalo hair and plant fibers in a twining technique, featuring designs of arrows, zigzags, and chevrons. Garments were frequently painted in various bright hues in solid colors, in stripes, or with figures and designs. Quillwork, with its typical geometric designs, was the traditional form of decoration; when beads came in, the Fox added extensively to the decoration until garments were virtually encrusted with beadwork, at first in geometric style, later floral. With the silk ribbons brought by the traders, the women made beautiful ribbonwork, applying it to dresses, shawls, leggings, and moccasins.

Face and Body Embellishment

Body painting was a favored form of decoration, especially if the colors were red and black. There is an early (1729) painting of Fox chiefs in a boat with their faces painted blue. Nesouaquoit, in a painting in the McKenney-Hall collection, looks ferocious with yellow, red, and black stripes on the lower half of his face. Hands painted on the body were indicative of foes killed in battle. Both sexes painted the face red on achieving adulthood. For special occasions, women painted the center part of the hair red.

Masks

Masks were seldom used by the Fox, but they donned a mask of fur, leather, hair, bone, and horn for the Crawling Around Man Dance.

Transitional Dress

The Fox quickly adopted European goods, especially cloth. The men continued to wear the otter-fur turbans, now with beadwork on the tails, grizzly bear–claw necklaces, beaded bandolier bags, beaded breechcloths, garters, leggings, and moccasins. In the early nineteenth century women were wearing cloth dresses in the European style. Metal ornaments became popular—silver armbands, earrings, peace medals, gorgets, brooches, and brass or tin tinklers.

Key Sources

Callender, Charles. "Fox." In *Handbook of North American Indians. Vol. 15: Northeast.* Pp. 636–647. Washington: Smithsonian Institution.

Forsyth, Thomas. "An Account of the Manners and Customs of the Sauk and Fox Nations of Indian Traditions." In *The Indian Tribes of the Upper Mississippi Valley and Region of the Great Lakes.* Vol. 2. Emma H. Blair, ed. Cleveland, OH: Arthur H. Clark, 1912.

Gearing, Frederick O. *The Face of the Fox.* Chicago: Aldine, 1970.

Hagen, William T. *The Sac and Fox Indians.* Norman: University of Oklahoma Press, 1958.

Jones, William. "Ethnography of the Fox Indians." Bureau of American Ethnology *Bulletin* 125.

Michelson, Truman. "Contributions to Fox Ethnology." Bureau of American Ethnology *Bulletin* 85, 95.

———. "Fox Miscellany." Bureau of American Ethnology *Bulletin* 114.

Huron

The Huron were the largest tribe of the northern Iroquois. Living on the east side of Lake Huron, between Georgian Bay and Lake Simcoe, they were the great traders of the north country. From the Subarctic peoples to the north they obtained winter clothing, beautifully tailored. From the tribes west of Sault Ste. Marie they bought buffalo skins, robes, and native copper. From the Neutral Indians to the south they acquired black squirrel skins that they made into robes, which were in turn traded to the Algonquians as prized items. As their own hunting became less productive, the Huron turned more and more to trade, getting furs and skins from others, which they made into snowshoes, moccasins, mittens, and fur caps; these were in turn bartered for European goods. Although extensive traders, they were basically sedentary farmers, gatherers, and fishermen. The origin of their name is open to question; some say that the roach or bristle of hair they wore reminded the French of a *hure,* or wild boar, while others say the name came from a French word meaning "ruffian" or "unkempt person." The Huron formed a loose confederacy—the Wyandot, including such peoples as the Erie, the Neutral (so-called because they refused to become embroiled in the long-standing Huron-Iroquois feud), the Tobacco Indians or Petun, and other smaller groups. Bitter enemies of the Iroquois, the Huron were attacked by them and almost annihilated; the survivors scattered widely, some to Michigan, later Oklahoma, and some to Quebec where they became known as the Lorette Huron.

Men's Basic Dress

Men wore a fitted breechclout with flaps to the mid-thigh hanging in front and back. Thigh-length leggings were tied to a belt with thongs. In cooler weather a piece of skin with an opening for the head was worn, or a sleeveless tunic was made of two skins fastened on the shoulders and at the sides; detached sleeves could be secured with a cord tied at the back and in front.

Women's Basic Dress

In early times, the Huron women wore fringed wraparound skirts, mid-calf in length, leaving the breasts bare, adding in fall and spring a poncho-like garment and gartered knee-length leggings of deerskin. At the time of contact they were wearing the strap-and-sleeve dress made of two deerskins held in place by shoulder straps; detachable sleeves could be added as desired, fastened with ties.

Footwear

The Huron moccasins were soft-soled, carefully puckered into the vamp in a style called "bullnose," or else with a seam from toe to instep that was covered with a decorative strip. Like others of the Iroquois family, they preferred buckskin that had been dyed black with their native black walnuts. Many favored a combination of quillwork and dyed moose-hair embroidery on the vamps and cuffs. In the heavy winter snows they wore snowshoes.

Outer Wear

Lightweight mantles were of deerskin, while winter robes were of black squirrel, bear, or beaver, secured at the front with thongs.

Hair Styles

Both sexes groomed the hair carefully, oiling, combing, and arranging it. The women usually wore it gathered into a single tress or braid that hung down the back, often wrapping it with fur or an eel-skin strip or tying it with thongs. Men wore the hair in a variety of styles; some had the roach, some shaved only half of the head, allowing the hair to hang free on the other side, while some wore the hair loose and at a natural length. Perhaps the most distinctive male Huron fashion was the wearing of the hair in two large rolls above the ears with the rest of the head shaved. Often a tuft of hair was left at the crown, along with the scalplock.

Headgear

A thong or cord was worn around the head by both sexes. A unique form of headdress was the feathered cap worn by the chiefs, with an embroidered headband rising to a peak at the front, which proclaimed the wearer the leader of the village. Although there was no mention of the fact, probably some sort of fur hood was worn during the winter.

Accessories

Pouches of black-dyed deerskin containing tobacco, charms, materials for fire-making, or other items were suspended at the back. Other pouches or bags and knife sheaths hung from the belt. Sashes, belts, scarves, and bracelets were finger-woven in a twining technique.

Jewelry

Women wore many strings of necklaces—around their necks and waists, around the arms and ankles,

A Huron embroidered a floral motif with moose hair on this late-nineteenth-century bullnose moccasin. Made in three pieces with a slightly puckered toe, it has a large vamp and flat cuffs.

and draped in festoons on the skirt fronts. Beads for these necklaces were fashioned of bird bones, red slate, small chunks of native copper, shells, stones, and pieces of turtle shells. Long beads were carved out of red slate in the forms of turtles and other animals. At celebrations a woman might wear as many as ten pounds of beads.

Armor

The Huron warriors wore suits of wooden slats laced together with thongs. They carried shields of cedar bark that covered the entire body, or used smaller shields made of rawhide. Around the head they wore a circlet of red moose hair and their legs were encased in fitted leather leggings. It was said that they wore their finest ornaments into battle so that if they were pursued, they could throw them off to divert the enemy's attention.

Garment Decoration

The Huron women gathered Indian hemp from which they made fibers used in a twining technique to construct bags, sashes, belts, and other items. Garments and moccasins were decorated with bands of quillwork or moose-hair embroidery in red and brown hues. Some garments were painted and had long fringes attached. Both quillwork and moose-hair embroidery were superseded by beadwork, but the typical floral designs of the Northeast were retained.

Face and Body Embellishment

Both sexes greased their bodies with animal fat as protection against cold, insects, and the sun. For special occasions most of the men painted their faces and bodies with geometric designs or representations of animals or humans. The principal colors were black (from soot), red (from red ocher and bloodroot), green, and violet; pigments were mixed with bear fat or sunflower oil for ease in application. Few men were tattooed; women were neither painted nor tattooed.

Transitional Dress

The usual European materials and fashions were adopted, earlier in the case of the Huron because of their extensive trading. Cloth and blankets (especially the Hudson's Bay Company blankets) replaced the tanned deerskin and fur robes of aboriginal times. By the mid-nineteenth century, the Huron were so scattered and so assimilated into other groups that all tribal distinctions in dress and decoration were lost.

Key Sources

Gringhuis, Dirk. "Indian Costume at Mackinac: Seventeenth and Eighteenth Century." *Mackinac History* 2(1).

Heidenreich Conrad E. "Huron." In *Handbook of North American Indians. Vol. 15: Northeast.* Pp. 368–388. Washington: Smithsonian Institution.

———. *Huronia: A History and Geography of the Huron Indians: 1600–1650.* Toronto: McClelland and Stewart, 1971.

Jenness, Diamond. *The Indians of Canada.* Toronto: University of Toronto Press, 1977. Reprint of 1932 edition.

Speck, Frank G. "Huron Moose Hair Embroidery." *American Anthropologist* 13(1): 1–14.

———. "Notes on the Material Culture of the Huron." *American Anthropologist* 13(2): 208–228.

Tooker, Elisabeth. "An Ethnography of the Huron Indians: 1615–1649." Bureau of American Ethnology *Bulletin* 190.

Trigger, Bruce G. *The Children of Aataentsic: A History of the Huron People to 1660.* 2 vols. Montreal: McGill-Queen's University Press, 1976.

———. *The Huron: Farmers of the North.* New York: Holt, Rinehart & Winston, 1969.

Iroquois

The Iroquois confederacy looms large in the history of the Northeast; the five tribes were extremely well organized and often successful in war. The name is subject to question; some say it is Algonquian for "real adders," others say it means "terrifying man," but the gist of the meaning is clear—frightening to the tribes they encountered. The confederacy, formed before European contact, united five tribes—Mohawk, Oneida, Onondaga, Cayuga, and Seneca—into the Five Nations. In the early eighteenth century the Tuscarora came up from North Carolina to join them, making the Six Nations. Their first recorded meeting with Europeans was with Jacques Cartier in 1534.

Men's Basic Dress

For everyday wear the Iroquois man wore a tanned leather breechclout with rather short ends hanging down in front and back. For ceremonial wear, he donned a kilt, knee-length, that was held in place with a belt. Leggings were different; somewhat loose, they were sewed up the front, often with an embroidered strip covering the seam. A curve at the bottom from front to back left an opening over the instep. They were gartered above or below the knee and were rarely fringed. These leggings were so long they partially covered the moccasins, dragging on the ground. A simple tunic for wear in cooler weather was made of two pieces of tanned buckskin fastened at the shoulders, mid-thigh-length, ending at the bottom with a fringe.

Women's Basic Dress

The Iroquois women dressed much like their Algonquian neighbors: the rather long wraparound skirt of brown-dyed deerskin, mid-calf in length, decorated with white quillwork or moose-hair embroidery, and gartered knee-length leggings. In summer they went bare-breasted, but the rest of the year they added a shapeless upper garment with fringes on the bottom.

Footwear

Moccasins were the same style for both sexes and were much like the Algonquian, but featured a squarish flap. They were soft-soled, of tanned deerskin, and either the one-piece type with the seam down the front or the two-piece style with an oval or U-shaped insert over the instep, the sole gathered in to fit. The usual moose-hair embroidery or porcupine quillwork in curvilinear designs adorned the cuffs and/or the vamps. Some of the Iroquois took basswood fibers or the always available cornhusk and made summer slippers, the only Northeastern Indians known to do so. Anciently they made a boot of the hock of the hind leg of an elk, which was sewed with sinew at the lower end and tied about the ankles with thongs.

Outer Wear

Lightweight robes were of tanned deerskin; winter robes were of bear, buffalo, or elk hides, with the skin side often painted, showing figures of men and animals in black and red. Other winter robes were made of the pelts of small animals, such as beavers, martens, minks, squirrels, or rabbits, sewn together. Some of the southern Iroquois made robes of feathers fastened to a netting of woven bark or hemp fibers.

Hair Styles

Iroquois men, especially warriors, shaved off all the hair except for the scalplock at the back; many wore the roach (the "Mohawk") with a roach spreader of bone holding erect a feather that rotated freely with the man's movements. Girls wore the hair loose and flowing; married women braided it into one large braid at the back, which was doubled up and fastened with a buckskin thong.

Headgear

A unique form of headdress was made by using a skull cap on a frame and covering it with several overlapping layers of feathers that hung down all around, except for one feather (usually golden eagle) held upright and rotating in a bone socket. Important Iroquois men wore a crown of erect feathers, golden eagle if obtainable, otherwise turkey, which were fastened into a band decorated with quillwork. Summer hats were fashioned of braided grasses or split reeds. Fur hoods were worn in winter.

Accessories

Garters and armbands were woven strips enhanced with moose-hair embroidery or quillwork. Sashes were also finger-woven with arrowhead designs and were worn around the waist or across the chest. From a shoulder belt or sash hung a pouch for tobacco or other personal items; made of tanned leather, they were usually dyed black, a favorite color with the Iroquois, continuing even to the present day. Wampum belts were ceremonial objects; the Iroquois seem not to have used wampum beads for decoration as was the case with other Northeastern tribes. The two varieties of wampum held special significance for the Iroquois; the white represented peace and good will, and the purple typified war, disaster, or death. Tumplines to support the women's burdens were tightly woven of elm, basswood, or nettle fibers, decorated with moose-hair embroidery.

Jewelry

Necklaces and bracelets were of bear's teeth and claws; bird bones, beaks, and claws; or beads of shell or carved bone. Gorgets of freshwater-clam shells hung on the breast. Earrings were of shell, polished stones, or clusters of beads.

Armor

Armor was made of wooden slats bound together with buckskin thongs. Small wooden or rawhide shields were carried, as were the fearsome ball-headed tomahawks or war clubs.

Garment Decoration

Finger-weaving in arrow and chevron designs appeared as sashes, garters, and cross belts. A netting technique produced the bases for feather cloaks. Elm, basswood, Indian hemp, nettle, and cornhusks were the usual fibers. Quillwork and moose-hair embroidery featured curvilinear designs. When beadwork was adopted, it appeared in the distinctive Iroquois style of white lacy designs, usually of white beads, on a dark cloth background.

Face and Body Embellishment

Facial paint for war was a black rectangle or three stripes on each cheek. When first encountered, the Iroquois men sported spectacular tattooing of double-curve motifs, geometric designs, or clan crests.

Masks

The wooden masks of the Iroquois False Face Society with their twisted faces were used in curing rites. Considered supernatural beings, these masks were carved from living trees in order to capture the spirit of the god. They were made and worn only by men. Women made cornhusk masks, also a part of curing rites, which were worn by both sexes.

Two Iroquois wear carved wooden False Face masks used in curing rites, while a third wears a large mask of braided cornhusks; each holds a rattle.

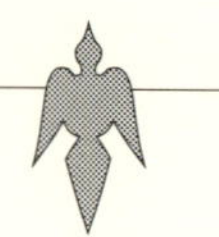

Transitional Dress

Later Iroquois dress was influenced as usual by European styles and materials. Blankets, cloth (both the heavy stroud cloth and the lighter weight cottons), needles, and scissors were adopted, as well as such sundries as vermilion for paint, glass beads, thread, yarn, shawls, silk ribbons, and handkerchiefs. The Iroquois learned silversmithing from the whites and became exceedingly proficient. Their specialty was the making of silver brooches, which were based on Scottish and English models, that featured such symbols as eyes, the sun, crucifixes, and the "two jaws interlocked," which became the Iroquois national badge. Armbands, headbands, and gorgets were crafted in silver. Women used stroud cloth for their long wraparound skirts, which eventually developed into calf-length tunics of cloth (especially dark-blue broadcloth) adorned with ribbons, beadwork, and silver brooches. Iroquois men wore a cap that was like the Glengarry bonnet of the Scots; made of black velvet, it was heavily beaded in floral designs and was fairly common from 1840 to 1870.

Key Sources

Bartram, John. *Observations on the Inhabitants, Climate, Soil, Rivers, Productions, Annals, and Other Matters Worthy of Notice, Made by Mr. John Bartram in His Travels from Pennsylvania to Onondago, Oswego, and the Lake Ontario, in Canada.* London: J. Whiston & B. White, 1751. Dover reprint, 1955.

Beauchamp, William M. "Wampum and Shell Articles Used by the New York Indians." New York State Museum *Bulletin* 41: 319–480.

Bloomfield, Julia K. *The Oneidas.* New York: Alden Brothers, 1907.

Carse, Mary (Rowall). "The Mohawk Iroquois." Archaeological Society of Connecticut *Bulletin* 23: 3–53.

Da Hanadisonkwe. "Native Dress and Designs among the Iroquois People." *American Indian Crafts and Culture* 7: 5–9.

Fenton, William. *The False Faces of the Iroquois.* Norman: University of Oklahoma Press, 1987.

———. "Iroquois Masks: A Living Tradition in the Northeast." In *American Indian Art: Form and Tradition.* Minneapolis: Walker Art Center, 1972.

———. "Northern Iroquoian Culture Patterns." *Handbook of North American Indians. Vol. 15: Northeast.* Pp. 296–321. Washington: Smithsonian Institution.

Gabor, R. *Costume of the Iroquois.* St. Regis Reservation, Ontario: Akwesasne Mohawk Counselor Organization, 1983.

Hislop, Cadman. *The Mohawk.* New York and Toronto: Rinehart, 1948.

Lyford, Carrie. *Iroquois Crafts.* Stevens Point, WI: R. Schneider, 1982. Reprint of 1945 edition.

Morgan, Lewis H. "Report on the Fabrics, Inventions, Implements, and Utensils of the Iroquois." New York State Cabinet of Antiquities *Annual Report* 5: 66–117.

Pratt, Peter P. *Oneida Iroquois Glass Trade Bead Sequence 1585–1745.* Indian Glass Trade Beads Color Guide Series 1. Syracuse, NY: Onondaga Printing Company, 1961.

Ritzenthaler, Robert. "Iroquois False Face Masks." Milwaukee Public Museum *Publications in Primitive Art* 3.

Schoolcraft, Henry R. *Notes on the Iroquois; or, Contributions to the Statistics, Aboriginal History, Antiquities and General Ethnology of Western New York.* Albany, NY: Bartlett and Welford, 1846.

Speck, Frank G. "The Iroquois: A Study in Cultural Evolution." Cranbrook Institute of Science *Bulletin* 23.

Thwaites, Reuben Gold. *The Jesuit Relations and Allied Documents. Vol. 14, Iroquois, Lower Canada, 1656–1658.* New York: Pageant Book Company, 1959.

Wilson, Edmund. *Apologies to the Iroquois.* New York: Farrar, Straus and Cudahy, 1960.

Menomini

The Menomini lived west of Lake Michigan and were hunters and fishermen, occasionally taking part in buffalo hunts, but were chiefly gatherers of wild rice, their major food resource. In fact, their name means "wild rice people." They spoke a dialect of Algonquian, different from the tribes to the east. Their first contact with the whites seems to have been Jean Nicollet in 1634. Catlin painted and

sketched some of the Menomini in 1836 and Paul Kane visited and painted them in 1845.

Men's Basic Dress

Men wore the tanned leather breechclout with mid-thigh-length flaps hanging down in the front and back. The deerskin leggings were somewhat loose, were fastened to the belt with thongs, were secured at the knees with large garters, and had fringes at the sides; they were often painted black and were embellished with colorful porcupine quillwork. A deerskin shirt of simple cut was added for cooler weather.

Women's Basic Dress

In early times women went bare-breasted, adding a poncho-type garment for warmth. Later they seem to have worn the strap-and-sleeve dress of tanned deerskin fastened at the shoulders with straps. Under this they wore a skirt of woven nettle fibers. Their leggings were knee-length and gartered. The garments, like those of the men, were adorned with beads, porcupine quills, and painting.

Footwear

The Menomini preferred soft-soled buckskin moccasins with a long, wide, decorated vamp and large flaps. Some moccasins were made with an especially high cuff that was turned up and wrapped around the ankle to give protection when harvesting wild rice. Snowshoes were indispensable to the men for winter hunting. They were of ash, steamed and bent into a rounded shape with the ends tied at the rear, a style that they called "catfish." Crossbars were added for strength and rawhide thongs were woven hexagonally to fill in the frame. Straps held the toes and heel in place.

Outer Wear

Tanned deerskin made lightweight robes. Winter robes of buffalo hides, obtained by trade from the west, were painted on the skin side in the Plains style. Small pelts such as beaver (the warmest and most desirable), marten, and squirrel were sewed together into warm robes. Rabbit skins were cut spirally into long strips and the strips then woven into robes, warm but fragile.

Hair Styles

Some men wore the hair naturally with one or two drooping feathers attached. Others wore a roach, but it was made of turkey beard instead of the usual porcupine guard hair. A favorite hair style among the Menomini men was made by shaving the head except for a large scalplock, which either fell from the crown or was coiled on top of the head with a feather or two stuck through it. Women wore the hair loose or in two braids which were pulled tightly to the back.

Headgear

The otter-fur turban, so typical of the Prairie tribes, was popular with the Menomini; it was worn with the tail extending out at the side or hanging at the back. Some men wore a feather headdress with the feathers sticking out at random. Both sexes wore fur hoods in the winter.

Accessories

The Menomini women made shoulder bags and pouches of dyed vegetable fibers, shredded bark, and buffalo hair; these rectangular articles were enhanced with porcupine quillwork and moose-hair embroidery, often with representations of thunderbirds and other sacred beings, as well as figures of humans and animals. Sometimes an eagle skin was suspended at the bottom. The women also finger-wove long sashes of various fibers; these sashes, ending in a long fringe, were worn around the waist or coiled on the head in a turban form. Garters, too, were made in this manner. Men often wore a knife in a sheath suspended at the neck.

Jewelry

Many strings of necklaces were worn, made of small chunks of native copper or of shells; especially popular were the hair pipe beads, long white tubes from the shell of the *Strombus gigas.* Both sexes pierced the earlobes in several places so that dangling ornaments could be placed in each hole. Hair pipe beads were also worn at each side of the face, suspended from the brow.

Garment Decoration

The superb twining technique of the Menomini women could be seen in the finger-woven sashes and bags; common fibers were nettle, shredded bark

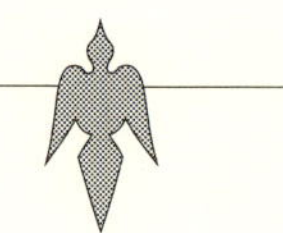

(especially basswood), and buffalo hair. They were adept at porcupine quillwork and moose-hair embroidery. Beginning about 1830 they changed from the earlier beadwork, based on the geometric designs of quillwork, to elaborate floral and realistic designs. Early in this century they learned the technique of ribbon applique, the strips being used on women's skirts, shawls, leggings, blouses, and men's breechcloths (which had taken on an apron form with extensive decoration). Some robes were painted in the Plains manner.

Face and Body Embellishment

Face paint (and some body paint) was used by the men in various ways, such as black parallel bars across the face, red designs on the cheek, or a part of the face painted black (the lower or upper part or one side). Women painted a round red spot on each cheek. Tattooing and skull deformation were not mentioned by authorities.

Transitional Dress

With European contact in the early seventeenth century and European trade articles available even earlier, the Menomini were quick to substitute cloth for buckskin, glass beads for porcupine quills and shells, and Hudson's Bay blankets for the cumbersome buffalo robes. However, the women continued to excel in weaving and their attractive shoulder bags were widely traded; they were often called "friendship bags" because they were frequently given as gifts. They also found their way to the Plains where they were traded for horses. Silver was made into brooches (attached in rows on women's blouses), men's armbands, earrings, and other ornaments for both sexes.

Key Sources

Hoffman, Walter James. "The Menomini Indians." Bureau of American Ethnology *Annual Reports* 3: 3–328.

Keesing, Felix M. "The Menomini Indians of Wisconsin: A Study of Three Centuries of Cultural Contact and Change." American Philosophical Society *Memoirs* 10.

Ray, Verne F. *The Menominee Tribe of Indians: 1940–1970.* Escanaba, MI: Photo Offset Printing Company, 1971.

Skinner, Alanson B. "Material Culture of the Menomini." Museum of the American Indian *Indian Notes and Monographs* 4.

———. "Social Life and Ceremonial Bundles of the Menominee Indians." American Museum of Natural History *Anthropological Papers* 13(1): 1–165.

Spindler, George, and Louise S. Spindler. *Dreamers without Power: The Menomini Indians.* New York: Holt, Rinehart & Winston, 1971.

Spindler, Louise. "Menominee." In *Handbook of North American Indians. Vol. 15: Northeast.* Pp. 708–724.

Miami

The Miami were the best known and most recorded of the tribes of the Illinois confederacy. The Illinois (or Illini) all spoke a Miami form of Algonquian and lived in northern Illinois, Indiana, and Iowa. Principal bands were the Kaskaskia, Kahoki, Michigami, Wea, Piankeshaw, Peoria, Mascouten, and the Miami; the last tribe is discussed here in some detail because of the availability of material, but the tribes were similar in dress and customs. The name *Miami* meant "people of the peninsula," referring to their original home near Green Bay, from where they worked their way down to what is now Chicago. Although they generally were not dependent on the fur trade, they were at a crossroads, so they were influenced early by the traders and their goods. First recorded white contact was that of Father Allouez in 1669. Several artists painted them. Joseph Wabin, illustrating a map of 1796, portrayed a Kaskaskia man—but already there were items of European manufacture. A portrait by Mrs. John G. Simcoe in the eighteenth century of a Miami man also shows manufactured items, such as silver ornaments and beads. James Otto Lewis painted Miami men at the Mississinewa Treaty of 1826. George Catlin lived among them, and painted and sketched from 1830–1832. George Winter, an Englishman, did watercolors in 1837–1839.

Men's Basic Dress

Miami men were called by the English "naked" or "tattooed men." In winter, despite the cold winds off

Lake Michigan, men wore only a deerskin shirt of simple cut, moccasins, and a breechclout painted red, a popular color with the Miami. During the summer only breechclout and moccasins were worn. Leggings, donned for special occasions, were gartered at the knees, some ending just above the knees, others at the thigh; embroidered bands decorated the front and the bottom of each leg.

Women's Basic Dress
Women wore a red deerskin wraparound skirt and loose knee-length leggings with decorative bands in a twining pattern down the sides and around the bottom. A simple poncho-like tunic was worn with this in cooler weather.

Footwear
Miami moccasins were soft-soled with a central seam in front and featured unusually large flaps that almost covered the toes, adhering to the typical Prairie styles of a different design on each side, usually repeating the designs on the other foot in reverse. The patterns on the flaps, elongated diamonds and triangles, were done with dyed porcupine quills (later beads and ribbon applique).

Outer Wear
Few robes were worn except for ceremony; lightweight tanned deerskin robes were painted, as were the occasional buffalo robes worn by the men. The simple geometric designs were similar to the "box-and-border" motifs of the Plains robes.

Hair Styles
The roach was commonly worn by the men, especially warriors; sometimes the entire head was shaved leaving only a tuft of hair at the crown. At the time of contact, men often wore the hair short except for long locks that dangled in front of and behind the ears. Women wore the hair loose and flowing, in two braids, or gathered into a clump at the back.

Headgear
Red feathers hung from decorative headbands, but the Miami did not wear many feathers nor did they give them the significance attributed by the Indians of the Plains.

Accessories
Pouches and bags contained necessities, such as sewing equipment, pipes and tobacco, fire-making material, and sacred, personal items. These and the ever-present knife sheaths were either attached to woven sashes or to leather belts.

Jewelry
Necklaces and bracelets of the usual shell beads were popular, as were clusters of beads hung from the ears and other elaborate ear ornaments. Shell gorgets were suspended from the neck by thongs. Women wore hair ties on the hair in back.

Armor
Warriors carried large shields of buffalo hide, large enough to cover almost the entire body.

Garment Decoration
Skins were dyed, generally red; they were also painted at times in the Plains manner. The women did porcupine quillwork, beadwork, and ribbonwork in the usual succession, so typical of the Prairie tribes. Finger-weaving, by twining, was done with the hair of the buffalo (available aboriginally in the area).

Face and Body Embellishment
Red facial paint was used extensively, sometimes with black added; the body was often painted brown. Women were lightly tattooed with parallel lines on the cheeks and chin, while men favored more elaborate designs. James Otto Lewis painted Brewett, a Miami chief, with seven parallel lines across the nose and cheeks and about ten on the chin.

Transitional Dress
By 1760 European garments were commonly worn, particularly by more prosperous Miami; by 1800 little evidence of Indian dress was retained except for robes and moccasins. Silver ornaments were extremely popular, especially ear wheels (round with a cutwork design), armbands, and gorgets in a crescent shape, sometimes as many as six being worn at one time. Silver headbands with feathers erupting from the top and cloth turbans were frequently worn.

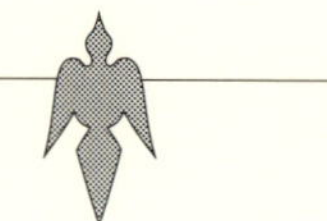

Key Sources

Anson, Bert. *The Miami Indians.* Norman: University of Oklahoma Press, 1970.

Callender, Charles. "Miami." In *Handbook of North American Indians. Vol. 15: Northeast.* Pp. 681–689.

Cole, Fay-Cooper. *Kincaid: A Prehistoric Illinois Metropolis.* Chicago: University of Chicago Press, 1951.

Ojibwa (Southeastern)

The Southeastern Ojibwa lived around Lake Huron, especially Georgian Bay, Manitoulin Island, and in the Upper Peninsula of Michigan. They did not practice agriculture but rather were food gatherers, particularly of wild rice and maple sap for syrup, as well as fishermen and hunters of deer and a variety of small animals. They spoke the eastern Ojibwa dialect of the Central Algonquian language. The terms *Ojibwa* and *Chippewa* are often confused, frequently being used interchangeably; as a general rule, *Ojibwa* is preferred by the Canadian people while the U.S. tribe is called *Chippewa.* First contact was probably with Champlain in 1615; by 1650 the Jesuit fathers had established missions among them and reported on their lifeways. The Ojibwa typically lived in relatively small groups for hunting and gathering and were more mobile than their Iroquoian neighbors to the southeast.

Men's Basic Dress

The men seem to have worn little in early times—only a fitted breechclout with flaps hanging in front and back and moccasins; a robe was added in winter. At the time of contact they wore a buckskin shirt, embroidered and painted, often trimmed with scalplock fringes (a suggestion of Plains influence). Their thigh-length or above-the-knee leggings of tanned deerskin were fringed at the sides, gartered at the knees, and decorated with porcupine quillwork and moose-hair embroidery.

Women's Basic Dress

The Ojibwa women anciently had worn a wraparound skin skirt, with a robe added for cooler weather. At the time of European contact they were wearing the strap-and-sleeve dress, a style that continued into the twentieth century. This dress was suspended by shoulder straps, was mid-calf in length, and featured detachable sleeves, tied on with thongs at the back and fastened at the wrists with no underarm seam. The dresses were decorated with red, black, and yellow paint; bird claws; porcupine quills; moose feet; and little chunks of native copper, and were girded with a sash or belt. Knee-length leggings were looser than the men's and featured quillwork along the sides. An underskirt of woven nettle fibers completed the costume.

Footwear

The one-piece tanned deerskin (sometimes moose hide) moccasins, preferably dyed black, either had a seam up the front from toe to instep, or had the skin puckered into a U- or oval-shaped vamp. A variation characteristic of the Ojibwa was the "partridge" moccasin, so-called because there was a straight seam across the toe into which the skin was puckered, which resembled a partridge's fantail; the seam up the instep was fringed, as was the heel seam. Moccasins were often trimmed with beaver fur. A simple form of moccasin was the "stocking" type made of two pieces of leather (later blanket cloth) cut in a foot shape and the pieces sewn together, which resulted in an uncomfortable seam along the sole. This type was sometimes used as a liner for winter moccasins. High moccasins were worn with snowshoes, which were necessary in the winter; the round or "bearpaw" snowshoe was worn by women and children, the tailed type by the men.

Outer Wear

Light robes of buckskin sufficed for spring and fall. Winter robes were made of the pelts of small animals such as beavers, martens, squirrels, and rabbits. The pelts were sewn together, except in the case of rabbit robes, which were made by cutting each rabbit pelt spirally into one long strip. The strips were then woven in a simple "in-and-out" manner to create a robe with fur on both sides. These were very warm but quite fragile.

Hair Styles

Men wore the hair in a variety of styles. Some allowed it to hang naturally, others fashioned it into two or four braids. Some, particularly warriors, shaved the head except for a brush or roach on top, with a scalplock hanging behind. Some warriors wore the

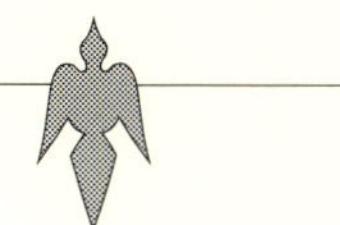

hair in braids but before a battle wound them in a coil on top of the head and wrapped it with bark to make it stand erect. Women often parted the hair in the center, pulled it to the back to make a single braid, and wrapped it with eel or snakeskin. Another style was to form two braids, which were wrapped with fur or worn plain. Both sexes often beautified the hair with red and yellow paint.

Headgear
Except for one or two feathers worn in the hair, the Ojibwa seldom wore anything on the head. A chief might wear the typical eastern headdress of a decorated band from which many feathers splayed out; eagle tail feathers were the most desired, reserved for those who had distinguished themselves in conflict. At times, a band of otter or beaver fur was worn around the head.

Accessories
Long finger-woven sashes, like the Assomption sashes, ended in a long fringe and featured diamond, arrow, and zigzag designs. Tanned leather belts were enhanced with porcupine quillwork, as were garters and deerskin pouches. Square or rectangular shoulder bags displayed geometric or stylized animal designs done in quillwork. The Grand Medicine Society of the Midewiwin was an important part of Ojibwa ceremonialism; the members (men) proudly displayed the bags of the society made of the entire pelt of an otter or a muskrat, with the paws and tail adorned with quillwork. These bags held body paint, amulets, and other personal and sacred items.

Jewelry
Ornaments were created from such available materials as shells, stones, teeth and claws of animals, and native copper that was pounded flat, cut, and rolled into beads; beads were also made of fossil crinoid rings. Gorgets of polished slate were suspended over the breast by means of thongs. Men wore nose rings. Both sexes pierced the ears in several places, or slashed along the lobe, in order to wear earrings in abundance, as well as feathers, bones, and other objects.

Armor
Armor to cover the torso was made of slats or rods of wood laced together with sinew; greaves to protect the shins were also made in this manner. Large round shields were of wood or rawhide.

Garment Decoration
Skin garments were frequently dyed black and edged with short fringes. Finger-weaving of long sashes, garters, and belts was done with buffalo hair mixed with vegetal fibers such as nettle. Both porcupine quillwork and moose-hair embroidery enhanced the aboriginal garments, superseded by beadwork.

Face and Body Embellishment
The Ojibwa were extremely fond of painting the face and body, using red ocher, charcoal or soot, and clay, in bars, patches, dots, and other simple designs. In summer, they plastered their backs with white clay; when it hardened, they painted figures on it or scratched out designs. Tattooing, especially of the men, was extensive, bodies often being covered with tattooed designs; the custom continued well into the nineteenth century. Women were tattooed lightly on cheeks and chin.

Transitional Dress
By 1700 the changeover to European styles, materials, and garments had begun. Cloth, either stroud cloth or lighter weight cottons, replaced deerskin. Blankets, especially from the Hudson's Bay Company, were used in place of fur robes; they were often made into *capotes,* the long hooded jackets girded with a sash wrapped several times about the waist. Glass beads brought by the traders became the favored form of decoration, at first repeating the geometric designs of quillwork, later adopting the floral style of the eastern tribes. Metal was eagerly sought; brass was made into "tinklers," little cones that jingled gaily with body movements; silver trade articles replaced the native shells and beads in such forms as headbands, armbands, brooches, bracelets, and gorgets. European-style ready-made garments were adopted—dresses, coats (particularly military coats), trousers, and, finally, shoes. By 1850 little remained of traditional Ojibwa dress.

Key Sources
Gringhuis, Dirk. "Indian Costume at Mackinac: Seventeenth and Eighteenth Century." *Mackinac History* 2(1).

Quimby, George Irving. *Indian Life in the Upper Great Lakes: 11,000 B.C. to A.D. 1800.* Chicago: University of Chicago Press, 1960.

Radin, Paul. "Ethnological Notes on the Ojibwas of Southeastern Ontario." *American Anthropologist* 30(4): 659–668.

Rogers, E. S. "Southeastern Ojibwa." In *Handbook of North American Indians. Vol. 15: Northeast.* Pp. 760–771. Washington: Smithsonian Institution.

Ottawa

The Ottawa lived in the Georgian Bay area and were speakers of a Southeastern Ojibwa dialect of the Algonquian language family. The name comes from a Cree word, *adawe,* meaning "to buy and sell," an appropriate name, for the Ottawa were great intertribal traders. Although they traveled extensively, they still grew corn and did some hunting, fishing, and gathering. At the time of contact they were joined with the Chippewa and Potawatomi in a confederacy called "the Three Fires." First European contact was with Samuel de Champlain in 1615, who reported on their lifeways. Information was also recorded by the fathers in the *Jesuit Relations.*

Men's Basic Dress

Men wore only a robe and moccasins as a rule, adding for dress occasions a fitted tanned-leather breechclout with flaps in front and back, decorated with quillwork. Thigh-length leggings, when worn, were simple tubes of hide, fringed on the outside seams, and gartered just below the knees.

Women's Basic Dress

Ottawa women in ancient times wore a simple wraparound skirt of tanned leather, with a poncho-like garment added when needed for warmth. At the time of contact they were wearing the strap-and-sleeve dress, consisting of two pieces of skin held in place with shoulder straps and usually belted; detachable sleeves were fastened at the wrists with no underarm seam, and were tied on at the back and front with thongs. Knee-length leggings were gartered with decorated bands just below the knees. A skirt of woven nettle fibers was worn under this dress.

Footwear

Moccasins were of deerskin, sometimes moose hide, and were one-piece, soft-soled, with a seam running from toe to instep and the sole puckered into it. This seam was often covered with a strip of quillwork. Cuffs were usually attached and could be worn down or up around the ankle and fastened with thongs. Rabbit fur or grass lined the moccasins in winter. Later styles featured the sole puckered into a U- or oval-shaped vamp. Snowshoes were necessary for travel in the deep snows of winter—round or "bearpaw" for women and children and tailed shoes for the men.

Outer Wear

Lightweight robes were of tanned deerskin, often embellished with painted designs. Winter robes were of the pelts of such small animals as beavers, martens, and squirrels, tanned and sewed together with the fur outside. Rabbit-skin robes were made by cutting a pelt spirally into one long strip and weaving the strips together in a simple weave; these were warm but fragile, and were especially worn by women and children.

Hair Styles

Some men, particularly warriors, wore the hair in a roach, with the head shaved except for a central tuft standing from front to back and with a scalplock hanging from the crown. Champlain called the Ottawa the *cheveux releves,* or "high hairs," because the hair was so high and upright at the forehead, diminishing in height to the back. The hair was often worn in two or four braids, which were sometimes wrapped with fur or thongs. Still others allowed the hair to hang loosely, or shaved it all except one little tuft at the crown. Women parted the hair in the center and pulled it to the back where it was fashioned into one braid and wrapped with fur or a snakeskin. Another style was to wear a braid at each side. For special occasions the part was colored with red or yellow paint.

Headgear

Although they were very fond of feathers, the Ottawa seldom wore more than two in the hair. Chiefs sometimes wore a headband decorated with quillwork from which many feathers cascaded. Most popular

were the tail feathers of an eagle, worn only by those who had shown great courage in battle.

Accessories

Belts were of tanned leather; dress belts were ornamented with porcupine quillwork. Sashes, garters, and armbands were finger-woven of fibers in various dyed colors and featured designs of arrows, zigzags, and chevrons. Shoulder bags, woven of nettle fibers, had a large opening at the top, and displayed designs of stylized animals and birds.

Jewelry

Ornaments were made of shell, bone, native copper, and teeth and claws of animals. The copper was pounded thin, cut, and rolled into tubes, or chunks of the metal had holes drilled in them for stringing. Beads were also made of sections of fossil crinoids, of wampum shells, and of dentalium shells from the Pacific coast, when available. Gorgets of polished slate had two holes in the top so they could be suspended from the neck by thongs. Both sexes pierced the ears in several places to insert feathers, clusters of wampum or other beads, or skewers of copper. Men wore nose rings; in fact, Champlain wrote: "I shall mention that the word, Ottawa, means Nation of Pierced Noses because they pierce their noses and attach a small prettily ornamented stone which comes to the middle of the mouth."

Armor

The Ottawa seem to have worn nothing in battle, but carried a huge shield, about four feet in diameter, of boiled leather (rawhide). The earliest picture we have of an Ottawa is of a naked warrior with the large shield.

Garment Decoration

Skin garments and the later cloth ones were enhanced with strips of quillwork, later beading. Finger-weaving, done with spun buffalo hair mixed with vegetal fibers such as nettle, produced sashes, garters, armbands, and belts.

Face and Body Embellishment

Tattooing by the men was common and continued well into the nineteenth century. Designs were of lizards, snakes, and geometrical figures, sometimes covering the entire body. Facial and body painting was also of great importance to the Ottawa, red, brown, green, and black being the most favored colors.

Transitional Dress

The Ottawa welcomed European products, especially cloth, beads, metal, and manufactured garments. Stroud cloth, red or dark blue, was made into breechcloths, skirts, dresses, and lightweight blankets. Hudson's Bay blankets were worn as blankets or made into the hooded *capote* jackets. Silver brooches, gorgets, bracelets, and peace medals were abundantly and proudly displayed. European coats, especially the military variety, were much sought after. Soon, manufactured garments, such as dresses, blouses, shirts, and jackets, took the place of those that had been made by the Indian women. Last to be adopted were the trousers, replacing breechcloths and leggings, and shoes.

Key Sources

Feest, Christian F. *Beadwork and Textiles of the Ottawa.* Harbor Springs, MI: Harbor Springs Historical Commission, 1984.

Feest, Johanna E. and Christian F. Feest. "Ottawa." In *Handbook of North American Indians. Vol. 15: Northeast.* Pp. 772–786. Washington: Smithsonian Institution.

Gringhuis, Dirk. "Indian Costume at Mackinac: Seventeenth and Eighteenth Century." *Mackinac History* 2(1).

Penobscot

The Penobscot were an Algonquian-speaking people who inhabited the coast of Maine and inland. They were a part of the Abenaki ("dawn land people") confederacy, which included other eastern Abenaki peoples, such as the Assagunticook, Pigwacket, Malecite, Passamaquoddy, and Micmac. The name "Penobscot" meant "it flows on the rocks," probably referring to the falls at Oldtown, a principal habitation. Verazzano visited them in 1524 and Champlain (1604) ascended the Penobscot River; he called these eastern Abenaki "Etchemin." A gentle, docile people, they did some farming but depended for sustenance mainly on coastal resources.

Men's Basic Dress

Men wore breechclouts of tanned deerskin, with flaps in front and back, or of a beaver pelt. Leggings were above the knee, gartered below the knee, and fastened to a belt with thongs; they were often fringed along the outer seams. A covering of deerskin was sometimes added, fastened on one shoulder and draped under the other arm. Or a hunter might be clad in a sleeveless belted tunic of skin.

Women's Basic Dress

Anciently women wore a wraparound skin skirt held in place by a belt. Before European contact they began to wear the "strap-and-sleeve" dress, made of two pieces of skin sewn together, held up by shoulder straps; sleeves were added when needed, tied on at back and front with thongs and fastened at the wrists, without underarm seams. Knee-length leggings were held in place by garters.

Footwear

Moccasins were of deer or moose skin in the typical one-piece, soft-soled eastern pattern of the sole puckered slightly into a narrow oval vamp. Some had a seam from toe to instep, covered with an embroidered strip. These were adorned on cuffs and vamp with moose-hair embroidery or porcupine quillwork. Snowshoes, constructed of white ash with a webbing of caribou or moose-hide strips, were made in a "pollywog" style, with shorter tails in back and the toe more pointed than rounded. Traditionally, a girl wove the cords of her betrothed's snowshoes.

Outer Wear

Both sexes in winter wore a knee-length tunic made of two moose skins, one for the front, one for the back, sewed up the sides and with or without sleeves; short fringes edged the neck opening and the sleeve tops. Robes of a moose hide or the pelts of smaller animals, such as beaver, otter, and muskrat, were winter wear. Birchbark served as a temporary rain cape. Later, under European influence, the men wore coats with a front opening, elaborately embellished with moose-hair embroidery in a floral manner.

Hair Styles

Men wore the hair loose, sometimes held in place with a leather band, or coiled on top of the head and fastened in place with thongs or a wooden skewer. Women, too, wore the hair loose, or they made two braids and coiled them on top of the head.

Headgear

Usually the Penobscot went bareheaded, but in winter or for special occasions men wore a large hood made of hide that covered the shoulders and often featured embroidery along the edges. One or two feathers (no more than two) were attached at the point of the hood. Women, too, wore a hood—high, conical, large, with a rounded lower edge, elaborately trimmed with moose-hair embroidery in the double-curve motif; at times a feather was added. Temporary rain hats were of birchbark. Sagamores (chiefs) wore crowns of deer bristles painted red, or of white bird skins with the feathers left intact. Important leaders also wore a high crown of upright feathers fastened into a headband.

Accessories

Pouches or shoulder bags were of moose hide or deerskin enhanced with moose-hair embroidery or quillwork; some bags were of woodchuck skins. Leather belts were decorated in a similar manner. Garters were strips of embroidered skin held in place with thong ties. Women later wore large collars extensively embroidered or beaded.

Jewelry

Little jewelry was worn by the Penobscot and other Eastern Abenaki. Necklaces and earrings of shells were major items. Small nose rings were worn into historic times.

Garment Decoration

The early porcupine quillwork and moosehair embroidery was replaced by beadwork, especially done in the double-curve motif so popular with New England Indians; this was often coupled with the European floral designs. The women's hoods were extensively decorated in this manner, also belts, shoulder bags, dresses, and coats (with the characteristic European front opening).

Face and Body Embellishment

No indication was found of tattooing, face and body painting, or skull deformation practices.

Masks

Hunters wore a mask made of a deer head including the antlers; this was not only worn as a disguise when hunting but also in dance ceremonies invoking the aid of the spirits in hunting endeavors.

Transitional Dress

Because of the coastal location, contact was early and frequent. Stroud cloth and cottons replaced tanned skins of moose and deer. Beadwork was eagerly adopted by the women. Not only hoods but belts, shoulder bags, dresses, coats, and large collars were all trimmed with bands of beadwork. Men continued to wear the typical headdress of upright feathers now set into a metal band with a pierced design, but it slowly shifted into a "warbonnet" style. By 1850 little of Penobscot traditional dress remained.

Key Sources

Eckstrom, Fannie (Hardy). "The Handicrafts of the Modern Indians of Maine." Lafayette National Park *Museum Bulletin* 3.

Erickson, Vincent O. "Maliseet-Passamaquoddy." In *Handbook of North American Indians. Vol. 15: Northeast.* Pp. 123–136. Washington: Smithsonian Institution.

Smith, Nicholas N. "Notes on the Malecite of Woodstock, New Brunswick." *Anthropologica* 5: 1–39.

Snow, Dean R. "Eastern Abenaki." In *Handbook of North American Indians. Vol. 15: Northeast.* Pp. 137–147. Washington: Smithsonian Institution.

Speck, Frank G. *Penobscot Man: The Life History of a Forest Tribe in Maine.* New York: Octagon Books, 1970.

Wallis, Wilson D. and Ruth S. Wallis. "The Malecite Indians of New Brunswick." National Museums of Canada *Bulletin* 148. Anthropological Series 40.

Potawatomi

The Potawatomi ("people of the place of fire") were closely related to the Ottawa and Chippewa, although their language is distinctively different, but still Algonquian; with them they formed a loose confederacy called "The Three Fires." They were also called Mascoutens. When first encountered by white men they lived near Green Bay, Wisconsin; later they moved south to the Chicago River area, then up into Michigan, where they became the Forest Potawatomi. Some moved farther south instead and became known as the Prairie Potawatomi, much influenced by the Plains culture. With the use of canoes, they were highly mobile, traveling the many rivers and lakes. They also raised maize, fished, and hunted (occasionally for buffalo). James Otto Lewis painted them in 1826, George Winter and George Catlin in the 1830s, and Paul Kane in 1845.

Men's Basic Dress

Men wore a tanned leather breechclout with quillwork bands at the bottom, with the flaps hanging down to the knees in front and back. Leggings, also of deerskin, were thigh-length, fringed down the side seams and gartered below the knees; some were embellished with strips of quillwork at the sides. Anciently, the Potawatomi men did not wear a shirt, but by the time of European contact, they were wearing unseamed pieces of tanned skin for shirts.

A Potawatomi man's printed cotton shirt made in the mid–nineteenth century has panels of woven beadwork on the front and on the shoulders, designs carried over from Plains warshirts.

Women's Basic Dress

The woman's dress consisted of two pieces of tanned deerskin fastened at the shoulders and at the side, reaching to below the knees, sometimes belted. Leggings, knee-length, were gartered just below the knees with strips of leather decorated with quillwork.

Footwear

The soft-soled one-piece moccasins had a seam up the front from toe to instep, usually with a decorated band over the seam; the cuffs were typical of the Prairie style—very large, extending almost to the ground, pointed at the front, and with designs symmetrically opposed for each cuff.

Outer Wear

A winter robe was of a bearskin or a buffalo hide. Warm robes were also made of the pelts of small animals such as otter, beaver, or squirrel sewed together. Rabbit-skin robes were made by cutting a pelt spirally into a long strip, then weaving the strips in a simple "in-and-out" manner. Lightweight robes were of tanned deerskin.

A Potawatomi woman's cotton blouse from the mid-nineteenth century has a bertha, or three-tiered flounced collar, edged with ribbon and decorated with silver brooches.

Hair Styles

Men wore the hair long, except when they were engaged in war, at which time they wore the roach, shaving the entire head except for an upstanding tuft from front to back on top of the head, with a scalplock hanging behind. Sometimes they constructed a roach of deer or porcupine hair dyed red, and attached it to the scalplock by means of a bone roach spreader. A single eagle feather was often added at the back. Women wore the hair in a single braid hanging down the back. Both men and women added many ornaments to the hair.

Headgear

Both sexes went bareheaded, the men occasionally adding a feather or two to the hair. Sometimes the tail of a small animal was worn at the nape of the neck. Men of importance wore an otter-fur turban, with the tail extending out at one side or hanging down the back. At times sashes were wound about the head in a turban fashion.

Accessories

The pelts of smaller animals were used to make pouches or shoulder bags. Belts were of tanned deerskin ornamented with quillwork. Finger-woven sashes, sometimes as much as eight inches wide, displayed designs of quillwork or moose-hair embroidery. Bags and pouches of skin or woven fibers contained such items as fire-making and sewing equipment, pipes and tobacco, and personal sacred objects.

Jewelry

Potawatomi costume was often highly decorative, and such devices as hair ornaments, bracelets, necklaces, armlets, and pendants were worn in abundance. Large gorgets of shell hung on the male chest. Beads and pendants were made from native copper imported from the Lake Superior area and from shells from as far away as the Gulf and Atlantic coasts.

Garment Decoration

Potawatomi women painstakingly created porcupine quillwork in geometric designs and moose-hair embroidery in modified floral designs, all characteristic of the region. Finger-weaving, using buffalo hair and other fibers, especially nettle, was

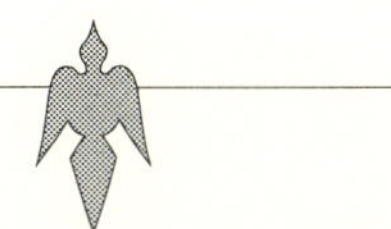

Potawatomi women replaced porcupine quillwork in geometric designs with ribbon appliqués on their garments during the nineteenth century. They also used metal brooches to decorate their blouses.

confined to the making of the wide sashes, belts, and garters using chevron, zigzag, and arrow designs. They were happy to adopt beadwork, continuing with traditional designs, but it was ribbon applique for which they were noted, and it appeared on almost all of their garments—leggings, moccasins, skirts, shirts, and shawls, as well as bags and pouches.

Face and Body Embellishment

Warriors painted their faces with red and black paint, especially the upper face, which might be all black, or black and red around each eye. Both sexes painted bodies and faces for ceremonial occasions.

Transitional Dress

Silver ornaments replaced the native copper jewelry. Cloth (stroud cloth and cottons) replaced tanned leather. Finally, the garments of the whites were worn instead of those of native manufacture. A distinctive item of clothing in the nineteenth century was the man's shirt of broadcloth with panels of ribbonwork on the chest and shoulders and often straight down the front like a European shirt. A characteristic woman's item was the blouse of trade cloth with a large ruffled collar or "bertha," which was adorned with many silver brooches and buttons.

A Potawatomi boy with a bow and arrows was photographed about 1856 near Chicago. He wears a cloth turban, ear ornaments, a shirt of buckskin fringed along the sleeves, and a yarn sash.

Key Sources

Claspy, Everett. *The Potawatomi Indians of Southwestern Michigan.* Dowagiac, MI: Braun-Brumfield, 1966.

Clifton, James A. "Potawatomi." *Handbook of North American Indians. Vol. 15: Northeast.* Pp. 725–742. Washington: Smithsonian Institution.

Connelley, William Elsey. "The Prairie Band of the Potawatomi." Kansas State Historical Society *Collections* 14: 488–570.

Deale, Valentine B. "The History of the Potawatomies before 1722." *Ethnohistory* 5(4): 305–360.

Edmunds, R. David. *The Potawatomis: Keepers of the Fire.* Norman: University of Oklahoma Press, 1978.

Landes, Ruth. *The Prairie Potawatomi: Tradition and Ritual in the Twentieth Century.* Madison: University of Wisconsin Press, 1970.

Lawson, Publius V. "The Potawatomi." *Wisconsin Archaeologist* 19(2): 40–116.

Ritzenthaler, Robert E. "The Potawatomi Indians of Wisconsin." Milwaukee Public Museum *Bulletin* 19(3): 99–174.

Skinner, Alanson B. "The Mascoutens or Prairie Potawatomi: Social Life and Ceremonies." Milwaukee Public Museum *Bulletin* 6(1).

Sauk

The Sauk (also spelled "Sac") and Fox tribes, although they were two distinctly different peoples speaking two distinct dialects of Algonquian, are sometimes treated as one tribe, particularly by the U.S. government. Possibly related to the Chippewa, the Sauk and Fox were united from about 1735 to 1804, and again from 1832 to 1852. The Sauk

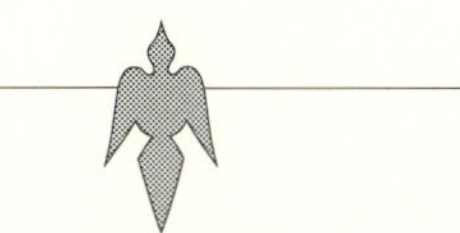

A delegation of Sauk, Fox, and Ioway chiefs, photographed in 1866, wear headgear that includes, from left to right, a cloth turban with roach, an otter-skin turban with a beaded tail, a cloth turban, and a fur turban with a shell-disk decoration. Their moccasins and leggings are beaded with either geometric or floral designs.

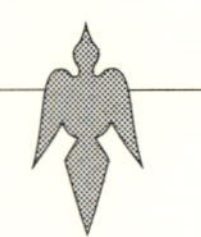

Sauk chief Keokuk's wife, painted in 1835, wears a wraparound skirt with ribbonwork at the hem, a cotton blouse decorated with silver brooches, and front-seam leggings with beaded edges and cuffs covering front-seam moccasins. Jewelry includes ear ornaments and hairpipe and pony bead necklaces.

were called "people of the yellow earth," also the "Nadowa." They moved from the upper Michigan area to Illinois, then westward, where they were strongly influenced by the cultures of the Great Plains. George Catlin painted some of their leaders in the 1830s, and Charles Bird King painted them in Washington in 1824 and 1837. John Jarvis in 1833 painted the famous Sauk leader Black Hawk and his son.

Men's Basic Dress

Aboriginally, the Sauk men wore only the breechclout and moccasins in summer, with a robe added in winter. The breechclouts, usually painted red, were typically of the fitted type without flaps, held in place with a leather belt or sash. By the time of European contact, hip-length leggings of deer or elk skin were being worn, made a lustrous white with white clay, and decorated with porcupine quillwork and fringes at the sides. Some, without fringes, were snug fitting, with flaps at the bottom to cover most of the foot. Another type of legging had a front seam, covered with a narrow band of quillwork, with a short hanging flap at the knee; this type often featured scalplock fringes. In cold weather breechclouts were of the tanned skins of raccoons, with the fur turned inward.

Women's Basic Dress

Anciently the Sauk women wore only a skirt of tanned deerskin, or fawnskin, and moccasins in the summer, adding a simple sleeveless shirt affair of tanned raccoon skin and knee-length skin leggings for cooler weather. These were beautified with painted designs or bands of porcupine quillwork. An underskirt of woven nettle fibers was often worn with this outfit. Sometimes in warm weather they wore a large collar (long enough to cover the breasts) of twined basswood bark painted red.

Footwear

The Sauk wore the typical Woodlands one-piece soft-soled moccasin with a seam from toe to instep, usually covered with a strip of quillwork. The flaps or cuffs of men's moccasins were exaggerated in size (unless the bottoms of the leggings were large) and were heavily decorated with porcupine-quill embroidery or quilled strips in geometric patterns;

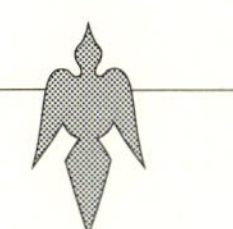

these designs were different for each flap, and were then reversed for the flaps of the other moccasin, a characteristic Prairie fashion. Snowshoes had been worn when the Sauk lived in the north, but were only a vague memory by the time they lived in Illinois.

Outer Wear

Lightweight robes or mantles were of tanned deer or elk skin. Bear, buffalo, or wolf robes were common for winter wear. Robes were also made of the pelts of beavers, raccoons, and muskrats sewn together and decorated with quillwork. In Washington in 1837 Keokuk, the great Sauk chief, and Wapella, another chief, wore white shawls or ponchos embellished with scalplocks, fringes, and eagle feathers.

Hair Styles

Most men, but especially warriors, wore the roach, shaving all of the head except for a tuft from front to back, which was painted red, and a scalplock hanging from the crown. Sometimes a roach was made of red-dyed deer hair, turkey feathers, or porcupine bristle, which was added to the tuft of hair, fastened by means of a roach spreader to the scalplock; or the

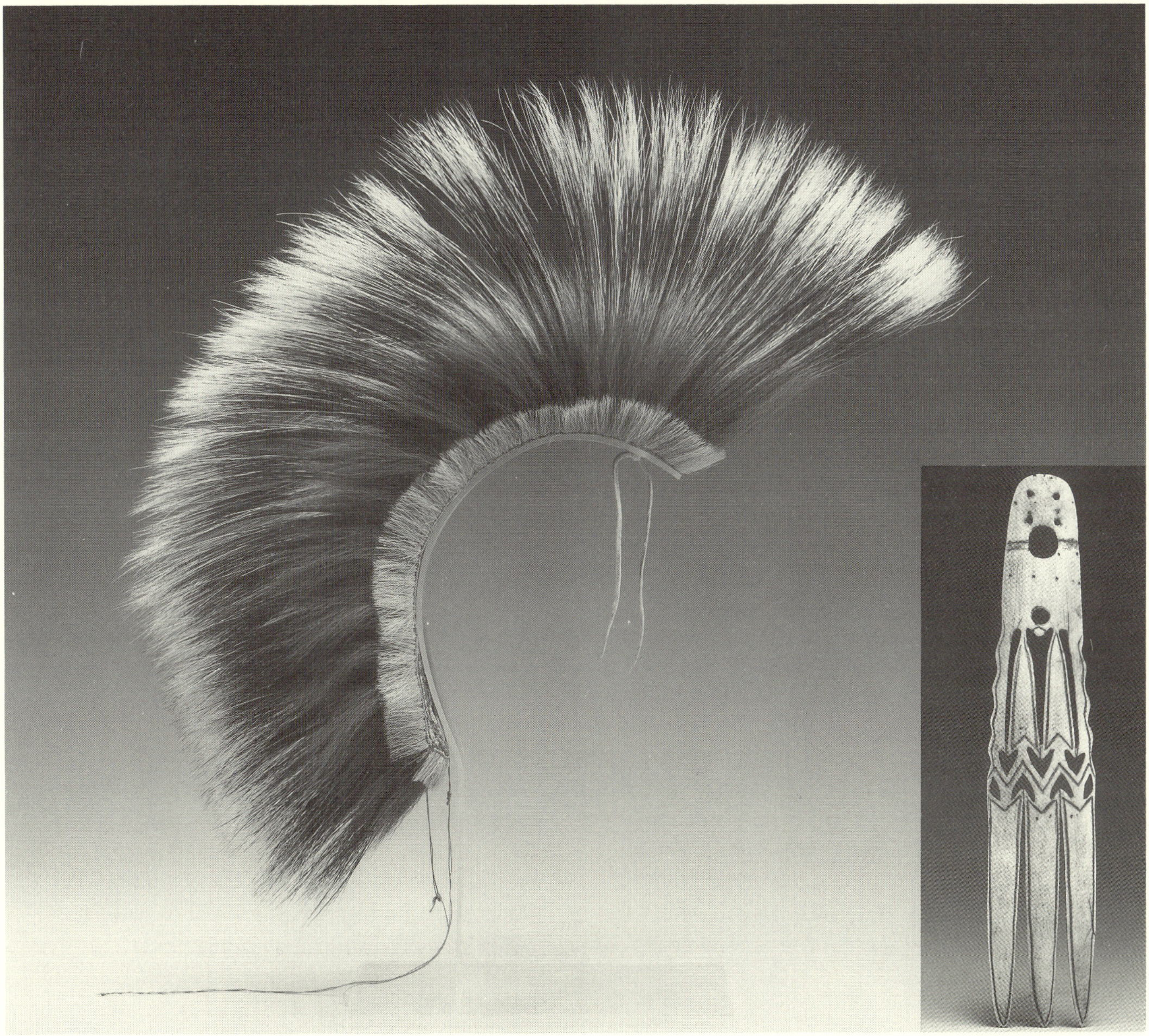

Made in 1910, this roach, made of porcupine and deer guard hairs, is over 11 inches long and 8 inches high. The roach was tied to the wearer's scalplock by means of a thong and a carved comb-like roach spreader, right.

tuft was shaved, the roach and scalplock left in place, and the bare scalp painted red. Women wore the hair in a single braid that was pulled to the back, wrapped in fur or leather, and adorned with a "hair tie" of a rectangular or hourglass shape, decorated with quillwork, later beadwork. Marrow from the shinbone of a deer was used for hair oil.

Headgear

The most common form of head covering was the otter-fur turban, using an entire pelt folded over, often with a long decorated streamer hanging down the back and with the tail usually extended horizontally at the side; a quillworked medallion was a frequent addition. Men also wore fillets or headbands made of the fur of bears, wildcats, or squirrels. Another form of headdress was a deerskin cap covered with feathers of hawks, owls, or eagles, in the eastern Woodlands fashion. Braves were given the right to wear eagle feathers for battle exploits, but at no time were the warbonnets of the Plains worn by the Sauk. Kishkekosh, a Sauk warrior, as seen in a painting by King in Washington, wore a cap of buffalo fur with horns attached—which he had taken in battle from a Sioux. Women usually went bareheaded, sometimes adding a woven headband.

Accessories

Accessories were those common to the Prairie tribes—medicine bags, fans, collars, sashes, and fur garters (simple thongs for the women); often a red flap was tied below the knee and left hanging. The finger-woven sashes were wrapped around the waist with the fringed ends trailing, worn over one shoulder in the bandolier style, or wrapped around the head as a turban. Pouches and flat envelope-type bags were made in the twining technique. Blackhawk, the great Sauk leader, wore a medicine bag made of the skin of a black hawk, and carried a fan of black hawk feathers. Typical of the extreme ornamentation of Sauk (and Fox) costumes, many accessories were worn at once and they were extensively embellished with paint and quills.

Jewelry

Grizzly bear–claw necklaces were greatly sought after, often being acquired from a fallen enemy in battle. Many shell bead necklaces were worn at the same time by both sexes. Ears were pierced in several places, then distended to accommodate earrings, hoops, clusters of shells, and feathers.

Garment Decoration

The geometric quillwork and abstract floral moose-hair embroidery gave way to beadwork and ribbonwork. Finger-weaving of bags, collars, sashes, and garters was done with buffalo hair and plant fibers such as nettle and the inner bark of basswood trees. Fringes edged many garments, some fringes being made of scalplocks in the Plains style.

Face and Body Embellishment

Painting of the face and body was of great significance to the Sauk, white and black pigments being most common. Sometimes white stripes were painted around the arms or legs. The eyes were often rimmed in red paint. Hands painted on the body were indicative, say some authorities, of enemies slain in battle. Women painted the center part of the hair red, as well as the jaws and neck.

Transitional Dress

Some forms of traditional Sauk costume were retained well into the mid-nineteenth century, combined with the materials available from the whites. But their great love for ornamentation prevailed. Men exchanged their breechclouts for beaded apron breechcloths. Silver ornaments were worn in profusion—gorgets, earrings, peace medals, headbands, armlets, neck rings, and bracelets. Beadwork was everywhere—on leather leggings and shirts, blanket robes, breechcloths, and moccasins, in geometric and floral patterns. The women created beautiful ribbon applique using the silk ribbons brought by the traders; the bands were used especially for women's skirts, leggings, and blouses. Instead of the gathered, flounced skirts of the pioneer women, the Sauk women wore a wraparound skirt of broadcloth in black, blue, or scarlet, with ribbonwork bands at the bottom and sides. Calico blouses displayed a profusion of silver brooches.

Key Sources

Callender, Charles. "Sauk." In *Handbook of North American Indians. Vol. 15: Northeast.* Pp. 648-655. Washington: Smithsonian Institution.

Forsyth, Thomas. "An Account of the Manners and Customs of the Sauk and Fox Nations of Indian Traditions." In *The Indian Tribes of the Upper Mississippi Valley and Region of the Great Lakes.* Pp. 183-245. Cleveland, OH: Arthur H. Clark, 1912.

Gilbert, Rolf. "A Sauk Chief's Gift: The Complete Costume of Moses Keokuk." *American Indian Art Magazine* (Winter 1986): 54–63.

Hagan, William T. *The Sac and Fox Indians.* Norman: University of Oklahoma Press, 1958.

Skinner, Alanson B. "Observations on the Ethnology of the Sauk Indians." Milwaukee Public Museum *Bulletin* 5(1, 3).

Shawnee

The Shawnee ("the south" or "southerners") wandered widely over the eastern part of the United States; by the time of contact, they were generally in southern Illinois and Indiana. Algonquian speakers, they were related to the Sauk and Fox. A hunting, gathering, and farming people, they were active in the fur trade, trading deerskins rather than beaver pelts. Because of their location and constant movement, they were transitional to the Southeastern culture. Tecumseh, the great Shawnee leader, attempted to unite all of the Indian tribes against the whites, but was defeated in 1811. After that time, he discarded his medal and all European attire, and urged his people to stop their dependence on trade goods, to reject all superfluous ornaments, and to go back to using skins for garments, but few listened to him. The Shawnee seem to have been well painted, from a watercolor by Joseph Wabin in 1796 to James Otto Lewis in 1823, George Catlin in the 1830s, and Charles Bird King in Washington in the 1820s and 1830s. The Shawnee, unlike many of the Prairie tribes, seem to have favored simple, undecorated garments.

Men's Basic Dress

Men wore the tanned leather breechclout, but it was rather small, just a short flap in front. Deerskin leggings were above the knee, gartered below the knee, with fringes along the side seams, and fastened to a belt with straps.

Women's Basic Dress

A deerskin wraparound skirt was the major item of dress of the Shawnee women. Leggings were short, gartered below the knee with a decorated band. A poncho-type tunic was added in cooler weather.

Footwear

Moccasins for both sexes were the Woodland type, soft-soled, one-piece, with a seam up the front from toe to instep, a quill-worked strip covering the seam, and a small turned-down cuff.

Outer Wear

Lightweight robes or mantles were of tanned deerskin. Heavier winter robes were of bearskin or buffalo hides, which the Shawnee did not paint in the Plains manner. Sometimes the men wore an animal hide over the shoulders with the claws still attached.

Hair Styles

The roach was not as common among the Shawnee as among neighboring tribes; occasionally men shaved the head in the front, and attached a feather or two at the rear. Women wore the hair loose, or in a single braid gathered at the back and fastened with a thong or a hair tie ornament.

Headgear

Few headdresses were worn. At times men wore a simple cap, almost like a nightcap, which may have been indicative of early European influence. Men sometimes wrapped the long finger-woven sashes around the head in a turban style.

Accessories

Accessories were typical of the Prairie tribes—medicine bags and pouches, sashes that were wrapped around the waist as well as on the head and sometimes crisscrossed on the chest, belts of leather to which articles could be attached, and fans for important personages.

Jewelry

Necklaces were popular with both sexes, consisting of many strings of beads made of hair pipes and other shells and native copper pounded flat and rolled tightly. Small nose rings were frequently worn. Earrings were the most prevalent form of decoration. The Shawnee

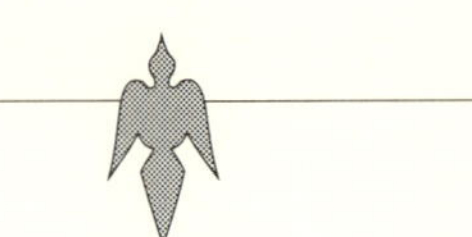

men slit the earlobes and distended the openings to great lengths, sometimes to the shoulders, by attaching weights; through these openings they hung huge hoops, rings, and ear wheels. At times they would pass a bunch of arrows or feathers through the orifice. Women pierced the ears, but did not distend the opening. Some men wore shell gorgets on the chest.

Garment Decoration
The simple garments of the Shawnee were at times edged with fringes, but little other decoration, until the women learned to do ribbonwork. The only weaving seems to have been the making of finger-woven sashes and belts in the typical arrow, chevron, and zigzag designs.

Face and Body Embellishment
Facial paint was usually red, although black and other colors were used. Some very fine lines may have been tattooed rather than painted.

Transitional Dress
Despite Tecumseh's urging, the Shawnee very early adopted European garments and styles, retaining, however, their use of ear ornaments and face paint. Women made garments of cloth but kept to traditional styles. They especially favored a black wraparound skirt, enhanced with bands of ribbonwork along the sides or down the front and around the bottom. Leggings, too, were edged with the ribbonwork. Blouses displayed silver brooches in quantity.

Key Sources
Callender, Charles. "Shawnee." *Handbook of North American Indians. Vol. 15: Northeast.* Pp. 622–635. Washington: Smithsonian Institution.
Harvey, Henry. *History of the Shawnee Indians, from the Year 1681 to 1854, Inclusive.* Cincinnati, OH: Ephraim Morgan and Sons, 1855. Reprinted by Kraus Reprint, New York, 1971.
Mooney, James. "Shawnee." *Handbook of American Indians North of Mexico.* Vol. 2. Pp. 530–538. Totowa, NJ: Rowman & Littlefield, 1975.
Trowbridge, Charles C. "Shawnese Traditions." Vernon Kinietz and Erminie W. Voegelin, eds. University of Michigan Museum of Anthropology *Occasional Contributions* 9.

Winnebago
The Winnebago Indians of northern Wisconsin occupied a transitional zone between the woodlands and prairie. This was reflected in their material culture, which incorporated elements usually associated with the Eastern Woodlands and the Plains. Their somewhat tailored skin clothing, moccasins, and snowshoes were of the Woodlands, but the design and decoration of garments reflected Plains fashions. They raised some maize, gathered wild rice, and occasionally crossed the Mississippi River to hunt buffalo, but were mainly a sedentary tribe. Unlike their neighbors, they spoke a dialect of the Siouan language. Their first contact with whites was with Jean Nicollet in Green Bay (1634). They engaged in the fur trade, but did not suffer the problems experienced by some tribes because they had substantial stores of corn. They were painted by James Otto Lewis and Peter Rindisbacher in the 1820s, by George Catlin in the 1830s, by Johann Baptist Wengler in 1851, and by Charles Bird King, who portrayed those who journeyed to Washington.

Men's Basic Dress
Early breechclouts were either of three pieces (an underpiece of thinner skin to cover the genitals and two apron flaps, front and back, well ornamented) or of one long piece also ending in flaps. They were of deer or elk skin painted red or black. Leggings were characteristically seamed down the front and fitted the legs rather closely (sometimes being laced up the front for a snugger fit), coming down over the foot in a point or cut squarely across the instep. Knee-length or above, these were also of deer or elk skin and were gartered below the knees. A poncho-type hip-length shirt was added in cooler weather. These garments were all finished off with the short fringes so typical of Winnebago dress.

Women's Basic Dress
Winnebago women in early times wore a shirt-like garment, usually to the thighs. At the time of European contact they wore the strap-and-sleeve dress. Women's leggings were knee-length and

gartered, the cuff on the upper part folded over and with no flap over the foot at the bottom.

Footwear

Winnebago moccasins, one-piece, soft-soled, and folded, were different from those of their neighbors. The men's were seamed down the front with a strip of porcupine quillwork, later beadwork, covering the seam; the rounded flaps on each side were similarly decorated. Women's moccasins had high front cuffs that featured quillwork or moose-hair embroidery and almost covered the toe. The style with an inset vamp was also used. Snowshoes were similar to those of other Forest tribes, but the two pieces of wood forming the "handle," instead of being tied together their whole length, were left unfastened at the end for several inches, a style called the "catfish." Women and children used the round "bearpaw" snowshoes.

Outer Wear

Winter robes were of buffalo or bearskin, or the pelts of small animals sewed together; these were worn over the left shoulder. Buffalo hides were tanned on the inner side and then painted in the Plains fashion.

Hair Styles

Men wore the hair in two long braids, or simply in a clump on each side, fastened with thongs. A few wore the roach, especially as a symbol of warfare, usually with a roach spreader and one or two feathers inserted in the swiveling socket. Women wore the hair in one braid at the back, often enclosed in a hair tie, a highly decorated rectangular piece of skin ornamented with quillwork or beadwork with many long embellished strips hanging down.

Headgear

The Winnebago usually went bareheaded, except to don fur hoods in the winter. Warriors sometimes wore the false roach made of deer hair dyed red. Influenced by the Plains concept of war honors, certain headdresses were reserved for certain exploits. For example, a red headdress with an eagle feather indicated that the man had counted first coup, or had scalped and killed a man in battle. An ankle band of skunk meant that the wearer had seen an enemy dead on the battlefield and touched him. One war headdress was made of grizzly-bear claws and buffalo horns on a rawhide base.

Accessories

A favorite accessory was the otter- or bobcat-skin medicine pouch, the *wayan,* used by those who belonged to the Midewiwin Society, and which was especially important in curing rites; the tail was decorated and the four paws were covered with squares worked in designs with porcupine quills. Bags, armbands, and garters were finger-woven or made of strips of fur. Belts of tanned leather were either left plain or decorated solidly in quillwork or beadwork.

Jewelry

Small, round shell gorgets were worn on the chest, suspended by a thong. Grizzly bear–claw necklaces were highly prized; other necklaces were made of shell beads, seeds, elk teeth, and some native copper. Both sexes pierced the ears in several places, but the men wore a greater number of earrings than the women.

Garment Decoration

The aboriginal crafts of porcupine quillwork and moose-hair embroidery gave way to beadwork and then to ribbon applique. The Winnebago women made beautiful bags of buffalo hair and plant fibers such as nettle in a twining technique, featuring stylized animals, thunderbirds, or abstract motifs of diamonds and zigzags.

Face and Body Embellishment

Facial and body paints were important to warriors and were applied according to the fancy of each individual. Red and black were the most common colors, signifying war and death respectively, with white denoting peace; green was also used frequently. Often a hand was painted on the face or the breast, usually indicating the killing of an enemy. Paul Radin, in his authoritative work on the Winnebago, tells of the various designs and symbols used in the facial burial masks and in the special war honors; for example, the legs painted white meant the man had been on the warpath in winter. Both sexes painted the center part of the hair red.

Transitional Dress

With European contact the emphasis shifted to cloth garments, especially stroud cloth (dark blue and red) and broadcloth, but the traditional styles prevailed.

The garments were heavily beaded with floral designs or embellished with ribbon applique. Cloth shirts appeared after 1800, at first of plain or printed cotton in the European style; later, bands of beading were added, across the shoulders or down the sides of the chest (like Plains shirts), or in a strip down the front. Later in the century heavily beaded vests were worn by the men. In the early nineteenth century the women wore a wraparound skirt of dark cotton with an opening down the front edged with bands of ribbonwork. A shirtwaist or blouse of cotton was worn outside the belt. A shawl or blanket was thrown over the shoulders. Still later in the century, printed cloth dresses in the pioneer style were adopted—full skirts ruffled at the bottom, a fitted bodice buttoned down the front, and full or plain fitted sleeves. These dresses were adorned with many silver brooches. Both sexes continued into the next century with European clothing, reserving "Indian" garb for ceremonies geared toward tourists.

Key Sources

Lanford, Benson L. "Winnebago Bandolier Bags." *American Indian Art Magazine* 9(3): 30–37.

Lawson, Publius V. "The Winnebago Tribe." *Wisconsin Archaeologist* 6(3): 77–162.

Lurie, Nancy Oestreich. *Mountain Wolf Woman: The Autobiography of a Winnebago Indian.* Ann Arbor: University of Michigan Press, 1961.

———. "Winnebago." In *Handbook of North American Indians. Vol. 15: Northeast.* Pp. 690–707. Washington: Smithsonian Institution.

Radin, Paul. "The Autobiography of a Winnebago Indian." University of California *Publications in American Archaeology and Ethnology* 16(7): 381–473.

———. *The Winnebago Tribe.* Lincoln: University of Nebraska Press, 1970. Reprint of 1923 edition.

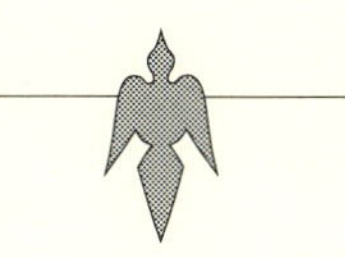

Chapter Three

Costume of the Plains

Above: Two Canadian Sarcis mix traditional attire with European-style clothing.

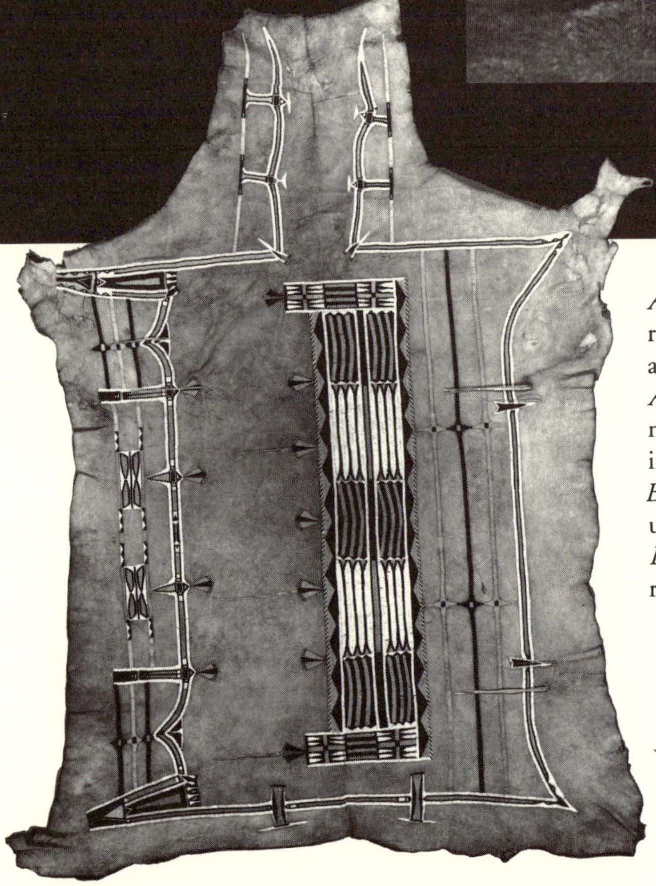

Above, left: An Oto chief wears an otter fur turban with a beaded rosette and band. His shirt is decorated with buttons and beadwork and two peace medals hang from his neck.
Above right: An Assiniboine medicine man wears a Fools Dance mask and holds a staff during a gathering at Fort Belknap, Montana, in the early 1900s.
Below: Sioux fetal amulets containing the wearer's umbilical cord ensured long life.
Left: This Sioux buffalo robe, its beaded box and border design reserved for a woman, was made circa 1870.

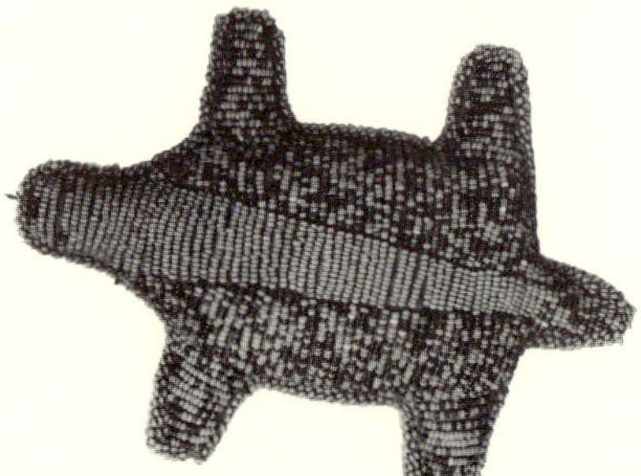

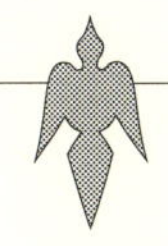

Plains

The Great Plains extend across the heartland of the North American continent. It is a land of violent contrasts—and monotony. The endless prairies, devoid of trees and even shrubs, are continually buffeted by strong winds that ruffle the abundant buffalo grass. In the heat of summer, crashing thunderstorms drench the earth, but the moisture evaporates quickly in the heat or sinks into the rocky or sandy soil. In the winter icy blizzards sweep across the plains, forming trackless wastes of driven snow. It is so arid that agriculture is possible only along the rivers and streams, especially on the eastern prairies. It is "big sky country," beautiful in its serenity, fearsome in its raging storms. It extends from the banks of the Mississippi to the foothills of the Rocky Mountains, from Texas into the Canadian plains.

There were hunters of big game on the Plains, perhaps as early as 10,000 B.C., but most settled along the rivers, making forays into the vast hunting preserves. The settlement of Europeans on the eastern seaboard beginning about 1600 pushed the Indians ever westward onto the Plains. In the late seventeenth century the horse appeared, spreading northward from the Spanish settlements of the Southwest. It was with the nomadic hunting tribes that this meeting had the greatest impact, leading to a horse/buffalo/Indian culture that was surprisingly short-lived, lasting little more than a century. By 1880, the buffalo had declined and whites had moved into the region, often violently, and the classic Plains Indian culture was gone. It left behind, however, a popular stereotype of the American Indian that persists today.

The early lifeways of the Plains Indians were extensively recorded. For many tribes the first contact was with members of the Lewis and Clark expedition (1805–1806), who kept extensive notes in their journals. Painters, such as George Catlin,

Peoples of the Plains

Arapaho, p. 88
Arikara, p. 91
Assiniboine, p. 93
Atakapa
Atsina
Blackfoot, p. 96
Blackfoot
Blood
Brule
Caddo
Cheyenne, p. 99
Coalhuitecan
Comanche, p. 104
Crow, p. 107
Dakota Sioux, p. 111
Gros Ventre
Hidatsa
Hunkpapa
Ioway, p. 114
Jumano
Kansa
Karankawa
Kiowa, p. 116
Kiowa-Apache
Lipan-Apache
Mandan, p. 119
Mdewakanton
Minneconjou
Minnetaree
Missouri
Oglala
Omaha, p. 124
Osage, p. 126
Oto
Pawnee, p. 128
Piegan
Plains Cree, p. 131
Plains Ojibway
Ponca
Quapaw
Sarci
Sisseton
Teton Sioux, p. 133
Texas, p. 141
Tonkawa
Two Kettle
Wahpekute
Wahpeton
Wichita
Yankton
Yanktonai

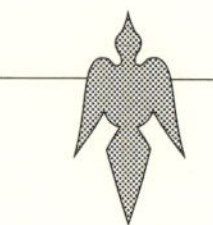

Karl Bodmer, John Mix Stanley, the Canadian Paul Kane, and the Swiss Rudolph Friederich Kurz depicted many of the tribesmen in costume that was not aboriginal (for the artists followed the traders), but had many elements of precontact dress. Catlin's notes, Maximilian's writings, and the in-depth observations of anthropologists give further information. Later came the photographers—William Henry Jackson, John K. Hillers, Alexander Gardner, Frank A. Rinehart, and, still later, Edward S. Curtis. Ewers has suggested that the Indian stereotype developed because of these artists and the wide distribution of their works.

Certain factors should be considered when discussing Plains dress. (1) Dress had to be easily transported, readily packed, and carried with ease, particularly in the case of the nomadic tribes. (2) Vast extremes of temperature meant that clothing must be adapted to the changes; this was usually handled by the addition or subtraction of articles of dress, but some items were of a seasonal nature. (3) Clothing was highly individualistic, reflecting not only tribal traditions but the wearer's taste and attainments. (4) Although tribal differences in dress are known, they are difficult to establish because of the continual trading, gift-giving, and intercommunication between the tribes, leading to a general similarity in Plains dress. (5) Plains costume was a costume of movement and sound—feathers and fringes streaming in the wind, tinklers and bells jangling, beads and shells rattling.

General Dress

Men's Basic Dress

The breechclout might be a buckskin apron or a piece of hide wrapped around the body. It is said that the traders may have brought in the fitted breechclout—a piece of skin 12 to 18 inches wide and 5 to 8 feet long, the ends passed under a belt, creating front and back flaps. Earlier breechclouts were plain, perhaps with a fringe or with quillwork for ceremonial occasions. The Indian was never without this item of attire, for it was a symbol of his sexual prowess; it was almost completely a male garment, although there are some rare examples of its being worn by girls before puberty. Thigh-length leggings were of tanned skin, folded over and tied together down the sides or sewed with sinew, the bottoms being left tattered or cut into fringes. Quillwork bands were sometimes added along the outside seams. Only in the extreme north did the Indians wear shirts aboriginally, and these were of a simple poncho type, the sides not sewn; later they were laced, loosely sewn, or tied with thongs. They were decorated with fringes, bands of quillwork, locks of hair, or strips of ermine. Most of these garments were made of deerskin, although elk and antelope skins were also used, prepared as white, natural tan, smoked brown, or dyed black.

Women's Basic Dress

Earliest attire for women was a simple wraparound skirt held in place by a belt, with a poncho-cape added for inclement weather. It was followed by the strap-and-sleeve dress, which consisted of two skins joined together at the sides to form a tube suspended by means of straps over the shoulders. Sleeves were added, if desired, tied on separately by means of thongs across the back of the neck and below the bust. A cape might be added to this. After being sewed, the excess leather was fringed. A transitional style of dress, which Norman Feder, the eminent art historian, has called the "side-fold dress," was made of one large hide folded around the body with a seam on one side; the top was folded down to produce a large flap, a vertical cut was made for the right arm, and a strap went over the right shoulder. The ensuing "two-skin dress" probably developed because of the greater availability of skins; the two skins were sewn together at the shoulders and at the sides, the excess leather was fringed, and the bottom was left uncut. This was followed by the "three-skin dress," in which two skins were sewn together at the sides and the top was made of one hide folded over and laced or sewn to the skirt, forming a large yoke with a neck opening. Knee-length leggings were gartered above or below the knees with thongs or strips of otter fur. Dresses and leggings were made of deer, elk, or antelope skins and featured such decorations as bands of quillwork, shells, rows of elk teeth, rows of thongs hanging in pairs, fringes, or the tail of the animal left intact.

Footwear

Plains moccasins were of two general types: (1) A soft-soled one-piece moccasin was like the eastern

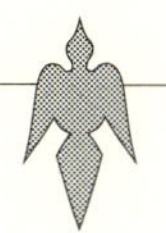

style in which the cut-out piece of leather was folded over so that one seam ran along the outer edge of the foot and another up the heel; there was a long tongue. In a variation of this pattern, the tongue was made separately and attached at the slit. (2) A second major type was the hard-soled two-piece style with the soles made of buffalo hide; these moccasins were either cut with a tongue or the tongue was added later. It is strange that the Indians wore right and left moccasins at a time when the whites were still struggling with the discomfort of shoes made alike. Cuffs were usually added, especially for winter, so they could be turned up and tied around the ankles with thongs; winter moccasins were made with hair left on and turned in or were made larger so they could be stuffed with grass, buffalo hair, or fur wrappings. Ceremonial moccasins were often painted and decorated with fringes and bands of quillwork. Women's moccasins were cut similar to the men's, but the ankle flap was more common on the women's.

Outer Wear

The buffalo robe was the great outer wrap of the Plains, worn in winter for warmth, but throughout the year as ceremonial garb. However, it was cumbersome, sometimes weighing as much as 90 pounds, and yet the Plains Indian was able to wrap himself in the robe with ease and grace. The fur being worn inside, the outside of the robe was commonly painted, usually in red, brown, and white. Certain forms of decoration were used for particular individuals: (1) The "feathered circle," also called the "black bonnet," worn by men but painted by women, was especially popular on the northern plains. (2) The women's robe, painted by them and worn only by them, featured geometric designs such as the "box and border" and, in some areas, the "hourglass and border." (3) The "exploit robe" was a pictographic record of a man's war deeds, painted by him and a male garment only; it consisted of stylized figures in battle scenes with many warriors, horses, and other animals. (4) Unmarried women's robes often had a row of medallions and pendants across the bottom. (5) Young unmarried men frequently wore robes with one horizontal strip of quilling and four large medallions. For an everyday robe, deer, elk, or antelope hide was used. Another outer wrap was the "chief's coat," which was a semi-military affair with brass buttons, gold braid, and sometimes epaulettes; much-sought-after items, used more for ceremony than for warmth, they had originally appeared in the form of gifts from traders to chiefs and were circulated widely.

Hair Styles

Men wore the hair in various ways, the most common style being the two braids (in the north) and hanging loose (in the south). Other styles: a forelock hanging down over the nose; the hair chopped in front and treated with clay to stand erect in a pompadour; the roach style, in which the head was shaved except for a brush standing erect on the top of the head from front to back; the hair pulled to the front and tied in a large knot on the forehead, a style usually reserved for medicine men. All had a scalplock, a long thin lock, usually braided, hanging from the crown, to which ornaments could be attached. Braids were sometimes wrapped with otter fur. Women generally wore the hair in two braids; unmarried women usually wore the braids hanging down the back, married women wore them forward over the shoulders. For formal occasions or times of great joy, the center part was painted with red ocher. On the southern Plains, the hair commonly hung loose. Bear grease was rubbed on the hair to make it glisten, and castoreum or sweet-smelling herbs were used as perfume.

Headgear

Except for occasional fur caps in the winter, the Plains Indians went bareheaded year-round. But they made use of ceremonial headgear. The best known is the famous feathered warbonnet, the trademark of many contemporary Indians, worn by some whose grandfathers never heard of it. It was a headdress of great distinction, for each feather of the "halo" and the trail behind represented a particular "coup" or war exploit, such as touching an enemy in battle, or saving a friend from death; each feather was awarded to the warrior by the tribal council. It was constructed on a leather skullcap base, with the feathers attached in a great circle; wing feathers (rarely tail feathers) of the golden eagle were the favored material. At the tip of each feather was a horsehair strand, the feathers representing men, the horsehair tips scalplocks. Further feathers were

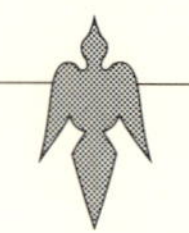

attached to the trailer, a long strip of buckskin; in prehorse days the trailer ended at the waist, later it reached the ground, depending upon the number of feathers to be added. From the peak of the bonnet a long plume extended to the back, an indication the wearer had participated in the Sun Dance. A forehead band, quillworked (later beaded), was adorned with ermine strips at the sides. A thong tied under the chin held the warbonnet in place while the wearer was riding or facing a strong wind. The buffalo horn headdress, a symbol of great strength and prowess, was worn only by warriors of the highest position; various items were added for decoration—seashells, pieces of animal skins or bones, feathers, braided horsehair tails, ermine skins—any articles that had special significance for the wearer. In the eastern and southern Plains the otter-fur turban was popular. Some headdresses were made of the entire skins of birds, or the head of an animal. Despite the popular conception, headbands were quite uncommon on the Plains. Men especially wore feathers in the hair, the number, size, color, and shape having significance to the wearer; however, there was no set "language" of the feathers, for indicators would differ from one tribe to the next, from one individual to the next. Shells, beads, animal claws, or bones might be added to the hair as ornament. The tall, black felt "Indian hat" was adopted by many Indian men in the late nineteenth century

Accessories

Men wore two belts, an inner thong that held breechclout and leggings in place, and a dress belt of rawhide put on over the thong but under a shirt when worn. From the outer belt hung such things as pouches, bags, tools, and weapons. "Medicine" bags were important because of the supernatural powers given to the wearer based on the articles within. "Strike-a-light" bags contained flint and steel. Knife cases were also attached to the belt. Women wore leather belts to carry important items such as awl cases and bags for paint. Belts were often painted and decorated with quillwork. Fans, carried by men, particularly older men, were of eagle feathers (tail and wing). After 1850 some Indian men wore breastplates, more for looks than for protection; these were fashioned of hair pipe beads two to five inches long, made from the shell of the *Strombus gigas,* which were strung into two, three, or four sections. The top of the breastplate had thongs to tie around the neck and the waist. It was ornamented with brass beads, shells, quilled or beaded decorations, and trade ribbons.

Jewelry

The Indians with their love for decoration wore much jewelry, arranging it with great care and taste; furthermore, it was a form of wealth easily transported. Necklaces were made of grass, seeds, shell beads, strings of fossil crinoids, animal claws, horns, antlers, and teeth, especially elk teeth. Grizzly bear–claw necklaces were magnificent and contained enormous medicine. Chokers were made of fur strips, dentalium shells (from the Pacific), rolls of otter skins stuffed and decorated with quillwork, and hair pipes; a popular addition was a large disk cut from a clamshell. Jewelry was suspended from the ears in profusion. Beads, shells, and hair pipes, totaling as much as half a pound in weight, might be hung from one ear. Shell gorgets or pectorals were suspended from the neck by thongs. A "hair bow" had a rawhide base in an hourglass shape, with beads or shells hung from it. Armbands and bracelets were formed from strips of quillwork. Nose ornaments were uncommon on the Plains. Silver peace medals were treasured by the chiefs; three to six inches in diameter, they had the image of the current president on one side and usually an eagle on the other. They were officially authorized by the president and minted by the U.S. government especially for gifts to chiefs.

Armor

Warriors carried large circular shields of heavy rawhide, taken from the neck of the buffalo, laced on a hoop, and painted. Some tribes decorated the shield itself with symbols of enormous power revealed in dreams, while others put designs on the buckskin covers that enclosed the shield proper. The Plains Indians did not wear armor as such, although in some areas heavy elk-hide or buffalo-hide shirts were worn in earlier times as a crude form of armor.

Special Costumes

There were no special costumes for chiefs; they dressed in warrior dress, including the warbonnet, but they did carry a wooden staff or lance, curved at the top, wrapped with otter fur and adorned with

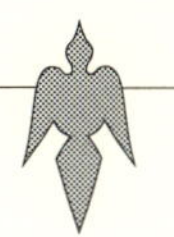

eagle feathers. Distinctive headdresses were worn by the members of the various warrior societies in their tribal dances. Shamans or medicine men often dressed differently from others, but in a highly individualistic manner.

Garment Decoration

Porcupine quillwork was important for garment decoration in early times, especially among the northern and central Plains tribes. Much work was done with bird quills, especially when green was desired, for they took dyes better. Red and yellow colors were fairly easily obtained. Black was often introduced by the use of maidenhair ferns. Designs were simple and geometric, typically done in a two-thread sewing technique. Beadwork began to be developed in the late eighteenth century, and for some time, the two techniques occurred together, often on the same piece. By the 1830s beadwork had become dominant. The late 1800s produced such a proliferation of beadwork that often entire garments were covered with beads, especially vests, moccasins, and leggings. In the early stages beadwork continued with the geometric designs of quillwork; later, the floral designs of the Northeastern Indians were adopted. The first major type of bead was the "pony bead," brought in by the traders on their ponies. The smaller seed beads in a great variety of colors appeared around 1840, followed by the medium-sized, often faceted, beads of the 1870s. The overlay stitch, in which beads on one thread were fastened down at frequent intervals by a second thread, was popular with many tribes. Other tribes preferred the "lazy" stitch, in which five or more beads were strung on a thread before being fastened in place, a good technique for filling in large areas. Little weaving was done by the Plains tribes. Painting was common on garments, either solidly or in strips and designs.

Face and Body Embellishment

Face and body painting was an important element in Plains culture, not only as a matter of ornamentation but also as great spiritual power, at times constituting a prayer to a supernatural being. Each warrior decided for himself the designs and colors in harmony with his attire, his purpose, and often his dreams and visions. Painting had different purposes:

(1) Painting acted as a talisman in war to protect the wearer; before a battle not only were the face and body painted but the horse as well. To signify war, women painted streaks down their noses, cheeks, and across the forehead. Warriors returning from a successful conflict painted the faces black, although the tip of the nose was usually left unpainted.
(2) Certain symbols and colors were indicative of membership in one of the secret military societies.
(3) The face and body were painted in preparation for certain ceremonies. For formal occasions, both men and women painted the part in the hair with red paint, symbolic of the earth and fecundity.
(4) Persons in mourning painted the face white.
(5) Painting was also used to shield the user from the sun, wind, snow, and insects; for this purpose, buffalo fat or bear grease was rubbed into the skin, then paint was applied over the grease. Tattooing was not generally found on the Plains except in the southern areas at times and in the far north.

Transitional Dress

Because of the elaborate trade network, European products found their way early on to the Plains. Commercial colors such as vermilion were imported as early as 1770. Glass beads quickly replaced the crude native beads that were so difficult to make. Early commercial beads, called "pony beads" because they were brought in by the traders in their pony pack trains, were immediately successful; these large beads, appearing about 1800, were superseded about 1840 by the tiny seed beads and other varied types. Beadwork became an outstanding characteristic of Plains decoration, used exuberantly and extensively into the modern period. Stroud cloth replaced tanned leather in breechclouts, dresses, leggings, and lightweight robes. Blankets, particularly the Hudson's Bay variety, slowly replaced the cumbersome buffalo robes, particularly as the buffalo diminished in numbers; these blankets, white with four colored stripes at each end, were marked with parallel lines at one side indicating the "point value," that is, the number of beaver pelts required in trade. They also appeared as *capotes,* the long hooded jackets of the French *voyageurs* girded with a long colorful sash. Buckskin warshirts were heavily beaded, as were the adopted vests of the white men. The tall, black felt hat with the flat brim appeared in the late nineteenth

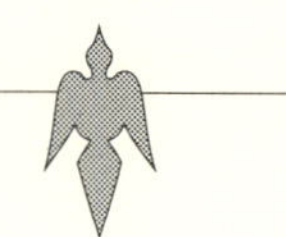

century. Metal was made into many ornaments. "Hair plates," long strips of rawhide with silver disks attached, were fastened into the hair, trailing down the back. Tin "tinklers," small metal cones, were used as ornament on dresses and shirts, cherished for their sound as well as appearance. Metal was also made into armbands, ball-and-cone earrings, and brooches.

Arapaho

The Algonquian-speaking Arapaho originally lived in the Red River Valley in earthen lodges; in the seventeenth century they moved onto the Plains to become horse nomads. They were closely associated with the Atsina (the Gros Ventre of the Prairies) and the Cheyenne, and were generally friendly with the whites. About 1780 they separated into the Northern and Southern Arapaho. The origin of the name is doubtful; some say it is a Pawnee word for "trader." Tall and handsome, the Arapaho men often had a prominent "Roman" nose, which led the Osage to call them "big nose people." Roaming the Plains, they established no permanent settlements and practiced no agriculture, spreading out in the areas of Nebraska, Wyoming, and Colorado. Catlin and Bodmer did watercolors and sketches of them in the 1830s, and Alexander Gardner photographed them in 1868.

Men's Basic Dress

The man's breechclout was often a simple apron of tanned deer or elk skin fastened in place with a thong belt; some authorities believe the breechclout was adopted after the traders came. Hip-length leggings of skin, added when desired, featured long fringes at the sides and were decorated for ceremonial wear with bands of quillwork. Shirts, when worn, were of tanned leather, cut in a simple poncho style with an opening for the head and tied at the sides with thongs. These, too, were adorned with quillwork bands and fringes at the bottom, sides, and the short "sleeve" ends; warriors' shirts were often painted with celestial symbols. It is questionable whether the Arapaho men wore shirts before the coming of the whites.

Women's Basic Dress

Women, aboriginally as well as historically, wore the simple skirt of leather, overlapping on the right side to form what has been called the "Algonkin split skirt." With this they added for warmth a poncho of skin or fur. The two-skin dress was popular later; it consisted of two deer or elk skins folded over to form a yoke at the top so that a tail hung in front over the breast and in back; shoulder seams were sewn or fastened, the sleeve ends being squared off in a characteristic fashion. Arapaho women later wore the three-skin dress in which two skins formed a skirt and the third skin was folded over to make a yoke that was fastened to the skirt. Yokes of both styles were decorated with bands of quillwork or rows of elk teeth; fringes and rows of thongs further ornamented the ankle-length dresses. Knee-length leggings were rectangular pieces of skin laced at the front on the inside of the leg and often painted with yellow ocher; they featured a wide area at the bottom, as much as eight inches wide, embellished with quilled bands, and were gartered below the knees.

Footwear

Moccasins were the typical Plains hard-soled type, with or without a cuff. Designs tended to be simpler than those of neighboring tribes, possibly because quillwork was used for decoration by the Arapaho long after others had adopted beading. They particularly favored such designs as the Maltese cross and longitudinal quilled stripes across the toe. They did not as a rule have the U-shaped insert above the instep. Southern Arapaho moccasins commonly had arrow designs. The women of the southern tribe tended to wear hard-soled boots, that is, moccasins and leggings attached together. Arapaho hunters wore snowshoes when tracking animals.

Outer Wear

The buffalo robe was worn by both sexes, despite its weight. It was often draped over the shoulders and tied in the front with thongs. The tanned side of the robe was adorned with painted designs or intricate porcupine quillwork. Lighter weight robes were of deer or elk skin.

Hair Styles

Women formerly wore the hair loose, with paint on it; later they adopted braids falling over the shoulders in front. Kroeber in his authoritative work on the Arapaho gives a detailed account of hair styles. He says that formerly the men had parted the hair on

Freckled Face, an Arapaho woman photographed in 1898, wears a long hairpipe neckpiece and a choker of small hairpipes and beads. Many rows of elk teeth decorate her dress.

each side and left a shorter length standing up in front, cutting it in a zigzag manner on the forehead. Later they, too, adopted the two-braids style. Older men at times gathered all the hair into a large knob on the forehead. Haircutting, like so many of the Arapaho activities, was a ceremonial rite, especially when young boys had the hair cut over the forehead and on one side.

Headgear

The Plains warbonnet was seldom worn by Arapaho warriors. Feathers were commonly worn by the men, fastened in clusters or singly to the scalplock at the crown of the head; feathers were ornamented with tufts of horsehair, dyed lightly with red or green colors. A common form of headgear was the eyeshade or sun visor; made of a piece of rawhide about a foot long, with a circular opening at one end with slits in it, when the visor was pressed on the head it stayed firmly and shaded the eyes from the sun. Visors were also made of a moose-mane or a horsehide-fringe circle.

An Arapaho man, photographed in 1875, wears leggings with beaded bands down the front and gartered below the knees; his moccasins are beaded with the buffalo track motif. He has a three-paneled, hairpipe bead breastplate, and he has wrapped his braids in fur.

Accessories

Older men carried fans of eagle wings; younger men sported fans of the tail feathers of hawks or eagles. Armbands were of tanned leather adorned with bands of quillwork and hanging quill-wrapped thongs or strips of fur. Rectangular "purses" were carried by the men, fringed at the bottom and embellished with quillwork. Lacking pockets, the Arapaho carried all sorts of pouches and bags for various purposes, usually attached to belts of thongs or leather straps. Hair pipe bone breastplates were worn by the men in the later nineteenth century.

Jewelry

Ear piercing, a ceremonial rite, was performed on the young; earrings of shell, bone, or feathers were worn by both sexes. The Arapaho were sometimes called Big Bead or Blue Bead Indians, because of the large blue beads they valued so highly; some authorities believe the beads may have been turquoise from the Southwest, which was widely traded even in prehistoric times. A small hoop or wheel adorned with quillwork was often worn at either side of the head. Warriors frequently wore necklaces that were based on their visions or dreams and were created using symbolic materials; for example, they would feature ammonites, shell fossils that were believed to contain the spirits of supernatural buffalos.

Armor

Large round shields were made of thick buffalo hide; these had a cover of tanned leather often painted with a turtle's image. Otter skins were believed to give protection, and so were often worn by warriors.

Special Costumes

Ceremony was central to the way of life of the Arapaho, and the Sun Dance was the most significant

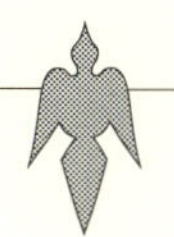

of these rites. On each of the four days, a participant wore different articles of dress and painted the face and body in certain ways, all indicative of complex symbolic meanings. Next in importance were the male age-graded societies, in which each individual worked up though the various levels. The third significant ceremony was that of the Women's Buffalo Society, for which particular regalia was worn. A period of mourning was indicated by the cutting of the hair, light gashing of the arms or legs, the wearing of old clothes, and a refraining from painting.

Garment Decoration

Arapaho moccasins and garments were decorated with quillwork long after other tribes had adopted beading. In their beadwork, they favored characteristic narrow beaded bands interspersed with small figures. There was much use of the Maltese cross and a central diamond shape with appendages. Scalloped lines of beading sometimes adorned the lower edges.

Face and Body Embellishment

Face and body painting was practiced, especially in the ceremonials; for the Sun Dance the face, torso, and arms were painted. Women painted streaks down the face, on the cheeks, nose, and forehead, to signify war. Both sexes painted the hair part ("the path of the sun") with red ocher, later vermilion. Old women indicated peace by painting a red spot on each cheekbone, one on the forehead, one between the eyes to signify a buffalo calf, and a line from the mouth down the chin to represent a road. Paint on the face generally signified happiness.

Transitional Dress

The Arapaho began to lose their tribal distinctions in dress as they started to adopt the warbonnet and warshirts of the Sioux and the beading techniques of many Plains tribes; however, they retained their symbolically spiritual approach to decoration. Women's dresses were in the Plains two-skin dress style, but were quite long (ankle length) and displayed elaborate beadwork. Blankets took the place of robes, but were finely beaded in the same manner as the buffalo robes had been quilled. As they entered the Reservation Period, slowly European fashions and garments took over.

Key Sources

Bass, Althea. *The Arapaho Way: A Memoir of an Indian Boyhood.* New York: Clarkson N. Potter, 1966.

Curtis, Edward S. *The North American Indian.* Vol. 6. New York: Johnson Reprint Company, 1970.

Kroeber, Alfred L. "The Arapaho." American Museum of Natural History *Bulletin* 18(1): 1–150.

———. *Arapaho: Decorative Art and Symbolism.* New York: American Museum of Natural History, 1902.

Mails, Thomas. "The Arapaho." In *Dog Soldiers, Bear Men and Buffalo Women: A Study of the Societies and Cults of the Plains Indians.* Pp. 189–212. Englewood Cliffs, NJ: Prentice-Hall, 1973.

Seger, John H. *Early Days among the Cheyenne and Arapahoe Indians.* Norman: University of Oklahoma Press.

Trenholm, Virginia Cole. *The Arapahoes, Our People.* Norman: University of Oklahoma Press, 1970.

Arikara

The Arikara were an offshoot of the Pawnee to the south, speaking the same Caddoan dialect of the Hokan-Siouan family of languages. Hodge says their name came from "ariki," a Skidi Pawnee word for "horn," referring to an early hair style in which two pieces of bone were twined in with the hair, which then stood up like horns on each side of a crest. Their name for themselves was Sahnish; they were also called Rees. Living on both sides of the Missouri River, they were semisedentary farmers, fishermen, and hunters. They brought corn or maize with them when they moved north, becoming proficient at raising and trading it; in fact, a sign-language symbol for them was the eating of an ear of corn. The grain was not only a matter of commercialism, but significant of deep spirituality, for many of their ceremonies were based on the raising of corn; they referred to maize as "Mother." The Arikara were bitter toward the whites, an attitude that seems to have been reciprocated, for the traders referred to them as "the horrid tribe." Denig said their habits were "more filthy than any other nation on the Upper Missouri" and that they had "thieving, shabby, ungraceful looks," while Lewis and Clark called them tall and well proportioned. First contact

seems to have been with Jean-Baptiste Trudeau, a French trader who wrote the first description of the Arikara in 1798. George Catlin and Karl Bodmer painted them in the 1830s. They were also recorded by the frontier photographer S. J. Merrow in the late 1860s.

Men's Basic Dress

The skin poncho was the early garment of these people, developing into a shirt with sleeves sewn only from wrist to elbow, with a triangular neck flap and decorative bands of quillwork, further embellished with paint and long hair locks. The tanned-leather breechclout was narrow and rather short. Leggings were cut in a "whole deerskin" pattern, which made for wide angular flaps at the lower edge, but which were snugly fitted otherwise. The Arikara obtained antelope-skin shirts and moccasins from the nomadic tribes to the west.

Women's Basic Dress

Both men and women wore garments of antelope as well as deerskin, tanned to a creamy white. Women went through the usual succession of wraparound skirt, the strap-and-sleeve dress, and the two-skin dress, which they were wearing at the time of contact. The two-skin dresses were decorated with long fringes at the bottom of the skirt and along the lower edges of the sleeves; quilled rosettes, dentalium shells, rows of elk teeth, and often the hooves of mountain sheep (at the shoulders) were further adornments. Leggings were frequently of antelope skin enhanced with quillwork.

Footwear

Early moccasins were of the soft-soled type, with the puckered toe gathered into a U-shaped insert above the instep. In some types of moccasins, especially the women's, the front was gathered into a seam, which was often covered with an embroidered or quillworked strip. The Arikara women especially liked to have their fitted leggings match the decoration of the moccasins. Later, the tribe adopted the hard-soled moccasins of the Plains. Snowshoes were worn for winter travel.

Outer Wear

Lighter weight robes were of deer or antelope skin. The buffalo robe for summer was without hair, while the winter robe was worn with the hair turned inside; the tanned side, worn outward, was painted. Catlin shows us the 12-year-old daughter of an Arikara chief wearing a robe of young buffalo hide with a sunburst design painted on it; it was also decorated with rosettes of quillwork. Men's robes often had a wide strip of quillwork with a quilled rosette at the end. Warriors' robes had painted symbols indicating such deeds as killing an enemy or counting coup on a fallen enemy.

Hair Styles

The roach was the common form of headdress for warriors; these were the artificial roaches of deer hair, porcupine guard hair, or turkey beard, kept in place by means of a roach spreader. Women wore the hair parted in the center and flowing loosely for special occasions, or fastened into braids for everyday work. Men wore the hair in various styles such as a pompadour; a forelock over the nose; two braids, which were often wrapped with fur; or worn loose with one to three feathers at the back.

Headgear

The Arikara braves wore the customary feathers in the hair designating certain exploits in battle, such as attacking an enemy during conflict or sustaining wounds. The characteristic warbonnet of the Plains was not adopted by them until well into the nineteenth century. Rawhide sun visors were worn.

Accessories

Tanned leather belts, decorated with quillwork or painted designs, were popular with both sexes. Decorated strips were also used as armbands and garters. Bags and pouches, hung from a belt or at the side, carried such things as pipes and tobacco, sewing equipment, paints and brushes, or sacred "medicine" articles. These, too, were enhanced with paint or quills.

Men, especially older men, carried eagle wing feather fans.

Jewelry

Hair cutting was semiceremonial, as was the piercing of the ears, all done "for the good of the child." The most popular ear pendants, says Curtis, were large blue clamshells. Grizzly bear–claw necklaces were

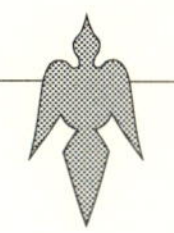

fastened to an otter skin, using the head and tail as decoration, further embellished with strips of ermine fur. The Arikara were said by Lewis and Clark to have invented the art of making glass beads. Actually, they seem to have learned, supposedly from some Spanish prisoner, the art of melting glass beads procured in trade and pouring them into molds of clay; the resultant beads were widely traded. Men wore the characteristic Northern Plains loop necklace and padded choker. A navel amulet, containing a baby's umbilical cord, was worn from infancy through life as a charm; it often featured a turtle or lizard effigy, symbols of longevity. Women sometimes wore elaborate necklaces of hair pipes.

Armor

Like other tribes of the Northern Plains, the Arikara wore no armor; for protection they carried a shield often painted with a buffalo symbol and with eagle feathers attached.

Special Costumes

Strongly concerned with ceremonialism, the Arikara had many societies, of both military and religious nature, including three women's societies. Regalia consisted of sashes of various colors, feathers, buffalo headdresses, shell breast ornaments, and other insignias of office. Mails, Curtis, and Lowie have all written extensively on these societies.

Garment Decoration

Little is mentioned about quillwork among the Arikara, except for the occasional use of quilled rosettes. They were famous for their ability to melt down the glass beads of the traders, casting them in clay molds to form pendants; these were unique and much desired for trading purposes. Beaded triangular neck flaps and arm and shoulder bands were significant elements on the men's war shirts. Cowrie shells and dentalium shells, obtained in trade from the far Pacific, were extremely popular for use in garment decoration and ornaments. Long fringes and the hooves of mountain sheep were further decorative elements.

Face and Body Embellishment

Face and body painting was widely used in the society ceremonials; for example, members of the Speckled male society painted themselves with dots of different colors. Red and black were the hues most frequently applied, with yellow and white used in some cases.

Transitional Dress

Because of their situation at the hub of northern trade, the Arikara, early in their history, adopted the dress of other Plains tribes as well as the products of the traders. Cotton and stroud cloth replaced deer and antelope skin. Hudson's Bay blankets were more satisfactory than the buffalo robes and beading was easier to do than quillwork and far more colorful. In the case of the latter, the Arikara preferred white backgrounds during the early pony bead period, changing to light blue backgrounds when seed beads became available. Peace medals, silver armbands, and hair plates were popular. Some men adopted the European turban style. By the 1870s the tribe was so decimated by diseases and other ills of the white culture that little remained of their own tribal culture.

Key Sources

Denig, Edwin Thompson. *Five Indian Tribes of the Upper Missouri: Sioux, Arikaras, Assiniboines, Crees, Crows.* Norman: University of Oklahoma Press, 1961.

Lowie, Robert H. "Societies of the Arikara Indians." American Museum of Natural History *Bulletin* 11(8).

Mails, Thomas E. "The Arikara. In *Dog Soldiers, Bear Men and Buffalo Women: A Study of the Societies and Cults of the Plains Indians.* Pp. 143–160. Englewood Cliffs, NJ: Prentice-Hall, 1973.

Stirling, Matthew W. "Arikara Glassworking." *Journal of the Washington Academy of Sciences* 38(8).

Works Progress Administration. *Arikara Indians.* Vermilion, SD: University Museum, 1941.

Assiniboine

The Assiniboine inhabited the region from the mouth of the Yellowstone River northeast to Lake Winnipeg. They were originally a part of the Yanktonai Sioux, from whom they separated in 1640; although constantly at war with them, they were greatly similar in language and appearance. They belonged to the Siouan linguistic family and also spoke the Dakota dialect. The name came from a Chippewa word meaning "stone boilers," referring to the common Indian method of heating stones and placing them in water to boil food; they were also called Stoney Indians. Predominantly traders and middlemen, they lived on the Plains with no permanent villages and without as many horses as neighboring tribes. It is difficult to categorize the Assiniboine; although they were similar in manners and dress to the Plains Cree and their allies in fighting the Sioux, their extensive traveling as traders, even as far as the Plateau, gave them opportunities to adopt the clothing of many of the tribes they encountered. But they never truly became nomadic horsemen of the high plains. Their dress and customs have been well documented for they were painted by Peter Rindisbacher (1821–1826), George Catlin (1832), Karl Bodmer (1833–1834), Paul Kane in 1842, and Rudolph Kurz in 1851.

Men's Basic Dress

Men's garments were fashioned of almost whole skins of deer or mountain goats rather loosely sewn together with little regard for fit. Breechclouts and leggings were the usual garb, with a shirt added as needed. Leggings of trapezoid pieces of hide were sewn up the sides, tapering to the bottom, and a short wide fringe was inserted along the seam. If painted or quilled with hoofprint designs, it indicated the wearer had stolen horses in the summer; white ermine strip fringes indicated a winter robbery. Shirts were of two types. One was the typical knee-length Northern Plains shirt; it had a boat neck, a large quilled rosette both front and back, and a rectangular piece, also quilled, at the neck. Fringes, quill-wrapped at the base, were added at the sides and down the arms. The other type of shirt showed influence of the Plateau where the Assiniboine traded; it was short-waisted, had rows of cut holes in circle designs, many dots of paint, and an elaborately cut bottom tab. Catlin did a meaningful painting of an Assiniboine warrior, Wi-jun-jon or Pigeon's Egg Head (also called The Light), going to Washington and returning. On his trip east he wore the buckskin fringed and decorated garments of his world; on his return he was dressed as a kid-gloved dandy in military dress and high-heeled boots—a sad commentary on the passing of beautiful garments.

Women's Basic Dress

Early dresses were probably the wraparound skirt with a poncho-like top, then the strap-and-sleeve dress. At the time of contact the Assiniboine women were wearing the two-skin dress, and it continued to be their favorite. The dress, to mid-calf in length, had a folded-over yoke at the top that was often laced down with a leather thong. Further decoration consisted of fringes down the side seams, rows of thongs, often many rows of elk teeth, and a quillworked strip down the top of each sleeve. The dresses were usually of mountain-goat skin and were often belted with many bags and pouches hanging from the belt.

Footwear

Early moccasins were of the Woodland soft-soled type with an oval or U-shaped inset. Hard-soled moccasins took their place, continuing with the shape and design of the earlier ones. Not only the instep but other areas were decorated with porcupine quillwork (later beadwork), usually with a blue background. Cuffs were attached, worn with the flaps down, or worn up and fastened with thongs for winter wear. In making moccasins, the women decorated the tops first, then sewed them to the rawhide soles. Warriors had wolves' tails trailing at the heels, indicative of enemies they had killed. Snowshoes were worn in winter.

Outer Wear

The buffalo robe was standard in the northern areas of the Plains, worn with the fur side in for winter. The tanned side was decorated; the Assiniboine commonly displayed a large rosette on the front and the back of the robe. Often the hide was split from head to tail for convenience in tanning; the two parts were then seamed together and the seam covered with embroidery or quillwork; so that the strip appeared in a horizontal position when the robe was worn.

Hair Styles

The Assiniboine, somewhat like the Crow, were inordinately fond of long hair; sometimes it reached to the ground. But Catlin found that usually such great length had been augmented by splicing in lengths of hair from other sources by means of glue. Often a forelock or a tiny braid was worn over the nose. At times the long hair was tied in a knot above the forehead or wound in a coil on top of the head. Some men wore small pompadours. Women wore the hair loose and flowing, taking pride in its length.

Headgear

The Assiniboine warriors were more inclined to wear the horned headdress than the halo warbonnet. Caps of wolf skin, especially white, were worn throughout the winter and even in the summer, despite the heat. At times these caps were smeared with red ocher. Some winter caps were of badger fur.

Accessories

Like most nomadic peoples, the Assiniboine wore belts from which hung many pouches and bags, such as "strike-a-lights" for carrying fire-making equipment, knife sheaths, cases for awls and other sewing needs, medicine bundles, and bags for painting materials. Of tanned leather, the belts were embellished with quillwork or embroidery; later, as metal became available, they were tack-studded in various designs. Fans of eagle or swan wing feathers were carried by dandies. Mittens, usually of fur and rarely worn by Plains Indians, were standard items with this tribe. Armbands and garters were strips of leather, embroidered or quillworked. Late in the nineteenth century the hair pipe breastplate was worn.

Jewelry

Necklaces were of grizzly bear–claws and strips of otter fur; of eagle or owl claws; of shells, such as dentalia from the Pacific coast; or of the bones or teeth of small animals. Some men wore the loop necklace common to the Plateau tribes. Many wore the navel amulet, containing the wearer's umbilical cord and featuring designs of turtles or lizards, symbols of longevity.

Armor

Warriors wore sleeveless jackets of moose leather of as many as six thicknesses. Generally shields of buffalo hide were carried, decorated with painted scenes of battle or images derived from the wearer's visions.

Special Costumes

The Grass Dance was performed by the Soldier Society of the Assiniboine; performers wore the roach headdress made of porcupine and deer-tail hairs. Most wore leggings with fringes of weasel skins or locks of human hair. The Kit Fox celebrants wore a coyote jawbone painted red or blue and fastened to a forehead band made of a strip of otter fur. These people also participated in the Sun Dance. There were many other dances and cults, some characterized by special dress, others a matter of individual choice.

Garment Decoration

Quillwork was used for the characteristic rosettes and rectangular patches on the front and back of the men's war shirts. Later these were accomplished with beadwork. Both the overlay and lazy stitch were used, with blue, at times even dark blue, backgrounds being favored. Popular designs were crosses, hexagons, horse hoofs, stepped triangles, and many small squares in the background. Fringes were frequently quill-wrapped at the base; some fringes were simply cut flaps in the Plateau style. Plateau influence could also be seen in the use of punctuated dot designs on short shirts. Women's dresses usually featured many rows of elk teeth or cowrie shells.

Face and Body Embellishment

Face painting was frequently resorted to by the men, especially those going into battle, red and black being the most common hues; black indicated an enemy had been killed. At times the eyes were rimmed with white clay. Tattooing is mentioned as being composed of two black stripes from the neck to the chest. Jenness quotes from *The Jesuit Relations* that this tribe tattooed representations of birds and animals, such as snakes, an eagle, or a toad, on their bodies. If so, this is unusual, for Indians rarely tattooed realistic designs. Women often had thin lines tattooed from the underlip to the chin.

Masks

Masks were seldom used in ceremonies on the Plains, but during their Fool Dance the Assiniboine wore masks made of rectangles of buckskin, fringed around the edges, with slits for the eyes and with an attached nose piece.

Transitional Dress

Slowly the Assiniboine changed their attire, beginning about the middle of the nineteenth century. They wore the hooded *capotes* made of the Hudson's Bay blankets. Buffalo robes were exchanged for blankets, tanned leather for stroud cloth or commercial leather. Quillwork gave way to beadwork, at which the Assiniboine women excelled; moccasins were fully beaded with bold color combinations and dark to medium backgrounds. Wide rawhide belts were studded with metal tacks. Hats, vests, cotton shirts, trousers, and full-skirted women's dresses had taken over by the end of the nineteenth century.

Key Sources

Denig, Edward Thompson. *Five Indian Tribes of the Upper Missouri: Sioux, Arikaras, Assiniboines, Crees, Crows.* Norman: University of Oklahoma Press, 1961.

Long, James Larpenteur. *The Assiniboines.* Norman: University of Oklahoma Press, 1961.

Lowie, Robert H. "The Assiniboine." American Museum of Natural History *Anthropological Papers* 4(1).

Mails, Thomas. "The Assiniboine." *Dog Soldiers, Bear Men and Buffalo Women: A Study of the Societies and Cults of the Plains Indians.* Pp. 339–352. Englewood Cliffs, NJ: Prentice-Hall, 1973.

Blackfoot

The Blackfoot Confederation consisted of the Blackfeet proper (Siksika), the Blood (or Kainah), the Piegan (also called the Pecunnies), and their allies, the Sarci to the north, and the Atsina or Gros Ventre of the Prairies to the southeast. They were Algonquian speakers except for the Sarcis, who spoke Athapaskan. These tribes lived on the high plains of what is now Montana and north into the province of Alberta. They were restless, roving buffalo hunters without permanent dwellings or villages, and were the largest of the tribes of the northern and western Plains. The origin of their name is not definitely known, but the most common belief is that it was a Cree term that referred to their custom of painting their moccasins black. Blackfoot traditions say that they originally came from the shores of a large lake to the north, possibly Lake Winnipeg, and there is some evidence of eastern cultural influences; but the confederation of the three major tribes seems to have persisted for some time, for one of the earliest contacts with whites mentions that their moccasins were often decorated with a three-pronged design to represent the three tribes. They were painted by Karl Bodmer and George Catlin in the 1830s and extensively painted by Winold Reiss in this century.

Men's Basic Dress

A Blackfoot man wore the usual Plains garb of breechclout, shirt, leggings, and moccasins. Breechclouts were about knee-length, the same length back and front, and decorated, if at all, with a short fringe. The knee-length shirts were of two deerskins, usually dyed dark brown or almost black, and were worn belted or unbelted. The hemline retained the ragged edge of the skins. Unusually long fringes hung under the arms and at the bottom. On the chest and the back appeared a large circular (rosette) or rectangular quillworked design; strips of quillwork were attached over the shoulders and down the tops of the sleeves. Other decorations were hair locks (quill-wrapped at the base) as fringes, rows of rolled ermine tails, and painted symbols. A black tadpole shape was popular with the Blackfeet and indicated the wearer had been wounded in battle. Dark horizontal lines were also symbolic of action in battle. Blackfeet men occasionally wore the short Plateau shirt, which featured punctuated designs. Dark-colored leggings were tapering tubes of tanned leather, tied at the sides with thongs; along the outer seams were bands of porcupine quillwork, rolled ermine tails, and fringes of scalplocks. Rectangular ankle panels were characteristic of the Blackfeet leggings.

Women's Basic Dress

Women's dresses were of the skins of deer, mountain goats, or mountain sheep. They were of four general types: (1) David Thompson in 1770 said that the Blackfeet and neighboring tribes wore the strap-and-sleeve dress to the ankles; by 1790 it was mid-calf length according to Mackenzie. (2) The side-seam (or side-fold) dress was worn; it particularly featured rows of porcupine quillwork in the Sioux style. (3) By 1830 the two-skin or deer-tail dress was common; the deer tail was attached at the center of the added-on yoke, which was often painted red and laced to the body of the dress with thongs. (4) The three-skin dress frequently had many rows of elk teeth, as well as rows of hanging thongs. At the center

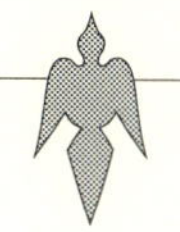

of this dress, both front and back, was a triangular patch (with the point at the bottom), symbolic of a buffalo skull or, some say, the uterus, while the square or rectangular patches at the lower corners were said to represent the woman's ovaries. Horizontal bands of quillwork or beadwork were applied all the way across the yoke of the three-skin dress, with a center dip, vestige of the deer tail. Women's knee-length leggings were square across the bottom, gartered below the knee, and either sewn at the top and tied at the bottom, or tied all along the sides. Panels at the sides were of quill or beadwork; horizontal stripes edged the bottom. Dresses were worn belted or unbelted.

Footwear
Moccasins were dyed almost black, fitted, and commonly decorated only on the toe. Early ones were the side-seamed type; later the typical hard-soled Plains moccasin was adopted. Ankle flaps were added for protection against brush and snow. Moccasins were often made from used, well-smoked lodge skins, and were stuffed with grass for warmth. Characteristic designs on the moccasins, as given by Koch, were the stepped chevron, the feather, the mountain, the cross, parallel bars, and the "Blackfoot-U" on the instep; these were usually made up of many small squares and rectangles. Designs made up of diamonds and triangles were also popular. Women's moccasins were similar to the men's; at times they were adorned with worked rosettes.

Outer Wear
Men's robes were of elk or buffalo hide with the hair left on. Lighter weight robes were of tanned mountain sheep hide. Catlin painted a Blackfoot boy wearing a robe of raccoon skins. Representations of battle scenes and symbols of war were painted on the robes or created in quillwork. Most popular were the "hourglass" figure indicating enemy wounded, hand shape (enemy killed in battle), and the horizontal battle stripes. *Capotes* were worn in the winter, made of the Hudson's Bay blankets obtained in trade. Blankets were also acquired from the weavers of the Southwest at the great trading center of Santa Fe.

Hair Styles
Bodmer studied the hair styles of the Blackfeet at Fort Mackenzie; some men had a bun in the back, some had upright hair in front in a pompadour fashion, stiffened with bear grease to stand erect and coated with white clay (for mourning) or red. The Sacred Medicine Pipe men, as well as older men, generally wore the hair in a topknot or large horn above the forehead. For some ceremonial rites the men wore the hair loose and flowing as a sign of humility. When feathers were worn in the hair, the Blackfeet preferred owl feathers to the eagle feathers of the Sioux. When braided, there was a braid at each side and one at the back; the ends were sometimes wrapped with fur. Some men wore a frontal lock over the nose. Women wore the hair in two braids or simply loose.

Headgear
Wissler maintains that the Blackfeet did not wear the typical Plains halo warbonnet; even before 1800 they wore their characteristic stand-up warbonnet of a circlet of erect feathers springing from a wide rawhide headband, with rolled strips of ermine at the sides. This high crown headdress was originally a part of the regalia of the Bull Society; it was considered better for windy weather and for riding than the halo bonnet and was also more conspicuous in battle and thus an indication of bravery. The buffalo-horn headdress was worn rarely, and then only by especially distinguished men. Fur hats, made of a simple band of fur, were for winter wear, usually from the pelts of coyote, badger, or otter. Rawhide visors were a protection from the summer sun.

Accessories
Large fans of eagle or owl wing feathers were carried by the men. Garters and armbands, often with strips of ermine fur attached, were common accessories. Mittens, made with the fur turned inward, were winter necessities. Shoulder bags and twined woven pouches were usually obtained in trade; few were made by the Blackfeet. Belts of tanned leather were ornamented with quillwork and beadwork. Later, as brass tacks became available, they were used to create designs on rawhide belts. The belts worn by the women were wider than the men's, sometimes as much as four inches wide. "Medicine" or sacred bags were made of the skins of small animals, birds, or reptiles, and ornamented in a variety of ways. A small bag containing an amulet or charm, usually

the wearer's umbilical cord, often hung around the neck. Other bags or pouches carried "strike-a-lights," tobacco, sewing equipment, or painting materials.

Jewelry

Loop necklaces of strings of bone disks, containing 8 to 14 loops, were highly popular with the men. The typical Blackfoot choker necklace, says Koch, was of light blue necklace beads alternating with cowrie shells or, less commonly, with elk teeth. Earlier, they had had a penchant for necklaces of odorous roots. Pieces of abalone shell, from the Pacific coast, were made into earrings and necklaces, as were other shells. The necklace of grizzly-bear claws with a band of otter fur was a highly valued possession, but did not have the otter tail hanging down the back as was typical farther south. Various ornaments were worn in the hair.

A Blackfoot, his hair in a pompadour, wears a 12-loop necklace of white seed beads wrapped around a muslin core and a hairpipe and pony bead choker with a large abalone shell disk and hairpipe pendant.

Armor

Before the introduction of firearms, the Blackfeet warriors wore a kind of armor made of very thick buffalo hide, which gave some protection against arrows. They preferred the shields made by the Crow to those of any others; these were carried outside of the left arm.

Special Costumes

Societies, which generally featured special regalia, were of great importance to Blackfoot life. The Dog Society members had their own headdress—a cap of various types of feathers with a beaded strouding strip hanging as long as five feet from the back of the head. The Buffalo Horn Society members wore a fur cap with long strips of ermine (18 inches or more) hanging from the cap; they also wore the high crown headdress. Warriors of the Kit Fox Society wore a hood for their special ceremonies. The shamans or medicine men wore the buffalo horn headdress, as well as, says Catlin, "the 'odds and ends,' and fag ends, and tails, and tips of almost anything that swims, flies, or runs, in this part of the wide world." The Motokik Women's Society wore distinctive headdresses of buffalo skins. Mails, in his superb work on Plains societies, gives exhaustive details on these special costumes. Mourners affected a disheveled appearance, cut off the hair in varying amounts, and slashed their arms or legs, or even cut off fingers. The Blackfeet danced the Sun Dance as well as the Grass Dance.

Garment Decoration

Little of Blackfoot quillwork survives; there is a much stronger emphasis on beadwork, particularly the use of the overlay stitch. Designs were bold and simple with strong contrasts; such motifs as the U-shape, tadpole design, and checkerboard patterns were common. Background colors tended to be white or light blue. Hole punctuation designs were sometimes found on shirts. Patches of cloth, triangular on women's dresses and rectangular on men's leggings, were popular. Floral beadwork appeared in the 1870s, but designs were highly simplified. The use of white ermine skins is almost a hallmark of Blackfoot costume. Fringes were unusually long, often 18 to 20 inches under the arms. Scalplocks were frequently used as fringe.

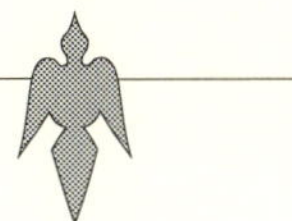

Face and Body Embellishment

Face painting was common, both for war and for ceremonial use; body painting was more to be found with the latter. A face painted black indicated a heroic deed of recent vintage. Stripes, circles, and dots were painted on the face in hues of blue, red, yellow, black, and white. Wissler, in his work on the material culture of the Blackfeet, gives the sources of many of these paints.

Transitional Dress

Commercial materials were adopted by the Blackfeet, although they still retained much of their traditional costume well into the Reservation Period. Paints and dyes from the traders took the place of the natural materials. Calicos, strouding, even velvet, were used for dresses, shirts, and leggings, but in the usual style. Pendleton and Hudson's Bay blankets replaced the buffalo robes, which were almost impossible to obtain after the buffalo declined. Some European garments were adopted, such as uniforms with gold braid and epaulettes, proudly displayed by chiefs. Round felt hats with feathers appeared in the mid-nineteenth century. The tall, black felt hat with the flat brim later became almost a trademark of the Blackfeet people. Gauntlets with heavily beaded cuffs were important accessories for the men. Metal was used for jewelry and other decorations. Heavy brass and copper wire was twisted into bracelets, necklaces, and armbands. Silver armbands and peace medals were much sought after. The glass beads of the traders were often used with quillwork, later alone. In their beadwork white predominated as a background color, with light blue a second choice. There was more emphasis on the overlay stitch and on the usual High Plains fondness for bold, simple, geometric designs. Stripes were common, as were checkerboards, small squares, rectangles, stepped triangles, long isosceles triangles, diamonds, and outlines of uniform width. The Blackfeet were among the few Plains people to use black in their beadwork. Winold Reiss in his superb decorative paintings of the Blackfeet has shown their colorful costumes in great detail since the 1920s.

Key Sources

Conn, Richard. "Blackfeet Soumak Necklaces." *Davidson Journal of Anthropology* 1(2).

———. "Blackfoot Women's Clothing." *American Indian Hobbyist* 7.

Curtis, Edward S. *The North American Indian.* Vol. 6. New York: Johnson Reprint Company, 1970.

Ewers, John C. *The Blackfeet: Raiders on the Northern Plains.* Norman: University of Oklahoma Press, 1958.

———. *Blackfeet Crafts.* Stevens Point, WI: Schneider, 1986. Reprint of 1945 edition.

Grinnell, George Bird. *Pawnee, Blackfoot, and Cheyenne.* New York: Scribner's, 1961.

Jenness, Diamond. "Sarcee Indians of Alberta." National Museum of Canada *Bulletin* 90.

Johnson, Michael G. "Blackfoot Bonnet." *Powwow Trails* 5(8).

Mails, Thomas. "The Age-Graded Societies, the Blackfoots as Examples." *Dog Soldiers, Bear Men and Buffalo Women: A Study of the Societies and Cults of the Plains Indians.* Pp. 77–142. Englewood Cliffs, NJ: Prentice-Hall, 1973.

Raczka, Paul M. "Blackfoot Artists: Rights and Power." *American Indian Art Magazine* 5(2): 30–35.

Reiss, Winold. *Blackfoot Indians of Glacier National Park.* St. Paul, MN: Great Northern Railway, 1958.

Spittal, William Guy. "Blackfeet Hair Ornament." *American Indian Hobbyist* 11(6).

———. "Blackfeet Horned Headdress." *American Indian Hobbyist* 11(8).

Wissler, Clark. "The Material Culture of the Blackfoot Indians." American Museum of Natural History *Anthropological Papers* 5(1).

Cheyenne

The Cheyenne, whom the Sioux called "Sha-hi-ye-na" ("people of an unintelligible language"), were Algonquian speakers, as were their allies the Arapaho. They seem to have lived at one time in the Great Lakes region, then slowly moved westward through southern Minnesota and onto the Plains; by 1755 they had acquired horses and had become nomads, roving as far west as Montana, Colorado, and Wyoming. About 1835 they split into two bands—the Northern Cheyenne and the Southern Cheyenne; although apart geographically, the culture and dress were similar in the two groups.

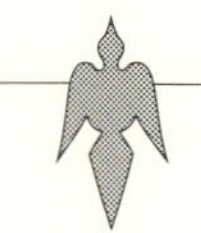

Possibly the most conservative of Plains Indians, the Cheyenne retained their social customs, traditions, and dress long after other tribes had largely assimilated European culture.

For primary source material we have the writings of George Bird Grinnell (who lived among them at times from 1885 to 1910), the paintings and sketches of George Catlin, the photographs of Edward Curtis, and also the "ledger drawings," made at Fort Marion, Florida, in the late 1870s by Indian prisoners there, some of whom were Cheyenne.

A Cheyenne, photographed in the mid-1870s, wears a breechclout with fringed leather leggings and a hairpipe breastplate; his beaded moccasins turn up at the toe.

Men's Basic Dress

Men's early clothing was the usual simple style—mountain sheep, deer, or antelope skins tied on with thongs. No shirts seem to have been worn until the whites came. Early breechclouts were simple aprons of skins. The Plains fitted breechclouts adopted later were long front and back; these were still worn under trousers (the flaps hanging out) until well into the twentieth century. Early leggings worn by the men were tied down the front with thongs; typical of those and later thigh-length leggings was a long loose triangular flap from the calf to the ground, which flapped noisily as the warrior walked, the sound augmented by buttons, shells, and deer hooves attached to the long side fringes. The inside of the flap was painted a bright red or orange, revealing shafts of bright color intermittently. When the Cheyenne adopted the war shirt, they wore it long (almost to the knees), painted with such symbols as thunderbirds, dragonflies, and celestial motifs; a long triangle at the neck was typically edged with a long fringe. Quilled bands, often with diamond designs, went over the shoulders and down the sleeves. The Southern Cheyenne warshirts did not usually feature these quilled or beaded bands of the northern group. The shirts were generally painted yellow, and were adorned with long dark green twisted fringes. Special war shirts were trimmed with scalps of enemies sewn along the seams.

Women's Basic Dress

The most ancient of the women's dresses consisted merely of two rectangular pieces of skin, tied together at intervals down the sides with thongs, and supported by straps over the shoulders; this was the "strap-and-sleeve" dress, in which sleeves were tied on as desired. An early nineteenth century garment was the "side-fold dress," which had a short right sleeve, a strap over the left shoulder, and a loose flap from the folded-over top. These were belted, were mid-calf length, were frequently worn with a cape, and were usually made from the supple leather of old lodges (tanned buffalo hide). Later the Cheyenne women wore the two-skin or three-skin dresses, with animal legs hanging from the sleeves (false legs if real ones were unavailable), and an unusual amount of fringing—long fringes at underarm seams, short fringes at the bottom of the yoke, fringes along the side seams and at the hem. They liked decoration in rows, particularly elk teeth; Denig says that with all the elk teeth, a single dress could weigh as much as 10 or 12 pounds. Shells (especially cowrie shells), teeth of other animals, thongs, or bead clusters were lined up in horizontal rows. Often the dresses were painted yellow. The edges of the yokes were square-cut, and decoration was straight across the yoke, lacking the "deer-tail" dip of many Plains dresses. Leggings were of native tanned deer or antelope hide painted yellow; they were fringed at the bottom and up the sides, and often had a side panel of quillwork. The Cheyenne were famous for the chastity of their women; it may have had something to do with the "protective belt" Grinnell tells about. This was a small rope or line, passed around the waist, knotted in front, then each end wound about the thigh nearly to the knee. Worn at night and when in the presence of men, it was a complete protection for her chastity, respected by all Cheyenne males.

Footwear

Old-type moccasins had the side seams and soft soles, with rawhide soles sewed on. After 1820 a one-piece upper was sewed to a rawhide sole; these were worn with or without ankle flaps, depending on the season. Ankle flaps of Southern Cheyenne moccasins had typically scalloped edges. Characteristic of the Cheyenne were the two "tails" of leather at the back of the heels; these were about two inches long and were of deerskin strips, or part of a buffalo tail, or tails of small animals. Geometric patterns (especially stepped triangles) in quillwork or beadwork and, later, tinklers adorned the moccasins. Cheyenne women wore "boots," really a combination of leggings and moccasins with rawhide soles. These were painted, trimmed with quill or bead work, and later featured metal medallions down the sides. Snowshoes were made by weaving strands of rawhide over a hoop. The Cheyenne were noted for their fine craftsmanship and well into the twentieth century Cheyenne moccasins were in great demand for powwows.

Outer Wear

Both sexes wore robes of tanned deer, elk, antelope, or buffalo hide. From the Sioux, they learned to tan a buffalo hide by cutting it in half, later sewing the two parts together and covering the seam with a quilled or beaded strip, which included medallions in the design. When stroud cloth became available, they sewed the white selvages together, making a white line down the center, sometimes covering it with a blanket strip in the traditional fashion. Like other Plains tribes they set a high value on robes of the white buffalo (which varied, as Mails says, "from a dirty gray to pale cream"). The quilling of robes was a sacred occupation, done only by the select women of the Quillers' Societies, encompassing great spiritual and symbolic actions and meanings. When porcupine quills became unavailable, the women worked with grasses, such as *Equisetum,* and later with dyed cornhusks.

Made in the 1870s for a Cheyenne girl, these boots are decorated with fringe and lazy stitch beadwork. The dark, heart-shaped patterns on each side of the front seam represent buffalo hoofprints.

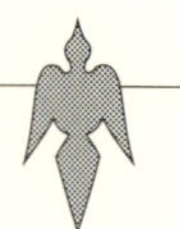

A Cheyenne, with a revolver and a studded knife sheath on his cartridge belt, wears a dentalium shell choker and a breechclout with long flaps.

Hair Styles

Men wore the roach fairly early, but before 1800 without a scalplock. Then came the pompadour, stiffened with clay and with long strings of shells at the sides of the face; the back hair was braided. Still later, the hair was cut off on one side of the head and braided on the other, with elaborate ear ornaments adorning the exposed ear. At times the men wore the northern Plains topknot, with the hair coiled over the forehead. Braids were often wrapped with otter fur. Grinnell gives some idea of the changing fashions in women's hair arrangements. Early it had been braided with fringed rolls of deerskin attached; later the braids were doubled up two or three times and tied behind the head. About 1830 the women began to wear a braid on each side, doubled up and fastened above and behind the ear. During all these periods, many of the women wore the hair simply loose and flowing.

Headgear

The Cheyenne men wore the halo warbonnet, as shown in paintings by Catlin in the 1830s, although earlier they had worn the straight-up headdress of the Blackfeet. The buffalo-horn headdress was also worn, but only by distinguished warriors. The famous Cheyenne chief Roman Nose wore a unique headdress with a browband from which issued a single buffalo horn. Men also wore headgear made of the stuffed pelt of a small rodent, as well as rawhide sunshades or visors.

Accessories

Accessories were many and varied. Fans of netted beading and trimmed feathers were carried by old men and shamans. Belts of tanned leather were tied with thongs and ornamented with quillwork. Garters, narrow, decorated leather straps, fastened the leggings in place and hung down on the outer side of each leg almost to the ground. Quill-decorated armbands were tied on with thongs. Many pouches and bags hung from the belt—cases containing awls and other sewing equipment, knife cases, bags to hold tobacco or paints and brushes—all beautifully adorned by the women with quillwork, fringes, and shells. After the 1850s the men wore the hair pipe breastplate.

Jewelry

An amulet, often in the form of a lizard, contained the umbilical cord of the wearer, and was usually worn throughout life. Necklaces consisted of strings of elk teeth, deer teeth, or fish vertebrae; some warriors wore necklaces of the fingers of enemies they had slain. The earliest bracelets were of native copper obtained from the Lake Superior area. Lewis and Clark noted brass rings among the Cheyenne; even then brass was available by means of trading. Aboriginally, nose rings of shell were worn, later of metal, but the custom did not continue long after European contact. The ears of both sexes were pierced in several places to display ornaments of shells or quillwork. At one time a long hole was cut in the cartilage all along the ear, then wrapped with beads strung on sinew. Long quilled ornaments, called "buffalo bull's tails" were fastened to a warrior's scalplock in the back. Women often wore long strings of shells hanging from the earlobes to the waist.

Armor

Shields were carried in battle. They had a special type—a hoop with crossed lacings that was ineffective against arrows, but was considered a form of magical protection. They liked Crow shields, obtainable in trade.

Special Costumes

The Sun Dance was an important ritual of the Cheyenne. Those who pledged to dance painted their bodies with great care, each mark being a specific symbol; they wore wreaths of sage on the head and a long skirt from waist to ankles. Members of the Kit Fox Society wore the roach headdress and a crescent badge, and painted their bodies yellow. Warriors of the Dog Men Society wore a long sash of tanned skin and a headdress of feathers fastened to stay erect; foremost members were permitted to fringe their leggings with human hair locks. The Cheyenne believed in the protective power of the Medicine Hat (bison-horn headdress with fur attached).

Garment Decoration

Quillwork was of great importance to the Cheyenne; in fact, Quiller Societies were formed especially to do the sacred work involved in the decoration of garments. Because of the scarcity of porcupine quills, various grasses were often substituted. With the adoption of beadwork in the nineteenth century, designs continued in the bilaterally symmetrical style of the past, done in the lazy stitch that produced results similar to quillwork. But all work was of high esthetic quality. Fringes and rows of thongs, elk teeth, or cowrie shells typically adorned garments. The Southern Cheyenne preferred green fringes twisted into thin cords and yellow painted buckskin. Crosses, circles, and rectangular shapes with diamonds enclosed were popular motifs.

Face and Body Embellishment

Besides painting for certain society rituals, face and body painting, especially by the men when preparing for war, was quite spectacular. Faces were painted in designs of red, blue, yellow, white, even black. Hair was often dressed with red earth.

Transitional Dress

The Cheyenne were slow to give up their traditional costumes, but they adapted European materials to their own styles. Dresses were made of cloth—and decorated with porcupine quillwork, beading, and the popular rows of cowrie shells, as well as ribbons of bright hues. The women of the Quiller Societies continued with their superb craftsmanship, even up to modern times. Moccasins and vests were heavily beaded with pictorial designs late in the nineteenth century. With the extinction of the buffalo, blankets were adopted—the Hudson's Bay variety; the Pendleton wools, especially the plaid type; and Santa Fe blankets. Metal, particularly German silver, was made into medallions, or "conchas," for ornamenting belts; these conchas were also made into hair plates, long leather straps to which the medallions were applied, often in diminishing sizes, and which were hung from the crown of the head. Tin tinklers decorated dresses and moccasins.

Key Sources

Cohoe, William. *A Cheyenne Sketchbook.* Norman: University of Oklahoma Press, 1964.

Conn, Richard. "Cheyenne Style Beadwork." *American Indian Tradition* 7(2).

Dorsey, George H. "The Cheyenne." Field Museum of Natural History *Anthropological Series* 9.

Grinnell, George Bird. *The Cheyenne Indians: Their History and Ways of Life.* New York: Cooper Square, 1962.

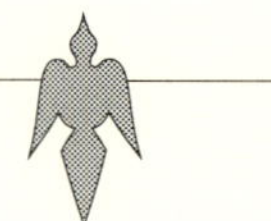

———. *Pawnee, Blackfoot, and Cheyenne.* New York: Scribner's, 1961.

Himmelfarb, Brenda. "The Cheyenne Way." *Native Peoples: The Arts and Lifeways* 5(1): 8–13.

Hoebel, E. Adamson. *The Cheyennes: Indians of the Great Plains.* New York: Holt, Rinehart & Winston, 1960.

Hoebel, E. Adamson and Karl N. Llewellyn. *The Cheyenne Way.* Norman: University of Oklahoma Press, 1941.

Mooney, James. "The Cheyenne Indians." American Anthropological Association *Memoirs* 1(6).

Powell, Peter J. *Sweet Medicine: The Continuing Role of the Sacred Arrows, the Sun Dance, and the Sacred Buffalo Hat in Northern Cheyenne History.* Norman: University of Oklahoma Press, 1969.

Seger, John H. *Early Days among the Cheyenne and Arapahoe Indians.* Norman: University of Oklahoma Press.

Comanche

Shoshonean speakers of the Uto-Aztecan language family, the Comanche were the historic offshoots of the Northern Shoshone, whose culture was similar. Traditionally they came from the mountains of Wyoming and Colorado; those who remained behind became Shoshone; those who left, the Comanche. Hunters and gatherers, they obtained horses by 1650 and a century later were in control of the southern Plains. They were top horsemen, highly successful horse breeders—and were known as the best horsemen around. They, along with the Kiowa, Shoshone, and sometimes the Ute, were known as Snake Indians. The word *comanche* is a Ute term for "enemy." Or the name may have come from the Spanish term *camino ancho,* which signifies "broad trail," referring to the extreme extent of land they traveled. Among the whites they developed a reputation for ferocity and fearlessness, and they were for years bitter enemies of the Texans. They had many bands, at least 12, that had similar cultural traits, but there were some differences; for example, some made garments of deerskin, others of antelope skin. Catlin said they were of medium height; heavyset, almost approaching corpulency; and ungraceful of movement—until they mounted a horse. But Texas pioneer Jenkins said they were "large, fine-looking men, and graceful." George Catlin painted Comanches in the 1830s.

Men's Basic Dress

The men's breechclouts had knee-length flaps front and back and were ornamented with shells, long fringes, bottom tabs, and narrow beaded edgings. Thigh-length close-fitting leggings were gartered below the knees, and had triangular flaps with long twisted fringes and bottom tabs, often with a bunch of eagle feathers at the sides, and were frequently painted blue. Shirts of any kind seem not to have been worn before the traders came; then tanned-leather shirts of deer, mountain-sheep, or antelope hide were worn until the end of the nineteenth century. These binary thigh-length shirts were contoured to fit the body; they displayed delicate twisted fringes, long fringes at the elbows or upper arms and around the triangle at the neck, and short fringes at the straight-edged side-slit bottom. Sleeves were close-fitting with short fringes at the cuffs. Shirts were often painted yellow or green, or a combination of the two hues.

Women's Basic Dress

The early garment for women was the knee-length skirt sewed up the sides with fringe along the seams and at the hemline. Over this was worn a poncho-like top made from one skin, with a narrow slit opening for the head, creating a high, straight neckline. This became the three-skin dress when the blouse and skirt were laced together. Porcupine quillwork seems not to have been used by the Comanche; they preferred the painting of dresses in a muted lemon color or buff, much fringing, pinked edges, occasional use of elk teeth, and, after beads were introduced, small bands of beadwork as edgings. Little girls, like those of many Indian tribes, wore a skin breechclout until puberty, then donned a buckskin dress. Knee-length leggings, secured with garters, were added for warmth; often these leggings were painted to match the moccasins.

Footwear

Comanche moccasins were in the typical Plains style with buffalo hide (later rawhide soles), but they were characteristic of the southern Plains in their use of large ankle flaps, painted uppers, and a limited use

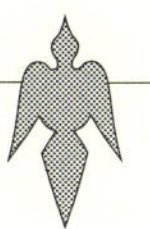

of ornamentation except for, later, narrow bands of beading; Wissler mentions a V-shaped insert on men's moccasins. These moccasins also had added tongues and very long fringes at the heels and along the front seam. A skunk tail was sometimes attached at the heel instead of the fringe. Southern Plains women combined leggings and hard-soled moccasins to form knee-high boots with tops that could be folded down; these boots were usually painted and featured narrow edgings of beading, as well as silver medallions down the side, the latter obtained in trade from the Southwest.

Outer Wear

Buffalo robes were made of prime winter pelts, which were very warm. Heavy robes for winter wear had the hair left on, while the hair was removed altogether for lighter robes. Because the buffalo hides were cut in half for ease in handling, there was a seam down the center, which was often painted red; otherwise, there was little decoration of robes except for robes of men or women of distinction, which displayed the "border and hourglass" design. Robes were also made of bear, wolf, coyote, or skunk skins, while rabbit fur was used for small children's and infants' wear.

Hair Styles

Women wore the hair loose, and cut or "hacked" it off, says Newcomb, paying little attention to the hair except to paint the part at times with red ocher. Men lavished much more attention on their locks, encouraging the hair to grow long, even augmenting it with horsehair or locks begged off a mourning woman. Sometimes the men braided the hair in two braids, leaving a scalplock at the back, to which was attached a yellow or black feather; the braids were often wrapped with otter fur. Other men would smear the hair with reddish clay, leaving it in a huge conglomerate mass. The part was painted white, yellow, or red. Most men plucked the facial hair, even the eyebrows. A few men sported mustaches. The roach seems not to have been worn by Comanche men.

Headgear

Both sexes usually went bareheaded except in bad weather, when the robe was pulled up over the head to form a hood. Fur caps were winter wear, made of buffalo calf or coyote skins. A characteristic form of headgear was a crownlike hat with a trail of eagle feathers reaching to the mid-thighs, and with ermine tails, obtained from the north, at each side of the

The daughters of Comanche Quanah Parker wear three-piece buckskin dresses and tall boots with German silver decorations. Painted buckskin and rows of fine fringing are typical of the southern Plains.

face. Ceremonial headdresses were also made of a cap of a buffalo scalp with feathers placed droopingly around it. The halo warbonnet was not as popular with the Comanche as with the northern tribes.

Accessories

Belts were worn not only for looks but for the carrying of various articles, such as pouches to carry powdered paint, bags for sewing supplies, awl or knife cases, and medicine bundles containing articles of sacred import to the wearer. Garters were leather straps with thongs for tying, decorated with fringe and shells. Men wore the hair pipe breastplate; Koch, basing his statement on Ewers's study of hair pipes, says that the Comanche probably invented them around 1850.

Jewelry

There was an early use of metal for jewelry—silver brooches, armlets, and hair plates—obtained in trade from the Indians of the Southwest. Old-time earrings were made of long, thin shells from Mexico; several holes were pierced in the ears for such earrings, as well as clusters of beads, shells, or bones. Quanah Parker, the famous Comanche leader, once wore a brightly colored stuffed bird in each ear. Hair pipe chokers, other necklaces, and bracelets were popular. Schoolcraft mentioned nose pieces of shell, bone, or silver. A boar's tusk was sometimes worn at the neck.

Armor

Warriors carried large shields made of two rawhide disks laced together and fastened within a circular wooden frame; the space between the rawhide disks was stuffed with feathers, grass, fur, even paper from discarded books of the pioneers. These shields were gaudily painted and adorned with feathers, which may have spoiled a foe's aim with their fluttering. Some warriors wore the buffalo-horn headdress.

Special Costumes

The Comanche did not develop soldier societies as such, but they had war leaders who wore a buffalo-scalp bonnet decorated with eagle and magpie feathers and ermine side fringes.

Garment Decoration

Porcupine quillwork was rarely done by the Comanche women. Beadwork, using the overlay or flat gourd stitch, was usually confined to simple small edgings, although some netting was done incorporating beads into the technique. Fringes were highly popular, particularly with attachments such as beads, shells, and teeth. Fringe was typically made by twisting the strands into cords and was often dyed green.

Face and Body Embellishment

Painting of the face and body, using many types of designs, was for special occasions. Red was popular, as were black, yellow, green, blue, and white. Women accentuated the eyes with red or yellow lines, painted the inside of the ears red, and embellished both cheeks with circles or triangles of red-orange. Tattooing was not conspicuous among the Comanche, but women tattooed the face and occasionally the breasts, and men tattooed the chest and emphasized their battle scars in that manner.

Transitional Dress

The Comanche wore Navajo blankets instead of the cumbersome buffalo robes. They added vests, felt hats, and bandana scarves, which they secured around the neck with a ring of buffalo bone. They got dyes from the traders—indigo, vermilion, and verdigris—to brighten their face and body painting. The peyote religion was strong among them, and they carried peyote fans of macaw or pheasant feathers (eagle feathers when obtainable). They continued the use of silver hair plates, adding such metal products as tin tinklers and silver brooches. Wallace and Hoebel, who have written so notably on the Comanche, give interesting sidelights on the clothing of the Reservation Period. Each man was given by the government a suit of clothing—pants, shirt, coat, hat, and a pair of socks. Women were allowed a woolen skirt, 12 yards of calico, 12 yards of other cloth, and one pair of woolen hose. Unfortunately, the material in the garments was shoddy and worthless, and sizes were not considered. Coats were made into vests by cutting off the sleeves, which children wore for leggings. The seats were cut out of pants to make them into leggings. Women merely wrapped the cloth around them instead of sewing garments. It was one of the government's answers to the "Indian question."

Key Sources

Ehrenback, T. R. *Comanches: The Destruction of a People.* New York: Knopf, 1974.

Evans, Dennis. "Southern Plains Women's Boots." *American Indian Tradition* 7(5).

Newcomb, W. W., Jr. *The Indians of Texas: From Prehistoric to Modern Times.* Austin: University of Texas Press, 1961.

Powers, William K. *Indians of the Southern Plains.* New York: Putnam's, 1971.

Wallace, Ernest and E. A. Hoebel. *The Comanches: Lords of the South Plains.* Norman: University of Oklahoma Press, 1952.

Crow

The Crow were a Siouan-speaking nomadic people living generally from the headwaters of the Yellowstone River to the eastern slope of the Rockies. They were once part of the Hidatsa, or Gros Ventre of the River. They called themselves Absarokas and were also known as the *Gens de Corbeaux,* "Kite Indians," and "Crow People." There were three divisions of the tribe: the River Crow, the Mountain Crow, and the Kicked-in-the-Bellies Crow. They were noted traders, particularly in shields, skin shirts, and buffalo robes. By 1790 they were in direct contact with European traders. François Larocque, the Canadian trader, wrote of them in 1805, providing much information on ceremonial dress but little on everyday clothing. William Wildschut and Robert H. Lowie later wrote about them. They were painted by George Catlin and Karl Bodmer in the 1830s, by Alfred Jacob Miller in 1837, and by Rudolph Kurz in 1851, and were photographed by Edward S. Curtis early in this century.

Men's Basic Dress

Breechclouts were seldom worn before 1800, but were universally worn by Catlin's time; Wildschut and Ewers say that the leggings were so made as to cover the male organ, the crossed flaps making a breechclout unnecessary. Hip-length leggings featured large flaps at the bottom and long fringes, but only the most distinguished warriors could wear fringes of hair locks. Skins used were mountain goat, mountain sheep, deer, elk, and antelope, tanned to a beautiful whiteness. Quillwork on these leggings used the plaited technique. Leggings were trimmed with painted stripes, fringed bottom tabs, and a rectangular patch at the bottom; quill-wrapped horsehair was often used as fringe. Shirts were heavily decorated. Fringes, of ermine tails more than of buckskin, or of hair bundles, were attached to the lower arms; longer fringes were twisted, resembling cords. Sometimes the shirts came to a point at the lower edge in front and back, indicative of influence from the Subarctic tribes to the north; the points were often edged with ermine. Also indicative of northern influence was the fact that the shirts were snug-fitting and had fitted sleeves with underarm seams. The usual sleeve and shoulder bands, marks of distinction, were heavily decorated with quills and/or beads. Pectoral units, circles or

Photographed in about 1890 with a cavalry saber, a Crow medicine man's shirt has beaded arm bands, shoulder bands, and rectangle at the neck with hair fringe on the sleeves.

rectangles, had ermine tails hanging from them. At times the shirts were painted in solid colors.

Women's Basic Dress

From the early wraparound skirt of tanned leather with accompanying poncho in cooler weather, the Crow women seem to have adopted the Plains deer-tail dress, the two-skin dress of deer, mountain-sheep, or mountain-goat skin with close-fitting sleeves. Dresses were longer (ankle-length) and narrower than those of neighboring tribes, and were often worn belted; later dresses of trade cloth followed the same style. Elk teeth were the most common decoration, with about three hundred being the usual number, but some had as many as a thousand teeth; these were applied in concentric arcs on both the back and front of the dress. Considering the fact that one hundred elk teeth

A Crow girl's dress is decorated with what appear to be cowrie shells, and her pony's trapping, including crupper and martingale, are elaborately beaded and fringed.

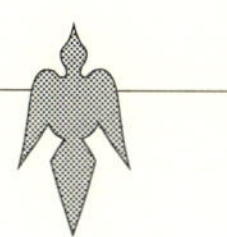

would buy a good horse, these were costly dresses, and it is not surprising that imitation elk teeth were made of bone. Dresses were fringed down the sides and trimmed with ermine, porcupine quillwork, and, later, beads. Patches were applied at the sides of the bottom. The umbilical cord was cut off a baby girl, put into a bag, and when she grew old enough to wear an elk-teeth dress, the bag with the cord inside was tied to the back. Knee-length gartered leggings were decorated with quillwork.

Footwear
Early Crow moccasins were the one-piece soft-soled type with side seams; later they adopted the hard-soled Plains moccasin. They liked longitudinal stripes on the forepart of the moccasins, especially red or green, bold geometric designs against solid-color backgrounds, the keyhole design, and the "Blackfoot-U" on the instep. For the warrior who had counted coup, wolf tails were attached to the heels.

Outer Wear
Buffalo- or elk-hide robes had the feathered circle design, the hourglass and triangle, and other symbols; a quilled blanket strip, which ran horizontally when the robe was worn, was a frequent adornment. Catlin sketched decorations from Crow robes, mostly of warriors on horseback.

Hair Styles
One of the most fascinating and distinctive aspects of Crow men's costume was their hair. They were proud of their long hair, which frequently reached the ground (often augmented by locks from others, especially women in mourning). Lowie tells about Chief Long Hair, whose hair was said to be over ten feet long; ordinarily it was wound with a strap and folded into a container, which was carried by the chief. Understandably, it was considered the chief's "medicine." Mails describes the method used by the Crow men to add strands of human hair or horsehair to their own locks with the aid of fine gum. Bodmer and others sketched the many styles of hairdressing used by the Crow men, variations such as the forelock, the pompadour, topknots, bangs, braids, loosely hung hair, and many little braids, including one at each side of the front to which "Crow bows" were attached. It is said that they used a heated stick for a curling iron and that they applied bear grease and buffalo dung to stiffen the locks, and cactus pith to give it a glossy sheen; they also perfumed the hair with castoreum or sweet grass. Many items were used for further adornment—beaded hairbows, heavy strings of beads or shells, and the usual feathers. Crow women wore the hair in two braids or hanging loosely; the hair was tied at night to prevent entanglement. Kurz said in the late 1840s that the women had hair reaching to the shoulders and cut in bangs in front. They often painted the hair part with red ocher.

Headgear
Crow warriors wore the warbonnet; in fact, some authorities claim the Crow invented it. However, more characteristic may have been the high-crown headdress, in which a complete circlet of feathers was attached to a leather browband; in one of Catlin's sketches, a crown precisely the same in pattern and material adorns the head of the warrior's horse. At times, buffalo horns or antelope horns were worn on the head, with long trails of feathers attached. Some used an entire bird, such as an eagle, as a headdress. Rawhide visors were used in summer as a protection against the sun.

Accessories
Large eagle-feather fans were carried by the men, especially chiefs. Belts of tanned leather, often with the long ends split and hanging, were painted in the typical Crow style—bold, simple shapes such as solidly colored rectangles, hourglasses, and diamonds and an extensive use of elongated isosceles triangles, all outlined with lines of varying width. Bags, pouches, and containers were decorated with painting rather than porcupine quillwork, and the traditional designs continued into the beadwork period. Bags and pouches held paints, sewing equipment, and tobacco. Cases held knives and awls. Garters were simple straps of leather tied with thongs.

Jewelry
Both sexes wore jewelry, but the men especially reveled in it with their bear-claw necklaces, strings of shells and beads, chokers of dentalium shells, loop necklaces, and dangling earrings. Both sexes had the ears pierced in many places although, unlike neighboring tribes, they had no particular ceremony for ear piercing.

Bluish green abalone shells from the Pacific were made into large iridescent earrings. According to Edward Curtis, men wore necklaces of polished and clay-daubed disks cut from the shoulder blade of a buffalo.

Armor

Before European contact, the Crow warriors had worn heavy, multilayered shirts of buckskin or buffalo hide as armor. These shirts fell into disuse with the introduction of rifles, but were often retained as ceremonial dress. The Crow made many shields, for themselves as well as for trade, for they were highly valued. These were usually made from the heavy skin of the buffalo's neck, and were painted in designs tending to show a single animal or bird with rows of zigzags. A soft buckskin cover for the shield was also painted. Further ornaments were rolled ermine strips or eagle feathers.

Special Costumes

In the old days almost every Crow belonged to a society, each of which displayed distinctive regalia, adornment, and behavior; Lowie made an intensive survey of these societies. Sashes, prominent in the Big Dog Society activities, were made of hide or, later, cloth; had a slit for the head to pass through; and were as long as 12 feet. Men of this cult also wore a cap of dried bear guts, and often a bear belt. The society was closely related to the Dog Dancers of the Hidatsa, drawn by Bodmer in 1833. Members of the Kit Fox Society roached the hair and wore a coyote skin as a neck piece, with the head in front and the tail behind. During the mourning period the face was daubed with paint, women chopped off their hair, and some men even cut off some of their own treasured locks.

Garment Decoration

Little quillwork has remained of Crow garment decoration, typically using a plaiting technique. Beadwork was developed by 1850, occurring often in conjunction with quillwork. The overlay stitch, sometimes called the Crow stitch, created bold geometric designs with solid-color backgrounds. Many different colors were used, often in subtle tones. Characteristic motifs were the hourglass, the keyhole or tadpole, the Blackfoot U, and elongated isosceles triangles. Ermine tails were extensively applied as trim. Also typical were rows of elk teeth; at times an entire dress would be covered with as many as 1,000 elk teeth in rows.

Face and Body Embellishment

Both sexes practiced tattooing to some extent, the women more than the men. The former had vertical lines on the chin, often a dot on the nose, and a circle on the forehead. Tattooing was done by pricking the skin with porcupine quills and rubbing in powdered charcoal. Men favored face and body painting. A face painted black indicated, as Mails says, "the fires of revenge which had burned out with the completion of a raid." But the usual custom was to paint the face red and add a tinge of yellow to the eyelids. Horizontal stripes, as symbols of war exploits, were painted across the chest and the arms.

Transitional Dress

Stroud cloth—red, blue, and green—was early adopted by the Crow. The blue cloth especially was

Fringes, ermine strips, feathers, and beadwork decorate this Crow buckskin shirt.

made into simple-cut dresses with the typical elk-teeth decoration; rectangular patches of contrasting color were added to the bottom of a dress as well as little patches of cloth to which thongs were attached. Cloth leggings were made of strouding for both sexes, the men preferring red and featuring a large, rectangular, decorated patch at the bottom. Men's stroud breechcloths were heavily beaded and worn in the apron style. Blankets, both Hudson's Bay and Pendleton, had beaded blanket strips down the center; *capotes* were made from the Hudson's Bay blankets, especially those with the red and white stripes. Beading was on everything—on gauntlets with beaded cuffs, vests, dress yokes, moccasins, and hair bows. Tinklers were added to many garments and accessories. Metal jewelry, such as bracelets and rings, was worn.

Key Sources

Charnley, Donn. "Crow Loop Necklace." *American Indian Hobbyist* 5(5, 6).

Curtis, Edward S. *The North American Indian.* Vol. 4. New York: Johnson Reprint Company, 1970.

Denig, Edwin Thompson. *Five Indian Tribes of the Upper Missouri: Sioux, Arikaras, Assiniboines, Crees, Crows.* Norman: University of Oklahoma Press, 1961.

Feder, Norman. "Crow Blanket Strip Rosettes." *American Indian Art Magazine* (Winter 1980).

———. "The Crow Indians of Montana." *American Indian Hobbyist* 5(5, 6).

———. "Of the Crow Nation." Bureau of American Ethnology *Bulletin* 151: 1–74.

Lanford, Benson L. "Parfleche and Crow Beadwork Designs." *American Indian Art Magazine* 6(1): 32–39.

Lessard F. Dennis. "Crow Indian Art: The Nez Perce Connection." *American Indian Art Magazine* 6(1): 54–63.

Lowie, Robert H. *The Crow Indians.* New York: Holt, Rinehart & Winston, 1935. Reprint edition, 1956.

Mails, Thomas. "The Crow." *Dog Soldiers, Bear Men and Buffalo Women: A Study of the Societies and Cults of the Plains Indians.* Pp. 283–306. Englewood Cliffs, NJ: Prentice-Hall, 1973.

Powell, Peter J., ed. *To Honor the Crow People: Crow Art from the Goelet and Edith Gallatin Collection of American Indian Art.* Chicago: Foundation for the Preservation of American Indian Art and Culture, 1988.

Taylor, Colin. "Costume Decorated with Quill-Wrapped Hair: Nez Perce or Crow?" *American Indian Art Magazine* 6(3): 42–53.

Wildschut, William and John C. Ewers. *Crow Indian Beadwork: A Descriptive and Historical Study.* New York: Museum of the American Indian, 1959.

Dakota Sioux

The Dakota Sioux, also called the Santee Sioux, were not the nomadic horsemen of the central and western Plains; they were village people living by the rivers and lakes of Minnesota and western Wisconsin, and engaging in a semiagricultural way of life. As Woodland Indians they had come from the east, pushed ever westward by the expanding economy of the whites; after 1700, some moved farther west to become the Teton or Lakota Sioux, the archetype of the Indian/horse/buffalo complex. The Dakota, so-called because they spoke the Dakota dialect of the Siouan language, exchanged the wild-rice economy of the tribes to the north and east for the planting of corn, which they traded to their kinsmen to the west. The Dakota consisted of four divisions: the Mdewakanton and the Wahpeton, who lived along the Minnesota River; the Wahpekute of southern Minnesota; and the Sisseton of the Lake Traverse area. There were minor differences in the costumes of these groups, but these differences are difficult to establish because there was much tribal intermingling and trade. George Catlin mentioned painting some of the Dakota leaders, including Sleepy Eye, chief of the Mdewakantons. Seth Eastman did watercolors in the Fort Snelling area in 1850. The Dakota were first mentioned in the *Jesuit Relations* of 1640; explorers, such as Radisson, Hennepin, and Peter Pond, also gave information on the Dakota.

Men's Basic Dress

Aboriginally, the Dakota made most of their garments from the hide of the readily available deer, a skin that was durable and, if properly smoked, would remain

soft and flexible even after being drenched in a sudden downpour. The man's breechclout of hide was passed between the legs, tucked under a belt in back and front, and the thigh-length flaps allowed to hang down. Thigh-length leggings, made of one piece of deerskin folded over, were fastened with thongs to the belt and tied or sewn at the sides. A poncho with a slit for a head opening was added for cooler weather. In winter, a form of sleeve was made by tying or sewing the underarm seams. Shirts and leggings were decorated with porcupine quillwork and short skin fringes; especially characteristic was a large quilled rosette on the front and back of the shirt. Dakota shirts were shorter and plainer than those of the Western Sioux.

Women's Basic Dress

Women in early times wore the wraparound skirt with a poncho added as needed. Later they wore the "strap-and-sleeve" dress, an influence from the Eastern Woodlands tribes, with straps over the shoulders and sleeves that could be tied on as needed. By the early nineteenth century they were wearing the two-skin dress featuring a fold-over yoke at the top that was edged with fringe and had the dip characteristic of the deer-tail dress. Later the three-skin dress with the separate yoke fastened to the two-skin skirt was adopted. Decoration consisted of rows of thongs; of fringing under the arms, on side seams, and at the hems; and of applied patches of quillwork.

Leggings, especially for dress occasions, were adorned in the same fashion; knee-length, they were secured with garters.

Footwear

The one-piece soft-soled moccasins reflected the Woodlands background of the Dakota; the seams were along the outer edge of the foot and up the heel. Some had a tongue cut separately and sewn in place. Another style had a seam up the front with the skin puckered into the seam, which was often covered with an embroidered or quillworked strip; some men wore moccasins with a long piece of buffalo hide trailing behind them. Cuffs might or might not be added. Winter moccasins were larger so they could be lined with grass, buffalo hair, or fur for warmth. Ceremonial footgear was beautifully embellished with quillwork, while those for travel or everyday wear were plain. Snowshoes were often made of pieces of rawhide, frozen after wetting in order to toughen them and make them smoother. Slabs of wood were also used as snowshoes. Some snowshoes were similar to the contemporary type—hoops of bent wood with a netting of rawhide strings, and fastened to the foot with leather straps; according to Catlin, some had pointed toes, curved at the end. Both sexes wore the same type of footwear.

Outer Wear

Buffalo robes, usually obtained in trade from the western tribes, were worn by men because of their great weight. Lighter robes were of deerskin, or of the skins of small animals, particularly beaver. Robes were embellished with quillwork or painted figures.

Hair Styles

Both sexes wore the hair loose or in two braids, which were at times wrapped with strips of fur or hide. Men had a third braid, the scalplock, that hung from the crown of the head, to which ornaments were fastened. After the mid-nineteenth century, roaches were worn by warriors. Hennepin commented that some men wore the hair short, well daubed with bear grease, and decorated with red and white feathers. Others had the down of feathers clinging to the bear grease. Some shaved the head leaving only a tuft of hair on top, which was greased and mixed with red ocher so it would stand on end.

Headgear

The Dakota Sioux seem not to have worn the halo warbonnet of the western Sioux, at least not until the adoption of the headdress by many tribes in the late nineteenth century. Nor did they wear the buffalo-horn headdress or the roach to any great extent. They usually went bareheaded. In cold weather caps of fur gave warmth; occasionally the entire heads of animals might be made into headgear.

Accessories

Since the Indians did not have pockets as we know them, they had many bags and pouches, which were usually attached to a belt and contained materials for painting, for sewing and quillwork, for starting fires, for tobacco, and for "medicine"—that is, objects of

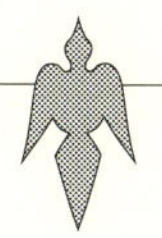

great personal spiritual value. Large feather fans were carried by men of distinction, made of eagle feathers when obtainable. In early days knives were carried in a sheath that hung around the neck; later they were attached to the belt on the left side at the back. Mittens were made of deer hide or fur. Armbands and garters of skin had long thongs for tying.

Jewelry

Jewelry was made from whatever was handy, and whatever pleased the eye of the wearer. Strings of shells, nuts, and stones were formed into necklaces or looped into earrings. Despite living so far inland, seashells obtained in trade were popular. Claws of animals or birds also graced necks, ears, and garments. Koch, in his excellent book on Plains costume, says that the Dakota Sioux made a necklace of the entire front paw of a grizzly bear, but this was quite rare.

Armor

Little mention is made of armor worn by the Dakota, but they did carry painted shields.

Special Costumes

Mails gives several societies important to Dakota life. The Badger Society members wore the war shirt, leggings, and otter-skin collar and carried a fan. Dancers of the Buffalo Cult wore the buffalo headdresses with horns and carried shields painted with buffalo symbols. The Sacred Bear Cult was particularly involved in curing rites; at their bear feasts they wore bearskins and painted the body red. The Dakota followed typical mourning customs—cutting the hair, gashing the flesh or cutting off fingers, and painting the face black. Some carried with them the bones of an important dead relative wrapped in skin, which was decorated with red and black quillwork.

Garment Decoration

Some simple quillwork was done by Dakota women but with light, not massive, designs. Beadwork, also, was not a strong tradition; late in the nineteenth century they adopted the floral style of the Northeastern Indians, but retained their traditional bilateral symmetry and stylized designs. The dragonfly was a favorite motif, also diamond shapes with appendages, eight-pointed stars, and small crosses and stars in the background. Fringes were short. Rows of quill-wrapped thongs and beaded patches were popular forms of decoration.

Face and Body Embellishment

Warriors smeared the face and body with paint in preparing for war. Paint was also used by both sexes for ceremonial occasions, red and black being the favored colors.

Transitional Dress

Contact with the white culture changed many aspects of Dakota life, often devastatingly, rarely beneficially. By 1775, cloth and blankets had replaced deerskin and buffalo robes. The cloth at first was the blue or red stroud cloth; cotton fabrics, printed calicos, ginghams, and broadcloth were widely used by the early nineteenth century. At first, women followed the styles of their aboriginal garments, but later they adopted European fashions. As early as the mid-eighteenth century, Dakota men were wearing white garments, such as the "chief's coat," a military uniform much valued for its gold buttons and gold braid. By the early years of the next century they were wearing the everyday garb of European style: shirts, coats, vests, trousers, and finally even shoes. Metal was a welcome addition, not only the treasured steel needles and scissors, but silver bracelets, brooches, and armbands. Tin "tinklers" decorated dresses, shirts, and moccasins. Dakota women were slow to practice the craft of beadwork, perhaps because of their Ojibwa neighbors, whose beautiful work was easily obtained in trade. Beading was used on moccasins, vests, and dresses. Ribbon applique, acquired in trade or learned from the Prairie tribes, appeared on stroud-cloth leggings, dresses, and breechcloths. Men liked to wear black neck scarves. By 1900 little of Indian clothing was retained except for occasional moccasins and blankets for everyday wear, and treasured heirloom costumes or newly made garments and accessories for ceremonial use.

Key Sources

Bray, Martha Colemen, ed. *The Journals of Joseph N. Nicollet: A Scientist on the Mississippi Headwaters with Notes on Indian Life.* St. Paul: Minnesota Historical Society Press, 1970.

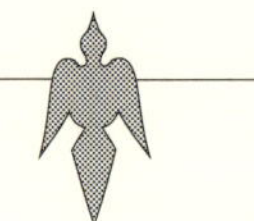

McDermott, John Francis. *Seth Eastman: Pictorial Historian of the Indian.* Norman: University of Oklahoma Press, 1961.

Mails, Thomas. "The Non-Graded Societies, the Sioux as Example." In *Dog Soldiers, Bear Men and Buffalo Women: A Study of the Societies and Cults of the Plains Indians.* Pp. 225–268. Englewood Cliffs, NJ: Prentice-Hall, 1973.

Meyer, Roy W. *History of the Santee Sioux.* Lincoln: University of Nebraska Press, 1967.

Pond, Samuel. "The Dakotas or Sioux in Minnesota as They Were in 1834." Minnesota Historical Society *Collections,* 1908.

Ioway

The Ioway were a small tribe of the Chiwere division of Siouan speakers settled primarily in present-day Iowa. At one time, along with the Oto and Missouri tribes, they seem to have been a part of the Winnebago, from whom they separated and moved southwestward. Their name comes from a Siouan word meaning "sleepy." The material culture exhibited strong Eastern Woodlands elements, coupled with Plains customs. They were painted by Rudolph Frederich Kurz, who was entranced by their friendliness and physical beauty, and by George Catlin and Charles Bird King.

Men's Basic Dress

The basic costume consisted of moccasins, breechclout, and leggings. Shirts, when worn, were of the poncho type with open sides, a triangular neck flap, and a ragged "deer leg" hem. Narrow breechclouts of deerskin were either of the fitted type with flaps hanging in front and back, or a wraparound kilt style; sometimes a long, bushy tail hung down behind. Front-seam thigh-length leggings, gartered at the knees, had large fringed flaps at the bottom covering much of the moccasins.

Women's Basic Dress

The early woman's costume was a skirt of tanned leather, belted or tied around the waist, with a poncho of hide added when needed or desired. A summer skirt might be made of dressed fawn skin, a winter top covering of raccoon skin. Knee-length leggings were fringed at the bottom and gartered. By 1844, they were wearing long cotton dresses with fringes at the bottom. Maximilian said the Ioway women dressed like the Sauk.

Footwear

Early moccasins had been of the soft-sole one-piece type with side seams, usually gathered to a central seam down the instep; ankle flaps were added, especially for women's moccasins, to be fastened with thongs for cooler weather. By the mid-nineteenth century this style was replaced by the Plains moccasin with the rawhide sole. Central Plains women not only liked to have their moccasins match the designs on their leggings, but also used reverse designs; that is, the outside left flap design would match the outside right flap design, and the inside flaps would match. Snowshoes were worn occasionally by the Ioway, the usual light hoops of ash wood laced with thongs.

An Ioway, photographed in 1900, wears a bear claw necklace and a George Washington peace medal. His otter-skin turban, with the otter tail at his right ear, has disk and feather decorations.

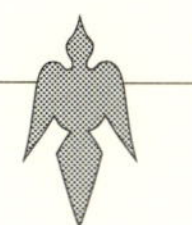

Outer Wear
Buffalo robes were prized by the Ioway. The fur on the outside being left on for winter robes, the inner hide was skillfully tanned and painted. They especially favored the "box-and-border" design (worn by women), and the "sunburst" of concentric circles made up of feather-like elements (worn by the men). Variations were indicative of local styles. Lighter weight robes were of tanned deerskin.

Hair Styles
Men shaved the head entirely except for a tuft on the crown and a scalplock in back, to which ornaments and feathers were attached for various dances and ceremonies. In 1848 the Ioway were still organized into clans, such as the Eagle, Bear, and Beaver, and the boys of each clan had a distinct hair style; however, adult men all wore the same tuft and scalplock. After the mid-nineteenth century some men simply cut the hair short and added an artificial roach, made of a combination of deer hair, porcupine hair, or horsehair painted red. Women wore the hair loose or in two braids; sometimes the braids were tied together at the ends and worn down the back.

Headgear
The tuft of hair worn by the Ioway men was often combined with a turban wrapped around the head beneath it; this might be of fur or a long sash woven of nettle or bark fiber. Some men wore the otter-fur turban with the tail extended straight out at the side; some fur turbans did not include the tail. Turbans of printed cloth from the traders were worn by some of the Ioway painted by Charles Bird King in Washington in 1837. Horn headdresses were occasionally worn, but not with the entire head of the buffalo, as was worn on the Northern Plains.

Accessories
Loosely twined storage bags were made by the women of basswood or nettle fiber, an indication of Southeastern influence. Pouches of tanned leather hung from the belt, containing articles for painting, sewing, and lighting fires, as well as tobacco and "medicine" items, sacred to the wearer. Garters and armbands, tied with thongs, had long fringes hanging; sometimes these were of wide bands of otter fur. Feather fans were carried by both sexes; preferably of eagle tail or wing feathers, they had a handle of painted hide. Some men wore a white wolf tail hanging down the back.

Jewelry
Grizzly-bear claws attached to thin bands of otter fur were prized necklaces. Other necklaces and chokers were made of many strings of beads; "wampum," Catlin called them, but he used the term loosely. Seashells, especially dentalium shells, were commonly strung for necklaces, chokers, bracelets, and earrings. Ears were pierced in many places to accommodate clusters of beads or long dentalium shells. Shell gorgets often adorned the men's chests.

Armor
At times a chest piece of leather was slipped over the head, hanging down the back as well; this may have been a form of armor.

Special Costumes
The Ioway had rival military clubs, but they were not as dominant in tribal life as was true of the Indians of the northern Plains. The Kit Fox Society members wore the roach. The Waiakida, guardians of public order, had the privilege of wearing the sacred bustle, and also of having their daughters tattooed. The period of mourning extended for six months, during which the mourner painted the face black; at the end of that time a feast was held, the black paint was removed, and red paint was used again.

Garment Decoration
Like other Plains tribes, the Ioway adopted beading, although they had never done much with porcupine quillwork. They preferred the lazy stitch, usually working in geometic designs, particularly the diamond-shaped feather motif. When floral beading became the fashion, they concentrated on abstract flower designs. Some finger-weaving was done in the form of woven sashes and bags of nettle or basswood-bark fibers. The sashes were later wrapped around the head as turbans.

Face and Body Embellishment
The Ioway painted the face and body profusely, with red being the most popular color, followed by white, green, black, and yellow. The men's shaved heads

were heavily painted with red. Vertical or horizontal lines adorned the cheeks; the shoulders were streaked and daubed with red. Handprints appeared on the torso. Tattooing, on the other hand, was a matter of rank and distinction. Skinner was told in 1912 that the Ioway wore tattoos as the whites wore diamonds. Blaine, in her fine work on this tribe, says that both sexes sported dots, diamond shapes, stars, lines, and feather symbols on the cheeks, necks, breasts, and legs. Only the wealthy could afford the process; it conferred nobility on the tattooed one.

Transitional Dress

Although the earliest contact with whites was in the early eighteenth century, the Ioway continued to wear traditional costume styles well into the nineteenth century, augmented by European garments and materials. By the 1840s they were wearing shirts, skirts, and blouses of printed calico; brightly hued trade blankets; and cloth sashes and turbans. Commercially tanned hide was adopted. Ribbon applique appeared on leggings especially, but it was probably obtained in trade, perhaps from the Osage, who were superb workers in this technique. Metal purchased from the traders was used for armbands and headbands. Tin tinklers jingled from moccasins, leggings, and dresses. Many of the men, especially those who went to Washington, displayed peace medals on their chests.

Key Sources

Blaine, Martha Royce. *The Ioway Indians.* Norman: University of Oklahoma Press, 1979.

Skinner, Alanson. "Ethnology of the Ioway Indians." Milwaukee Public Museum *Bulletin* 5(4): 181–354.

Torrence, Gaylord and Robert Hobbs. *Art of the Red Earth People: The Musquakie of Iowa.* Iowa City: University of Iowa Museum of Art, 1989.

Kiowa

The Kiowa were dominated by the Comanche and were allies of the Western Shoshone; all three tribes are often referred to as Snake Indians. They were closely associated with the Kiowa Apache. Their name is a word in their own language, "Kaigwu," signifying "principal people." They came originally from Montana, drifting down the Plains until they finally settled in western Oklahoma in the eighteenth century. Speakers of the Kiowa branch of the Uto-Aztecan language family, they were buffalo hunters, highly mobile, and practicing no agriculture. They were among the most bitter enemies of early white settlers, who often regarded the Kiowa as exceedingly predatory. Living in permanent villages much of the year, they moved far and wide in search of buffalo. There were Spanish records of them as early as 1732. George Catlin and Charles Bird King painted the Kiowa.

Men's Basic Dress

Tanned-leather breechclouts were of the fitted type with knee-length flaps in back and front. Leggings of skin were also snugly fitted, but with a wide triangular flap on the lower half; this flap was not only heavily fringed but was painted a bright red or orange, in contrast to the rest of the legging, which was painted yellow or a combination of yellow and green. The legging was long enough to cover much of the moccasin. The fringes on both the leggings and breechclout, as well as later shirts, were long and usually twisted into fine cords. The Kiowa did not wear shirts until cloth ones were introduced by the traders. Some men then wore hide shirts, which had long, tight sleeves, a triangular neck flap, and side slits at the bottom; the heavy, long fringes and and the yellow- or green-painted backgrounds were the only decorations, except for the occasional use of narrow beaded edgings, mescal beads, and some hair locks.

Women's Basic Dress

The early dress of the Kiowa women was simply the wraparound skirt, with a poncho of hide draped over it in cool weather. At the time of contact, probably during the eighteenth century, they were wearing the long deerskin dress with the fringed bottom, typical of the Southern Plains. Dresses were painted all over, either yellow or a combination of yellow and green; there was little other decoration except for occasional narrow beaded edgings. Leggings were knee-length and gartered. By the 1870s they had adopted the three-skin Plains dress, but with some tribal distinctions. It had a large squared yoke, often dyed yellow, decorated with cowrie shells, and with a scalloped design at the yoke bottom edge. The hem

Two Kiowas wear shirts with long, fine fringes and fringed leggings. The man on the right has fur-wrapped braids and button decorations on his shirt and breechclout.

of the dress was also scalloped with an added fringe. The legs were left on the underside of the sleeves, or false legs were attached. Kiowa women preferred to paint dresses or to decorate them by pinking or scalloping edges, by fringing, or by adding ribbons or rows of thongs. Beadwork was limited to edgings. Conn tells about distinctions between dresses for formal social and religious wear. The former had skin tabs, fringes, bead medallions, and pendants, giving it a "somewhat frivolous" air; the latter, with its white simplicity and sweeping fringes, had little ornamentation except for celestial designs painted on the bodice.

Footwear

Moccasins were unlike those of many tribes in that the leather uppers were sewn to the rawhide soles with the right side out, leaving an exposed seam allowance and giving the moccasins a tendency to curl up around the edges, a protection in the sharp underbrush; the toes often tended to be quite pointed. The seamed back ended in a long, heavy fringe at the heel. A long tongue, separately attached, was often forked and usually beaded along the edge. Uppers were sometimes elegantly painted or, later, in imitation of tribes to the north, fully beaded. The fringed rectangular cuff, generally split at the back, had a small beaded border. All exposed leather on these moccasins was painted. Women wore leg-moccasins (boots), early ones being soft-soled, later hard-soled. The uppers were extended to the thigh, sometimes being gartered just below the knee, with the top folded over. Beading was sparse, confined to edgings, but a favorite addition was a row of silver medallions or "conchas" down each leg, obtained in trade from the Southwest.

Outer Wear

Robes and blankets, in this warm climate, were used only in the winter when needed or for ceremonial occasions. Buffalo or deerskin robes were painted, with the "hourglass and border" design being the most common; other paintings were of scenes of war, the hunt, or ceremonies. The former geometric designs were painted by the women, the latter pictographic designs by the men. These Southern Plains tribes also wore self-fringed Navajo blankets obtained in trade.

Hair Styles

Both sexes wore the hair loose or braided or put up in one or more "clubs." Braids were often wrapped with otter fur. Occasionally men wore the forelock, a lock hanging down over the nose. Like the Crow in the north, the Kiowa men cherished long hair, often augmenting it to reach to the ground. By the 1820s men were wearing hair plates obtained in trade from Mexico or the Southwest; these were silver disks or conchas fastened to leather straps and worn at the back of the head, some of these hair-plate strips being so long they reached the ground.

Headgear

The Kiowa went bareheaded most of the time. Occasionally the men wore the otter-fur turban, so common on the Central Plains; a folded otter skin was wrapped around the head, sometimes with the tail left extending straight out at the side, down the back, or simply tucked in. Beaded or quilled medallions or conchas were added as decoration.

Accessories

Fans were made of feathers, eagle feathers when obtainable. Armbands and garters were straps of leather fastened with thongs, unadorned until beadwork was introduced; these were often painted, especially in yellow or green tones. Belts for both sexes were adorned with conchas or silver medallions obtained in trade, later made by the Kiowa themselves. From the belts hung the usual Plains articles—bags containing paint and painting equipment, awl or knife cases, a small case for the navel amulet or charm of the umbilical cord of the wearer, a strike-a-light case, and a pouch for sewing materials.

Jewelry

Earrings and necklaces of shells and beads were common; a unique design was that of a stylized crawdad or crayfish. Hair pipe beads were used as earrings, hair ornaments, and pendants on garments; because they were fragile and easily broken, the short pieces were used further in necklaces and other forms of jewelry. Another unique form of necklace popular in the Southern Plains was made of the ball-and-socket joint bones of land turtles, which created interesting patterns. Round brooches and pectoral ornaments were created by the Kiowa silversmiths.

Armor
Large shields were carried by the Southern Plains warriors, and their armor, for both men and horses, was of tough rawhide.

Special Costumes
The Kiowa had six men's and two women's societies. The highest military order, the Real Dogs or Horses, consisted of the bravest warriors of the tribe; their insignia was a long sash of rawhide (later of cloth). Mooney gives the types of sashes—the leader's of elk skin colored black, three of red cloth, and six of elk skin dyed red. The mourning period extended for a year, during which mourners painted the face black, cut the hair, and slashed the skin of arms and legs to show their sorrow.

Garment Decoration
The Kiowa did little or no quillwork, probably because porcupine quills were not available except through trade. Beadwork usually took the form of small edgings on garments, even following some scalloped edges. They developed a distinctive type of stylized floral design, typically done in the overlay stitch. They also made a form of bead netting, often called the "gourd" stitch or "peyote" stitch (when used on peyote accessories and costumes). Fringes were popular, with the thin strands carefully twisted to resemble cords. Garments, especially dresses, moccasins, and leggings, were painted solidly in yellow or green, and celestial symbols used as further decoration.

Face and Body Embellishment
A warrior often painted his face, his shield, and his horse all the same color. In general, painting was done with solid colors. Tattooing appeared as a circle on a woman's forehead, considered a tribal mark.

Transitional Dress
Women made dresses of cloth, at first of stroud, later cotton; especially popular with the Kiowa woman was the ankle-length red dress, fringed and beaded, later copied by many Indian women for ceremonial use. Still later, white was used for this type of dress. Men added black kerchiefs to their vests and shirts. Hair pipe breastplates (no longer of bone pipe pieces, but often of plastic), peace medals, silver armbands, and the roach were all used for special occasions. For everyday wear, men adopted the cowboy's high-heeled leather boots with chaps. The Kiowa were strongly influenced by the Ghost Dance of the 1890s, and created dresses and shirts to participate in the dance; they continued their use of native tanned leather, however, and their typical use of many fringes and painted backgrounds. The Kiowa have emerged today as superb craftsmen and artists, especially in their work with silver and their silk-screen prints.

Key Sources
Jacobson, Oscar B. *Kiowa Indian Art: A Portfolio of Serigraphs.* Nice, France: Szwedzicki, 1929.
Lowie, Robert H. "Societies of the Kiowa." American Museum of Natural History *Anthropological Papers* 11(11).
Mayhall, Mildred P. *The Kiowas.* Norman: University of Oklahoma Press, 1962.
Powers, William K. *Indians of the Southern Plains.* New York: Putnam's, 1971.

Mandan
Of the Upper Missouri tribes the Mandan were the most populous and prosperous; they were agriculturists, living in earth lodges in well-fortified villages. Their name, according to Prince Maximilian, was given to them by the Sioux and may be a corruption of the word *mawatoni;* some say it meant "people on the bank." They were closely allied with the Hidatsa, who also spoke a Siouan language. They were visited by Sieur de la Verendrye in 1738, by Lewis and Clark in 1804, and both George Catlin and Karl Bodmer painted them in the 1830s. They were terribly reduced by smallpox in 1837. White traders called them "the polite and friendly Mandans."

Men's Basic Dress
Like the Crow, the Mandan were splendidly dressed, especially the men, and their ceremonial costumes were even more elaborate than those of the Sioux. Ewers suggests that, like many of the Plains tribes, they wore no breechclouts aboriginally; later, probably after 1830, they adopted the typical Plains

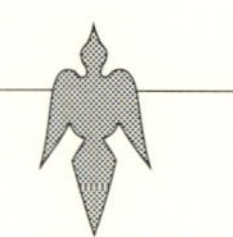

style of the fitted skin breechclout with flaps hanging fore and aft. Thigh-length leggings were fitted, with quilled or beaded strips to the side of the front, and with long fringes, hairlocks, or feathers at the side seams; at times they were painted with horizontal stripes. Fringed at the bottom, they usually extended well over the instep of the moccasins. War shirts, usually reserved for ceremonial use, were earlier quite long (knee-length), but were shortened in the early nineteenth century, and the quilled or beaded shoulder and armbands were made larger. These binary shirts, of antelope, deer, or mountain-goat skin, were minimally tailored with partly open or loosely stitched seams. A large beaded or quilled rosette or a painted sun symbol commonly adorned the chest. They were often painted with stars, crescent moons, buffalo hooves, or other devices. Ermine tails and quill-wrapped scalplocks were added and the bottom was frequently edged with fur. Both Catlin and Bodmer did superb paintings of Mah-to-to-pa, the Mandan chief.

Women's Basic Dress

Verendrye said in 1738 that the Mandan women wore only a skin apron in the front; at times dresses were worn that were of simple cut, unfitted, belted, and sometimes with a cape-like piece over the right shoulder; these may possibly have been "side-fold" dresses. Later, women wore the long deer-tail two-skin dress, with a dip in the yoke; this garment was made from a large deer or mountain-sheep skin. Trimming consisted of rows of elk teeth or cowrie shells, with dewclaws, rows of thongs, fringes under the arms and down the side seams, and applique patches of red cloth at the bottom. Often quilled rosettes adorned the yoke. Leggings of skin, knee-length, were gartered.

Footwear

The Mandan wore the one-piece soft-sole moccasin with the side seam. Later, probably in the early nineteenth century, these were attached to rawhide soles; usually the upper was sewn to the sole from the inside, then turned right-side-out with a stick. Another type of moccasin had the upper gathered into a front seam, which was often covered with a quilled or beaded piece. The large ankle flaps were worn up or down. Winter moccasins were made larger so they could be stuffed with grass or fur for

Draped in robes, Mandan women of the White Buffalo Cow Society wear fez-like hats made of rare albino cow bison fur. One woman, right of center, wears a full-length white robe, and holds branches and a bird-wing fan

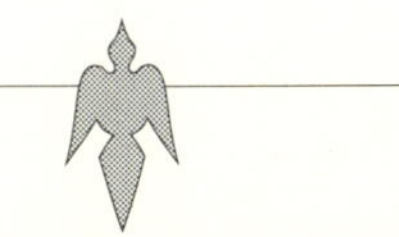

Mah-to-to-pa, Four Bears, a Mandan chief, painted by George Catlin in 1832, wears a shirt decorated with porcupine quill bands, rosettes, and paintings of his exploits. His long feather warbonnet has a profusion of ermine skins and a set of bison horns.

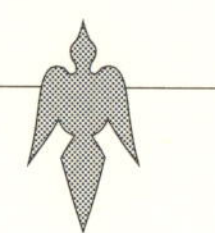

warmth. A warrior had the honor of wearing strips of skunk fur or a wolf tail trailing at the back of his moccasins.

Outer Wear

Robes were made of the skin of a young buffalo bull, with the fur left on the outside and the inner side tanned. It was worn by wrapping around the body and was kept in place either by belting or by holding it with the left hand, leaving the right arm free; it was not pinned or tied. Men's robes were ornamented with paintings depicting their war exploits, or a feathered circle, or a beaded or quilled strip with rosettes at intervals. Women's robes were not painted, but were often ornamented with a strip of rosettes. Lighter weight robes were of deerskin. Some men wore an otter-fur shawl.

Hair Styles

The men cherished their long hair, augmenting it with human locks or horsehair, so that it reached to the calves or even to the ground. They made a "fall" by dividing it into plaits or slabs two inches wide, which were fastened together with sinew, filled in with glue, and then the entire assemblage was painted red; these falls, once they were set, remained unchanged from year to year. The hair was worn in two braids, or with a forelock (which usually sloped outward), or twisted into a knot above the forehead, or with small braids at the side of the face. Many allowed the hair to hang loose, especially as a sign of humility and spirituality. A few men allowed a sparse beard to grow. Women wore the hair as long as they could cultivate it, had a center part, and often wore it in two large braids. At times, after braiding, they would undo the hair and allow it to spread over the shoulders in a "crinkled" fashion.

Headgear

The Mandan men, especially those of great distinction, wore the feathered warbonnet, but not the usual "halo" type; rather, the eagle feathers cascaded from the top of the head down the back; this headdress was surmounted by buffalo horns that

Mandan men brandish spears, shields, and rifles during a bison dance. They wear bison heads, manes, and skins, and some have painted stripes, usually reserved for war, on their bodies.

had been shaved to almost a third of their thickness. Ermine tails were added in abundance. The horned headdress was also worn without the eagle feathers at the back. Polished and painted wooden sticks were bound together and worn on the head. Mah-to-to-pa wore in his hair six wooden sticks representing musket wounds suffered or prisoners captured, as well as a carved wooden knife symbolic of a bloody conflict he had had with a Cheyenne chief. Men also wore feathers in the hair, singly or in clusters. Fur caps or turbans were worn in the winter.

Accessories
Large fans of eagle or turkey feathers were carried by the men. Some carried a fly brush attached to the wrist. Garters and armbands were of fur with feathers hanging down. Looking-glass boards, small mirrors set in wooden frames, obtained from the traders, were hung around the neck or attached to garments. Small pouches, fringed and decorated with quills or beads, hung from the leather belt. Medicine bundles, containing articles sacred to the wearer, were often made of ermine or beaver fur. Knives and awls were kept in sheaths. Women's sewing supplies and equipment and paints were kept in pouches.

Jewelry
Hair pipes and beads and valuable strings of dentalia hung at the sides of the face along with hair bows, which Ewers says may have been a Mandan invention. Necklaces were of beads, shells, grizzly-bear claws, and odorous roots. Stuffed, padded buckskin chokers, worn in pairs, were usually of blue and white beads. Ears were pierced to accommodate rings, clusters of beads, hair pipes, or pieces of abalone shell. Occasionally bracelets and gorgets were obtained in trade. Clothing was decorated with deer or antelope hooves, which made nice clacking sounds; jinglers of native copper were also cherished for their sounds.

Armor
Catlin describes Mah-to-to-pa's shield—made of the hide from the buffalo's neck, hardened with glue from the hooves, covered with the skin of a "polecat" and fringed with rows of eagle quills and antelope hooves. No mention is made by Catlin or Bodmer of armor.

Special Costumes
The Mandan had a complex system of age-graded societies with ceremonies, regalia, songs, and costumes for each; several of these were women's societies. In the dance of the Buffalo Society, a frenzied dance to attract buffalo, some of the men wore buffalo heads on their own heads; others had fur and horns on the heads and/or feathers of owls, ravens, eagles, or swans. Feathers hung down the back representing bulls' tails. The only other articles of dress were breechclouts and moccasins from which trailed foxtails. The legs and arms were painted, usually in horizontal stripes. The important society of the Mandan women was the White Buffalo Cow Society, in which the lead woman wore a white buffalo robe; considering that only one in 100,000 buffalo was albino, the skins understandably commanded an incredible price. Other women in the dance of this society were wrapped in robes adorned with quilled or beaded rosettes and strips, and wore a hussar-type hat of white buffalo skin with owl or raven feathers splaying out the top. Members of the Kit Fox Society had a coyote jawbone, painted red or blue, fastened to a brow band of otter fur; they also roached their hair, rare among the Mandan. Catlin did a painting of a shaman, Old Bear, dressed in a robe of white wolf skins and his body daubed with clay. The women chopped off the hair as a sign of mourning, but the men spared only a lock or two to show grief.

Garment Decoration
Some plaiting was done with porcupine quills, but beading was a significant element in the magnificent Mandan costumes. Rosettes, arm and shoulder bands, and women's dress yokes were adorned with beading in geometric designs, particularly based on celestial symbols—stars, crescent moons, and sun symbols. Like the Arikara, the Mandan were said to have made their own beads and pendants by melting down glass traders' beads and casting the molten liquid in clay forms. Garments were also adorned with rows of thongs or elk teeth, quill-wrapped hair locks, many fringes, ermine skins, and red cloth patches.

Face and Body Embellishment
The Mandan practiced face and body painting, using red ocher, yellow ocher, white clay, and charcoal. A

blackened face indicated a warrior had killed one of the enemy. Sometimes one eye was painted one color and the other was of a different hue. Forehead and jaws were often painted red. A hand painted on the chest represented an enemy taken prisoner; yellow horizontal stripes also meant prisoners taken. These were all symbolic of war exploits, and the women were permitted to paint in like manner. Women often painted the left cheek and eye red, and placed two blue spots on the temple near the right eye. There was a little tattooing on the part of the Mandan—the men on the breast and upper arms, the women on the lower part of the face.

Transitional Dress

The Mandan engaged in such extensive trading that they were early exposed to white culture, but they retained tribal distinctions in their costumes. The major evidences of borrowing from the whites were their use of beads (they were especially fond of blue and white beads) and a limited use of red cloth as patches and as strips for decoration. The tribe was so decimated by smallpox that few were left to be assimilated into the alien culture.

Key Sources

Bowers, Alfred W. *Mandan Social and Ceremonial Organization.* Chicago: University of Chicago Press, 1950.

Bruner, Edward. "Mandan." In *Perspectives in American Indian Culture Change.* Pp. 187–287. Chicago, 1961.

Catlin, George. *O-Kee-Pa: A Religious Ceremony and Other Customs of the Mandans.* John C. Ewers, ed. New Haven, CT: Yale University Press, 1967.

Curtis, Edward S. *The North American Indian.* Vol. 5. New York: Johnson Reprint Company, 1970.

Lowie, Robert H. "Societies of the Crow, Hidatsa and Mandan Indians." American Museum of Natural History *Anthropological Papers* 9(3).

Mails, Thomas. "Mandan." In *Dog Soldiers, Bear Men and Buffalo Women: A Study of the Societies and Cults of the Plains Indians.* Pp. 175–188. Englewood Cliffs, NJ: Prentice-Hall, 1973.

Will, G. F. and Herbert J. Spinden. "The Mandans: A Study of Their Culture, Archaeology, and Language." *Harvard University Papers* 3(4).

Omaha

The Omaha were Dhegihan speakers of Siouan, a dialect also used by the Ponca, Osage, Kansa, and Quapaw. Their name meant "going against the wind" or "downstream people," indicative of their territory along the Missouri River above Omaha. Great wanderers, they had come originally from the Ohio Valley, then to the Great Lakes region, then roamed the plains of South Dakota, finally settling in northeastern Nebraska to become corn-raising agriculturalists living in earth lodges. Karl Bodmer and George Catlin painted them, as did Charles Bird King, the latter portraying some of the Omaha leaders who went to Washington in 1821 and 1836. Taylor says the Omaha tended toward corpulency. Dress was similar to that of the Ponca and the Osage.

Men's Basic Dress

Omaha men wore the typical Plains breechclout of skin with flaps hanging in front and back. Thigh-length leggings with front seams were gartered below the knees; they were often painted green and had fringes and feathers hanging down the sides, as well as quill-worked bands down the front or down the sides in front of the fringes. Large flaps at the bottom often covered much of the moccasins. A chief's leggings sometimes had round dots punctured into the tanned skin. War shirts seem to have been adopted from the tribes to the north early in the nineteenth century. They were the "deer leg" type with broad shoulder and armbands, a fringed triangular flap at the neck, and decorations of quill or bead designs, many hair locks, and fringes.

Women's Basic Dress

Anciently, the women wore a wraparound skirt of tanned deerskin with a simple poncho-type covering for warmth. By the early nineteenth century they were wearing the three-skin Plains dress—with the top of one skin folded over for a yoke and fastened to the two-skin skirt, either being loosely laced together or sewn with sinew. Later they made the dresses of stroud cloth, blue or red, with the white edge showing as a part of the design. Knee-length leggings were gartered.

Footwear
Early moccasins were of the soft-sole one-piece variety with the front seam characteristic of the Woodland background of the Omaha. Later they added the usual rawhide sole of the Plains, but they retained the front seam, covering it with a decorated band. Cuffs were typically large and floppy. As was true of many tribes, the infants wore moccasins with a small hole in the sole of one, to indicate to the spirits of the underworld that the child was not ready for death because its moccasins were worn out; new moccasins were given the child at a "turning" ceremony, a puberty rite, signifying that the child was now ready for life's journey.

Outer Wear
Long buffalo robes were worn with the hair outside, done, as Mails relates, "in recognition of the transmission of life from the buffalo to man that the latter might live." Lighter weight robes were of deerskin. Some rabbit-skin robes were worn by women and children.

Hair Styles
Men wore the hair plain, parted in the center, generally about shoulder length. Some men, especially warriors, wore the roach, a three- or four-inch tuft left standing from the front of the head to the back. With this was worn a scalplock, one lock from the crown allowed to grow full length, usually braided, to which feathers and ornaments were attached. An artificial roach was made from deer hair dyed red and horsehair; other materials used were porcupine guard hair, skunk hair, or turkey beard. This was attached by means of a roach spreader. The Omaha observed a symbolic cutting of a young boy's hair, the style of cut depending upon the gens of the father. Koch (based on Fletcher) gives many of the cuts, and Bodmer did a painting of a young Omaha showing his tonsure. The young boy wore his hair in this particular manner until the second set of teeth came in; then it was allowed to grow, but the scalplock was always kept separate and braided. Women arranged the hair in two braids, which were often tied together at the ends to hang at the back.

Headgear
The feather warbonnet was worn by the Omaha, but with an odd custom; the young man who received it (often from an antagonist) was expected to start on a war trail immediately and not return until he had killed an enemy, or he must take an exposed position in the next conflict, both alternatives extraordinarily dangerous for a young and untried warrior. A feather cap was also worn by the Omaha men composed of the feathers of owls and birds of prey. A fur cap was worn in winter, made of a band of fur from a smaller animal such as a coyote, a badger, or an otter. These caps had no tops and were ornamented with quillwork or designs painted on rawhide; feathers often were fastened to stand erect at the back. The otter-fur turban was also worn with the tail extended stiffly to the side or worn down the back.

Accessories
Otter-skin bags, like those of the Prairie tribes, were used to hold "medicine" items, personally sacred to the wearer. Pouches of deerskin were decorated with quillwork. The women made finger-woven scarves, belts, garters, and turbans of nettle fibers. Belts and shirts were often decorated with silver disks or "conchas," obtained in trade from the Southwest. Garters had brass bells attached, to add to the rhythm and sound of the dance. A wolf-skin collar was sometimes worn by a warrior. Some men carried a fly brush fastened to the wrist.

Jewelry
The grizzly-bear claw necklace was popular, with the claws attached to an otter-fur choker with a decorated tail hanging down the back. Ears were pierced in several places to accommodate clusters of beads, rings, or shells. Necklaces and chokers were formed of beads, cowrie, and other shells.

Special Costumes
Mails, basing his work on Fletcher, says there were two classes of Omaha societies: (1) The social societies had both warrior societies and some strictly social groups. (2) The secret societies dealt with supernatural mysteries. There were no women's groups. Of the first group, the Thunder Society was the most important; its members wore only a breechclout with a bunch of braided grass in back,

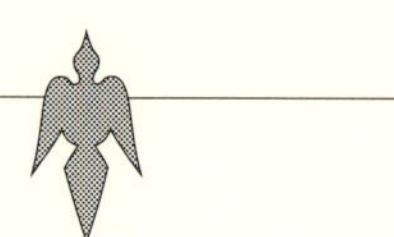

symbolic of scalps taken in battle. This later became the Grass Dance or Omaha Dance, one of the most popular dances of the next hundred years, in which the "crow" or bustle was worn. In the secret Bear Society, one member wore the entire skin of a grizzly bear; others wore bear-claw necklaces. Various designs and colors of painting were displayed.

Garment Decoration

The Omaha women pounded the fibers of the nettle plant until they were soft and pliable, then braided them into strips to make belts, sashes, and garters. Quillwork, using a technique of two threads with diagonal folding, produced fine work of soft, subtle hues. Beadwork was used on war shirts (adopted from the Sioux to the north), the otter-fur bags and turbans, and for bandelier bags, at first in geometric designs, later in floral patterns and even realistic images. Some ribbonwork was done. Deer hide for garments was frequently stained or painted green, a favorite color with the Omaha. At times leather garments were punctuated, the dots forming a casual design.

Face and Body Embellishment

Body paint was applied as an appeal or as a prayer of thanksgiving, black being indicative of victory; returning warriors who had taken scalps painted the face black. A leader of a war party displayed diagonal lines on the face representing tears, weeping for lost braves. Red stripes or solid-red areas were painted on foreheads, chins, and cheeks. Women were tattooed on the forehead with a black circle (to represent the sun) and a four-pointed star on the back and the breast (symbolizing the night), representing war honors of a husband or father. Men frequently had tattooed dots on the face.

Transitional Dress

The Omaha, with their central position on the Plains, early adopted materials and fashions of the white culture, but retained much of their traditional style of dress until late in the nineteenth century. Blankets or stroud cloth replaced the unwieldy buffalo robes. Metal was made into armbands, earrings, and brooches. Cloth turbans were worn, adorned with feathers. The otter-fur turban continued in popularity, but was decorated with ribbon applique, beads, and ermine trim. By the early years of this century little was left of distinctively tribal costume.

Key Sources

Fletcher, Alice C. and Francis La Flesche. "The Omaha Tribe." Bureau of American Ethnology *Annual Reports* 27.

Mails, Thomas. "The Omaha." In *Bear Men, Buffalo Women and Dog Soldiers: A Study of the Societies and Cults of the Plains Indians.* Pp. 269–282. Englewood Cliffs, NJ: Prentice-Hall, 1973.

Powers, William K. *Indians of the Southern Plains.* New York: Putnam's, 1971.

Osage

The Osage, related linguistically to the Omaha, Kansas, Ponca, and Quapaw, spoke the Dhegihan dialect of the Siouan language. They were great wanderers—from the Ohio River to the Great Lakes, to Missouri, Kansas, and finally to Arkansas and Oklahoma. Their name seeems to have been a French corruption of their name for themselves—Wazhazhe. Semisedentary, they raised corn, hunted the buffalo, and seemed always to be at war. The first record of the Osage is from Marquette's journal of 1673. The French refugee artist Balthazar Fevret de Saint Mémin painted them in 1804, as did George Catlin and Karl Bodmer in the 1830s. They were divided into three bands: the Great Osage, the Little Osage and the Arkansas Band.

During the first half of the twentieth century the Osage were one of the wealthiest nations per capita in the world—garnering $300,000,000 in royalties in gas and oil, which money they managed carefully for the greater benefit of the tribe as a whole.

Men's Basic Dress

Tanned leather breechclouts had very short flaps, so short that the fitted part through the crotch was exposed. Leggings had front seams, often covered with a quilled band and with long scalplock fringes from the band or from the sides; the garters, beaded strips of skin below the knees, also had long scalplock fringes hanging at the sides. Leggings were either split over the moccasins or covered them in the style of spats. In their warm climate, the Osage usually went with torsos bare, but depended for extra warmth on lightweight robes.

Women's Basic Dress

The early woman's garment was the wraparound skirt of tanned leather; with this was worn a skin cape in the Woodlands manner, or a poncho, sleeveless, without seams, and with only a slit for the neck opening. Knee-length leggings had a front seam and were gartered. Later they adopted Plains type dresses, the two-skin and three-skin.

Footwear

Older one-piece soft-sole moccasins had a seam running the entire length of the sole; these were also worn by the Quapaw, a closely related tribe. Later the Osage adopted the hard-sole moccasins of the Plains, which were beaded and painted, and continued with the front seam. Men's moccasins had no cuff, while the women's displayed a large cuff.

Outer Wear

Although buffalo robes were occasionally worn by chiefs, the usual robe was of tanned deerhide, draped over the shoulders and tied in the front, a manner attributed only to the Arapaho and the Osage. Koch says these front-tied cloaks were typically worn by officials of one of the men's societies.

Hair Styles

Some men wore the hair long like the Ponca. Others shaved the hair, except for a scalplock and a short tuft of hair, which was then augmented by a roach of deer hair or horsehair dyed red. Later some men wore the hair clubbed in the back. Women wore the hair loose or in braids.

Headgear

Some men wore a wide otter-fur headband with a feather at the back. The otter-fur turban was also worn, with such distinctive decorations added as minutely figured disks and bands of netted beading on the pendant at the back. Fur caps for winter wear were from the pelts of coyotes, otters, or badgers.

Accessories

Woven garters often had brass bells attached to them to add to the sounds and rhythms of the dance. Neck bands, and later hatbands, were woven of horsehair and beaded in a diagonal beading technique. Mirrorboards, small looking glasses set in wooden frames, were attached to garments. Small pouches, attached to the belt, contained articles and equipment for painting, sewing, tobacco, and personal, sacred "medicine" items. Wide leather belts, as much as six inches wide, were popular with both sexes.

Jewelry

Catlin tells about the Osage slitting the ears in several places and hanging an abundance of ear ornaments from them. He attributes this to the wearing of the roach, but the women also wore many earrings; these were large clusters of beads and shells. Necklaces were of long strings of beads, so long they were sometimes worn under one arm and over the other shoulder. Chokers had a large round shell at the front. Large shell gorgets were occasionally worn. Some men pierced the septum and inserted a nose ring.

Garment Decoration

The Osage women were famous for their beautiful garments adorned with ribbon applique; this was the southernmost extent of this type of decoration, and their skill in this technique has continued to the present. Frequent designs were the hourglass, the double-fork design, and rows of hand images. Blankets, leggings, and shawls were enhanced with ribbonwork. Some beadwork was done, especially with blue and white beads; the women also used the technique of adding beads during the finger-weaving process when making sashes and similar articles of dress.

Face and Body Embellishment

Men daubed red paint around the hair, the eyes, and the eye sockets. Both sexes displayed tattooing, which had ritualistic as well as social and esthetic bases. Common designs were horizontal lines on the chest, concentric circles on the shoulders, and vertical lines on the face. A warrior could gain distinction by deeds of valor, which could also be reflected in the tattooing of his wife or a daughter. If the keeper of the sacred pipe had killed an enemy in battle, he was entitled to have a skull tattooed on his back or breast. Catlin mentions the head as being flattened at the back and

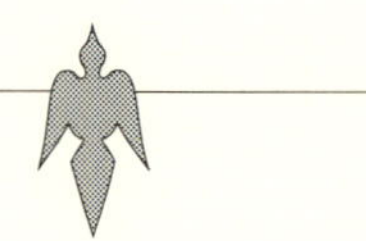

somewhat "elevated" at the top, but only moderately; this seems to have been due to their manner of tying infants into cradle boards.

Transitional Dress

The Osage were determined not to yield their culture to that of the whites; however, they early adopted many of the materials offered by the traders, such as cloth, blankets, blue and white beads, German silver, and even peacock feathers. By 1830 women were making or buying dresses of calico or broadcloth with blouses and full skirts. Men wore black scarves, tied at the neck. Vests were decorated with ribbonwork or heavily beaded. In the late nineteenth century, a striking use of the military coat was as a "wedding coat"; this was further embellished with beadwork, silk ribbonwork, and German silver ornaments. Metal was used for many items such as earrings, armbands, bracelets, and hair plates, which were attached to fur or leather straps and worn as belts or hair ornaments. Peace medals on ribbons were proudly displayed by the chiefs.

Key Sources

Mathews, John J. *The Osage: Children of the Middle Waters.* Norman: University of Oklahoma Press, 1961.

Welsch, Roger. "The Old Villagers: The Omaha and Ponca." *Nebraskaland Magazine* 62(1): 16–20.

Whiteford, Andrew Hunter. "Tapestry-Twined Bags, Osage Bags, and Others." *American Indian Art Magazine* (Spring, 1978: 32).

Pawnee

The Pawnee were a powerful tribe living in their earth lodges in villages along the River Platte. Their language was of the Caddo family of the Hokan-Siouan stock. They were related to the Arikara, speaking the same language and exhibiting many of the same customs. The name comes from the way they used to wear the hair—the scalplock was stiffened with paint and fat and curved to resemble a horn or "pawnee." They were divided into four bands—the Grand Pawnee, the Tappage Pawnee, the Republican band, and the Skidi or Wolf (Loup) Pawnee. Originally farmers of the Southeastern Woodlands, they had been pushed west and north until they finally settled in central and western Nebraska, where they took to hunting buffalo. They were first mentioned by Coronado in 1541; by 1720 they had acquired horses, and by 1750 they had made contact with the French fur traders. There were many skirmishes between the Pawnee and the settlers, but no full-blown warfare. In fact, many of the men became valuable scouts for the U.S. Army, especially in the Indian Wars of 1865–1885.

Samuel Seymour painted a Pawnee council meeting in 1819. Charles Bird King painted members of a Pawnee delegation to Washington in 1821; also that year John Neagle did portraits of some of the Pawnee. George Catlin visited and painted them in the early 1830s.

Men's Basic Dress

The men's breechclout *(auzeum)* of tanned skin had rather long flaps. Leggings, worn only in colder weather or for gala occasions, had side seams (later front seams), often bottom tabs, and were gartered at the knees; painting on the leggings included horizontal lines, hands, and especially celestial symbols, favorite images with the Pawnee. The hair fringes were quill-wrapped and braided and, as Maurer tells, had an interesting significance, for the hair was that of friends intertwined with that of the wearer, signifying support and friendship. The occasional "deer leg" shirt was fairly plain, but sported very long fringes under the arms.

Women's Basic Dress

Women wore the combination of the poncho (or cape) and the skin skirt, which was fringed at the bottom. Conn says the style may have come from the Apache to the southwest, for the Pawnee often raided them, but Lowie says he believes it to have been an eastern influence. Garments were painted with the customary celestial designs, highly important to the Pawnee. In the eighteenth century this style of dress was modified by sewing the poncho directly to the skirt top. Gartered leggings were knee-length.

Footwear

Early moccasins were the typical one-piece soft-sole variety; later the hard sole, often made of used pieces of rawhide, such as from parfleches or lodges, was adopted. Moccasins had front seams that were usually

Lone Chief, a Pawnee, wears strouding leggings with large side flaps and beaded bear paws. He wears a hairpipe breastplate and two peace medals over a cloth shirt, and his braids are wrapped beaded tubes.

covered with a quilled or beaded strip and often had fringes or feathers attached, hanging to the sides; a forked tongue was sometimes added. Very large ankle flaps were worn, and the moccasin was often tied around the ankles.

Outer Wear

Robes, when worn, were of buffalo hides painted with representations of warfare, such as warriors on horseback. Lighter weight robes of deerskin were also worn.

Hair Styles

The most common hair style among the Pawnee men was the "roach," in which the head was shaved leaving a tuft of hair from front to back, stiffened with fat and red paint, and a long, braided scalplock at the back. The roach was augmented by a strip of deer or porcupine hair, also stiffened and painted red, which was held in place by a "roach spreader" of carved elk antler. Those who did not wear the roach wore the hair loose. Women wore the hair flowing or in two braids down the back, the parting being painted red for special occasions. Men plucked both beard and eyebrows.

A Pawnee man holds a large feather fan. He has a feather headdress and wears a heavily fringed shirt and leggings with beaded bands.

Headgear

Few headdresses were worn; however, we have a portrait of Petalesharo, Pawnee chief, painted by King in 1821, wearing an eagle-feather headdress, much like the Sioux warbonnet except, instead of the beaded browband, there is a small red fringe with short ermine tips hanging beneath it over the forehead; long ermine tails hang at the sides of the face. This chief had saved a woman about to be sacrificed in the Pawnee Morning Star ceremony; after his daring rescue of the maiden, the sacrifice was abandoned but not the ceremony. Some otter-fur turbans were worn by the men.

Accessories

Long fans, of turkey or goose feathers, were carried by men of distinction. Lacking pockets, the Indians carried necessary articles in bags or pouches attached to the belt. These contained such items as painting equipment and paint, sewing materials for the women, awls, knives, cases, and "medicine" objects of sacred importance to the wearer. Some bags were made of woven fibers, such as grass or buffalo hair, in a simple twining technique; brightly hued sashes—red, green, and yellow—were also woven in this manner. Mirror boards, small looking glasses set in wooden frames, were carried or attached to garments.

Jewelry

Bear-claw necklaces were worn with otter tails; Ewers says that the Pawnee alone retained both the otter head and the tail as adjuncts to these items. Other necklaces were of beads and shells. At times a choker was made of a band of quillwork. Ears were pierced in many places, with earrings worn in abundance, the most common types being clusters of beads and shells or drops.

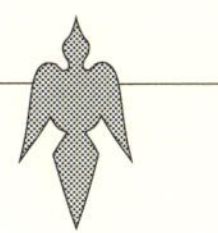

Armor

The usual battle dress of the Pawnee warrior was a coat of paint, a pair of moccasins, and a breechclout or a long sash tied about the waist. Large oval or round shields, painted with symbolic images, were carried.

Special Costumes

The Pawnee had a highly complex and extensive scheme of religious organizations, each with its own special regalia and ceremonies, which Murie has recorded so well. The medicine man, whose power was given to him by the bear spirit, wore the entire skin of a grizzly bear.

Garment Decoration

Very little quillwork was done. Beadwork, created in the lazy stitch technique, appeared on war shirts, as wide bands on leggings, and as ornament on otter-fur turbans. Sashes and garters were finger-woven of grass or buffalo-hair fibers. Celestial designs were painted on leggings and other garments.

Face and Body Embellishment

Painting of the face and body was of great importance to the Pawnee. Men painted their bodies with red and yellow stripes, carefully tipped the eyelids with red paint, and painted the entire face or the upper half with red. The Pawnee scouts painted their faces white because, as Mails points out, it symbolized the wolf whose medicine was considered the greatest aid in scouting. Catlin painted The Buffalo Bull, Pawnee chief, with his totem, the head of a buffalo, painted on his chest and on his face. In the Morning Star ceremony, the girl to be sacrificed was painted, the right half of her body red, the left half black. Tattooing was rarely practiced by the Pawnee.

Transitional Dress

The materials of the whites were quickly adopted by the Pawnee. They began to wear blankets—preferably white with a large colored stripe. The women wore the cloth dresses in the fashions of the day. Both sexes wore black cloth turbans tied around the head. Metal armbands, peace medals, and "ball-and-cone" earrings were popular. By the late nineteenth century little remained of tribal dress.

Key Sources

Dunbar, John B. "The Pawnee Indians." *Magazine of American History* 4, 5, 8.

Grinnell, George Bird. *Pawnee, Blackfoot, and Cheyenne.* New York: Scribner's, 1961.

Hyde, George E. *Pawnee Indians.* Denver: University of Denver Press, 1951.

Murie, James R. "Pawnee Indian Societies." American Museum of Natural History *Anthropological Papers* 11(7).

Plains Cree

The Plains Cree, also known as the Kristenaux or Knistenaux, were allies of the Assiniboine and occupied much the same territory on the prairies of Alberta. Related tribes were the Woodland Cree of southern Canada and the Swampy Cree of Keewatin. Algonquian speakers, they were constantly at war with the Sioux and the Blackfeet.

The Plains Cree were divided into the "River People" and the "Lowlands People," which groups were in turn divided into 12 small bands whose members were in general rather poor, owning few horses. First mentioned in the *Jesuit Relations* of 1640, the Plains Cree originally had been a part of the Chipewyan nation much farther north; before 1700 they had lived around Great Slave Lake, and with the coming of the Hudson's Bay Company's trading posts had turned to trapping beaver.

Maximilian said their dress was like that of the Assiniboine. The Plains Ojibwa were similarly dressed.

Men's Basic Dress

Early shirts, seldom worn anciently, were made from one skin (so they were short-sleeved), and were well decorated with porcupine quillwork, for which the Plains Cree were famous. Later shirts were in the Plains style, but were longer than those of their neighbors; they were made of deer or elk skin, occasionally of buffalo hide. Usually they had fitted sleeves and were decorated with fringes on the sleeves and at the hem, as well as rosettes of quillwork, a large one on the chest and on the back or smaller ones on the upper sleeves. These shirts were painted with linear designs such as stripes or horseshoes, both indicative of war exploits. Breechclouts of tanned

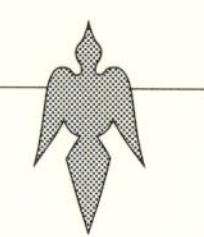

leather were the fitted type with flaps front and back. The hip-length leggings were gartered at the knees with strips of leather or of fur. Quillworked strips were placed down the outside of the leggings, coupled with long fringes that were quill-wrapped at the base. Occasionally shirts like those of the Plateau tribes were worn—short, with tabs at the bottom and with painting and/or perforations in a tadpole design. Wolfskin leggings with long fringes were worn in the wintertime.

Women's Basic Dress

Cree women anciently wore a simple skirt with a skin cape or poncho thrown over it when desired. The next style was the strap-and-sleeve dress, first of skin, then of cloth. Although Isham reported the use of cloth as early as 1743, skin continued to be used, for Kurz sketched skin dresses in 1851. Whatever the material, the basic shape remained the same; a wraparound skirt was held in place by straps over the shoulders and there were separate sleeves that could be tied on. The strap dress was most common, but side-fold dresses were also worn. The Cree-type side-fold dress, as Feder has designated it, was made of one large hide with a seam down the left side. The top was folded down to make a flap hanging almost to the waist; then a cut was made on the folded edge to form an armhole, with a strap added to fit over the right shoulder. The seamed left side hung down lower and had two tabs at the bottom. Decorations consisted of small horizontal rows of quillwork, and fringes at the bottom and sometimes down the left seam. The dress seems to have disappeared by the 1830s, but the strap-and-sleeve dress (sketched by Kurz in 1851) continued, along with the "deer-tail" or two-skin dress adopted from the tribes to the south (as painted by Bodmer in 1833). The Cree women wore knee-length gartered leggings with front seams that extended to the moccasin tops or over them.

Footwear

Moccasins of deer, moose, or elk skin were at first the Woodland type made of one piece of skin with a soft sole, a seam up the front and at the heel, and a U-shaped insert on the instep; the pointed toe was gathered to the insert and flaps were so high they could be wrapped around the ankle and secured with thongs, a style welcome for its warmth in a cold climate. Another soft-sole style had a side seam, which was worn until the 1870s; in winter they were made of buffalo hide with the hair turned inward. Later the Cree adopted the hard-sole Plains moccasin. Fringed moccasins were the prerogative of the warrior. Snowshoes were necessary for winter hunting; these were usually of an oval shape. The Arapaho and the Plains Cree were the only Plains tribes to use snowshoes extensively.

Outer Wear

Robes of buffalo hide with the hair turned inward were knee length and tied close to the chin in cold weather; at other times the left shoulder was left bare. The robes were painted or embellished with beautiful quillwork; long horizontal stripes on a robe signified a long war trip, a cross stood for a peace parley, and the sun symbol was sometimes used. Robes were also made of beaver fur and rabbit skin, the latter worn particularly by women and children. The blanket-coat, called the *capote,* was adopted very early by the Cree, after the Hudson's Bay Company established their trading posts. Made out of the company's white blankets with large colored stripes, they featured long hoods ending in a tassel, a front opening, and a belt or a long sash to hold it closed.

Hair Styles

Men wore the hair loose, in two or more braids, with a forelock hanging down over the nose, or in a pompadour fashion. A single stick worn in the hair indicated that the man had been wounded in battle. Women wore the hair in two braids as a rule, sometimes with bangs on the forehead.

Headgear

Buffalo horned hoods were used as an animal disguise when hunting buffalo. Winter caps of fur, covering the face except for the eyes and nose, were often decorated with feathers or horn-like tufts of fur. Any kind of fur was used for caps—dog, coyote, rabbit, or beaver; these were made in the form of a band around the head with the tail hanging in back. Some winter hats were made of a ring of buffalo hide with the hair up; this cap was gathered into a peak with sinew. Some men wore the leather cases of their bows wound about the head like a turban. Rawhide visors protected the eyes from the summer sun. Cree

women wore a hood in winter, tied under the chin, and with a long tail that was fastened to the belt in back.

Accessories
Mittens were made of rabbit fur or tanned skin, the latter displaying quillwork. Garters, too, were adorned with quillwork. Bags and pouches, some of deerskin, some of woven nettle fiber and buffalo hair, carried such items as apparatus for making fires, shot, tobacco, paint and painting equipment, and sewing materials. Awls and knives were in leather sheaths attached to the belt. The belt was either a leather strap or a long woven sash. Carrying straps or tumplines were worn across the chest.

Jewelry
Hair pipes, long, white tapering tubes made from a marine shell, were popular as ornaments, either worn in strings at the sides of the face or as necklaces, earrings, or pendants. The ears of both sexes were pierced in several places to provide a place to hang earrings; these were often clusters of beads or shells. A popular necklace was the choker, two rolls of stuffed hide decorated with blue and white beads and tied on at the back with thongs. Grizzly-bear claws, strung on a folded piece of fur or skin, made necklaces that were highly valued by the Cree men. Loop necklaces, more common on the Plateau and among the Blackfeet, were also popular. Large, circular shell gorgets with two holes for suspension were worn on the chest.

Garment Decoration
The Cree women were famous for their quillwork, which appeared on robes, leggings, and other garments. They quickly took to beadwork, using the overlay stitch; at first designs were geometric, similar to quillwork, with white backgrounds. Later floral work became prevalent, at first in a linear style, then in a luxuriant naturalistic manner. The women also did fine ribbonwork. Ball fringes of yarn were a popular form of decoration. Some painting was done, particularly on robes.

Face and Body Embellishment
Tattooing was common for both sexes, the men displaying vertical stripes on the arms and the chest, the women having vertical lines on the chin. Face painting, too, was common, often red with black stripes or perhaps just the upper half of the face was painted. Women painted the center part of the hair red for special occasions.

Transitional Dress
Besides the hooded jackets mentioned above, the Cree gladly adopted blankets for outer wear instead of buffalo robes. Otherwise they continued with traditional dress until the changeover in the late nineteenth century to white garments. The greatest change seems to have been in adornment, with the predominant use of beadwork instead of the fine quillwork.

Key Sources
Denig, Edwin Thompson. *Five Indian Tribes of the Upper Missouri: Sioux, Arikaras, Assiniboines, Crees, Crows.* Norman: University of Oklahoma Press, 1961.

Feder, Norman. "The Side Fold Dress." *American Indian Art Magazine* (Winter 1984) 48–55, 75, 77.

Howard, James H. *The Plains-Ojibwa or Bungi.* Reprints in Anthropology 7. Lincoln, NE: J & L Reprint, 1977.

Johnson, Michael G. "A Note on Plains Cree Bonnets." *American Indian Crafts and Cultures* 5(7).

Mandelbaum, D. G. "The Plains Cree." American Museum of Natural History *Anthropological Papers* 37.

Skinner, Alanson B. "The Plains Ojibway and Plains Cree Indians." American Museum of Natural History *Anthropological Papers* 11(6).

Teton Sioux

The name *Sioux* comes from the French traders who called them "Nadowessioux," meaning "lesser enemies" (the Iroquois were the "true enemies"). The language was one of the Siouan family of languages of Siouan-Hokan stock. There were three major divisions of the Sioux: (1) the Eastern or Santee Sioux who spoke the Dakota dialect and should therefore be termed the Dakota Sioux, and are treated elsewhere; (2) the Central or Yankton Sioux who spoke the Nakota

A Sioux man, feathers in his hair, has beaded ear decorations. His fringed shirt has beaded bands on the shoulders and sleeves.

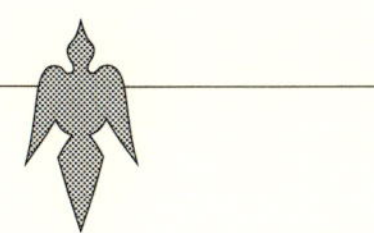

dialect; (3) the Western or Teton Sioux who spoke the Lakota dialect. The Teton Sioux divisions were seven in number: the Minneconjou, the Oglala, the Hunkpapa, the Sans Arcs or Broken Bows, the Two Kettles, the Blackfeet (not to be confused with the Blackfoot confederacy farther west), and the Bois Brules or Burnt Woods.

The first mention of the Sioux appeared in the *Jesuit Relations* of 1640; at that time they lived in Minnesota as relatively sedentary agriculturalists. By 1700 they had left the Santee Sioux and had begun to move westward; by 1750 they had acquired horses and by the end of the century they had established themselves on the Plains as the very embodiment of the buffalo/horse/Indian culture.

The large role played by the Sioux in the late–nineteenth-century history of the Western frontier became the subject of an extensive popular literature and later film. The resulting stereotype of the American Indian is still widely accepted today.

Artists were strongly attracted to the Teton Sioux; George Catlin, Karl Bodmer, Alfred James Miller, and James Otto Lewis all painted them extensively.

Men's Basic Dress

The breechclout was commonly worn to mid-thigh and was usually longer in back; earlier, some had worn a kiltlike affair of fur and feathers, which was particularly characteristic of the Bear Dance. Thigh-length leggings of dressed deer or antelope skin had side seams and a fringe at the sides; sometimes large flaps hung over the moccasins. Often the entire legging was painted red and various symbols painted over this—black horizontal stripes for coups, red vertical stripes for a battle wound, horseshoes for a successful horse raid. Skunk skins were often worn around the knees in lieu of leggings. Quilled strips were common on old men's leggings. Shirts worn in earlier times were simple affairs of one hide tied or sewn under the arms to form a loose sleeve. The warshirts of the nineteenth century were signs of rank, worn only by leaders, especially the "Wicasas" or "shirt wearers." Sleeves were half-sewn, tailored to fit the arm somewhat, and with long fringes of buckskin thongs or hair locks, sinew-wrapped at the bottom, or ermine tails wrapped with red stroud attached down the sleeves. Denig, in 1853, said the hair for hair locks was sometimes that of an enemy, or of a friend, or the warrior's own locks, or horsehair. Fringes also edged the quilled or beaded bands over the shoulders and down the arms. Triangular patches at the neck, both front and back, were symbolic of the knife sheaths worn earlier; these patches might also be either rosettes or rectangular pieces, quilled or beaded. Painted shirts were worn only by the Wicasas, and usually in two colors; some painted the upper half blue and the lower yellow, while some preferred the upper part red and the lower green, or any other combination. Often the shirts were painted all yellow with perhaps green vertical stripes. The usual symbols were present—the hands to represent slain enemies, horseshoe shapes to indicate horses stolen, and such. Long tail pieces were left to hang at the sides. These war shirts changed little over the years and continue to the present day in the gala dress of the Indian male.

Women's Basic Dress

The average Sioux woman prided herself not only on the workmanship of her sewing, quilling, and beading, but also on the individuality of her garments. The earliest type of dress was the simple wraparound skirt with a poncho top. The next style was the strap-and-sleeve dress made from one hide wrapped around the body and suspended from the shoulders by thongs or straps; to this was added, when desired, sleeves tied on with thongs and a belt. The side-fold dress came next, and Feder, in establishing the two general types of this style (Sioux and Cree) gives the characteristics of each. The Sioux type was made of two pieces of skin sewn together horizontally and the folded-down top commonly covered the seam; there may have been painted designs on the top. The left side was longer, usually with decorated tabs at the lower edge. A strap went over the right shoulder only. Horizontal quilled strips (generally of bird quills) covered the bottom half of the skirt. A flounce, decorated with pony beadwork, was often added at the bottom. This was transitional to the "deer tail" dress or the two-skin dress on which, later, a dip was left in the center of the yoke to indicate where the tail had been; these garments were typically cut straight across the

A Sioux mother and daughter, photographed at Rosebud, South Dakota, in the late 1890s, wear cloth dresses. The woman's dress, tied with a leather belt decorated with metal disks, or conchas, has rows of dentalium shells on the yoke and pearl button crosses at the hem. Her cloth robe, probably of strouding, has a decorative beaded blanket strip, and her moccasins are beaded with a buffalo hoof design.

bottom. The three-skin dresses, as they came into style in the early nineteenth century, often had fringes attached at the bottom, but the Sioux women liked fringing on all seams. This type of dress had the separate, fully beaded yoke, which Wissler calls "capelike." Other forms of decoration were rows of dentalia or cowrie shells, or elk teeth, the last most prized because a mature elk has only two canine teeth, which last much longer than the life of a man and were therefore symbolic of longevity. Koch says that the Sioux dress had a characteristic notched sleeve. The knee-length leggings were quilled or beaded on the lower half and tied at the sides with thongs. Little information is available regarding undergarments except for the "chastity belt" commented on by some authorities; this seems to have consisted of a thong or strip of leather passed through the crotch and attached to the belt, considered inviolate by Sioux men.

Footwear

Early moccasins were the one-piece soft-sole Woodland type with quilled decoration. Later ones were the hard-soled two-piece Plains moccasin cut straight along the inside edge. These moccasins were fitted and, for ceremonial occasion, had fully beaded uppers and sometimes even beaded soles, the latter for burials and also special gifts. Tongues and cuffs were added and were left plain or decorated to match the moccasin. Winter footwear was of dressed buffalo skin with the hair left on and worn inside, and with thick soles of elk skin. Foxtails were often attached to the heels, and dandies sometimes even had the entire pelt of a skunk dragging along behind the heel. Mails mentions that Sioux moccasins often had the top quilled in long red and green triangles and the edges beaded in white with red, yellow, or blue stepped triangles. Thunderbirds and dragonflies were popular designs. Women's moccasins were like the men's, beaded around the lower edge and with beaded strips down the front or fully beaded. Like other northern Plains tribes, the Sioux used snowshoes in winter, some of wood, some consisting of flat pieces of rawhide that had been frozen after wetting. Catlin tells of snowshoes made of hoops bent round for a frame with a netting of rawhide thongs and fastened with rawhide straps.

Outer Wear

The buffalo robes worn by the Sioux were highly individualistic; that is, the design painted on the robe indicated the age, sex, marital status, and rank or privilege in the tribe. The robe with a "box-and-border" design was made and worn only by women; they also liked the design of two facing E's with four legs. The women painted and the men wore the "sunburst" or "feather" design robes, said to be symbolic of their feather warbonnets. Men painted and wore robes with stylized depictions of people and animals engaged in conflicts. Young men wore a "courting" robe featuring a horizontal strip of quillwork or beading with four large medallions on it; this design was later transferred to the courting blankets of stroud cloth. Red hands on a robe symbolized being wounded in warfare; black hands indicated an enemy killed in battle. Lightweight summer robes had the hair carefully scraped off and the hide shaved to a remarkable

A Teton Sioux woman wears a buffalo robe painted with a box and border design over her side-fold dress, which is fringed and decorated with metal ornaments at the bottom. Based on drawings by Karl Bodmer, an engraver later added an Assiniboine girl to the scene.

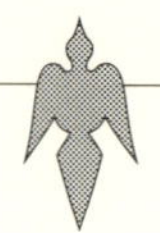

thinness; winter robes were warm with the hair left on and worn inside.

Hair Styles

Like other Plains Indians the Sioux wore the hair in many different styles. The two braids with the center part was most common for both sexes; actually with the men it was three braids, for the scalplock hung from the crown of the head in back, a defiant gesture in warfare. Braids were wrapped with otter fur, trade cloth, or narrow quilled bands and were sometimes lengthened with added strands of human hair or horsehair. Some men shaved the head, leaving the scalplock; this was especially true of those in mourning. A few men wore the pompadour. Miller, in an 1837 painting, depicted a Sioux warrior in a roach headdress, but this was uncommon among the Sioux. Some men gathered the hair into a club at the back and tied into it a whistle made of the wing bone of a raven. Wanata in 1825 wore 19 small sticks in his hair, emblematic of the 19 enemy scalps he had taken. Some men wore the forelock hanging over the nose. Others had the hair cut to the jawline in front and gathered into a clump at the back or left hanging. Catlin tells about One Horn, who wore his long locks coiled across the top of his head, giving the appearance of a turban. Mails tells us that the free-flowing style of hairdress was reserved for ceremonials as a sign of humility and reverence before the Great Spirit. Women wore the hair long, parted in the center, either hanging over the shoulders or gathered into a bag at the back. Some women wore the hair clubbed into large locks and piled over the temple in a cushion shape, somewhat like One Horn's hair style. Often the women waved the hair by dampening their braids and, when dry, combing the hair out. Men wore feathers in the hair, each feather representing some deed of courage; but the symbolism of coup feathers was not as obvious as some believe, for there were varying symbols adopted by different bands or tribes, while a few were a matter of significance only to the individual. However, some meanings were fairly general; for example, a horizontal feather indicated a slain or living enemy touched in battle, and an upright feather meant an enemy killed.

A pipe in his left hand, a Sioux wears a feather and stick headdress and a fringed shirt with a beaded triangular inset at the neck.

Headgear

The most characteristic headdress was the huge warbonnet, worn only by the bravest men of the tribe, for each feather represented an exploit, a deed of great courage; braves who wore it among the Sioux were members of the Akichita Society. These warbonnets were considered "medicine" or great protection in battle; at the same time they represented the highest courage, for the wearer of this colorful headgear was the focus of attention. If a warrior showed cowardice in battle, his headdress was taken away and he was expelled from the Society. The greatest men of all wore buffalo horns with the warbonnet. Some warriors wore an eagle head and feathers atop the head. In winter both sexes wore a turban of animal skins.

Accessories

The pocketless Indians wore many pouches, bags, and other containers attached to the belt. In earlier times these were adorned with porcupine quillwork; later this was replaced with beautifully executed

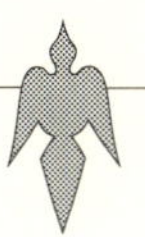

beadwork that still retained the geometric designs of precontact days. Pouches of buffalo fur, tanned leather, or the pelts of small animals held "medicine" articles sacred to the individual wearer, materials for face and body painting, or sewing equipment for the woman. Knife sheaths and awl cases were richly decorated. Quilled or beaded leather armbands often had feathers attached as well as thongs for tying. Navel amulets, quilled or beaded in the turtle design, held the umbilical cord of the wearer. Eagle-feather fans were carried by important men of the tribe. Hair pipe breastplates were worn after 1870, more as a symbolic shield than as a protective device.

Jewelry

Jewelry for both sexes took many forms. Men wore the grizzly bear–claw necklace with otter-fur bands, but without the otter tail hanging down behind. Necklaces of hair pipe beads were especially popular with the Sioux women, becoming even more elaborate and extended after 1890. Some men wore chokers of dentalium shells obtained from Pacific Coast tribes. Shell gorgets were also popular, hanging from the neck on a ribbon or thong. Both sexes wore many strings of beads, some of elk teeth or cowrie shells, and long, heavy earrings. Men later wore silver hair plates, round disks attached to a leather strip, often in graduated sizes; these were suspended from the crown or made into belts. They also adorned women's belts. Long ornaments hung at each side of the face, made of hair pipe beads, dentalium shells, or other beads.

Armor

Some shirts in earlier times were of very heavy buckskin, worn as a type of armor, but for the most part the Sioux warriors wore nothing in battle except a breechclout, belt, moccasins, and headgear. However, some men wore their finest regalia, considering it the right way to die in battle. Heavy shields made of tough buffalo hide were carried into conflict; these were decorated with otter fur, eagle feathers, and eagle down; they were painted with significant symbolic designs or figures. Shield covers were made of deer hide on a wooden frame and decorated like the shields; these were sometimes carried in battle instead of a shield, considered powerful enough medicine to protect the carrier.

A Sioux woman, her blanket robe with its beaded blanket strip draped to show the yoke of her dress with its rows of dentalium shells, wears a large hairpipe and trader's bead necklace. The disks at her side may be German silver.

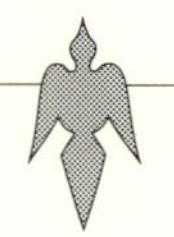

Special Costumes

Mails, who has written extensively on the Sioux societies, gives two types of organization: (1) the dream societies composed of men who had dreamed of the same animal, and (2) the military societies, some of which were police societies. For the most part the members of these societies wore their regular ceremonial garments (war shirts, leggings, warbonnets), adding certain society regalia, such as otter-skin collars and society sashes. The Tall Ones Society wore an owl-feather headdress. The men of the Kit Fox Society wore a headdress of wolf hide, a kit-fox skin around the neck with the head in front and the tail in back, and a coyote jawbone, painted red or blue, fastened to an otter-fur headband. The Crow Owners Society wore the stuffed skin of a crow around the neck. The Omaha Dance Society members wore the otter-skin collar, a "crow" bustle, and a roach headdress. For the Bear Dance, a medicine man wore the entire skin of a bear over his body. The Sun Dance costume consisted of a skirt of painted hide reaching from waist to ankles, wreaths of sage on the head, and rings of sage held in the hands or tied on the wrists. Mourning customs were similar to those of other tribes; the hair was cut off, sometimes a man shaved his head, no ornaments were worn, nor was painting of the face or body engaged in, except for white.

Garment Decoration

Although glass beads had been available from the traders for a long time, Sioux beading did not replace quillwork until the nineteenth century; during the latter part of the century, in the time of the Reservation Period, beadwork proliferated to the extent that garments were heavily encrusted with beads, especially dress yokes, vests, moccasins, and gauntlet gloves. The earlier geometric designs were replaced by realistic images featuring American flags, flowers, and battle scenes. Fringes appeared on almost all garments, some quill-wrapped, some beaded.

Face and Body Embellishment

Face and body painting, like much of Sioux attire, was highly symbolic. Red, made from red ocher, later vermilion, was the sacred color. Black, a mixture of grease and charcoal or soot, was a face paint for victory. White clay was a symbol of mourning. Family totems were shown by animals painted on the body. Warriors and members of societies could be distinguished by special face and body painting. Tattooing was occasionally practiced, usually by women; it was done as a blue dot on the forehead or two lines on the chin "so upon death their ghost will not be pushed off the Ghost Road."

Transitional Dress

The Sioux were quick to adopt the dress of traders and settlers and by 1825 had already appeared in the frock coats and neck scarves worn by the whites, but they kept to their traditional ornamentation. Vests, worn by men extensively after 1885, were at first cut straight, later fitted in the European manner with points in front. The European style of coat or jacket with the front opening was adopted. Blankets, both the Hudson's Bay and the Pendleton types, replaced buffalo robes; lighter blankets of stroud cloth were decorated with the customary blanket strip and medallions. Dresses were made of stroud cloth, but not in the traditional form; rather they were cut in two pieces, a front and a back, with square "wings" for sleeves and a long gusset at each side. Cowrie shells were affixed to the top part in many rows of arcs or straight across the top. Silver chest ornaments and peace medals were cherished. Tin tinklers and thimbles appeared on every garment and accessory possible. Men, after 1870, wore the hair pipe breastplate, and elaborate, long neck pieces of hair pipes were worn by both sexes.

Key Sources

Blish, Helen. *A Pictographic History of the Oglala Sioux.* Lincoln: University of Nebraska Press, 1967.

Conn, Richard. "Western Sioux Beadwork." *American Indian Hobbyist* 6, 9, 10.

Denig, Edwin Thompson. *Five Indian Tribes of the Upper Missouri: Sioux, Arikaras, Assiniboines, Crees, Crows.* Norman: University of Oklahoma Press, 1961.

Dyck, Paul. *Brule: The Sioux People of the Rosebud.* Flagstaff, AZ: Northland Press, 1971.

Hassrick, Royal B. *The Sioux: Life and Customs of a Warrior Society.* Norman: University of Oklahoma Press, 1964.

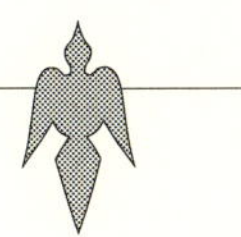

Hyde, George E. *A Sioux Chronicle.* Norman: University of Oklahoma Press, 1956.

Johnson, Michael G. "Western Sioux Man's Costume, 1880–1910." *Powwow Trails* 6(1, 2).

Lessard, F. Dennis. "Pictographic Art in Beadwork from the Cheyenne River Sioux." *American Indian Art Magazine* 16(1): 54–63.

Little, Shan. "A Sioux Woman's Dentalium Shell Dress." *American Indian Crafts and Culture* 2(10).

Lyford, Carrie A. *Quill and Beadwork of the Western Sioux.* Boulder, CO: Johnson Publishing Company, 1979. Reprint of 1940 edition.

Powers, William K. "The Art of Courtship among the Oglala." *American Indian Art Magazine* 5(2): 40–47.

Taylor, Colin. *Warriors of the Plains.* New York: Arco Publishing, 1975.

Tucker, Michael S. "Old Time Sioux Dancers." Panorama City, CA: Tyrone H. Stewart, 1969.

Wissler, Clark. "Decorative Art of the Sioux Indians." *American Museum of Natural History* 13.

Texas

Newcomb, in his excellent book on the Indians of Texas, says that the physical variations among these tribes were minor, but that they were culturally quite diverse. The coastal tribes along the Gulf of Mexico were the Atakapa, the Karankawa, and the Coalhuitecan, all three being marginal to the culture of the Southeastern Woodlands. Inland were the Tonkawa, who exhibited many Plains costume features. Across the Pecos River were the Jumano, whose material culture showed strong influences from the Southwest.

Information on these tribes is meager. Cabeza de Vaca in 1535 and Espejo in 1583 recorded early details about these tribes, as did the later Spanish explorers and the fathers who established missions. Different languages were spoken by these peoples—Tonkawan, Tunican, and Uto-Aztecan for the most part. These tribes were all extinct or had disintegrated by the nineteenth century. It is said that cannibalism was practiced, but the extent of it, and its place in ritual or religion, is not known. Some practiced agriculture, but the soil was poor and production difficult. Some, especially the Tonkawa, depended on the buffalo for subsistence.

Men's Basic Dress

The breechclout to the knees or longer, of tanned deer or buffalo skin, was usually the only article of dress in this warm climate (although some authorities mention total male nakedness); sometimes a small stuffed animal was thrust into the top of the breechclout, and sometimes the men tied herbs near the genitals. Later, the Plains leather shirt of simple cut was adopted. Leggings of tanned skin, when worn, often had many horizontal rows of fringe below the knees. Young children wore nothing as a general rule, although some authorities mention that boys sometimes wore only a tiny pink bow on the penis.

Women's Basic Dress

Women wore a simple wraparound skirt of tanned deerskin tied at the sides with thongs; for cooler weather a skin was trimmed into a circular shape, a hole cut for the head, and it was fastened around the waist with thongs. Some women, particularly those in coastal Texas, wore the double apron of the Southeast, draped and fringed; a fringed cape was added to this when desired. Also in this area some women wore a skirt of Spanish moss and a breechclout of hay or grass. Some women wore a double apron of skin, with the back apron trailing on the ground and covered with sound-producing items, such as shells, nuts, and bones. Leggings, when worn, had fringes at the sides.

Footwear

Often called "barefoot Indians," these tribes seldom wore moccasins; when worn, they had front seams and flaps or cuffs. Occasionally fiber sandals are mentioned.

Outer Wear

In the sixteenth century, cotton blankets were observed, probably acquired in trade from the Puebloans to the west. Other robes were made of deerskins, of strips of rabbit fur, of coyote hide, or probably any fur obtainable. Winter robes, especially for the men, were of buffalo hide, well tanned, with the tail of the buffalo trailing behind; these were painted on the inside with geometric designs in red and black.

Hair Styles
Men parted their long hair in the middle and braided it or tied it with strips of fur; some had a scalplock to which they fastened feathers of geese, cranes, hawks, or other birds. Warriors were said to have cut off the hair on the left side to the jawline, leaving the right side to grow as long as possible; the long hair was then often folded and tied up with a thong. Men frequently plucked the beard and eyebrows. Women wore the hair parted in the center and either let it hang loose or had one long braid down the back.

Headgear
Both sexes went bareheaded, but the Jumanos were recorded as wearing "bonnets" made of many colorful macaw feathers, which they said came from the direction of the sea (a possible Mexican article of trade).

Accessories
Belts were made from ropes of bison hair. Strips of leather or fur were worn below the knees, around the ankles, as armlets, and as wristlets. Pouches and bags of tanned leather were carried or attached to the belt.

Jewelry
Ornaments of shell, bone, feathers, or pretty stones were worn as earrings, necklaces, and hair adornment. They also had jewelry of copper (from the north), coral, and turquoise (from the tribes of the Southwest). Labrets were attached through a hole pierced in the lower lip; these were of stone, bone, wood, or shell. Some men bored the nipple, inserting a piece of cane through the perforations.

Armor
There is some indication that armor, of heavy leather painted blue, was worn into the eighteenth century, but shields are not mentioned.

Garment Decoration
The Texas Indians, with their scanty garments, did little in the way of decoration. Sashes and some belts were finger-woven, using buffalo hair or grass fibers.

Face and Body Embellishment
The Texas tribes painted and tattooed their faces and bodies extensively. Black and red were the preferred colors of paint, while green and yellow were also used. Stripes were painted across the face, the mouth, the nose, the back, and the breast. Some women painted black stripes in concentric circles around each breast. Some painted bodies indicated marital state. Tattooing and scarification were done with charcoal rubbed into punctures made in the skin, with resin applied to set the tattoo. Tattooing may have been used to indicate tribal affiliation as well as age and sex. Because infants were kept tied in cradle boards, there was some head flattening, but not in an extreme manner.

Transitional Dress
Because of the decimation and final extinction of the Texas tribes with European contact, there was little of transitional dress. However, they did acquire blankets from the traders as well as such items as skirts, jackets (including leather military jackets), shirts, hats, belts, and ornaments.

Key Sources
Berlandier, Jean Louis. *The Indians of Texas in 1830.* Washington: Smithsonian Institution, 1969.

Bollaert, William. "Observations on the Indian Tribes in Texas." *Journal of the Ethnological Society* 2.

Campbell, T. N. "Coalhuitecans and Their Neighbors." In *Handbook of North American Indians. Vol. 10: Southwest.* Pp. 343–358. Washington: Smithsonian Institution.

Gatschet, Albert S. "The Karankawa Indians, the Coast People of Texas." Peabody Museum *Archaeological and Ethnological Papers* 1-2.

Newcomb, W. W., Jr. *The Indians of Texas.* Austin: University of Texas Press, 1961.

———. "Karankawa." In *Handbook of North American Indians. Vol. 10: Southwest.* Pp. 359–367. Washington: Smithsonian Institution.

Powers, William K. *Indians of the Southern Plains.* New York: Putnam's, 1971.

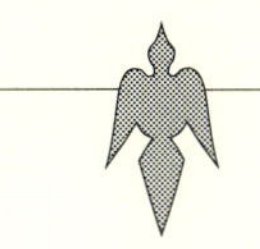

Chapter Four

Costume of the Southwest

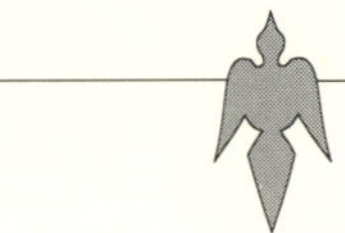

Above: Armed Apaches led by Geronimo wear traditional clothing, including headbands and large, white breechcloths.
Below, right: A Zuni Pueblo woman photographed in 1897 with pottery, baskets, a woven blanket, and sheep skins. She wears a plaid cotton dress below her manta, which is belted and decorated at the hem; she wears a dark blanket robe over a shawl; socks replace moccasins.
Below: Woven by a Jemez Pueblo woman in the late 19th century, this handspun cotton shirt was made in sections. The embroidery is red and indigo wool.

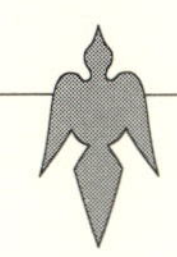

Southwest

The Southwest is an arid, inhospitable land, but one of great diversity where some mountains are as high as 12,000 feet and where deserts may be barely above sea level, creating a great variation in temperature. It is a spectacular land of towering, overhanging cliffs, great mesas flat as tables, and strange rock formations, all in violent hues of red, pink, orange, and yellow, splotched and streaked. But the land thirsts for water. Dry rocks and sand abound with prickly thorns and cactus. There are rivers, a few permanent ones such as the Rio Grande, the Pecos, the Gila and Salt, and the Colorado, and there are washes everywhere, dry gullies that swell with raging torrents after the occasional violent thunderstorms. Eventually, the Indians settled along the rivers where they could farm the rich soil and be assured of a constant supply of water. From this developed a sedentary life, especially among the Puebloans. Early in their history these people sought to control the water, both by religious intervention and with check-dams and other irrigation techniques. The continuing dry climate has been a boon to archaeologists for it has meant that artifacts of past centuries have remained remarkably intact. The forbidding land has also meant that remote areas have remained relatively untouched. Thus ancient evidence of the distinctive traditional cultures of the Southwest has survived to a greater extent than almost anywhere else on the North American continent.

People have inhabited the Southwest since about 12,000 B.C., and there is tantalizing evidence that occupation may have started even earlier. The Anasazi, forerunners of the modern Pueblo peoples, were established in the region by about 400 B.C., and were centered in the Four Corners area. The Hohokam culture of the Gila and Salt rivers experienced a parallel development, but collapsed after 1400. Some authorities believe they were the

Peoples of the Southwest

Acoma, p. 151
Apache, p. 153
Chiricahua, p. 156
Cibecu
Cochiti
Havasupai
Hopi, p. 158
Isleta
Jemez, p. 162
Jicarilla, p. 164
Laguna
Maricopa
Mescalero, p. 167
Nambe
Navajo, p. 169
Northern Tonto
Papago
Picuris
Pima, p. 174
Pueblo, p. 177
San Carlos
Sandia
San Felipe
San Ildefonso
San Juan
Santa Ana
Santa Clara
Santo Domingo
Southern Tonto
Taos, p. 182
Tesuque
Walapai
Western Apache
White Mountain
Yavapai
Zia
Zuni

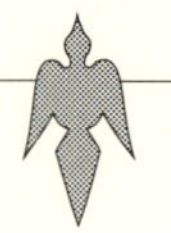

ancestors of the present-day Pima and Papago. The Mogollon culture of west-central New Mexico arose about A.D. 700, but also disappeared long before European contact.

The Spanish under Coronado invaded the region in 1540 and were followed by more Spaniards who looked for gold, ruled the Indians harshly, often cruelly, and attempted to replace their "pagan" religion with Catholicism; the Indians superficially accepted the Spanish religion, meanwhile going "underground" with their own beliefs and ceremonies. In 1821 Mexico achieved her independence from Spain, and the Southwest became a part of the Mexican Republic. Mexico bestowed full rights of citizenship on the Indians, but was so busy consolidating her independence that the Indians were little disturbed by Mexican rule. In 1848 the United States, victorious in the Mexican War, took the Southwest.

The treatment of the Indians was often brutal, displaying a great lack of understanding of Indian beliefs and lifeways. The situation was somewhat relieved in the 1930s when John Collier was appointed Commissioner of Indian Affairs in Washington. Attempts to understand Indian cultures were aided by the increasing work of anthropologists. In the last few decades many of the tribes have become more secure economically, have discovered the monetary benefits of tourism, and have developed a greater interest in their own tribal cultures. Despite exposure to the devastating effects of European diseases and superior weapons, and the forcible relocation of some groups, the Southwest Indians have managed to keep much of their culture intact.

Southwestern Indian costume is distinctive in several ways, and there is a better sense of the continuity of traditional dress from earliest times to the present than one encounters elsewhere. Not only are articles from the past to be seen in museums (sometimes very well preserved by the dry climate), but some of the same types of garments are in use today, especially in ceremonial dress. Dancers may wear kilts and headresses almost identical to those of the Archaic period, and the audience, too, particularly the women, may wear garments quite similar to those of their ancestors. In fact, this is one of the very few places on the North American continent (north of Mexico) where true native costume has survived to the present day.

The Southwest is the only North American culture area that featured the use of garments made from cloth woven on a true loom (a "true loom" being defined as one with heddles that provide a "shed" through which the weaver may easily pass threads). Indians of other cultures wove cloth but not with looms; rather, they used twining, braiding, or other finger-weaving techniques. Furthermore, by A.D. 1200 the Southwesterners were cultivating cotton and weaving with its fibers, the only Indians who did so before the coming of the Europeans.

Ritual plays a very significant part in Southwestern Indian life. This is not the individualistic ceremonialism of the Plains Indians, but a group participation—re-creating through the same dances, music, and costumes the ceremonies of centuries past.

The Southwest Indians may be divided on the basis of costume into four distinct groups: (1) the Apache, both the eastern ones in New Mexico and the western group in Arizona; (2) the Navajo, Athapaskan speakers, as were the Apache, but wearing different garb; (3) the Pueblo Indians, both the eastern groups along the Rio Grande and the western ones along the New Mexico–Arizona border; and (4) the rancherias of western Arizona. The tribes of the lower Colorado River area (Mojave, Chemehuevi, Yuma, and others), although often included with the Southwestern Indians, wore clothes much more characteristic of the California tribes. Inevitably, areas overlap, not only within the Southwest region, but they also encroach upon other major culture areas, including the Plains and the Great Basin.

General Dress

Men's Basic Dress

In early times men wore tanned, deerskin breechclouts; later, after A.D. 1000, the breechcloths were of woven cotton. These may have been of the apron type, hanging in the back and front and tied at the sides, or they may have been fitted, passing through the crotch and under a belt. Some authorities say a kilt was worn over this; certainly kilts were worn, since they appeared in many of the later dances. An early skin poncho gave way to a woven cotton shirt, a rectangular piece of cloth with a hole in the center for the head, and square-cut sleeves; these were tied at the sides and under the arms rather than being sewn. Early leggings were of skin or woven yucca or other fibers; some were made of human hair woven in a coiled netting technique. Heavy leggings of hide were worn in the past and continue to be worn in some places today for protection in the desert.

Women's Basic Dress

Women wore fiber aprons made of strips of yucca or other fibers twined from a cord or of woven rectangles, fringed and decorated; the women were adept at manipulating fibers, not only yucca (both the fine inner fibers like threads and the long, coarse blades) but also *Apocynum* (dogbane or Indian hemp, a relative of milkweed), fur, feathers, mountain-sheep wool, and human hair. To the east, especially in the mountains, wraparound skirts of tanned leather were worn, often with a decorative border at the hemline, and with a poncho added for cooler weather.

Footwear

Few articles of footwear of the American Indians surpassed the beautiful sandals made by the Southwestern craftsmen. They were made of various fibers, but especially yucca and Indian hemp, and were of two general types—the square-toed and the round-toed. The earlier square-toed sandals, usually of yucca fiber, were woven back and forth across the sole and were held on either by a toe and heel cord, or by a cord passed through loops at the edges of the sandal. The later round-toed sandals were often made in two layers—an upper layer of finely woven fiber frequently decorated with colored strands in geometric patterns, and a bottom layer coarsely woven to create traction. These, too, were held on the foot by thongs in various ways. Some woven sandals had flaps, almost becoming moccasins. Except in the eastern areas, which were influenced by Plains culture, leather sandals were rare because a rawhide sole would dry to an uncomfortable shape in wet weather; however, buckskin moccasins with ankle flaps were worn by a few. Some socks were worn, with a yucca-fiber sole and an upper part of

Laguna men and women posed in the mid-1880s. Men wear cloth headbands, silver jewlery, cotton shirts and trousers with woven belts, as well as leather leggings gartered at the knee. Two women wear dark wool mantas over cotton blouses and woven belts and blankets.

A Zia Pueblo Snake Society member, photographed in 1888 or 1889, wears a kilt with a snake design, a bear claw necklace, and a long sash, probably woven on a belt loom. He holds two feathers and a gourd rattle.

cotton and mountain-sheep wool, finger-woven in a loop technique.

Outer Wear

Mantles or robes were of four different types. (1) A wraparound robe of tanned deerskin was worn in the northern regions, with thongs to fasten it at the chest. (2) Rabbit-fur robes were made of strips cut in a spiral from the rabbit pelt and woven on yucca cords in a simple cross weave; these were also popular as burial wrappings. (3) Feather mantles were worn in the south, made from feathers of domesticated turkeys; the feathers were stripped carefully from the vanes and the shafts wound around cords, then woven in a simple cross weave. (4) Some twill-weave cotton blankets were made, with designs woven in of black, red, or rust, and other naturally dyed fibers.

Hair Styles

Generally the men wore the hair long; in early days it was divided into three clumps, one at each side and one at the back, each tied with a cord. A few wore a scalplock in the style of the Indians to the east. Women often cut the hair short; it seems to have been used for cordage, for many items were woven of human hair. Mails calls it a "renewable crop."

Headgear

The Indians usually went bareheaded, but a few types of headgear were worn. Some wore a close-fitting basketry cap, particularly in the northern areas, as an influence from the early Anasazi or Basketmaker peoples. Some headbands were created from turkey feathers. In the south magnificent headdresses of macaw feathers imported from Mexico were cherished.

Accessories

Beautiful sashes were made, like those to be seen today in Pueblo ceremonies; braided or twined in a finger-weaving technique, these were about three inches wide and six to nine feet long. They were created in designs with variously colored dyed fibers and usually had a fringe strung with shells. Belts and burden straps (tumplines) were woven of yucca fiber and painted with mineral paints. Flexible bags, which served as containers, were made of twined yucca fiber and also featured colored decorations.

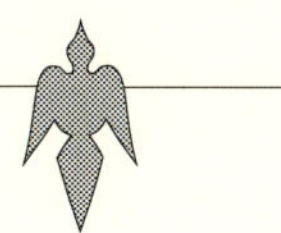

Jewelry
Stone and shell beads were in great abundance, including beads of olivella and abalone shells. After A.D. 500 there was an increasing use of turquoise; some necklaces were made of thousands of beautifully finished turquoise beads. Other bead materials were catlinite (pipestone) from faraway Minnesota and coral from the Gulf of Mexico. Pendants were created of polished pieces of abalone shell, as well as mosaics made from tiny bits of turquoise glued onto the abalone shells with mesquite gum or asphaltum. Strings of beads were also worn as earrings. Some nose plugs and ear plugs were displayed as ornament in early times.

Armor
Early Pueblo warriors used basketry for armor and wore a close-fitting cap of tanned skin, ventilated with numerous holes and decorated with feathers. Early Navajo warriors used thick coats of toughened hide as a form of armor.

Garment Decoration
Articles such as belts, straps, and sandals were decorated with dyed fiber strands in geometric designs. Cotton fibers were dyed in various hues, then woven into simple patterns. Fringes were used on the edges of garments, often with shells strung on the cords.

Face and Body Embellishment
No body painting or tattooing seems to have been indicated among early Southwest tribes. There was some unintentional skull deformation due to the practice of strapping infants to flat wooden cradle boards.

Transitional Dress
With the coming of the Europeans, Southwestern tribal costume developed in different directions; these postcontact changes are discussed below in the sections on individual groups.

Acoma

The name *Acoma* means "people of the white rock." Keresan speakers, they lived, and still live, on a spectacular mesa that rises abruptly out of the surrounding plain, and has always been difficult to access. Called "The Sky City," it has been inhabited for at least 1,000 years; they vie with the Hopi in claiming to live in the oldest inhabited village in the United States. It remains a closed system even today; visitors are tolerated, but prohibited from taking pictures, sketching, or making notes unless specifically permitted. They are closely allied to the Laguna, sharing many costume similarities.

Men's Basic Dress
Early breechclouts were of tanned deerskin, in the fitted style with flaps hanging before and behind. Later breechcloths were of woven white cotton in a basket weave, the ends decorated with embroidered bands; weaving was done by the Acoma men, while the women created the embroidery. An everyday breechcloth of cotton was passed through the crotch and tucked into a thong tied about the hips. After the Spaniards came, breechcloths were of dark blue or black wool woven in a diagonal twill pattern. Instead of, or occasionally in addition to the breechcloths, kilts were worn, a wraparound style from waist to knee, also in woven cotton or wool, with a band of decoration at the lower edge. Early poncho-type shirts of tanned leather gave way to shirts of woven cotton in a square-cut style, with or without sleeves, two pieces for front and back, a folded piece for each sleeve; these shirts were not sewn but tied under the arms and at the sides. Leggings were essentially a footless stocking of snug fit, calf-length, and held in place by a strap under the instep. These were made in a loop twining technique; later, beginning in the nineteenth century, they were crocheted. Also in that century men adopted the Mexican-style white cotton trousers.

Women's Basic Dress
The *manta* or mantle was both a shawl and a dress. When worn as a dress it was wrapped around the body with the open edge on the right, fastened on the right shoulder, and passed under the left arm. It was sewn part way down the side and held in place with a red, or red and green, woven belt. Usually the manta was of black wool, the center area being done in a diagonal-twill weave; at the top and bottom a wide indigo blue band was woven in a diamond-twill weave. Sometimes bands were sewn to the manta, embroidered in red, blue, and (frequently by the Acoma) yellow and green. As commercial cloth became available in the

nineteenth century, a white cotton underdress was worn, with a lace edging that showed below the upper dress. In the last century white lace aprons, at times in back as well as in front, were added to the costume. Some early mantas were of white cotton woven in a plain basket weave; tassels were used as decoration. Today the traditional black wool mantas are occasionally worn, but most dresses in the traditional manta style are made of commercial fabrics; flowered blouses and printed cotton aprons are worn with them.

Footwear
Men wore calf-high boots of tanned leather (buckskin) with painted rawhide soles. Women wore ankle-high boots, also with painted rawhide soles, and wrapped their legs with strips of leather, whitened with clay, in a "puttee" manner.

Outer Wear
Robes or mantles were made of deerskin or buffalo hide. The mantas mentioned above were worn as shawls over the head or on the shoulders. Later shawls were of commercial fabric such as stroud cloth or printed cotton. Rabbit-skin robes were made of strips cut spirally from the rabbit pelt, wrapped around a yucca core, and woven in a simple cross weave.

Hair Styles
Both sexes let the hair grow long and usually bound it up in a *chongo,* the characteristic Southwestern hair style, in which the hair is coiled at the back in a figure eight and bound at the crossing with ties. Often bangs were worn in front. Some men bound and wrapped a clump of hair that then hung down in back. In the last hundred years, most men have cut the hair at the jawline or the shoulders and held it in place with a cloth headband.

Headgear
Except for ceremonial attire, the Acoma went bareheaded, at least in earlier times. With the advent of commercial cloth, men sometimes wrapped a large strip in a turban style, tying it at the front.

Accessories
Belts, tightly woven of cotton or wool and dyed in various designs in red, black, or green, were worn by both sexes. Embroidered sashes ended in tassels rather than a fringe. Headbands were of woven strips. By 1900 no weaving was done by the Acomas. Plaited yucca rings were worn by the women to support the jars carried on the head; tumplines of plaited fiber or woven cotton helped in carrying heavy loads. Canes of office were carried by dignitaries; these were silver-headed canes given by the Spaniards and later President Lincoln to the Pueblo chiefs, and were handed down to each succeeding chief.

Jewelry
Early beads were made of shell (especially abalone and olivella) and pieces of turquoise. An early Spanish explorer said the Acoma Indians wore earrings and nose pendants of turquoise. Coral beads were popular

An Acoma woman wears a traditional dark manta, wrapped boots, and silver and turquoise jewelry.

for necklaces, imported from Italy by the Spaniards. Necklaces of silver beads often featured silver crosses interspersed with the beads. Bracelets and rings were worn, but were not as large or elaborate as those of other groups. The Acoma did not do silversmithing or fine jewelry work, rather obtaining such items in trade.

Special Costumes

The major Acoma ceremonial was (and is) the Feast Day of St. Esteban, their patron saint, held on 2 September and observed with a Corn Dance in the plaza. The men dancers wore white cotton kilts with embroidered fringed sashes, the leather calf-high moccasins with rawhide painted soles, and garters at the knees with fringed loops hanging. Branches were inserted into armbands. Symbolic designs were painted on the chest and the cheeks. Women danced barefoot, wearing the traditional black manta; on their heads they wore a thin wooden *tablita.*

Garment Decoration

Weaving, first of cotton, later of wool, was carried out in plain, diamond-twill, or diagonal-twill patterns. Kilts, breechcloths, shirts, sashes, and mantas woven of cotton were decorated with bands of embroidery done with wool yarn, and featured geometric designs in red, blue, green, and yellow. Later mantas of wool also had embroidered bands attached. Fringes and tassels were added to belts and sashes. Leather was painted, as in the soles and uppers of moccasins and the whitened leg bindings.

Face and Body Embellishment

The Acoma did not paint the face or body except for ceremonial occasions, and they also painted the faces of the dead for burial.

Key Sources

Curtis, Edward S. *The North American Indian.* Vol. 16. New York: Johnson Reprint Company, 1970.

Douglas, Frederic H. "Acoma Pueblo Weaving and Embroidery." Denver Art Museum *Indian Leaflet Series* 89.

Garcia-Mason, Velma. "Acoma Pueblo." In *Handbook of North American Indians. Vol. 9: Southwest.* Pp. 450–466. Washington: Smithsonian Institution.

James, H. L. *Acoma, the People of the White Rock.* Glorieta, NM: Rio Grande Press, 1970.

Mails, Thomas E. "Acoma History and Life." In *The Pueblo Children of the Earth Mother* 1: 256–276. Garden City, NY: Doubleday, 1983.

Mera, Harry Percival. *Pueblo Indian Embroidery.* Santa Fe, NM: William Gannon, 1975.

Minge, Ward A. *Acoma: Pueblo in the Sky.* Albuquerque, NM: University of New Mexico Press, 1976.

White, Leslie A. "The Acoma Indians: People of the Sky City." Smithsonian Institution *Annual Report, 1929–1930.*

Apache

Athapaskan speakers, the Navajo and Apache migrated from the north (probably northwestern Canada), settling in the Southwest perhaps as late as A.D. 1500. Fierce warriors and raiders, they were called "apaches de nabahu" or "enemies of the cultivated fields" by the Zuni and other Puebloans. About 1640 the two groups acquired horses, and about 1700 they separated and developed different cultures. The Apache were mountain folk, exhibiting great mobility in their hunting of game (including buffalo) and their gathering of wild foods in the canyons and on the mesas of New Mexico and Arizona. The wandering bands suffered constant harassment and encroachment from the Spanish *conquistadores,* from the Mexicans, and from the equally nomadic Comanche. Under American rule, conflicts broke out into continuing warfare and "Apache" became the most dreaded name in the West, particularly when referring to Geronimo's band.

The Eastern Apache were the Chiricahua, the Jicarilla, the Mescaleros, the Lipan-Apache, and the Kiowa-Apache; they were all influenced by the Plains tribes in their dress, but especially the last two tribes, who are usually considered Plains Indians. The Western Apache were the White Mountain, San Carlos, Cibecue, and the Northern and Southern Tonto bands. Edward S. Curtis took some photographs of the Apache, as did many other photographers of the nineteenth and twentieth centuries.

Men's Basic Dress

The Apache men exhibited three overlapping periods of dress. The first, the Tanned Skin Period, was

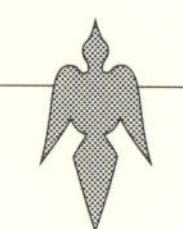

heavily influenced by the Plains tribes to the north and east; they wore the tanned-leather shirt of deer or buffalo hide (poncho in the early days) with beaded strips over the shoulder and down the arms, plentiful fringing, and buckskin leggings. Yellow-ocher staining of the skin, as found on the southern Plains, was characteristic. As happened increasingly elsewhere, a great scarcity of game developed just about the time commercial cloth became available; this was welcomed by the Apache because with so much movement and warfare, they had little time to tan what skins they obtained nor did they have a knowledge of weaving. The Mexican Period began early in the nineteenth century when the men began to wear Mexican garments—the breechcloth of white cotton cloth, very large and hanging to the knees in front and back, the loose, white cotton pants and the white cotton shirt that hung out over the top of the pants, as did the cotton breechcloth under it. The Transition Period began in the late-nineteenth century with the adoption of more Anglo attire, often creating a mixture in their own garb, wearing dark vests or colored-print cotton shirts with white cotton pants, and men's suit coats.

Women's Basic Dress

Women very early wore the wraparound skirt with the simple poncho of tanned leather added when desired. This was followed by the Plains-type three-skin dress with the two-skin skirt and the top (one skin) folded over into a yoke and attached to the skirt. Long fringes finished off the sleeves and the hems and the dresses were often painted a solid color. During the nineteenth century the women began to wear an Indian version of the Victorian dress; usually called the "camp dress," this consisted of a full skirt of cotton cloth, print or plain, and a loose, almost hip-length overblouse of the same material with short, full sleeves to above or below the elbows gathered into a cuff. The round-necked square-yoked blouse had bands of braid, rickrack, or bias tape in a contrasting color; the bands were repeated at various levels on the skirt. Under this they were said to wear the full-length petticoats and bloomers of the white women.

Footwear

Early moccasins were of the simple two-piece soft-sole Plains type with a front seam; these were ankle-high and sometimes tied at the front. Later the rawhide sole was added. By the mid-nineteenth century the Apache were wearing the moccasins and leggings combined to form a boot. These were knee-high and had rawhide soles, buckskin uppers, and pointed, curved-up toes; the soft tops were gartered at the knee and often folded down to form convenient pockets. Decoration consisted of short fringes or silver conchas down the sides, painted leather, or small strips of beading. During the Mexican Period, instead of leggings men wore heavy wool socks (which seem to have been of U.S. government issue).

Outer Wear

Shawls of skin were worn by both sexes and were tied at one shoulder or in front; some were in the form of ponchos of a rectangular shape sporting fringes and sometimes rows of thongs; later shawls were of heavy cloth, such as strouding, fringed. Blankets obtained in trade were popular from the early 1800s into the present century; often the blankets featured the blanket strip with medallions, as found on Plains robes. The Mexican *serape* was also worn by the men.

Hair Styles

During the early period, both sexes wore the hair loose and flowing or in two braids, often with bangs. Apache maidens wore (some still wear) a distinctive hair style in which the hair was pulled back and tied at the nape of the neck with a *nah-leen,* a flat dumbbell-shaped ornament covered with red cloth and often studded with brass tacks or brass buttons; long cloth streamers hung down the back. During the Mexican Period, the men cut the hair to shoulder length and held it in place with a cloth headband. Usually men plucked the facial hair.

Headgear

A large kerchief headband for the men and, later, a beaded headband for the women were the usual items of Apache headgear. Among the eastern bands a Plains warbonnet was sometimes worn by warriors. Some men began to wear the Mexican *sombrero* during the nineteenth century; the large Western hat is often worn today.

Accessories

Women wore wide leather belts, sometimes as wide as ten inches, embellished with brass tacks and/or

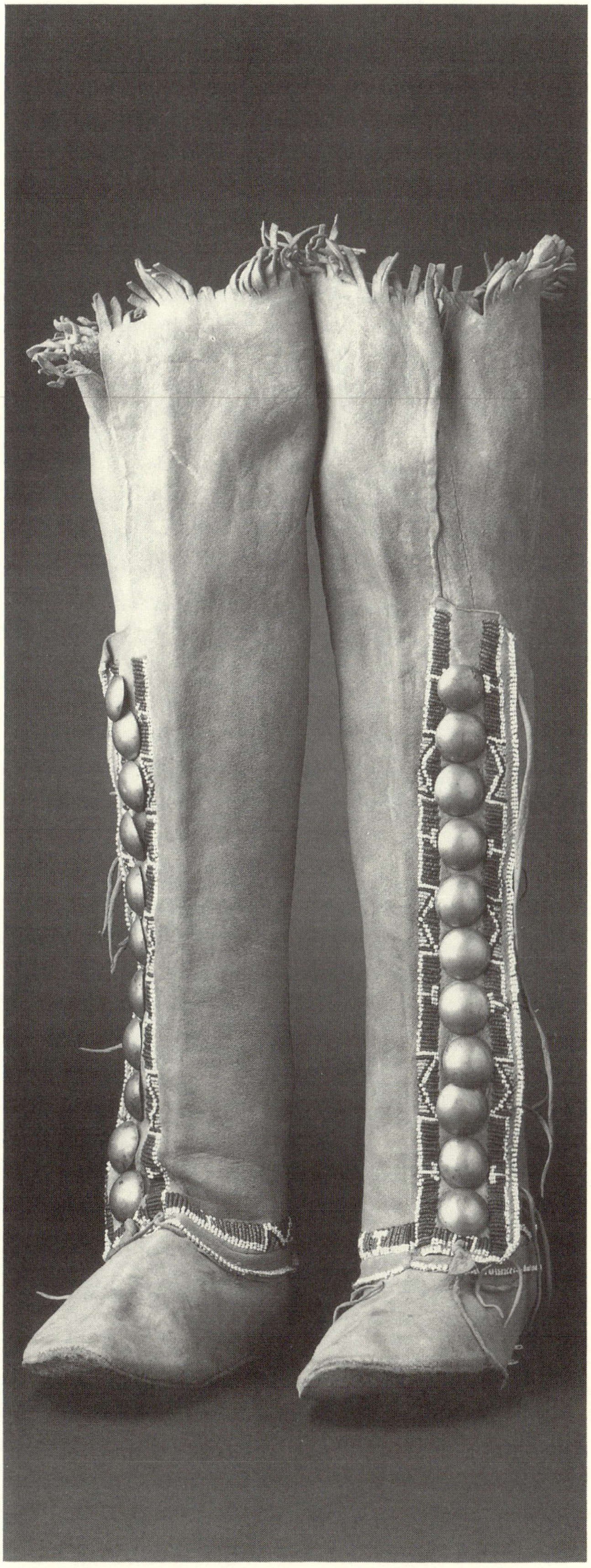

The thigh-high boots of an Apache woman have silver concha decorations and beadwork.

metal conchas. Men's shirts were belted with leather belts or one or two cartridge belts—loaded. Colorful cloth kerchiefs were tied about the neck. Pouches were carried by the women; these were of deerskin in a rectangular or a U-shape and had beaded fringes at the bottom.

Jewelry

Chokers of hair pipe beads with suspended metal disks were the most common type of ornament, but many strands of metal or shell bead necklaces were also worn, as were a few silver rings.

Armor

Shields were made of painted cowhide, decorated with a few feathers, and held over the arm by means of one or two straps. Many fighters, especially leaders, wore war caps—leather helmets adorned with crow or turkey feathers, conchas, horns, or any other items that struck the wearer as having a protective quality.

Special Costumes

The major ritual of the Apache was the Girl's Puberty Rite, a ceremony at which the masked Mountain Spirits or Gan Dancers performed. There were some differences in the costumes of the girls as well as the dancers, so these will be discussed under separate Apache groups. The Gan Dancers also performed at curing rites.

Garment Decoration

Beadwork was done in the geometrical style of the Plains; there was some use of beaded fringes, particularly on pouches. Some leather garments were painted a solid color, yellow being most popular. Fringes were much used, especially in later periods when they became exceedingly long on the girls' ceremonial costumes. Conchas decorated boots, belts, and some dresses; other belts had designs formed with brass tacks. The camp dresses used (and do use) much braid, rickrack, and lace.

Face and Body Embellishment

Women at times painted a red spot on each cheek, especially when taking part in rituals. Black was also used on the face by both sexes. Men preparing for war greased the body and painted the face in various symbolic designs determined by the individual.

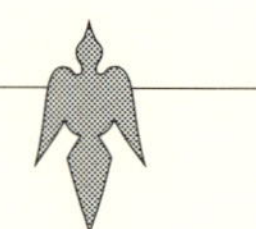

Masks
Deer or antelope head masks were worn by hunters in order to get closer to their quarry. Black cloth masks were, and are, worn by the Gan Dancers during the Girls' Puberty Rite.

Key Sources

Baldwin, Gordon. *The Warrior Apaches.* Globe, AZ: Dale Stewart King, 1965.

Basso, Keith H. and Morris E. Opler, eds. "Apachean Culture, History and Ethnology." University of Arizona *Anthropology Papers* 21.

Cramony, John C. *Life among the Apaches (1850–1868).* Glorieta, NM: Rio Grande Press, 1970.

Dutton, Bertha P. *Navahos and Apaches: Indians of the American Southwest.* Englewood Cliffs, NJ: Prentice-Hall, 1975.

McCoy, Ronald. "Gan: Mountain Spirit Masks of the Apaches." *American Indian Art Magazine* 10(3): 52–58.

Mails, Thomas E. "The Costume of the Apache Indians." *Encyclopedia Britannica Library Research Service* 6.

———. *The People Called Apache.* New York: Promontory, 1974.

Opler, Morris E. *An Apache Life-Way.* Chicago: University of Chicago Press, 1941.

———. "The Apachean Culture Pattern and Its Origins." In *Handbook of North American Indians. Vol. 10: Southwest.* Pp. 368–392.

Whitaker, Kathleen. "Na Ih Es, an Apache Puberty Ceremony." *Masterkey* 45(l).

Worcester, Donald E. *The Apaches: Eagles of the Southwest.* Norman: University of Oklahoma Press, 1979.

Chiricahua Apache
The Chiricahua Apache live around the southern New Mexico/Arizona border and into Mexico. They were composed of three bands: (1) the eastern or "red paint people," so-called because warriors painted a red band across the face; (2) the central or "Wild Apaches"; (3) and the southern or "Enemy Apaches." These bands all fought unceasingly against the Spanish and carried on a bitter war of revenge with U.S. troops from 1848 to 1886 when Geronimo, the last holdout, surrendered. Highly mobile hunters, raiders, and gatherers, the Chiricahua Apache did no farming; indeed, the different bands were seldom in one place long enough to have planted or harvested crops. Deer and pronghorn antelope were extremely important game animals, not only for food but also for their hides, which were made into rawhide and tanned skins for clothes. *Chiricahua* is an Apache term for "great mountain." The Chiricahua artist Allan Houser has done many fine paintings of his people in traditional dress. There are some useful photographs from the nineteenth century, especially of Geronimo and his men.

Men's Basic Dress
Early garments were of tanned skin—a breechclout, which was sometimes a kilt shape rather than a fitted clout, a poncho, and simple leggings. Since they lived near the Mexican border, frequently escaping across it, it is little wonder that the Chiricahua adopted and clung to the Mexican style of clothing, especially the men. The situation is further complicated by the fact that little is known about very early clothing of the Chiricahua, and it is not known when they first began wearing Mexican-style clothes. What lingers in the mind are the photographs of the fighters taken during the height of the bloody conflicts of the nineteenth century. These men usually wore a white cotton shirt girdled with a leather belt or one or two cartridge belts. Occasionally they wore a buckskin shirt with a laced neck closing. Over the shirt a black vest or coat was often worn, indicative of the changeover to Anglo clothing. To distinguish themselves from others, says Dutton, the Warm Springs men wore a buckskin band over the right shoulder, colored yellow with the sacred pollen of the cattail. Leggings were really a part of the moccasins, forming boots. An unusually large, white cotton breechcloth hung in front and behind; a particular Chiricahua feature was that the breechcloth was pulled around so it almost covered the entire back. Pants were of the loose, Mexican type made of white cotton; by the end of the century, dark trousers were generally substituted.

Women's Basic Dress
A short skirt of tanned skin was worn in the early period; with this was worn an upper garment of one skin with the deer legs left as appendages at the corners and a hole in the center for the head. By the

end of the nineteenth century Apache women were wearing the long-sleeved blouses and long, full skirts with a ruffle at the bottom, adopted from the Anglo women's garments; this seems to have been transitional into the characteristic Apache camp dress—the long, full-sleeved, hip-length blouse with the square yoke and the full skirt with the decorative bands and/or a flounce at the bottom.

Footwear
From the simple two-piece soft-soled moccasin with the separate skin leggings of the early days evolved the Apache legging/moccasin with the turned-up toes; some had the elevated disks at the toes, like the moccasins of the Western Apache, and many had a beaded strip around the bottom edge. The soft legging top, thigh-length, often painted, was gartered at the knee, was frequently fastened with thongs about the ankle, and could be folded down to form a pocket for carrying necessary items, such as paints or a knife. The rawhide soles were sometimes tanned with the hair left on for extra padding and warmth. The little Apache boy just learning to walk experienced the "putting on moccasins" ritual, in which he donned new moccasins and was led on a pollen-strewn path to the east, accompanied by prayers for a long and successful life.

Outer Wear
The tanned skin poncho of early days developed into a rectangular capelike affair with fringes, beadwork, and tin tinklers, sometimes worn for warmth but particularly seen at ceremonial occasions. Winter robes were made from furs, including badger, beaver, and otter. Blankets were quickly adopted by the Chiricahua, especially in plaid or striped patterns. Women wore a woven fringed shawl, also often plaid, tied in front or on one shoulder. Large, loose deerskin coats were worn by some men in the winter.

Hair Styles
Both sexes wore the hair long and flowing or in two braids. By the late nineteenth century the men were cutting the hair to shoulder-length or shorter. Women wore the *nah-leen,* a leather ornament in an hourglass or figure-eight shape, usually studded with brass tacks that held the coiled hair in place with ties. Some women parted the hair and wound each side over a willow hoop; these were then arranged over the ears in the Hopi manner.

Headgear
Men wore a cloth headband tied in the front. A famous Chiricahua headdress was made of fur and curved antelope horns with long locks of human hair hanging at the back; it was used both as a war cap and as an item of ceremonial dress. In the nineteenth century the men adopted Anglo or Mexican hats.

Accessories
A cloth neckerchief, often fastened with a concha, was a popular item with the men. Buckskin awl cases made by the women were embellished with tin tinklers, beadwork, and fringes. Both sexes wore amulets of unpainted wood, of particular personal spiritual significance.

Jewelry
Necklaces were made of long strings of shells, colored Mexican-bean beads, fetishes, or commercial beads, sometimes finished off with a star pendant, or they were of the choker type made of hair pipe beads. Abalone shells from the Pacific coast made attractive earrings. Some men sported a bear-claw necklace, but not necessarily of grizzly-bear claws.

Armor
Armor, as such, was not worn by the Chiricahua warriors, but they carried a shield of painted rawhide or cowhide with a few feathers attached. Some wore painted war shirts of leather.

Special Costumes
With her first menstruation the Chiricahua girl was ready for the Puberty Ceremony, a four-day ritual. Her dress was in the traditional style, made of four buckskins or doeskins, two for the top, two for the skirt. The top piece had a rounded yoke, edged with a beaded strip, from which hung long cord fringes; long fringes also hung from the sleeve ends. At the back hem of the top piece was suspended the tail of a black-tailed doe. The skirt had the deer legs hanging at the sides (as did the top) and rows of shorter fringes at the hem and above. The dress was colored yellow, the hue of sacred pollen, and was decorated with beaded or painted designs—symbols of the

morning star, the sun, the moon, and an arc for a rainbow. The girl's boots were knee-high and had the painted, often beaded, turned-up disks at the toes. The Gan dancers, their torsos bare, wore skirts of tanned leather painted yellow, held in place by a belt and fringed in various ways. They also wore the usual Apache boot with the turned-up toe. On their heads were headdresses made of thin wooden slats or agave stalks, symbolic of the four sacred directions. The face was covered with a simple buckskin mask painted black with holes for the eyes and mouth. Gan dancers today continue to wear this traditional costume.

Masks

Except for the black cloth masks of the Gan Dancers, the Chiricahua Apache did not use masks in their ceremonials.

Transitional Dress

The Chiricahua men changed in the late nineteenth century from their Mexican-style garments to North American–style dress: trousers, cotton shirts, vests, and shoes. Some adopted "Western" garb, including cowboy hats, Levi's, plaid shirts, and cowboy boots. Women wore the full, ruffled cotton skirts and fitted blouses of the late nineteenth century, following white fashions with purchased clothing to the present; a few still wear the Apache camp dress. Chiricahua dress is still seen in such ceremonials as the puberty rites; both spectators and participants are apt to wear traditional clothing.

Key Sources

Hoijer, Harry. *Chiricahua and Mescalero Apache Texts, with Ethnological Notes by Morris E. Opler.* Chicago: University of Chicago Press, 1938.

Mails, Thomas E. "The Chiricahua Apache." In *The People Called Apache.* Pp. 207–283. New York: Promontory, 1974.

Opler, Morris E. "Chiricahua Apache." In *Handbook of North American Indians. Vol. 10: Southwest.* Pp. 401–418. Washington: Smithsonian Institution.

Hopi

The Hopi live in six pueblos on high mesas in northeastern Arizona on a reservation that is completely surrounded by the Navajo reservation. They are the only Shoshonean-speaking people among the Pueblo Indians. The word *Hopi* comes from *Hopitu,* meaning "the peaceful ones," and characteristically they have never had a cult of war. Despite conflicts with the Spanish, the Navajo, and the white Americans, they have been able to retain their traditional culture to a remarkable degree. They practice a specialized kind of agriculture in the valleys below the mesas, but moisture is minimal and the farming is precarious. Edward S. Curtis, A. C. Vroman, Ben Wittick, and other photographers of the Southwest depicted them extensively; today they are represented in many paintings by contemporary Southwest Indian artists, of whom Fred Kabotie is perhaps the best known.

Men's Basic Dress

The breechclout of tanned leather in the early days was superseded by a cotton breechcloth, which was black with end borders of blue and came to mid-thigh. By 1900 wool replaced cotton, but the same colors were used; it was worn outside the white cotton pants adopted from the Mexicans, which were knee-length and gathered at the waist. Or dark woolen pants were worn, often with silver buttons up the sides. Early shirts were of antelope hide with long tails in back. The later shirt was of a simple rectangular cut, one piece for the main part with a center hole for the head and a piece for each sleeve; this was of blue wool woven in a diagonal-twill weave or of white cotton in the same style, and was not embroidered as was the custom in the other pueblos. Footless stockings or leggings, usually worn for ceremonies but sometimes for everyday, were knit of black, white or blue yarn in a plain stockinette stitch or with cables. Some leggings were of tanned leather simply wrapped around the legs and held in place by garters. Occasionally men wore kilts woven of black or indigo-blue wool.

Women's Basic Dress

The *manta* or blanket dress was the basic garment of the Hopi women. A rectangular garment, woven of dark blue in a diagonal-twill weave with woven borders of blue or black in a diamond or zigzag weave, it was folded and sewn up the right side with an opening at the top for the right arm; knee-length, it was fastened on the right shoulder leaving the left shoulder and arm bare. At times there was an overfold

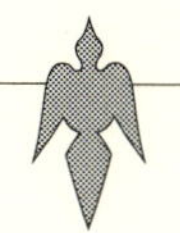

at the top. The manta was girded with a woven belt. Some mantas were white with borders of red and blue. By 1900, encouraged by the missionaries, a printed cotton blouse was added, or a dress that covered the arms and showed below the hem of the manta; sometimes a white petticoat was worn so the lace showed at the hem.

Footwear

Early sandals were plaited or woven of yucca fiber like those of the Basketmaker ancestors of the Hopi. Later moccasins were of deerskin fashioned in one of two styles: (1) A long toe piece was attached to the black rawhide sole around the front end, with the flap folded over for a tongue. A long piece of leather was then attached around the rest of the sole and carefully wrapped around the leg to the knee and tied with thongs. For everyday wear for both sexes, the deerskin was left in its natural color, but the moccasins and long wrappings for the women to wear on ceremonial occasions were whitened with kaolin. (2) Deerskin, dyed a brick-red color with mountain mahogany, was sewn to the black-painted rawhide sole all around, wrapped around the ankle, and fastened on the outside of the foot with thongs or silver Navajo buttons. The hard sole of both styles was crimped so it turned up, giving added protection against cactus, sharp rocks, and prickly shrubs.

Outer Wear

When the Spaniards came to the Southwest, they reported that the Hopi were wearing deer or buffalo hide robes. These were replaced by woven blankets or shawls of various types, worn over the shoulders and tied in front with thongs, or pinned, or worn over the head. A smaller version of the dark manta was used as a shawl, tied in front, usually a part of women's wear. Maidens commonly wore the white shawl of cotton; done in a twill weave, it featured bands of red and indigo-blue embroidery or weaving. A woven blanket of dark wool with white stripes was called a "Moki-stripe." Around the turn of the century plaid shawls were popular—black-and-white plaid for the men, brown-and-white for boys. Rabbit-skin robes have been made by the Hopi for centuries, the weaving done by Hopi women; the rabbit pelt was cut spirally in one long strip, which was twisted around a cord, wrapped around a simple loom in one continuous warp, and twined with other strips. These were made in various sizes mostly for women and children. Earlier in this century many women cherished Czechoslovakian wool-challis shawls, obtained from traders, square in shape and with a deep fringe all around. Since World War II, they have been unobtainable, and women now enjoy shawls in checks and plaids made by the Pendleton Mills.

Hair Styles

Men wore the hair in the *chongo* style, in which the hair is gathered to the back, coiled in a figure-eight manner, and tied with thongs or a "hair tie"; the hair at the sides was cut to the jawline. With white influence in the last century, the Hopi cut the hair shoulder-length and held it in place with a cloth headband. Bangs were cut in the front as desired. Infants had the hair cut only once a year—just before the Bean Dance festival in February—except for necessary cutting of the bangs.

To indicate their arrival at a marriageable age, young girls wore the characteristic Hopi hair style called the "squash blossom" or "butterfly." To achieve this, the hair was parted in the center and each side was wound around a wooden, U-shaped "hair bow" in a figure-eight, tied with a thong, and then spread out in a whorl shape or disk about eight inches in diameter. When the girl was married, the bride's mother would, after the completion of the marriage ceremony, form the bride's hair into two clumps that were wrapped with a loop at the end, the badge of the married woman. Bangs were not so common among Hopi women as they were at other pueblos.

Headgear

The Hopi, both men and women, went bareheaded most of the time. Some men wore the Mexican hats of the nineteenth century. A cloth headband (often red), a strip of rabbit fur, or a woven headband was used by the men to keep their hair in place. Headdresses were worn only for ceremonials. Sun visors for weavers were made of leather stretched over a wooden frame.

Accessories

Belts, garters, or headbands were woven of red, green, and black wool on a belt loom in a floating-warp technique, using cotton string as warp. These were worn primarily by women and were wrapped more than once about the waist with a long fringe (18 inches long) hanging at the side. They were made by women on a belt loom. Pouches, made of tanned hide in the early days, were later woven of wool yarn.

Jewelry

Many substances were used for necklaces—shells, turquoise, bird bones, mica, even coal in the form of lignite, polished and shaped for use. Since 1898, when the Hopi began to learn silversmithing from the Navajo and Zuni, silver and turquoise jewelry has been popular; earlier they had obtained it in trade. After 1935 they worked in a "cut-out overlay," making cutout designs in the silver and soldering it to a base which had been oxydized for contrast. Like the Zuni, they use turquoise sparingly, in small pieces, in jewelry that is finding a profitable market today.

Armor

The Hopi had conflicts with the Apache, Navajo, and others, and at times of active fighting, the Warrior Society functioned. The men went into battle wearing moccasins, a white kilt, and sash and their torsos wrapped in several layers of deerskin, adding caps made from mountain lion or wildcat skins, with eagle feathers for decoration. Black and white paint was applied to the arms, legs, and head. Whiteford says that shields were decorated with representations of spirits, which provided protection.

Special Costumes

There are many ceremonies and festivities in the Hopi villages today, ceremonies that are solidly based in tradition. Most of them involve the *kachinas,* human symbolic representations of the many gods in

Photographs taken in 1901 show two Hopi hair styles: that of a married woman, left, and an unmarried woman. Both women wear mantas fastened at the right shoulder.

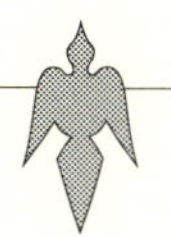

the Hopi pantheon; there are about 30 major gods and over 200 lesser ones. Because of the infinite variety, kachina dolls are created to teach the children how the different kachinas are dressed. The major ceremonies of the year are: the Bean Dance in February to bless the bean sprouts in the fields, the Kachina dances from April through late July, the Snake Dance, and the Flute Dance, the last two in August. "Mudheads," or *koshares* are clowns that add fun, often satire, to the festivities; the Hopi clowns usually wear black kilts and have their torsos painted brown. Masks and headdresses are the most important items of kachina dress. The kilt is the basic ceremonial garment of the men; it is made of different materials and types and is decorated in many ways. Mails gives extensive information on the Hopi ceremonies illustrated by many excellent drawings.

The wedding ritual is a significant part of Hopi life. The groom and other men of the village weave the white wedding robe and the plaited cotton sash ("rain sash") with long fringes and braided balls. White leggings and white ceremonial moccasins are worn. The bride carries a reed bundle that contains a second, larger wedding robe and the white sash. The bride's large white cotton robe is kept for her burial, and helps to insure her passage into the world beyond. A man's body may be wrapped in deerskin or a blanket woven in a diamond-twill pattern, often with a plaid design.

Garment Decoration

Anciently, both cloth and leather were painted, but this custom has virtually died out. The most common form of garment decoration was "brocading," a

A finished whorl hair style for maidens is worn by the young woman, right. A wooden hairstick, grass-stem brush, and cup are to her right.

technique in which the weft elements are wrapped around the warp threads or cords to create a design on the top surface. Panels were embroidered and applied to mantas, kilts, and other garments. Hopi men did most of the weaving and embroidery. Fringes on sashes were decorated with wood and/or cornhusk rings. Both Kate Peck Kent and Nancy Fox have done extensive work in Pueblo embroidery and weaving.

Face and Body Embellishment
Face and body paint was used considerably in ceremonial costumes and by warriors going into conflict. Colors used were red, black, yellow, blue, brown, and white. The paints consisted of earth ochers and plant stains. There was some flattening of the skull noted in the past, but it was caused by binding infants into cradle boards.

Masks
The vast array of masks was used as an integral part of the Hopi ceremonies; there was also some use in curing rites.

Key Sources
Curtis, Edward S. *The North American Indian.* Vol. 12. New York: Johnson Reprint Company, 1970.
Fox, Nancy. *Pueblo Weaving and Textile Arts.* Santa Fe: Museum of New Mexico Press, 1978.
James, Harry C. *The Hopi Indians.* Caldwell, ID: Caxton, 1956.
Kent, Kate Peck. "The Braiding of a Hopi Sash. *Plateau* 12(3): 46–52.
"Living Spirits of the Kachinas." *Arizona Highways,* June 1971.
Mails, Thomas E. *The Pueblo Children of the Earth Mother.* Garden City, NY: Doubleday, 1983.
McGibbeny, J. H. "Hopi Jewelry." *Arizona Highways,* July 1950: 18–25.
Miller, Sheryl F. "Life in the Balance: The Hopi Way. A Current Exhibition at the Southwest Museum." *American Indian Art Magazine* 17(2): 52–61.
Museum of Northern Arizona. *Hopi Indian Arts and Crafts.* Flagstaff: Northern Arizona Society of Science, 1951.
O'Kane, Walter Collins. *The Hopis: Portrait of a Desert People.* Norman: University of Oklahoma Press, 1953.
Parsons, Elsie Clews. "Hopi and Zuni Ceremonialism." American Anthropological Association *Memoirs* 39.
Pendleton, Mary. *Navajo and Hopi Weaving Techniques.* New York: Collier Books, 1974.
Roediger, Virginia More. *Ceremonial Costumes of the Pueblo Indians.* Berkeley: University of California Press, 1991. Reprint of 1941 edition.
Simpson, Ruth DeEtte. *The Hopi Indians.* Southwest Museum *Leaflet* 25. Reprint of 1953 edition.
Waters, Frank. *Book of the Hopi.* New York: Viking, 1963.
Wright, Barton. *Hopi Material Culture: Artifacts Gathered by H. R. Voth in the Fred Harvey Collection.* Flagstaff, AZ: Northland; Phoenix, AZ: Heard Museum, 1962.
Wright, Margaret Nickelson. *The History and Hallmarks of Hopi Silversmithing: Hopi Silver.* Flagstaff, AZ: Northland, 1972.

Jemez

The Jemez are the only remaining Towa speakers; Towa is a branch of the Kiowa-Tanoan language family. They stubbornly resisted the Spaniards of the seventeenth century, and they continue the resistance today to Anglo encroachment and influence. They lived (and live) on the east bank of the Jemez River, a tributary of the Rio Grande. Like the Acoma, the Jemez inhabited their lofty mesas, protected by sheer cliffs; they tended their extensive gardens in the lower fields, trading their vegetables and fruit for deerskin, cloth, silver belts, turquoise, and other desirable items. Parsons has written the major work on the Jemez pueblo. The dress of the Jemez people is characteristic of others of the Rio Grande pueblos.

Men's Basic Dress
Anciently, men wore the breechclout and poncho of tanned leather. They adopted the white cotton pants of the Mexicans in the nineteenth century, loose and baggy in the early days, closer fitting in this century, with slits up the sides to the knees. With this was worn the cotton shirt, formerly of woven cotton, in this century of commercial cloth; this shirt was belted and worn outside the trousers. A white woven-cotton breechcloth was often embroidered and displayed tassels at the ends. Like many of the Pueblo peoples,

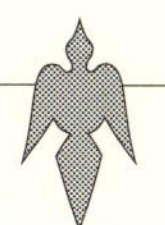

they lost their textile arts when commercial cloth flooded the trading posts; however, they have continued to make and embroider their distinctive shirts, handwoven with characteristic crosses on the body of the shirts and the sleeves, embroidered in red and black yarn, and with tassels hanging from the sides of the waists and at the ends of the sleeves. Today these are still embroidered, but made of white commercial cloth. For special occasions the men might wear snug-fitting, fringed deerskin trousers.

Women's Basic Dress

From the simple wraparound skirts and ponchos of early days, the women adopted the typical Pueblo dress, the *manta* of woven black wool, folded around the body, sewn up the right side, and fastened on the right shoulder, leaving the left shoulder and arm bare; later a blouse or underdress was worn. The manta was belted with a long sash woven of red and green yarn, wrapped around the waist one or more times, and with long fringes at the ends. With this they wore the white leather wraparound leggings of the Pueblo Indians.

Footwear

Moccasins were the regular Pueblo type—of brick-red tanned leather with a black sole, fastened at the outer sides with thongs or silver buttons. Some crocheted or knitted stockings were worn. The women wore white moccasins with black soles and the long white wrappings of buckskin, tied with thongs at the knees.

Outer Wear

There is some evidence of feather robes in the early days. Also, the Jemez hunted buffalo twice a year, and buffalo robes were a part of their attire. With the decline of the buffalo, the woven shawl (smaller version of the manta) became the usual outer garment, worn over the head or over one shoulder. This was replaced to some extent by the commercial blanket, usually a Pendleton or Navajo product. In this century, women have worn a square of commercial cloth tied on the shoulder, often belted. Some rabbit-skin blankets were woven by the women.

Hair Styles

Both sexes wore the *chongo,* the Southwestern hair style in which the hair is parted, drawn to the back, coiled in a figure-eight, and fastened at the crossing with a thong or hair tie; the hair is worn in bangs in front and is cut at the sides at the jawline. Many men have worn their hair cut shoulder-length or shorter and held in place with a cloth headband.

Head Gear

Headbands, as noted above, were worn by the men, often of white cloth, tied at the side. No other headgear was worn except for the elaborate headdresses worn by ceremonial dancers.

Accessories

Cotton and wool belts, garters, and hair-ties were woven by the men, as were long ceremonial sashes. For a long time weaving died out among the Jemez; in the 1920s women began to weave again, and by the 1950s there was a strong revival in the art. The governors of Jemez, like those of other pueblos, carried canes of office. These were of two types: (1) a wooden Spanish cane with a silver head and an engraved cross, given by the Spaniards, and (2) a similar cane given by Abraham Lincoln. These are passed on from one governor to the next and displayed at ceremonials.

Jewelry

Early beads were of stone (particularly turquoise), bird bones, and shells, as well as the teeth and claws of such animals as grizzly bears, coyotes, and wolves. The Jemez people do not do silversmithing, so in recent times their turquoise-and-silver jewelry has been obtained in trade from the Navajo.

Armor

Shields were made of two layers of tough buffalo rawhide sewn together; a painted deerskin cover was ornamented with eagle feathers.

Special Costumes

The Jemez had a busy ceremonial year; besides the festivities participated in by all pueblos, the Jemez observed the Old Pecos Bull Dance on 2 August, the Corn Dance on 12 November, and the Matachine Dance on 12 December. In the Bull or Buffalo Dance, the dancers wear huge buffalo heads with horns, a knee-length kilt, fringed and painted, and moccasins to the knees. For the Dance of the Matachines the dancers wear Western-style coats with rather full, white,

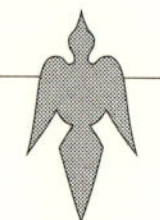

cotton pants; their hats support a colored framework. In the Jemez funerary rites, all buttons were cut off from the dead person's garments and the clothing was removed and placed under the corpse. Stockings and shoes or moccasins were placed by the feet, and the body, bundled up in a blanket tied with the mother's sash. For a specified length of time the mourners had to wear a shawl at all times, over the shoulders or around the hips.

Garment Decoration

Many articles of ceremonial wear were embroidered—kilts, shirts, rain sashes, and belts. Characteristic colors were black, red, green, and white.

Face and Body Embellishment

Painting of the face and body in many colors was done for ceremonial dances. Warriors painted the face with black horizontal lines.

Masks

Masks were worn by participants in the various festivals. The guards in the Easter ceremonial wore huge flaring masks edged with feathers. The chief dancer of the Bull Dance wore a mask made of a wooden frame covered with a dark cloth spotted with rings, formed into a stylized bull's head with horns and a protruding red tongue.

Key Sources

Mails, Thomas E. "Jemez Pueblo." In *The Pueblo Children of the Earth Mother* 1: 388–396. Garden City, NY: Doubleday, 1983.

Parsons, Elsie Clews. *The Pueblo of Jemez.* Andover, MA: Phillips Academy, 1925.

Sando, Joe S. "Jemez Pueblo." In *Handbook of North American Indians. Vol. 9: Southwest.* Pp. 418–429. Washington: Smithsonian Institution.

Jicarilla Apache

The Jicarilla Apache live in northern New Mexico; an eastern band, the Llaneros ("plainsmen"), live east of the Rio Grande and have been much influenced by Plains culture, and a second band, the Olleros ("potters"), live west of the river, taking on more of the Pueblo ways. A third influence has been that of the Southern Athapaskan, for they spoke that language as did the other Apache and the Navajo. Some say the name *Jicarilla* means "little basket," but more authoritative information is that the word comes from the Spanish for "little chocolate cup-shaped hill," referring to a hill in the area. The Jicarilla carried on some agriculture, but mainly they were hunters and gatherers. They hunted buffalo, antelope, deer, mountain sheep, and elk, as well as smaller animals. There were many conflicts with the Spanish and later the United States government, leading

Photographed in the late 1870s, this Jicarilla Apache wears a fringed shirt with beaded arm and shoulder bands. His leather cross belt is studded with tacks and his breechcloth is made of trade cloth.

almost to the destruction of the Jicarilla in the early years of the twentieth century. There has been a slow recovery and some economic stability, especially since the 1950s. Written sources on the Jicarilla are few, with Opler and Mails being the most helpful in terms of costume and ceremonialism. Edward S. Curtis photographed them, as did others.

Men's Basic Dress

A poncho-type shirt of tanned skin (usually of mule-deer hide) was worn well into modern times; sleeves were attached, not sewn under the arms, but rather tied in places. There was an especially long triangular neck flap both in front and back, painted yellow, edged with a short fringe, and with wide shoulder bands beaded in a plain geometric style. Fringes along the shoulders and arms were quite long and, in characteristic Southern Plains style, grouped in bunches along the arms. Leggings of buckskin were close-fitting with tabs at the bottom, flaring side flaps, and long fringes. A long breechclout, originally of skin but later of commercial cloth such as strouding, reached to the ankles front and back; often beaded designs or cloth applique edged the bottom.

Women's Basic Dress

The Jicarilla woman's dress, usually of the skin of a black-tail mule deer, was a two-skin dress, sewn along the shoulders and down the sides, belted, simple, and relatively unornamented except for fringing at the side seams and along the hem. It could be turned quickly into more formal wear with the addition of a fringed and beaded yoke-type cape, with longer extensions over the arms than down the front. Leggings of deerskin had wide bands of beading across the bottom. The Jicarilla women never adopted the "camp dress" worn by other Apache women, but in the nineteenth century they wore "pioneer" dresses—long, one-piece dresses of printed cotton with full ruffled skirts and snug bodices and sleeves.

Footwear

Early moccasins of deerskin had a slit down the front and a pointed toe. By the late 1800s both sexes were wearing the Plains-type moccasin with a low cuff, fringe at the heel, and a tongue; it was either plain, or decorated with a beaded band around the edge or solid beading over the instep in simple geometric

A Jicarilla Apache, photographed in Dulce, New Mexico in 1950, wears a fringed buckskin dress designed for a puberty ceremony. She also wears a wide leather belt studded with brass tacks and a beaded necklace with a large shell disk which was used during the ceremony.

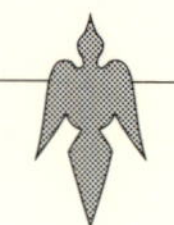

designs. Soles were rawhide, often turned up at the toe in the typical Apache fashion, and the leather was whitened. Women's moccasins were like the men's, only plainer. Some women adopted the Southern Plains moccasin/legging combination with a beaded band up the sides. Beading designs were similar to Ute beadwork. Snowshoes were used by the Jicarilla in the mountain snows; they were simply made of bent wood, tied at the heel end and rather loosely laced.

Outer Wear

Until the buffalo declined, buffalo robes were common wear among the Jicarilla. Navajo blankets were adopted in the eighteenth century; after 1900, Pendleton blankets with Indian-inspired designs were adopted. Some blankets of dark stroud cloth had a Plains-style strip across the center with the characteristic beaded medallions. Men often wore these wrapped about the waist. Women donned shawls of printed cotton and other cloth.

Hair Styles

Both sexes wore braids in the Plains fashion, the men often wrapping theirs with cloth or otter fur, the women tying theirs with yarn or cloth strips. If the hair was not braided, men sometimes encased it in a beaded hair tube. Women occasionally wore hair ties, leather beaded ornaments in an hourglass shape.

Headgear

Both sexes normally went bareheaded. However, the warriors often wore war bonnets; Mails describes the two types: (1) the characteristic Plains bonnet with the beaded band and the halo of golden eagle feathers, with or without the tail of feathers; (2) the Pueblo type, which had a single row of eagle feathers over the head and halfway down the back, sometimes with cow or buffalo horns added at the sides. Winter caps were of beaver or other animal fur. The wide-brimmed Mexican hat (felt or straw) was adopted in the nineteenth century, and later the Stetson style of hat, both being worn into the contemporary period.

Accessories

Women wore a broad leather belt, at times as wide as 16 inches, decorated with brass tacks or buttons; to these belts were attached knife cases, awl cases, pouches, and other items. Navajo concha belts were also worn. Pouches were often of deerskin with a drawstring top, beaded and fringed. Ceremonial eagle-feather fans featured a beaded bird-skin handle. Men wore armbands of brass or silver, or beaded leather strips. Hair tubes or hair ties kept the hair in place. Some men displayed the hair pipe breastplate, so popular on the Plains in the late nineteenth century. Beaded leather wristguards were often seen on both wrists. Cloth neckerchiefs were tied in front, cowboy fashion.

Jewelry

The particularly favored piece of jewelry for both sexes was the choker, which consisted of hair pipe beads with spacers of glass beads or shells; loops and clusters of beads dangled from some chokers. Women also wore many strings of beads. Some women had a large shell gorget on the breast. A brass or silver concha frequently adorned the man's triangular neck flap. The most popular type of earring for men was a large silver hoop with one large silver bead hanging from it. Bracelets were of trade brass or copper. Some men wore long loops of beads slung over one shoulder and under the other arm.

Armor

In the early days the warriors wore buffalo-hide tunics as a form of armor, but this ended with the decline of the buffalo. War shields were made of rawhide in the Plains style and decorated with paint and feathers.

Special Costumes

Curing ceremonies took place, in which Hactcins or masked Mountain Spirits danced the Bear Dance wearing kilts of woven yucca fiber; spruce branches were carried or inserted in armbands and legbands. Clowns, wearing only breechclouts and moccasins, had the faces and bodies painted in black and white horizontal stripes. The Relay Race in mid-September was an important festival; runners wore short buckskin kilts, headbands of yucca, and belts of otter skin. The most important festival was the Puberty or Adolescence Rite; the ceremony celebrated the girl's first menstrual period, and an adolescent boy was an important adjunct to the four-day ritual. She wore an uncolored dress of buckskin, heavily fringed, a splendid cape that was beaded, fringed and painted

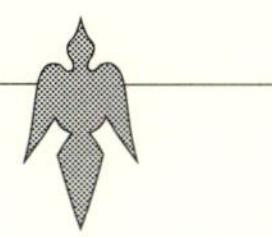

yellow, and yellow leggings and moccasins. He wore buckskin moccasins, leggings, a shirt with two weasel pelts attached at the shoulders, a wristguard, and a beaded armband. Sacred yellow pollen was sprinkled on them, and their faces were painted with black and red markings.

Garment Decoration

There was some painting of garments in solid colors, especially yellow. Fringing was added to many garments; either the garment was fringed at the edge, or a fringed piece was sewn on. Beadwork was common after 1850, following Plains and, particularly, Ute styles of designs; especially favored were large compositions with monochrome backgrounds. Rows of tin cones or tinklers edged some garments.

Face and Body Embellishment

Elaborate traditional and highly symbolic designs were painted on the faces and bodies of participants in the ceremonials. Some painting was applied in other situations. Children had the cheeks painted red to protect them from witchcraft. Women often had a red spot on each cheek. Men painted vertical stripes on the cheeks.

Transitional Dress

By the late 1800s the Jicarilla were wearing a combination of Anglo and Indian clothing. Men wore dark vests with cotton shirts, the shirttails hanging out; hats were Western or Mexican, as they are today. Some older women still wear the long, full-skirted and flounced dresses of the nineteenth century, girded with the wide leather belts, but most women wear the customary clothes of today. A few of both sexes have their hair in braids.

Key Sources

Curtis, Edward S. *The North American Indian.* Vol. 1. New York: Johnson Reprint Company, 1970.

Douglas, Frederic H. "A Jicarilla Apache Beaded Cape." Denver Art Museum *Material Culture Notes.*

———. "A Jicarilla Apache Woman's Skin Dress." Denver Art Museum *Material Culture Notes.*

Dutton, Bertha P. *Navahos and Apaches: The Athabascan Peoples.* Englewood Cliffs, NJ: Prentice-Hall, 1975.

Mails, Thomas E. "The Jicarilla Apache." In *The People Called Apache.* Pp. 348–403. New York: Promontory, 1974.

Opler, Morris E. *Childhood and Youth in Jicarilla Apache Society.* Los Angeles: Southwest Museum, 1946.

———. "A Summary of Jicarilla Apache Culture." *American Anthropologist* 38.

Tiller, Veronica E. "Jicarilla Apache." In *Handbook of North American Indians. Vol. 10: Southwest.* Pp. 440–461. Washington: Smithsonian Institution.

VanRoekel, Gertrude B. *Jicarilla Apaches.* San Antonio, TX: Naylor Company, 1971.

Mescalero Apache

The Mescalero Apache have occupied the same territory in southeastern New Mexico and into Texas and Mexico since the seventeenth century. They were named for their extensive use of and dependence on the mescal plant for food (not to be confused with the mescal bean or peyote). Hunters and gatherers, living in small bands, they were extremely mobile. They suffered like the other Apache under the cruel tyranny of the Spaniards and the encroachment of the settlers in the nineteenth century. They belong to the southern branch of the speakers of Athapaskan. Opler and Mails are the two best sources on the Mescaleros, and the photographs of Ben Wittick have been the most useful.

Men's Basic Dress

The men dressed much like their Jicarilla brothers during the buckskin period, both influenced by Plains dress. They wore the buckskin shirt, decorated with fringes in bunches along the arms and at the lower edge, in the Southern Plains manner. Triangular neck pieces, in front and at the back, were also fringed. Some shirts had the beaded shoulder bands. Red and/or yellow paint was often rubbed into the buckskin. It is referred to as a "war shirt," but since almost all men were considered warriors, it was practically standard dress. A small leather breechclout was worn, sometimes decorated with beadwork. Leggings of tanned leather (later of strouding or other cloth) had wide flaps, like chaps, that often displayed bands of beading. In the nineteenth century they adopted the cotton shirts and dark vests of the Anglos.

Women's Basic Dress

The early attire was the poncholike top and the wraparound skirt, both of tanned deerskin that was often painted yellow. Sometimes knee-length leggings were worn with this. With the availability of cloth, the women began to wear the "Mother Hubbard" dresses—a one-piece garment with a long sweeping skirt. They did not, as a rule, adopt the "camp dress" of the other Apache tribes. Meanwhile, the buckskin dresses were retained for the ceremonial Puberty Rite.

Footwear

Some sandals were made from the fibers of the mescal plant. But most men and women wore the low-top moccasin of deerskin, with the rawhide soles and with a front seam over the instep often covered with a beaded band or triangle, and with short fringes and tin tinklers added. When a child was just starting to walk, he was given new moccasins to wear, then led to the east along a trail of footprints edged with yellow pollen.

Outer Wear

In the early days, robes were made of deer, elk, bighorn sheep, or buffalo hide. In the early-nineteenth century, blankets came into use, especially the Pendleton blankets with the plaid or Indian designs, often with self-fringes. The manner of wearing was either over the shoulders or around the hips. Carter mentions "buckskin coats," but these may have simply been war shirts.

Hair Styles

Both sexes usually wore the hair in two braids; men wrapped the braids with fur or, later, cloth. Sometimes the hair was simply tied in clumps at the sides. A few women and children wore the hair in bangs on the forehead. When a child's hair was first cut, prayers were said for good health and long life, and the hair was often cut in little tufts to encourage growth.

Headgear

Women rarely wore any type of head covering. Warriors almost invariably wore a turban-style cap of fur or trade felt, which featured beaded strips, feathers, and often large crosses or squares laid out in white buttons. Turbans of fur, especially otter fur, frequently had the tail of the animal hanging in back. Hats of felt or straw in the Anglo or Mexican fashions were adopted in the nineteenth century.

Accessories

Some pouches were made of buckskin with a drawstring closure and attached to a belt; other bags or pouches were woven of mescal or other plant fibers. Belts were simple leather affairs; some men during the conflicts with the U.S. troops wore cartridge belts. Men sometimes wore a bandolier of fur over one shoulder, which carried an amulet pouch ornamented with beadwork.

Jewelry

Jewelry was not common with the Mescaleros. A few dentalium-shell earrings and necklaces of beads or tinklers were to be seen. Occasionally a piece of abalone shell on a string was displayed. Peace medals were proudly worn by some men.

Armor

Some warriors covered their chests with hair pipe breastplates, more for symbolic strength than actual protection. A popular war cap was the turban of fur or trade felt mentioned earlier with the addition of cow horns and golden eagle feathers. Painted rawhide shields with feathers and other medicine appendages were carried by those who possessed them.

Special Costumes

The major, in fact almost the only, ceremony of the Mescaleros was the Puberty Rite, held during the first week in July; it is still being observed today. It was established to commemorate a young girl's coming of age, and followed traditional activities and costumes. The girl wore a two-piece buckskin dress with a square or round yoke at the top, from the edge of which hung long fringes. The buckskin skirt had rows of fringes as well as fringes at the sides, and tabs at the lower edges. Often there were rows of thongs and/or rows of tin tinklers. Both skirt and top piece were painted yellow, as were the buckskin moccasin uppers. The girl also wore a long necklace of hair pipe beads. The Gans or mountain spirits, who danced at the ceremony, wore heavily fringed yellow buckskin skirts, leggings, high leather moccasins with the upturned toe, black hoods of cloth or buckskin, and headpieces of thin slats of wood in a cross-piece fashion.

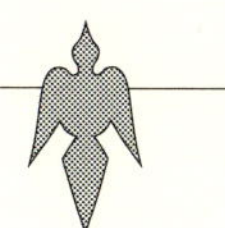

Garment Decoration

Fringes, long and short, were the most typical form of garment embellishment. Some beadwork was done, but it was simple in design and done sparingly, usually in the form of bands on moccasins, war shirts, leggings, and caps. Garments were often painted, especially yellow.

Face and Body Embellishment

Some painting was done, but only for the Puberty Rite participants. The body of the girl was painted yellow, symbolic of growth, and red, the color of blood and life. The Gan Dancer's body and arms were painted black, with symbolic designs painted over these colors in yellow, white, or red. A few warriors wore facial paint, but designs were a matter of individual decision.

Masks

The special masks worn by the Mescaleros were those of the Gan Dancers in the Puberty ceremonial; these were of buckskin (later cloth), painted black, and had a shell on the forehead. A hunter often wore a mask of an antelope or deer head with the horns attached, so he could sneak up on his prey.

Key Sources

Dobyns, Henry F. *The Mescalero Apache People.* Phoenix, AZ: Indian Tribal Series, 1973.

Hoijer, Harry. *Chiricahua and Mescalero Apache Texts.* Chicago: University of Chicago Press, 1938.

Mails, Thomas E. "The Mescalero Apache." In *The People Called Apache.* Pp. 284–341. New York: Promontory, 1974.

Opler, Morris E. "The Apachean Culture Pattern and Its Origins." In *Handbook of North American Indians. Vol. 10: Southwest.* Pp. 368–392. Washington: Smithsonian Institution.

———. "Mescalero and Apache Texts." American Folklore Society *Memoirs* 31.

———. "Mescalero Apache." In *Handbook of North American Indians. Vol. 10: Southwest.* Pp. 419–439. Washington: Smithsonian Institution.

Sonnichsen, C. L. *The Mescalero Apaches.* Norman: University of Oklahoma Press, 1958.

Navajo

The Navajo, Athapaskan speakers, probably arrived in the Southwest with the Apache sometime in the late fifteenth century, trekking down from their original home in northwestern Canada. Some of the migrants probably came down along the eastern edge of the Rockies; others took the route west of the mountains through Nevada and Utah. They began raiding the pueblos, at the same time adopting many elements of Pueblo material culture. About 1700 they seem to have separated from the Apache; their names come from *apaches du nabahu,* a Spanish term meaning "raiders of the fields" or "enemies of the cultivated fields." Their name for themselves is *Dine.* Today, as in the historical past, many are semisedentary pastoralists, taking care of their flocks of sheep and numerous horses, and occasionally farming wherever moisture is adequate. They live in small family groups without tribal community and, until recently, without a central authority.

They were not a peaceful folk, making a name for themselves as raiders and plunderers, fighting the Pueblo Indians, the Spanish, the Mexicans, and the Comanche. Finally, in the 1860s, the United States government forced them to walk the many miles to Ft. Sumner in eastern New Mexico in what is still called "the long walk of the Navajo." There, at Bosque Redondo, they lived for four years under miserable conditions, starving, ridden by disease. The government finally realized its tragic mistake and permitted them to return to their homelands in northern Arizona and New Mexico. Slowly and painfully they rebuilt their lives.

Today the Navajo are the largest single tribe in the country, living on 16 million acres, and with a vigorous tribal council at Window Rock, their capital. They have been extensively photographed during this century. Their arts and crafts are well represented in many museum collections throughout the country.

Men's Basic Dress

In the early period, we may assume that the men wore the tailored buckskin garments of the Subarctic when they first started their southward movement. Some of them adopted the early Plains garments (breechclouts, leggings, poncho-type shirts, and moccasins, all of buckskin, and buffalo robes). Others took on the clothing of the Desert Culture through which they passed—breechclouts of shredded cedar bark or yucca fibers and rabbit-skin robes. After the Pueblo Revolt of 1680, many of the Pueblo Indians took refuge with the Navajo and there were strong cross-cultural currents from the Pueblos and the Spaniards. The women (not the men) learned to weave, and the men wore shirts of dark blue or black wool or white cotton; these shirts were simple rectangles with an opening for the head and with sleeves, also rectangles, sewed in separately. By 1824 loose, white cotton pants were worn, slit to the knees on the outside, showing Spanish influence. Also Spanish were the close-fitting leggings of tanned leather with rows of silver buttons. Some men wore knitted leggings with a cable stich down the outside; both types of leggings were gartered. With these a breechcloth was worn, either dark wool with a brightly colored edging or, when worn with the cotton pants, of white cotton. With the advent of commercial cloth, the typical "Navajo" costume was developed: a long-sleeved hip-length shirt of cloth, especially velveteen or corduroy in a bright color, worn with dark or white pants, and girded with a concha belt.

Women's Basic Dress

Like the men, the women in the early days adopted the leather garments of the Plains (wraparound skirt, the poncho top, and knee-high leggings) or the fringed double apron of yucca or other fibers of the Desert Culture; this meant a short skirt to the knees in front and a longer one in back. The Navajo women also had a Pueblo-Spanish period in which they learned to weave and to wear the dark woolen dress (called the "bil" or sometimes the "tilma"); unlike the Pueblo women, they did not wrap one piece around the body, but used two pieces of woven material, fastened at the shoulders, with slits for the head and arms, and cinched at the waist with a woven belt or sash (later a concha belt). The center portion of the dress was of black or dark blue with designs woven in red at the top and bottom as wide borders; a few were of gray with black trim. The shoulders were sewn with large stitches or fastened with brass or silver pins. These woven dresses were rarely seen after 1900. With these dresses were worn the wrapped leggings of the Pueblo women, made of buckskin whitened with clay. After the desperate period at Ft. Sumner, women began to wear the characteristic long, full cotton skirts and velveteen blouses we tend to identify as "Navajo." Some authorities say the women were influenced by the dress of the officers' wives at the fort. However, Underhill presents convincing arguments otherwise. She says there were few women at the fort, nor did the Navajo women know how to sew at the time. Rather, she believes there were two influences: (1) Traders began to set up posts in the 1870s; their shelves were filled with cheap commercial cloth, and their wives were there to offer help and models of dresses. (2) During the 1870s and 1880s many of the women who had been sold as slaves to the New Mexican ladies were returned to Navajo land; these women had been taught to sew by their mistresses, who deplored the Navajo woven dress with its open sides and lack of underwear beneath.

In addition, the railroads that came into the area about this time brought a flood of goods including sewing machines (which were not extensively used, however, until after 1900). The blouses were cotton at first; after the 1890s velveteen replaced cotton. The garment had long fitted sleeves, a high neckline with a collar, and was fitted by means of tucks; the blouse was about hip-length and was worn over the top of the skirt. Silver buttons made from coins were used for ornament everywhere—down the front opening, around the collar, down the sleeves, and around the cuffs. Skirts were full, often in two or three tiers, at times with a wide ruffle at the bottom; at first these skirts were of printed calico, later of brightly colored plain cotton.

Footwear

In the early days both sexes wore low-top Plains moccasins, one-piece and hard-soled, or they wore sandals woven of yucca fiber. By the mid-nineteenth century they were wearing the rust-colored moccasins with light-colored soles, ankle-high, with one or more silver buttons at the side for closure. Men sometimes wore the moccasins knee-high, in which case they were fastened with a row of silver buttons down the outside.

Outer Wear

Early Navajo robes were of deer or buffalo hide or rabbit skin, the latter provided with loops to pull the robe close to the body for warmth. Underhill says they also might wear a skin of deer or antelope tied in front by means of the forelegs. After the women learned to weave, they produced the beautiful "chief" blankets; these blankets, featuring simple geometric patterns of stripes, diagonal lines, terraced diamonds, and triangles in dark blue, white, and red, were produced for wearing as shoulder blankets; red was especially favored and the women unraveled the trade cloth called *bayeta* to get a brilliant red yarn. After 1865, blankets were woven strictly for trade, for the Navajo could not afford to wear them. From there it was but a step to weave the larger and heavier rugs for the traders instead of blankets, and the Navajo adopted Pendleton blankets for wear, preferring those with vertical stripes. Occasionally striped Mexican *serapes* were worn by the men; these sometimes had a slit for the head in the poncho manner.

Hair Styles

Originally the Navajo must have worn the loose, flowing hair style of the Apache. With Pueblo contact they adopted the *chongo.* The hair was parted in the center, pulled back, coiled into a figure-eight, and the intersection tied with thongs or lengths of handspun native yarn; women frequently wore a large white scarf tied into the chongo, while the men preferred a colored cotton kerchief about the head. During the

An exhibit includes five styles of Navajo wool blankets made between 1840 and 1880. From left to right are a classical style poncho serape made before 1890, a diamond blanket of the early 1870s, and a chief blanket, right, from the 1840s.

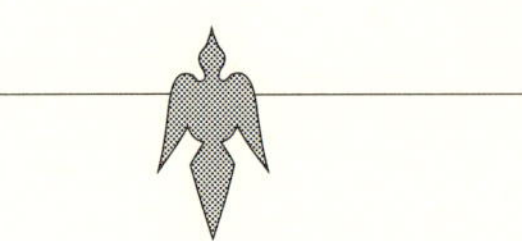

Two Navajo women, a child nearby on a cradleboard, work at a loom in Arizona at the turn of the century. They wear their hair twisted into a chongo.

1860s and 1870s the United States government forced many of the Navajo men to cut off their long hair, a great blow to them because it was significant to their ceremonials. By the turn of the century, they were again wearing long hair coiled into chongos; these could be seen even into the 1960s; however, many of the men wore the hair in the shoulder-length Pueblo style, often with bangs. A cotton kerchief was tied about the head whether the chongo, the bobbed hair, or the contemporary short hair style was worn.

Headgear

The cotton headband has been the most common form of headgear for the Navajo men; in this century many have adopted the light-colored Western hat of felt or straw with the curved brim, or the straight-sided flat-brimmed hat. Women have always gone bareheaded.

Accessories

Accessories were few. The "concha" belts were a most important article of attire. Leather backed, they featured either 1 to 3 large silver conchas or medallions, or 6 to 12 smaller ones; after 1920 turquoise might be added, a small piece in the center of each concha. A large silver buckle was generally used for fastening. Some belts, as well as garters, were woven on a belt loom, typically in red, green, and white yarns. Some men wore a bandolier-type belt, hanging diagonally across the chest and ending in a leather pouch fastened with a silver ornament, in which were carried such things as tobacco and fire-making equipment. A bow guard or *ketoh* might encircle the left wrist; this was often adorned with turquoise and silver work. Originally made of leather, it was used to protect the wrist from the snap of the bowstring; many men continue to wear a bow guard as ornament.

Jewelry

Navajo jewelry has a worldwide reputation for craftsmanship and art. It is highly important to the Navajo concept of harmony and beauty in life; turquoise, to them, is a reflection of water and the sky, both essential elements of their spirituality. The jewelry takes many forms—necklaces, bracelets, rings, earrings, hatbands, and buttons. Necklaces have been formed of beads of silver, turquoise, coral, and shell, worn as multiple strings. Often a *jaclah* is added—loops of strung beads hung in clusters from other strings. The most famous is the squash-blossom necklace, with floral elements said to represent the blossoms of the squash; but some authorities say it was really the Spanish pomegranate blossom that was being imitated. Others say the elements represent the *datura* blossoms, held sacred for their hallucinogenic properties. At the bottom of the necklace is the *naja,* a crescent-shaped silver piece said to ward off the evil eye. Some earrings featured single or double crosses of silver to represent the morning star. Earrings, usually worn by men, were simple hoops in the nineteenth century with one or two silver beads hanging; in this century simple turquoise pendants are preferred. Silverwork was not an ancient craft but was learned by the Navajo in the mid-nineteenth century, probably from the Mexicans; turquoise was not used to any great extent until after 1900. Most silverwork consisted of casting, hammering, filing, and stamping. Jewelry was, and is, worn in great abundance by the Navajo.

Armor

Like his Athapaskan ancestors, the Navajo warrior wore, with his customary garments, a heavy shirt of three or four thicknesses of hide; with that was worn a war cap, made of tanned leather and decorated with shell buttons and a plume of owl or eagle feathers. A quiver of mountain-lion fur was slung around his

A Navajo woman, photographed in 1981, spins wool that she has carded. She wears silver and turquoise jewlery and a longsleeved blouse over a full skirt.

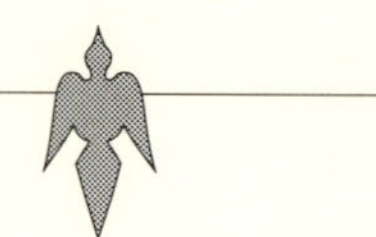

neck, and on his left wrist was a leather bow guard. Rawhide shields were painted with sacred designs to provide further protection. These shields and war caps were not worn after 1870.

Special Costumes

The major ceremonials of the Navajo are the curing rites, performed by medicine men to restore the balance of nature, during which they sing "chants" or "ways." Accompanying these chants are the *yeis,* masked figures of both sexes representing natural forces, such as wind and thunder. The *Yeibichai* or Night Way, the major curing rite, is held during the winter; women wear their customary garb, while the men wear kilts. Both wear masks.

Garment Decoration

In the early days of their migration the tanned leather clothing was decorated with porcupine quillwork, but this was discontinued as they got out of the range of the porcupine. Weaving, with women the sole weavers, was done usually in the regular weave, also the double and the two-faced weave; major decoration was the use of colored bands and designs during the weaving process. Little other decoration was applied to apparel except the staining of boots with mountain-mahogany dye and the extensive use of silver buttons in rows on the blouses especially.

Face and Body Embellishment

The only use of paint was on the participants and patients in the curing ceremonials, done in an individualistic manner. There was some flattening of the skull, but it was unintentional, due to the hard surface of the cradle boards used for infants.

Masks

Buckskin masks were decorated in various ways to represent gods in the curing rites; these were whitened or otherwise painted, with circular holes cut out for the eyes and mouth, often with a fringe of hair added, a collar, or feathers at the top. The masks were removed at the end of the ceremony so the children would know these were people they knew, not really gods.

Key Sources

Amsden, Charles A. *Navajo Weaving: Its Technic and History.* Glorieta, NM: Rio Grande Press, 1971.

Bedinger, Margery. *Indian Silver: Navajo and Pueblo Jewelers.* Albuquerque: University of New Mexico Press, 1973.

Curtis, Edward S. *The North American Indian.* Vol. 1. New York: Johnson Reprint Company, 1970.

Dutton, Bertha P. *Navahos and Apaches: The Athabascan Peoples.* Englewood Cliffs, NJ: Prentice-Hall, 1976.

Hegemann, Elizabeth Compton. *Navaho Silver.* Los Angeles: Southwest Museum, 1962.

Kaufman, Alice and Christopher Selser. *The Navajo Weaving Tradition: 1650 to the Present.* New York: Dutton, 1985.

Kent, Kate Peck. *Navajo Weaving: Three Centuries of Change.* Santa Fe, NM: School of American Research Press, 1985.

———. *The Story of Navaho Weaving.* Phoenix, AZ: Heard Museum, 1961.

Kluckhohn, Clyde C. and Dorothy Leighton. *The Navajo.* Garden City, NY: Doubleday, 1962.

Kluckhohn, Clyde C., W. W. Hill, and Lucy Kluckhohn. *Navaho Material Culture.* Cambridge: Belknap, 1971.

Mera, H. P. "Navajo Textile Arts." Santa Fe, NM: Laboratory of Anthropology, 1947.

Mills, George. *Navajo Art and Culture.* Colorado Springs: Taylor Museum of the Colorado Springs Fine Arts Center, 1959.

Roessel, Ruth. "Navajo Arts and Crafts." In *Handbook of North American Indians. Vol. 10: Southwest.* Pp. 592–604. Washington: Smithsonian Institution.

Underhill, Ruth M. *The Navajos.* Norman: University of Oklahoma Press, 1983. Reissue of 1956 edition.

Watkins, Thomas E. *The Navaho.* Southwest Museum *Leaflet* 16.

Wheat, Joe Ben. "The Navajo Chief Blanket." *American Indian Art Magazine* 1(3): 44–53.

Pima

The rancheria peoples of southwestern Arizona consist of the Pima, the Papago, or Tohono O'odham, and the Maricopa living in communities or "rancherias" along the Salt and Gila rivers, with the Papago extending down into Mexico. All three groups

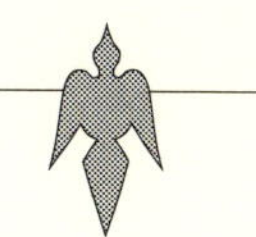

are treated here because their costume is almost identical. The Pima, probably descendants of the ancient Hohokam peoples, lived in permanent villages in the summer and were nomadic hunters and food gatherers in the winter. The name means "No" or "I don't know" in a Mexican dialect. The Papago ("bean people") were also seminomadic, with summer "field villages" and winter "well villages." They speak Pima, an Uto-Aztecan language. The Maricopa (the name is an abbreviation of *Cocomaricopa,* which is their name for themselves) are related to the Mojave. Although they spoke a different language (Yuman, a branch of the Hokan language), they took refuge with the more populous Piman groups in the mid-nineteenth century when Apaches threatened to destroy them, and have settled in comfortably with the Pimans. First European contact in this area was with the introduction of Christianity in 1539 by Father de Niza. Information on these tribes has come from the early Spanish padres, the later Protestant missionaries, and from the many photographers of the nineteenth century—Edward S. Curtis, Ben Wittick, and Adam C. Vroman especially.

Men's Basic Dress

Early breechclouts were of tanned leather, later of woven cotton, and small, almost like a bikini, with little or no flaps. Anciently the Maricopa men wore a breechclout of woven strips of willow bark. Crude leggings were worn for protection in the desert—simple pieces of deerskin wrapped around the legs and gartered with a strip of leather. In this hot climate little other clothing was needed; rarely a skin shirt of a poncho style might be worn. During the Mexican period some men adopted the white cotton pants. When commercial cloth became available, men often wore a short breechcloth of cotton (especially red, a favored color with these peoples) attached to a wide cloth belt.

Women's Basic Dress

Women in the early period wore either the wraparound skirt of deerskin or home-woven cotton cloth, or the one-piece fringed fiber skirt of the Desert Culture (different from the double-apron skirt of California), using fibers of the inner bark of cottonwood or willow trees; these seem to have had padding under the skirts, forming "bustles" all around. Later, probably due to missionary influence, they wrapped their body in commercial cotton in a sarong-type fashion, covering the breast and extending to the ankles. The next step was the adoption of the "camp dress" of the Apache—a long, full skirt with a bottom ruffle and a full-sleeved blouse hanging over the skirt; again, red was the preferred color.

Footwear

The Pimans usually went barefoot but when traveling, especially in the desert, they wore rawhide sandals similar to those of the Mexicans. In fact, the Navajo name for these people was "foot gap ones," referring to the sandals they wore with thongs between the toes. Some sandals were of the twisted fibers of willow bark, similar to those of the Desert Culture. The Pimans did not wear moccasins.

Outer Wear

Few wraps were necessary in this hot climate, but desert nights were cool, and blankets were worn or used for bedcovers. Rabbit-skin robes were woven by the men, who did all of the weaving. Cotton was handspun and woven into plain undyed blankets, with an occasional red weft thread for decoration. Women wore the blankets over the shoulders or the head; men wore them around the waist, or folded and thrust over the shoulder like a Mexican *serape.* Hopi blankets of black wool with white stripes were obtained in trade.

Hair Styles

Women wore the hair long and loose with bangs in the front almost to the eyes as a protection from sun glare. About once a week they washed the hair in amole suds and applied a dressing of black river mud mixed with mesquite; this was left on overnight, then combed out or brushed. It was said to make the hair a lustrous black and to get rid of vermin. Men wore the hair in bangs and prided themselves on its length, sometimes adding horse or human hair to increase it. They rolled the long hair into twists that were then coiled around the head in a turban-like fashion, similar to the style of the Yuma to the west; over this they often wound a headband to make the mass even larger. Some rolls or twists might hang down the back, and often a braided ear lock hung at each side

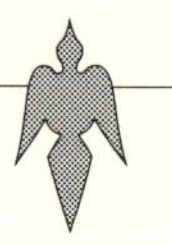

of the face. Eagle down or an eagle feather at the back completed the hair style.

Sometimes the Maricopa women wore the hair gathered on top of the head and tied so it was allowed to splay out like an umbrella.

Headgear

Hats were unknown to the Pimans until the nineteenth century. However, they did wear the turban mentioned above, which was made of long bands woven on a belt loom, ending in braided fringes. Some men wore a bonnet which was made of a deer-hide hood with eagle feathers projecting outward; strings under the chin held it in place. This headgear was said to signify bravery.

Accessories

Few accessories were used by these tribes. Women wore a head ring of woven fibers to cushion the round-bottomed water jars they carried on the head. Bands woven on the simple looms were used as headbands, as belts or sashes, and as crosspieces on the chest, these crosspieces being worn during ceremonies.

Jewelry

Silver was not worked by the Pimans, but some turquoise was made into ear pendants; such ear ornaments, and others of stones, shells, or glass beads, hung below the ear, sometimes to the collarbone, worn by both sexes alike. Necklaces, worn more by the men than the women, were of shells, later of glass beads. Some men wore nasal ornaments of bone or a blue shell.

Armor

Shields were made of a heavy fabric painted black with white spokes, a design that was supposed to have power over the enemy when rotated.

Special Costumes

Piman ceremonials were predominantly curing rites performed by shamans (who wore a top hat as a status symbol in the nineteenth century). Rainmaking dances and corn rituals were annual rites. Participants painted the faces white and had white dots on the legs. Women wore long, white, belted gowns. At some ceremonies there were masked clowns. At others, women wore white blouses and skirts with basketry designs on them, in the "camp dress" style of the Apache. There was much variation in the rituals and attire. A girl's puberty rite was held, for which the grandfather made special soft sandals of buckskin for his granddaughter, who was dressed in bright printed calico. After a death in the tribe, mourners wore a form of sackcloth for a month and the bereaved woman cut the hair short to the jawline; instead of a dress she wore a blanket wrapped around the body up to the armpits, leaving the arms bare.

Garment Decoration

Except for an occasional band of another color sewn to the bottom of a skirt, the Pimans did not decorate garments.

Face and Body Embellishment

Face and body painting was reserved for special occasions. Typically, women painted white vertical lines down the cheeks. Men removed the sparse facial hair in order to paint more effectively. Both sexes tattooed the face. Girls, as a part of the puberty rite, were tattooed on the lower eyelids (but not the Maricopa girls) and with three lines from the mouth to the chin. The tattooing was performed with cactus spines and charcoal.

Key Sources

Dobyns, Henry F. *The Papago People.* Phoenix, AZ: Indian Tribal Series, 1972.

Dutton, Bertha P. *The Rancheria, Ute, and Southern Paiute Peoples.* Englewood Cliffs, NJ: Prentice-Hall, 1976.

Ezell, Paul H. "History of the Pima." In *Handbook of North American Indians. Vol. 10: Southwest.* Pp. 137–148. Washington: Smithsonian Institution.

Fontana, Bernard L. *Of Earth and Little Rain: The Papago Indians.* Flagstaff, AZ: Northland, 1981.

Joseph, Alice, Rosamund B. Spicer, and Jane Chesky. *The Desert People: A Study of the Papago Indians.* Chicago: University of Chicago Press, 1949.

Russell, Frank. *The Pima Indians.* Tucson: University of Arizona Press, 1975.

Shaw, Anna Moore. *A Pima Past.* Tucson: University of Arizona Press, 1974.

Spier, Leslie. *Yuman Tribes of the Gila River.* New York: Dover, 1973.

Underhill, Ruth. *The Papago Indians of Arizona.* Lawrence, KS: Haskell Institute Press, 1955.

Pueblo

The Pueblo Indians (the name is Spanish for "town") live in their "high-rise" homes in the pueblos, which are strung like beads along the Rio Grande River and to the west into Arizona. The homes are made of stone and adobe, cubic in shape and compact, rising several stories in places, and centering around a plaza, the focal point of their ceremonial life, so significant to their culture. There is a variety of environments—mountain, riverine, desert. The Puebloans are a surprisingly homogeneous people, despite the fact that they represent different subsistence patterns and a bewildering assortment of languages. The eastern pueblos along the Rio Grande are predominantly agricultural, while the western pueblos of the Hopi, Zuni, Laguna, and Acoma, living in areas where farming is precarious, tend toward sheep and cattle grazing. Four linguistic stocks are present: (1) Uto-Aztecan (Hopi); (2) Penutian (Zuni); (3) Keresan (Acoma, Cochiti, Laguna, Santa Ana, San Felipe, Santo Domingo, and Zia); and (4) Tanoan-Kiowan, which in turn is divided into three dialects: (a) Tewa (Tesuque, Pojoaque, Nambe, San Ildefonso, San Juan, and Santa Clara); (b) Towa, spoken only at Jemez; and (c) Tiwa (Taos, Isleta, Sandia, and Picuris). The unpredictability of rain in this dry climate has led to an intricate system of ceremonials concerned with the production of rain and favorable circumstances for crops, especially corn.

Considered descendants of the Anasazi, the Puebloans integrated elements of that culture with that of the Spanish who first visited the region in 1540 under Coronado. The Indians fought stubbornly to retain their ancient ways in the face of Spanish colonialism; the conflict culminated in the Pueblo Revolt of 1680. Later, under Mexican control, the Puebloans adopted some elements of Mexican dress. When the United States government took over in 1848, they attempted to change Pueblo customs, attitudes, and dress. Another factor forcing change in dress was the influx of railroads into the region bringing commercial cloth and other trade goods in great abundance. By 1920 the European manner of dress was fairly well established—at least in everyday wear. However, the Puebloans brought forth their traditional garments to the ceremonials and wore them joyously and reverently.

There is a large volume of source material on the Pueblo Indians. Written records began with the Spanish explorers and padres, followed by missionaries and such anthropologists as Bandelier, Cushing, and Stevenson, with later writers such as Dutton, Underhill, and Mails. They were extensively photographed by Curtis, Wittick, Vroman, and others.

Men's Basic Dress

Early breechclouts were of tanned leather or of woven cotton, the latter with fringes, tassels at the corners, and with the ends richly embroidered. Embroidered kilts were often worn in place of breechcloths, but these disappeared after the mid-nineteenth century except for use in ceremonials. The early shirt of deerskin made in the simple rectangular poncho style, with or without sleeves, changed to a woven cotton shirt well before Spanish times; this was frequently beautifully embroidered. With the wool from the sheep brought by the Spaniards, dark blue or black shirts were made, commonly without decoration, although occasionally fine red or blue stripes were woven in horizontally. When, in the late 1800s, commercial cloth was available, shirts were made of unbleached muslin or dark printed cotton. Velveteen shirts became popular in the late nineteenth century and have continued in use to the present day. At some of the pueblos, Mexican-style white cotton shirts were worn; these typically had openwork panels in the front. Leggings were simple pieces of leather wrapped around the legs for desert travel. Footless stockings were knitted or crocheted of cotton yarn; these techniques replaced the earlier finger-weaving. The white cotton pants adopted from the Spaniards were of two pieces sewn together, the crotch being left unsewn and covered with the breechcloth; later a gusset was inserted so no breechloths were necessary. These pants were often flared at the bottom and slit to the knees on the outside seams.

Women's Basic Dress

Pueblo women's clothing has changed little over the centuries since the Spaniards came; they were little affected by Spanish styles perhaps because they saw only Spanish men. The *manta,* the basic dress of the Pueblo women (the word is Spanish for "piece of fabric"), has been retained with remarkably little change since prehistoric times; always woven by the men, it consists of a large piece of handwoven dark blue or black wool in a diagonal-twill weave, with large borders of indigo blue in a diamond-twill weave. Red and green cords are twisted and woven into the junction between the center part and the borders. The piece is folded over and sewn up the right side, with an opening for the armhole and a section sewn for the shoulder; the left shoulder and arm is left bare. Some women use silver pins to fasten the right side; a woven belt holds the garment in place. During the 1880s, a cotton-print underdress was worn under the manta; it was long-sleeved, high-necked, and long enough to show an inch or two beneath the manta. This style may have been forced on them by puritanical Anglos as a matter of modesty, or they may have adopted it to avoid the scratchiness of the wool; the style continues to be worn to the present. Knitted or crocheted leggings of white cotton yarn were worn by some women. For dress-up, a white apron with lace edging was often added.

Footwear

Anciently, yucca sandals were worn, but Pueblo footwear typically takes three forms, which have all been worn in the past and are worn today for ceremonials. The knee-high boot is worn by the men either for work in rough terrain or for special ceremonies. It has a rawhide sole, which is often dyed black, and a buckskin upper that may be tied with thongs or it may have a row of silver buttons down the outer sides for fasteners. It is gartered at the knees with a woven tie and is dyed a rich red-brown with mountain mahogany. A second type of footwear is the ankle-high moccasin, also with a rawhide sole and buckskin upper, usually dyed red-brown. Worn by men and women alike, it is generally fastened at the side overlap with one silver button. The third type of Pueblo footwear is worn only by the women and is common throughout the pueblos. The rawhide sole is white or is blackened with soapweed combined with charcoal, which gives a shiny polished surface to the sole. The long, wide strip of buckskin whitened with clay that forms the upper is fastened to the sole, then wound around the leg to the knee, making a bulky "puttee" (the more bulky, the more prestige), and is tied with attached thongs. These are worn only for special occasions. In cold and snowy weather, a piece of skin (now usually goatskin with hairy side inward) is wrapped about the foot for warmth.

Outer Wear

The turkey-feather robes of their Anasazi ancestors were abandoned long ago by the Puebloans. Rabbit-skin robes, woven by the women and worn from time immemorial, lingered until well into the twentieth century, and are still worn at some ceremonial dances. The manta was worn as a shawl, as well as a dress, with a little adjustment. Other mantas were used as shawls, such as a homespun, woven, white cotton manta with woven red and blue borders or with embroidered borders, knotted and fringed (the "maiden shawl"). A woven, blue wool manta featured red embroidered borders. "Back shawls," squares of printed cotton worn by both sexes, hung down the back and were held in front or tied at the neck. In the nineteenth century the Pendleton Mills of Oregon began making blankets inspired by Indian designs, which were extremely popular in the pueblos until the mid-twentieth century. Before World War II, Czechoslovakian shawls with deep fringes and heavily embroidered patterns were also highly regarded by the women, but war cut off the importation.

These Basketmaker fiber sandals from the 700s were found in Cañon del Muerto, Arizona. Their geometric pattern is similar to designs woven into baskets of the time.

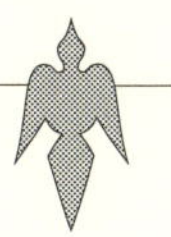

Hair Styles

Both sexes wore the hair in the *chongo* fashion made by fastening the hair in back into loops of a figure-eight and tied with a strip of cloth or a handwoven hair tie at the crossing; usually the hair was cut in bangs over the forehead, and cut at the sides at the jawline. Some men wore the hair shoulder-length and held in place with a cotton headband. The Hopi "butterfly" hair style, an indication of maidenhood, was occasionally to be seen at other pueblos. In the northern and eastern pueblos, some wore the hair in braids in the Plains style.

Headgear

Except for the cotton headbands mentioned above, headgear of any sort was worn only for ceremonies.

Accessories

"Floated warp" belts were woven on a belt loom or a narrow upright loom. The Hopi style of belt had red, black, and green warps with black cotton wefts. The Navajo style using red and green wool warps and white cotton warps and wefts was worn by both Navajo and Pueblo Indians. Garters and hair-ties were woven in a similar fashion but were smaller and narrower. Sashes were made in embroidery weaving (often called "brocading"), a technique in which colored yarns floating on the surface are wrapped around some of the warp threads, thus forming the pattern. A different type of upright loom was used in a braiding technique, often called "sprang," in which parallel stretched threads are braided. In the late 1800s, concha belts were worn, gained in trade from the Navajo, later made by the Pueblo silversmiths. Leather belts and wristguards, often ornamented with silver pieces, were items of male attire. Drawstring bags and pouches were made of buckskin or of cotton in a finger-weaving manner. An important accessory in the pueblos was the "cane of office" carried by each succeeding governor of a pueblo. From 1620 on, metal-tipped canes inscribed with a Spanish cross and adorned with tassels bespoke the authority of that elected official. When Mexico won its independence from Spain in 1821, new staffs, silver-thimbled, were given to the governors. Ten years after the Gadsden Purchase, in 1863, Abraham Lincoln presented the pueblo governors with black ebony canes, silver-crowned and inscribed with his own signature. At any ceremony of a civic nature, the Spanish and Lincoln canes are borne as symbols of authority.

Using a pump drill, a San Felipe Pueblo man, photographed in the early 1880s, demonstrates a turquoise and shell bead drilling technique. He wears a cotton shirt and scarf, a blanket robe, and leather gaiters fastened at the knee.

Jewelry

Jewelry in abundance has been worn by the Puebloans since earliest times; often a family's entire wealth may be on display in the jewelry worn, particularly the silver and turquoise pieces. A favorite necklace has been made of small pieces of turquoise, perforated and smoothed, alternating with larger pieces of shell, the rare shells cherished because they had to be imported from Mexico or California. Ear pendants were and are made in the same fashion. The Navajo "squash blossom" necklace with its pendant *naja* has been a great favorite with the Puebloans. Fetish necklaces, featuring small, exquisitely carved animals of stone (usually birds or bears), have been cherished for their beauty as well as their symbolism. A necklace form unique to the Puebloans, prescribed by the early padres, and sometimes called the "sacred heart" necklace, displayed a large silver double cross of Lorraine and tiny silver beads between smaller silver crosses.

Armor

Although breastplates made of rib bones have been found in archaeological sites of the Archaic period, the Pueblos did not continue such use. However, they

A 1953 watercolor by Santa Clara artist Pablita Velarde shows a young Pueblo girl dressing for her first dance. She wears a black manta, fastened at her right shoulder, and wrapped, white leggings; the two women in attendance wear blouses below their mantas.

sometimes carried shields, two thick pieces of leather stitched together and painted with significant symbols.

Special Costumes

At most ceremonies, men wear white, woven cotton kilts extending from the waist to the knee and overlapping on the right side; the ends are embroidered in black, red, and green. It is tied on with cords, and tassels of colored yarns decorate the lower corners. With the kilt is worn a "rain sash," a long, white, woven cotton sash with long fringes to represent the falling rain. Special ceremonial moccasins are painted blue and feature a strip around each heel adorned with geometic designs created with white porcupine quills and black horsehair. Women wear the black mantas and the "maiden shawls" (white with blue and red borders). *Tabletas,* flat, upright painted plaques of wood, tower above the women dancers' heads. Some authorities say that at the time of death the woman's black manta is reversed on her body so the right shoulder is bared instead of the left. Hair has usually been worn loose at the rituals, as a further symbol of rain; ceremonial wigs of black wool with bangs of wool or natural hair were sometimes worn by the men. The Puebloans have an extensive annual ceremonial calendar with many traditional costumes donned by the participants, especially those worn by the kachinas. It is impossible to give much information here, but the subject has been extensively treated especially by Roediger and Mails.

Garment Decoration

Major decoration was in the weaving, done by Pueblo men; weaves used were plain, tapestry, and various twill weaves. Embroidery done during the weaving process was usually called "brocading" or "false embroidery"; if embroidery was done on the woven fabric itself, it was a woman's task. No painting or dyeing of fabrics seems to have been common, except for a few items of ceremonial wear, and beadwork was rarely created and applied to garments except occasionally in those pueblos in the northern areas. Designs were highly conventionalized and traditional, usually representing natural forms, such as rain, clouds, and lightning.

Face and Body Embellishment

Face and body painting was extensively used in the ceremonials, but not otherwise. The clowns *(koshares)* had huge black and white stripes on their bodies. The "mudheads" painted the entire body a pinkish brown. Other paintings depended on the particular character being impersonated. There was no tattooing among the Pueblos, and no skull deformation except for that brought about inadvertently by the use of hard cradle boards.

Masks

Masks were used to represent gods in the ritual dances. Huge helmet masks fitted over the heads of some participants; others wore half-masks with a fringe of horsehair at the bottom. A white cloth mask with openings for the eyes and mouth was placed on the head of a deceased person, tied around the forehead with a cord.

Transitional Dress

Women dropped the scratchy wool mantas in favor of cotton dresses in the same style. They added white aprons with lace edgings. Men adopted the Anglo dark vest, worn with cotton shirts that hung out over the dark pants or the white cotton pants still worn by many. Some men retain the shoulder-length hair style with the cotton headband. Few chongos are seen today. Sneakers or tennis shoes and other "store-bought" shoes are the usual footwear, although most men like to wear cowboy boots and favor the Western look with cowboy hats and Levi's.

Key Sources

Bandelier, Adolph F. A. and Edgar L. Hewitt. *Indians of the Rio Grande Valley.* Albuquerque: University of New Mexico Press, 1937.

Bedinger, Margery. *Indian Silver: Navajo and Pueblo Jewelers.* Albuquerque: University of New Mexico Press, 1973.

Burr, Alexander Hartley. *Pueblo Indian Painting.* Scottsdale, AZ: Folio, 1980. Reprint of 1932 edition.

Curtis, Edward S. *The North American Indian.* Vols. 12, 17. New York: Johnson Reprint Company, 1970.

Dozier, Edward P. *The Pueblo Indians of North America.* New York: Holt, Rinehart & Winston, 1970.

Dutton, Bertha P. *The Pueblos.* Englewood Cliffs, NJ: Prentice-Hall, 1976.

Fox, Nancy. *Pueblo Weaving and Textile Arts.* Santa Fe: Museum of New Mexico Press, 1978.

Hewett, Edgar Lee, and Bertha P. Dutton. *The Pueblo Indian World.* Albuquerque: University of New Mexico Press, 1945.

Mails, Thomas E. *Pueblo Children of the Earth Mother.* 2 vols. Garden City, NY: Doubleday, 1983.

Ortiz, Alfonso. *The Tewa World.* Chicago: University of Chicago Press, 1969.

Roediger, Virginia More. *Ceremonial Costumes of the Pueblo Indians.* Berkeley: University of California Press, 1991. Reissue of 1941 edition.

Sando, Joe S. *The Pueblo Indians.* San Francisco: Indian Historian Press, 1976.

Stevenson, Matilda Coxe. "Dress and Adornment of the Pueblo Indians." Manuscript No. 2093 in the National Anthropological Archives, Smithsonian Institution, Washington.

Underhill, Ruth. *Pueblo Crafts.* Phoenix, AZ: Pueblo Indian School, 1945.

Wright, Barton. "Tabletas, a Pueblo Art." *American Indian Art Magazine* 1(3): 56–65.

Taos

Taos ("in the village") is the most northern and eastern of the pueblos, with a consequent influence from the Plains culture and the Ute tribes, which can be seen in their garments. The people speak Tiwa, a branch of the Kiowa-Tanoan language family, as do their neighbors of the Picuris pueblo, with whom they share many similarities including costume styles. The high altitude (over 7000 feet) means a short growing season, so they are unable to grow cotton and must get their woven textiles from other pueblos; there is thus little emphasis on agriculture but more hunting and gathering and a preoccupation with horses and cattle. In the nearby Sangre de Cristo Mountains deer have been plentiful, and the Taos people have long had a reputation for producing beautifully tanned hides. Due to the development of the Taos Art Colony in the early years of this century, many artists have painted the colorful Taos people, frequently offering much ethnographic and costume information, despite tendencies toward romanticism.

Men's Basic Dress

Anciently the men of Taos may have dressed like the Anasazi peoples to the west, although it has been difficult to establish their origins. One could assume breechclouts of tanned leather rather than fibers because of the availability of deer in the mountains; later, as commercial cloth became available, heavy flannel was used for breechcloths. They may have worn the woven kilts of the other pueblos, but since they were not weavers, these would have been obtained in trade. Poncho-style shirts of deerskin were typical. Taos men seem to have gone east to the Plains to hunt for buffalo sometime late in the eighteenth century, in the course of which they adopted items of Plains dress. Shirts were made of elk or deer hide with fitted full-length sleeves and the long, fine fringes of the Southern Plains falling from the sleeves; two or three ermine tails as well as fringes hung from the triangular neck flap. Some shirts displayed beaded shoulder and sleeve bands. Thigh-length leather leggings had flaps at the sides with fringes and often a row of beading along the edge of each fringe; commonly a row of tabs was added to the bottom of the cuff.

Women's Basic Dress

Women, too, by the late-eighteenth century were wearing Plains garments—a binary dress with cape sleeves of a square cut, with yellow paint and rows of thongs as decoration. The undulating hem, says Conn, may have reflected the shape of the skins in earlier dresses. By the late nineteenth century, there was a strong movement in the pueblo rejecting outside influences, both Plains and white, with resultant strict regulations as to dress; so the Taos women returned to the Pueblo manta of dark wool, cinched with a belt, often with a cotton dress underneath that covered the otherwise bare left arm and shoulder, a style that continued well into the twentieth century. Some wore the white cotton manta with wool embroidery on the top and bottom edges.

Footwear

The typical men's moccasin was one-piece and hard-soled and had an added fringed tongue; the sole was at times painted black using soapweed mixed with charcoal, at other times left its natural color. Early soles had been of buffalo hide with the hair left on. Men generally wore the Pueblo-type moccasin with the upper dyed rust-colored and fastened with a silver button. The women in all of the pueblos wore the hard-soled boot/moccasin with the wrapped leggings of clay-whitened buckskin attached. The Taos women however, were unique in that the white wrappings were in four or five deep folds, creating a voluminous leg covering (the larger the more prestigious); this folded upper could be unfolded, raised to the thigh, and tied with a cord for protection when horseback riding. This type of boot was worn by the older or married women.

Outer Wear

Heavyweight buffalo robes were winter wear, with lighter weight deer- or elk-skin robes for warmer wear; these robes were occasionally painted and beaded, but the decoration was done by the Ute or Plains Indians rather than the Taos people. Rabbit-skin robes were made aboriginally, a craft that was revived by the women in 1970. Women wore a woolen shawl or blanket, usually obtained from other Puebloans or the Navajo; in addition, a square of cotton or silk cloth was often tied at the front and hung down the back. Before World War II they were wearing silk shawls with deep fringes, most of them imported from Czechoslovakia. The Taos men wore a unique blanket of white, always worn in a characteristic fashion, across the forehead and swathing the entire figure, with the end thrown over the left shoulder; at times the blankets were knotted around the waist. The origin of this white Taos blanket is unknown; it does not seem to have been aboriginal. Later, Navajo blankets or commercial white cloth or sheets have been substituted.

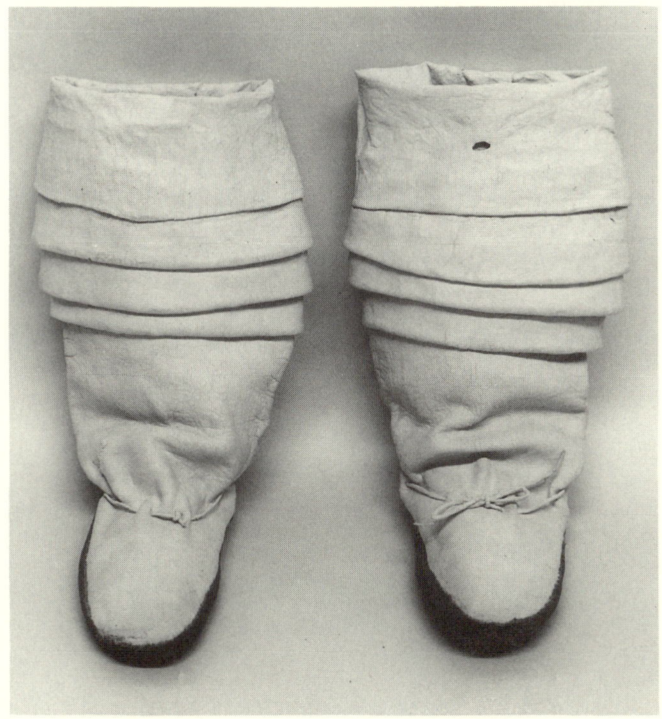

Deerskin boots, made in the mid-1950s, belonged to a married woman of the Taos Pueblo. The soft leather wrappings, here in folds, could be pulled up for riding horseback.

Hair Styles

Women wore the hair banged to the eyebrows in front, cut off at the ears on the sides, and gathered to the back where it was tied in a loose bunch with a cloth or thong; occasionally maidens wore the side whorls common to the western pueblos, but they were not as large or distended. Men, unlike other Puebloans, wore their hair in the Plains style—two braids that were wrapped with bright cloth or even ermine strips.

Headgear

No hats or headbands were worn at Taos except for the use of wreaths of leaves worn during the summer to ward off the heat of the sun. Headdresses were confined to ceremonial wear.

Accessories

Garters and belts were anciently made of leather; woven strips were later obtained in trade from the pueblos to the west, especially from the Hopi. The "canes of office," both Spanish and Lincoln, were a significant part of ceremonies, always carried by the current governor of the pueblo.

Jewelry

Men wore shell gorgets on the chest occasionally. But the Taos people were not workers in metal, so any jewelry they wore was acquired in trade from the Hopi and Navajo to the west; this took the form of bracelets, rings, and silver hoop earrings in this century. Multiple necklaces of shells and pieces of turquoise were often worn. A popular necklace in Taos, as in many of the pueblos, was one with silver crosses and the large double-armed cross of Lorraine pendant at the center. The hair pipe choker of the Plains has been and is still worn today.

Special Costumes

Taos pueblo, because they were not dependent on corn-growing and rain, did not participate in the elaborate ceremonials to be seen in the other pueblos. They celebrated the transferring of the governor's canes on 1 January. They observed many of the saints' days, as was characteristic of all pueblos, during which there were masked dancers in costume, but there was not the rigid ritual to be found in the western pueblos. They did have the clowns, or "chiffonetis" as they were termed in Taos, with the black and white horizontal stripes covering the entire body.

Garment Decoration

Only the Plains-derived garments, which continued to be worn well into the twentieth century, featured such decoration as fringes, beadwork, and painting.

Face and Body Embellishment

Except for the dancers in the ceremonials, no face or body painting was practiced.

Masks

Masks for dancers took the forms of half-masks, full face masks or helmet masks. In Taos, the masks were decorated in a more individualistic manner than elsewhere. As was true in most tribes based on hunting, animals masks were used not only to aid in hunting the prey, but also in such performances as the Deer Dance and the Buffalo Dance.

Transitional Dress

Early in this century the rulers of Taos pueblo enforced strict regulations on dress in an attempt to suppress white influence. Men were not permitted to wear pants purchased from the traders, but a compromise was effected whereby the seat was cut out, creating leggings. Nor were they allowed to wear "store" shoes, but the heels were removed, turning them essentially into moccasins. Furthermore, the Pueblo hair styles of braids for men and the bangs and side-cuts for women were enforced. However, many white articles of dress, such as dark vests and cotton shirts, were more commonly adopted. Frequently the white cotton Mexican pants were worn. Some of the women adopted the "camp dress" of the Apache, with its full cotton skirt and colorful cotton overblouse. Today some semblances of traditional garb may be seen at the ceremonials and festivities, but they are customarily donned by the elders of the pueblo.

Key Sources

Bodine, John J. "Taos Pueblo." In *Handbook of North American Indians. Vol. 9: Southwest.* Pp. 255–267. Washington: Smithsonian Institution.

Parsons, Elsie Clews. *Taos Pueblo.* New York: Johnson Reprint Company, 1971.

Reno, Phillip. *Taos Pueblo.* Chicago: Swallow, 1963.

Roediger, Virginia More. *Ceremonial Costumes of the Pueblo Indians.* Berkeley: University of California Press, 1991. Reissue of 1941 edition.

Trenton, Patricia and Patrick Houlihan. *Native Faces: Indian Cultures in American Art.* Los Angeles: Los Angeles Athletic Club and Southwest Museum, 1984.

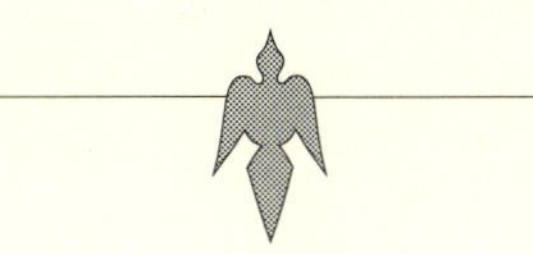

Chapter Five

Costume of the Great Basin

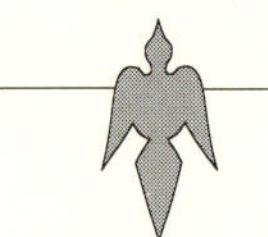

Above: Owens Valley Paiutes wearing ceremonial skirts of magpie feathers and eagle down.
Right: Ute girls played with dolls and learned the elements of design and decoration from them.

A Shoshone man wears his hair in a pompadour. His loop necklace reflects a style borrowed from Plateau costume.

A Shoshone buffalo robe recounts the story of a buffalo hunt.

Great Basin

The Great Basin, lying between the Rocky Mountains to the east and the Sierra Nevada to the west, is an arid land predominantly within the states of Colorado, Utah, and Nevada. There are deserts, spectacular rock formations, mountains, and vast plains with sparse vegetation. Because of the internal drainage, the few rivers, such as the Humboldt, simply sink into the ground. Lakes, such as the Great Salt Lake, are usually saline. Summers are hot and dry, winters bitterly cold. Although the native inhabitants of the Great Basin were frequently described by the whites with the pejorative term "Digger Indians," actually the eking out of a bare subsistence from this forbidding land required great resourcefulness, as well as an extensive knowledge of where and when food could be acquired through gathering and hunting. The land could sustain only a limited population, so the small bands, composed of one or two families, traveled long distances in their annual rounds of seasonal harvesting. Because of the sparse vegetation, the area was lacking in big game; there were only a few antelope or deer, but jackrabbits were abundant, a significant source of food and clothing. In times of famine, the Basin people resorted to insects and reptiles for food. The peoples of the Basin spoke Shoshonean, a branch of the Uto-Aztecan language family. Regarding the dress of these people, there was no Great Basin costume, as such. There were strong influences from the Basketmakers to the south and east in the Four Corners area and from the Fremont culture in Utah and northwestern Colorado. But clothing remained unchanged for centuries, until the horse appeared, and some of the eastern tribes, like the Ute, adopted some of the Plains modes of life.

Peoples of the Great Basin

Bannock
Gosiute
Mono
Northern Paiute, p. 191
Panamint
Shoshone, p. 193
Southern Paiute, p. 197
Washo
Ute, p. 200

General Dress

Men's Basic Dress

In summer men and children went naked in the searing heat. In winter, men wore a breechclout or a kilt, and roughly wrapped leggings of crudely tanned deerskin when available. Usually, however, they were dependent upon garments woven of grass or shredded bark. Tunics were sometimes made of woven rabbit-skin robes, hip-length and belted.

Women's Basic Dress

In summer, women wore an apron in front fastened to a braided belt or cord; this was made of buckskin, if available, or strips of sagebrush, juniper bark, or yucca fibers; if not in strips, the fibers were woven. In cooler weather, two aprons were worn, in front and back, and a crude poncho or tunic would be added. When available, buckskin was fashioned into long dresses with fringes at the bottom and at the ends of the sleeves. Iridescent magpie feathers and shell pendants at times added their beauty to the skirts.

Footwear

Usually the Basin peoples went barefoot, but footwear was necessary at times. Anciently it was of two basic materials, fiber or leather. Sandals were made of twisted sagebrush bark, yucca leaves, or other fibers in a plain weave or open-twined weave. These sometimes had an inner sole, and were tied to the foot with thongs in various ways. Ancient moccasins of leather sometimes took the form of "hock" moccasins, in which the hock of the animal's leg (a bison, if possible) was removed in the form of a tube, and one end sewed to form the toe; thongs were tied around the ankle to keep the moccasin in place. A second form was the Fremont moccasin, made from three pieces cut from the foreleg of a deer or antelope; one piece was cut in the shape of a sole; the second, longer piece was sewn to the sole, folded back, and sewn on one side to the sole again, back to the heel. The third piece was attached at the heel, along the sole, and to the second piece at the front. Dewclaws on the soles acted as hobnails for traction, and thongs were used as fastenings. A third type of leather moccasin was a one-piece affair, sewn up the front to the instep and up the heel; these had a separate outer sole attached and often cuffs pulled up for leggings. When horses entered the Basin, moccasins with rawhide soles were made similar to those of the southern Plains. Snowshoes, for use in the mountain snows, were simple affairs, round or oval with a fiber netting.

Outer Wear

Warm outer garments were necessary for protection against the bitter cold of winter. A buffalo robe, no matter how worn or moth-eaten, was treated as a rare treasure. But reliance was placed on the rabbit-skin robe; these robes were found almost everywhere on the North American continent, but they were of the greatest importance in the Basin because it was almost the only animal fur regularly available to them. The pelt was cut spirally into long strips and woven into a warm, but fragile, lightweight robe; the weaving was done on a frame of two parallel poles placed a few inches above the ground. It required as many as 100 rabbit pelts to make one man's robe. Robes were occasionally made of other materials. Anciently, there had been feather mantles, like those of the Basketmakers. Some robes were woven of cedar-bark strips, some of the feathered skins of ducks or other waterfowl; others were of woodchuck, beaver, or other small animal hides, even of meadow-mouse skins, sewn together into blankets.

Hair Styles

Little was done with the hair. The men wore it long. The women brought it forward over the shoulders and tied it with cords. The eastern tribes, such as the Ute and the Bannock, influenced by the Plains, wore the hair in braids, the men often wrapping them in otter fur.

Headgear

The Basin people went bareheaded most of the time; however, in winter it is said they donned crude caps made of fur. The women of the tribes marginal to the California culture, such as the Northern Paiute, occasionally wore the basket hats of that area; the Basin basket hat tended to be shallower than those to the west, and often ended in a little peak at the top.

Accessories

These wandering people had few accessories. A few woven belts and sashes were done in the Basketmaker tradition, and a few belts were made of leather. Some pouches of buckskin were made, but they were unornamented as a rule. The Ute and Shoshone adopted some of the Plains accessories.

Jewelry
Ear pendants and necklaces were made of stone, shells, bones, seeds, and feathers. The shells, such as olivella and abalone, were obtained through a casual trade network from the Pacific coast. Obsidian, made into bangles and pendants, came from the Northwest and turquoise was obtained from the mines in Arizona.

Armor
Historically, armor is unknown in the region, but there is archaeological evidence for the use of large, decorated shields in the Fremont complex of Utah (A.D. 550–1450).

Garment Decoration
Decoration was simple—a few pendants, feathers, or shells sewn on garments. The Ute and Shoshone, marginal to the Plains, adopted beadwork in the nineteenth century; the Ute did especially fine work with this material.

Transitional Dress
By the late eighteenth century, the eastern tribes were adopting Plains garments as well as elements of Anglo dress. The tribes in the center of the Basin maintained their traditional culture until the appearance of emigrants in the 1840s. By 1875 they were forced onto reservations and by the end of the century had adjusted almost completely to European-style clothing.

The Shoshone and Bannock are closely related, are marginal to the Plateau, and will be treated here together. The Mono, Panamint, and Washo groups are discussed in the chapter on California.

Northern Paiute

The Paiute (the name is said to mean "Water Ute" or "True Ute") consisted of the Northern Paiute (sometimes called Paviotsos) and Southern Paiute. The former spoke Northern Paiute, a form of Shoshonean, a branch of the Uto-Aztecan language family. They seem to have come into the area as late as A.D. 1000. They lived in a vast area of western Nevada to the Sierra Nevadas and north into Oregon; they included the Mono and Owens Valley Paiute of California (who, however, were more attuned to the California culture), all of whom were related linguistically. The small family groups were seminomadic and lived by hunting, fishing, and mainly gathering; they were generally called by the name of their major food resource, such as "pine nut eaters," "fish eaters," or "sheep eaters." The horse was introduced into the area in the late eighteenth century, and mounted bands practiced raiding. In the mid-1800s the Northern Paiute were overrun by miners and settlers, who destroyed their subsistence resources. By the 1860s they were forced into reservation life and a wage-labor economy.

Men's Basic Dress
In summer, men went naked or wore a breechclout either of tanned leather, with fringed flaps fore and aft, or of twined sagebrush bark. A shirt was added in cooler weather; this might be made of one piece of skin in a poncho style seamed at the sides, or of two skins with side seams and shoulder seams, and was often fringed at the bottom. Preferred hides were those of deer, antelope, or bighorn sheep, but some use was made of bobcat, marmot, or coyote hides. Other materials were used for shirts, such as rabbit skins, twined bark, or braided tule grass. Leggings were made of strips of buckskin, bark, or badger pelts, reaching to the knees or higher.

Women's Basic Dress
In warm weather women wore a knee-length apron suspended from a belt in front, or a double apron, using such materials as twined sagebrush bark or the skin of the coyote, rabbit, deer, or badger. A short cape or poncho was worn with the apron as necessary. In cooler weather, dresses were worn; these were ankle-length, belted, often with bell-shaped sleeves, and sometimes ornamented with plain fringes. In the northern areas they were of buckskin; in the marsh areas, grasses such as tule were used. In some sections, the skins of coots or other ducks were twisted into strands, to be twined and formed into fringe or woven garments. In the southern part of the area the Northern Paiute used shredded sagebrush bark.

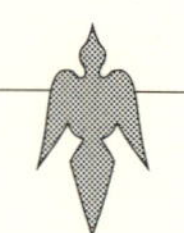

Knee-length leggings were made of material available. By the mid-nineteenth century the women were adopting the two-skin dress of the Plains, with the undulating yoke and the attached deer tail.

Footwear
In areas where deer were abundant, moccasins were made of buckskin, either one-piece or two-piece, the only decoration being short fringes; men's moccasins were ankle-high, the women's higher than that in the winter. Sagebrush bark was twined or braided to make sandals for summer or overshoes for winter. In the mountain areas, snowshoes were necessary for winter travel. Rabbit-skin socks and badger-skin boots were also reported as winter wear.

Outer Wear
The abundant rabbits furnished the most readily available fur for the Paiute, the only drawbacks being that rabbit robes attracted vermin and wore out quickly. The skin was cut spirally into a strip 10 to 15 feet long that was dried so that it twisted into a fur rope. Using hemp or other native cordage as warp, the men wove the rabbit strips into large pieces for robes or smaller ones for capes or other garments; the simple loom was made of two to four willow sticks fastened horizontally to the ground with stakes. Other animal furs were used for robes, but they were scarce and the Paiute had to depend upon the rabbit.

Hair Styles
Hair was worn loose and flowing. By the 1880s some of the Northern Paiute had adopted the Plains style of two braids, especially the men, who sometimes attached shell ornaments to the braids. But most left the hair uncut. Women at times used a thong to hold the hair in place.

Headgear
With their superb skill in basketry, the women made fine basket hats, similar to those of California; these were useful not only to keep a tumpline from chafing when carrying heavy loads, but also to protect the head from pitch when harvesting pine nuts. Basin hats were typically shallower and less decorated than those of California or the Plateau. Winter hats for the men were made of coyote, badger, or any kind of fur available; these were ornamented with the topknots of quail or other feathers. Both sexes wore headbands of skin, sagebrush bark, or tule.

Accessories
Belts of fur strips, leather, or braided fibers were worn by both sexes. Pouches and bags for transporting necessary articles were of leather with drawstrings or woven of fibers. In the late nineteenth century the women learned beadwork from the Plains people, and beaded strips in simple geometric designs appeared as decoration on dresses, cradle boards, bags, and hats.

Jewelry
Necklaces of shell and bone beads were worn for special occasions. Some acquired the California custom of using white disk shell beads as a medium of exchange. Shell and stone pendants hung from pierced ears.

Special Costumes
The "War" Dance of the Walker River Northern Paiute featured participants wearing kilts fashioned from fur strips or feathers, magpie-feather caps with head rings made of eagle down, and lavish face and body painting.

Garment Decoration
Occasionally paint in solid colors was applied to parts of garments, or pendants were attached. Later, beaded strips were used as decoration. Although proficient basketmakers, the Northern Paiute did no weaving except for the hats and the crudely woven sagebrush-bark garments.

Face and Body Embellishment
Body and face paint was worn at ceremonial gatherings, especially dances; colors were red, black, yellow, and white, made from ochers and clays. Some simple tattooing was practiced, such as lines on the face.

Transitional Dress
Although the Paiute resisted white culture and encroachment, by the late nineteenth century they were wearing blankets of the Pendleton type, long "pioneer" dresses, scarves on the head or neck, felt hats, and, finally, "store" shoes.

Key Sources

Davis, Emma Lou. "An Ethnography of the Kuzedika Paiute of Mono Lake, Mono County, California." University of Utah *Anthropological Papers* 75, *Miscellaneous Papers* 8: 1–55.

Euler, Robert C. *The Paiute People.* Phoenix, AZ: Indian Tribal Series, 1972.

Fowler, Catherine S. and Sven Liljeblad. "Northern Paiute." In *Handbook of North American Indians. Vol. 11: Great Basin.* Pp. 435–465. Washington: Smithsonian Institution.

Gifford, Edward W. "The Northfork Mono." University of California *Publications in American Archaeology and Ethnology* 31(2): 15–65.

Riddell, Francis A. "Honey Lake Paiute Ethnography." Nevada State Museum *Anthropological Papers* 4.

Steward, Julian H. "Ethnography of the Owens Valley Paiute." University of California *Publications in American Archaeology and Ethnology* 33(3): 233–350.

Steward, Julian H. and Erminie Wheeler-Voegelin. "The Northern Paiute Indians." In *American Indian Ethnohistory: California and Basin-Plateau Indians.* New York: Garland, 1974.

Stewart, Omer C. "Culture Element Distributions, XIV: Northern Paiute." University of California *Anthropological Records* 4(3): 361–446.

Wheat, Margaret M. "Notes on Paviotso Material Culture." Nevada State Museum *Anthropological Papers.*

Shoshone

Shoshonean speakers of the Uto-Aztecan linguistic family, the Shoshone were marginal to the southern Plateau and to the Plains. There were three general groups: (1) The Western Shoshone, of central and northeastern Nevada and adjacent Utah, were Indians of the Basin culture, continuing with their traditional lifeways until recent times; they were unskilled in tanning, were poorly armed, and had no horses. The Gosiute of northwestern Utah were considered Western Shoshone. (2) The Northern Shoshone of southern Idaho were rich in horses and exhibited Plains influence after 1800. Sacajawea, the woman who aided Lewis and Clark in their 1805 expedition, was a Northern Shoshone. The Bannock, a detached band of Northern Paiute, joined the group and despite language differences settled in comfortably with them. (3) The Eastern Shoshone of western Wyoming were strongly influenced by the Plains material culture; they had early traveled to the Plains on foot and by 1700 had acquired horses and adopted Plains dress. About that time the Comanche had split off from these people and settled on the Plains. Lewis and Clark described the Shoshone as rather short with broad faces and dark complexions. They, along with the Comanche, were called Snake Indians by many tribes and the whites. Lewis and Clark gave much information on the Shoshone in their journals. Lowie (1909) and Steward (1938) have been the significant contemporary sources concerning these people.

Men's Basic Dress

In the hot Basin summers, the men went naked or wore a breechclout of woven fiber, skin, or fur. In cooler weather leggings and a shirt were added. The thigh-length shirts were of antelope, bighorn, deer, or, rarely, elk hide. Particularly in the eastern and northern areas they featured underarm and side-seam fringes; the bottom retained the forelegs of the animal, and often displayed quillworked shoulder bands. Leggings were thigh-length and instead of fringes had flaps at the sides. They were of skin, especially antelope, close fitting, and often had a rectangular piece of contrasting color with two square panels sewn on at the bottom. Lacking skin, the leggings were of woven sagebrush or juniper bark.

Women's Basic Dress

In summer, an apron of skin or woven fibers, such as sagebrush or juniper, sufficed; a back apron might be added. A calf-length gown with elbow-length sleeves was worn as the weather became cooler; this was either made of two skins or of woven fibers and was belted. The sleeves were only partially fastened and the waist side seams were left open, particularly for nursing mothers. The dress was ornamented with such items as rows of thongs, feathers, hooves, bird claws, elk teeth, or cowrie shells. Bodmer has left us a painting of a Snake or Shoshone woman wearing a

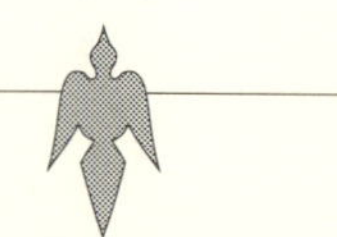

A Shoshone man, his hair in a pompadour, holds a revolver. He wears a breechcloth, metal armbands, and a loop necklace.

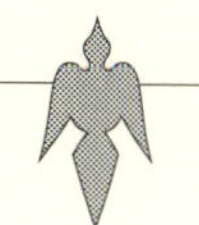

dress featuring strips of light-blue and white pony beadwork down the sleeves and around the neck; the deer tail is retained. Frequently the dresses had little square patches of red trade cloth edged round with beads at the hem. Later in the nineteenth century the three-skin dress was adopted. Southern and Western Shoshone women continued to wear the traditional Basin garments. Knee-length leggings were gartered.

Footwear

Most Shoshone men and women went barefoot for much of the year. Moccasins, when worn, were of the one-piece soft-sole type with a seam along the outer edge, and were made of deer, elk, or buffalo hide; some were attached to rawhide soles. In the winter moccasins were of hide with the hair left on, and grass or fur was stuffed inside for warmth. Some moccasins were of twined sagebrush bark or of fur. Dandies liked to cover the moccasin with the skin of the polecat, leaving the tail to trail at the back. In the late 1800s, women often wore high-top moccasins, like the boot of the Southern Plains, decorated with tin cones and beadwork. Snowshoes were round or oval shape with a netting of fiber and thongs at the center to attach the foot.

Outer Wear

The rabbit-skin robe was the most common outer wrap; it was usually woven of strips cut spirally from the rabbit pelt; sometimes the skins were sewn together, as was true also of the skins of beaver, marmot, and other small animals. Winter robes were also created from bighorn, deer, or antelope hides; a buffalo hide, when available, made a highly treasured robe that often had a beaded blanket strip across it, in the manner of the Crow or Cheyenne Indians. Dressed elk hide with the hair removed made a summer robe. The Western Shoshone, lacking in animal hides, had to depend on rabbit-skin robes or those of twined sagebrush bark. Lewis and Clark tell about a "tippet" worn by the Shoshone women, the "most elegant article" they had ever seen; this seems to have been a cape with a collar of otter fur and suspended from it 100 or more rolls of ermine fur reaching to the waist. By 1900 Pendleton blankets had replaced the robes of native manufacture.

Hair Styles

Men wore the hair in various styles, such as the pompadour; the forelock; two braids wrapped in otter fur or, later, cloth; hanging loose with bangs on the forehead; or two small braids at each side in front, the rest loose. Women let the hair hang loose as a rule; in the nineteenth century they adopted the two braids of the Plains women. The hair was cut short as a sign of mourning.

Headgear

The women in areas near California wore the typical round basketry hat, while in those areas closer to the Plateau they wore the higher basketry hat of that region. The Western Shoshone women wore helmets or hats of twined sagebrush bark or willow. Men usually went bareheaded, but in the mid-nineteenth century they adopted headdresses characteristic of the Plains tribes. The warbonnet, with its beaded headband and "halo" or "stand-up" circle of eagle feathers with cloth trailers (some with a forked trailer), was worn for special occasions. Other feathers, such as red-tailed hawk, magpie, swan, or even peacock (acquired from the traders), adorned the headdresses. Horns and ermine tails were further embellishments. Some men wore a strip of otter fur around the head. Fur hats provided warmth in the wintertime.

Accessories

Accessories were many, especially in the northern and eastern areas. Buckskin bags and pouches were painted with geometric designs, later beaded. Armlets of fur, iron, or brass were worn above the elbow. Cloth neckerchiefs were held in place with an abalone-shell ornament. Some men, late in the nineteenth century, wore hairpipe breastplates and carried beaded bandolier bags. Painted rawhide visors were fastened with thongs tied under the chin. Lewis and Clark mentioned collars of twisted sweetgrass ornamented with porcupine quills, or of shells or elk teeth. Belts worn by both sexes were of fur or leather. Some snow goggles were constructed of rawhide.

Jewelry

Necklaces of various types were treasured. Anciently, tubular beads of bone or animal teeth, especially elk teeth, were most popular. The claws of the brown bear were strung on a thong interspersed with beads. The loop necklace consisted of many strands of beads attached to rawhide sidebars. Chokers were made of hairpipe beads. Both sexes pierced the ears in order to suspend clusters of beads or pieces of abalone shell. Hair ornaments were also of abalone, or of other shells. Some men pierced the nasal septum to insert a bone nose pin, but the custom died out after European contact. Lewis and Clark commented on the amount of metal the Shoshone used for ornament, such as bracelets of iron, copper, tin, or brass; pewter buttons; and earrings, brooches, and other ornaments constructed of sheet copper, brass, or wire. Toward the end of the century pectoral ornaments of German silver, especially in crescent-like forms, were popular with the men.

Armor

The Sioux called the Shoshone "Big Shields" because, before the advent of horses, the warriors fought behind huge shields that completely covered them; in battle, the men faced the enemy with the shields touching each other, forming an unbroken wall. The shields, made of tough buffalo hide, were round and

A Shoshone buffalo robe records a bison hunt.

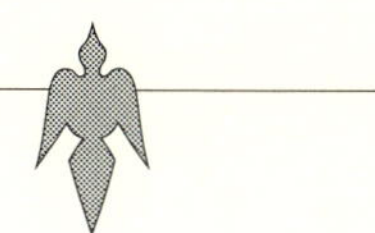

had a painted buckskin cover. The warrior wore a leather tunic—a sleeveless shirt made of six layers of antelope hide; between the layers was often spread a mixture of sand and glue held in place by quilting. This armor was well-nigh impervious to arrows, but as guns spread across the Plains, the Plateau, and the Basin, the armor fell into disuse and had disappeared by 1805.

Special Costumes

The Grass Dance of the Plains was known as the Wolf Dance among the Shoshone; the dancers painted bears or snakes on their torsos, and wore costumes that were heavily beaded—kilts, bandolier bags, moccasins, breechclouts, and leggings—richly decorated with feathers of all kinds. Dancers of the Sun Dance (adopted 1890) painted a buffalo on the torso. Women in the Scalp Dance were privileged to wear, for this one occasion, an article of male attire—the huge halo warbonnet. Mourning was indicated by cutting the hair, gashing the legs, and, in the case of women, blackening the face and even the torso with tar or pitch.

Garment Decoration

Fringes, rows of thongs, and porcupine quillwork were the most common forms of decoration before Plains influence set in, at which time the women began to create beadwork using both the overlay and lazy-stitch techniques; they were fond of blue-gray beads, and late in the nineteenth century worked in floral patterns. Tin tinklers and silver medallions were also acquired later through trade.

Face and Body Embellishment

For special occasions the face was painted, the pigments being mixed with marrow, and the hair daubed with red or white clay; this painting was quite complex and symbolic with its realistic representations of snakes, bears, painted hands, wavy lines, horseshoes, and other designs. Faces were blackened for war. Women were frequently tattooed on the chin; however, both sexes might be tattooed on the face, arms, and legs.

Transitional Dress

With cloth available, dresses, leggings, breechcloths, and shirts were made of strouding, calico, broadcloth, and other types of fabric. In the early twentieth century Anglo store clothes were purchased. Women wore cotton headscarves and fringed plaid shawls with their long skirts or dresses. Pendleton blankets from the mill in Oregon were worn by almost all the Shohones. The men adopted the tall "Indian hat" of black or white felt. Gauntlets with heavily beaded and fringed cuffs were worn, but were mainly created as items for trade.

Key Sources

D'Azevedo, Warren L., ed. *Handbook of North American Indians. Vol. 11: Great Basin.* Washington: Smithsonian Institution, 1986.

Feder, Norman. "Shoshone Split-Horn Bonnet." *American Indian Hobbyist* 6(3, 4).

Lowie, Robert H. "The Northern Shoshone. American Museum of Natural History *Anthropological Papers* 2(2): 165–306.

———. "Notes on Shoshonean Ethnography." American Museum of Natural History *Anthropological Papers* 20(3): 185–314.

Madsen, Brigham D. *The Northern Shoshone.* Caldwell, ID: Caxton, 1980.

Malouf, Carling. "The Gosiute Indians." University of Utah *Anthropological Papers* 3.

Murphy, Robert F. and Yolanda Murphy. "Shoshone-Bannock Subsistence and Society." University of California *Anthropological Records* 16(7).

Steward, Julian H. "Culture Element Distributions, XIII: Nevada Shoshone." University of California *Anthropological Records* 4(2): 209–360.

———. "Culture Element Distributions, XXIII: Northern and Gosiute Shoshoni." University of California *Anthropological Records* 8(3): 263–292.

Trenholm, Virginia C. and Maurine Carley. *The Shoshonis: Sentinels of the Rockies.* Norman: University of Oklahoma Press, 1964.

Southern Paiute

The Southern Paiute were Shoshonean speakers of the Uto-Aztecan language family. They inhabited the arid mountains and deserts of southern Utah and southern Nevada into California; they included the Kaibab Paiute north of the Grand Canyon and the

Chemehuevis of California, who were strongly influenced by the Mojave. The Southern Paiute were not a tribe but were rather small groups of extended families foraging for the limited plant foods of the area; they practiced some agriculture. Aside from the ubiquitous rabbits, there was little game available to them. The coming of the Mormons into the area in 1847 had negative effects, for their subsistence food was destroyed with cattle grazing and agriculture by the settlers, and by 1869 they had been placed by the government on a reservation. John Wesley Powell and the photographer John K. Hillers (1873) recorded valuable information on the group; the major contemporary source has been Julian H. Steward.

Men's Basic Dress

Breechclouts were made in the simple apron style or as wraparound kilts; these were of twined sagebrush bark. Deerskin was also used for this purpose, but it seems not to have been aboriginal. Shirts were poncho-style of the same materials, as were leggings for cooler weather. By the early nineteenth ccentury, the Plains influence had reached the Southern Paiute, as shown by the use of fringe on the buckskin shirts and leggings. Later in the century some beadwork was applied, but it was minimal.

Two Paiutes, dressed for cool weather, wear belted leather dresses with bell-shaped sleeves, characteric of the Great Basin. Warm weather attire was a knee-length apron suspended from a belt. Skilled in basketry, they wove hats and utilitarian items for gathering and storing seeds, nuts, and edible roots.

Women's Basic Dress

Women wore the apron of twined sagebrush bark, of deerskin when available, or of rabbit fur; if desired, a back apron was added. Dresses were made of twined willow or sagebrush bark. By the nineteenth century calf-length dresses for cooler weather were made of two deerskins, folded into a yoke at the top, with bell-shaped sleeves added if the skins were small, and with the bottom left uneven; a leather belt or thong held the dress in place. Later, small fringes were added to the skirt hems, down the side seams, and at the underarm seams and ends; sometimes narrow beaded strips decorated the sleeves. Knee-length leggings, commonly of twined sagebrush bark, were kept in place with garters.

Footwear

Usually the Southern Paiute went barefoot, but in rough terrain and colder weather they wore sandals of bark or yucca fibers; these were made with twining or braiding techniques. In the southwestern part of the area, some wore rawhide sandals, probably copied from the Yuma. Simple foot mittens or socks of badger or squirrel skins kept the feet warm in winter; also, for use in snow, a sole made of a slab of the inner wood of the Joshua tree was added to the sandals. With the Plains influence from their neighbors, the Ute, they later began to wear buckskin moccasins with a welted toe seam and a tongue.

Outer Wear

Throughout the Basin both sexes wore the rabbit-skin robe; the pelt was cut spirally into thin strips that were dried and twisted to be used as weft in the weaving of the blankets. Warp was made of fiber cordage. Capes were also made of a single deerskin, or of the pelts of small animals sewn together.

Hair Styles

Both sexes commonly wore the hair loose with a center part, sometimes held in place with a thong; occasionally the front hair was cut into bangs. In the southwestern area, some men affected the Mojave style of long ropes or rolls. Later, braids were adopted by a few. For special occasions, eagle down or one or more upright eagle feathers adorned the hair.

Headgear

The Southern Paiute women were fine basketmakers, and their basket hats were much prized by other tribes; these hats were rounded or of a mammiform shape, and were made in a twining technique. Men wore skin caps embellished with magpie or red-tailed hawk feathers, or a tuft of quail topknots.

Accessories

Accessories were few among these nomadic people. A few drawstring pouches of deerskin or bags of twined sagebrush bark sufficed to carry sewing or painting equipment. Belts were thongs or strips of leather.

Jewelry

Jewelry, also, was minimal. Ears were pierced, not so much for earrings as to assure longevity and a proper crossing after death into the spirit world. A few shell or bone beads created necklaces or earrings. Some men in the western areas pierced the nasal septum for the wearing of a bone, shell, or turquoise ornament.

Garment Decoration

Aside from the later use of small fringes and a few beaded strips, clothing was largely undecorated.

Face and Body Embellishment

The face was painted black and the hair red for combat. Red paint was also applied to the face and body for special situations, such as the birth of a child, a girl's first menstruation, and festivals. A few

Paiute men of California's Owens Valley wear ceremonial skirts of magpie feathers and twisted eagle down for a dance staged in 1932. Their headdresses are made of magpie feathers with a ring of eagle down. Three dancers wear moccasins, a Plains influence, while the fourth, right, wears sandals.

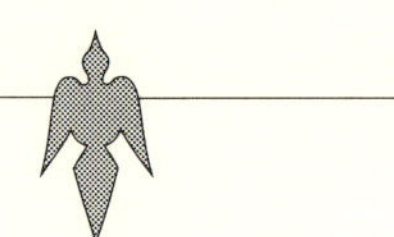

groups practiced tattooing on the face, but rarely on the body.

Transitional Dress

Although the nineteenth century brought the Plains influence in matters of dress, this was short-lived; with the influx of Mormons and other settlers, the Southern Paiute became more and more accustomed to the dress of the whites, and by 1900, there was little of traditional dress remaining.

Key Sources

Clements, Lydia. *Indians of Death Valley.* Hollywood, CA: Cloister, 1975.

Driver, Harold E. "Cultural Element Distributions, VI: Southern Sierra Nevada." University of California *Anthropological Records* 1(2).

Euler, Robert C. *The Paiute People.* Phoenix, AZ: Indian Tribal Series, 1972.

Euler, Robert C. and Catherine S. Fowler. "Southern Paiute Ethnohistory." University of Utah *Anthropological Papers* 78.

Kelly, Isabel T. "Southern Paiute Ethnography." Glen Canyon Series 21. University of Utah *Anthropological Papers* 69.

Kelly, Isabel T. and Catherine S. Fowler. "Southern Paiute." In *Handbook of North American Indians. Vol. 11: Great Basin.* Washington: Smithsonian Institution.

Manners, Robert A. "Southern Paiute and Chemehuevi: An Ethnohistorical Report." In *American Indian Ethnohistory: California and Basin-Plateau Indians.* New York: Garland, 1974.

Stewart, Omer C. "Culture Element Distributions, XVIII: Ute-Southern Paiute." University of California *Anthropological Records* 6(4): 231–356.

Wallace, William J. and Edith T. Wallace. *Desert Foragers and Hunters: Indians of the Death Valley Region.* Ramona, CA: Acoma Books, 1979.

Ute

The Ute ("Blue Sky People" or "Rulers of the Shining Mountains") were an important division of the Shoshonean speakers of the Uto-Aztecan language family, closely related to the Paiute and the Bannock. There were three major divisions: (1) the Uncompahgre of southern Colorado, (2) the White River Ute of northern Colorado, and (3) the Uintah of eastern Utah. Basically hunters (antelope, rabbits, deer, and elk) and gatherers (roots and seeds), they practiced little agriculture. They were skillful traders, especially adept at tanning and selling fine deerskins. First European contact was with the Spaniards in 1626, and by 1680 they had acquired horses, one of the first Indian tribes to do so, becoming noted horsemen and horse breeders. By 1800 they were traveling out on the Plains to hunt bison, but never settled there. With the arrival of many settlers in the mid-nineteenth century, and the gold miners in Colorado in the 1860s, they were pushed out of their high-country territories. Although quite removed from other tribes, they had close relations with the Jicarilla Apache of New Mexico. Their dress reflected their Great Basin background as well as Plains and Southwestern characteristics.

Men's Basic Dress

Aboriginally, the men had worn a short breechclout of native tanned leather with flaps in the front and rear. The Uintah of Utah also wore breechclouts of woven fibers such as sagebrush bark. In the mid-nineteenth century, the Ute wore breechcloths of commercial cloth, very long, ankle-length, usually dark, with a light-colored band at the bottom. Some were only knee-length. Early shirts were simple poncho-type garments of tanned leather; after 1800, the Ute copied the Plains attire, wearing buckskin shirts that were usually shorter than the Plains shirts and had long fringes under the arms in bunches in the Southern Plains style. Wide, beaded shoulder bands and beaded bands down the sleeves further duplicated Plains shirts, as did the long, triangular neck flaps, also fringed. Later cloth shirts, dark, white, or plaid, were similarly decorated with beaded bands and hung down to the mid-thighs. Late in the 1800s some of the men wore a biblike affair adorned with embroidery or beadwork. Thigh-length deerskin leggings (some snug-fitting, some loose), commonly had flaps at the sides, although some were fringed on the lower half of the flap and were cut square across the bottom. Some leggings had war exploits painted on the flaps, and others had a row of brass tacks or

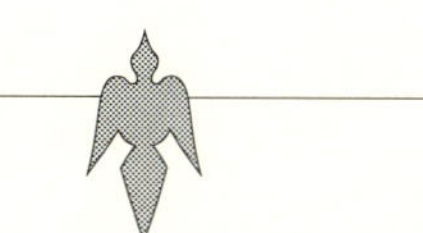

Utes photographed in 1874 wear finery that includes, for the man standing, sixteen German silver hair plates and fringed leggings with beaded panels. The seated Ute, a Hudson's Bay Company type blanket robe draped about him, has a beaded strip over his left shoulder, a large neckpiece, and a hairpipe-bead necklace.

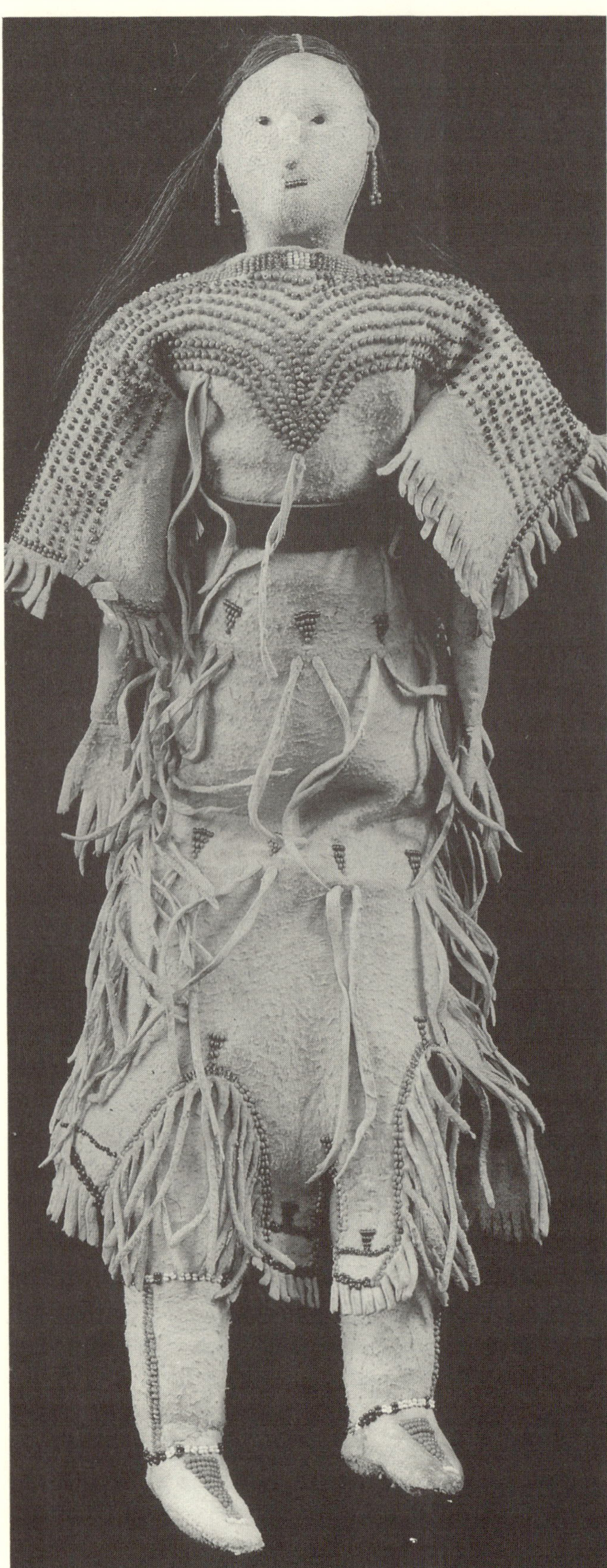

A Ute doll, just over 18 inches tall, has a fringed dress with a heavily beaded shoulder yoke. Girls played with such dolls and learned crafts necessary for making garments.

bells down the sides. The skin leggings were later converted to trousers by the addition of a seat of native tanned leather.

Women's Basic Dress

Women in summer wore short skirts or aprons of shredded sagebrush bark or, in the eastern areas where deer were abundant, they wore wraparound skirts or dresses of native tanned leather. Preferably of doeskin, although antelope or mountain-sheep hide were acceptable, the dresses were constructed of two skins with a folded-over yoke at the top. Like the Plains dresses that they were copying, these retained the deer-tail dip in the yoke. Later in the nineteenth century, the women adopted the three-skin dress, with the folded-over yoke sewn to a two-piece skirt. With the wraparound skirt mentioned above, the women sometimes wore a poncho-like top of deerskin or, in the western areas, a top covering of sagebrush and tule fibers. With the acquisition of commercial cloth, the women made dresses in the traditional patterns; in the west they reflected the bell-shaped sleeves, in the east they copied the yoked style. With the yoked dresses, they wore long-sleeved printed-cotton blouses. Wide belts were customary. Half-leggings of deerskin were tied at the knees and decorated with brass bells down the sides or with fringes.

Footwear

Most Ute went barefoot, but when traveling in rough terrain or in cold weather, they wore sandals of yucca fiber or simple soft-soled buckskin moccasins. After they became horsemen, particularly the eastern Ute, they adopted the two-piece Plains moccasins with the soles of buffalo hide or rawhide, and uppers of elk or deer hide; a long, narrow tongue was either sewn on or omitted. Muskrat or beaver insoles and sagebrush stockings provided warmth for winter. Moccasins were beaded with simple designs of squares, triangles, stepped triangles, or zigzags, often with the buffalo-hoof design on the front. Later beadwork was of a floral nature. The cuffs were not beaded as a rule. The snowshoe, so important in this mountain environment, was a circle of bent wood with a netting of rawhide thongs, which still retained the fur and loops for anchoring the foot to the frame.

Outer Wear

Ute robes, like those of the Plains, were of bear, elk, or buffalo hides; lighter weight robes were of deerskin. Often a beaded strip with beaded rosettes adorned the center of the robe. The Uintah and other western Ute made the rabbit-skin robes of strips of rabbit pelt woven into a wrap or covering that was fragile but very warm; this was done in a simple cross weave on a crude two-bar frame. Later, blankets from the traders were adopted—plaid or striped, mainly from the Pendleton Mills of Oregon. The women wore shawls with deep fringes. By 1900, the Ute men were favoring buckskin fringed jackets with a front opening.

Hair Styles

Men wore the hair loose, braided, or in "clumps"; it was often parted on the side rather than the center, and frequently combed up in a pompadour. The braids were often wrapped with strips of otter fur. During the late 1800s, men encased the clumps of hair or braids in white beaded cylinders or hair tubes. Women wore the hair loose and flowing or in two braids. A few men sported sparse mustaches.

Headgear

Commonly the Ute went bareheaded, but the men wore winter caps of beaver or weasel pelts. A rawhide visor was worn as an eye shield in the bright sunlight. A few men adopted the warbonnet headdress of the Plains in the late nineteenth century, but they did not attach the symbolic significance to the feathers that their Plains neighbors did; headdresses had the characteristic long cloth trailers with feathers, and some included buffalo horns. Also about that time they were wearing the Mexican sombrero or the tall, flat-brimmed "Indian hat." At the Denver Exposition of 1882, a few Ute men proudly wore silk top hats. Some men wore a cluster of feathers on the top of the head, and occasionally women wore a feather or two in the hair. A few women in the western or northern areas wore woven basket hats, which featured colored designs as a product of the weaving, not as false embroidery or pigment appplication.

Accessories

Accessories were abundant, especially with the eastern groups. Hairpipe breastplates were popular after the 1870s; some, which may have been constructed earlier, had large glass beads strung on thongs instead of the hairpipe beads. Wide leather belts, often four or five inches wide, were worn by the women late in the century; these belts were embellished with large silver conchas or brass tacks in geometric designs. Some leather straps were painted; braided belts were also worn. Bags of various types were carried or attached to a belt; these ranged from small buckskin drawstring pouches for carrying paint and other sundries to very long, elaborately beaded bandolier bags slung over the shoulder; the latter, of buckskin or strouding, were adopted by the men in the 1870s and by the women after 1900. Fur bands encircled the ankles or the elbows, often with feathers attached. Some men wore hair plate bands, long strips of leather with medallions of brass or tin attached, hanging from the back of the head; after 1860, the medallions were made of German silver. Some of these hair ornaments were so long they trailed on the ground.

Jewelry

The most popular necklace was the choker of pipe beads or dentalium shells interspersed with glass beads. Some neck ornaments were of hairpipe beads

A Ute family, photographed in 1915, wears a mix of traditional and European-style clothing. The woman carries a cradleboard on her back.

in rows; these were worn by women and were sometimes so long that they even reached the knees. Iridescent abalone shells from the Pacific coast were made into large earrings, added to neck ornaments, or simply worn on a string at the neck. A traditional "four-winds" silver cross on a necklace was spiritually symbolic of the four directions. Men who had been given peace medals by the government wore them on a thong or a ribbon. Some men wore the treasured bear-claw necklaces; one example even had human finger bones used as spacers. A tiny polished bone was occasionally worn in a pierced nasal septum.

Armor

Armor, as such, is not mentioned by the authorities consulted, but warriors carried a shield made of two thicknesses of buffalo hide with a cover of buckskin painted white and ornamented with feathers. This was held on the arm by leather straps.

Special Costumes

The Dog company of the Ute was the only society comparable to those of the Plains; Mails tells that the members wore a distinctive neck piece made from a slit wolf skin. Mourners wore no special costume, but they cut their hair and wore ragged clothing to show their grief.

Garment Decoration

Aboriginally, garment decoration consisted of such simple adornments as fringes, rows of thongs, cowrie shells, or elk teeth. After the eastern Ute went out on the Plains for buffalo hunting, they learned beadwork, although there was little of it done before 1850. They were influenced by Cheyenne techniques, such as the lazy stitch and some overlay. The women created intricate, beautiful beadwork, much sought after in trade. It was characterized by elongated geometric shapes, a preference for blue or pink backgrounds, and little use of white except to outline shapes. Later beadwork tended toward the floral mode. From the traders the women obtained brass tacks, brass bells, and silver medallions to decorate garments.

Face and Body Embellishment

Face painting was practiced using such colors as red, yellow, white, blue, and green in many designs, somewhat symbolic. For battle, warriors painted the body with yellow and black stripes. For special occasions, women painted dark circles on the cheeks, a white circle on the forehead, and the hair part red. Some facial tattooing was practiced, using cactus thorns dipped in cedar-leaf ashes. The Ute tended to have flat, wide faces, due to being strapped into hard cradle boards as infants.

Transitional Dress

By 1900 men were wearing "store-bought" clothing, such as vests, trousers, coats, hats, and shoes. Women were making their own dresses, but in the prevailing white mode. Today they still like to wear shawls and blankets, and wear the hair in braids. In their ceremonial dress, the Ute can scarcely be distinguished from the Plains or other Indians. Today almost all traces of Ute tribal clothing characteristics have been lost.

Key Sources

Callaway, Donald, Joel Janetski, and Omer C. Stewart. "Ute." In *Handbook of North American Indians. Vol. 11: Great Basin.* Pp. 336–367. Washington: Smithsonian Institution.

Daniels, Helen Sloan. *The Ute Indians of Southwestern Colorado.* Durango, CO: Durango Publishers, 1941.

Delaney, Robert W. *The Southern Ute People.* Phoenix, AZ: Indian Tribal Series, 1974.

Hafen, LeRoy R. *The Indians of Colorado.* Denver: State Historical Society of Colorado, 1952.

Hughes, J. Donald. *American Indians in Colorado.* Boulder, CO: Pruett, 1977.

Marsh, Charles S. *The Utes of Colorado: People of the Shining Mountains.* Boulder, CO: Pruett, 1982.

Opler, Marvin Kaufmann. *The Southern Ute of Colorado.* New York: Appleton-Century, 1940.

Pettit, Jan. *Utes: The Mountain People.* Colorado Springs: Century One, 1982.

Rockwell, Wilson. *The Utes: A Forgotten People.* Denver: Sage Books, 1956.

Smith, Anne M. Cooke. "Ethnography of the Northern Ute." Museum of New Mexico *Papers in Anthropology* 17.

Uintah-Ouray Ute Tribe. *Ute Ways.* Fort Duchesne, UT: Uintah-Ouray Ute Tribe, 1977.

John

Selish-Delaware. 3.

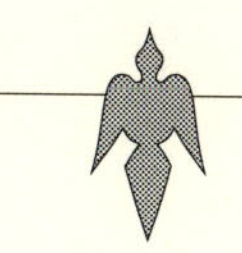

Chapter Six

Costume of the Plateau

Right: Women of the Columbia Plateau, such as this Yakima mother and daughter, wove basketry hats and cornhusk friendship bags.

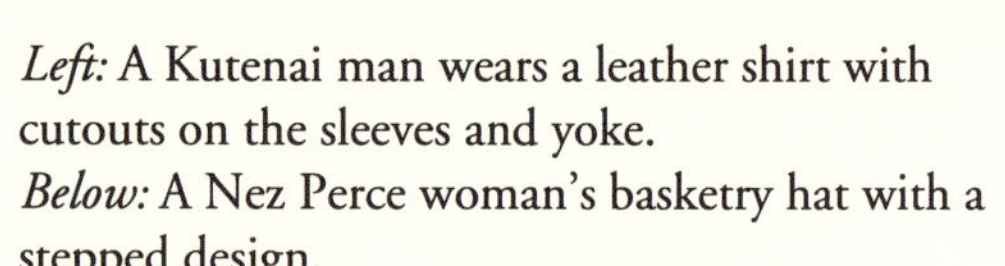

Left: A Kutenai man wears a leather shirt with cutouts on the sleeves and yoke.
Below: A Nez Perce woman's basketry hat with a stepped design.

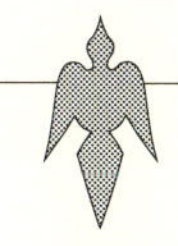

Plateau

The Columbia Plateau lies between the Rockies and the Cascade Mountains of Washington and Oregon and runs north into the mountains of British Columbia. Historically, it was less isolated than the Great Basin because of the many rivers, particularly the Columbia and Fraser river systems. In the southern portion the tribes, as might be expected, were marginal to the Basin culture. The land is characterized by high plains, sagebrush desert, mountain valleys with pines and firs on the upland slopes, and some marsh areas. Little or no agriculture was practiced. Chief food sources were salmon (a staple) and other fish, roots (especially camas), berries, small game and waterfowl, mountain sheep, deer, and elk. For the purpose of looking at costume, the land may be divided into three areas: (1) the eastern Plateau of western Montana and Idaho, (2) the western Plateau extending into eastern Washington and Oregon. and (3) the northern Plateau of southeastern British Columbia.

Languages varied. In general, Salishan was spoken in the northern areas and Washington, and the Shahaptian language in the southern part of the region. The Wishram/Wasco spoke Chinookan. The Kutenai were Algonquian speakers. Finally, many of the tribes used the Chinook trade jargon.

A diversified hunting and gathering culture developed in the area as early as 5000 B.C. and persisted in some places into historic times. Small communities engaged in fishing, hunting, and gathering. However, trade was vigorous, for archaeologists have found turquoise from the Southwest and shells, such as abalone, dentalium, and olivella, from the Pacific coast. The many small tribes were known as energetic middlemen; slaves were one of the most common commodities. Horses reached the Plateau in the early eighteenth century and elements of the Plains culture were adopted,

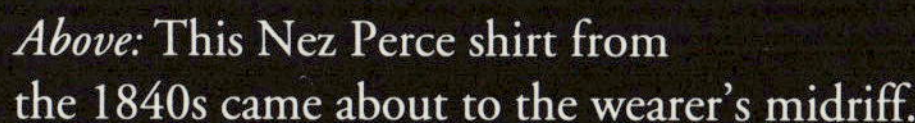

Above: This Nez Perce shirt from the 1840s came about to the wearer's midriff.

Peoples of the Plateau

Cayuse, p. 213
Coeur d'Alene
Columbia River, p. 216
Colville
Flathead, p. 218
Interior Salish, p. 220
Kalispell
Kutenai, p. 223
Lake, p. 220
Lillooet, p. 220
Nez Perce, p. 225
Nicola
Okanagon, p. 220
Palouse
Sanpoil/Nespelem, p. 230
Shuswap, p. 220
Spokane
Tenino
Thompson, p. 220
Umatilla
Walla Walla
Wanapum
Wasco/Wishram, p. 231
Wenatchi
Yakima, p. 235

particularly by the Kutenai, the Nez Perce, and the Flathead. Fur traders penetrated the Plateau in 1811 and were succeeded by missionaries and settlers; it was the usual story of encroachment, conflicts, and the forcing of the native peoples onto reservations.

Early documentation of Plateau tribes appeared in the journals of the Lewis and Clark expedition (1805–1806) and the writings and paintings of Nicholas Point, S.J. (1840–1847). Photographers late in the century added to our knowledge of costume, not only Edward S. Curtis, but also Lee Moorhouse of Pendleton, Oregon, and Dr. Edward Latham, the Indian Agency physician at the Colville Reservation. The peoples of the Plateau lacked both the emphasis on rank found among the Northwest Coast Indians and the driving war culture of the Plains. Their wide-ranging trade activities created contacts with varied cultures, and there were many examples of the assimilation of costume elements from other areas.

General Dress

Men's Basic Dress

The costume of the Indian men of the Plateau was scanty, even in the north, sometimes consisting simply of a breechclout, robe, and moccasins. The buckskin breechclout seems to have arrived late, possibly early in the nineteenth century; it had flaps, front and back, in some areas was rather long, and there was little decoration, except for fringes. Leggings were also of deerskin, gartered at the knee, usually thigh-length, and sometimes fringed, with large buckskin flaps at the sides. Later cloth leggings had characteristic rectangular patches at the bottom and flaps at the sides. Around 1900 angora chaps were highly popular. The tanned deerskin shirts were shorter than those of the Plains, waist-length as a rule. Early ones were poncho-style; later shirts were seamed up the sides with fringes in the seams, and occasionally short sleeves were added. They exhibited the typical Plateau embellishment of rows of holes punctured in the buckskin with an awl. Some authorities have attributed this to a desire for ventilation, but the fact remains that it was done in a decorative fashion. Koch says that some Plateau and early Plains shirts had life forms painted on them, such as buffalo and otters.

Women's Basic Dress

The earliest attire was a simple wraparound skirt and poncho top, both of skin. Later they wore the strap-and-sleeve dress, and may have worn the side-seam dress. By the early nineteenth century, the Plateau women were wearing long (ankle-length) binary dresses, using the skins of mountain goat, black-tailed deer, or elk, left in their natural shape. These were simple in shape and construction. The typical two-skin dress was sewn up the sides and across the top with the folded-down yoke that retained the deer tails in front and in back. Side seams would be left open to the waist for nursing mothers. Later, leather pieces were added to the bottom to make an even hemline. The yokes of these dresses were decorated with wavy bands of quillwork or, later, beadwork, which reflected the lines of the deer tails and the yoke edge. When cotton superseded deerskin and even stroud cloth, the characteristic Plateau dress evolved; usually of striped or plain fabric, it was a T-shaped garment with the seams of the square-cut sleeves left unsewn. The sleeves, the top, and sometimes the hem were typically edged with a band of contrasting color. These dresses were girdled with a sash or leather belt, and a printed-cotton blouse was usually worn beneath the dress. Down the Columbia River, in the western part of the region, shredded bark skirts and capes were common. Leggings were either front-seam or side-seam construction.

Footwear

Some moccasins were simply of deerskin with the hair inside, folded around the foot with a seam up the front. However, more commonly the moccasins were of one piece of leather folded along the inside of the foot with the seam along the outside; these had a right and a left moccasin. Before being sewn they were beaded on the instep. The tongue was frequently slashed in a V-shape. A cuff was added as well as thongs, which were long enough to tie around the ankle one or more times. Some moccasins were adorned with porcupine quillwork and painted red.

Outer Wear

Robes were of buffalo hide or simple pieces of buckskin thrown over the shoulder. In most areas rabbit-skin robes were worn and in the southern part

A Palouse man, photographed in 1890, wears a shirt with heavily beaded sleeve and shoulder bands and fringed with strips of ermine. He wears his hair loose rather than in braids, a common practice among Plateau people. The broad front flap of his breechclout rests on his knees.

of the Plateau mantles were woven of sagebrush bark and other fibers. When the buffalo were depleted, Pendleton blankets, often with fringes, were substituted.

Hair Styles

Both men and women wore the hair loose or in two braids, which were often wrapped with strips of otter or weasel fur. The men at times adopted hair styles from the Plains tribes such as pompadours, a coiled knot above the forehead, or a forelock hanging over the nose.

Headgear

A popular headdress was the warbonnet of the Blackfeet with its circle of upright feathers and strips of ermine at the sides; actually, some authorities say the style was first worn by the Kutenai men and other eastern Plateau tribesmen, and later adopted by the braves of the northern Plains. Many of the Plateau men wore visors or sunshades to protect the eyes against the strong sun; these were flat pieces of rawhide with a hole cut for the head, or a circle formed from the long mane of the moose. The brimless twined-basketry hats of the women were typically taller than those of California, somewhat fez-like. They were either covered with false embroidery in natural brown-tone fibers or were painted. Later, the designs were created in commercial yarns of bright hues.

Accessories

A characteristic accessory with the Plateau dress was a twined-cornhusk bag, sometimes called a "friendship bag." The warp was of Indian hemp or, later, a commercial binder twine used for agricultural

Four Spokane women wear Plateau-style dresses made of cloth, with square cut sleeves bordered by a contrasting color. Their hair is braided and each woman wears abalone shell disks as decoration. The friendship bags are made of cornhusks and embroidered with yarn.

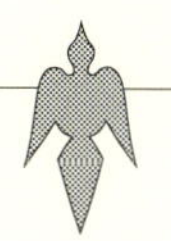

purposes and the weft of cornhusk. The fibers were woven into complex geometric designs. Later bags were occasionally decorated with yarn or had fully beaded panels covering the front of the bag. These cornhusk bags were carried by the men as well. Simple drawstring pouches of buckskin were designed to carry paints and similar necessities. Belts of leather were covered with quillwork, later beadwork. Armlets and some belts were made of strips of fur.

Jewelry

Early necklaces were made of copper tubes and pendants, combined with shell disks, or of dentalia and other shells and bones. Earrings were characteristically large round or square pieces of abalone shell, one at each ear, or they might be set in the hair at ear level. Three-strand chokers were especially popular, combined with necklaces of disk-type beads. Loop necklaces consisting of many strands, 8 to 14, fastened to a rawhide strip at the side, were worn by the men.

Armor

Armor was made of the stiffest hide obtainable, such as elk or buffalo; it was soaked until soft, then shaped as desired. Usually two or more layers were required for protection from enemy arrows.

Garment Decoration

The Plateau women seem to have learned porcupine quillwork from the Plains craft workers. Beadwork, introduced as early as 1810, brought by the traders from the east, was of a geometric style, reflecting the earlier quillwork. Between 1810 and 1860 a simplified floral beadwork was introduced featuring symmetrical compositions with stylized designs and frequent use of the double-curve motif. Usually this was created in a combination of overlay and lazy-stitch techniques. By the late nineteenth century the symmetry and the double curve had vanished, the beadwork taking on a character of its own with asymmetrical designs of naturalistic flowers and animals.

Face and Body Embellishment

There was constant conflict over sources of paint; many of the Plateau men painted the face (red was most admired), and found themselves fighting with the Blackfeet for possession of the sources. An iron clay found near Helena, Montana, offered vermilion, and some Indians traveled to California to obtain red cinnabar. Chrome yellow was made from a yellow stone found along the river of that name. Black paint from Canada may have had a petroleum content. Green mineral deposits were to be found on the South Fork of the Blackfoot River, probably a copper stain. Head flattening was found in the western areas into the historic period but disappeared by the mid-nineteenth century.

Transitional Dress

By 1875, the men had adopted white garments; they wore trousers, dark vests (heavily embellished with beadwork), cotton shirts and neck scarves, "ranger" hats, and gauntlets, also richly beaded on the cuffs. However, commercial blankets, especially those of the Pendleton Mills, continued to be worn almost to the present day. Women were slower to change, wearing the typical Plateau dress well into the 1930s; but then they, too, began to purchase European-style clothing.

Cayuse

The name of the Cayuse—renowned, formidable horsemen—has come to be associated with horses throughout the West. Their name came from the French *cailloux,* meaning "people of the stones." In early times they lived at the headwaters of the John Day River near Mount Hood in Oregon, later moving north and east. Traders rather than producers, they allied themselves with the Nez Perce, even adopting their language, which was more fluid and less complex than their own (a Shahaptian collateral tongue, Waiilatpuan). Copying the Nez Perce in culture as well, they began to hunt buffalo on the Plains and to wear Plains clothing. Culturally, they were similar to the Nez Perce, the Walla Walla, the Umatilla, and the Yakima.

The first contact between whites and the Cayuse seems to have been the Lewis and Clark expedition (1804–1806). The Cayuse were often troublesome to white settlers; the conflicts culminated in the Cayuse War of 1847, which in turn led to the Whitman Massacre. Gustavus Sohon sketched them in 1855. The best single source on the Cayuse is Ruby and Brown (1972).

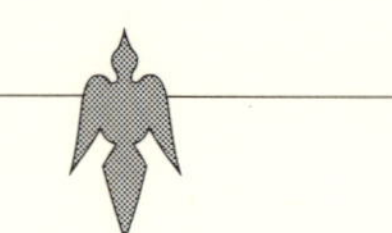

Men's Basic Dress

The men wore long breechclouts, often trimmed with horizontal bands of quillwork; preferred skins were those of deer, antelope, or elk. Later of cloth, some breechcloths were dark with white edges and embellished with floral beadwork. The men liked white deerskin shirts and leggings; the thigh-length shirts were adorned with porcupine quillwork, painted designs, and often fringing on the outside seams, and were girdled with a sash or a black leather belt. The thigh-length leggings were also decorated with quillwork and fringes.

Women's Basic Dress

Early primitive garments were the wraparound skirt of skin, with an added poncho, also of skin. Later, the women wore the two-skin dress with the deer-tail yoke; this was adorned with porcupine quills, then pony beads in the early nineteenth century, and by the middle of the century the small seed beads. Fringes were added at the hem and at the ends of the sleeves. As cloth became available, they wore the characteristic Plateau dress of a cotton print, belted, with square-cut elbow-length sleeves, a blouse showing beneath, and decorative bands of a contrasting color. Knee-length leggings were gartered below the knee.

Footwear

Moccasins, of deer, elk, or antelope skin, often painted red, were of one piece with a seam along the outer sides; these were soft-soled, but later, with

Cayuse finery in this early 1900s photograph shows two styles of warbonnets: a halo style with bison horns worn by the horseman, and a standup warbonnet worn by the man holding the heavily fringed rifle scabbard. Trappings for the horse, a reflection of its value to the owner, include a feather bustle and beaded neckpiece.

Plains influence, a rawhide sole was attached. Winter moccasins, with the hairy side retained and turned inward, featured cuffs, that could be turned up and bound with thongs.

Outer Wear
Early robes were of elk or antelope skin with the hair retained; lighter weight robes or mantles were of tanned deerskin. In the nineteenth century the men copied the Plains buffalo robe, worn more for status than for warmth. The Pendleton blanket with fringes was worn commonly by both sexes from the end of the century well into the twentieth century. Ruby and Brown mention a chief in full regalia wearing a "hooded cloak."

Hair Styles
The hair was long and thick, generally worn in two bunches, one at each side of the head. Like the Crow Indians, the men made it longer and thicker by the addition of human hair or horsehair. When actively engaged, the warrior might coil it and knot it on the top of the forehead. Men wore many types of ornaments in the hair—quillwork, beadwork, strips of ermine fur, pieces of metal, anything available that was polished or shiny. Some wore braids wrapped in beaver or otter fur, with the front gracefully combed up in a pompadour. Women usually wore the hair in two braids with a large piece of abalone shell fastened into each braid at ear level.

Headgear
Some of the men wore the horned halo warbonnet of the Plains with pendant ermine strips at the sides, others displayed wolf-skin caps ornamented with bear claws and feathers. Sohon in 1855 sketched some Cayuse men wearing flat fur hats. Women wore the tall truncated-cone basketry hat with the geometric designs often done in the imbrication technique. In this century, many have exchanged the basket hat for cotton headscarves tied at the back.

Accessories
Belts for both sexes were of leather, often painted black. Bags were the most common accessory. Women made bags of cornhusk with geometric designs in dyed husks. Later bags were of leather with beadwork; late in the nineteenth century they were decorated with floral designs showing eastern influence. The cornhusk bags are still made today and are a popular trade item.

Jewelry
The loop necklace was the most frequent type of necklace worn; it consisted of many strands of flat,

A Cayuse woman wears a buckskin dress with a lazy-stitch beaded yoke. Her tall basketry hat, a truncated cone shape, is typical of those worn by Plateau tribes. She holds two friendship bags: in her left hand, a cornhusk bag with embroidered geometric designs; in her right, a beaded bag with a floral design.

white disk beads fastened to rawhide straps at each side, and tied about the neck with thongs. These were worn by the men, often with chokers of dentalium shells. Women wore many strands of beads and the large dentalium shells at each ear. A popular necklace for both sexes consisted of a mirror in a small wood frame suspended by a thong.

Garment Decoration

Some porcupine quillwork was used for garment decoration, followed by the use of the large glass pony beads, later the small glass seed beads; beadwork at first was done in the geometric patterns of quillwork, but later in the nineteenth century floral designs were adopted. Beadwork was done in the lazy-stitch and overlay techniques. The basketry hats were twined, often with imbrication designs added after the hats were finished. Some of the buckskin shirts had painted designs.

Face and Body Embellishment

Both men and women beautified themselves with face paint in red, green, black, and white hues. Lampblack was used to line the eyes and to make a line from the corner of the eye to the ear. The Cayuse Indian painted his horse using the same designs and colors he used on himself, creating an even closer relationship with the animal. Women, especially those from aristocratic families, were often subjected to head flattening in their infancy; this was done by binding the head closely with cords over pieces of folded hides.

Transitional Dress

Early in the nineteenth century the men were wearing European garments; they especially liked to wear the scarlet coats and breeches of the English soldiers. Later in the century, they wore plaid or dark cotton shirts, and dark vests and trousers. Women wore the Plateau dress almost to the mid-twentieth century. Moccasins were the last item of traditional wear to be dropped, replaced by "store" shoes.

Key Sources

Ruby, Robert H. and John A. Brown. *The Cayuse Indians: Imperial Tribesmen of Old Oregon.* Norman: University of Oklahoma Press, 1972.

Columbia River

The Columbia River Indians present a particular problem in the study of their early dress. The tribes were many, small in number, and roamed widely along the rivers, leading to much contact and trading and many intermarriages; most of these tribes lost their tribal identity in the nineteenth century and many simply dissappeared. The situation is further complicated by the fact that the tribes were called by various names, not only the names they gave themselves, but also the names given by European explorers, traders, and settlers. In this western Plateau area, we move away from the Plains influence and, with the effects of the huge trading activities at The Dalles of the Columbia River, there is much more impact from the cultures of the Great Basin, California, and the Pacific Northwest.

Lewis and Clark (1804–1806) provided extensive information on these peoples in their journals, commenting frequently on the similarity in dress. Paul Kane, the Canadian painter, was among them in 1847. Major tribes discussed here are the Teninos (also called Warm Springs Indians), the Umatilla, the Walla Walla, the Wenatchi, and the Wanapums, all of whom spoke Shahaptian, except for the Wenatchi, who were Salishan speakers.

Men's Basic Dress

Men wore a breechclout either of tanned deerskin or of the pelt of an animal such as a fox, hanging in front like an apron; sometimes only breechclouts and robes were worn. Buckskin shirts were longer than those worn upriver, at times reaching the knees; these were ornamented with porcupine quills, shells, strips of ermine or rabbit fur, and beads, which they obtained early through their extensive trading. Thigh-high leggings were gartered at the knees with strips of fur. A favored item of attire was the pelt of an animal, especially an otter skin, hung around the neck so that the tail hung down over the chest.

Women's Basic Dress

Some women wore scanty clothing. Lewis and Clark mention that "the [Wanapum] females have no other covering but a truss or piece of leather tied around the hips and then drawn tight between the legs." That sounds like a breechclout. They mention this same style elsewhere for other tribes, and also a form of

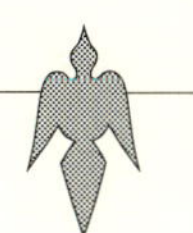

wraparound skirt of skin. This may have been worn with a poncho top. As deer became more plentiful, and as the men acquired horses in the eighteenth century and could hunt farther afield, women began to wear long dresses of deer or elk skin, suggesting Plains influence; early types were of the strap-and-sleeve or side-seam types, later developing into the two-skin style with ornamentation on the yoke, which retained the deertail as decoration, and which was further ornamented with the large pony beads in the lazy-stitch technique, rows of thongs, and some fringing. Some dresses had few ornaments; others featured the highly valued dentalium shells from the Pacific coast and even thimbles brought by Lewis and Clark. As commercial cloth became more common, the women adopted the T-shaped Plateau dress of printed or solid-color cotton with its large square-cut sleeves, open underarm seams, bands of contrasting color, and a cotton underblouse.

Footwear

The typical moccasin of the area was of one piece of deerskin or buffalo skin folded and sewn along the outside edge of the foot; before sewing, they were beaded, usually with pony beads, on the instep area. They often had a forked tongue. In the mountainous areas snowshoes were worn; they had a unique shape, almost like a teardrop.

Outer Wear

In an area teeming with game, robes were made of the skins of deer, antelope, wolves, elk, wildcat, bighorn sheep, and, for children, gray squirrel; they were especially fond of otter fur, for which they would pay a great price. Lewis and Clark mentioned robes of scarlet and blue, which may possibly have been from the Hudson's Bay Company traders. They also wrote of small robes worn by the women, about three feet square, that covered the neck and shoulders, reached the waist in back, and were attached to the belt in that place. Another type of outer wear they recorded was a "tippet," probably what we would call a cape, worn by one of the chiefs: "formed of human scalps, and adorned with the thumbs and fingers of several men slain by him in battle." After 1895, when the Pendleton Woolen Mills were established in Pendleton, Oregon, those blankets were worn by both sexes, the men's blankets having a felt edge, the women's a long fringe; these were worn well into the mid-twentieth century.

Hair Styles

Both sexes wore two braids in the Plains style or wore the hair loose; some women made it wavy by braiding it, wetting it, drying it, and then unbraiding it. Another style was to cut it in bangs over the forehead, cut locks square at the sides at ear level, and tie the rest into two queues or clumps that were brought forward over the shoulders. Some men, especially older men, coiled the hair into a knot on the forehead. Occasionally, small braids were worn at each side of the face, the rest of the hair hanging loose. Ornaments were seldom worn in the hair, at least at the time that Lewis and Clark were there; later the women adopted the Plateau style of a large, rectangular piece of abalone shell in each braid at ear level.

Headgear

Women's brimless basketry hats were made of bear grass and cedar bark, later of cornhusk material; typically a short buckskin fringe edged the bottom of the hat. Men wore a headband of fox or otter skin, with or without the fur. They also wore caps decorated with fur and feathers.

Accessories

The most common accessories were bags or pouches woven of bear grass, cedar bark, silk grass, and other fibers; these may have been obtained in trade from the Wasco, who were most adept at making twined bags. Later, as cloth and beads became readily obtainable, bags were made of those materials. Belts were of leather, also later adorned with beadwork. Plateau women favored the large pony beads for beadwork, and the horse was a popular animal design. Because of the large trade network centered around The Dalles, metal was early available; armbands, as well as other items of adornment, were made of brass or copper.

Jewelry

Large blue and white pony beads were widely used by these peoples. They were made into necklaces, earrings, and bracelets, and were attached to garments; these

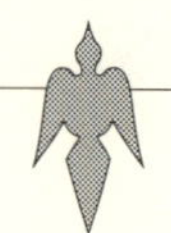

beads were not only favored for ornamentation, but were also used as a medium of trade. Bracelets were also made of brass, copper, and horn. Some trinkets were fashioned from shells, fish bones, and feathers. Collars of bear claws were worn by the men. Men also pierced the nasal septum, inserting a dentalium shell therein for special occasions. Lewis and Clark recorded that one chief brought out 14 fingers taken from enemies killed in battle, and said that such items were sometimes "worn around the waists and necks as amulets against any real or imaginary evils."

Garment Decoration

Weaving was done, but only of fibers such as bear grass, silk grass, cedar bark, and tule, made into the Plateau brimless hat and the twined bags for carrying items. Some porcupine quillwork was created and beadwork was made, with blue and white pony beads being most favored.

Face and Body Embellishment

Skull flattening was practiced by many of these tribes; in the mountains only the women underwent this operation, while downriver some men also exhibited this characteristic. This was done by pressing the infant's head between two boards, resulting in a profile of a straight line from the nose to the crown of the head. Very little tattooing seems to have been practiced, although Lewis and Clark mentioned one tribe near The Dalles in which the women had lines of dots from the ankles to the calves, which would seem to imply tattooing. Very little painting of the face or body seems to have been performed.

Transitional Dress

In the late-nineteenth century, after the period in which Plains influence was apparent in garments, the men and women wore the Plateau "reservation" garments. Women wore the Plateau dress of printed or solid cotton cloth with the square-cut sleeves, and the men wore the long cotton shirt and skin or cloth leggings with typical square patches or panels of a contrasting color at the bottom. Vests were adopted, beaded elaborately or decorated with white pearl buttons. Braids, worn by both sexes, were the most common form of hair style. Many men wore the tall "Indian" hat with the flat brim. "Store-bought" garments became prevalent, finally shoes replaced the beaded moccasins, and all tribal distinction was lost in the garments of the Columbia River Indians.

Key Sources

Biddle, Nicholas, ed. *The Journals of the Lewis and Clark Expedition.* 2 vols. New York: Heritage, 1962.

Gogol, John M. "Columbia River/Plateau Indian Beadwork." *American Indian Basketry Magazine* 5(2): 4–28.

Gridley, M. *With One Sky above Us: Life on an Indian Reservation at the Turn of the Century.* New York: Putnam's, 1979.

Flathead

The Flathead were Salishan speakers living in the fastnesses of the Bitterroot Mountains of western Montana. The name "Flathead" has caused much confusion. Some early explorers said they were called that because they practiced skull flattening like the Chinookan tribes to the west; actually there is no record of such ever having been the case. Some authorities say they were given the name because they did *not* deform the skulls, so that the heads looked flat compared to the tapered heads of the tribes who felt such heads were indicative of proper upbringing. The name may have come from the French, who called them "Tetes plattes," possibly because of the flat fur caps worn by the men. The Flathead combined traits of the Plains, the Plateau, and the Great Basin cultures, and some of their ceremonials were similar to those of the Northwest Coast. They hunted buffalo on the Plains, and exchanged buffalo products with the Columbia River tribes for dried salmon, a staple in their diet. They also ate camas root, gathered berries and other foods, hunted, and fished. Their first white contact seems to have been Lewis and Clark in 1805. De Smet later said they were a peaceable folk with few quarrels and few enemies. Alexander Henry called them "brave and virtuous." Ruby and Brown say there was little difference in dress between the Flathead and the Shoshone. Gustavus Sohon did sketches of the Flathead in 1854. Curtis photographed them in the early years of this century.

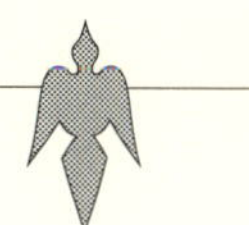

Men's Basic Dress

Men wore long knee-length shirts of native tanned hide (usually deer or buffalo hide); later, they adopted the Plateau style, that is, short (barely waist length) and with punctured holes in various designs. Maurer explains that this type of decoration was common among the Chippewa and others of the eastern Plains before 1830, later emerging as an important style for war garments among the Crow, Blackfoot, and Plateau tribes. These shirts were further adorned with owl or eagle feathers, or ermine strips hanging from the shoulders and arms. Breechclouts of skin were narrow with flaps in front and back, flaps that were at times mid-calf in length, at other times much shorter. Thigh-length leggings of tanned leather were ornamented with quillwork in early times, later with beadwork, or a combination of the two. In the late nineteenth century they were of stroud cloth, usually blue. The hides used for these garments were of buffalo or deer, and, occasionally, elk.

Women's Basic Dress

At the time of the Lewis and Clark expedition, women seem to have worn a long wraparound skirt of skin reaching to the ankles and tied at the waist, leaving the torso bare; in cooler weather a poncho-type covering was added. Later they adopted the dresses of the Plains, at first the strap-and-sleeve dress or the side-seam dress, later the two-skin dress with the yoke showing the characteristic "deer-tail" dip and long fringes under the arms and along the bottom of the yoke; this was followed by the three-skin dress. These dresses were of deerskin, which was superseded by cloth, particularly red or blue stroud cloth. By the mid-nineteenth century they were using solid-color cotton cloth, often lining the dresses with a cotton calico and bordering the hem with a band (or bands) of a contrasting color. Leggings, also added for warmth or protection, were knee-length, gartered, and adorned in the same manner as those of the men.

Footwear

Moccasins were one-piece with a side seam; these were soft-soled, with rawhide soles added later in the century. The long rectangular tongue was about six inches in length; the cuff was from six to eight inches tall and long enough to fold over the tongue in front. Long thongs, 36 inches in length or more, were tied around the cuff several times. Snowshoes were worn by the men when hunting or trapping.

Outer Wear

Robes for the men were of buffalo hide, when available; the rabbit-skin robe was made by the women and worn by them and by children. Women wore their robes draped over the left shoulder or fastened in front. Lewis and Clark said that "the Flathead threw white robes over their shoulders"; this is somewhat ambiguous, for it may have referred to white blankets or to skin robes tanned to a whiteness. Some men wore the *capote* of the French *voyageurs,* made from Hudson's Bay Company white blankets with the broad colored stripes. After 1900, Pendleton blankets with Indian-inspired designs were worn by both sexes.

Hair Styles

The hair was worn loose as a rule; however, men displayed various styles for ceremonial occasions. For one popular style, a bunch of hair was gathered over the forehead, combed to the back and tied in with the rest of the hair, then pushed forward to form a pompadour. Some wore a forelock over the nose, others had a tiny braid at each side of the face, and still others wore the hair in two braids wrapped with strips of otter fur. Women wore the hair loose or in two braids.

Headgear

Most Flathead men went bareheaded as a rule. However, Sohon showed one of the men wearing a flat cap of fur. He also did a drawing of a chief wearing a top hat. But the warbonnet of the Blackfoot type, with its circle of stand-up feathers placed in a rawhide headband, was much more common, as was the buffalo-horn headdress.

Accessories

Cylindrical cases were used to carry the warbonnets mentioned above; these were of painted rawhide with fringes added. Both sexes carried bags and pouches, in lieu of pockets, to hold such items as paint, fire-making or sewing equipment, amulets or charms, and tobacco. These were of buckskin, either drawstring or flat cases, ornamented with quillwork,

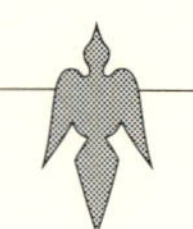

beadwork, or both, and fringes. A medicine bag might contain forefingers stripped from enemies slain in battle. Belts were of leather embellished with beadwork. Late in the nineteenth century, some men wore the hair pipe breastplate. Garters and armbands of leather were adorned with beadwork.

Jewelry

Brass ornaments, such as pendants and tinklers, were made from brass kettles obtained from the traders. The most popular type of jewelry was the loop necklace, made from white clamshell disks from California, or thongs wrapped with beading. These often featured large pieces of abalone shell and were frequently worn with chokers of dentalium shells.

Armor

There is little mention of armor, but the Flathead carried the typical war shield of the Plains, the round disks made of two or more layers of tough buffalo hide, painted and embellished with feathers.

Special Costumes

Koch says that dancers of this tribe wore feather rosettes at the back of the head. Flathead ceremonials were more akin to those of the Northwest Coast Indians; they did not practice the Sun Dance, but they had a Camas Dance, a Blue Jay Dance, and some curing rites. The dead were dressed in their finest robes and placed on scaffolds until burial took place.

Garment Decoration

Since the Flathead were greatly influenced by Plains customs, they did little or no weaving. Quillwork and beadwork were the usual types of garment decoration. At first beading was done in geometric designs; later, floral forms took over.

Face and Body Embellishment

Little painting was practiced by these Indians; occasionally face painting was used by warriors preparing for battle, but this was not as extensive as that done by Plains men. For dress occasions, women painted the part of the hair with red ocher and red spots on the cheeks.

Transitional Dress

Although some women adopted the Plateau dress with its square-cut sleeves, more commonly the three-skin dress, now made of cloth, was worn. During the Reservation Period of the late nineteenth century, men began to wear purchased white garments, while the women made their own cloth dresses in white styles. The vests were heavily beaded by the women in floral designs. By the turn of the century there was little left of Flathead dress, as such.

Key Sources

Curtis, Edward S. *The North American Indian.* Vol. 7. New York: Johnson Reprint Company, 1970.

Fahey, John. *The Flathead Indians.* Norman: University of Oklahoma Press, 1974.

"Gustavus Sohon's Portraits of Flathead and Pend d'Oreille Indians, 1854." Smithsonian Institution *Miscellaneous Collections* 110: 1–66.

Johnson, Olga Weydemeyer. *Flatheads and Kootenay: The Rivers, the Tribes, and the Region's Traders.* Glendale, CA: Arthur H. Clarke, 1969.

Ronan, Peter. *Historical Sketch of the Flathead Nation.* Minneapolis, 1890.

Turney-High, Harry Holbert. "The Flathead Indians of Montana." American Anthropological Association *Memoirs* 48.

Interior Salish

The Indians of the northern Plateau were predominantly of the Interior Salish group, consisting chiefly of the Lillooet, the Thompson Indians of the Fraser River Valley, the Okanagon, the Lake Indians, and the Shuswap, five tribes that were similar in culture but battled constantly with one another. They inhabited the mountainous regions of southern British Columbia and northern Washington and Idaho. They were dissimilar in many ways from the Coastal Salish, but tended to follow their caste system and the use of slaves. They traded with the coastal Indians, offering skins, hemp, cedar bark, and goat's wool in exchange for shells, smoked salmon, and slaves. With the acquisition of horses in the late-eighteenth century, they began to adopt a Plains lifeway. James Teit, an anthropologist, worked most extensively with the Interior Salish groups.

Men's Basic Dress

Men were attired only in knee-length breechclouts of deerskin in the summer. In colder weather they added leggings and shirts of dressed leather, such as elk, deer, mountain goat, or antelope hide. The shirts had earlier been the short Plateau type, often with punctuated decoration; later they were longer, about thigh-length, with short, wide fringing. Thigh-length leggings with wide flaps were gartered below the knees; some had the typical Plateau patch of a contrasting color at the bottom. Later breechcloths were of dark-colored strouding or other cloth with beadwork in floral designs.

Women's Basic Dress

Little is known of early women's dress, for their earliest contact, Simon Fraser, sent out by the Hudson's Bay Company in 1808, gave little information on dress. Their early garments were probably a wraparound skirt with a top covering of a skin with a hole cut for the head. Early explorers mention "tunics" for the women, probably a two-piece dress, belted. Later a fringed and beaded cape was added. The Plateau dress was later adopted by some Salish women, with its square-cut sleeves, contrasting bands of color, and cotton underblouse. Leggings of skin were knee-length with beaded strips and small fringes.

A young Interior Salish woman braided her hair to mark the end of adolescence. Tab-like fringe, characteristic of the Columbia Plateau, edge the yoke of her dress.

Footwear

Moccasins were of the soft-sole one-piece type with tall cuffs added in the winter, wrapped securely with thongs. Early moccasins were plain, later ones beaded. The Lillooet and the Shuswap made sandals of fur or hide tied onto the foot with thongs; Driver says these sandals were historically independent of those worn in the South, and were worn by those too poor to afford tanned-leather moccasins. Snowshoes, introduced in 1780, were small and round, unlike the beautifully designed and constructed snowshoes of the Subarctic tribes to the north. Some tribes, such as the Okanagon, wove socks of rush fibers.

Outer Wear

Like the Coast Salish, the Interior Salish wove blankets of goat wool, but not dog hair (as Gustafson states, it was more likely coyote hair); these followed the same designs as those on the coast. Some cloaks were made of sagebrush, Indian hemp (dogbane), or nettle stalks, instead of the cedar bark of the moist coastal areas. Blankets were also made of strips of rabbit fur, cut spirally from the pelt, and woven in a plain weave; these were especially worn by women and children. Fur robes were worn in the winter, made of the hides of deer, elk, beaver, and other small animals; a few buffalo robes were obtained in trade from the Plains.

Hair Styles

Both sexes wore the hair loose and flowing. After the acquisition of horses and the resulting Plains influence, they wore the hair in two braids; some men wore a tiny braid at each side of the face, or a bunch of hair at each side, brought forward over the shoulders like braids and often wrapped. Women had

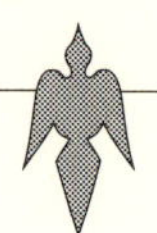

a special type of ornament worn at the ends of the braids to indicate puberty.

Headgear

Usually men went bareheaded, but a few wore the warbonnet of the Plains, of the upright ring of feathers style rather than the halo type, and with ermine strips hanging at the sides; some examples showed a band of medallions rather than the typical beaded headband. Around 1900, men favored an angora goat–hair "medicine hat," in shape like a shako, and displaying feathers erupting from the top. Some women, particularly those in the southern areas, wore the Plateau basketry hat woven with a hemp warp, hemp grass and yarn weft, and decorated with geometric designs done in an imbrication technique, in which strips of colored grass or bark were fastened to the surface of the coiled basketry hat. Fur caps were worn by both sexes in the winter.

Two Interior Salish of Canada's Thompson River group show Plains Indians influence by the style of their feathered warbonnets and beaded and fringed warshirts.

Accessories

Some bags were made of twined grasses or bark, others of skin, either decorated with quillwork, beadwork, or a combination of the two. Belts were of leather, often beaded in geometric designs, later in the nineteenth century with floral designs. Large cuffs, like gauntlet cuffs, were also beaded, especially in floral designs, since they were a late accessory appearing after the turn of the century. Some mittens are mentioned; those would seem to have been in the northern areas, and a late addition. Eagle-feather fans and metal armlets were popular items.

Jewelry

The most valued piece of jewelry for men was the loop necklace, sometimes reaching to the waist with its many "loops" of beaded thongs or white disk beads strung on a thong. Often abalone shells adorned these necklaces. Often, too, they were worn with a choker of dentalium shells. Earrings and nose ornaments were also made of dentalium shells. Women frequently wore a large round or square piece of polished abalone in each braid at ear level.

Armor

Some rod-and-slat armor was worn, held together with sinew or thongs. In some places elk-skin armor was used, made of several layers of tough hide, laced together with thongs. Most shields were small and round like those of the Plains warriors; however, Fraser mentioned that the Lillooet had shields "large enough to cover the whole body, composed of splinters of wood like the ribs of stays and neatly enclosed with twine made of hemp."

Special Costumes

Girls were isolated at the time of their first menstrual period; when they came out in public they wore fir or pine boughs on their heads and were wrapped in a Salish blanket. The dead were wrapped in woven-grass matting, fur robes, or blankets woven of

mountain-goat hair; widows and widowers cut their hair short and wore old clothes as a sign of bereavement.

Garment Decoration

The Interior Salish women excelled in coiled basketry, in some areas making the conical hats, adorned with colored fibers in an imbrication technique, whereby the design was achieved after the weaving was completed; fibers were dyed with natural dyes until the availability of aniline dyes late in the nineteenth century. Some garments were woven of sagebrush bark, especially where cedar or spruce bark was not obtainable. The Plains-type Salish blankets were woven using mountain-goat wool in natural colors—black, brown, and white—with white backgrounds predominating; later, when commercial cloth became available, thin fabric strips were used in the weaving, particularly red flannel. Small fringing appeared on garments, which were also decorated with porcupine quillwork, beadwork, or a combination of the two. Early designs were geometric, later floral. Ermine tails and dentalium shells were also popular forms of garment decoration.

Face and Body Embellishment

Teit has written extensively on the face painting and tattooing of the Thompson Indians. Face painting was performed by women of other tribes as well, but it was not extensive, being confined mostly to circles or lines on the cheeks. Tattooing was practiced by most of the tribes; almost all the Lillooet women had their wrists and arms tattooed.

Transitional Dress

Because of the early appearance of traders, the Interior Salish wore trade goods and white garments in the first half of the nineteenth century. The men wore coats, vests, cloth shirts, and top hats, but retained tribal attire for ceremonial occasions. The women were much slower to adopt white fashions; the Plateau dress was worn by some of them well into the twentieth century.

Key Sources

Curtis, Edward S. *The North American Indian.* Vol. 7. New York: Johnson Reprint Company, 1970.

Dawson, George M. "Notes on the Shuswap People of British Columbia." Royal Society of Canada *Processes and Transactions* 9(2).

Teit, James A. "The Lillooet Indians." American Museum of Natural History *Memoirs* 4(6).

———. "The Middle Columbia Salish." University of Washington *Publications in Anthropology* 2: 83–128.

———. "The Salishan Tribes of the Western Plateaus." Bureau of American Ethnology *Annual Reports* 45: 23–396.

———. "The Shuswap." American Museum of Natural History *Memoirs* 4(7): 443–789.

———. "Tattooing and Face and Body Painting of the Thompson Indians of British Columbia." Bureau of American Ethnology *Annual Reports* 45: 397–439.

———. "The Thompson Indians of British Columbia." American Museum of Natural History *Memoirs* 2.

Kutenai

The Kutenai (also spelled "Kootenay") have been a puzzle to linguists, for they spoke a language very different from that of any other North American tribe. Sapir, the linguistic expert, suggested "hesitantly" that it was of Algonquian-Wakashan stock; later authorities have adopted the term "Kitunahan speakers." The name *Kutenai* may have come from the Athapaskan word for "people of the waters or lakes," or it may simply have been a name for themselves. Living in southern British Columbia and northern Montana and Idaho, they were divided into two groups: the Upper and Lower Kutenai. The Upper Kutenai frequently crossed the mountains to hunt buffalo on the Plains and took on much of the Plains culture; the Lower Kutenai, farther removed from the mountains, subsisted largely on fish and were more influenced by the neighboring Salish. The Kutenai were the first Plateau tribe to deal with white traders, meeting them in the late 1700s. Both George Catlin and Karl Bodmer painted Kutenais in the early 1830s, and Edward Curtis photographed them in the early 1900s.

Men's Basic Dress

Men wore clothing similar to that of the Mandan and other northern Plains tribes. They produced beautifully tanned deer hides and were famed for their white elk and mountain-goat skins. Their breechclouts were of tanned leather with flaps front and back and were ornamented with fringe. Shirts were like Plains shirts, but not as long, barely hip-length, and more closely fitted at the waist and down the sleeves. Some shirts had a circular yoke, similar to shirts of the Subarctic. The most common decoration was fringing, often quite long, on the upper arms, in the seams at the sides, and across the bottom; some porcupine quillwork was done, but the Kutenai seemed to prefer cutouts on the leather or punctuated designs. Leggings of deer or elk hide had side flaps, were gartered at the knees, and were adorned with quillwork or, later, beadwork. When commercial cloth became available, leggings were of dark stroud cloth and often featured two rectangles at the bottom edged in white, creating a white strip down the lower center front.

A Kutenai man wears a shirt decorated with leather cutouts on the sleeves and yoke. He carries a Colonial Salish blanket over his left arm.

Women's Basic Dress

Information is lacking on early Kutenai dresses, but they probably wore a buckskin wraparound skirt with a top made of a piece of skin with an opening for the head. The women also cherished the beautifully tanned white buckskin for garments. They wore what some called a "shift," which may have been the side-seam dress or the two-skin dress with its deer-tail yoke embellished with long fringes. They do not seem to have adopted the Plateau dress with its square-cut sleeves to any extent. Leggings of skin were knee-length and gartered, later of cloth beautifully beaded.

Footwear

Moccasins were of the center-seam type, with an elongated U-shaped vamp that also served as the tongue. Cuffs were added, which could be worn up in the winter and bound with long thongs that were threaded through the top of the moccasin proper. Footwear, like other attire, was handsomely decorated with quillwork, later beadwork.

Outer Wear

The Upper Kutenai wore buffalo robes, either from the buffalo they hunted on the Plains, or in trade from Plains Indians. Lower Kutenai tended to wear Salish blankets obtained from their Interior Salish neighbors. Elk hide and deer hide with the hair left on made suitable robes for winter; when tanned they made lighter weight mantles. Rabbit pelts were cut spirally and the strips woven into warm but fragile cloaks, used especially by the women and children. Some men in the mountains wore the blanket-coat of the Hudson's Bay Company. After 1900 women liked to wear plaid blankets and shawls of the Pendleton type.

Hair Styles

Some of the men wore the hair straight up, an old-time style used by warriors for its grotesque effect; with the use of bear grease or buffalo dung, they stiffened it to stand in a point or to curve into a horn shape. This was often painted. Some men wore the frontal lock with the rest of the hair hanging loose; others wore the typical two braids of the Plains, often wrapped with strips of otter fur or cloth, and with a scalplock at the back hanging from the crown of the head. Women wore the hair loose or in two braids. Weasel tails were sometimes fastened into the braids of both sexes.

Headgear

Some warriors wore the elaborate Plains headdresses, but these were more like the Blackfoot style with the upright circle of feathers; it was not until modern times that they adopted the halo headdress. Usually the men wore one or two feathers in the hair. Some women, particularly those of the Lower Kutenai, wore the tall basket hat of the Plateau; later, women exchanged the basket hat for cloth headscarves, tied in the back. Both sexes wore simple fur hats in winter.

Accessories

Belts were of leather; later, women wore cloth sashes. To the belts were fastened the usual bags and pouches. Some bags were of tanned leather, heavily fringed and colorfully beaded. Pipe bags had long fringes and beaded sections. Lower Kutenai women wove bags of grasses, such as tule, or roots, decorated with animal designs. Armbands and garters were beaded strips of leather or cloth. A few men carried eagle-feather fans. Fur mittens were worn in early days; in the late nineteenth century gloves (gauntlets) were made with large, heavily beaded cuffs.

Jewelry

Loop necklaces were extremely popular with the men, so long that some almost reached to the crotch; often worn with these loop necklaces were chokers of pipe beads, dentalium shells, or padded, beaded rolls. Men often wore hair ornaments dangling at the sides of the face, fashioned of pipe beads or bead clusters; hair bows were also an item of male jewelry. Women wore abalone shells, square or round, in the braids at ear level, or one shell near the part on the left-hand side. Necklaces were also made of strands of shells or beads.

Garment Decoration

Quillwork was not as common among the Kutenai as beadwork, which was at first of geometric designs, later floral, showing the influence of the Iroquois men who came among them in the nineteenth century. A favorite beadwork motif was the Oregon grape. Punctuated leather designs on men's shirts were further embellished with fringing and scalloped edges. Another popular decoration was the application of "cut-out" pieces of leather painted in a contrasting color. Some garments were painted with realistic figures, often those seen in dreams. Feathers, ermine tails, and squirrel tails were also added for decorative effect.

Face and Body Embellishment

The Lower Kutenai practiced face painting occasionally, but tattooing was somewhat rare. However, Bodmer painted a Kutenai man with the lower part of his face tattooed black.

Transitional Dress

By 1900 Kutenai men had adopted European-style garments for everyday wear, retaining tribal clothing for ceremonial wear. Women wore the Plateau dress well into the twentieth century, also retaining it for special occasions. However, little of Kutenai dress remains today. For powwows and tourist attractions, the typical Plains style predominates.

Key Sources

Baker, Paul. *The Forgotten Kutenai.* Boise, Idaho, 1955.

Boas, Franz. "The Kootenay." *Annual Archaeological Report.* Appendix to the Report of the Minister of Education, Ontario, Canada. 1905.

Curtis, Edward S. *The North American Indian.* Vol. 7. New York: Johnson Reprint Company, 1970.

Johnson, Olga Weydemeyer. *Flathead and Kootenay: The Rivers, the Tribes and the Region's Traders.* Glendale, CA: Arthur H. Clark, 1969.

"The Kootenay." *British Columbia Heritage Series* 1(8). Victoria, British Columbia: Department of Education.

Turney-High, Harry H. "Ethnography of the Kutenai." American Anthropological Association *Memoirs* 56.

Nez Perce

The Nez Perce received their name from the French for "pierced noses," a misnomer for, so far as is known, they were never given to that practice.

Shahaptian speakers, they roamed the area from the Bitterroot Mountains of western Montana to the Blue Mountains of eastern Washington. The Upper Nez Perce lived along the Salmon River and, having acquired horses in 1750, often went onto the Plains to hunt buffalo; they were famed as horsemen and horse breeders. The Lower Nez Perce inhabited the area around the Snake River and were primarily fishermen. Lewis and Clark met the Nez Perce in 1805, describing their dress and commenting that they were attired much like the Shoshone. Soon explorers and trappers entered the area, followed by fur traders, then missionaries, and finally settlers in the 1850s. With land so rich in natural resources, the government wanted to open up the region for development, offering to establish a reservation for the Nez Perce. Chief Joseph refused to recognize a treaty of 1863 by which the whites were permitted to enter Wallowa Valley, the ancient home of the Nez Perce. When the government attempted to enforce the treaty, Chief Joseph and his followers resisted; finally, after bitter battles, Joseph led his people, about 200 warriors and their families, on a thousand-mile retreat, hoping to escape to Canada. With his people freezing and starving, many of them killed, he was forced to surrender within 20 miles of the Candian border. It was a bitter capitulation, but Chief Joseph became renowned for his heroic leadership. George Catlin painted some of the Nez Perce in the 1830s and Gustavus Sohon sketched them in the 1850s. Edward Curtis and other photographers have recorded their lifeways.

A Nez Perce man wears beaded leggings and an "octopus" shoulder bag.

Men's Basic Dress

Nez Perce men wore the short skin shirt of the Plateau with its punctured decoration. Often worn over this shirt was a collar consisting of an entire otter skin with the tail hanging down in front. Koch says that the Nez Perce used deerskins dyed to a salmon color. Catlin painted two of the chiefs, Rabbit Skin Leggings and No Horns on His Head, who were visiting the Sioux and whose attire shows strong Sioux influence. Shirts had beaded bands over the shoulders and down the arms, as well as beaded rosettes or rectangles on the chest and back. Later shirts, like those of the Sioux, were thigh-length. Breechclouts were of skin with fringes; later they were of cloth, ankle-length, with vertical bands of beading. Late in the nineteenth century long plaid breechcloths were favored. Thigh-length leggings of deerskin, mountain-goat skin, and even of rabbit fur, had side flaps and fringed bottom tabs, and were frequently painted with horizontal stripes. Later made of cloth, especially blue strouding, the leggings had side flaps edged with white, as well as rectangles at the bottom with white edgings. Some later leggings were made from Hudson's Bay Company blankets. Shirts and leggings were often embellished with quill-wrapped horsehair fringes, a characteristic type of decoration found especially among the Nez Perce and the Crow.

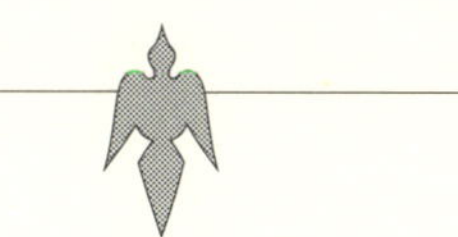

Standing next to a tipi door decorated with animal pelts, a Nez Perce woman holds a cornhusk friendship bag and wears a belted deerskin dress with a beaded yoke and rows of thongs on the skirt. In addition to a basketry hat she wears long loops of bead and shell necklaces and feather and shell earrings.

Women's Basic Dress

When Lewis and Clark met them in 1805, the Nez Perce women wore ankle-length skin dresses without a belt, decorated with beads, shells, and little pieces of brass. By the mid-1800s they were wearing the two-skin dress with the deer tail retained front and back. Later dresses had the dip in the yoke without the tail. The yoke was heavily beaded in the Plains style; long fringes edged the yoke, the side seams, and the uneven hemline, often with dewclaws strung into the fringes. Rows of thongs were also used as ornament on dresses. A decorated belt was usually a part of the deer-tail dress. Often, too, an underblouse was worn, precursor of the Plateau dress. By 1900 the yoke was decorated in a "Plateau" style with long loops of beads forming a modified swag pattern, a style that had persisted since 1800 among the Nez Perce. Also by 1900 the Plateau T-shaped dress, with its contrasting bands of color and square-cut oversleeves, was worn by many of the women, a style that continued well into the new century. Leggings were knee-length and gartered with bands of leather or cloth, handsomely beaded.

Footwear

Moccasins were the soft-sole type with the seam along the side of the foot, earlier decorated with porcupine quillwork, later with beadwork or a combination of the two. Maurer shows a Nez Perce moccasin with a popular design of a long beaded trapezoid emanating from a circle or a bar with flanking bars; diagonally striped bands and eight-pointed stars also seem to have been common features. Conn tells about the use of "scatter beading" in Plateau moccasins, in which the beads were sewn individually to a backing in simple figures or a polka-dot pattern; this was generally used as a way of creating a mottled surface or a variation in texture. Typically moccasins were painted red. Snowshoes were necessary for hunting in the deep snows of winter.

Outer Wear

Robes were of deer, elk, or buffalo skin decorated with shells, beads, and paintings. Some robes were of rabbit fur, the pelt cut into strips and woven in a simple weave; warm but fragile, these were commonly worn by women and children. Some men wore the *capotes* of the French traders, front-opening coats made from the white Hudson's Bay Company blankets with their broad colored stripes. After 1900 Pendleton blankets were favored, particularly appealing because the designs were loosely based on those of the Southwest tribes; women preferred the blankets with long fringes.

Hair Styles

Most men wore an upswept or pompadour hair style, typically combined with the rest of the hair hanging loose or in two braids; white thongs were often twined into the braids or else the braids were wrapped with otter fur. Some men took a wide lock at the front, coated it with bear grease and buffalo dung, and folded it back in a loop over the forehead. Some men wore the forelock, cut square on the forehead, but not as long as those of the Cree or Sioux to the east. Women wore the hair loose or in two braids.

Headgear

The "stand-up" warbonnet (not the "halo" type), made of eagle feathers set in a beaded leather band, and with strips of ermine fur at the sides, was generally worn by the Nez Perce warriors, or else they donned a cap made of an entire wolf's head with the ears standing erect; this was adorned with bear claws, bird feathers, and other decorations. Some wore the

Made of cotton string, cornhusks, and native fiber in the 1960s, this Nez Perce woman's hat shows the traditional technique of wrapped twining and use of a stepped design.

horned headdress. Flat fur caps were often donned in the winter. Visors, as protection from the sun or snow, were made of a strip of skin from a moose's mane and worn by both sexes. Women wore the tall basket hat of the Plateau, fez-shaped and typically ornamented with designs woven in; it was made of Indian hemp in a wrapped twining technique with bear grass dyed in dark colors to carry the design. The designs were in zigzags with three points at the top and three at the bottom. Later hats were made of cornhusk with trade yarn to fill in the designs of "stepped feet."

Accessories
Wolf furs were treasured, the pelts hanging over an arm or wrapped around the waist. Belts, especially those worn by women, were wide and heavily beaded. Garters were beaded strips or leather thongs. Women all carried one or two of the "friendship bags," made first of grasses, then of cornhusk with designs in commercial yarns, still later of jute string and yarn. The false-embroidery designs consisted mainly of arrows, eight-pointed stars, triangles, and similar geometric forms. Later, abstract floral shapes were common. Some "octopus bags," with their eight tabs at the bottom, were acquired in trade. Men wore bandolier bags, in the style of the women's friendship bags.

Jewelry
The loop necklace was a favorite with the men, usually combined with a choker of dentalium shells or strands of beads. At times the cascading strands of beads were further ornamented with large pieces of abalone shell or large pony beads. Squarish or round pieces of abalone were also worn at the neck (on a cord) or tied into the braid at ear level (women) or as earrings (men). Also worn in the ears were fur strips, conch shells, clusters of beads, or metal hoops. Necklaces of bones were popular, as were those of bear claws. Lewis recorded in his journal (1806) that the Nez Perce men wore in their noses "a single shell of wampum," which was probably dentalium. Later authorities claim they did not wear nose ornaments. Lewis and Clark also reported that the women wore bracelets of brass and copper, as well as dress decorations of brass, the brass seemingly obtained from trade kettles.

Armor
Small round shields of elk skin were painted and adorned with feathers. Armor was made of layers of tough elk skin or buffalo hide; the Nez Perce were also said to have worn helmets of elk skin.

Garment Decoration
Using beargrass and Indian hemp, the Nez Perce created fine basketry, as seen in their high fez-like hats and their bags. Possibly because of this craft, they did little with porcupine quills. But beadwork was highly valued by them, using designs done in false embroidery on their basketry items. Later they developed typical designs in abstract floral patterns; Gogol, in describing their contour bags, says they used the double-curve motif (showing eastern influence) in the early bags, later developing abstract florals in a three-part division, both horizontally and vertically, with the beads sewn to the fabric or buckskin in an applique stitch. Their

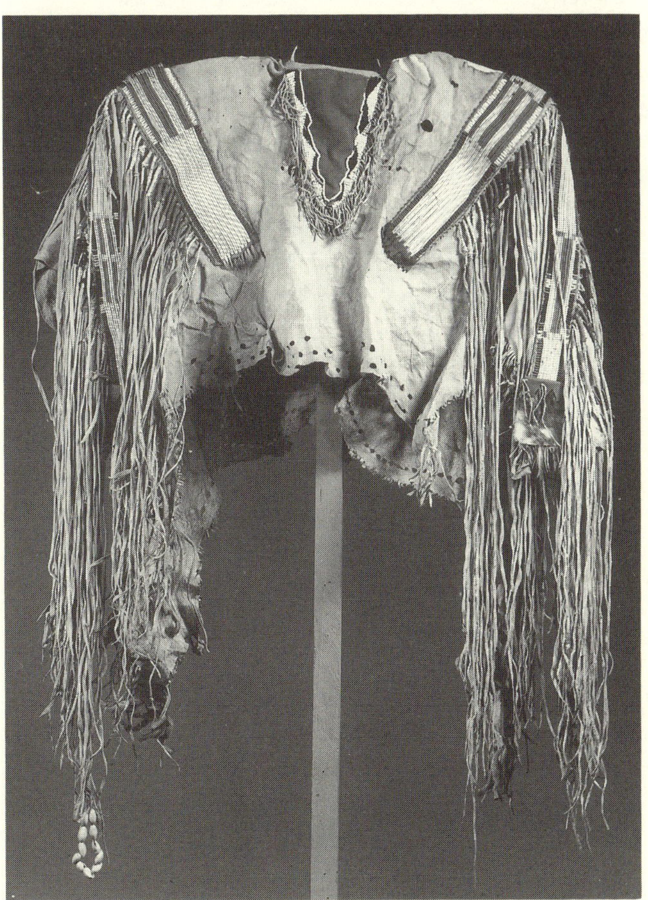

This leather Nez Perce shirt from the 1840s, decorated with porcupine quills, horsehair, and pony beads, has strouding at its neck. Shirts of the period tended to be short, coming to about the midriff.

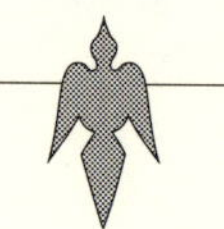

wrapping of horsehair with quills for use in fringes was typical of this tribe and the Crow, from whom they also adopted beadwork patterns and techniques.

Face and Body Embellishment

Aside from decorating the face and the center part of the hair with red paint for special occasions, little other means of embellishment was used.

Transitional Dress

It was the usual Plateau story in the transition to white attire. Early in this century the men were wearing purchased garments, such as trousers, coats (even Prince Albert coats), hats, and top hats, but adorning them with beads, feathers, and shells. The women continued to wear the cloth Plateau dress with square-cut sleeves and bands of contrasting color, although some adopted the long, full skirts and cotton blouses of the white women. Cotton neck scarves were popular with the men, and the women wore the scarves as headscarves, tied at the back. Shawls were also the usual female outer wrap. For ceremonial wear, they embraced the Plains garb, so universally adopted.

Key Sources

Alcorn, Rowena L. *Last Trail to Bear Paw: Flight of the Nez Perces, 1877.* Tacoma, WA: Western Media, 1977.

Curtis, Edward S. *The North American Indian.* Vol. 8. New York: Johnson Reprint Company, 1970.

Gogol, John M. "The Archetypal Columbia River Plateau Contour Beaded Bag." In *Eye of the Angel: Selections from the Derby Collection.* Northampton, MA, 1990.

Haines, Francis H. *The Nez Perces: Tribesmen of the Columbia Plateau.* Norman: University of Oklahoma Press, 1955.

Josephy, Alvin M., Jr. *The Nez Perce Indians.* Lincoln: University of Nebraska Press, 1979.

Shawley, Stephen Douglas. "Nez Perce Dress: A Study in Culture Change." Master's Thesis, University of Idaho, 1974.

Spinden, Herbert J. "The Nez Perce Indians." American Anthropological Association Memoirs, 1908.

Taylor, Colin. "Costume Decorated with Quill-Wrapped Hair: Nez Perce or Crow?" *American Indian Art* 6(3).

Sanpoil/Nespelem

The Sanpoil and Nespelem of eastern Washington, Salish speakers, lived in cultural isolation, avoiding all conflict possible. Living on the banks of the Columbia River above Big Bend, the two tribes were closely associated, often being considered one people. The Chelan and Colville were neighboring tribes who shared much of their material culture. These peoples were at odds both with the social caste system of the Northwest Coast and the glorified warriors of the Plains; however, they did adopt some features of Plains dress. Lewis and Clark reported on these tribes in their journals (1804–1806).

Men's Basic Dress

Early men's attire was scanty, often just a breechclout of woven hemp, with little more added in the winters. About 1700 Plains dress began to have an impact in the area, and breechclouts and leggings were made of deerskin or of fur. Ponchos of woven grasses and other fibers were replaced by deerskin shirts. With white contact of the early-nineteenth century, and with cloth available from the traders, garments were made of strouding and other cloth. Leggings displayed the patches edged with white at the bottom. Plaid breechcloths were popular.

Women's Basic Dress

Aboriginal clothing seems to have been an apron, front and back, made of woven Indian hemp or of bark mixed with deer hair. Ponchos, woven of hemp, were added for cooler weather. With influence from the Plains, these garments were replaced by a buckskin wraparound skirt and poncho of the same material. Leggings were of woven hemp, later of skin. In the late nineteenth century the Plateau dress was adopted with its square-cut sleeves, contrasting bands of color, and cotton underblouse.

Footwear

Footwear may have been absent in the earliest times; possibly skins, grass, or fur were simply wrapped about the foot when necessary. Skin moccasins seem to have been introduced later; they were simple and unadorned, and of the soft-sole, side-seam type. Crude snowshoes were worn by hunters in winter.

Outer Wear
Aboriginal robes were of woven grass, with robes of animal fur, such as fox or wolf pelts, for winter wear. The ubiquitous rabbits furnished robes for women and children. As the Plains influence became more marked, buffalo robes were occasionally acquired in trade. By 1900 both sexes were wearing the blankets manufactured by the nearby Pendleton Mills; women also favored their plaid shawls with the deep fringes.

Hair Styles
The hair was worn loose or in two braids as a rule; however, there were several hair styles for both sexes, including the pompadour for men. Women adorned the ends of their braids with silk ribbons from the traders. Both men and women plucked the eyebrows to form a straight line, and the men used bone or wooden tweezers to pluck out the scant facial hair.

Headgear
No headgear was worn by these people until fur caps were introduced from the Plains along with other items of attire. Some women adopted the tall basketry hat in the nineteenth century.

Accessories
Belts, garters, and armbands were made of strips of leather, sometimes decorated with quillwork or, more commonly, beadwork. Large, finely woven rectangular bags were a popular item with both sexes. In the early days, these were of grasses, such as Indian hemp; later, as the Sanpoil and Nespelem began to practice some agriculture, cornhusk was used with colorful designs created with commercial yarns; often these designs were like the quilt patterns of the period. Fringed pouches of buckskin were also a favored form.

Jewelry
Men wore the loop necklace with its multiple strands of swags, often adorned with a large piece of abalone shell in the center of each swag; with this was worn a choker, generally of several rows of dentalium shells interspersed with glass beads. Men wore earrings of abalone shell; the women usually wore one in each braid at ear level. Women also wore chokers, as well as other necklaces of beads and shells.

Armor
These were peaceable folk, and wore no form of armor.

Special Costumes
The Sanpoil believed that the dead were in a land located at the end of the Milky Way; the body was wrapped in deerskins and buried with personal items. Mourners cut their hair very short to show their grief.

Garment Decoration
Quillwork was known, but little was done. The women became expert beadworkers, using the technique to decorate garments and accessories for ceremonial purposes. They were also experts in basketry, making finely woven, flat, rectangular bags with designs applied in a form of false embroidery.

Face and Body Embellishment
The only type of adornment practiced by these tribes was the occasional use of red face paint. They did not engage in skull deformation as was done by their Chinookan neighbors.

Transitional Dress
Despite their desire for isolation, these people were visited by traders, trappers, and settlers after the Lewis and Clark expedition opened the way to the coast, so they were early exposed to white garments, accessories, and techniques of manufacture and decoration. By 1900 all traces of tribal clothing had vanished except for the Plateau dress worn by the women, and the Plains-type ceremonial costumes donned by the men for special occasions.

Key Sources
Ray, Verne F. "The Sanpoil and Nespelem." University of Washington *Publications in Anthropology* 5.

Wasco/Wishram
The Wishram lived near The Dalles of the Columbia River, and across the river on the south bank were the Wasco, close friends and allies. The Wasco name meant "cup or small bowl of horn," referring to a cup-shaped rock nearby; Wishram was a name given to them by the Yakima and Klickitat Indians. The Wasco were called Echeloot by Lewis and Clark. Both

Photographed in 1901, a Wasco man wears leggings attached to a belt, a breechclout, and feather bustle. He has attached a roach and wears his hair in braids.

tribes spoke Chinook, as well as the Chinook jargon, so important for trade at The Dalles. Because of the influx of traders in their area, both tribes adopted elements of Basin, Plateau, and Northwest Coast dress. Trade was brisk in buffalo robes, shells from the Pacific coast, and glass beads and ornaments from the traders to the east. However, due in part to raids from the Paiute and Shoshone, the area was depopulated and the Wasco and Wishram, much diminished in numbers, eventually settled on reservations.

Men's Basic Dress

Clothing was scanty aboriginally; men wore a breechclout of skin or of a fur pelt, unlike their Chinook neighbors to the west who wore breechclouts of woven cedar bark. With this a fur robe sufficed in winter. But with Plains influence, the men began to wear deerskin garments—a long breechclout with flaps front and back, thigh-length leggings with side flaps, and a long shirt, almost to the knees. These were decorated with beads, sometimes porcupine quillwork. Some were belted. Later, in the mid-1800s, they began to wear cloth garments in the usual Plateau styles—a long breechcloth with broad horizontal or vertical stripes, leggings with white-edged rectangles at the front or on the sides, and a long, dark cotton shirt with fringes at the shoulders or beadwork panels.

Women's Basic Dress

Early primitive garments were of fibers (cedar bark or bear grass) or skin, consisting of a double apron. Later, reflecting Plains influence, the women wore an ankle-length dress of tanned leather in the two-skin style, with the deer tail retained in the yoke; this was usually belted, had fringes at the sides and the bottom, and often rows of thongs. The yoke was heavily beaded in a lazy-stitch technique. In the late nineteenth century, during their reservation days, the Wasco and Wishram women adopted the cloth Plateau dress with its square-cut sleeves, contrasting bands of color, and cotton underblouse.

Footwear

Although in the early days little or no footwear was worn, plain moccasins with cuffs were later made in the soft-sole side-seam manner. A few wore front-seam moccasins with tongues. This footwear was often painted red and adorned with beadwork. Simple snowshoes were worn by the men to track deer and elk in the winter.

Outer Wear

Robes were of deer, elk, or wolf skins. The fur was retained for winter wear; both sides were tanned for lighter weight robes. Gray-squirrel pelts were sewn together to make warm, attractive robes for the children. Rabbit pelts were cut spirally into long strips, which were woven in a simple fashion into robes for the women. Some men wore the buffalo robes obtained in trade.

Hair Styles

Hair was worn loose, in braids, or in two rolls brought forward over the shoulders. Some braids were wrapped, especially by men. Some men wore a small braid at each side of the face, the rest of the hair hanging loose. Another style featured bangs on the forehead, the hair cut at the sides at ear level, and the rest loose.

Headgear

Beautiful wedding caps were made of multicolored beads and dentalium shells, displaying the family wealth; from a velvet crown the beads and shells were festooned in long strands down the back and at the sides. Worn with the cap was a wedding veil, also of beads and dentalium shells, as well as bells, coins, and other trinkets. Women wore the twined basketry hat made of *Apocynum* and decorated with dyed grasses. Men went bareheaded, except for fur pelts used as caps in winter.

Accessories

Both the Wasco and the Wishram developed a remarkable art style, readily seen in the fine baskets and bags they wove decorated in shades of brown on natural cream-colored fibers (usually *apocynum).* Belts were of leather, as were garters and armbands.

Jewelry

The most popular adornment for men was the loop necklace with its many swags of beads; these were often of white clamshell disks from California, and were usually worn with a choker of dentalium shells interspersed with the large glass pony beads. The white clamshell disks were also used in making necklaces for the women. Large square or round

A Wishram bride wears a loop necklace, a dress with six broad rows of lazy-stitch beading on the yoke. She has three strands of white disk shell beads, used as currency, as a necklace. The front of her wedding cap has a row of Chinese coins.

pieces of abalone shell were fastened into the women's braids at ear level, or at the center part. In early times both sexes were said to have worn a dentalium shell thrust through the nasal septum.

Garment Decoration

Very little beadwork was done by these peoples until the nineteenth century, despite the vigorous trading at The Dalles; some authorities think the later development of beading may have come from Iroquois Indians entering the area from the east. But the beaded figures continued the unique style as found in the famous woven bags; a distinctive motif was that of a skeletal figure with a large hexagonal head. Abstract animals were also favored. No painting on garments is mentioned, except for the red moccasins.

Face and Body Embellishment

Skull flattening was practiced by many tribes in this region, particularly the Chinook. Lewis and Clark reported that the Echeloots (Wishram) flattened the heads of their children, and observed that the males as well as the females were subjected to this practice, but among the mountain tribes the custom was confined to females. No mention is made of tattooing. There are passing remarks about some painting of the faces.

Transitional Dress

Because of the pitifully small group of Wasco and Wishram left when they entered reservation life, they could hold onto little of their heritage. They adopted the Plateau type of garments, followed by complete transition to European-style clothing.

Key Sources

Schlick, Mary D. and Kate C. Duncan. "Wasco-Style Woven Beadwork: Merging Artistic Traditions." *American Indian Art Magazine* (Summer 1991): 36–45.

Spier, Leslie and Edward Sapir. "Wishram Ethnography." University of Washington *Publications in Anthropology* 3.

Yakima

The Yakima inhabited the area from the Cascade Mountains of Washington as far as the Columbia River basin to the east, living especially on the lower course of the Yakima River. There were 14 or more tribes or bands and all three languages were spoken—Salishan, Shahaptian, and Chinook; it is difficult to establish how many were true Yakima and how many were members of other tribes. They hunted deer, bear, and smaller game; they had many horses, were highly mobile, and traded vigorously at The Dalles. Their first white contact was with Lewis and Clark in 1805. They fought the Yakima War in 1858; lost horses, lands, and possessions; and were removed to a reservation. Despite their reverses the Yakima have retained much of their native culture.

Men's Basic Dress

Yakima men easily made the transition from the early primitive fiber and skin garments to the elaborate skin garments of the Plains and finally the nineteenth-century reservation wear, influenced so strongly by European-style clothing. Their basic costume was scanty, just a skin or fiber breechclout, with other garments added as the weather turned colder, or as people dressed for special occasions. Sometimes a fur kilt or fur apron was worn as a breechclout. Fringed leggings of skin were thigh-length, fastened to a belt or thong around the waist; later cloth leggings, usually of dark-blue stroud cloth, had the characteristic panels edged with white at the bottom. Shirts of skin, sometimes sleeveless, commonly rather short and decorated with fringing, were added in winter; these later had the beaded chest medallions and the beaded shoulder and sleeve bands of the Plains shirts. Later shirts were of dark cloth but retained the beadwork. Later breechcloths were also of dark cloth with horizontal or vertical stripes of a contrasting color and with added fringes, or of fringed wool plaid. For ceremonial wear, most men liked to have a pelt (preferably wolf skin) hanging over the arm or attached to their garments.

Women's Basic Dress

In the summer the early Yakima woman wore a short wraparound skirt or a double apron of woven fiber, adding knee-length skin or fiber leggings, and a short poncho-type cape as needed. Early skin dresses, indicating Plains influence, were either a strap-and-sleeve dress or a side-seam dress, later developing into the two-skin dress with the deer tail retained. These

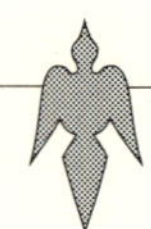

skin dresses were adorned with quillwork, beadwork, or a combination of the two, as well as rows of thongs and fringes. In the Reservation Period they adopted the T-shaped cloth Plateau dress with the square-cut sleeves, the bands of contrasting color at sleeve ends and the hem, and the cotton underblouse. These were made from a rectangular piece of cloth, folded for the shoulders, cut in a T so the sleeves were elbow length, and with triangular gussets inserted at the sides. The yoke area featured rows of glass beads in lazy stitch, often with beaded fringes at the bottom.

Before European contact, Yakima wore few items of clothing. By 1901 many, including this man, adapted attire influenced by the Plains tradition, including leggings with wide flaps, hair braided and wrapped in fur, and a loop necklace with many swags.

Footwear

Moccasins were worn by the Yakima, but mostly in the winter; these were of buckskin of the side-seam type with an added sole of rawhide and with tall cuffs wrapped with rawhide thongs. Moccasins for ceremonial wear were without cuffs and were decorated with quillwork or beadwork, the latter in a floral style. Small, round snowshoes worn by the hunters in winter were laced with thongs and attached to the foot with leather straps.

Outer Wear

Early robes were of bighorn-sheep and mountain-goat skins, but these had disappeared by the time of Lewis and Clark. Fox skins were popular, as were elk, wolf, and deer; some of these were like capes, being merely waist length. Buffalo robes were obtained from the Plains through trade. The warm but fragile rabbit-skin robes were woven by the women from spirally cut strips of fur, and worn by the women and children particularly.

Hair Styles

The hair was worn loose in the early days. With Plains influence in the nineteenth century, the men began to wear braids, often fur-wrapped, or pompadours with loose or braided hair. Sometimes the hair was parted on the left side; otherwise the center part was customary. Women wore two braids. During the reservation days, benefits were sometimes withheld from the Yakima unless the men cut their hair, a source of great irritation and friction.

Headgear

Except for fur hats for winter wear, headgear was not worn by the Yakima men until they began to adopt Plains wear in the nineteenth century. Then some men wore the horned bonnet adorned with many ermine tails; others wore the huge halo headdress of the Plains warriors, but the decoration remained essentially Yakima in character. Later some men wore a beaded headband with one or two erect eagle feathers. Women wore the basket hat of the Plateau, about ten inches high and four inches in diameter at the top; it was ornamented with designs using colored grasses in the overlay technique, designs with three points at the top and three at the bottom. This was

Photographed in 1900, a Yakima mother, right, and daughter, whose face is painted, display friendship bags.

worn even after Plains dress styles were adopted. A unique Plateau form of headgear was the bridal headdress; Conn shows a magnificent example adorned with treasured dentalium shells from the Pacific coast, large pony glass beads, and Chinese coins, which were a favored form of decoration that had come into the area in the mid-nineteenth century.

Accessories

Armlets, wristlets, and garters were fashioned of fur or strips of beaded leather tied with thongs. Some men wore a band diagonally across the chest with ermine tails hanging from it. Bandolier bags were also popular, decorated with elk teeth, buttons, and "mother-of-pearl" disks (which may have been the white clamshell disks acquired in trade from California). Around 1900 some men were wearing

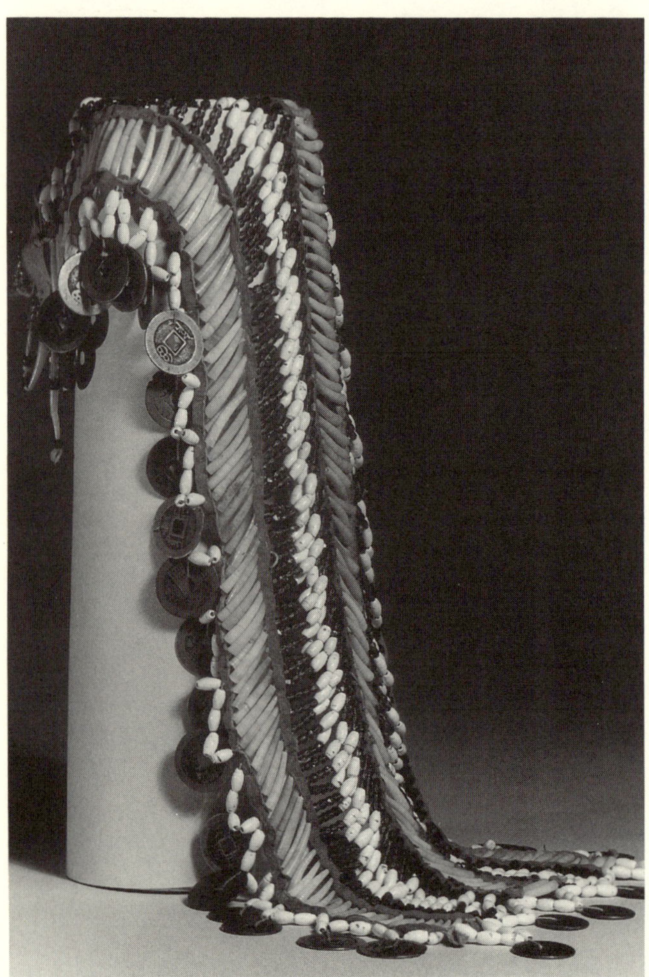

A Yakima bride's headdress represented her family's wealth with its three vertical rows of dentalium shells. Chinese coins, traded inland from the Pacific coast, edge the piece.

the hair pipe breastplate of the Plains. Pouches were of deerskin decorated with beadwork and fringe. Some fiber bags were obtained from the Wasco and Wishram tribes to the south.

Jewelry

The loop necklace made of white clamshell disk beads and often decorated with large pieces of abalone shell was usually worn with a choker made of rows of dentalium shells interspersed with large pony beads. Bear claws and teeth were formed into highly valued necklaces. Strings of beads and shells, especially olivella and cowrie shells, were also worn around the neck. Pieces of abalone, round or square, became earrings for the men or were worn by the women in their braids at ear level.

Garment Decoration

Daugherty, who has been the major authority for this tribe, says that the Yakima had a "highly sophisticated and conventionalized art style," reaching its zenith just before white contact. Although they adopted Plains attire, their decoration of it was distinctly their own. The women's yokes were beaded in long lazy-stitch swags, edged with beaded fringes. Typical colors of Yakima garments were black and white, and the large pony beads were preferred over the smaller seed beads. The women knew the basic weaving techniques—twining, coiling, and plaiting, as shown in their skillfully made basket hats and rabbit-skin robes. They knew quillwork, but it was not as commonly created as their beadwork. Other decorations were ermine tails, rows of thongs, and rows of buttons.

Face and Body Embellishment

There is some indication of the use of red and yellow paint for facial decoration. Oddly, despite their closeness to the Chinook and the fact that some of the Yakima spoke Chinook, there is no record of their having practiced skull deformation.

Transitional Dress

Men changed to European-style garments earlier than the women; by 1900 they were wearing cotton shirts, trousers, vests, and coats. The women continued with the Plateau dress well into the century, and finally, they too changed over to purchased garments, both

sexes retaining what Yakima garb they had for ceremonial occasions.

Key Sources

Curtis, Edward S. *The North American Indian.* Vol. 7. New York: Johnson Reprint Company, 1970.

Daugherty, Richard D. *The Yakima People.* Phoenix, AZ: Indian Tribal Series, 1973.

Gridley, M. *With One Sky above Us: Life on an Indian Reservation at the Turn of the Century.* New York: Putnam's, 1979.

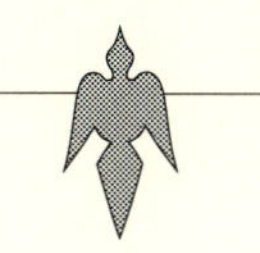

Chapter Seven

Costume of California

Above, left: A Tolowa woman wears a buckskin dance apron decorated with shells and tinklers.
Above, right: Hupa Jumping Dancers wear deerskin aprons and tall headdresses of woodpecker scalps attached to deerskin bands.

Below, left: A Hupa man wears a deerskin kilt.
Below, right: One of the few remaining items of traditional Chumash clothing, this woman's skirt was found in a cave near Santa Barbara, California.

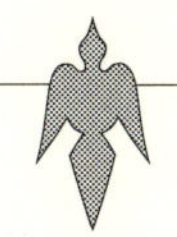

California

Any discussion of California seems to lead to superlatives. The state has the highest mountain—Mt. Whitney—in the lower 48 states, as well as the lowest elevation, in Death Valley. It has the tallest trees (the giant sequoias and the redwoods) and some of the oldest trees (bristlecone pines). It has the longest coastline of any of the lower 48 states, while its valleys, particularly the San Joaquin and Imperial, make California the leader in the production of many fruits and vegetables.

When discussing the California Indians, the superlatives continue. The aboriginal population was the densest of any of the North American culture areas. The languages spoken were the most widely varied of any area, and included 6 major language groups, 21 distinct language families, and over 100 dialects; "the greatest aboriginal diversity in the world," according to Hodge. Tragically, the destruction of the region's Indian people following white appearance and encroachment was the most rapid and brutal on the continent. From an estimated population of over 300,000 at the time the first mission was established in 1769, 100 years later barely 20,000 survivors were left.

To understand better the costume of these peoples, it may help to look more closely at their environment and history. The state has two major mountain ranges—the Sierra Nevada and the coastal ranges. The northern part of the state has great forests with towering trees, many rivers, and a rocky coastline with craggy cliffs. The central area is a large fertile valley ringed with mountains and to the west the rocky seacoast and San Francisco Bay. The southern area is mountainous and arid, with few lakes or rivers and with a coastline of many fine beaches. The eastern strip, the land west of the Sierra and continuing south to the lands bordering the Colorado River, is reminiscent of the Great

Peoples of California

Achomawi
Athapaskan, p. 247
Atsugewi
Cahuilla
Cato, p. 247
Chemehuevi
Chilula, p. 247
Chimariko
Chumash, p. 249
Cocopa
Costanoan, p. 251
Cupeno
Diegueño, p. 261
Essalen
Fernandiño
Gabrieliño, p. 261
Halchidoma
Hupa, p. 253
Juaneño, p. 261
Karok
Kawaiisu
Klamath/Modoc, p. 257
Koso
Lassik, p. 247
Luiseño, p. 261
Maidu, p. 259
Mattole, p. 247
Mission, p. 261
Miwok, p. 265
Mojave, p. 267
Mono
Nongatl, p. 247
Panamint
Pomo, p. 272
Salinan
San Nicoleño
Serrano
Shasta, p. 274
Sinkyone, p. 247
Tolowa, p. 247
Tubatulabal
Wailaki, p. 247
Washo
Whilkut, p. 247
Wintun, p. 276
Wiyot
Yana/Yahi, p. 278
Yokuts, p. 280
Yuki, p. 282
Yuma, p. 283
Yurok, p. 286

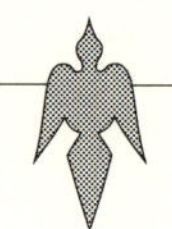

Basin with its high and low deserts, much of it virtually uninhabitable. In fact, almost one-third of California was, and is, extremely inhospitable because of its peaks and vast deserts, able to support only a very small population in many areas.

The Indians of California typically lived in autonomous villages, traveling a few miles to higher elevations on foraging expeditions in the summer and descending to the valleys in the winter. It was an economy based on gathering, especially the abundant acorns; some fishing, particularly salmon in the north; and hunting.

California has been inhabited 10,000 years and possibly longer. Archaeological sites have yielded evidence of a remarkably stable economy that persisted into the historical period. There was widespread trade, with beads of olivella and other shells functioning as a kind of currency in some areas.

European voyages of exploration began with Cabrillo in 1542. In 1769 the first mission was established in San Diego, with 20 more being built by 1823. Russians came in 1809, lured by the prospect of hunting sea otters, but they had little effect on Indian lifeways. There was a brief Mexican period, when the missions were secularized. Gold was discovered in 1848, and it was the beginning of the end for the California Indians, as the native people were subjected to diseases for which they had no immunity; brutal killings, massacres in some cases, also played a role in their demise. Some attempt was made to establish reservations, but the entire program was a failure. In the 1870s, as anthropology began to make its mark as an established science, there was a strong effort made to observe carefully the few specimens left of a vanishing race.

The warm climate obviated the necessity of much clothing on a daily basis. However, the Indian people did wear some garments, and not just for ceremonial occasions. Their clothing may be classified as (1) aboriginal, (2) white-influenced, and (3) mission clothing. The aboriginal dress changed little over the centuries of prehistory and during the historical period until the last half of the nineteenth century. The white-influenced garb will not be discussed here, for there was no pattern to it; the Indians adopted any article of European-style dress and wore it with their own traditional garments.

General Dress

Men's Basic Dress

Men went naked normally, especially older men, but for colder weather or for dances they donned a piece of buckskin, worn in a kilt style, to the mid-thighs or longer. Some wore a breechclout of leather, but without flaps in front or back, simply held in place by a belt. In the northern areas men sometimes wore a poncho affair of skin or fur. Skin leggings were worn only in the mountain snows.

Women's Basic Dress

Women were usually bare on top, especially before the whites came. Their major garment was a two-piece skirt, made of a small apron in front and a larger one in back, both tied on by thongs. It was of shredded bark or fiber of various kinds, depending on local vegetation, or of deerskin. Buckskin denoted wealth, and only poorer women wore a complete fiber skirt. If of leather, it would be a back piece overlapping a front fiber skirt, or both pieces would be of skin. Fiber skirts were twined together at the top for several inches. Ornamentation consisted of pine nuts, shells, beads, and other objects fastened to the strands of fiber or buckskin fringes at precise intervals so a horizontal pattern emerged.

Footwear

Moccasins were used only for traveling; these were one-piece and unsoled, seamed at the heel and up the front, ankle-length or higher, uncuffed. In the southern areas sandals of leather or of agave were worn. Snowshoes were used in the central and northern Sierras, but these were crude affairs that could be made in half an hour. They were round wooden hoops, often strung with grapevines, and had no tailpiece, as well as no provision for the heel.

Outer Wear

Rabbit-skin robes for cooler weather were fairly prevalent, but they tended to be shorter than those of the Southwest, more in the form of a cape thrown over the shoulders, or wrapped around the body, at times over one arm and under the other; they were secured in front with thongs. Occasionally armholes would be cut out. Feather robes were also worn. These were sometimes of bird skins, woven like rabbit robes, or the feathers were inserted into a netting.

A Karok deerskin dance hat has a crest of flicker feathers tipped by goldfinch breast feathers.

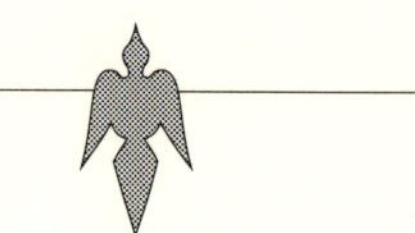

Furs were used as covering also; particularly prized were the sea-otter robes.

Hair Styles
Men and women wore the hair long and loose, at times with bangs, especially in the south. In some areas the men wore their long hair fastened on the top of the head with bone pins. Many men wore hair nets to hold the hair in place.

Headgear
Men generally went bareheaded, except for participation in ceremonies. The typical basketry hats, usually quite rounded, varied somewhat from one locale to another. In the north they were made with a straight overlay twining technique, were rounded in shape, and were worn at all times by the women and by the men when carrying a load, to ease the strain of the tumpline. In the central area the few caps worn were done in a coiling technique. In the south they were typically higher, like a truncated cone, and were donned by women for load-carrying; these were also made by a coiling method. Most caps were decorated with geometric designs colored by means of the natural colors of the fibers used. In a few places false embroidery was used to create the designs, and in some southern tribes, designs were painted on the hats.

Accessories
A few finger-woven fiber bags were produced. In the northern half of the state some men wore belts or sashes of netted fibers, using the folds to insert necessary articles for carrying. Most belts were simply thongs; a few were leather straps. Men with long hair in the north/central sections used hairpins to hold the hair in place on the top of the head.

Jewelry
Ornaments consisted predominantly of necklaces of beads, made of shell (olivella, abalone, dentalium, and others), stone, bone, magnesite, or steatite, as well as less permanent materials—pine nuts, seeds, cones, and twisted and braided straw. Gorgets of abalone pieces were popular with some tribes, as were earplugs or spools of steatite or bird bones. Small bones, rings, loops of beads, feathers, or sticks were inserted in pierced ears or noses.

Armor
Body armor of rods twined with string was worn for fighting, but since these were peaceable folk, there was little need for armor. In the north, tough elk hide was also used for armor as well as rods. Generally, no helmets were worn and no shields were carried.

Special Costumes
Large feathers, especially those of the turkey vulture, bald eagle, raven, yellow-bellied magpie, great horned owl, and California condor, were in great demand and added significantly to the spectacular appearance of dance costumes. Headbands, plumes on sticks, and headdresses used the yellow quills of the flicker, the red quills of the pileated woodpecker and the red-breasted sapsucker, as well as the blue quills of the Steller's jay. Headdresses formed a dazzling array, varying from tribe to tribe. Dance skirts, also, were often startling in their beauty. Throughout California mourning rites were important ceremonies; it was customary for the bereaved to cut off or singe the hair as a sign of sorrow. A widow blackened the face with pitch, which was allowed to remain until it wore off, at which time she was ready for remarriage.

Garment Decoration
Porcupine quillwork was not done by the California tribes except infrequently in the far north, nor did they work with glass beads except for the netted/beaded collars of the Mojave and some glass beadwork in the north during the late-nineteenth century. Feathers, besides being used for robes, were attached to the body and/or to the clothing. Eagle down was often inserted into the men's hair nets and into the strips of the dance skirts. Some false embroidery and painting was done on the basket hats, which also represented the only type of weaving done for garments, with the exception of the rabbit-skin robes. Some netting was done by the northern tribes.

Face and Body Embellishment
Tattooing was practiced by most tribes, more often by women than men, and more commonly on the face than the body. A few men, such as the Mojave, often were extensively tattooed. Painting of the face and body was popular everywhere, black, white, and red

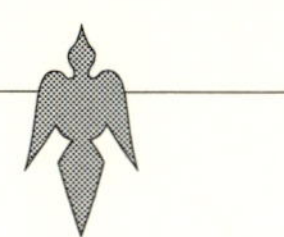

being the most favored colors. Bright-red cinnabar, which was mined in California and widely traded, is a dangerous pigment (sulphide of mercury), and some authorities believe it may have led to the diseased bones found in some burial sites. Painting was usually reserved for ritualistic occasions.

Transitional Dress

As the whites flooded into the area, the Indians abandoned their aboriginal clothes and quickly adopted European-style dress. Little remained but the ceremonial attire. By the early twentieth century, the surviving Indian population could scarcely be distinguished from the whites by their dress.

Athapaskan

The Athapaskan speakers of northern California may be divided into two groups: (1) The northern group consisted of the Hupa, Tolowa, Chilula, Whilkut, and the Mattole. (2) The southern group included the Nongatl, Lassik, Wailaki, Sinkyone, and the Cato. Culturally they followed the customs of the tribes to their west, with the emphasis on wealth, especially the display of that wealth in the form of obsidian blades, woodpecker scalps, and dentalium shells. These were hill people, small tribelets inhabiting permanent homes on the river banks; herds of elk and black-tailed deer roamed the area. Most of these people were rather dark of skin, short in stature, and quite round of face. Their first white contact was with the miners of the early 1850s and the results were devastating. Many tribes were decimated and became extinct. However, Edward S. Curtis managed to take some fine photogaphs of the Athapaskans, especially of the Tolowa and Hupa.

Men's Basic Dress

In hot weather the men went naked. The breechclout, when worn, was either an apron style, a wraparound kilt to the mid-thighs, or fitted through the crotch without flaps but held in place by a belt; usually of buckskin, it was occasionally of fur. At times a cape or poncho of deerskin was added.

Women's Basic Dress

Women wore the usual double-apron skirt, the front one of fibers, the back one, which overlapped the front, of skin; wealth was shown by wearing *both* aprons of skin. The torso was commonly bare, until after the whites arrived; then cloth bandeaus or blouses were added. An excellent photograph by Ericson (c. 1890) gives fine details of this costume, showing a buckskin overskirt with *Glycymeris* shell decorations and fringes with obsidian tinklers. The front underskirt was usually made of braided bear grass *(Xerophyllum tenax)* and was adorned with shells, beads, and pine nuts in patterns of horizontal rows, with a fringe of abalone-shell tinklers.

Footwear

Moccasins, when worn, were the typical California type—a one-piece soft shoe of buckskin with a front seam and a heel seam. Long ties held the tall cuffs in place. Moccasins were worn only for long journeys, for wood gathering, and for winter wear, at which time they were often lined with grass for warmth.

Outer Wear

A lightweight mantle of deer or elk skin was sometimes worn. The Sinkyones, especially, wore rabbit-skin robes, the pelt cut spirally in long strips that twisted as they dried and were then woven in a plain cross weave. These were shorter than the robes of colder areas, often being only waist-length.

Hair Styles

Both sexes wore the hair shoulder-length or longer; some gathered the hair into two masses in front of the shoulders, tied with thongs. A strip of mink fur adorned with woodpecker scalps was sometimes fastened into the hair. Women at times wore braids, wrapping them with strips of cloth or fur, and occasionally attaching shells or thimbles to them. Men, particularly, bound the hair into nets of iris fiber, using bone hairpins to keep the net and hair in place. Woven headbands were also worn.

Headgear

The overlay twined basket cap was worn habitually by the women, at times by the men; these caps, round like a bowl, made of hazel shoots and conifer roots, twined with bear grass or maidenhair ferns, were decorated with geometric designs made from the

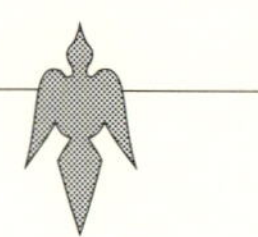

natural colors of the fibers or red-dyed with alder bark. The Wailaki, who preferred a somewhat flat-topped hat, represent the extreme southern limit of the use of the twined technique for hats. Woven headbands tended to be a later addition. Flat fur hats were occasional winter wear.

Accessories

Belts were a necessary item; these were either thongs or tanned leather straps, often heavily decorated with shells and tinklers, and featuring tassels at the ends. Some belts were simply strips of netting tied around the waist, which were handy repositories for necessary items. Other accessories were for ceremonial attire. Carved elk-horn purses in a long, cylindrical shape held various items, but especially the woodpecker-scalp headbands for dance wear.

Jewelry

Deer-hide bracelets were worn by both sexes. Men had the nasal septum pierced and inserted a dentalium shell, denoting wealth; the dentalium from northern tribes of the Pacific coast and the clamshell disk beads from southern tribes, both indications of wealth, were highly important to these people. Necklaces, consisting of strings of the disk beads, were choker length or longer, at times reaching to the waist. Obsidian pendants, also a sign of wealth, were attached to garments and made into jewelry in earlier times; later they were replaced by trade beads, thimbles, metal tinklers, and coins, particularly the perforated Chinese coins. Popular ear ornaments were pieces of *Haliotis* (abalone) shell.

Armor

Most men went to war naked or clad only in a breechclout, but the important warriors had the protection of a slat-and-rod corselet, held together with sinew. Armor of several thicknesses of tough elk hide was also reported. A thick cap of fur or elk hide protected the head. Sometimes the hair was coiled into a knot on top of the head and spikes were thrust through to keep enemies from grabbing for the hair. Only the Wailaki carried shields of tanned elkskin, thick and tough; this was worn at the back to leave the hands free, and when a warrior saw an arrow coming, he simply turned his back.

Special Costumes

There were many special ceremonies, such as the Feather Dance, Acorn Dance, Clover Dance, and the Black Bear Dance (when a bear was killed). Dance skirts and capes were made of the feathers of large birds, such as the condor, fastened into a net base of *Apocynum* (Indian hemp) fibers. Flicker quill headbands were typical of central California. For these rituals, sticks were carried, ornamented with feathers, tinklers, and tufts of down. Throughout these ceremonies, there was a conspicuous display of wealth in obsidian blades, woodpecker scalps, and dentalium shells. Mourning was indicated by cropping the hair and smearing pitch on the face or forehead, not to be removed until the end of the mourning period. The bereaved also wore a braided necklace for a year or the extent of the mourning period.

Garment Decoration

Weaving techniques consisted of twining and braiding, as seen in the basketry hats and the fiber skirts. The few rabbit-skin robes were woven in a cross weave. Netting, especially of iris fiber, was used as waistbands and as bases for dance skirts and capes. Decoration added to garments was of shells (particularly abalone and dentalium), tinklers, beads of nuts and seeds, later trade beads, and feathers.

Face and Body Embellishment

Tattooing was the only form of embellishment used. Most women had three vertical lines tattooed on the chin; some had more extensive tattooing on the nose and cheeks. It was optional among all the tribes on the forehead, cheeks, chin, chest, wrists, or legs. Mattole men tattooed a small, round blue spot on the middle of the forehead.

Transitional Dress

By the mid-nineteenth century European garments were commonly worn, especially by the men. Women used the cloth offered by the traders at first for dresses made in the traditional style, but later they, too, adopted garments of commercial manufacture. By the end of the century both sexes dressed like the whites. A few prized costumes were treasured and brought out for the ceremonial dances.

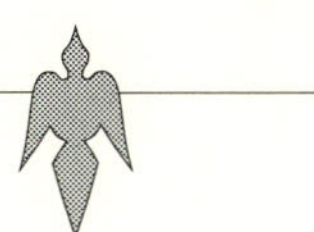

Key Sources

Curtis, Edward S. *The North American Indian.* Vol. 13. New York: Johnson Reprint Company, 1970.

Drucker, Philip. "The Tolowa and Their Southwest Oregon Kin." University of California *Publications in American Archaeology and Ethnology* 36(4): 221–300.

Elsasser, Albert B. "Mattole, Nongatl, Sinkyone, Lassik, and Wailaki." In *Handbook of North American Indians. Vol. 8: California.* Pp. 190–204. Washington: Smithsonian Institution.

Goddard, Pliny E. "Notes on the Chilula Indians of Northwestern California." University of California *Publications in American Archaeology and Ethnology* 10(6): 265–288

Gould, Richard A. "Tolowa." In *Handbook of North American Indians. Vol. 8: California.* Pp. 128–136. Washington: Smithsonian Institution.

Wallace, William J. "Hupa, Chilula, and Whilkut." In *Handbook of North American Indians. Vol. 8: California.* Pp. 164–169. Washington: Smithsonian Institution.

Chumash

The Chumash people lived along the Santa Barbara Channel of Southern California on the mainland coast, the adjacent islands, and interior valleys. The first European contact with the Chumash was Cabrillo's expedition in 1542, but more than two centuries passed before Spanish soldiers and colonists began to move into the region, a process heralded by the Portola overland expedition of 1769. The Chumash were largely gathered into Franciscan missions by the first years of the nineteenth century, and both their society and population quickly collapsed. By the early twentieth century their numbers were reduced to a mere handful.

Although nudity was prevalent in the warm climate, there was some use of warmer clothing for winter and an abundance of ceremonial attire, displaying considerable social significance.

Men's Basic Dress

Men wore a wraparound buckskin kilt, when they wore anything. Around the waist was a sash of netting, into which necessary items could be thrust, or to which ornaments could be attached.

Women's Basic Dress

Women wore the two-piece skirt, commonly of tule or sea grass, or sometimes the shredded bark of willow or sycamore trees. Small globules of asphaltum were attached to the ends of the fibers to weight the skirt down against the wind.

Upper-class women wore a knee-length wraparound skirt of deerskin, with fringes on which shells were strung; these hide skirts were sometimes painted with designs.

Footwear

Generally, the Chumash of both sexes went barefoot. Occasionally hide sandals were worn, consisting of a sole of tough hide bound to the foot and ankle with thong ties. Some sandals were of yucca fiber or tree bark.

Outer Wear

The rabbit-skin robe was replaced in this area with a feather robe (much more common throughout southern California); narrow strips of birdskin were bound with a cord and woven in the same manner as the robes of rabbit skin. These were waist length, except that men of higher status wore ankle-length robes. Some robes or cloaks were of fur, such as bearskin or sea-otter fur; deerskin was also made up into mantles. Shell or bone pins were used as fasteners.

Hair Styles

Women wore the hair long and loose with a center part; some wore bangs on the forehead. Men wore their long hair loose; sometimes part of the hair was coiled into a topknot and a bone pin thrust through it to anchor it securely. Occasionally men plucked the beard with a clamshell tweezer.

Headgear

Basketry hats were plain, but were woven in a superb coiled technique, probably of *Juncus;* no examples have come down to us, but it would seem they would follow the typical southern California shape of a truncated cone, somewhat higher than the hats of the north. Some women wore a headband adorned with ornaments.

Accessories

Pouches and bags to carry necessary items were of hide. Tubes made from cane or elderberry wood were used to contain tobacco or medicines. Many pins of bone or wood functioned as fasteners of capes and hair; some of these pins were as much as a foot and a half in length. Miller, in his excellent book on the Chumash, shows some of these hairpins.

Jewelry

In their ornaments the Chumash made much use of steatite (soapstone), which was obtained from a mine on Santa Catalina Island. Earrings, nose plugs, and necklaces were created using the steatite as well as various shells and bones. Asphaltum, found on the beaches, was used to make ornaments of pieces of abalone shell inlaid in the pitch. Keyhole limpet shells made delicate hair ornaments, and olivella shells were fashioned into beads. The shells of the giant Pismo clam were ground into disks and drilled so they could be strung into necklaces; these white clamshell disks were used as a form of money throughout much of California, but they were much more desired as an ostentatious display of acquired wealth. The Chumash seem to have been the principal manufacturers of these clamshell disks, trading them widely. Some men wore a slender tube of clamshell in the perforated nasal septum. Dark wooden rods were worn in the pierced earlobes.

Special Costumes

Ceremonies featured the Swordfish Dance, with its headdress adorned with a long "sword" of fishbone; the Barracuda Dance; the Seaweed Dance; and the

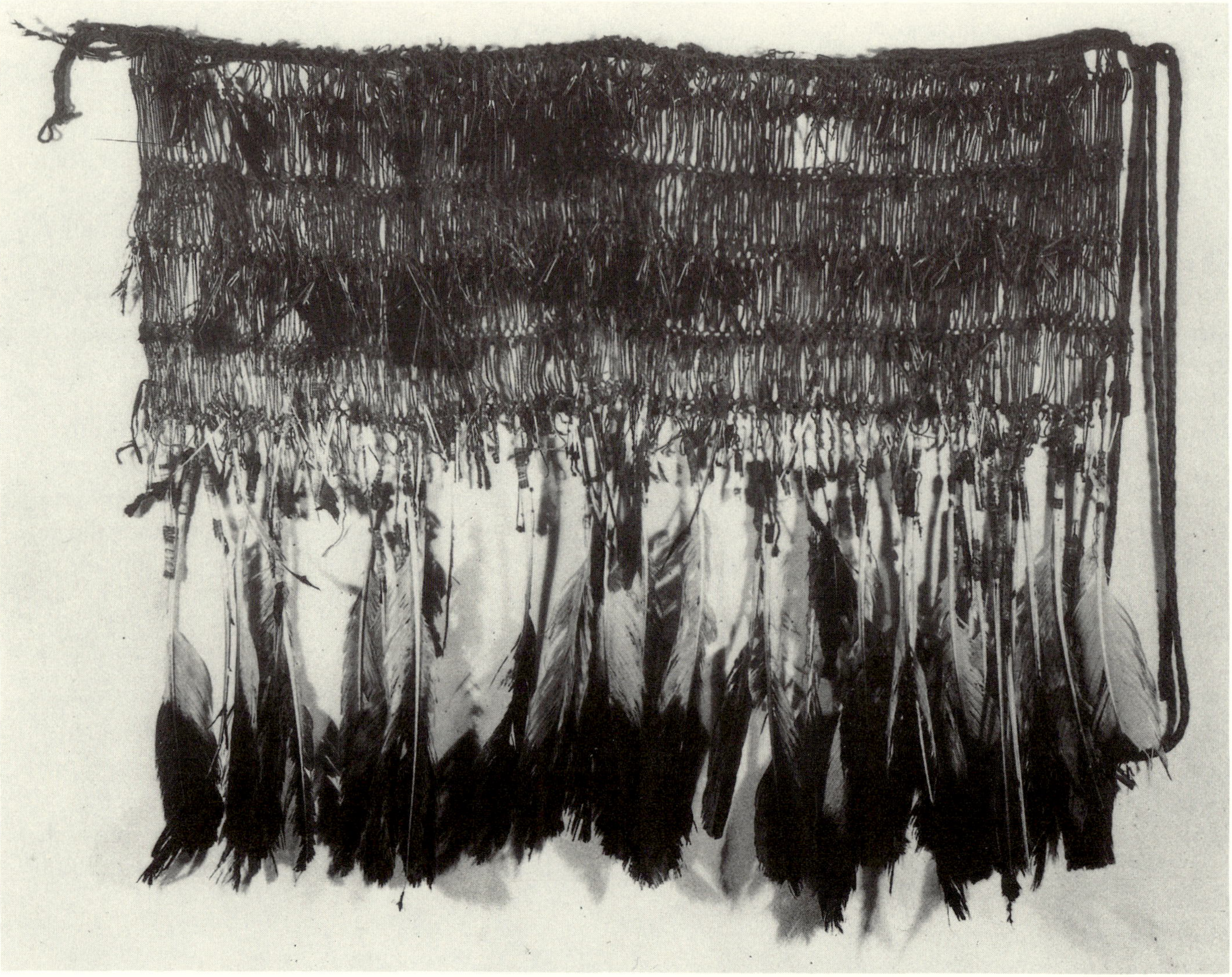

A woman's ceremonial dance skirt, one of the few remaining items of early Chumash clothing, combines eagle and crow feathers. Found in a cave near Santa Barbara, California, the skirt is 33 inches wide and ties around the waist.

Shoshonean Condor Cult. Shamans often wore a dance skirt of strings of milkweed fiber with eagle down twisted into the strings, and with feathers of the eagle or condor attached at the bottom. Some shamans wore a belt of deer hooves. Hudson et al., in *The Eye of the Flute,* illustrate some of the headdresses and face painting used in ceremonials.

Garment Decoration

The coiling technique used in making the basket hats, the simple weaving of feather robes, and some twining in the fashioning of the tule or sea-grass skirts were the only fiber techniques used by the Chumash. Their simple garments were generously decorated with beads and pendants of steatite, bone, and shell. Feathers were a major form of adornment, particularly those of the condor, the eagle, and the flicker. No paint was used on garments.

Face and Body Embellishment

Face painting in designs of stripes, zigzags, and checkers were a significant part of ceremonial dress. Black and red pigments, obtained from the north, were mixed into a brown hue; white clay was also used. Some dancers would cover the entire face with red ocher, then apply dots of black and white paint. Colors and designs often indicated status. Women painted the bodies with red ocher to prevent sunburn.

Transitional Dress

The early Spanish explorers affected Chumash culture only fleetingly. But the missions destroyed that culture rapidly, so rapidly that it is pointless to discuss transitional dress, since there was so little of it.

Key Sources

Anderson, Eugene N., Jr. "A Bibliography of the Chumash and Their Predecessors." University of California *Archaeological Survey Reports* 61: 25–74.

Campbell, Grant. *The Rock Paintings of the Chumash: A Study of California Indian Culture.* Berkeley: University of California Press, 1965.

———. "Chumash: Introduction," "Eastern Coastal Chumash," "Island Chumash." In *Handbook of North American Indians. Vol. 8: California.* Pp. 505–508, 509–519, 524–529. Washington: Smithsonian Institution.

Greenwood, Roberta S. "Obispeño and Purisimeño Chumash." In *Handbook of North American Indians. Vol. 8: California.* Pp. 520–523. Washington: Smithsonian Institution.

Hudson, Travis, et al. *The Eye of the Flute: Chumash Traditional History and Ritual as Told by Fernando Librado Kitsepawit to John P. Harrington.* Santa Barbara, CA: Santa Barbara Museum of Natural History, 1977.

Landberg, Lief C. W. *The Chumash Indians of Southern California.* Los Angeles: Southwest Museum, 1965.

Miller, Bruce W. *Chumash: A Picture of Their World.* Los Osos, CA: Sand River Press, 1988.

Costanoan

The Costanoans (Spanish for "coast people") inhabited the seacoast from Point Sur to the Golden Gate and inland to the San Joaquin Valley. Of Penutian stock, their closest language relatives were the Miwok. They were not a single tribe, but rather a number of tribelets clustered around San Francisco Bay. Because of their position, we have quite a bit of information on their aboriginal manner of dress, as reported by various explorers and traders. Vizcaino, in 1602, and Portola, in 1769, described their culture. In 1795 José Cardero and Tomas de Suria did drawings of the Costanoans. In 1806 Wilhelm von Tilenan, a German artist with Kotzebue's expedition, depicted them. Louis Choris, in 1816, did many watercolors and drawings of these Indians, but by that time they had been devastated by the six missions in the area; their culture and population were almost destroyed. In 1971 the descendants of these people formed the Ohlone tribe of today.

Men's Basic Dress

The men went naked. Later, under the influence of the missions, they wore a small-fitted breechcloth without flaps held in place by a belt. In cool weather they daubed themselves with mud for warmth.

Women's Basic Dress

The double apron skirt was of netted grass, such as milkweed fibers or braided tule in front, and the rear

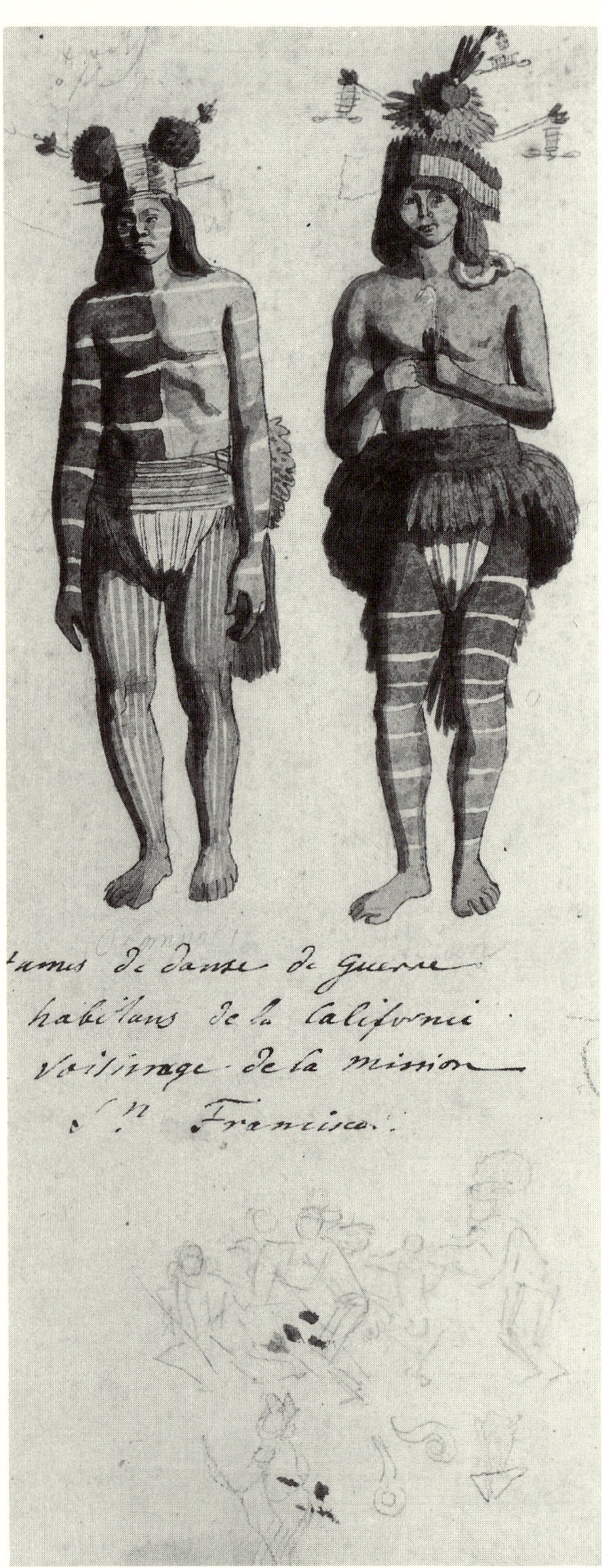

Two barefoot Costanoan men dressed for a War Dance wear feather headdresses, fitted breechclouts, and body paint.

skirt was of deerskin. Women went barebreasted at all times, except when they donned outer wear for warmth.

Footwear

No sandals or shoes were worn by the Costanoans.

Outer Wear

Since rabbits were procured in great numbers, the rabbitskin robe was the most common article worn for warmth; the pelt was cut spirally, the strips dried so they twisted, and those strips woven in a simple cross weave. Deer, bear, elk, and antelope skins were also used. Otter-skin cloaks were most highly treasured, as were woven feather mantles.

Hair Styles

Women wore the hair long and loose. Men, also, wore the hair long, but they often coiled it on top of the head, fastening it in place with a four-pronged "comb" or a hairpin. Another hair style for men was to bind it with hair nets made of milkweed fiber. Many of the men had beards and mustaches; others plucked the facial hair with clamshell tweezers.

Headgear

The coiled basket hat was worn, but usually only to cushion the strain of a tumpline when carrying a large load. Otherwise nothing was worn on the head except for dance rituals.

Accessories

Since the Costanoans were always on the move for hunting, fishing, and gathering, few accessories were worn or carried. Thongs were worn as belts. Pouches of deerskin sufficed to carry any necessary items, such as paint or tobacco.

Jewelry

Necklaces of shells were often adorned with eagle down. Dentalium shells were eagerly sought from traders to the north, while the clamshell disk beads, used for money as well as ostentation, were obtained from the Chumash peoples to the south. Abalone shell was cut into pleasing shapes, polished, and perforated, to be strung into necklaces or worn as earrings. Ears and noses were pierced in infancy, so

that long plugs of wood or incised bone could be inserted.

Armor
Neither armor was worn nor shields carried by these people, but when engaging in warfare, the entire body was painted with red ocher, and feathered headdresses and bear-claw necklaces were worn.

Special Costumes
There were dances for all occasions—the First Grass Dance, the Acorn Dance, the Coming-of-Age Dance, the Mourning Dance, and others. Both sexes donned feathers and painted the face and body for dancing. Some men wore bands on the forehead made of flicker shafts and some wore dance skirts of raven or crow feathers. At the time of death mourners singed the hair and blackened the face with asphaltum, which remained until it wore off.

Garment Decoration
Weaving was confined to the few basket hats worn and the rabbit-skin and feather robes. Netting with milkweed fiber was used for hair nets. Almost all decoration consisted of feathers and shells.

Face and Body Embellishment
Face and body paint for dancers was made from white clay, red ocher or cinnabar from nearby mines, and charcoal dust. Men painted the arms, legs, and chest with white vertical and horizontal lines, as well as other designs. A girl was tattooed in designs of red, blue, or green hues at the time of her first menstruation. The dots and lines had special significance, proclaiming her lineage and tribal relationships, which were of importance in establishing which mate she could marry, for she could not marry within the tribelet or certain relatives. The women sometimes tattooed a collar around the neck, and both sexes often tattooed a line from the chin down onto the chest. Some men had measuring marks tattooed on the arm in order to measure accurately the strings of clamshell disks used in trading.

Masks
As was true of many hunting societies, the men wore deer-head masks for camouflage when approaching their prey.

Transitional Dress
Early Spanish explorers had little effect on Costanoan costume. More changes came about under missionization (see Mission Indians). The destruction of their culture by the missions left few survivors, who faded into other tribes in the area leaving no traces of Costanoan dress.

Key Sources
Choris, Louis. *San Francisco 100 Years Ago.* San Francisco: A. M. Robertson, 1913.

Heizer, Robert F., ed. *The Costanoan Indians.* Cupertino: California Historical Center, 1974.

Levy, Richard. "The Costanoans." In *Handbook of North American Indians. Vol. 8: California.* Pp. 485–495. Washington: Smithsonian Institution.

Margolin, Malcolm. *The Ohlone Way: Indian Life in the San Francisco–Monterey Bay Area.* Berkeley, CA: Heyday Books, 1978.

Hupa

The Hupa lived in a secluded valley on the Trinity River where it meets the Klamath River, still called the Hoopa Valley today. Fortunately for them they were far from the missions and their valley contained little gold, so they remained isolated in their inaccessible valley. Athapaskan speakers, they subscribed to the wealth-oriented culture of their northwest California neighbors, a culture that was in turn related to that of the tribes of the Pacific Northwest. Wealth was indicated by the ostentatious show of woodpecker-scalp headbands, red or black obsidian blades, and the use of dentalium shells for money and display. In the late nineteenth century when California was setting up reservations, one was established in the Hoopa Valley, so the Hupa did not have the problems of displacement experienced by other tribes. Today they are the largest of the California tribes, possessing a strong ethnic identity and a stable economy. More clothing was worn here than in the warm coastal region, but there was still a pronounced similarity to that of other tribes in the area.

Men's Basic Dress
Men wore the breechclout, either of deerskin or of the skins of small animals sewn together; this was draped about the hips as a form of kilt. By 1890,

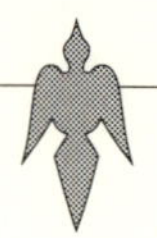

according to Ericson, who photographed the Hupa from 1890 to 1900, the men had substituted cloth for the deerskin wrapping; with this a waistband of dentalium shells and perforated coins (Chinese) was worn. For special occasions a tunic was worn made of two deerskins with the hair left on, seamed along one side, joined on the left shoulder, and held in place by a belt; sometimes these were made of panther skins. Knee-length leggings of skin, sewed up the front with sinew, were worn only for hunting in snow-covered mountains.

Women's Basic Dress

Women wore the double-apron costume. The front apron was usually of fiber, such as bear grass, braided or twined into a long fringe, with shells, beads, and pine nuts hung in a manner that created designs in horizontal rows. The back apron was of deerskin and overlapped the front part; for ceremonial purposes, often a peplum or folded-over yoke of skin was added to the skirt, tied in front, and decorated in a similar manner, especially with abalone pendants. Wealthy women displayed their status by having both aprons made of skin, in which case the front apron was made into long fringes, also embellished with seeds, nuts, and shells. With this skirt, a cincture about four inches wide, adorned with similar materials was worn. Women went bare on the top, covering the breasts only with many strands of beads.

A Hupa man wears a headband, strings of dentalium shell necklaces, and a deerskin kilt.

Footwear

Buckskin moccasins were worn only for long trips; it was the usual California moccasin of one piece with a seam up the front to the instep and at the heel. Occasionally elk-hide soles were added.

Outer Wear

For added warmth, both men and women wore robes or capes of deerskin or of wildcat fur, with the hair on the inside; for rainy weather the hair side was turned outward. Some robes were painted.

Hair Styles

Both sexes wore the hair long. Women often wore it in two bunches at the sides, sometimes wrapped with mink or other skins, or covered with red woodpecker crests, and perfumed with *yerba buena,* a form of mint. The men bunched it in two rolls hanging at the front over the shoulders or sometimes in a single one in the back. For ceremonial wear and as a status symbol, they wore a hair net of iris fiber, often ornamented with feathers. The knotting technique was similar to modern macrame. A few men displayed scanty beards, but most plucked the sparse facial hair with clamshell tweezers.

Headgear

Men went bareheaded except for ceremonial headdresses; some men wore a mink headband for special occasions. Women wore the bowl-shaped close-fitting basketry hat; this was woven in a twining technique of available fibers, commonly bear grass. Decoration consisted of geometric designs in overlay work done with red, white, and black colors; white

came from the bear grass, black was obtained from maidenhair ferns, and red was created from giant fern stems colored with alder bark.

Accessories

The major accessory of the Hupas was the elk-horn purse; this was a cylinder of horn with an opening along the side, incised with designs of triangles, diamonds, and lines, into which charcoal was rubbed to make the designs stand out. In this purse the men kept their "money," strings of dentalium shells placed end to end, shells that were obtained from the tribes to the north. Bags and pouches were made of deerskin. Necessary items were also carried in netted bags of iris fiber.

Jewelry

All Hupas pierced the earlobes, inserting shell ornaments, such as abalone pendants and dentalium shells with tassels of woodpecker feathers; hair ornaments were also of abalone pendants with strings of clamshell disk beads attached. Noses were not pierced. Necklaces were often strings of the white clamshell disk beads, acquired in trade from the central California peoples, who used them as money, but the Hupas preferred dentalia for their currency. Other necklaces featured pieces of abalone shell, cut into squares or circles and polished to a beautiful sheen.

Armor

Men wore corselets of the "rod-and-slat" variety or a tunic of several layers of tough elk hide. These were effective at stopping arrows, but extremely awkward to wear. No shields were carried. Some warriors wore a headband of a roll of deerskin filled with grass.

Special Costumes

The Hupas wore magnificent costumes for their various ceremonies. In the Puberty Dance the men wore leather headbands thickly set with sea-lion teeth. For the Jumping Dance in the autumn, they wore the woodpecker-scalp headdress, made on a band of deer fur, taken from the animal's belly and attached to this was as many as 50 woodpecker scalps, preferably those from the pileated woodpecker. Bare-chested, with innumerable strings of dentalium shell beads, and with horizontal tattoo marks on each cheek, the dancers wore aprons of deer or civet skins. The White Deerskin Dance was a part of the same festival; here the dancers wore wolf-fur headbands, buckskin or civet–cat fur kilts, with condor plumes in the hair. Some of the men wore chaplets or crowns of sea-lion tusks and waved great obsidian blades. Valuable albino deerskins, with the heads and necks stuffed, were brandished aloft, fastened to high poles; a narrow strip of woodpecker feathers was sewn to the ear tips of the deer's head, around the eyes, and as a representation of a tongue. The major dancers wore hair nets from the forehead to the middle of the shoulders, with a feather fringe. Mourners blackened the face with pitch and singed the hair; widows wore

In this 1890s photograph a Tolowa woman wears a buckskin dance apron decorated with *Glycymeris* shells and abalone and obsidian tinklers. Tinklers also enhance the ends of her cloth-wrapped braids, and she wears a basketry hat.

a basket hat that was plain except for thin brown horizontal lines.

Garment Decoration

Weaving was used by the women to make their basketry hats; no mention was made of rabbit-skin robes. The hats were woven in a twining technique, usually of bear grass, with decorations in an overlay manner, done in simple geometric designs of black, red, and white colors. The white was bear grass, the black came from the stems of maidenhair ferns, and the red was produced by dyeing giant fern stems with alder bark. Twining and braiding were used to make the fiber skirts. A netting technique using iris fibers was practiced. Some featherwork was done, particularly for dance headdresses. Garments were decorated with shells, especially olivella, abalone pendants, and dentalia, as well as feathers, pine nuts, seeds, and glass beads, the latter in the red, white, and black color combination so favored by the Hupas. Some crocheting was done late in the nineteenth century.

Face and Body Embellishment

Adult women had three vertical lines tattooed on the chin; occasionally marks were made at the corners of the mouth. Men had ten lines tattooed on the left arm below the elbow in order to measure precisely the strings of dentalium shells valued as money as well as for ostentation. Face painting was practiced only by men for ceremonial purposes.

Transitional Dress

By the early 1800s the Hupas had obtained such things from the traders as cloth, blankets, and beads.

Hupas, photographed in the 1890s by A. W. Ericson, participate in the White Deerskin Dance. Some hold albino deer skins on poles; two dancers, foreground, carry large obsidian blades and wear deer-skin skirts and crowns spiked with sea-lion teeth.

Late in the century the men were beginning to wear the clothes of the whites—the trousers, vests, cotton shirts, and some hats. Women adopted the "pioneer" dress with its long sleeves, fitted bodice, and full skirt, but both sexes were reluctant to put shoes on feet accustomed to going barefoot. By the turn of the century almost all traces of Hupa traditional wear had disappeared, except for the ceremonial garments, many of them kept and treasured as heirlooms; these were brought out and donned for reenactments of their ritual dances, performances still being given today.

Key Sources

Curtis, Edward S. *The North American Indian.* Vol. 13. New York: Johnson Reprint Company, 1970.

Goddard, Pliny Earl. "Life and Culture of the Hupa." University of California *Publications in American Archaeology and Ethnology* 1(1): 1–88.

Goldschmidt, Walter R. and Harold E. Driver. "The Hupa White Deerskin Dance." University of California *Publications in American Archaeology and Ethnology* 35: 103–142.

Wallace, William J. "Hupa, Chilula, and Whilkut." In *Handbook of North American Indians. Vol. 8: California.* Pp. 164–179. Washington: Smithsonian Institution.

Klamath/Modoc

The Klamath and the Modoc tribes of northeastern California were closely allied and were so similar in dress that they will be discussed together here. The Klamaths, "people of the lake," lived around Upper Klamath Lake in Oregon; the Modocs ("southerners") inhabited the area around Lower Klamath Lake and Clear Lake in California. Both tribes were Lutuamian speakers of the Shapwailutan language family. The Modoc had severe conflicts with the whites, leading in 1872–1873 to the remarkable Modoc War (in which the Klamaths remained neutral), fought in the barren lava beds of the area. Atrocities on both sides left a legacy of bitterness. Regarding clothes, they shared some elements with both the Plateau and California tribes. They made extensive use of tule and bulrush for garments and accessories.

Men's Basic Dress

Men wrapped a piece of deerskin about the hips as a breechclout. In winter they wore knee-high, gartered leggings made of small mats of tule grass. A poncho-type shirt of skin was also worn in cooler weather.

Women's Basic Dress

Aboriginally, the women wore a wraparound skirt with a foldover at the top; a poncho of skin was added in cooler weather. Later, some women wore simple tunics of deerskin, sleeveless and belted at the waist, probably winter wear. Others wore the double-apron skirt of California, with the front made of the soft inner bark of willow or cottonwood trees and the overlapping back of buckskin or, in the lower Klamath region, of braided bear grass decorated with pine nuts; with the double-apron skirt, they went bare-breasted. Women, too, wore the knee-high leggings of tule grass in the winter.

Footwear

Moccasins were of twined tule strands lined with grass for winter wear. For summer, moccasins were of deerskin in the three-piece style (sole and uppers of one piece, U-shaped tongue insert, and cuff), commonly with a drawstring in front. It was a style unlike the usual California type, reflecting influences from the east and from the north. The snowshoe was a round hoop of ash or other wood with a few thongs lashed across the circle; a smaller shoe of this general type was worn in the marshes for wading.

Outer Wear

A cape or blanket of shredded tule or sagebrush was worn by the women when warmth was desired. Skin and furs were also fashioned into robes. Powers tells about particularly fine robes, on which brilliantly colored duck scalps, such as mallards, were sewn in various patterns, forming a beautiful, but rather smelly garment.

Hair Styles

Both sexes left the hair hanging loose and natural; in an attempt to "civilize" these Indians, the government agents tried to get the men to cut their hair short. A compromise was reached whereby they cut it "halfway down." For this they were given hats.

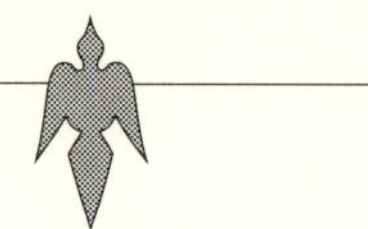

Headgear

Basket hats, worn regularly by women and occasionally by men followed the rounder California style rather than the tall hats of the Plateau. Many of these tended to be larger to the point where it is difficult to see how they could stay on the head unless the hair was tucked into the hat; some had a little peak to them, and others were flat-topped. They were woven chiefly of *Xerophyllum* (bear grass) in a plain twining technique with the weft of fine strands of tule; a limited amount of overlay twining in simple geometric designs formed the decoration. In some cases, especially with later Plains influence, some porcupine quillwork adorned the hats. Eye shields, much like the crownless visors of the Plains, were used by the men in the winter to avoid snow blindness.

Accessories

Accessories were few. Belts were either thongs or straps of tanned leather or rawhide; later belts for the Modoc, at the time of the Modoc Wars, were cartridge belts. Pouches of soft leather, fringed, carried necessary items such as equipment for sewing (awl and sinew), for making fires, for tobacco, and such.

Jewelry

Jewelry was minimal. A few ornaments of shell were worn in the hair. Some dentalium shells were obtained in trade from tribes to the north; these were used in making necklaces and chokers, along with glass beads.

Armor

Armor was of two types: (1) cuirasses of slats, similar to the "rod-and-slat" armor of the Northwest and (2) a corselet of two or more layers of tough elk hide. Both of these were extremely awkward to wear but effective in stopping arrows. No mention was made of shields.

Special Costumes

The Klamath and Modoc did not perform elaborate ceremonials; they had a few dances, but the costuming was highly individualized in nature, rather than following the rigid, traditional styles of many of the California or Northwest tribes. Mourning was minimized; chief mourners simply cut the hair to show grief.

Garment Decoration

Weaving was confined to simple twining and overlay for the basketry hats; no mention was found of rabbit-skin robes, although they may have fashioned them from pelts. A fleeting comment was made about porcupine quillwork applied to hats, probably after Plains influence became more evident, but the technique seems not to have traveled farther into California. Very litle mention is made of garment decoration by the people of these simple cultures.

Face and Body Embellishment

Men and women painted their faces for ordinary daily life with various pigments made from clay, rotten wood, and ocher. There was some skull deformation, a custom adopted from the tribes to the north, for this was not typical of California tribes; this was deliberate on the part of the Modoc especially, for they carefully bandaged the infant's head in order to achieve the desired distortion. Tattooing was practiced to a limited extent, created by rubbing charcoal into cuts made in the skin.

Transitional Dress

After the mid-nineteenth century, the Modoc and Klamath men showed white influence with their cloth breechcloths, cloth tunics with sleeves, cartridge belts, stroud-cloth leggings, and a red cloth tied around the head. The women wore long cotton dresses and plaid shawls with fringes. However, the basket hats were retained into the present century.

Key Sources

Barrett, Samuel A. "The Material Culture of the Klamath Lake and Modoc Indians of Northeastern California and Southern Oregon." University of California *Publications in American Archaeology and Ethnology* 5(4): 239–292.

Murray, Keith A. *The Modocs and Their War.* Norman: University of Oklahoma Press, 1959.

Ray, Verne F. *Primitive Pragmatists: The Modoc Indians of Northern California.* Seattle: University of Washington Press,1963.

Spier, Leslie. "Klamath Ethnography." University of California *Publications in American Archaeology and Ethnology* 30.

Stern, Theodore. *The Klamath Tribe: A People and Their Reservation.* Seattle: University of Washington Press, 1965.

Maidu

The Maidu (their name for themselves), of the Penutian family of languages, lived in the grasslands along the Feather, American, and Sacramento rivers and east to the foothills and high peaks of the Sierras. Subsistence was based on gathering, hunting (particularly wildcats and mountain lions), and some fishing. They used clamshell disk beads for money. There were three divisions: (1) the Southern Maidu or Nisenan, who lived in the mining region and who were so degraded by the flood of incoming miners that in a few years they were destroyed as a viable culture; (2) the Northeast Maidu or Mountain Maidu; and (3) the Northern or Konkow ("meadowland") Maidu.

Men's Basic Dress

The men wore little or nothing, both summer and winter; rarely, they donned a kilt of deer or puma skin or of pounded wire grass or *Juncus* (small bulrush). Deerskin leggings, with the hair left on and turned inward, were tied above the knee and wound around the legs with thongs; these were used only in the deep mountain snows. A robe took the place of a shirt or poncho.

Women's Basic Dress

The double-apron skirt of the women was made of shredded willow or maple bark, or of wire grass, tule, or other grasses; the mountain women preferred buckskin two-piece skirts, the front part fringed. These skin skirts were said to be less profusely decorated with pine nuts than those of other tribes.

Footwear

Moccasins, for traveling only, were the typical California type—a one-piece upper with a seam up the front and at the back, reaching above the ankle, and tied with thongs; these were stuffed with grass for warmth. Snowshoes were made of circular hoops of willow or redbud with two crosspieces tied with sinew.

Outer Wear

The Mountain Maidu wore rabbit-skin robes, which involved 40 or more rabbit pelts, spirally cut into strips, that were dried until twisted, then woven in a simple cross weave using a framework of pegs on the ground; these were often trimmed with ground-squirrel tails. Bird-feather robes were common, especially in the Sacramento Valley because of the many water birds there—wood ducks, mallards, and Canada geese. Conn tells about a Maidu robe woven in 1830 of duck feathers on a base of braided leather strands; since it took six women four months to make such a robe, and because of their fragility, few examples remain today. "Shawls" of round-stemmed tule grass or of pieces of skin were thrown over the shoulders for warmth. Men, and those generally shamans, wore a mantle of eagle or hawk feathers attached to a foundation of net, hanging at the back to the knees.

Hair Styles

In the north, men wore the hair long and loose; in the valley it was tucked under a netted cap or held back by a band of fur or a thong. Konkow men wore the hair shorter. Women often cut the hair at half-length; it either hung loose or was bound with a thong. The Konkow men plucked the facial hair, while other Maidu men allowed sparse mustache hair to grow.

Headgear

The Maidu women seem not to have worn the basket hat, except possibly in the north, where they were said to have been flat-topped like those of the Modoc; these hats or caps were made of hazel shoots, bear grass, or maidenhair fern in a twining technique with a full-twist overlay. Many women twined shredded tule leaves to make a headband, often decorated with tiny pieces of abalone shell. Men wore netted hair nets, which were necessary to anchor headdresses, but may not have been worn habitually.

Accessories

Some pouches were made of buckskin, but the netted bags were more common; these were made of milkweed-fiber cords with an attached leather strap for carrying. Six-inch-wide belts of buckskin were worn by the women; for dance purposes, they were covered with woodpecker scalps and abalone pendants.

Jewelry

Clamshell disks, obtained in trade from the south, perforated and strung on thongs, formed necklaces that served as both money and as an overt display of wealth; sometimes several yards long, the necklaces were looped many times around the neck. Abalone and olivella shells were popular for use in ornaments, but dentalium shells were rarely to be found. Steatite from the south, pine nuts, seeds, and tiny cylinders of "red alabaster" or magnesite were also fashioned into necklaces. Women, especially, pierced the ears and inserted cut and polished pieces of abalone shell, incised bird bones, or polished sticks. Men, and some women, pierced the nasal septum and inserted feathers or feathered sticks. Men sometimes wore large gorgets or chestpieces of abalone shell.

Armor

An elk-hide tunic from the shoulder to the knees was worn as armor in the valley; corselets of rods of mountain mahogany were more common at the higher elevations. The corselet was said to have had a high collar, into which the head could be withdrawn to avoid a shower of arrows. Powers says that when the warriors were going into battle they would wax and twist the hair into two "devilish-looking horns"; in addition they wore feathered headdresses, and painted their breasts black.

Special Costumes

Boys and girls had puberty rites; other ceremonies were the Kuksu Dance, the 1872 Ghost Dance, and the Acorn, Flower, and Coyote dances. The men's netted caps were indispensable for the ceremonies because the headpieces had to be fastened into the tightly contained hair; these caps or nets were done in an openwork single-knot technique of milkweed or wild hemp-fiber cords, and were embellished with down or small feathers. Kroeber gives an excellent chart of the costumes worn in the Kuksu rituals: the feather capes, headdresses, woodpecker-scalp headbands, netted caps, and such. The feathered headbands were usually of the stripped red quills of the red-shafted flicker; the feathers of the yellow-shafted flicker, a rare bird in California, were particularly worn and treasured as a symbol of good luck. The vanes were stripped from the feather shafts, the upper portion being retained to create diamond shapes; the quills were then strung on finely-rolled hemp cords and twined. For mourning, men shortened the hair; a widow cut or burned the hair off close and covered it with pitch, which was left until it wore off, at which time she could remarry. The Mountain Maidu widows wore a buckskin thong with beads of pitch. A "mourning necklace" was worn by some widows.

Garment Decoration

The Konkow used simple twining to make the basket hats. Netting techniques for the hair nets were carried out with a single cord (of milkweed or hemp) knitted or looped on itself. The featherwork technique of the woodpecker headbands was unique with the Maidu in its use of twining rather than gluing of the feathers.

Face and Body Embellishment

Women tattooed the chin with three, five, or seven lines and had diagonal lines from the corners of the mouth to the outer edges of the eyes. The Maidu were on the edge of the tattooing tribes of the north; to the east and south, the practice diminished. Men had no distinctive marks, but both sexes sometimes tattooed lines and dots on breasts, arms, and hands. The marks were made with fish bones, pine needles, bird bones, or obsidian splinters, and were rubbed with wild-nutmeg charcoal or a reddish pigment. Body painting for ceremonial dances was done with white clay, red ocher, or charcoal, applied in dots or lines. At her puberty rite a girl had five vertical lines of alternating red and black painted on each cheek; one was erased each morning, upon which she was eligible to marry.

Transitional Dress

The transitional period was brief; the tremendous influx of miners and later settlers destroyed the Maidu culture, and almost the people. They quickly adopted white garments—trousers, vests, cotton shirts, coats and jackets, cotton dresses, and shoes. But they retained the accoutrements of their ceremonial life, some of which may be seen even today.

Key Sources

Bates, Craig D., and Brian Bibby. "Collecting among the Chico Maidu." *American Indian Art Magazine* Autumn 1983.

———. "Flicker Quill Bands of the Maidu: Ceremonial Art of Central California." *American Indian Art Magazine* Autumn 1980: 62–67.

Beals, Ralph L. "Ethnology of the Nisenan." University of California *Publications in American Archaeology and Ethnology* 31(6): 335–414.

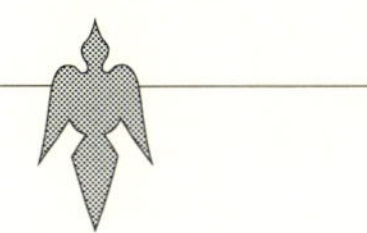

Curtis, Edward S. *The North American Indian.* Vol. 13. New York: Johnson Reprint Company, 1970.

Dixon, Roland B. "The Northern Maidu." American Museum of Natural History *Bulletin* 17(3).

Kroeber, A. L. "The Patwin and Their Neighbors." University of California *Publications in American Archaeology and Ethnology* 29(4): 253–323.

Potts, Marie. *The Northern Maidu.* Happy Camp, CA: Naturegraph, 1991. Reprint of 1977 edition.

Riddell, Francis A. "Maidu and Konkow." In *Handbook of North American Indians. Volume 8: California.* Pp. 370–386. Washington: Smithsonian Institution.

Wilson, Norman L. and Arlean H. Towne. "Nisenan." In *Handbook of North American Indians. Vol. 8: California.* Pp. 387–397. Washington: Smithsonian Institution.

Mission Indians

The first of the Spanish missions was built at San Diego in 1769; from there the padres worked northward, building missions along *El Camino Real* ("the King's Road"), a day's journey apart by horseback, to the last of the 21 missions, San Francisco Solano, built in 1823 at Sonoma. Spain had a dual purpose in founding the missions: (1) There was an abundance of heathen souls to be brought into the benevolent fold of Christianity, as represented by the Catholic Church. (2) With the establishment of the missions, presidios were also built, representing a military jurisdiction that would ensure the dominance of Spain in the region. In order to keep the missions functioning, many hands were needed, which need would be supplied by the Indian converts, whether or not they desired to work.

Although the fathers believed they were bringing "civilization" to these "heathens," they found peoples with cultures that were eminently suited to the southern California environment, and already filled with ceremony and ritual. They intended to "clothe" these poor souls, who already wore garments made from native materials, showing a close relationship between the environment, the climate, and their lifeways.

There were many Indian tribes along the coast that were affected by the establishment of the missions, but the earliest and the ones with the gravest impact were as follows: (1) The Diegueño (Yuman speakers of the Hokan language stock, called by anthropologists the Ipais) were under the domination of the San Diego mission, but they put up a stubborn resistance, which led to conflict in which one of the padres was killed, the only Franciscan martyr in the history of this movement. (2) The Luiseño (Shoshonean speakers of the Uto-Aztecan language family) were named after San Luis Rey. (3) The Juaneño, living in the San Juan Capistrano area, were similar in speech and culture to the Luiseño and the Gabrieliño. (4) The Gabrieliños, named for the San Gabriel Arcangel mission and considered by many to be among the most populous and the wealthiest of the California tribes, included the Fernandinos and the San Nicoleños of San Nicolas Island; they were all speakers of the Shoshonean branch of Uto-Aztecan. (5) The Serrano group ("mountaineers") spoke Takic, a dialect of Shoshonean, lived in the San Bernardino Mountains, and were under the influence of the San Gabriel, San Fernando, and San Buenaventura missions. It may help to look at the aboriginal costumes of these Indians when the padres first saw them.

Men's Basic Dress

Men and children usually went naked. Sometimes men wore a waist cord or a braided girdle of agave fibers to carry items of personal use. In cooler weather they would don a poncho-type shirt of deer, mountain-sheep, or antelope skin.

Women's Basic Dress

Women wore the double-apron skirt. The back apron, which overlapped the front, might be of deerskin or it might be of the inner bark of the willow or cottonwood tree. The front apron was commonly of Indian hemp or milkweed strings, which were often netted or braided. On San Nicolas Island the last surviving member of the San Nicoleños was discovered by traders, having lived in solitude from 1835 to 1854; she was wearing a

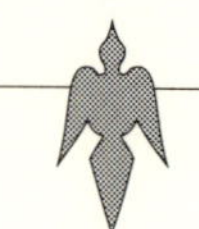

gown made of square pieces of bird skin sewn together.

Footwear

Usually everyone went barefoot. However, the Serrano often wore "Apache" boots or the California moccasin—a one-piece soft-soled affair with a front seam up the instep and a heel seam. High cuffs were wrapped with thongs in colder weather. Farther south, yucca-fiber sandals were worn, especially for travel on rough, thorny, or hot ground; these had thick soles of fibers being worked back and forth over a looped cord, and were attached with thongs.

A Mission Indian wears Mexican-influenced clothing: a cloth garment, sandals, and straw hat. He has a bow and quiver and uses a tumpline to carry a basket.

Outer Wear

Rabbit-skin robes were made, as were some of willow bark; mantles of tanned deerskin were also common. Bird-skin blankets were created with the feathers still attached to the skin. Sea otter capes were the most treasured of outer garments.

Hair Styles

Women wore the hair long and loose, often with bangs, and frequently adorned with flowers or garlands. Men also wore the hair long and loose; a few braided it into one braid at the back, others coiled it on top of the head, where it was held in place with a large pin. In the south some men adopted the long, thin hair rolls of the Yumans to the east. Both sexes plastered the hair with mud for 24 hours, then washed it with yucca suds, to keep it glossy and clean and free of parasites.

Headgear

The Serrano wore a feathered cap similar to those of the Plateau; some of the Serrano wore finely coiled basket hats with stepped diagonal designs. Throughout much of southern California, basket hats were used mainly for easing the burden of carrying loads with a tumpline; these were of *Juncus* or a stiffer fiber, often with a peak on top, and typically with a design painted on or woven in. They seem to have known both types of cap or hat, for Spier says that the diagonally twined cap was for women, and the coiled cap was for men.

Accessories

Accessories for everyday wear were few with these simple costumes, consisting of belts of leather straps or thongs and some pouches of deerskin or woven fibers. Some bags were of netted milkweed fibers.

Jewelry

The ledges of Santa Barbara Island provided steatite (soapstone) for ornaments, often inlaid with pieces of abalone shell by the use of asphaltum. Ornaments were also formed from shells, bones, clay, bear claws, deer hooves, and, later, glass beads. Some semiprecious stones were found in the area and used for ornamentation—quartz, jasper, topaz, agate, garnet, and opal. Girls had the ears pierced at puberty and wore round deer shank bones in the ear. Boys had the nasal septum perforated also at puberty, inserting a cane or a shell pendant therein.

Special Costumes

At puberty the girl had her face painted with red and white spots and black stripes on the cheeks. Boys, at puberty, had ceremonies involving the use of *datura,* a strongly hallucinogenic plant. The annual mourning rituals were of great importance; mourners blackened the face with pitch and singed or cut the hair. For the Eagle Dance and other rituals, men wore a knee-length kilt of eagle or condor feathers. Headdresses were simple, often of spotted-owl or hawk feathers at each side of the head, held in place by a band.

Garment Decoration

Decoration, too, was simple, mainly consisting of the addition of feathers. Weaving was used for making the rabbitskin robes and the basket hats (in the coiling technique), which were worn typically only for carrying burdens. Some netting was done as bases for feather dance kilts and for girdles for carrying items. Skirt fibers were often twined or braided.

Face and Body Embellishment

Many painted the face daily using red ocher, white clay, and charcoal. Some of the men painted spots and broad horizontal stripes on the body. Tattooing was common. As a part of the puberty rites, girls were tattooed with a vertical line on the forehead and three lines on the chin; later, tattoos were added, often with a circle on each cheek, with bands encircling the wrists, and geometric designs on the upper chest. Boys at puberty were also tattooed, especially with horizontal or vertical lines on the forehead. A cactus spine or a flint sliver was used to

California Indians who lived near missions established by Roman Catholic priests in the 1700s became known as Mission Indians. Traditionally, these peoples had worn few clothes, but the priests introduced Mexican-style shirts or tunics of cloth woven and dyed at the missions. Here Mission Indians, wearing woven clothing, gamble at Mission Dolores near San Francisco in 1816.

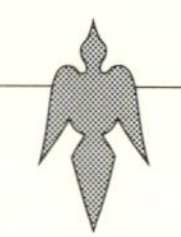

make the marks and agave charcoal was rubbed in for the color.

Transitional Dress

The clothing the Indians wore at the missions was distinctly different from that worn by the Indians outside the missions; the garments appeared different because they were basically Mexican in style, but the main difference was that "real" cloth was used, cloth woven on the mission looms. These first true looms (true in that they had heddles to make "sheds" for easier and faster weaving) were brought from Mexico, and in 1773 Father Palou brought Mexican Indian women to teach spinning and weaving to their California sisters. From 1790 to 1795 instructors were also brought in, who taught not only the craft of weaving, but also the construction of spinning wheels and looms.

In her well-researched book on the missions, Webb tells about the varieties of fabrics woven—the wool blankets and *mangas* (ponchos) for the shepherds, lighter loincloth material, cotton clothing fabric, and a coarse type of cotton serge *(sayal Franciscano)* from which the gray Franciscan habits were made for the padres. She also tells about dyes used, most of which were imported from Central American countries. A few native dyers had used mountain mahogany and rabbit bush, but the aboriginal inhabitants had little actual knowledge of dyes before the Spaniards came.

In 1814 a questionnaire was sent out from Spain requesting the mission fathers to give all facts of mission life, and from these we learn much about the mission clothing of the time. It was said that each year a suit of clothing was given to each "neophyte," a suit that was often sold, given away, or gambled away, The clothes were colorful: blue, blue and white, gray (black and white mixed), red (especially popular), yellow, green, and purple. Some striped material was woven. Louis Choris, an artist with a Russian expedition in 1816, left sketches of some of the Mission Indians.

The men wore a loincloth or a kilt *(taparabo)* of cotton or wool, about a yard and a half long and half a yard wide, secured by means of a thong about the waist. In addition to this, or instead of it, was worn a *coton,* or shirt, a sort of tunic of narrow cloth, that came to below the thighs, made of printed cotton or of wool. A sketch of a Diegueño in 1857 shows him wearing a cloth tunic almost to the ankles, edged with small tassels of yarn, with an undertunic showing beneath. Mexican-style trousers made of soft leather were worn by the men who rode horseback to tend the sheep or cattle.

The women wore the same type of tunic as the men, only shorter, with a skirt of cotton or wool. A French trader wrote in 1827 that at the mission of San Luis Rey the girls were dressed all alike, with red flannel petticoats and white blouses, and the same style of garment was worn at San Jose that year. This sounds as though the padres were adopting Mexican dress for both sexes.

No shoes were worn by either sex, except for sandals for travel and the Mexican shoes worn by the horsemen.

Short woolen blankets were tossed over the shoulders on occasion, sometimes worn folded in the manner of Mexican *serapes.*

Women continued to wear the hair long and loose, sometimes wearing a chaplet of flowers and at times gathering it into a knot on top and binding it with a thong. Men also wore the hair long, although some men cut it at the shoulders; often, particularly while working, they coiled it on top of the head and fastened it with thongs or a large pin.

The Mission Indians seem not to have worn the basketry hat to any great extent; it may have been worn when carrying heavy loads. Headbands of woven fibers were frequently worn. A drawing of 1827 shows a man wearing a tall, flat-topped woven fiber hat with a brim.

Flat fiber bags carried necessary personal items. The Indians were fond of the *panos colorados* (large red handkerchiefs) given as gifts by the padres to their charges; these were worn around the neck or the head. Thongs or strap belts held some of the tunics or shirts in place.

The missions discouraged all "pagan" rites. However, Kotzebue, the Russian explorer, in 1816 reported that after a religious service, the Indian men danced, adorned with "feathers and girdles ornamented with feathers and bits of shells," their bodies painted with "regular lines of black, red, and white."

Using the natural colors of the wool and imported dyes, the cloth woven at the missions was often striped in patterns of broad and narrow bands;

occasionally plaids were created on the looms. Webb reports that the women made drawn work and lace, but these seem to have been made to be sold rather than worn.

Key Sources

Bean, Lowell John, and Florence C. Shipek. "Luiseño." In *Handbook of North American Indians. Vol. 8: California.* Pp. 550–563. Washington: Smithsonian Institution.

Bean, Lowell John, and Charles R. Smith. "Gabrieliño." In *Handbook of North American Indians. Vol. 8: California.* Pp. 538–549. Washington: Smithsonian Institution.

Blackburn, Thomas C. "Ethnohistoric Descriptions of Gabrieliño Material Culture." University of California Archaeological Survey *Annual Reports* 5: 1–50.

Cuero, Delfino. *The Autobiography of Delfino Cuero: A Diegueño Indian, as Told to Florence Shipek.* Banning, CA: Malki Museum Press, 1970.

Curtis, Edward S. *The North American Indian.* Vol. 15. New York: Johnson Reprint Company, 1970.

Engelhardt, Zephyrin. *The Missions and Missionaries of California.* 4 vols. San Francisco: James H. Barry, 1908–1915.

Geiger, Maynard, and Clement W. Meighan. *As the Padres Saw Them.* Santa Barbara, CA: Santa Barbara Mission Library, 1976.

Johnson, Paul C., ed. *The California Missions: A Pictorial History.* Menlo Park, CA: Lane.

Johnston, Bernice E. *California's Gabrieliño Indians.* Los Angeles: Southwest Museum, 1962.

Robinson, Alfred. *Life in California, a Historical Account of the Origins, Customs, and Traditions of the Indians of Alta-California.* Oakland, CA: Biobooks, 1947.

Sparkman. Philip S. "The Culture of the Luiseño Indians." University of California *Publications in American Archaeology and Ethnology* 8(4): 187–234.

Spier, Leslie. "Southern Diegueño Customs." University of California *Publications in American Archaeology and Ethnology* 20(16): 295–358.

Webb, Edith Buckland. *Indian Life at the Old Missions.* Lincoln: University of Nebraska Press, 1982.

Miwok

The Miwok (a native word signifying "people") lived along the coast north of San Francisco Bay, in the southern basin of Clear Lake, and on the western slopes of the Sierra Nevadas—the Coast, Lake or Central, and Interior or Eastern Miwok, respectively. Hunters, gatherers, and fishermen, they all spoke Miwok, a subdivision of the Penutian language family. They were the first of the California Indians to come in contact with English-speaking foreigners; in 1579 Francis Drake spent five weeks among the Coast Miwok. In 1599 the first depiction of California Indians—an engraving published by Theodor de Bry, an illustration of the Indians welcoming Drake—was made. Louis Choris, with the Kotzebue expedition of 1816, did sketches of the Miwok. During the Mission Period and after, the Miwok were often kidnapped for slave labor at the nearby missions and on the ranches. The appearance of miners, settlers, and new diseases added to their destruction. It is the typical California story, and today the Miwok and their culture have virtually disappeared.

Men's Basic Dress

Men generally went naked, especially along the coast, but in the interior they wore a loincloth of buckskin or tule grass; this breechclout may have been of a double-apron type, or it sometimes must have had flaps, for an "unhandy ankle length" is mentioned. A form of shirt was a sleeveless piece of deerskin thrown over the shoulders, seemingly a poncho.

Women's Basic Dress

The Miwok themselves said that in primitive times both sexes went entirely naked; if true, it is most unusual, for Indian women always wore at least an apron. Along the coast the women generally wore double-apron skirts of shredded tule. The Central Miwok women wore the front and rear aprons of grass fibers and/or deerskin. The women in the Sierra area wore a wraparound dress of buckskin, with the hair side out, unfringed and open on one side.

Footwear

Normally the Miwok went barefoot. However, moccasins were worn in cold weather or on long rough trips; these were the California style, made of one piece of deerskin, seamed up the back and in front with milkweed-fiber thread or sinew. Tall overlapping cuffs were bound around the ankles with thongs. They were lined with shredded cedar bark for warmth.

Outer Wear

In cold weather both sexes wore robes of skin (deer, bear, mountain lion, coyote, and sometimes even buffalo acquired in trade from the east). Short or long robes were also made of rabbit skin, the pelts cut spirally into strips that were dried until they twisted, and were then woven into robes, loose and fragile but very warm. Feather capes were worn only by the very wealthy women; these were woven of ropes made by wrapping feathers around a cord, then woven in the same technique as a rabbit skin blanket. Mallard, snow geese, and Canada geese feathers were most sought after for these cloaks.

Hair Styles

Both sexes allowed the hair to grow long and to hang loosely. At times the men, especially when working, bunched the back hair into a knot, which was pinned in place with a large hairpin or bound with thongs. One native informant on the Coast Miwok said the women wore three braids; if so, it would be most unusual for a California Indian. A headband of beaver skin, a chaplet of flowers, or feathers were popular ornaments. After cloth became available, a cloth headband was customary. The hair net was worn, but only by those men of a higher rank. Occasionally the hair was worn in bangs over the forehead; cutting was done with an obsidian blade, or the hair was singed off with a burning stick. Some men cultivated sparse beards and mustaches.

Headgear

The Miwok seem not to have worn basket hats; when carrying heavy loads with a tumpline, a protective pad of tule grass or other fiber was worn on the forehead.

Accessories

Few accessories were worn or carried; occasionally a small leather pouch was used to carry necessary items such as paint. Simple leather or fiber belts girded garments. Feathered wristlets were a pleasing dress-up item.

Jewelry

The white clamshell disk beads were favored as ornament, but found more value as currency; abalone shell pieces, cut in round or square shapes and highly polished, were made into necklaces or earrings, never used as currency. Necklaces also consisted of cylinders of magnesite, scarce and valuable, and olivella shells from the coast. A boy's nasal septum was pierced at puberty and nose sticks of polished bone or dentalium shells were inserted. Both sexes had pierced ear lobes in which the youngsters wore flowers, women wore bead and shell earrings, and the men wore ear plugs of bird bones or feathers.

Special Costumes

No puberty rites took place. The Lake Miwok performed the "Big Head Dance," but seemingly not the other Miwok. They followed the Kuksu rites, so widespread in central California; in the Kuksu Dance performers wore a cape of feathers attached to a netted base. Dance skirts of feathers were also worn for ceremonies. The First Fruits Dance was held in the spring, at which men, women, and children danced carrying flowers and wearing them in the hair. A dance costume of the Coast Miwok was a "coat" made of pelican skins with the feathers still attached, tailored to fit, and closed with abalone "buttons." Headdresses were of three types: a forehead strip made of woodpecker scalps; a headband of upright black feathers, possibly condor; and a cap with horn-like "tremblers." An annual mourning rite was held. Widows cut or burned the hair as a sign of bereavement, covering the short hair with a mixture of white clay and asphaltum. Pitch was also mixed with powdered bone to form a substance which was applied to the face and left on until the end of the mourning period.

Garment Decoration

The Miwok made superb baskets, but seem to have done no other weaving; the rabbit skin robes may have been made by them, but it is also mentioned that they obtained them in trade from the Mono

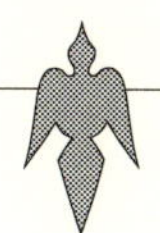

Lake Paiute. Netting was done as a base for feather garments and to create the men's hairnets. Shells, feathers, and flowers seem to have been the major items of decoration.

Face and Body Embellishment

Faces and bodies were painted for ceremonials, particularly in hues of black, red, and white—created from charcoal; ocher, which was obtained from the Eastern Mono; and a local clay respectively. Broad horizontal bands of white were popular for dance array. Tattooing appeared with both sexes, especially exhibiting vertical and zigzag lines on the chin and cheeks and, in some cases, on the neck; some older people had the chest tattooed. Green oak galls made a blue-black ink for the color, applied with a sharp piece of bone or a sliver of obsidian. To make a desired short flat head, the Eastern Miwok used a hard cradle board, pressing from the center to the sides; mothers also pressed an infant's nose to ensure a desirable flattened effect.

Masks

A simple face covering was reported for the Kuksu Dance.

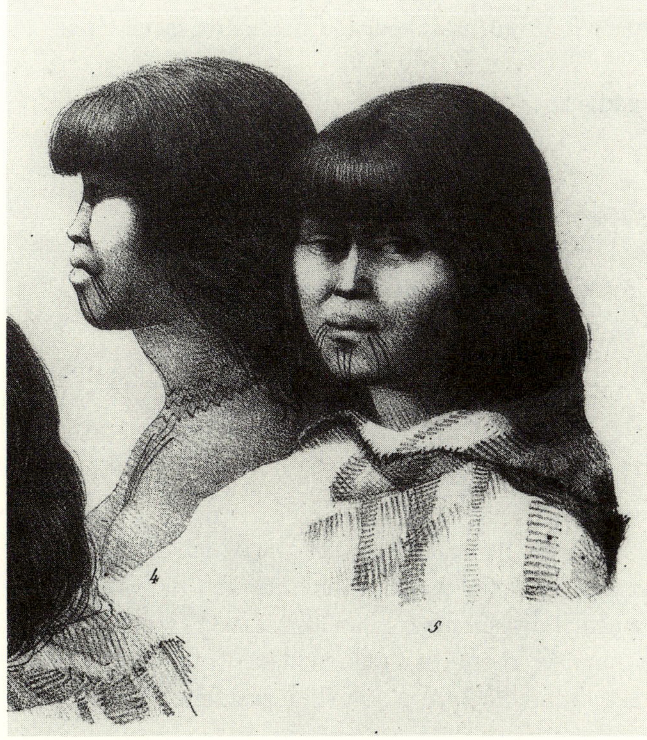

Saclan Miwok women, their hair worn loose, have chin and neck tattoos for tribal identity in this 1816 watercolor by Louis Choris.

Transitional Dress

By the early-nineteenth century the Coast Miwok were contacted by whites, but this had little impact on their dress until the end of the nineteenth century. The Eastern and Lake Miwok were devastated by the miners and the settlers of mid-century and later; what few Miwok were left quickly adopted European-style dress, retaining little of their traditional garb, except for a few ceremonial costumes.

Key Sources

Barrett, Samuel A., and Edward W. Gifford. "Miwok Material Culture." Milwaukee Public Museum *Bulletin* 2(4): 117–376.

Callaghan, Catherine A. "Lake Miwok." In *Handbook of North American Indians. Vol. 8: California.* Pp. 264–273. Washington: Smithsonian Institution.

Godfrey, Elizabeth. *Yosemite Indians.* Yosemite Natural History Association, 1941.

Kelly, Isabel. "Coast Miwok." In *Handbook of North American Indians. Vol. 8: California.* Pp. 414–425. Washington: Smithsonian Institution.

Levy, Richard. "Eastern Miwok." In *Handbook of North American Indians. Vol. 8: California.* Pp. 398–413. Washington: Smithsonian Institution.

Mojave

The Colorado River Indians included the Mojave, the Halchidoma, the Yuma, and the Cocopa. The Mojave (the Fort Mojave Council has officially adopted this spelling) were the largest of these tribes; the name is said to mean "three mountains," referring to the sharply pointed peaks near Needles. The annual flooding of the river led to extensive agriculture, although they had no arrangements for irrigation. The Mojave were great travelers; this activity seems to have satisfied their curiosity, for they were not particularly interested in trade. However, warfare was a consuming passion with them. The Spaniards came in 1604 but had little impact, for they established no missions in the area but brought wheat, which the Mojave began to raise. In the mid-nineteenth century explorers, trappers, immigrant parties, and finally the railroads came into southern California. Jedediah Smith traveled through the region in 1826 and kept a journal of his

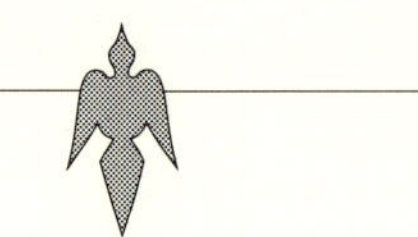

experiences, as did Lt. Whipple in 1854, a valuable record. H. B. Mollhausen, accompanying an 1857–1858 exploring expedition, did some fine drawings of the Mojave, and Ben Wittick took some excellent photographs in the 1870s and 1880s.

Men's Basic Dress
It was too hot for clothes most of the time, so the men went naked. Some wore narrow breechclouts of woven willow-bark strips that passed between the legs and under a thong belt so that a small flap hung in front and a longer one in back. After white contact they wore cloth loincloths with long panels hanging in front and behind. Later, too, they wore small fitted breechcloths held in place by a cloth girdle about the hips. No leggings were worn.

Women's Basic Dress
Women wore the front and back aprons of willow bark, the back section being especially twined to stand out in a "bustle" effect; the first two or three rows of the skirt were done in simple twining to hold the strips of bark in place. When commercial cloth was available, the Mojave women unravelled long strands of red and dark blue to twist into cords for the front apron. Under the front skirt or apron was worn a short underapron of finer bark at all times. Women went bare-breasted, even for a long time after white contact. A part of an upper-class woman's costume was the famous Mojave collar, which may have been based on an earlier prototype of fiber, but the well-known ones were of blue and white glass beads obtained from the Mission Indians on the coast. The collars had patterns using diamonds, triangles, hexagons, and at times the Greek fret motif. The body was of netted openwork of blue and white seed beads with a drawstring at the neck and with three-inch fringes made of strands of seed beads. Both men and women made these collars, particularly in the late-nineteenth century, the only articles made by them of fine craftsmanship. Until the whites came the women wore nothing on the upper torso but the collar; later, plaid shawls and then cotton blouses were added.

Footwear
Normally the Mojave went barefoot, only wearing fiber sandals for traveling; these were fashioned from untwisted bundles of mescal that were woven back and forth over a looped cord forming a thick sole. Later, rawhide sandals were worn, but since deer were scarce, these were soon replaced by "store" shoes.

Outer Wear
The women wove rabbit-skin robes or, more likely, acquired them from the Paiute or the Walapai to the east. Some wool ponchos were obtained in trade from the Navajo; these were about 18 inches wide, with an opening for the head.

Hair Styles
Women wore the hair long, occasionally with bangs on the forehead. Men let the hair grow waist-length, taking special pride in its glossy sheen, which was achieved by plastering it with mud and boiled mesquite bark, leaving it on overnight, then washing it out. They then rolled it into 20 or 30 rope-like strands; at times these were pulled to the back and tied with a thong, or they would be wound on the top of the head into a huge turban-like arrangement. Both sexes sometimes painted the hair with white clay. Occasionally a feather or two was fastened to the crown of the hair. A few men sported beards or mustaches, but most plucked the sparse facial hair.

Headgear
The Mojave used no head covering.

Accessories
Bags or wallets were woven of fibers, later of commercial yarns. Some braided or finger-woven belts were made. A band was worn on the forehead to ease the strain of the tumpline. When traders brought in cotton bandanas, the men wore them as neckerchiefs.

Jewelry
Other than the beaded collars, the Mojave were adorned with the usual ornaments—strings of clamshell disk beads (which also served as a form of money), bead and/or shell necklaces (often worn in great abundance), earrings, shell pendants in the nasal septum of the young men, and feathered articles. Many old women wore a clamshell ornament at the throat, cut in the form of a frog.

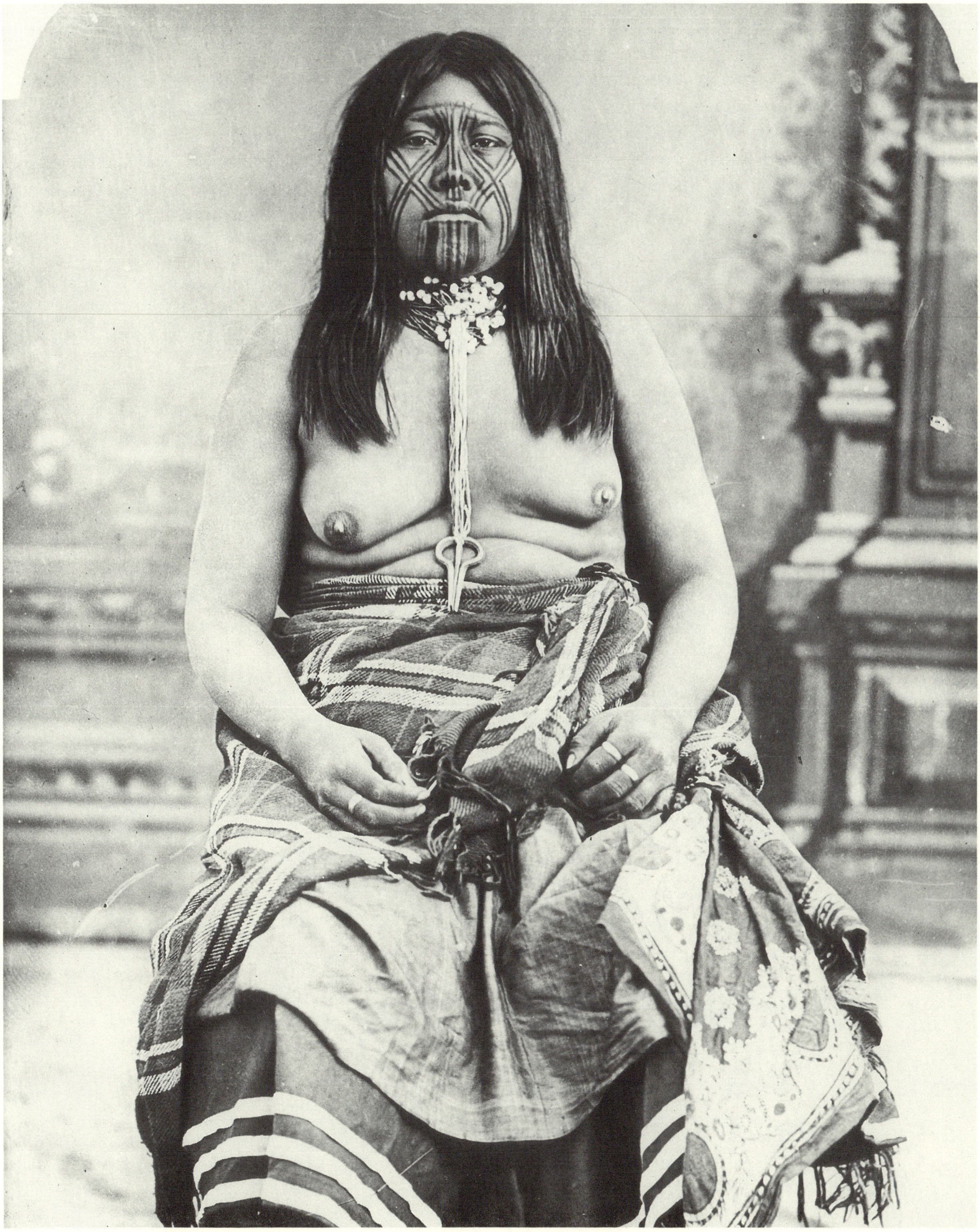

Mojave women went bare-breasted and continued to tattoo themselves well after contact with whites. This woman, her tattoos enhanced for a mid-1880s photograph, wears a shawl wrapped around her waist, a short cloth skirt, and a Jew's harp as a pendant.

In the 1880s a popular item of jewelry was a Jew's harp hanging on a thong; this may have been only for show, not use. Turquoise was obtained from the tribes to the east. Glass beads, particularly blue and white, were strung into necklaces that were coiled in thick masses around the neck. Chokers of beads featured one long strand hanging down over the chest.

Armor

The Mojave men wore no armor but protected themselves with round, unornamented hide shields.

Special Costumes

The Mojave had few ceremonies—an occasional bird dance, song cycles based on individual dreams, and, most important, the annual mourning rites. To show

A Mojave woman wears a netted collar, a wrapped-cloth belt, and a full, cloth skirt; her hair is painted in stripes. She poses with a man identified as a runner who wears a vest, a long-sleeved shirt with armbands, and a tightly wrapped cloth girdle.

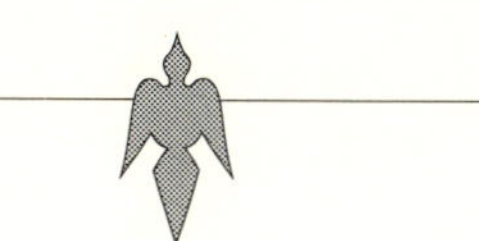

bereavement, the women cut the hair to a little below the ears, while the men clipped a bit off the ends of their rolls. All personal belongings, including garments, even the beaded collars, were buried with a corpse.

Garment Decoration

The Mojave were not weavers, but they were superb beadworkers, as shown by the beautiful collars. Because the climate was so hot and so little clothing was worn, decoration consisted almost entirely of face and body painting and tattooing.

Face and Body Embellishment

The Mojave painted the face and body daily with the usual red, white, and black pigments, the black being used especially to indicate readiness for warfare. Women often painted red and yellow designs on the face. The body was decorated with large horizontal or vertical stripes on the arms, the torso, and the legs. Women sometimes painted concentric circles on the breasts, the men on the chest. The Mojave painted themselves more than any other California tribes. Tattooing was also universal with both sexes; there was a strong belief that the untattooed person did not go into the afterworld, but rather into a rat's hole at death. Both boys and girls were tattooed at puberty, but no standardized designs were used. Women commonly had lines on the chin, but they varied in pattern. Kroeber gives many of the tattooing designs in his *Handbook of the Indians of California.*

Transitional Dress

The men were happy to change over to breechcloths of cotton, which were worn with cotton sashes. White cotton shirts were added toward the end of the nineteenth century, usually without trousers; in the next century they began to wear the typical western dress—large hats, Levi's, and cowboy boots. Women, too, were delighted to change to cotton, more comfortable than the fiber skirts; they wore full skirts of printed cotton with wide ruffles or flounces at the bottom, topped by a cotton sash. Plaid fringed shawls were a favored form of wrap for cool weather, otherwise a cotton-print square shawl was tossed over the shoulders and fastened in front. Shoes are still seldom worn.

Key Sources

Smith, Gerald A. *The Mojave Indians.* San Bernardino County Museum Association, 1977.

Mojave women adapted glass beads made in Europe to their traditional techniques of netting collars. This collar of dark blue and white beads, 22 inches in diameter, was made in the late nineteenth century.

Spier, Leslie. *Yuman Tribes of the Gila River.* New York: Dover, 1978. First published 1933.
Stewart, Kenneth M. "Mohave." In *Handbook of North American Indians. Vol. 10: Southwest.* Pp. 55–70. Washington: Smithsonian Institution.
Taylor, Edith S. and William J. Wallace. *Mohave Tattooing and Face-Painting.* Los Angeles: Southwest Museum, 1947.
Tsosie, Michael Philip. "Historic Mohave Bead Collars." *American Indian Art Magazine* (Winter 1992): 36–49.

Pomo

The Pomo ("earth people") lived north of San Francisco Bay along the coast and inland to the coastal range. Their customs were much like those of their neighbors, the Wintuns, to the east. They were north of the northernmost missions so, although some of the Pomo were captured for slave labor, they actually had little contact with the padres. They were Hokan speakers, with seven distinct languages called Pomo and seven distinct geographical groups. They were, and are, famed for their basketry, some of the finest in the world. They were noted for their "minting," that is, the making of clamshell disk beads for currency. Through the twentieth century the Pomo have been notably active in the Indian rights movement, including the dramatic occupation of Alcatraz Island during 1969–1971.

Men's Basic Dress

Men went naked almost all of the time; occasionally they wrapped a skin around the hips, or even wore a breechclout fashioned from rabbit fur. Leggings of skin or of tule fibers were used for traveling in mountain snows.

Women's Basic Dress

The Pomo women wore the two-piece skirt of fiber; this was of tule grass in the lake region, of willow bark in the interior, and of the inner bark of the redwood tree along the coast. Some of the skirts, especially the rear ones, were of deerskin; if the front skirts were of skin they were slit into fringe. In the winter heavier bark was used for the apron-skirts.

Footwear

Generally the Pomo went barefoot. However, a simple soft-soled skin moccasin was worn for traveling in rough country; these were lined with grass for warmth. In the lake country where tule was available everywhere, moccasins and even crude leggings were twined from the fibers.

Outer Wear

Mantles were created, depending on the region, of shredded tule grass (lake), of redwood-tree inner bark (coast), or of willow bark (inland Pomo). People of wealth wore mantles of deerskin. Where rabbits were available, robes were made that had openings for the arms, were fastened in front with wooden skewers, and were held in place with a rope belt. Along the coast a few displayed robes of seal or sea-otter fur. At times, the pelts of animals, such as puma, wildcat, or gopher, were sewn together into cloaks. Feather robes are mentioned, but as being worn only by very wealthy men.

Hair Styles

Both men and women bound their long hair in a knot at the nape of the neck and fastened it with one or more decorative hairpins. Some men bound the hair with nets of milkweed fiber, which were adorned with beads for ceremonial occasions.

Headgear

No caps or hats of any sort were worn by the Pomo.

Accessories

Shoulder bags were made of fiber in a looped openwork technique and decorated with shell pendants. Small pouches were made of the pelt of a small animal such as a squirrel. For carrying, a woman used a large netted bag that had a broad woven band in the net with a pad of tule or moss underneath, easing the strain on the forehead; sometimes small-polished shell beads were placed so as to roll over when the load swayed, preventing sidewise chafing. Decorated belts and neck bands were not only accessories but also displays of status and wealth.

Jewelry

Ornaments were many and varied, usually indicating the status of the wearer. Clamshell disk beads, abalone pendants, feathers, and magnesite cylinders

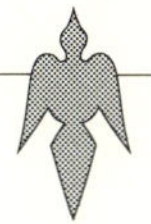

were fashioned into necklaces. The magnesite, which looked like creamy-white chalk, turned a delicate salmon color when roasted in the ashes; often referred to as "Indian gold," magnesite was an important item of trade and the Pomo, with their significant deposits of the mineral supplied much of central California. Hairpins, earrings, and earplugs were beautifully and delicately made of quail, bluebird, woodpecker, or mallard feathers fastened to crane wing bones with tiny bits of shell added. Men frequently wore a shaft of abalone shell as nose ornament. These articles of jewelry were not only a part of ceremonial attire, but were visible evidences of wealth.

Armor

Body armor was made of willow or hazel shoots closely twined with cords in two layers; the outer layer was of vertical rods and the inner layer of horizontal rods. The armor may have been effective against arrows, but it definitely reduced the warrior's mobility. Shields were not used by these people.

Special Costumes

Contrasting with their scanty everyday attire, the Pomo had brilliant, elaborate ceremonial costumes. The headbands of orange and black flicker (yellow-hammer) feathers were spectacular. A pair of "plumes," made of two slender rods tipped or wrapped with feathers, swayed with the movements of the dancers. The "Big Head" headdress was also worn; this consisted of many thin dogwood rods tipped with feathers, sticking out in all directions like a huge pincushion almost four feet in diameter; the ends of the rods were tipped with feathers or poppies. Women had two types of dance headdresses: (1) a headband with pieces of abalone shell hanging down over the face and (2) a fur headband ornamented with glass beads, feathers, and shells. A buckskin kilt decorated with feathers was worn for the ritual dances; men wore hair nets embellished with eagle down. One ceremonial item was a long magnificent mantle of black eagle (or owl or hawk) feathers fastened to a netted base. Brown mentions reed breastplates as a part of ritual costume. Powers tells of an unusual mourning custom: the widow mingled ashes of her husband with pitch, which mixture was then applied in a band about two inches wide at the edge of the (previously cut) hair, creating a "chaplet."

Garment Decoration

The fine artistry and craftsmanship of the Pomo could be seen in the decoration of garments, especially those for ceremonies. Delicate featherwork and shellwork adorned all costumes. A netting technique created bases for feather mantles and hair nets. Although the Pomo were extremely adept at twining and coiling techniques of basketry, the only "weaving" of garments seems to have been the making of armor, rabbit-skin robes, and the garments and accessories of tule. Glass beads were used as a form of embellishment rather than as "beadwork."

Face and Body Embellishment

Tattooing was sparingly done. Many women displayed the vertical lines on the chin. Few of the Pomo men were tattooed. However, Powers tells of a warrior who tattooed his chest and arms, including a fine representation of a sea otter—a most unusual

A Pomo's chin-to-hip armor, made of two layers of willow and hazel shoots, offered protection from arrows at the expense of mobility.

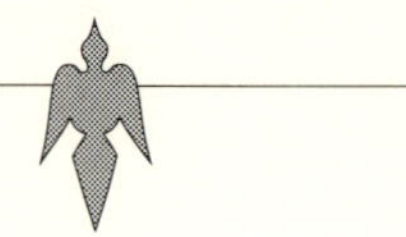

motif for California, as designs were almost always geometric. Powers tells further that a woman of this or neighboring tribes often tattooed a rude picture of a tree or other object on the abdomen. Face and body paint was applied extensively for ceremonies in the usual red, white, and black colors.

Transitional Dress

Although the women continued to wear the fiber skirts for some time, by mid-nineteenth century many were wearing calico dresses in the typical white fashions. These were made by them at first, later purchased. Men adopted the vests, trousers, cotton shirts of the whites. But shoes were only slowly acquired by the barefoot Pomo. Their magnificent ritual costumes in all their glory have continued even to the present day.

Key Sources

Barrett, Samuel A. "Ceremonies of the Pomo Indians." University of California *Publications in American Archaeology and Ethnology* 12(10): 397–441.

———. "The Ethnogeography of Pomo and Neighboring Indians." University of California *Publications in American Archaeology and Ethnology* 6(1): 1–332.

———. "Material Aspects of Pomo Culture." Milwaukee Public Museum *Bulletin* 20(1–2).

Bean, Lowell John and Dorothea Theodoratus. "Western Pomo and Northeastern Pomo." In *Handbook of North American Indians. Vol. 8: California.* Pp. 289–305. Washington: Smithsonian Institution.

Brown, Vinson and Douglas Andrews. *The Pomo Indians of California and Their Neighbors.* Healdsburg, CA: Naturegraph, 1969.

Gifford, Edward W. "Ethnographic Notes on the Southwestern Pomo." University of California *Anthropological Records* 25: 1–47.

Gifford, Edward W. and Alfred L. Kroeber. "Culture Element Distributions, IV: Pomo." University of California *Publications in American Archaeology and Ethnology* 37(4): 117–254.

Loeb, Edwin M. "Pomo Folkways." University of California *Publications in American Archaeology and Ethnology* 19(2): 149–405.

McLendon, Sally and Michael J. Lowy. "Eastern Pomo and Southeastern Pomo." In *Handbook of North American Indians. Vol. 8: California.* Pp. 306–323. Washington: Smithsonian Institution.

McLendon, Sally and Robert L. Oswalt. "Pomo: Introduction." In *Handbook of North American Indians. Vol. 8: California.* Pp. 274–288. Washington: Smithsonian Institution.

Shasta

The Shasta (the name was probably that of a chief) were a group of small tribes that lived on the upper Klamath River and other rivers of northern California, and into the Oregon area; in fact, they may be considered more related to the Oregon tribes, but there were strong influences of California in their costume. They treasured both the woodpecker scalps of the northwest tribes and the clamshell disk beads of the central California tribes. They spoke a Shastan form of the Hokan language family, which was also shared to some extent, with the Achumawi, or Pit River Indians, who lived to the east of Mt. Shasta, and the Atsugewi ("pine tree people"), who lived south of the Achumawi in the area of Lassen Peak. Although these tribes were similar in culture, there were some differences in attire, which will be indicated. Between the Gold Rush and the Rogue River Wars of 1850–1857, the Shastan peoples suffered severe disintegration of their culture attributable both to European diseases and the violence of white settlers.

Men's Basic Dress

Men wore a crude overtunic of skin with a hole cut out for the head and the sides fastened together below the armpits; this was often belted. With this was worn a kilt or apron of skin and, for travel, deerskin leggings, which were fringed, decorated with shells, and painted the typical California colors—red, white, and black. Poorer men wore a tule mat around the hips and knee-length tule leggings. Since this was one of the coldest regions of California, warmth was important.

Women's Basic Dress

Women wore the two-piece skirt of fiber (especially the front apron) and/or deerskin. With this was worn a sleeveless tunic of deerskin made in the casual poncho style. The Achumawi women wore a one-piece wraparound skirt of skin; reference is made to the fact that these women at times wore a sleeveless gown, extending from shoulders to knees. Poorer women wore skirts made of bundles of tule fibers, which were sewn or twined together. No mention is made of leggings, but they probably donned either skin or fiber leggings in the winter.

Footwear

Moccasins, used only for travel, had heavy soles of bear or elk skin added to the one-piece moccasins. In the winter, the inner soles were cut out so the foot rested on fur. Winter moccasins were made large so that grass or moss could be stuffed in for warmth. The Atsugewi did not wear the typical California one-piece moccasin, but rather they wore a three-piece affair consisting of the moccasin proper, a U-shaped insert that became a loose tongue, and a tall cuff that could be wrapped with thongs to keep out the snow. Poorer people wore twined tule slippers stuffed with grass in winter. A kite-shaped snowshoe was worn by the hunters in winter.

Outer Wear

Fibers such as tule and juniper bark were shredded and made into cloaks. Robes were also made of buckskin with the hair left on for warmth. No rabbit-skin robes are mentioned by the authorities consulted; however, it would be unusual if the Shasta peoples did not avail themselves of this widespread form of covering.

Hair Styles

Men wore the hair long and loose, occasionally gathered into a coil on the top of the head and skewered with a bone or wooden pin. Some men of the Shasta Valley wore the netted hair net. Women followed the Yurok style of two bunches of hair, sometimes wrapped with fur, hanging in front over the shoulders. Children to the age of three had all the hair singed off close to the head. This was continued with boys until adolescence; girls had a strip of hair left from the forehead to the nape of the neck until puberty.

Headgear

Only the women wore the basketry hats, done in a twining technique, often made of shredded willow bark; Powers comments that these small, round, closely-fitting caps were occasionally used as drinking cups. The Maidu said that the Achumawi wore a flat-topped basket hat much like that of the Modoc and Yana. Men wore fur hats or buckskin caps in winter. The adolescent girls, secluded for ten days during their first menses, wore visors of bluejay feathers to shield the eyes.

Accessories

A sort of glove was reported, made by winding a strip of rabbit fur about the hand and wrist and up the forearm. Belts were frequently adorned with dentalium shells. Some women's belts were made of bunches of strands of hair intertwined with buckskin, or of buckskin alone, decorated with beadwork or porcupine quillwork, which would imply a fairly late date in the nineteenth century. Early bags or pouches were embellished with shell or stone beads, later with quill or beadwork, which was done by the Shasta Valley women mainly.

Jewelry

Ornaments for both sexes were made of beads, shells, and feathers. Noses were perforated and a dentalium shell was inserted as ornament. Earrings were of pieces of abalone shell or dentalia. Necklaces were made of a variety of materials—clamshell disk beads, bear claws, elk teeth, abalone pendants, and pine nuts. The Klamath River people also used bear teeth or bird claws for necklaces, while their children wore deer-hoof necklaces.

Armor

Long body armor was made of layers of tough elk or bear hide. Short waistcoat-length armor was made of rods twined together with hemp cord; the edges were bound with deerskin, and shoulder straps were of fur. Four horizontal bands of red paint adorned the front; a checkerboard portion in the back was woven with strands of human hair. No shields were mentioned.

Special Costumes

The Shasta had few rituals, as the people to the northwest observed; the major rite was the girl's puberty dance, at which the girl wore old moccasins and woven wristlets of buckbrush. Boys also had a

puberty rite, at which time they wore skunk brush belts. Flicker quill headbands were displayed at the ceremonies, also a netted fiber dance cap of tule grass, on which abalone pendants and glass beads glistened; the cap was held on during dancing by a red flannel chin strap. As was generally observed throughout California, a widow cut or singed the hair, blackened the face, and cropped hair with pitch; after her hair had regrown, she was free to marry her dead husband's brother. A mourning belt of her own hair or of willow bark was also displayed as a sign of bereavement.

Garment Decoration

Pine nuts, shells (especially abalone and dentalia), and feathers were commonly used for decoration. Quillwork, seldom found in California, was occasionally done by the Achumawi women; it was probably learned from the Modoc and Klamath, and did not extend to other California tribes. Beadwork, too, was not typical of those tribes, but was made by the Achumawi and the Atsugewi. A quail-feather motif, sometimes found in the beadwork, was characteristic of basketry designs of northern California.

Face and Body Embellishment

Tattooing was optional with both sexes; it consisted of parallel lines on the chin, forehead, cheeks, chests, wrists, or legs; most women had the three vertical lines on the chin. Many practiced skull deformation by compressing the forehead of an infant by means of a flat piece of wood or a tight binding, as was done by the tribes to the north. Face and body paint was a mixture of grease and marrow with red, black, white, and yellow pigments. Powers says the Shasta smeared their faces daily with chokecherry juice, to give themselves a "bloody corsair look."

Transitional Dress

Powers, in 1872, wrote about the Shasta men and how they adopted such articles of dress as dainty calf-boots, fancy shirt fronts, breastpins, rings, and such; he said there was not another tribe in the state "going out of existence so rapidly, in such good clothes, and with more elegance." However, the women were not included in this; they wore dark cotton skirts, cotton blouses, and cloth headscarves. By the end of the century almost all remnants of tribal costume were gone except for a few ceremonial garments.

Key Sources

Curtis, Edward S. *The North American Indian.* Vol. 13. New York: Johnson Reprint Company, 1970.

Dixon, Roland B. "The Shasta." American Museum of Natural History *Bulletin* 17(5): 381–498.

Garth, Thomas R. "Atsugewi." In *Handbook of North American Indians. Vol. 8: California.* Pp. 236–248. Washington: Smithsonian Institution.

———. "Atsugewi Ethnography." University of California *Anthropological Records* (14)2: 129–212.

Holt, Catherine. "Shasta Ethnography." University of California *Anthropological Records* 3(4): 299–349.

Olmsted, D. L., and Omer C. Stewart. "Achumawi." In *Handbook of North American Indians. Vol. 8: California.* Pp. 225–235. Washington: Smithsonian Institution.

Silver, Shirley. "Shastan People." In *Handbook of North American Indians. Vol. 8: California.* Pp. 211–224. Washington: Smithsonian Institution.

Wintun

The Wintun (their native name for "people") lived on the upper Sacramento River and the upper Trinity River in northern California. They spoke a dialect of the Penutian language family. The northern Wintun were called the Wintu, the central group the Nomlaki, and the southern Wintun were the Patwin. There was much seasonal shifting of population for the gathering of acorns, hunting, and fishing for salmon; the furs acquired included fisher, marten, bear, elk, deer, and sea otter.

In the early nineteenth century the Wintun were increasingly influenced by the Franciscan missions at San José, Delores, and Sonoma. Their population, thought to have been about 14,000 at the time of white contact, declined precipitously through the nineteenth century as European diseases and the social disorder engendered by white settlement took a terrible toll.

Among the Wintun, a particular form of wealth was the pelt of the black bear, which also served as a burial shroud. Clamshell disk beads were also accounted wealth, as were cylindrical magnesite beads, furs, woodpecker scalps, and obsidian blades. They typically had oval faces and wide foreheads; the women usually had small hands and feet, and a small frame.

Men's Basic Dress

Men usually went naked or draped a hide around the hips.

Women's Basic Dress

Women wore an apron of tule or of the shredded inner bark of the maple or cottonwood tree; a back apron might be added of the same material. For special occasions, a fringed doeskin or fawn-skin skirt was added in the back, and occasionally substituted for the front fiber apron. Often the deerskin was slit in front into long fringes, with pine-nuts and bits of shell placed on each strand.

Footwear

Generally the Wintun went barefoot. Some mention is made of sandals (not moccasins) of elk hide. For those men hunting in the foothills in the winter, a round snowshoe was constructed of a hazelwood frame laced with grapevine or deer-hide thongs.

Outer Wear

Some mantles were made of tanned deer hide; others were woven from strips of rabbit pelt, cut spirally, dried, and twisted into a cord for weaving. Capes were made of fox skins when available.

Hair Styles

Women wore the hair long and loose; unmarried girls had long bangs on the forehead down to the eyebrows. Men also wore the hair long, sometimes coiling it into a knot on top of the head and fastening it in place with a wooden skewer; they occasionally donned a hair net, also anchoring it with a bone or wooden pin. A few men allowed a sparse beard or mustache to grow, but generally the facial hair was plucked with clamshell tweezers.

Headgear

Basketry hats were worn only by the northern Wintus, done in a closework twining technique. The only other headgear was for ceremonial use.

Accessories

Some men wore belts of human hair decorated with porcupine quills, rare and highly prized; quillwork, seldom done, was in conjunction with *Xerophyllum* (bear grass) and maidenhair fern. Some belts, made only by certain privileged families, were of red-headed woodpecker scalps. Wide belts, sometimes of checkerboard pattern, were important dance items. When beadwork came into the area, pouches for shot and tobacco were made, displaying bicolor designs based on triangles and arrows.

Jewelry

Piercing of the nasal septum was rarely performed; it was achieved with the use of a porcupine quill and into the perforation a bone or a dentalium shell was inserted. Ears were also pierced for the wearing of earrings. Necklaces were of olivella or abalone pendants (obtained from the Yurok or Karok), magnesite cylinder beads and clamshell disk beads (from the Pomo), dentalia from the north, and pine nuts.

Armor

Elk-skin armor was worn. The Patwin wore armor of vertical slats or rods, held together with sinew; both types of armor made movement difficult, but would stop arrows. No shields are mentioned.

Special Costumes

The "Big Head" Dance "to save the Earth" was probably originated by the Wintun; it combined the Ghost Dance of the 1870s, war dances, and dream dances, and was of comparatively recent development, based on the earlier Kuksu cult. A pincushion-like headdress was made of slender rods exploding in all directions; the rod ends were tipped with poppies or feathers, and fastened at the back were two long bands embellished with the quills of flickers. Some dancers wore headdresses made of the feathers of white-headed woodpeckers or great horned owls. Kilts of shredded maple bark swayed and rippled with the movements of the dance. Performers also wore magnificent mantles made of feathers of various birds, arranged in patterns of rings and bands. Hair nets adorned with eagle down were worn by the men at ceremonials, as were headbands of flicker feathers and strips of fox,

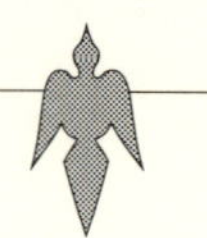

mink, otter, or the white belly hair of a wolf. Initiation dances were held for girls at puberty. At death, a body was clothed in deerskin and wrapped in a bearskin that was then bound with sinew. A widow cut her hair short and smeared her face with a mixture of pitch and charcoal, which was left on, until it was removed as a signal she was ready for remarriage.

Garment Decoration

The fringes of women's skirts were decorated with shells, nuts, and beads. Weaving was represented by the rabbit-skin robes and the twining of hats in the northern area; netting was used for hair nets. Quillwork was rare; it featured the usual geometric designs, which appeared in the later beadwork. Some fine featherwork was done for ceremonial costumes.

Face and Body Embellishment

Men were rarely tattooed. Women usually had three vertical lines on the chin; the tattooing was done in early adolescence, using an obsidian sliver and charcoal. Occasionally, women were tattooed on the breast or stomach. A menstruating girl had vertical lines painted on her cheeks with charcoal or red and blue pigments. Some face paint was applied for dances.

Masks

During the Kuksu dance, the face was disguised or concealed, not by a mask per se, but with a "curtain" of feathers or a heavy coat of paint on the face.

Transitional Dress

There was little of transitional dress; with white contact, the men quickly adopted contemporary clothes, while the women were slower to wear the full skirts and blouses of cotton worn by the pioneer women. By 1900, there was almost no Wintun tribal dress remaining, except for the ceremonial costumes brought out for festivals and dances.

Key Sources

Curtis, Edward S. *The North American Indian.* Vol. 14. New York: Johnson Reprint Company, 1970.

DuBois, Cora A. "Wintu Ethnography." University of California *Publications in American Archaeology and Ethnology* 36(1): 1–148.

Goldschmidt, Walter. "Nomlaki." In *Handbook of North American Indians. Vol. 8: California.* Pp. 341–349. Washington: Smithsonian Institution.

———."Nomlaki Ethnography." University of California *Publications in American Archaeology and Ethnology* 35(8): 303–443.

Johnson, Patti J. "Patwin." In *Handbook of North American Indians. Vol. 8: California.* Pp. 350–360. Washington: Smithsonian Institution.

Knudtson, Peter M. *The Wintun Indians of California and Their Neighbors.* Happy Camp, CA: Naturegraph, 1977.

Kroeber, Alfred L. "The Patwin and Their Neighbors." University of California *Publications in American Archaeology and Ethnology* 29(4): 253–423.

LaPena, Frank R. "Wintu." In *Handbook of North American Indians. Vol. 8: California.* Pp. 324–340. Washington: Smithsonian Institution.

Yana/Yahi

The Yana and the Yahi of the upper Sacramento Valley spoke a peculiar form of the Hokan language; the sexes spoke differently—men used the women's form when conversing with them, but among themselves they spoke the male form, while the women spoke only the female form at all times. Their first contact with whites was in 1821. They were almost exterminated by disease, loss of access to hunting and gathering territory, and a massacre by white miners in 1864. On 29 August 1911, a starving, shivering Yahi man was found, destitute, in Oroville, California. He was fed, given clothing, and lodged in the jail for a few days, until it could be decided what was to be done with him. The problem was solved by two anthropologists from the University of California, T. T. Waterman and Alfred L. Kroeber. They took him to the university and lodged him in the Museum of Anthropology, where he stayed until his death in 1916. They called him "Ishi," the word for "man" in his language. Kroeber's wife, Theodora, told about him in her book, *Ishi in Two Worlds.* A gentle, obliging man, he provided a wealth of information

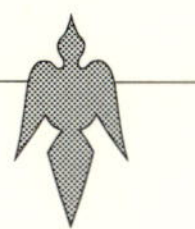

to the anthropologists he met and worked with, and we are greatly indebted to him for our knowledge of aboriginal techniques of creating and using artifacts, as well as facts about dress.

Men's Basic Dress

The Yana and Yahi wore the typical northern California clothes—a buckskin kilt, leggings of skin from hip to ankles, and, occasionally, a poncho-style shirt also of skin. Poorer men wore only a simple wraparound deerskin kilt or apron.

Women's Basic Dress

Women wore a front apron of shredded bark or tule grass, with a back apron of fiber, that hung down from a string of buckskin; wealthier women wore skirts of skin with leather tassels braided with grass in front, often strung with pine nuts. Although it is not mentioned, the women may have worn a casual poncho-style covering in cooler weather.

Footwear

The characteristic deerskin moccasin was worn; this was the one-piece type with a seam up the back and one up the heel.

Outer Wear

Robes were simply made of deerskin (with the hair left on for winter), wildcat fur, coyote fur, and bearskin. The rabbit-skin blanket was made from strips of the spirally cut pelt, then woven in a simple cross weave.

Hair Styles

Both sexes wore the hair long. Men tied it in back with a thong, or coiled it on top of the head and skewered it with a large bone or wooden pin. Women usually wore two braids or rolls in front of their shoulders, often wrapped with mink or buckskin strips. The men plucked out the facial hair with a sharp splinter of wood.

Headgear

The basket cap was worn by the women, but this was the juncture of the northern twining with the overlay technique, usually of *Xerophyllum* (bear grass), and the southern technique of coiling and twining without overlay. The Maidu said the Yana wore flat-topped basket caps or hats. The weaving was not well done; the warp was of hazel or willow switches and the weft of pine roots or sedge. Overlay was worked with white, black, and red strands against the brown of the pine roots. Men wore elk-skin hats in the winter.

Accessories

Some belts were made of human hair; some were of leather adorned with woodpecker scalps. Bags and pouches were simply made of buckskin.

Jewelry

Both sexes pierced the earlobes and fastened in them ornaments of shell, or strings or loops of beads. Men's and women's necklaces were of dentalium and olivella shells, beads, juniper berries, nuts, and clamshell disk beads, the latter most important. Magnesite cylinders were obtained in trade and favored as ornament. Men pierced the nasal septum and inserted a dentalium shell.

Special Costumes

Ceremonies among the Yana and Yahi were not elaborate. They participated in the Kuksu cult, wearing feather garments and the headbands of woodpecker scalps. At puberty the ears were pierced for earrings, and boys had the nasal septum perforated.

Garment Decoration

The only weaving done was the rabbit-skin robe and the basketry hats with their overlay designs in red, black, and white colors. Some featherwork was done for ceremonial dress. But in general the Yana and Yahi women were not craftspeople.

Face and Body Embellishment

Some women were tattooed with the three vertical lines on the chin, but this was not common. Some paint was used on the face and body, but this, too, was rare.

Transitional Dress

The Yana and Yahi were so decimated with white contact that they were little able to maintain their traditional manner of attire. Ishi, when found, was wearing some cast-off white garments, and that was, in general, the fate of the tribe.

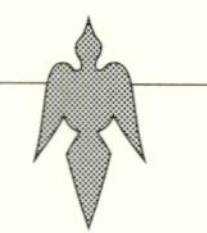

Key Sources

Gifford, Edward W., and Stanislaus Klimek. "Culture Element Distributions, 11: Yana." University of California *Publications in Archaeology and Ethnology* 37(2): 71–100.

Johnson, Jerald Jay. "Yana." In *Handbook of North American Indians. Vol. 8: California.* Pp. 361–369. Washington: Smithsonian Institution.

Kroeber, Theodora. *Ishi in Two Worlds.* Berkeley: University of California Press, 1970.

Sapir, Edward, and Leslie Spier. "Notes on the Culture of the Yana." University of California *Anthropological Records* 3(3): 239–298.

Waterman, Thomas T. "The Yana Indians." University of California *Publications in American Archaeology and Ethnology* 13(2): 35–102.

Yokuts

The Yokuts (their name for themselves) were Penutian speakers who inhabited the San Joaquin Valley and the adjacent foothills of the Sierra Nevada. The Spaniards called them Tulareños, or "people of the cane breaks," for they were surrounded by abundant plant and animal life, particularly tule grass which grew as tall as 10 or 12 feet; they hunted, gathered, and did some fishing, but like most California Indians practiced no agriculture. The Yokuts consisted of three groups: the North Valley, the South Valley, and the Foothill Yokuts. They exhibited a remarkable political solidarity; a rarity among California Indians, they were organized as tribes rather than tribelets, each with a name, a territory, and a dialect. The Spaniards tried to conquer the interior, but did not succeed; many of the runaways from the Franciscan missions took refuge with the Yokuts. Their history following European contact was the usual tragic California story—encroachment, exploitation, disease (especially malaria in 1833), and murder—yet somehow the Yokuts managed to survive; some live today on the Tule River Reservation.

Men's Basic Dress

Men usually went naked, or they had aprons of deerskin hanging in front and in back, or they wrapped a skin around the hips in a kilt-like manner; some wore a deerskin breechclout with flaps in front and rear.

Women's Basic Dress

Women wore the two-piece skirt, the front of willow bark or tule, and the overlapping back of deerskin or even of coot skins. Heizer mentions a breechclout for the women of skin with flaps hanging in front and back.

Footwear

The typical California moccasin of elk hide or deerskin was worn—of one piece with a seam up the front and at the heel. Some sandals were made of several layers of tough hide to form a sole, held on with thongs. These and the moccasins were worn only by men and for travel in rough country. Some rude moccasins of bear fur were reported for use in winter.

Outer Wear

Cooler weather meant robes of fur, rabbit skin, or coot skins, fastened in front with wooden or bone skewers. The rabbit pelts were cut spirally in strips which were dried so they twisted into a fur-covered strip; these were then woven in a simple cross weave. Coot skins were handled in the same manner. Robes were also made of the skins of ground squirrels, ducks, and quail.

Hair Styles

Hair was full length, worn loose, except when gathered into a clump in back, or coiled into a topknot and fastened with a large wooden or bone hairpin. Some men displayed a sparse mustache.

Headgear

No head covering was worn by the men, but the women wore a coiled basket hat, of a conical shape like the hats of the south rather than the short, rounded caps of the north; the hat was worn only when carrying a heavy load with a tumpline.

Accessories

Accessories were few. Simple belts were made of thongs or of straps of tanned leather. Bags and pouches were of deerskin or elk skin.

Jewelry
Treasured necklaces were of golden-eagle claws or bear claws, strung with shells such as olivella and abalone, secured in trade from the Costanoans. Long strings of clamshell disk beads were proudly displayed; these were cut from the long perforated cylinders of huge clams, probably obtained from the Chumash on the coast. At puberty boys and girls had the earlobes pierced for the wearing of ornaments of wood, bone, or shell. The nasal septum was perforated for the insertion of bone or wooden pins. Spier says there is some conflict among authorities as to which sex followed the custom; probably both sexes had the option.

Armor
Armor is not mentioned, but warriors painted their faces red and adorned themselves with feathers before going into conflict.

Special Costumes
The Yokuts had no rites for adolescent girls, but boys had an initiation ritual that involved the drinking of an infusion of *datura* (jimsonweed), which gives hallucinatory reactions and is typical of southern California rituals. The Yokuts had a war dance, but they were a peaceable people and seldom went to war. A Rattlesnake Dance was performed in the spring, and the 1870 Ghost Dance was adopted by them for a short time. Eagle down was an important element of ceremonial costumes and was much sought after. Flicker quill headbands were worn, but more characteristic were the dance skirts of strings of milkweed fiber cords wrapped with eagle down and feathers. Also popular was a tall headdress made of crow and magpie feathers, fastened to the head by means of a head net commonly worn by dancers. Sticks tipped with quail feathers were inserted in the pierced earlobes. For an important mourning ceremony, widows and other mourners singed off the hair in varying amounts, depending on the extent of bereavement. Women blackened the face with pitch, which was retained until it wore off.

A Chulamni man, or Northern Valley Yokuts, has tattoos on his chin and wears his hair loose with a cloth headband.

Garment Decoration
Weaving was practiced by the Yokuts only for the coiled basket hats and the rabbit-skin and coot-skin robes. Featherwork was demonstrated in their ceremonial attire, as well as by the coot robes mentioned above.

Face and Body Embellishment
Tattooing was practiced more in the north than in the south, and it was fairly common for women but rare for men. Women tattooed the chin with the characteristic vertical lines plus some zigzag lines and rows of dots. The tattooing procedure was to rub charcoal into cuts made with an obsidian blade.

Transitional Dress
With the annexation of California by the United States and the influx of settlers into the rich farmlands of the San Joaquin Valley, the Yokuts culture was almost totally extinguished. The few who were left took on European-style dress—the trousers, shirts, vests, cotton blouses and skirts, the headscarves, the hats—scarcely distinguishable from poor whites. Very little of their ceremonial costume survived into the present century.

Key Sources
Curtis, Edward S. *The North American Indian.* Vol. 14. New York: Johnson Reprint Company, 1970.

Gayton, Anna H. "Yokuts and Western Mono Ethnography." University of California *Anthropological Records* 10(1–2): 1–302.

Latta, Frank F. *Handbook of Yokuts Indians.* Bakersfield, CA: Kern County Museum, 1949.

Spier, Robert F. G. "Foothill Yokuts." In *Handbook of North American Indians. Vol. 8: California.* Pp. 471–484. Washington: Smithsonian Institution.

Wallace, William J. "Northern Valley Yokuts." In *Handbook of North American Indians. Vol. 8: California.* Pp. 462–470. Washington: Smithsonian Institution.

———. "Southern Valley Yokuts." In *Handbook of North American Indians. Vol. 8: California.* Pp. 448–461. Washington: Smithsonian Institution.

Yuki

The Yuki—the name is a Wintun word meaning "enemy"—are commonly divided into four groups: the Yuki proper, the Coast Yuki, the Huchnom, and the Wappo. The language is simply called Yuki; it has no known linguistic relatives. The Yuki were hunters, fishers, and gatherers, living along the Eel River and the coast. They had a remarkably dense and stable population with a relatively simple material culture and an elaborate ceremonial tradition. The Huchnom were the "mountain people"; the Wappo were so-named from an Americanization of the Spanish word *guapo,* meaning "brave," indicative of their fierce resistance to Franciscan missionization. They represented the southernmost influence of the Northwest Coast culture area and the beginning of the California culture area. Their first contact with whites was in 1856, and by 1864 they were almost exterminated by the settlers who were encroaching on their land. A few Yukis live today on the Round Valley reservation in California.

Men's Basic Dress

Men generally went naked; if anything was worn, it was a deerskin wrapped around the loins.

Women's Basic Dress

Women wore the fringed double-apron skirt, usually of deerskin, and often decorated the front fringe with pine nuts and shells.

Footwear

No moccasins or sandals were worn by the Yuki.

Outer Wear

A deerskin was used for warmth; rabbit-skin robes are scarcely mentioned, except for the Wappo, but it was difficult for them to get enough pelts, so they wore short capes rather than robes. Chiefs or other headmen proudly wore robes of seal or otter skin. Some mention is made of capes of tule grass worn by the Wappo, who also worshipped the owl and the hawk, conciliating the birds with offerings and wearing mantles of their feathers.

Hair Styles

Women wore the hair long and flowing. Men also wore the hair long but bundled it up into a topknot, which was held in place with large wooden or bone pins. A hair net made of milkweed or iris fibers was woven with large meshes and was drawn tight with a string around the edge; this was used by men only when working and for holding ceremonial headdresses in position. The Huchnom men and women wore the hair only to the shoulders. No beards or mustaches were displayed by the men.

Headgear

The only form of headgear was the hair net mentioned above. Although the women were superb basket weavers, they wore no basket hats.

Accessories

The Yuki had few accessories—belts of thongs or a strap of leather and a few bags or pouches of deerskin. These were typically undecorated except for use in ceremonies.

Jewelry

Men frequently wore a small bone or a dentalium shell in the pierced nasal septum. Only the women wore necklaces, commonly of pieces of abalone shells or strings of clamshell disk beads, the latter a measured display of wealth. Earlobes were pierced for the insertion of the salmon-colored cylinders of magnesite, which were also used in necklaces. Women's wrist bangles were made of abalone-shell pendants.

Armor

No armor was worn, but warriors going into battle decorated their hair nets with white osprey down and generally wore the whole wing of an eagle in the hair.

Special Costumes

Yuki ceremonial life was costumed with great elaboration. They celebrated a war dance, a Feather Dance, a girl's puberty rite, a boy's initiation rite, and a Green Corn Dance in which, as Powers tells us, the men wore a breechclout and a mantle of the black tail feathers of an eagle, reaching from under the chin down to the thighs but not encumbering the arms. Men wore the string hair nets filled with eagle down, flicker quill headbands, netted feather capes, and deerskin kilts, and carried forked feather plumes. Gifford, who wrote extensively on the Yuki, says that they performed a Condor Dance in which the entire skin of a condor was used, with the wings tied over the arms and the head worn over the dancer's head. Powers gives a vivid description of the Acorn or Thanksgiving Dance in which the women had tall plumes in the hair and the men were decorated with cowls or garlands of white owl down in the hair and wore mantles of eagle, buzzard, or hawk tail feathers. These feather mantles were common to this region, but the garland of white down was peculiar to the Yuki and the Wailaki to the north. Some of the Yuki adopted the Kuksu cult, wearing the "Big Head" headdress. They participated in the Ghost Dance in 1872. Girls, during their first menses, left the hair long in front over the eyes so they could not see from right to left; they also wore a large basket over the head wherever they went. A widow cropped the hair closely and smeared it with pitch.

Garment Decoration

Little weaving was done except for the rabbit-skin robes. Featherwork was of fine artistry, as displayed in their ceremonial garments and accessories.

Face and Body Embellishment

Both men and women were tattooed with pitch-pine soot and a sharp splinter of deer bone. Tattooing, which was done in various lines, zigzags, and diamonds, appeared especially on the women's cheeks and chins. The Yuki women did not have a prescribed design for each tribe, as in the Northwest, but exhibited great individual variety. Body and face paint was applied only for dances; charcoal, red ocher, and white clay were the most commonly used pigments.

Masks

As was true of so many Indian tribes, the hunters used deer-head masks as disguises when approaching their prey.

Transitional Dress

The Yuki were almost wiped out in such a short time after white contact that transitional dress scarcely existed. The few survivors took on European-style dress of purchased garments—the trousers, vests, shirts, blouses, skirts, and head-scarves or neckerchiefs. They still clung to the vestiges of ceremonial wear.

Key Sources

Curtis, Edward S. *The North American Indian.* Vol. 14. New York: Johnson Reprint Company, 1970.

Driver, Harold E. "Wappo Ethnography." University of California. *Publications in American Archaeology and Ethnology* 36(3): 179–220.

Foster, George M. "A Summary of Yuki Culture." University of California *Anthropological Records* 5(3): 155–244.

Gifford, Edward W. "The Coast Yuki." Sacramento Anthropological Society *Papers* 2.

Miller, Virginia P. "Yuki, Huchnom, and Coast Yuki." In *Handbook of North American Indians. Vol. 8: California.* Pp. 249–255. Washington: Smithsonian Institution.

Sawyer, Jesse O. "Wappo." In *Handbook of North American Indians. Vol. 8: California.* Pp. 256–263. Washington: Smithsonian Institution.

Yuma

The Yuma spoke a Yuman dialect that was a part of the Hokan linguistic family. They called themselves "Quechans," meaning "those who descended," perhaps referring to their own account of the Creation. They lived in rancherias along both sides of the lower Colorado River, practicing a kind of floodwater agriculture; they were growers and gatherers rather than hunters. The Yuman culture was similar to that of the Halchidoma to their north and the Cocopa to the south. Since the possessions of a deceased person were abandoned, there was little development of material goods. Unlike other California tribes (except at the missions), the Yuma rode horses, which they obtained in trade from the Southwest. Although there was much trading with peoples to their east, their clothing was more like that of the California tribes, especially similar to that of the Mojave. The Yuma were among the tallest of American Indians, the men averaging almost six feet in height. Their first known European contact was with the Spanish missionary Father Kino in 1702. Forbes has written extensively on the Yuma.

Men's Basic Dress
Forbes says that when the Spaniards first came to the area, they found most of the Yuma men going about entirely nude; even as late as 1774, the Quechan men were still reluctant to cover the genitals. About the early 1800s they began to wear a small loincloth. After 1849, European-style clothing was worn but the legs were usually bare. Some wore a girdle of bark or twine with a breechcloth of a trade handkerchief (bandana type) fastened under the girdle. At times a small G-string was worn attached to a belt or thong.

Women's Basic Dress
Women wore the two-piece skirt, the front one of strips of the inner bark of the willow, the rear one of the same material tucked up into a "bustle" effect. Earlier they seem to have worn feather skirts.

Footwear
Generally the Yuma went barefoot; however, rawhide sandals are mentioned, probably for travel over rough, hot, thorny ground.

Outer Wear
For warmth both sexes wore rabbit-skin robes, or crudely woven blankets of bark fiber. Some obtained blankets from the Hopi in trade. Generally, robes were short, more like shoulder capes. One writer, Duflot de Mofras, in 1842 said that the Yuma planted cotton "which they spin and weave into fine cloth," a statement that is not borne out by other writings. Coronel, around 1830, said the Yuma made blankets from the hair of wild sheep, which sounds somewhat more plausible. But the Yuma were not adept weavers; the blankets may have come from the Pima to the east.

Hair Styles
Both sexes let the hair grow long. Males were particularly proud of their long hair, sometimes plastering it with a reddish mud or pinon gum to arrange the hair in crowns or horns, or else they rolled it into long rolls which were treated with mesquite sap or gum. At times these curls were rolled up on top of the head in the form of a turban, even further covered with a cloth turban. Bunched up feathers occasionally hung from the hair. In the nineteenth century, both sexes wore bangs on the forehead and tended to wear the hair shorter. At times the dark hair was painted with white horizontal stripes.

Headgear
The turbans mentioned above were made of cloth strips about three inches wide wound around and around the head; what with the rolls of hair also worn

Photographed about 1885, a Yuma woman at the San Carlos Reserve, Arizona, has chin and cheek tattoos. Her hair is painted with horizontal stripes, and she wears a cloth dress with full sleeves and skirt, and beaded necklaces.

on top, these "turbans" were gigantic affairs. Forbes mentions a piece of deerskin worn like a helmet and adorned with a small crest of feathers.

Accessories

Belts of thongs or woven fibers were replaced by girdles or sashes when commercial cloth became available. Cloth bandanas were used as neckerchiefs or headscarves, or hung in front as a sort of (male) breechcloth. Woven-fiber head rings were used to hold carrying jars on the head. Narrow bands were wound around the arms for armbands.

Jewelry

Men perforated the nasal septum, inserting rings, sticks, or loops of beads; these ornaments were sometimes so ponderous that the facial features became distorted. Multistrand necklaces, bracelets, and earrings of glass beads and shells were worn by both sexes. The Yuma made pierced beads from small, red conch shells, similar to coral, obtained from the Gulf of California. Abalone shells were acquired in trade from the Pacific coast and made into gleaming pendants.

Armor

No armor was worn or shields carried, but warriors painted their faces coal black with a red stripe down the center and the rest of their bodies were painted in large horizontal stripes. Their hair was painted with a red pigment, indicating warlike intentions.

Special Costumes

There were a few rituals, such as for adolescent girls and boys. The boy's puberty rite included use of a drink made from *datura* or jimsonweed, a hallucinogen. There were also annual mourning ceremonies. But no special costumes were donned for these rites.

Garment Decoration

Little or no weaving was done, except for the rabbit-skin robes on a crude upright loom, and some finger-weaving of girdles, robes, or skirts. They had no cotton, using only grass fibers, rabbit pelts, or bark.

Face and Body Embellishment

Women and girls tattooed the chin with dots and stripes in black or blue pigments and with circles of black around the eyes. Forbes says the men occasionally tattooed even in the 1850s. However, face and body painting was far more important to the Yuma. Many pigments are mentioned, such as red, white, black, blue, yellow, and green; women and girls especially were fond of red and yellow face paint. Father Font (1775) said the Yuman men painted all over with red hematite, charcoal, a shiny lead-colored earth, white clay, and other substances, the pigments being mixed with grease so they could be easily removed. Alarcon (1540) reported that some men covered their faces almost entirely with streaks; others had their faces blackened on one half with soot. Some men painted the arms and legs with wiggly vertical stripes.

Masks

Masks are briefly mentioned as being black in color and shaped like the face; they were probably used for warfare in order to attain a ferocious aspect.

Transitional Dress

Soon after white contact, the Yuma were adding bits and pieces of Anglo dress to their own costumes. Men wore coats (especially desirable were the military variety with epaulettes), vests, cotton shirts, and plaid trousers, although usually the legs were bare. Cloth bandanas were popular, to be used as neckerchiefs, breechcloths, headbands, or armbands. Some women wore large pieces of cloth as dresses in a sarong fashion. They often wore the bandanas as headscarves. This mixture of Yuman and Anglo dress lasted well through the nineteenth century. Interesting sources of Yuman costume are the clay figurines—the small dolls made for tourists dressed in the traditional garb.

Key Sources

Bee, Robert L. "Quechan." In *Handbook of North American Indians. Vol. 10: Southwest.* Pp. 86–98. Washington: Smithsonian Institution.

———. *The Yuma.* New York: Chelsea House, 1989.

Cleland, Charles F. "Yuman Dolls." *American Indian Art Magazine* Summer 1980: 36–41ff.

Drucker, Philip. "Culture Element Distributions, XVII: Yuman-Piman." University of California *Anthropological Records* 6(3): 91–230.

Forbes, Jack D. *Warriors of the Colorado: The Yumas of the Quechan Nation and Their Neighbors.* Norman: University of Oklahoma Press, 1965.

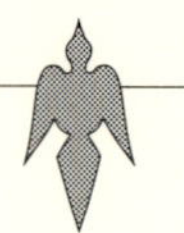

Forde, C. Darrel. “Ethnography of the Yuma Indians.” University of California *Publications in American Archaeology and Ethnology* 28(4): 83–278.

Kroeber, Alfred L. “Yuman Tribes of the Lower Colorado.” University of California *Publications in American Archaeology and Ethnology* 18(8).

Trippel, Eugene. “The Yuma Indians.” *Overland Monthly* 13: 561–584; 14: 1–11.

Yurok

The Yurok lived along the coast near the mouth of the lower Klamath River; their name means “downstream” in the Karok language. The Yurok language has been tentatively identified as Algonquian in origin, but controversy persists in the matter. Although using a different language from the neighboring Karok and Hupa, they shared many culture elements. The Yurok and their neighbors put great emphasis on wealth and possessions, on property rights, and on a class system where wealth and social status were bound together. Their first European contact was in 1827 with Hudson’s Bay Company fur traders, but there was little impact on the Yurok lifeways. The Gold Rush of the mid-century brought in miners and settlers, leading to much conflict and destruction of Yurok people and culture; many of them became wage-laborers. From an estimated 2500 individuals in 1770, the number had dwindled to less than 700 by 1900. George Gibbs made some sketches of the Yurok in 1851.

Men’s Basic Dress

Nakedness was common among males, particularly with the older men; otherwise, a piece of buckskin was draped around the hips held in place with a thong or leather strap. A sketch by Gibbs shows a man wearing a fringed deerskin kilt and below it a pelt, possibly of a cougar. In cooler weather or for travel, a man might wear a sleeveless skin poncho. For hunting in mountain snows, knee-length buckskin leggings were worn.

Women’s Basic Dress

Women wore the double-apron skirt, both aprons of deerskin; the front one was about a foot wide, was deeply fringed, and the strands were wrapped with *Xerophyllum* (bear grass) or maidenhair ferns or strung with pine nuts and shells in horizontal designs. The deerskin of the overlapping rear skirt was folded laterally to create a double thickness with a peplum. Wealthy women had heavy ornamentation of abalone shells, clamshell beads, and obsidian pendants, all of which jingled and jangled in a satisfactory manner. These beautifully decorated skirts were displayed especially at ceremonials, and were considered family heirlooms of great monetary value, sometimes being stored in bank vaults for their protection. Poorer women had to be content with double-apron skirts of the shredded inner bark of the maple. The upper torso was usually left bare with a covering only of multiple strands of beads.

Footwear

The usual footwear was the one-piece moccasin of deerskin, seamed up the front and at the heel; this was normally without decoration, being worn only for travel. Kroeber tells about an odd manner of having a thong (self-knotted inside) come out at the sole edge, then lashing it at the instep and the heel, a device impractical for traveling or even daily wear. A crude snowshoe was formed of a round hoop with a few cross ties of grapevine.

Outer Wear

For cold weather, the everyday robe was made of two deerskins sewed into a cape. Or a wrap might be made of the pelts of small animals pieced together. Because rabbits were scarce in Yurok country, the rabbit-skin robe, so common elsewhere, seems to have been unknown to them. The whole skins of large birds such as the turkey, vulture, bald eagle, yellow-billed magpie, raven, great horned owl, or California condor were carefully sewn together to create elegant and warm, but fragile, mantles. “Good rain gear,” probably made of tule or other grasses, is mentioned by some authorities.

Hair Styles

The men wore the hair somewhat long; when working they tied it with a thong in back or coiled it into a bundle, skewered with a bone splinter. The women gathered the hair into two bunches, which fell to the front over the shoulders; for

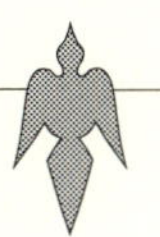

A mannequin displays ceremonial attire of a Yurok woman of the early 1900s: a basketry hat, a shell necklace, and a leather and bear grass skirt decorated with beads, abalone, clam, and *Olivella* shells.

special occasions these bundles were wrapped with mink-fur strips, adorned with tiny woodpecker scalps.

Headgear

Men wore nothing on their heads, except for dances or other ceremonies. Women made basket caps of willow twigs and pine roots; these twined caps were round and low and featured triangles or rhomboids, using a half-twist overlay technique. The designs were created with native dyes or with hazel stems, redwood, or bear grass. A cap made of rawhide and ornamented with viburnum seeds and paint was often worn by a woman shaman.

Accessories

The Yurok measured their wealth in strings of dentalium shells, carefully graded by size and condition; for carrying and safekeeping, purses, six or seven inches long, were made of carved elk antler incised with geometric designs. A small sack of finely meshed netting was used to carry small objects; it was typically trapezoidal in shape and had a deerskin carrying strap. Another bag, unique to this area, was a pouch made of a piece of folded deerskin, with the hair side out, fastened with a stick for closure; it was flat and could be carried conveniently under the upper arm. Small mats of finely woven tule grass were formed into pouches for carrying pieces of obsidian. Simple thongs or straps were used as belts.

Jewelry

Dentalium shells were used for both money and ornament; when displayed as currency, only the longest were used and they were placed butt end to butt end, pointed end to pointed end, so the shells would not "telescope." Since the value, and thereby the status of the individual, depended on the length, they were strung on a string and carefully measured. Shorter dentalia were used only as ornament, in necklaces and other items of jewelry. Abalone pendants were popular for earrings, as well as being strung on skirt fringes. Other materials used for necklaces were olivella shells, pine nuts, viburnum seeds, clamshell disk beads, steatite pendants, and, occasionally, turquoise. The Yurok did not pierce the noses or the ears.

Armor

Armor took two forms: (1) a tunic made of one or more layers of tough elk hide; (2) a cuirass made of rods or slats bound together with sinew. The latter, especially, was unwieldy in battle, but it would stop an arrow.

Special Costumes

The two major ceremonies of the Yurok were the Deerskin Dance and the Jumping Dance. The Deerskin Dance presented the opportunity to display the albino deerskins, the ultimate treasures of the Yurok; the dancers wore aprons of civet or deerskin draped about the hips, multiple strands of dentalium-shell beads, and forehead bands of wolf fur. Rods holding eagle or condor feathers rose from the crown of the head. Each dancer held a stick aloft, that supported a deerskin, preferably a white albino skin, the head stuffed. Some of the dancers had a wolf-fur strip around the head; attached to this were the canine teeth of sea lions, forming a crown-like headdress. For the Jumping Dance, the dancers were resplendent in buckskin headbands, flapping at the sides, on which were mosaics of fifty or more woodpecker scalps; from the crown of the head a rod tipped with a white plume waved with the dancer's movements. A deerskin was wrapped about the waist and the chest. Men dancers and spectators wore hair nets of fine meshed wild iris fiber often adorned with eagle down. Women spectators wore their finest attire embellished with seeds, beads, abalone pendants, and dentalium shell necklaces.

Garment Decoration

Weaving was shown in the basketry caps, which were twined of willow twigs and pine roots; the decorations were done with hazel stems, bear grass, and redwood. Some simple weaving was done with tule grass, which was made into mats and occasionally into small, flat purses. Fine-meshed netting with iris

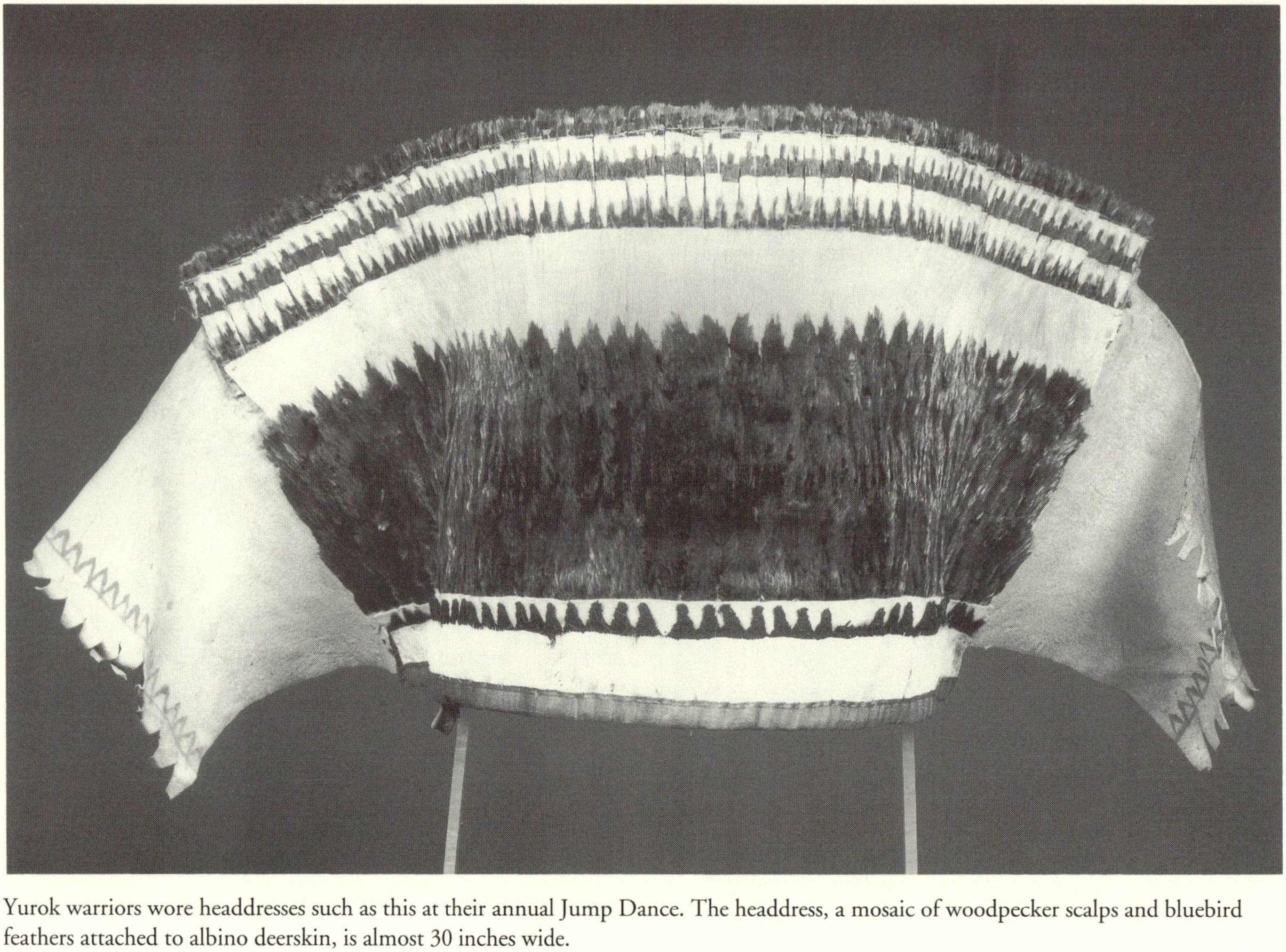

Yurok warriors wore headdresses such as this at their annual Jump Dance. The headdress, a mosaic of woodpecker scalps and bluebird feathers attached to albino deerskin, is almost 30 inches wide.

fibers created the men's hair nets. Featherwork appeared in the birdskin mantles and the magnificent headbands of woodpecker scalps for the Jumping Dance and other ceremonies. The long fringes of the women's skin skirts were wrapped with bear grass or maidenhair ferns and adorned with seeds, shells, nuts, and pendants of abalone, obsidian, steatite, and turquoise. These all made for pleasurable sights and sounds.

Face and Body Embellishment

Women had the chin tattooed either solidly or in three broad, vertical lines; it was not a matter of individual taste, but rather tribal affiliation. The Yurok felt that an untattooed woman looked like a man when she grew old. The men had marks tattooed on the arms for the purpose of measuring the strings of dentalium shells. No painting of the face and body was practiced, nor was skull deformation done.

Transitional Dress

The Yurok were decimated rapidly with the appearance of miners and settlers in their territory, and the transitional period in dress was brief. They quickly adopted white garments—trousers, vests, cotton shirts for the men, and cotton blouses and skirts for the women. Scarves were worn as neckerchiefs by the former and on the head by the latter, although the basket hat was retained well into the twentieth century. Ceremonial costumes were kept and cherished; the women added blouses to their heavily decorated skirts and wore shoes, but otherwise the rites were celebrated in the early fashions.

Key Sources

Kroeber, Alfred L. *Handbook of the Indians of California.* New York: Dover. Reprint of 1925 edition.

Pilling, Arnold R. "Yurok." In *Handbook of North American Indians. Vol. 8: California.* Pp. 137–154. Washington: Smithsonian Institution.

Thompson, Lucy. *To the American Woman: Reminiscences of a Yurok Woman.* Berkeley, CA: Heyday Books, 1991.

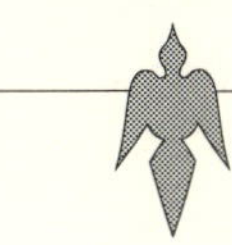

Chapter Eight

Costume of the Northwest Coast

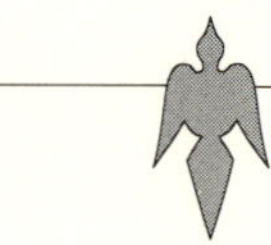

Above: Haida dancers in ceremonial attire, including Chilkat blankets, carved frontlet headdresses (center), hold masks (right), and a drum (left).
Below, right: A Kwakiutl Hamatsa, or Cannibal, Dance Society member wears a large, articulated bird mask. His cape is made of shredded cedar bark.
Below: A trade cloth blanket, collected on the southwestern coast of Alaska, has abalone shell decorations recalling the family crest of the Russian imperial family.

Northwest Coast

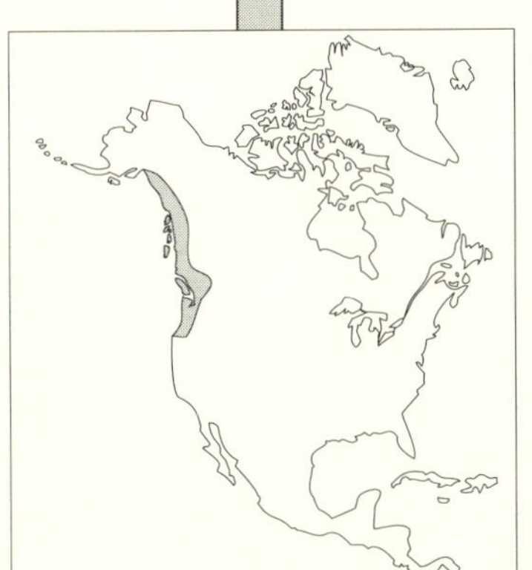

The Pacific Northwest Coast Indians inhabited a land as dramatic as their culture. The jagged mountains rise precipitously from the Pacific. In the narrow strip of land extending from Yakutat Bay in southeastern Alaska to the southern Oregon coast, there are innumerable fjords rivaling Norway's in their majesty. Thousands of islands dot the coastline. The region has a mild climate, warmed by the Japan current, but the sea remains cold, a condition that brings on fog and heavy rains. The heavy rainfall creates a true rain forest with dense stands of fir, cedar, and hemlock. From ancient times even to the present the native peoples have exploited the products of the sea and forest.

The inhabitants of this area and their culture differed significantly from those of other culture areas. There was no agriculture—no room for it—nor was there any necessity for farming, for they were abundantly supplied with food, shelter, and clothing from the sea and the forests. There was no pottery and no domestication of animals. Their diet stressed animal fats; few vegetables were eaten except in the southern areas where camus roots were available and, farther south, acorns. Their particular form of transportation was the canoe, which became to them what the horse was to the Plains Indians. It was a wood culture, which reached its highest attainment with wood carvings such as totem poles and masks, and in the carving of utilitarian objects. The distinctiveness of their culture was due in part to the fact that they were isolated from other Indian tribes, particularly by the Coast Ranges and, farther south, the Cascades; only in the north was there some communication with the Athapaskans of the interior.

The Northwest Coast differed also in its social structure. A hereditary aristocracy placed tremendous emphasis on wealth. This wealth was

Above: A carved wooden mask used by Bella Coola dancers.

Peoples of the Northwest Coast

Bella Bella
Bella Coola, p. 301
Chilkat (Tlingit)
Chinook, p. 305
Coast Salish, p. 307
Eyak
Gitksan
Haida, p. 310
Haisla
Heiltsuk
Kwakiutl, p. 313
Nootka/Makah, p. 317
Oregon Coast and Interior, p. 321
Puget Sound, p. 324
Quileute
Quinault, p. 326
Tlingit, p. 329
Tsimshian, p. 334
Washington Coast, p. 338

displayed, and much given away, at the famous "potlatches," feasts at which individuals established their claims to wealth and prestige by acts of conspicuous consumption. Slavery was common, forming a large (one-third) segment of the population. But there was no class system as such; rather, it was a graded system in which an individual knew his own place, but was able to move up or down the social scale depending upon material losses or gains. This led to intense rivalry; it also aided in developing one of the greatest art styles in the world, one which Kehoe calls "disciplined exuberance." Talented specialists in arts and crafts turned out an abundance of material possessions, filled with vitality and sophistication. It was dramatic and exciting, but it was almost destroyed by the encroaching white culture; however, there has been a renaissance in Northwest Coast art during the 1970s and 1980s with a spirited revival of traditional elements in modern forms.

From the standpoint of costume, the Northwest Coast area divides roughly into north and south, the north being the center of the culture and the home of the Tlingit, Haida, Tsimshian, Kwakiutl, Bella Coola, Nootka, and Coast Salish. South of these were a multitude of small tribes (really language groups) that are treated here as the Puget Sound, Washington Coast, and Oregon peoples.

Many languages were to be found in the Northwest, the major ones being (1) Penutian, including Tsimshian and Chinook; (2) Nadene, an Athapaskan form including Haida and Tlingit; (3) Wakashan-Algonquian in the northern area, which included the Kwakiutl and Nootkan languages; (4) the Salishan languages of northern Washington and southwest British Columbia; and (5) the many diverse languages of the Washington and Oregon coasts, so diverse that there is no point in enumerating them here.

Archaeology in this area is young; it was only in the early 1940s that serious excavation attempts were made, most of them along the Columbia and Fraser rivers. Much uncertainty and controversy persists over the earliest habitation in the region, the guesses ranging from as early as 9000 B.C. Part of the problem is that perishable items, such as wood and cloth, usually are not preserved well in the damp climate. An important archaeological discovery, however, was that of Ozette, a village on the coast of northern Washington that was buried under a massive mudslide about A.D. 1450, leaving many of the remains of everyday living in a remarkable state of preservation.

The Pacific Northwest was one of the last continental coastlines to be explored by the Europeans. In 1741 Vitus Bering, a Dane with a Russian crew, began fur trading with the natives of the Aleutian Islands. In 1774 Spanish explorers (Perez, Heceta, and Bodega) reached Alaska and took possession in the name of the King of Spain. In 1778 Captain James Cook landed at Nootka Sound on the west coast of Vancouver Island; he collected many artifacts and works of art as well as a quantity of sea-otter skins, which were traded with the Chinese at a satisfactory high price. This began a period of intensive trading; posts were established by the English at Nootka Sound and by the Russians at Kodiak, Alaska. In 1793 Alexander Mackenzie of the British Northwest Company finished his trek across Canada dedicated to the establishment of suitable trading posts. Between 1799 and 1802 an estimated 48,500 sea-otter skins were shipped. Lewis and Clark (1804–1806) were followed by scores of land traders. By 1821 the Hudson's Bay Company and the Northwest Company merged, creating a string of posts along the coast; the sea otter began to disappear. Spain and Russia withdrew their claims, and in 1846 the British and Americans established the international boundary at the 49th parallel. As elsewhere on the continent, trade brought troubles—alcohol, guns, and diseases. However, it also brought metal, which was a boon to the woodworking craftsmen.

Next came missionaries, Protestant and Catholic, to convert the Indians and to attempt to change the native culture to that of the whites. Following them came the settlers with the customary conflicts over gold, land, and the environment, and the Indians were forced into the position of second-class citizens. Fortunately they were able to remain on their ancestral lands in many cases, but reservation life was a crushing experience to most of them, and many attempted to settle on the outside. In 1916 the first of many lawsuits was filed against the United States government, demanding the return of stolen lands. In 1946 the government agreed to the claims of some of the Oregon Coast Indians, and other claims have been filed since then.

Northwest Coast costume differed from that of other culture areas in several respects. There was little borrowing. No footwear was worn except for occasional trading trips into the interior. The most common textile was woven shredded cedar bark; only the northern Tlingit used tailored deerskin garments, such as shirts, moccasins, leggings, and breechclouts, and they were usually obtained in trade from the Athapaskans of the interior. There was a great difference between everyday dress and ceremonial costume; furthermore, costume, especially ceremonial, established one's position. Sumptuary laws restricted the use of certain materials, such as abalone and dentalium shells and sea-otter furs, to persons of validated distinction. There was little difference in attire between the sexes; many garments were worn by both men and women with minor changes, even in the case of ceremonial garb.

General Dress

Men's Basic Dress

In this gentle climate, men generally wore nothing. In the winter they sometimes wore tunics of woven cedar bark, edged with rabbit or other fur to reduce the scratchiness of the fibers; these tunics were rectangular shapes that were folded over, passed under the left arm, fastened on the right shoulder, and girdled at the waist; they were generally knee-length. Leggings were known, but were worn only by the northern tribes when traveling into the interior.

Women's Basic Dress

For everyday wear, women donned an apron of lengths of cedar bark attached to a waistband and tied at the back. Over this, when desired, a knee-length wraparound skirt was worn; in the north, it was often of deerskin, in the central area of woven cedar bark, and in the south of lightly shredded or split cedar-bark fibers. In place of a skirt, they occasionally wore a tunic similar to those worn by the men, of woven cedar bark edged with fur.

It may be well at this point to explain the process of making cedar-bark garments, a woman's task. The fibrous inner layer was stripped from the outer layer of the bark of either the red or yellow cedar; the red was more common in the north, the yellow in the southern part of the area. The yellow-cedar bark was tougher, but also was more difficult to process. This inner bark was dried, then split either in length or in width, depending on the final product. It was then shredded, using a bark shredder made of bone, wood (generally yew), or the nasal bone of a whale; the bark lengths were laid over a sharp edge, such as that of an old canoe paddle, then pounded with the shredder until they were separated into fine strands. Weaving was done on a simple two-bar loom using a twining technique. Everyday garments woven were (1) the woman's apron; (2) a conical cape; (3) a blanket, which was worn in several ways; and (4) some of the basketry hats, although they were more commonly woven of spruce roots.

Footwear

Everybody went barefoot most of the year, even in snow; moccasins were known, but only worn when traveling into the interior over the mountain passes. Snowshoes, again for mountain travel, were simple round or oval forms, without toe or heel bars, but with rawhide rope and loosely woven netting.

Outer Wear

Everyday clothing for both sexes was minimal, but outer wear was required either for protection against the chills of winter or against the frequent rains. Capes of shredded cedar bark were waist-length, of a conical shape with an opening for the head, and finished off with a fringe at the bottom or edged with strips of fur at top and bottom; these were often in two layers—the outer layer soft and closely woven, the inner layer more loosely made. Cedar-bark blankets were warm, soft, and water-repellent; they were either rectangular in shape or rounded at the bottom, and were finished off with a fringe of bark. Occasionally they featured painted heraldic designs, or patterned edgings of mountain-goat wool, but elaborately decorated garments were usually reserved for ceremonial use. These blankets and capes were superb rain gear, along with the basketry hats. Fur robes were donned, sea otter being the most prized fur, but bearskin (the entire skin) was popular; also used were marten, marmot, fur seal, hair seal, and

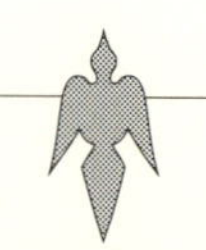

A young Tlingit with a fringed headgear wears a button blanket, so-called because buttons were sewn in a pattern, draped around his shoulders.

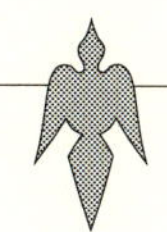

everyday furs such as raccoon and bobcat. Some robes were made of the skins of such birds as ducks or loons, flattened or sewn together, or, as with rabbit robes elsewhere, the skin was cut spirally into long, thin strips that were twisted, often with fiber for strength, and woven with a weft of nettle fiber. In the hands of a skillful weaver, the different shades of the bird skins were combined into handsomely designed robes. Robes were held in place with thongs or with long blanket pins of wood or bone, the heads often delicately carved. Two famous woven blankets were those of the Coast Salish and the Chilkat division of the Tlingit; these were widely traded along the coast and well into the interior.

Hair Styles

Men wore the hair loose and long, or coiled into a bun on the top of the head. Women fashioned the hair into one or two braids, worn down the back, often ornamented with carved wood or shell pendants. Men wore full mustaches and often goatees.

Headgear

The famous basketry hats of the Northwest Coast were twined of spruce or cedar root or shredded cedar bark; they were of various shapes—some with wide brims to shed rain, some with knobs on top to denote the status of a chief, some dome-shaped, and, in the far south, women's hats were in the truncated cone shape of the Plateau or the small, rounded form of northern California. Many were painted in conventionalized designs of birds, fish, or animals, while others were decorated in the twining process by the use of dyed fibers. An inside headband of braided fibers and ties to go under the chin kept the hat firmly in place. Early hats, collected at the time of the eighteenth-century explorers, were small in diameter and depth, often painted blue on the brim and the sides; nineteenth-century hats were larger, with sizable designs often covering an entire hat. Some clan hats in the north were carved of wood in the shape of a crest animal; these, like the frontal headdresses, were especially for ceremonial occasions. A few winter hats were fashioned of fur.

Accessories

Pouches, especially to hold dentalium shells representing currency, seem to be the major, perhaps the only, accessories carried by these people or attached to belts; these were of diagonally plaited cedar bark and, in the north, were of leather occasionally decorated with porcupine quillwork. Belts were usually braided strips of bark fiber or of leather, the latter ornamented with shells, teeth, and claws. Some armbands of fur or braided fibers were worn.

Jewelry

Jewelry and ornaments worn by the peoples of the Northwest Coast depended for their amount and richness on the status of the wearer. Aboriginal ornaments were fashioned predominantly of bone, antler, wood, and shell. Shells were most popular, particularly the dentalium, which functioned both as ornament and currency; these dentalia, called *hiqua,* were extremely hard, tusk-like, milky white in color, an inch or two long, and tapered at one end. Gathered along the coast, they were especially sought when very large, and were traded widely, even as far east as the Plains. They made beautiful necklaces and chokers and were used extensively as decoration on garments. Olivella shells—smooth, polished, ranging in color from lavender to dark purple—made beautiful beads for necklaces. Although abalone shells could be found in the waters off Vancouver Island, they were inferior to the shimmering blue and green beauty of the California variety, which were brought to the area by the fur traders of the nineteenth century. The abalone was cut into sections for pendants to hang on garments and headdresses, inlaid on frontal headdresses, or as eyes and teeth in a mask. Necklaces were also formed of animal teeth and claws, pieces of bone, antler, or thin copper rolled into tubular beads—all these later interspersed with the glass beads of the traders; rarely, tubular beads of cannel coal were to be seen. Dentalium shells were gathered in clusters and suspended from the multiple ear perforations or fashioned into headbands; square or round pendants of abalone also adorned the ears. Early bracelets were of copper, occasionally iron, or mountain-goat horn. Men, and a few women, pierced the nasal septum and inserted a piece of abalone, a dentalium shell, or, later, a silver ring. The "labret," peculiar to the northern tribes and perhaps adopted from the Eskimos, was an elliptical plug of bone, wood, or ivory that was inserted into the lower lip.

A bearded Tlingit man displays his wealth and status at the turn of the century by wearing a Chilkat blanket and a tall headdress with carved figures on the front; other ornamentation includes strands of ermine skin, abalone shell, and sea lion whiskers.

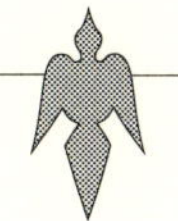

These labrets took various forms, some being a round button shape, others oval or squarish, some small for little girls as their first labrets, others successively larger; some had perforations for the attaching of beads or other ornaments. Only young girls and women wore labrets. They were worn anciently, but under the influence of the nineteenth-century missionaries the "heathen" practice was stamped out (although earrings were permitted).

Armor

Armor was of three styles: (1) a cuirass of overlapping slats or heavy wooden rods strung together with sinew, often called "rod-and-slat" armor, a type that severely restricted mobility; (2) a sleeveless tunic of several thicknesses of tough elk hide or deer hide, sewn or tied at the sides and on the shoulders with sinew and often painted; and (3) heavy cord or rope wrapped around the torso. Slat-and-rod armor was reserved especially for chiefs, who also, in the north, wore carved wooden helmets, representations of crest animals, depicting horrifying faces, set-in eyes, and a visor to protect the face. Some helmets are mentioned as being a bag-like mask of elk skin with holes for the eyes. Additions to the armor were a high neck protector or collar of wood, also painted, and greaves of wooden slats. Common warriors wore no special clothing, but wound their hair on top of the head so it could not be grasped easily by the enemy. Garfield, in writing about the Tsimshian, mentions shields of beaten copper. It is thought that the introduction of firearms made armor obsolete.

Special Costumes

Unlike the everyday clothes, ceremonial garb was spectacular, as showy and as colorful as the individual could attain, for it was a matter of pride and wealth to be dressed in spendid garments. There were two types of ceremonies—the social rituals, such as the "potlatch," and the secret-society rites. The core of the potlatch was a feast at which the giver claimed certain rights, based on prestige and wealth; those who feasted were witnesses, their presence thereby validating the claims. Elaborate presents were distributed to the guests; as a sign of conspicuous consumption, the host burned articles by throwing them into the flames, or cut up blankets into strips to be distributed among the guests, or threw items into the depths of the sea. Rites of passage were featured at the potlatches—name bestowing, the piercing of the ears or the nose for ornaments, ritual tattooing, and puberty recognition. The ceremony grew excessively and out of bounds due to the accumulation of wealth and goods from white contact in the nineteenth century; it was made illegal in 1884, but was continued in secret. The ban was lifted in 1951 and new vigor was infused into social life as the potlatch returned, now with the distribution of many nontraditional goods.

Ceremonials, the second type, were those conducted by the secret societies and other dancing groups, designed, as Gunther says, "to establish or renew relations with the supernatural." Often called Winter Dances, they were performed during the cold season when the food quests were diminished, and they featured the use of masks, rattles, and musical instruments.

On ceremonial occasions, the finest of costumes were worn. The magnificent Chilkat blanket was particularly displayed, along with the tunic, leggings, and dance apron, all of the same woven material with

A Tlingit man wears a sleeveless shirt painted with his family's totem of a bear.

the characteristic crest emblems. The oldest tunics or shirts had been of tanned leather painted with crest symbols, but these had disappeared by the time of the eighteenth-century explorers. The conical hat woven of spruce root and painted was worn by participants; a chief's hat might be surmounted by a number of basketry rings, indicating the numbers of potlatches he had given. It was a further matter of prestige to wear the "frontlet" headdress, which had a carved wooden plaque of the face of a crest animal, ringed with pieces of inlaid abalone shell, and surmounted by upstanding sea-lion whiskers; at the sides were ermine skins, and at the back was a cloth trailer covered with rows of ermine skins. A flap of moose hide inside the crown was used for scattering eagle down during dances. Participants sometimes wore a large, stiff neck ring of cedar bark; strands of cedar bark, twisted and braided, hung from the neck ring, adding further movement to the dance. During the nineteenth century, "button blankets" were a popular item at the ceremonials. Shamans wore leather or Chilkat dance aprons, often with the addition of a crown of grizzly-bear claws. Deer hooves, puffin beaks, and, later, thimbles were added to the costumes for their sound effects.

Garment Decoration

The Northwest people had a distinctive style of art, especially in woodcarving, painting, and weaving, a style that permeated their costumes. It was vigorous, assertive, primarily heraldic in subject matter, and the designs generally covered the entire surface area. Certain shapes were used repeatedly—the "eye" form, squared-off ovals, lines swelling and tapering to a point, and elongated triangles as fill-ins. Color was flat and was limited to a few hues, mostly black, red, green, blue-green, and yellow. Weaving reached a high point of excellence in the area. Porcupine-quill decoration was found only among the most northern tribes, and may have been obtained in trade from the Athapaskan peoples. Beadwork developed to some extent in the twentieth century, usually as delineation of traditional patterns.

Face and Body Embellishment

Face painting was common with both sexes; it was practiced daily for protection against the wind and sun, and for warmth. Far more elaborate face painting was customary for ceremonies; in the north, especially, the painting took the form of heraldic crests. In the north, too, small, carved wooden stamps were used to paint repeat patterns. Three colors were used most often—black (from soot or charcoal), white (from diatomaceous clay), and red ocher—the pigments being mixed with bear fat or whale oil for ease in application. For some occasions, tiny flakes of glittering mica were applied to well-greased skin. so that the performer sparkled in the firelight as he twirled in the dance. All tribes in the area knew tattooing, but most preferred face painting. The tattoos were made by drawing soot-blackened thread through the skin just below the surface. Girls had their first tattoo marks made at puberty, at which time a family crest was tattooed on the hand. Both sexes were tattooed on many parts of the body—face, chest, front of legs, back of arms, and elsewhere, often with inherited designs that only the owners were permitted to use. In the southern part of the area the women tattooed their chins with three vertical lines, typical of northern California tribes. Tattooing was discontinued in the early nineteenth century.

Head deformation was a sign of aristocracy; slaves did not usually display any kind of skull-flattening. It took two forms: (1) the principal type, in which the deformation was achieved by attaching a diagonal board to the infant's head in the cradle, causing the forehead to slope backward to a peak; (2) a style found among the Kwakiutl and the Nootka for which pressure was applied by bandages, elongating the head to a shape called a "sugar loaf." This beautification was practiced from the Kwakiutl as far south as the Siuslaw on the Oregon coast and up the Columbia River among the Chinookan tribes; occasionally it was observed among the Shahaptian tribes of the interior.

Masks

Masks, used particularly for the Winter Dances, were the highest art form created by the Northwest artist/carvers. They evidenced a variety of forms, sizes, and purposes; many represented powerful spirit helpers, such as crest animals and mythical creatures. Some were human faces, occasionally reaching a startling degree of realism. Carved of wood and painted, the masks frequently used such additional

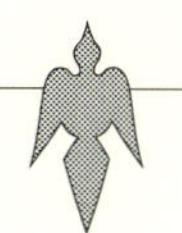

materials as abalone shell, fur, human hair, and operculum shells as teeth. Transformation masks were especially a part of Kwakiutl ritual; these could be manipulated by the wearer by means of strings, so that huge tails and fins could be moved, beaks of large birds could be opened and shut, gaping jaws of animals created fearsome images, and human faces could be transformed into other creatures. These transformation masks were large but lightweight to enable the wearers to handle them with ease; a cedar bark fringe also covered the wearer's torso so the manipulation could pass undetected.

Transitional Dress

With the arrival of European explorers in the late eighteenth century, the natives of the Pacific coast were intrigued with their clothing, and sought them in trade. But they wore them in their own manner, adding decorations of traditional materials and patterns. It was not until 1875 that the cedar-bark garments were replaced by European-style attire, which, incidentally, was not as suited to the rainy climate. The blankets of the Hudson's Bay Company were greatly appreciated, but they put their own stamp on them, making them into the famous "button blankets." These were of black or dark-blue stroud cloth or lightweight blanket cloth, with a border and central applique of red cloth (usually flannel or felt); the central figure was typically that of a crest animal, and was embellished with rows of white buttons. These blankets reached their classic form about 1850 and began to replace the Chilkat blanket in ceremonials. The designs were also applied to shirts, leggings, and dance aprons, all for ceremonial use. They are still made and worn today, but no longer are the crest animals the sole property of certain individuals and families; rather, they are adopted as the maker and wearer desires.

Silver, gold, and brass appeared with the traders in the late 1700s, and were eagerly acquired to be made into items of jewelry, particularly bracelets and rings; European-style engraving techniques were followed. Thimbles replaced deer hooves and puffin beaks as costume sound effects. Glass beads were sought in trade, but beadwork as such did not become dominant in Northwest Coast decoration, rather, the beads simply augmented the traditional forms of embellishment.

Today, European-style clothing is worn all along the Northwest Coast—Levi's, cotton dresses, sea boots and shoes, and cotton headscarves—although some still wear the basketry hats in a downpour. The life of ceremony is still strong among these people and is still characterized by magnificent costumes and accessories.

Bella Coola

The Bella Coola (a Kwakiutl term of unknown meaning), hemmed in on three sides by the Kwakiutl, lived on the Dean and Bella Coola rivers, and were influenced by the culture of the Athapaskans of the interior as well as that of the Kwakiutl. Their preferred name for themselves today is Nuxalk, meaning "caught in the web of a net," the name of a village at the mouth of the Bella Coola River. They were Salishan speakers who had possibly broken away from the Salish to the south about A.D. 1400 and trekked over the mountains. They were excellent hunters, particularly of the mountain goats that abounded in their high country. They were on friendly terms with the neighboring Bella Bella, frequently engaging in intermarriage. Their first European contact was with George Vancouver in 1793. There followed the usual pattern of fur traders, diseases, a Hudson's Bay Company post, and missionaries. In 1885 a group of nine Bella Coola went to Germany, offering their traditional dances and songs to enthusiastic audiences; among those present was Franz Boas, who was inspired to begin his lifelong interest and work among the Northwest Coast Indians. In the 1970s, with a revitalized interest in traditional culture, a troupe of Bella Coola dancers and singers traveled throughout British Columbia, again performing before enthusiastic audiences. Because of their active trade with the Carrier and Chilcotin of the interior, they have always acquired handsomely tanned deerskins for their apparel.

Men's Basic Dress

Men went naked in warm weather, adding a cedar-bark or tanned-leather tunic as needed, knee-length in front, to the heels in back. Mackenzie said that the bark garments often had strips of otter fur woven in for warmth; these garments were decorated along the lower edge with geometric designs in black and yellow.

Women's Basic Dress

Women wore an apron of shredded cedar bark in front, nothing behind, for warm weather. For cooler weather they wore a tunic similar to that of the men—of woven cedar bark, to the knees in front, to the heels in back, often woven with strips of sea-otter fur for warmth. This sleeveless tunic was fastened over one shoulder and belted or worn loose.

Footwear

Generally the Bella Coola went barefoot, but for traveling they wore moccasins of dressed moose or caribou skin, which they obtained in trade from the Carriers. For snowshoes, they made either a temporary pair from a single cedar limb, or a more permanent pair made of *babiche* lacing stretched over a wooden frame, usually of maple.

Three Bella Coola from British Columbia, photographed in 1885, wear ceremonial garments. The man standing, center, wears a Chilkat tunic woven of mountain goat wool and other fibers; the central design is a family crest. His companion, kneeling at right, has wrapped a Chilkat blanket around his shoulders, and the man to the left wears a pillbox-style hat. All wear moccasins and leggings.

Outer Wear

Robes were of woven cedar bark, rectangular in shape, often with a lower rounded edge; these were worn under the right arm and fastened on the left shoulder, wrapped around the waist, or draped over the shoulders and tied under the chin. The robes were often edged with sea-otter fur, or had braided borders with mountain-goat wool worked into the braids; often warps were left to form a deep fringe on the bottom. A circular (really conical) cape made of woven shredded cedar bark with an opening for the head made an excellent rain cape. A few robes were of whole skins, tied on with thongs and belted.

Hair Styles

The hair was worn short or long. When long, it was braided and smeared with oil and red ocher. The women often fastened ornaments into the braids.

Headgear

Basketry hats, worn for protection against sun glare or rain, were woven of spruce root or cedar fibers in the shape of a truncated cone with a flaring brim; they were often painted in bird or animal designs carefully adapted to the shape of the hat. Fur hats were occasionally donned for winter wear.

Accessories

Accessories were few. Leather pouches carried a few necessities, such as tobacco, painting or sewing equipment, or the dentalium shells used for currency. Belts were of braided cedar bark or strips of tanned leather, sometimes painted with bird, animal, or geometric designs. Some bags were of woven cedar bark.

Jewelry

Jewelry was beautifully made and extensively worn. Ears and noses were pierced at puberty, so that nose rings, early of abalone, later of silver, and ear ornaments could be worn; earrings were of many materials—shark teeth, bone, abalone shell cut into round or square shapes, clusters of dentalia, and thin copper rolled into tubular beads. When silver became available it was fashioned into earrings, nose rings, and finger rings. Bracelets in early days were of mountain-goat horn or copper, later of trade brass or silver, still later of gold. Necklaces of dentalium shells

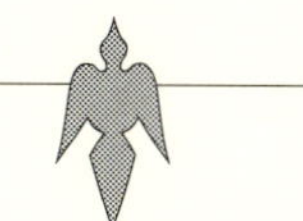

This Bella Coola dancer, his face painted, wears ceremonial garb that includes a cap made of fur and feathers, a cedar-bark neck ring, and a cedar-bark cape edged with fur.

were popular, combined with glass trade beads as they became available. Labrets, worn by the women, were made of carved wood or bone or, according to Mackenzie, of copper; they were either small buttons at each corner of the mouth, or a large central labret below the lower lip. Heavy collars or neck rings were worn, made of twisted iron acquired in trade from the interior or from ships' blacksmiths.

Armor

Warriors wore slat armor made of maple or birch; they carried shields of tough moose hide.

Special Costumes

Typical of the Bella Coola was a rich and complex ceremonialism; their major events were two dancing societies—the Sisaok, during which family and clan crests were presented in connection with potlatches, and the Kusiut winter dancing society, involving the initiation of younger members. Chiefs who had them wore carved and painted wooden helmets, at the top of which were the basketry rings showing the number of potlatches given. Some chiefs wore the frontlet headdress, characteristically painted with blue and vermilion designs on a background of unpainted wood; the typical Bella Coola frontlet had a carved bird with a jutting, upthrust beak as the main figure. Baleen splints were often substituted for the usual sea-lion whiskers. Some wore a collar of shredded cedar bark decorated with strips of ermine. They wore an unusually large number of feathers in the hair at their ceremonies.

A carved Bella Coola mask, 15 1/2 inches high, was designed to be tied on; masks were painted in strong colors such as red, blue, and orange.

Garment Decoration

Shredded cedar bark was woven into garments, often with sea-otter fur woven into the strands for warmth. The bark was also formed into fringes or braids for added decoration. Paint, particularly blue and vermilion, was applied to hats, garments, helmets, and frontlets. Abalone pendants were attached to some women's tunics, as well as to ceremonial garb.

Face and Body Embellishment

There was little tattooing and face painting among the Bella Coola. Skull flattening was practiced to some extent; like their neighbors, the Kwakiutl, they tied a pad over the head of the infant in the cradle, wrapping it with bands of hide, producing the tall "sugar loaf" elongation.

Masks

Bella Coola masks displayed their makers' superb abilities in carving. These were enormous masks, sometimes five feet long and often with movable parts, such as beaks. Basic motifs were of natural elements—sun, moon, birds, flowers, thunder, and so forth. The colors were unusual—dark and light green, orange, red, black, and, especially, a bright blue. Holm points out the typical bulbous faces and strongly sculptural nature of the carving.

Transitional Dress

Although more isolated in their mountainous homeland than their neighbors, the Bella Coola were affected by the goods of the traders. In the second half of the nineteenth century, they replaced the Chilkat blankets with the button blankets and those of the Hudson's Bay Company. They adopted

European-style dress: the cotton blouses and skirts for women, the trousers, boots, and flannel shirts for the men. But they retained the magnificent costumes of their ceremonials.

Key Sources

British Columbia Department of Education. *Bella Coola.* British Columbia Heritage Series 1. Our Native Peoples 10. Victoria, British Columbia: Don McDiarmid, Queen's Printer, 1953.

Davis, Philip W. and Ross Saunders. *Bella Coola Texts.* Heritage Record 10. Victoria: British Columbia Provincial Museum, 1980.

Kennedy, Dorothy I. D. and Randall T. Bouchard. "Bella Coola." In *Handbook of North American Indians. Vol. 7: Northwest Coast.* Pp. 323–339. Washington: Smithsonian Institution.

Kirk, Ruth. *Wisdom of the Elders: Native Traditions on the Northwest Coast.* Vancouver, British Columbia: Douglas & McIntyre, 1986.

Kopos, Cliff. *Bella Coola.* Vancouver, British Columbia: Mitchell Press, 1970.

McIlwraith, T. F. *The Bella Coola Indians.* 2 vols. Toronto: University of Toronto Press, 1948.

Chinook

The Chinook proper lived just north of the mouth of the Columbia River. Often included with the Chinook are the following tribes speaking the Chinookan language and clustered along both sides of the river, as indicated by Swanton: north of the river in the present state of Washington were the Cathlamet, Cathlapotle, Chilluckittequaw, Skilloot, and the Wishram; on the south side of the Columbia in the present state of Oregon were the Clackamas, Clatsop, Clowwewalla, Multnomah, Wasco, and the Watlala. They were all similar to the Chinook in their culture and dress. They were extensive traders, their industry giving rise to the "Chinook jargon," used by explorers, traders, Indians, and others in the Northwest and beyond; the *lingua franca* of trade, it was a combination of Chinookan, Nootkan, English, French, and a few Russian words. First European contact was with Robert Gray in 1792. Peter Carney in 1814 and Paul Kane in 1846 drew and described the Chinook, but it is to the journals of Lewis and Clark (1805) that we must turn for information on the appearance and aboriginal clothing of the many small Chinookan tribes along the river. The journals list the items of trade as: Hudson's Bay Company blankets, scarlet and blue stroud cloth, buttons, copper and brass in sheets and wire, and sailors' clothes such as hats, coats, trousers, and shirts. The Chinook culture was heavily disrupted by the fur traders, the diseases brought by whites, and finally by the pioneers of the Oregon Trail who became settlers. In the early-twentieth century, Curtis photographed Indians who were remnants of the early Chinookan peoples.

Men's Basic Dress

Men went naked except for ornaments. In cooler weather they donned robes.

Women's Basic Dress

Women never went naked, but wore a fringed front apron of fibers; these were of finely twined strands of cattail leaves or of shredded cedar bark, silk grass, or rushes, often knotted at the ends of the strands. Some authorities mention a complete skirt of these fiber strands, knee-length in front and calf-length in back. Lewis and Clark commented on a "vest" or "corset" of fur, tied at the back and without shoulder straps to hold it up. They also recorded that the women of the tribes up the river wore a dressed skin from the neck to the waist in front, along with a "bandage" that passed between the legs, which sounds like a type of breechclout. Some deerskin gowns were worn inland.

Footwear

The Chinook peoples went barefoot, although some of the inland tribes were able to obtain tanned-leather moccasins and simple snowshoes from the tribes to the east and north.

Outer Wear

Some robes were made of antelope, deer, elk, or goat skins; furs from smaller animals, such as beaver, muskrat, squirrel, sea otter, and rabbit were cut in strips (usually spirally), dried and twisted to produce furred cords, and woven in a simple cross-weave technique, or the small pelts were sewed together with sinew. The sea-otter robes were most esteemed. Rabbit-skin robes were seldom made by the Chinook, but were more often obtained in trade from the

Plateau. Bird skins, especially those of the wild geese, were treated in the same manner to make lightweight, warm coverings and robes. Mats of woven tule grass or shredded cedar bark made effective rain capes. Men generally wore the robes over the shoulders and tied in front; women draped a robe under one arm, fastened it on the other shoulder with wooden pins, and often belted it to stay in place. As the traders brought in cloth, blankets were made of scarlet or blue strouding. The blankets woven by the Coast Salish of dog hair and mountain-goat wool were also obtained in trade.

Hair Styles

The hair of both sexes was parted in the middle and worn long and loose over the shoulders and down the back. The men plucked out all facial hair.

Headgear

Lewis and Clark purchased a whaler's hat from the Chinook, but it was undoubtedly obtained in trade from the Nootka or Makah to the north; it was the knobbed style with whaling designs on the brim. The more common headgear of the Chinook was the simple domed hat, often with a wide black brim, typical of the Washington Coast tribes. On the upper Columbia the Chinookan women wore the tall, truncated cone hats of the Plateau.

Accessories

Aside from a few pouches or bags of tanned leather or woven cedar bark, and belts of the same material, accessories were almost nonexistent.

Jewelry

Ears were perforated in several places; especially desired as earrings were the dentalium shells acquired in trade from Vancouver Island and the northern coast; these shells were not only favored as ornament, but were important items of trade. The nose, too, was pierced, and adorned with an inserted dentalium shell or the quill of a goose or swan. Necklaces were of bone, dentalia or other shells, feathers, and beads; the most highly sought items were the large blue and white china beads, called "chief" beads, which were widely traded and, like the dentalia, used as a medium of exchange. Lewis and Clark commented on the strange custom of the women of wearing strings of sinew tied tightly around the ankles to make them smaller; however, it tended to enlarge the legs enormously. Later the women wore copper anklets, sometimes five or six at a time.

Armor

The Chinook made some of the finest elk-hide armor on the Northwest Coast; it was in great demand and was traded widely. Some of the warriors wore rod-and-slat armor of wooden strips fastened together with sinew; the most desirable wood used was tough "ironwood." They wore cedar-bark helmets and a few, probably inland fighters, carried shields of elk hide.

Special Costumes

The potlatches and elaborate ceremonials of the northern tribes did not extend to the Columbia River region. The Chinook observed a First Salmon Dance, but ceremonial dress was lacking in their observance.

Garment Decoration

The Chinookan peoples were tradesmen, not craftsmen; whatever they desired in the way of decoration, they were able to acquire through trade. Aside from their highly esteemed elk-skin armor, they made and decorated few articles of clothing that demanded more than simple sewing or decorating.

Face and Body Embellishment

Painting was usually limited to the face, and reserved for the death of a relative or as preparation for war. White clay was especially favored for paint. Some anointed their bodies with seal oil and red ocher. Tattooing was practiced to a limited extent, mostly by women on the arms, legs, or cheeks; designs consisted mainly of circles or dots in parallel rows. Skull deformation was practiced on infants of both sexes by many of the Chinookan tribes, a custom that extended from the Columbia River north as far as the Kwakiutl. Captain Clark has left a sketch of an infant lying in a wooden cradle, with a padded board bound against the forehead, producing a forehead sloping back from the eyebrows. A flattened skull was considered a mark of beauty as well as prestige, consequently denied to slaves.

Transitional Dress

Lewis and Clark had brought European-style garments to the Chinook, which became much in

demand and began the transition away from traditional clothing. By the 1850s only the older women were wearing the traditional cedar-bark skirts; rather, printed cloth dresses, ankle length, were the usual female attire. The men wore shirts and trousers. Only the efficient basketry hats were retained as rainwear. By the early 1900s, Edward Curtis was having great difficulty finding subjects in traditional dress for his photographs, and the Chinook had nearly been destroyed.

Key Sources

Biddle, Nicholas, ed. *The Journals of the Lewis and Clark Expedition.* 2 vols. New York: Heritage Press, 1962.

Curtis, Edward S. *The North American Indian.* Vol. 8. New York: Johnson Reprint Company, 1970.

Ray, Verne F. "Lower Chinook Ethnographic Notes." *University of Washington Publications in Anthropology* 7(2): 29–165.

Ruby, Robert H. and John Brown. *The Chinook Indians: Traders of the Lower Columbia River.* Norman: University of Oklahoma Press, 1976.

Silverstein, Michael. "Chinookans of the Lower Columbia." In *Handbook of North American Indians. Vol. 7: Northwest Coast.* Pp. 533–546. Washington: Smithsonian Institution.

Coast Salish

The main body of Coast Salish lived on both sides of the Strait of Georgia, in British Columbia and on Vancouver Island; they were members of the Salishan language family, and included the Cowichan, Comox, Pentlatch, and Sechelt groups. They are sometimes divided into the North, Central, South, and Southwest Salish (the latter two are discussed under Puget Sound and Washington Coast tribes), all speakers of Salish. Swanton uses the term "Stalo" in referring to the two northern groups. Actually, the terms *Salish* and *Salishan* are not aboriginal but have been devised by students of linguistics. First white contact seems to have been Simon Fraser in 1808; the Hudson's Bay Company set up a post in the 1820s. These contacts were followed by the usual scourge of epidemics and by miners, settlers, and missionaries, all of which led to cultural changes, leaving little of the original culture except some ceremonials. Their subsistence was based on salmon and the products of the dense forests, the abundant sea and land mammals, and waterfowl. The Hudson's Bay Company records, Gunther, and Jenness have been the major sources of information. Paul Kane sketched them in 1847.

Men's Basic Dress

Nakedness was the normal condition of the men in warm weather, with a robe in winter or a shirt-like garment woven of down and nettle fiber. For hunting inland, skin garments such as shirts and leggings were worn.

Women's Basic Dress

The skirt of cedar-bark strips, sometimes reaching to the ankle, was the common attire of the women. Like the men, they sometimes added a shirt of woven down and nettle fiber. Haeberlin (translation by Gunther) mentions a shirt (dress?) from the shoulders to below the knees, sometimes with long sleeves, usually short ones, and adorned with strings of shells under the arms and often strips of otter fur around the neck; with this garment, knee-length and gartered leggings gave warmth. This attire was worn inland and during colder weather, and was of buckskin in the winter, doeskin in the summer.

Footwear

Ordinarily both sexes went barefoot. However, in cold weather as well as inland, skin moccasins were worn. Simple snowshoes were used by hunters when traveling in the mountains.

Outer Wear

Common robes were of deer or elk skin or of woven shredded cedar bark (in the northern area); these were worn over the shoulders or draped under one arm and fastened on the other shoulder with one or two large pins of bone or wood. Rarely, feather robes were made and worn, consisting of strips of bird skin, dried, twisted with shredded cedar bark to create warp cords, and woven in a simple cross weave. For wet weather a poncho or hip-length cape was donned; this was woven of shredded cedar bark or cattail leaves. But the Salish blanket was the major form of outer wear, woven by the women of the

Coast Salish tribes along the Strait of Georgia and well into the Puget Sound area.

For these fine Salish blankets, mountain-goat wool was the best weaving fiber; they used nonviolent methods of gathering the wool—picking the shed wool from bushes and deserted nests. Other fibers used were Indian hemp, nettle, shredded cedar bark, duck or goose down, animal hair, and fireweed "cotton"; each of these had its own unique qualities, establishing the particular texture of the finished product. Alone among the North American Indians, the Coast Salish and their neighbors wove with wool aboriginally, and alone among them they used spindles for spinning; spindles had huge whorls made of wood, steatite, or whale bone, carved by the men into stylized designs of animals, birds, or humans. A "true" loom was not used; more correctly it is called a "fixed warp frame," for they wove with a continuous warp wrapped around the top and bottom crosspieces. It did not have the heddle and rod of a true loom to raise particular threads during the weaving process. It has long been accepted that a chief component of the Salish blanket was dog hair, said to be sheared from small white dogs carefully kept and bred for the purpose. Vancouver mentioned this fact in 1792, as did other reporters of the time. Paul Kane painted a picture from sketches done in 1847 showing Salish women weaving at a loom and a small white dog nearby. However, Paula Gustafson, who has done extensive research on this question, says that of all the so-called "dog blankets" in museums today, she could find none that tested as dog hair; rather, she says that fibers analyzed from blankets were found to be coyote hair and that, furthermore, dog hair is difficult to spin because of its twisting properties. She says she "cannot concur with the reported extensive use of dog hair as a primary weaving yarn."

Gustafson classifies the Salish blankets as follows: (1) "Plain" blankets using a twill weave (over two, under one) with a warp and weft of animal hair and warp or weft threads of contrasting color, creating patterns of lines or plaids; (2) "Organized" blankets (sometimes called "nobility"), which she further divides into three types—classic, colonial, and hybrid. Classic blankets, woven from 1778–1850, showed little outside influence and concentrated on strong horizontal patterns. Colonial blankets (1850–1900) usually had a square or diamond shape in the center and may have been influenced by the patchwork quilt patterns of the pioneer women. The hybrid type (after 1850) basically used a twill technique for the main body of the blanket, with the side borders twined into geometric designs. Dyes for the Salish blankets were natural ones—alder bark for red, lichen for yellow, hemlock bark for various shades of brown, the Oregon grape for a golden yellow, and oxidized copper for blue-green; black was achieved by burying the fibers in iron-rich mud for a time. These Salish blankets were quite heavy, often had long fringes, and were usually reserved for ceremonial occasions; smaller blankets functioned as shoulder blankets. Found at Ozette was a box containing a folded blanket which was originally blue-black plaid with a white background; it is the oldest known specimen of Northwest weaving, being 300 to 500 years old. With the coming of the Hudson's Bay blankets, weaving died out among the Salish peoples, but it was revived during the 1970s, creating some weaving of superb quality with a return to the fibers and techniques of the past.

Hair Styles

Men let the hair grow long, held in place with a cedar-bark headband or gathered into a clump at the back, fastened with a bone or wood hairpin. Women wore the hair parted in the middle and loose or in two braids. Only slaves or mourners wore the hair short. Some men plucked all the facial hairs, others sported a mustache, while a few had scraggly beards.

Headgear

Some women's peaked basketry hats were tall, brimless, and of split cedar bark, similar to those of the Plateau. Other hats, worn by both sexes, were mushroom-shaped, often of double construction, generally of spruce root, and had chin ties to anchor them firmly in rough weather; some were painted, but usually the pattern was shown in the weave. These brimmed hats afforded protection against the frequent rains as well as the glare of the sun on water. In winter fur caps or pointed hoods of skin were worn by the men.

Accessories

Accessories were few. Pouches were made of skin, while flat bags were of woven shredded cedar bark.

Some braided-fiber belts held robes in place; other belts were of mountain-goat wool, woven in the same technique as the blankets. Mittens are mentioned as being worn by hunters in the mountains.

Jewelry

Bone or mountain-goat horn were favored materials for bracelets; these had elaborate all-over designs engraved on them. Bracelets were also made of brass, copper, antler, leather, dentalium shells, even iron and tin in the late eighteenth century. Necklaces of dentalium and abalone shells, nose ornaments (usually a dentalium shell in the pierced nasal septum), and earrings (often several in the multiperforated earlobes) adorned the wealthy men and women. To these aboriginal articles were added the glass beads and the Chinese and Portuguese coins of the traders.

Armor

Warriors wore a knee-length tunic of two or more layers of elk hide or deerskin.

Special Costumes

Ceremony among the Salish peoples was based on a quest for an individual guardian spirit. At the rituals some wore their own Salish blankets; others donned Chilkat blankets. Unlike their Kwakiutl neighbors, the Salish participants wore less elaborate costumes. Some dancers wore headdresses of long strands of shredded cedar bark or mountain-goat hair. High, conical hats made of human hair and crowned with duck or loon feathers made their appearance at ceremonies; these were called "sharpheads" and the feathers fluttered with the slightest movement of the dancer. Paul Kane has left us a painting of Salish dancers in a "Medicine Mask Dance" (1847), in which one wears a Chilkat blanket and they all wear masks of various types. (Oddly, several wear breechclouts, which do not seem to be mentioned in the literature.) During potlatches at which young boys and girls were given hereditary names, they wore a multitude of strands of mountain-goat wool, a sacred material in the rituals. Another watercolor by Paul Kane shows us a chief wearing a medicine cap made of feathers and human hair said to have been taken from the heads of persons killed in battle.

Garment Decoration

Garments were decorated with fur trim, particularly otter, strings of shells, and long fringes. A few hats were painted. Weaving techniques were twining or twilling, or the two in combination, as well as a plain cross weave.

Face and Body Embellishment

Some face painting occurred, at times with designs representing the individual's guardian spirit; the painting was done with red ocher, charcoal, and powdered mica. Red and white paint was used on the bodies. Skull deformation was general (except by slaves and lower class persons); it was done by a pad, a piece of shredded cedar bark wrapped in buckskin, tied in place over the forehead of the infant, resulting in a broadened forehead and a wedge-shaped head. This custom was practiced as late as 1850. A few women had lines tattooed on the chin and cheeks, and both men and women sometimes tattooed the arms and legs.

Masks

Coast Salish dancers wore distinctive masks, often with moving parts like those of the Kwakiutl; in fact, a few masks were obtained from those neighbors. Feathers would flap, birds would open their beaks, and some human faces had different mouths to be attached. The Sxwayxwey dancers wore masks with enormous protruding eyes, horns, and feathered crests. For secret-society dances, wolf masks with fearsome jaws and eyes appeared.

Transitional Dress

By the 1850s Hudson's Bay Company blankets replaced those woven by the Salish women; they were especially useful for gifts at potlatches because of their relative cheapness and their availability. But the wearing of Salish blankets continued for ceremonial use well into the twentieth century; these were the plain type—all white with occasional red lines. Button blankets, probably acquired in trade, were also popular. During the 1860s the Scottish employees of the Hudson's Bay Company introduced sheep and taught the Salish people to knit, resulting in heavy sweaters and jackets that were often embellished with pieces of fur and deep fringes at the bottom. The men also wore beaver-skin hats similar to shakos. Women adopted the long cotton dresses or blouse/skirt combinations of the white women. They bound cotton scarves tightly around the head. A few basketry hats were used for rain gear.

Key Sources

Barnett, Homer G. *The Coast Salish of British Columbia.* Eugene: University of Oregon Press, 1955.

British Columbia Department of Education. *Coast Salish.* British Columbia Heritage Series 1. Our Native Peoples 2. Victoria, British Columbia: Don McDiarmid, Queen's Printer, 1952.

Curtis, Edward S. *The North American Indian.* Vol. 9. New York: Johnson Reprint Company, 1970.

Duff, Wilson. *The Upper Stalo Indians of the Fraser Valley, British Columbia.* Anthropology in British Columbia, Memoir 1. Victoria: British Columbia Provincial Museum, 1953.

Gustafson, Paula. *Salish Weaving.* Vancouver, British Columbia: Douglas & McIntyre, 1979.

Hill-Tout, Charles. *The Salish People.* Vancouver, British Columbia: Talonbooks, 1978.

Horse Capture, George P. and Richard A. Pohrt. *Salish Indian Art: From the R. Simplot Collection.* Cody, WY: Buffalo Bill Historical Center, 1986.

Kennedy, Dorothy I. D. and Randall T. Bouchard. "Northern Coast Salish." In *Handbook of North American Indians. Vol. 7: Northwest Coast.* Pp. 441–452. Washington: Smithsonian Institution.

Kissell, Mary L. "Organized Salish Blanket Pattern." *American Anthropologist* 31(1): 85–88.

Maud, Ralph, ed. *The Salish People: The Local Contributions of Charles Hill-Tout.* 4 vols. Vancouver, British Columbia: Talonbooks, 1978.

Suttles, Wayne. "Central Coast Salish." In *Handbook of North American Indians. Vol. 7: Northwest Coast.* Pp. 453–475. Washington: Smithsonian Institution.

Wade, Edwin L. "The Art of the Salish Power Dances." *American Indian Art Magazine* 1(4): 64–67.

Wells, Oliver N. *Salish Weaving: Primitive and Modern.* Sardis, British Columbia: Oliver N. Wells, 1969.

Haida

The Haida ("the people" in their language) lived in splendid isolation on the Queen Charlotte Islands with one group, the Kaigani, on Prince of Wales Island. Dependent on the sea for their livelihood, they made perilous voyages in their magnificent canoes, trading seal and sea-otter furs for Chilkat blankets, copper, slaves, eulachon oil, and moose and caribou hides. They were the only tribe of the area to carve the argillite (a glossy black slate) found on their islands. The Haida constitute the only members of the Skittagetan linguistic family, which resembles the Athapaskan language. First contact with Europeans seems to have been with the Spaniard Juan Perez in 1774, followed by many other explorers and traders. The usual problems of epidemics, encroaching whites, and missionaries led to the depletion of the Haida; however, their traditional culture continues vigorously today.

Men's Basic Dress

For everyday wear the men clothed themselves in skin breechclouts, or a skin thrown over one shoulder, or a sleeveless tunic of deerskin (probably caribou) with several rows of small fringes at the sides and displaying human figures painted in red and black. They rarely went naked like so many of the Northwest Coast men.

Women's Basic Dress

The women wore a tunic of tanned leather reaching from the neck to the calves. It is said that they also wore a small apron from the waist to the knee; this was probably of shredded cedar-bark fiber. Gunther says they wore this fiber apron *over* the skin dress.

Footwear

The Haida went barefoot in their mild climate. Simple skin moccasins were worn only in the coldest weather.

Outer Wear

The most prized cloaks were of sea-otter fur, but other types were to be found. They traded their fine canoes for Chilkat blankets, worn especially for ceremony. Shredded yellow–cedar-bark robes were woven in checkerboard patterns. Some cloaks of mountain-goat wool had narrow strips of sea-otter fur woven into them so the appearance was that of an entire otter skin. Blanket pins were of carved wood, bone, or native copper, later of silver. Caribou-skin robes were painted with designs similar to those of the Chilkat blankets, all executed in red and black pigments.

Hair Styles

The coarse black hair of the Haida was allowed to grow long; some men coiled it up into a knot on the top of the head, securing it with a wooden or bone pin. Often the hair was matted and covered liberally with red ocher; it was sometimes augmented with hair cut from the heads of victims of conflict.

Headgear

Some of the hats woven of finely split spruce root or shredded cedar bark had a narrow brim and were tied under the chin; others had a wider and taller brim. Designs on the hats were of painted birds or animals done in the characteristic "split" manner, so they could be adapted to the shape of the hat; typical colors were red, blue, and black. Decoration also consisted of raised lines of twill weave.

Accessories

Flat bags were plaited from the inner bark of the cedar. Woven belts, collected in 1774, were edged with black-dyed wool, which may have been mountain-goat wool, although that animal is not native to the Haida islands.

Jewelry

Haida women (not the men) wore labrets made of wood, bone, shell, or the black slate (argillite); these were single labrets under the lower lip. The custom died out by the 1880s. Argillite was also carved into earrings, rings, bracelets, and nose rings. Some of the armorers on the early trading ships made rings of twisted iron to be worn as bracelets, neck rings, or anklets. These were also made from native copper acquired in trade from the north.

Armor

"Rod-and-slat" armor was worn by the Haida warriors; this consisted of wooden rods that were woven together with a cord of nettle bark; thigh guards were made of the same material. Under this they wore a tunic of elk skin. With the armor they may have worn helmets as well. Armor of this sort would stop an arrow and even a musket shot from moderate range.

Special Costumes

The Haida had a rich and varied ceremonial life that centered around feasts, potlatches, and dances; these served to celebrate or commemorate events such as births, puberty, marriages, death, the installation of a new lineage dwelling, or the inauguration of a new chief. Ritual garments were beautiful and costly, rich in decoration, and tapestried with symbolic meanings. Chilkat blankets with long fringes sweeping the ground were evidence of trade with their northern neighbors. Some robes were of skin

A nineteenth-century Haida clan hat woven of spruce root has a twilled design on the brim. The ten basketry rings atop the hat may each represent a potlatch given by the wearer.

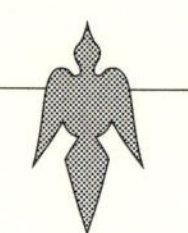

painted with crest figures; others were the famous "button blankets," made of dark-blue stroud cloth with a large crest-figure applique of red flannel or felt, outlined with white pearl buttons or white seed beads; dance shirts, made of the same material and ornamented in a similar fashion, had an opening at the top for the head and were unsewn at the sides. Dance capes, too, featured red appliques with white button outlines. Headdresses took various forms as well. Clan helmets were carved of wood and painted, often blue, representing crest figures; these and the twined basketry hats were sometimes surmounted by rings woven of cedar bark, one ring for each potlatch given by the wearer. "Frontlet" headdresses displayed a carved figure of a crest animal or bird above the forehead, surrounded on both sides and the top with large squares of abalone shell; the same shell was used as inlay for teeth, eyes, even nostrils. Strips of ermine, feathers, and sea-lion whiskers were further adornments. Shamans and other dancers wore dance aprons of skin or dark cloth, similar to those of the Tlingit, with their several rows of fringe, Chinese coins, or puffin beaks. Neck rings of woven cedar bark were festooned with multiple strands of bark. Shamans wore neck rings hung with charms with mystic meanings.

At puberty the girl was secluded, required to avoid many taboos and to wear a headdress of woven cedar bark covering the head with an opening for the face. At death the corpse was cleansed and costumed, and the face was painted by a close relative; mourners cut the hair short and blackened the face with pitch.

Garment Decoration

The painting of crest figures on skin was popular with the Haida, although they tended to use color sparingly. The basketry hats were also painted with crest animals and birds. This was done in the characteristic style of the northern tribes—the curvilinear lines, the avoidance of right angles and open spaces, the use of "eye" symbols to indicate joints, and a fluidity unparalleled in most Indian art. Except for the long fringes of the (imported) Chilkat blankets, fringes were small. Weaving was mainly a matter of twining, although some twilling was done to create raised surfaces on the hats, and a checkerboard technique was used for bags and some robes. Feathers, strips of ermine, shells (especially abalone), sea-lion whiskers, puffin beaks, and the traders' white buttons were additions to many of the Haida garments and headdresses.

Face and Body Embellishment

Face painting was common, particularly for ceremonies; heraldic crests adorned the faces, or else solid areas of color were painted. However, tattooing was stressed to a greater extent by the Haida. Using both red ocher and charcoal, tattoos of family crest figures enhanced the arms, legs, back of hands, cheeks, back, and even the insteps. The tattooing process was executed at special name-giving ceremonies. The Haida did not practice skull flattening.

Masks

Many of the dance masks of the Haida were portrait masks, some showing old women with labrets and face painting. Transformation masks were also used, in which parts of the mask moved to reveal other faces or creatures, showing the dual nature of man and nature. The masks were of painted wood, some with copper or abalone-shell inlays, and often with many strands of shredded cedar bark.

Transitional Dress

The Haida acquired trade goods early, in the late eighteenth century; at first they esteemed articles of European clothing, but later they demanded cloth in exchange for their sea-otter furs. By the mid-nineteenth century they had made the complete transition to European clothing, except for a few basketry hats, and even that craft was almost lost. They were decimated by the diseases brought by whites, but those left continued with their rich ceremonialism, adopting especially the button blankets and some of the decorated skin clothing of the Tlingit. A few craftsmen turned their talents to metalwork, creating beautiful bracelets in silver and then gold. They continued to carve their argillite.

Key Sources

Blackman, Margaret B. "Feastwear: Haida Art Goes Couture." *American Indian Art Magazine* 17(4): 56–65.

———. "Haida: Traditional Culture." In *Handbook of North American Indians. Vol. 7: Northwest*

Coast. Pp. 240–260. Washington: Smithsonian Institution.

———. *Window on the Past: The Photographic Ethnohistory of the Northern and Kaigani Haida.* Mercury Series, Canadian Ethnology Paper 74. Ottawa, Ontario: National Museums of Canada.

British Columbia Department of Education. *Haida.* British Columbia Heritage Series 1. Our Native Peoples 4. Victoria, British Columbia: Don McDiarmid, Queen's Printer, 1952.

Curtis, Edward S. *The North American Indian.* Vol. 11. New York: Johnson Reprint Company, 1970.

Swan, James G. "The Haidah Indians of Queen Charlotte's Island, British Columbia, with a Brief Description of Their Carvings, Tattoo Designs, etc." Smithsonian Institution *Contributions to Knowledge* 21(4): 1–18.

Swanton, John R. "Contributions to the Ethnology of the Haida." Publications of the Jesup North Pacific Expedition 5. American Museum of Natural History *Memoirs* 8(1): 1–300.

Kwakiutl

The Kwakiutl occupied the northern and eastern areas of Vancouver Island and the British Columbia mainland opposite. They prefer to be termed "Kwagiulth" or "Kwa-kwa-ka'wakw," which translates as "those who speak Kwakwala," but the traditional name will be used here. They were Wakashan speakers, along with their neighbors the Nootka. There were about 30 autonomous groups, the major ones being the Heiltsuk/Bella Bella in the north and the Haisla in the south. They had the usual Northwest Coast dependence on marine life; sea otters were particularly cherished because of their use in ceremonial attire. Kwakiutl art is flamboyant, brilliant in color, and nonrestrictive in form.

First European contact was with a British trader in 1786. Although there was much intertribal violence and even head-hunting in some cases, conditions were stabilized by the 1850s. The Hudson's Bay Company set up posts in Kwakiutl territory in the 1830s. White encroachment, resultant epidemics, and missionary activities disrupted Kwakiutl society. The government banned potlatches, which were most important to these people, but the rituals simply were practiced underground until the 1920s, when a few were held openly. The potlatches were revived in strength in the 1970s. Much of our information on the Kwakiutl is based on the pioneering work of Franz Boas around the turn of the century. Drucker, Holm, and Hawthorn have contributed extensively, especially on Kwakiutl art. Edward Curtis made numerous photographs of them, as well as a film.

Men's Basic Dress

Men went naked most of the time, adding when desired a tunic of woven, shredded cedar bark (usually yellow cedar), that was edged with white fur, had sleeves to the biceps, was below the knees, and was belted; if not worn as a tunic with an opening for the head, it was worn under one arm and fastened on the opposite shouder, or simply wrapped as a rectangular piece about the waist.

Women's Basic Dress

In warm weather women wore an apron or a skirt of multiple strands of shredded cedar bark, an efficient material for it would shed rain, dry quickly, and retain its shape. When cooler weather came, the women donned a tunic like that of the men, made of woven, shredded cedar-bark strands; like them, they often wore it under one arm and fastened it on the other shoulder.

Footwear

The Kwakiutl, like most of the peoples on the Northwest Coast, went barefoot.

Outer Wear

Both sexes wore robes of woven yellow cedar bark, which sometimes had strips of sea-otter fur added to the weaving, creating a garment that looked like fur. The early trader Lisiansky mentioned blankets embroidered in squares and adorned with tassels, which sounds like one of the Salish blankets often collected by trading (or raiding) on the part of the Kwakiutl. The choicest cloaks were of sea-otter fur, reserved for chiefs or men of high standing. Marmot skins, considered almost as valuable as sea-otter skins, were sewn together with fibers of nettle to make a robe; robes were also made from marten, deer, mink, and black-bear skins. Capes of bark and hats of woven spruce protected both men and women from the frequent rains.

Hair Styles

Men wore the hair long, gathered at the back, sometimes in a knot; a headband of fur or bark kept it out of their eyes when they were working. Small cedar twigs were often fastened into the hair as ornament. Women wore their long hair parted and hanging loose or braided into two plaits. Many of the men displayed mustaches and a few had beards. The hair was black, but it was anointed with so much red ocher and grease that it was difficult to determine the color.

Headgear

Hats of finely woven spruce roots tended to have a sloping brim up to a high crown that was flat on top; these were usually decorated with painted crest designs all around the brim. Men wore a distinctive hat or head ring of fur in a "pillbox" shape, adorned with pieces of abalone shell to indicate wealth. A few headbands of fur strips or woven cedar bark were worn.

Accessories

Soft pouches of tanned leather or woven cedar bark carried important personal items such as painting or sewing equipment. Belts were of leather, or braided fiber, or of cordage. Some armlets were of fur.

Jewelry

Both sexes pierced the nasal septum for the insertion of such ornaments as dentalium shells, rings of abalone, later of metal, or small cedar rods. Bracelets and anklets were of carved polished horn or of copper; later, as metal became available from the traders, they were of twisted iron or brass, followed by silver and then gold, finely crafted. Necklaces were not commonly worn; however, one source mentions a necklace made of the toenails of dead people, probably obtained in raids; the necklace was given by a chief to his son so he would become a brave warrior. Hair ornaments and earrings were made of clusters of the valued dentalium shells. Some of the women wore

This carved cedar mask of four bird beaks, made in 1938, is almost four-feet long. The Kwakiutl Hamatsa Society Dancer who wore the mask needed considerable strength and dexterity to manipulate the beaks.

labrets, fastened by means of a perforation in the lower lip; these were of bone or wood.

Armor

The men wore an unusual type of armor as shown in a Curtis photograph of a Kwakiutl warrior; strands of rope were bound around the torso and over the shoulders to form a sort of breastplate. A wraparound skirt of woven, shredded cedar bark was worn beneath this. They also made armor from elk hide and from wooden slats. The warrior went barefoot and bareheaded. No shields were mentioned by sources consulted.

Special Costumes

The Kwakiutl had a rich ceremonial life with the typical Northwest Coast ritual costumes plus the use of fantastic masks, many with transformation devices built into the structures. There were mourning rituals and dancing society affairs at which novices were initiated, all of which were dramatic representations of ancestral supernatural experiences, each rite with its own spectacular costume. The best known was the Hamatsa Society Dance, sometimes called the Cannibal Dance; it is doubtful that human flesh was actually eaten, but it seems that dog flesh, abhorred by the Kwakiutl, was consumed, creating a terrifying experience for the participants and watchers. The costumes of the dancers featured elaborately woven head pieces, large neck rings, arm and leg ornaments, and much use of strands of cedar bark dyed red with alder bark. Coppers were carried in the ceremonies; these were symbols of wealth and each had a name that indicated the extent of its value. The symbolic shape of the copper also appeared on blankets and dance aprons, and was carved on rattles, staffs, and headdresses. The headband was a turban-like affair of plaited red-cedar bark with a cloth lining, often adorned with abalone-shell pieces, fur, and feathers. Head rings were thick rolls of twisted or braided cedar bark, ornamented with pendant knots and fringes of bark. These were worn with the Chilkat leggings, tunics, and blankets, and later the button blankets. Many of the spectators and participants wore the basketry hats embellished with "potlatch rings" on top, each woven basketry ring representing a potlatch given by the wearer. The "cannibal" dancers wore kilts of hemlock boughs, with boughs around the head, the neck, the wrists, and the knees. The "frontlet" headdress was an important ceremonial item adopted in the second half of the nineteenth century from the Tlingit and Tsimshian to the north; it consisted of a carved wooden face attached to a head ring of cedar bark, painted in hues of green, black, and red, with an edging at the sides and across the top of squares of abalone shells. Eyes, teeth, even nostrils were often pieces of inlaid abalone shell. Ermine tails appeared at the sides and in rows on a cloth trailer down the back. Sea-lion whiskers stood upright at the top, from which down would float with each of the dancer's movements; down represented peace. In some dances only the cedar-bark rings, adorned with abalone-shell pieces, were worn on the head. The costume was completed with cedar-bark neck rings and a blanket. The Chilkat robe of the Tlingit as well as the "button blankets" of the nineteenth century were seen at all ceremonial occasions. The button blankets were of dark-blue stroud cloth or other heavy material, with a central applique of red flannel in a crest figure, outlined with white pearl buttons. Shamans wore dance aprons for rituals; these were

A Kwakiutl double mask of red cedar represents Tsonoqwa, the Cannibal Woman. The outer mask, 16 inches high and 13 inches wide, is a human face with heavy eyebrows and a bearskin mustache, while the inner mask is thought to show Tsonoqwa's human qualitites and a human's abalone shell necklace.

like the Tlingit garments—made of skin with rows of fringe ending in puffin beaks, which made a satisfying clacking during the dance.

Garment Decoration

The Kwakiutl made fine utilitarian garments, but acquired the Chilkat and Salish blankets in trade for the most part. Their decoration of costumes was bold, colorful, and distinctive, not dependent on the filling in of all available spaces. For paints, they used red ocher, white made from burnt clamshells, blue from a blue clay or a copper oxide, black from ground-up charcoal mixed with salmon eggs, green from copper sulfide, and a brilliant red from cinnabar, when available. These colors were used to paint basketry hats, masks, and headdresses. Strands of shredded cedar bark, often dyed red with alder bark, were not only used for garments but appeared as decoration. Major weaving was that of the cedar-bark garments and the hats of twined spruce root. Fur edgings, abalone-shell pieces, and dentalium shells further adorned garments and accessories.

Face and Body Embellishment

Skull deformation was practiced by the Kwakiutl; the process (a pad tied over the forehead, wrapped in bands of hide) produced a cone-shaped head that came to a high point in back, sometimes called a "sugar loaf" form. This process meant that the head and face were narrower than those of the Salish and Chinook peoples to the south. There was little of tattooing and not much face painting, except that spectators at ceremonials sometimes painted their faces black.

Masks

The superb Kwakiutl wood carvers made a bewildering array of masks for the winter ceremonies. Both Gunther and Hawthorn, writing on Kwakiutl art, have cataloged masks extensively. The masks were beautifully carved of wood with powerful, dramatic features of bird, animal, human, or insect figures. Painted in brilliant colors, typically black, white, and red, some had copper or abalone insets for eyes or teeth, or copper bands across the forehead. Transformation masks were a specialty of the Kwakiutl; by the use of strings and other forms of manipulation, wings could flap, beaks could open and shut, and one face could flow into another face. The huge masks were fastened in place by means of a harness on the shoulders; long strands of shredded cedar bark hung from the mask and shoulders in the form of a cape-like garment that covered the dancer.

Transitional Dress

The Kwakiutl took the goods of the traders and fashioned them into articles that reflected their own artistic concepts, as can be seen in the famous button blankets, which used trade pearl buttons and wool to create unique garments. After 1850, the Hudson's Bay Company flooded the area with their characteristic blankets; they were cheap (only 50 cents apiece), and became a unit of value as gifts at the potlatches, but they did not replace the Chilkat and button blankets at the ceremonies. By the 1880s European-style clothing was worn generally, often combined with ceremonial dress. The basketry hats were replaced with felt hats worn by the men, while the women wore cotton scarves tightly bound about the head. In the 1970s and 1980s, popular headbands were beaded with alternating black and white vertical rectangles.

Key Sources

Boas, Franz. "Ethnology of the Kwakiutl." Bureau of American Ethnology *Annual Reports* 35.

———. *Kwakiutl Ethnography.* Chicago: University of Chicago Press, 1966.

———. "The Kwakiutl of Vancouver Island." American Museum of Natural History *Memoirs* 8(2).

———. "On the Use of Masks and Head Ornaments of the Northwest Coast of America." *Internationales Archiv fur Ethnographie.* Leiden, 1890.

British Columbia Department of Education. *Kwakiutl.* British Columbia Heritage Series 1. Our Native Peoples 7. Victoria, British Columbia: Don McDiarmid, Queen's Printer, 1953.

Codere, Helen. "Kwakiutl: Traditional Culture." In *Handbook of North American Indians. Vol. 7: Northwest Coast.* Pp. 359–377. Washington: Smithsonian Institution.

Curtis, Edward S. *The North American Indian.* Vol. 10. New York: Johnson Reprint Company, 1970.

Goldman, Irving. *The Kwakiutl Indians of Vancouver Island.* Boston: Beacon Press, 1961. Reprint of 1937 edition.

Gunther, Erna. *Art in the Life of the Northwest Coast Indians: With a Catalog of the Rasmussen Collection of Northwest Indian Art at the Portland Art Museum.* Portland, OR: Portland Art Museum, 1966.

Hawthorn, Audrey. *Kwakiutl Art.* 2d ed. Seattle: University of Washington Press, 1988.

Holm, Bill. "Kwakiutl: Winter Ceremonies." In *Handbook of North American Indians. Vol. 7: Northwest Coast.* Pp. 378–386. Washington: Smithsonian Institution.

Rohner, Ronald P. and Evelyn C. Rohner. *The Kwakiutl Indians of British Columbia.* New York: Holt, Rinehart & Winston, 1970.

Waite, Deborah. "Kwakiutl Transformation Masks." In *The Many Faces of Primitive Art: A Critical Anthology.* Douglas Fraser, ed. Pp. 266–300. Englewood Cliffs, NJ: Prentice-Hall, 1966.

Nootka/Makah

The Nootka lived on the west coast of Vancouver Island; across the Strait of Juan de Fuca on the extreme northwest tip of Washington lived the Makah, closely related in language and culture, so the two will be treated here as one group; the modern name of the two tribes is Nuu-chah-nulth, meaning "mountains in a row." They inhabited an area lashed with storms, drenched with rains, dense with lush forests, and shadowed by rugged mountains. These peoples were the major whalers of the Pacific Northwest; the killing of the whale was of vital concern to them, and special rites and attire were connected with the chase of the great creatures of the sea. They both spoke Nootka, a branch of the Wakashan language family. They embraced much of the Northwest culture but did not believe in competitive potlatches. Their subsistence was based on whales, salmon, and seals. They had an almost complete monopoly in dentalium shells, which were obtained on the sea floor off the coast, and were widely traded.

There is information on early European contacts with both peoples; John Webber, the artist with Cook on his third voyage (1778), and Jose Cardero and Tomas de Suria, two artists with the Alejandro Malaspina expedition (1791–1792), all made detailed drawings of the Nootka and Makah. The tribes took part in the trade of sea-otter skins, which ended in the early 1800s. In the second half of that century they conducted a lively trade in dogfish oil. They were decimated by diseases and repressed by the missionaries who came in 1875. Despite government regulations, they managed to keep much of their culture alive. During the 1970s the Makah came into prominence with the excavation of the Ozette village, which was buried under a mud slide over 500 years ago.

Men's Basic Dress

Men usually went naked. In cooler weather they donned a tunic of woven cedar bark, worn under one arm and fastened on the opposite shoulder. Another type of garment was a rectangular mat or robe of cedar bark that was wrapped around the hips and held in place with a belt. Both items of dress were edged with white fur, or if the individual was wealthy, strips of sea-otter fur.

Women's Basic Dress

Women did not go naked, but wore an apron or a skirt of strands of shredded cedar bark or tule rushes or of deerskin. When necessary for warmth they added, like the men, tunics of woven cedar bark, either exposing one arm, or fastened on both shoulders. A belt held the garment in place. Sometimes they wore a wraparound skirt of woven cedar bark and a cape on top, waist-length, of the same fibrous material.

Footwear

The Nootka and Makah, like most of the other Northwest Coast people, went barefoot. However, Captain Cook said that "a few have a kind of skin stockings which reach halfway up the thigh." These sound rather like leggings. Moccasins were used by both sexes in the coldest weather, probably obtained from the Salish people in trade. They hunted elk and deer in the mountain snows wearing simple snowshoes of circular frames laced with hide thongs.

Outer Wear

Although basic garments were minimal or nonexistent, outer wear was of many types. Robes of sea-otter skins were displayed by wealthy individuals; lesser folk wore robes of mink or marten skins sewn together. Great bearskin robes were worn by the whalers. Cedar bark was the basic material for many wraps. The short, circular shoulder capes with fur edgings at top and bottom were woven double at times, and made excellent rain gear; sometimes they had a patterned border at the top and a fringe at the bottom, and were rubbed with red ocher. Some robes of twined, shredded cedar bark were rectangular in shape with a rounded bottom edge; versatile garments, these could be draped over the shoulders and tied under the chin, or folded around the body and fastened on one shoulder, or worn as a skirt by either sex. Some ponchos of cedar bark were finely woven in a checkerboard pattern; others, especially for fishermen, were of seal gut. Some robes were of strips of downy bird skins such as mallard, twisted around bark fiber to use as weft; these were warm, soft, and light, but fragile. Captain Cook collected a mantle (1778) from the Nootka, but the origin is not established; they may have acquired it in trade. It is of woven yellow cedar bark and nettle fibers, the latter mixed with mountain-goat wool; it is painted in red and black, showing a raven, a fish, and human faces. The oldest specimen of Northwest Coast weaving is a blanket found at the excavation at Ozette; it is twill-woven with white and blue-black plaid stripes.

Photographed in 1910, a Nootka girl newly entering womanhood wears her hair in wrapped braids with dangling metal, beaded, and fringed ornaments. A comb pinned to her robe allows her to scratch her head without violating ritual restrictions.

Hair Styles

The hair was worn shoulder-length by the men or, when on whaling expeditions, tied up in a coil on the top of the head and further embellished with sprigs or wreaths of hemlock or spruce. Women wore two braids or "clumps" at the sides or one braid down the back. Hair was adorned with red ocher, held in place with bear grease; sometimes bits of down were added. Despite the matted condition of the hair, the Nootka had beautifully carved combs of cedar wood that were used in rituals. Men, in general, had more facial hair than most Indians, and the Nootka men displayed it in beards and/or mustaches.

Headgear

Nootka and Makah hats were of two major types: (1) The well-known "whaler's hat" was of twined spruce root with a bulb-shaped extension at the top, and with designs of whaling activities worked into the weaving by means of an imbricated technique using dark-brown grasses; sometimes these hats were lined with a headband of braided cedar-bark strands, to which thongs could be attached so the hat could be tied under the chin in rough weather. These hats were worn by both sexes as a sign of high status and were not made after the eighteenth century; there are not more than 20 of these hats known in the world today. At times feathers protruded out of the top of the hat instead of the knob. (2) A second type of hat, in shape like a shallow dome, woven often of cedar bark instead of spruce roots, was plain or had simple, bold designs painted in red and black on the brim. Some featured a broad black band on the lower section of the brim. Cook mentioned hats with basketry potlatch rings on top, but these were probably obtained from tribes to the north.

Accessories

Whalers wore fur anklets. Both sexes at times wound strands of shredded cedar bark around the knees and ankles; anklets were also of elk hide. A few chiefs carried feather fans. Belts were usually of braided or woven cedar bark. Bags were made in a twilled technique of fine strands of bark or of wider strands in a checkerboard weave. Fishermen carried their hooks and other equipment in a pouch of deerskin or finely twined cedar bark.

Jewelry

Nose rings were of copper or abalone shell; long pieces of shell, wooden rods, bones, or even a quill were inserted through the pierced septums of the men; women wore smaller nose pins, often dentalium shells, or a wooden rod. Necklaces or chokers of dentalium shells were popular, as were trader beads, olivella shells, bear claws, and beaver teeth. Hair ornaments were often long, magnificent affairs of dentalium shells combined with large glass trade beads, sometimes reaching half way down the back.

Nootka, known as whalers, used an overlay of surf grass to show boats, harpooners, and whales in this conical hat collected in 1794. Not more than 20 of these hats survive.

In the drawings of Tatooche and his two wives, we see many ornaments, including a headband of dangling dentalia, bead and shell necklaces, and long earrings; earrings were also made of metal cones and pieces of abalone shell from the California coast, much superior to the local abalone shells. Bracelets were of carved mountain-goat horn or of worked native copper from the northern tribes. Shell or wooden labrets were worn by a few men, especially Makah.

Armor

Chiefs wore armor of double layers of elk skin, occasionally strengthened by wooden rods sewn to the outside; these were often painted. Although elk hide seems to have been the most common form of armor, some examples of Nootka armor have been preserved that are of the "slat-and-rod" type. Warriors painted their faces black. No helmets were used.

Special Costumes

Two winter ceremonies occupied the Nootka and Makah—the Wolf ritual and the Doctoring ritual; in the latter the shaman wore undyed yellow-cedar bark. Hide robes, painted in red and black, were to be seen at the ceremonies, also neck rings and head rings of shredded cedar bark. A wooden frontlet exhibited a carved wooden face on the front, wooden slats at the sides, and an abundance of shredded cedar bark below. For the Wolf Dance, a forehead mask, which should really be termed a "headdress," was unique to this area; it was made of thin boards joined together in a framework that was very light and quite large, and was tied under the chin with cords. It was painted in red, black, blue, and gray colors on a white background. Dance aprons of hide were bedecked with rows of tinklers; early tinklers were made of deer hooves or carved wooden cones, while later ones were tin cones or thimbles, all of which added to the rhythmic sounds of the dance. At puberty, a girl wore a special hair ornament of rows of dentalia, one on each braid. Mourning for a near relative's death was demonstrated by blackening the face, cutting the hair short, and wearing the poorest of garments.

Garment Decoration

Pieces of abalone shell, dentalium shells, brass buttons, and, later, pearl buttons were favored forms of decoration. Weaving on a two-bar loom was mainly with a twining technique, although some flat bags were plaited in a checkerboard manner; weaving found at Ozette was mentioned as being twilled. Various things were added to the wefts for weaving —feathers, twisted bird skins, mountain-goat wool (which had to be obtained in trade), and some cattail and other fibers. The famed whaler's hat had a warp of finely twined spruce root and a weft of thin strands of cedar bark dyed black; an overlay of white surf grass or bear grass created the designs. The art style was simple, whether using realistic or geometric forms, with a tolerance for open space that was not a feature of art farther north.

Face and Body Embellishment

Faces were painted with red, blue, and white paint; warriors and chiefs covered the faces with black paint and spread glittering powdered mica over that to create what they hoped was a terrifying effect. John Webber, the artist with Captain Cook, said that the Indians were painting their faces differently each day and that they would sometimes turn up in the afternoon with a design totally changed from the one used in the morning. Faces were painted all over for everyday weather protection and were designed with painted crest animals or checkerboard squares for ceremonies. Body and arms were sometimes painted red. The tattooing of women was quite general, most common designs being the vertical lines on the chin. Skull flattening was practiced, but less than among the Kwakiutl; they differed, too, in that they applied a padded board to the infant's head in the Chinook manner, creating a slanting forehead and a broadened face. Infants' legs were also bandaged to create bulging calves, marks of beauty.

Masks

Most of the masks worn by these peoples were forehead masks, which did not hide the face; however, some masks were humanoid, worn over the face. The Nootka and Makah were splendid carvers, making masks for many of the tribes to the south; from the Kwakiutl they learned the art of transformation masks, which operated with a network of strings to open and shut beaks, extend rays of a sun-like face, shift eyes from side to side, and to accomplish other changes through manipulation.

Transitional Dress

European contact was early (1788) and frequent after that point, but this had little effect on native culture. There was a great desire for articles of European dress, but these were worn with their own traditional clothing in various ways. By the mid-nineteenth century the cedar-bark garments, which required so much time and skill to make, were replaced with trade blankets, cotton dresses, raincoats, and flannel shirts. Shoes and boots were adopted. Ceremonial dress has been retained in many respects, particularly the button blankets and forehead masks. Few items of tribal distinction are worn today, although it may be noticed that men and women at contemporary social functions often wear a unique headband, beaded with alternating black and white vertical rectangles.

Key Sources

Arima, Eugene Y. *The West Coast People: The Nootka of Vancouver Island and Cape Flattery.* Special Publication 6. Victoria: British Columbia Provincial Museum, 1983.

Arima, Eugene Y. and John Dewhirst. "Nootkans of Vancouver Island." In *Handbook of North American Indians. Vol. 7: Northwest Coast.* Pp. 391–411. Washington: Smithsonian Institution.

British Columbia Department of Education. *Nootka.* British Columbia Heritage Series 1. Our Native Peoples 5. Victoria, British Columbia: Don McDiarmid, Queen's Printer, 1952.

Colson, Elizabeth. *The Makah Indians.* Minneapolis: University of Minnesota Press, 1953.

Curtis, Edward S. *The North American Indian.* Vol. 11. New York: Johnson Reprint Company, 1970.

Drucker, Philip. "The North and Central Nootkan Tribes." Bureau of American Ethnology *Bulletin* 144.

Heizer, Robert, ed. *Narrative of the Adventures and Sufferings of John R. Jewitt while Held as a Captive of the Nootka Indians of Vancouver Island 1803 to 1805.* Ramona, CA: Ballena, 1975.

Hill-Tout, Charles. "Report on the Ethnology of the South-eastern Tribes of Vancouver Island, British Columbia." *Journal of the Royal Anthropological Institute of Great Britain and Ireland* 37: 306–374.

Kirk, Ruth. *Hunters of the Whale.* New York: Harcourt, Brace and Jovanovich, 1974.

Marr, Carolyn J., Lloyd Colfax, and Robert D. Monroe. *Portrait in Time: Photographs of the Makah by Samuel G. Morse, 1896–1903.* Neah Bay, WA: Makah Cultural and Research Center, 1987.

Renker, Ann M. and Erna Gunther. "Makah." In *Handbook of North American Indians. Vol. 7: Northwest Coast.* Pp. 422–430. Washington: Smithsonian Institution.

Sendey, John, comp. *The Nootkan Indian: A Pictorial.* Port Alberni, British Columbia: Alberni Valley Museum, 1977.

Swan, James. "The Indians of Cape Flattery." Smithsonian Institution *Contributions to Knowledge* 16(8).

Oregon Coast and Interior

The Oregon coast is a narrow area between the steep-cliffed mountains and the sea; the interior is a land of rivers, particularly the Willamette, Rogue, Umpqua, and Coquille rivers, between the Coastal Range and the Cascade mountains. Beyond that range the land is lower, often desert, to the eastern edge of Oregon where the tribes merge into the Plateau culture. There are few tribes in the eastern area except for those along the Columbia River. These peoples of western Oregon were seminomadic, for they lived in winter homes and summer camps. In the north, especially along the coast, there were many manifestations of the Northwest Coast culture, while the southwestern groups, predominantly Athapaskan speakers, were similar in their material culture to northwestern California groups. The Oregon groups, as given by Ruby and Brown, were, from north to south along the coast: the Clatsop, Tillamook, Affalati, Siletz, Yaquina, Alsea, Siuslaw, Umpqua, Hanis Coos, Miluk Coos, Tututni (Rogue River Indians), Coquille, and Chetco peoples. Inland were the Chilwitz, Klatskanie, Clackemus, Tualatin, Northern Molala, Yamel, Luckiamute, Mary's River, Kalapooia, Santiam, Chelamela, Yoncalla, Southern Molala, Chastacosta, Takelma, Gallice, and Applegate River peoples. There were five major language groups: Penutian, Hokan, Aztec-Tanoan, Athapaskan, and Salishan families with innumerable dialects. Subsistence was based on salmon, land mammals, sea mammals, shellfish, roots, and berries. Most individuals were freeborn; there were a few slaves and few chiefs. In the southernmost groups there was a strong class system based on wealth, indicative of the California influence. First European contacts were with the trading ships of the late-eighteenth century; a strong trade was developed, but native culture was little influenced except by the adoption of articles of cloth and metal. More devastating were the diseases brought by the early ships, followed by the encroachment of the settlers and miners of the mid-nineteenth century, treaties and broken treaties, and finally the reservation life of the tattered remnants of the bands.

Men's Basic Dress

The men wore skin garments (when they wore any) in the form of breechclouts or aprons; some wore small aprons covered with feathers. In cooler weather they added closely fitted deerskin or elk-hide leggings and tunics or shirts, belted at the waist. Lewis and Clark mentioned that some of the lower Columbia River Indians wore, as a sole garment, a small blanket fastened across the chest with a cord.

Women's Basic Dress

For everyday wear women wore fringe skirts of shredded cedar bark (or maple or hazel bark) with a cold-weather cape (waist-length) of the same material; some were attired in the double-apron style of bark skirt with beaded fringe as found in California, with the large back apron overlapping the front. For special occasions they had knee-length leather tunics decorated, depending on their wealth, with buckskin fringes, bear-grass tassels, quillwork, pine seeds, dentalium shells, and pendants of abalone shell, along with short skin leggings. Lewis and Clark recorded wraparound skirts of buckskin.

Footwear

Generally these Indians went barefoot, but for traveling or with snow on the ground they wore deerskin moccasins, which covered the ankles and had a front seam. Simple round snowshoes were worn by the hunters in the mountains.

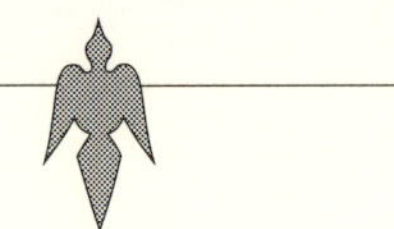

Outer Wear

Colder weather meant for both sexes capes or robes of otter or weasel skins, sewn together, or lighter weight deerskin mantles. Women's capes were of tule grass, deerskin, elk skin, or woven strips of rabbit skin. Rain capes were of twined cedar bark or cattails, made warm and soft by weaving in strips of rabbit fur. Some rain capes were made of fur.

Hair Styles

Women parted the hair in the center, making two shoulder strands or two braids. Men allowed the hair to grow long and gathered it at the back, or they chopped it off at the shoulders. Along the northern coast the men carefully plucked out the facial hairs with clamshell tweezers; along the southern coast mustaches and sparse chin whiskers were more common. In some areas face and hair were coated with elk or bear grease.

Headgear

The women's brimless basketry hats or caps were of two types: a flat-topped shape was found from Coos Bay northward, while the southern caps were of the half-sphere California type. These were done in an overlay twining technique of spruce root or wild-hazel bark with the overlay in red, white, and black; bear grass was used for the white strands, was dyed red with alder, or might be buried in mud for a black hue. Some of these hats were obtained from the Shasta. Dentalium shells and red pileated-woodpecker scalps were special adornments. Caps for winter were of handsome whole skins of loons or other waterfowl or of the skins of small animals such as raccoons or weasels; fur hats were also made of the heads of bears or deer, with the ears left intact. A headband of fur, dressed leather, or cedar bark kept loose-flowing hair in place; some wealthy men in the southern area attached scalps of red-headed woodpeckers to their leather headbands.

Accessories

Belts were of dressed leather or braided or woven grass fibers; they were sometimes embellished with shells or beads. Pouches of deerskin held tobacco, fish hooks, painting or sewing equipment, or other personal necessities. Southern groups adopted the California "purse," made of antler horn, often nicely carved, and with a slot in which valuable objects such as dentalium shells could be secured.

Jewelry

Ears were pierced at an infant's special naming ceremony, and pendants, plugs, and shells, both abalone and dentalia, were worn in the ears. Necklaces were made of dentalia strung with beads of seeds or shells. A navel amulet was made of a baby's umbilical cord placed in a small beaded pouch and worn by the child until five or six years old as protection against evil. Nose ornaments, usually worn by men, were pendants or dentalium shells skewered through a perforation in the nasal septum. Hair ornaments, bracelets, and armlets featured shells, feathers, and quillwork.

Armor

Warriors wore tunics of double layers of elk hide, often fastened to sticks of wood; designs were painted on the hides. The men of Coos Bay sewed strings of deer hooves over the chest and the back for greater protection. The Clatsops had an abundance of elk skin and made some of the finest armor along the entire coast. Hide helmets were commonly worn.

Special Costumes

Various ceremonies were performed, including the First Salmon feast, the winter dances, mourning rites and rites for other occasions, and in the extreme south the Deer Dance of the Californians. However, ceremonial costume was not as rigid nor as elaborate as that of the tribes farther north. Feathered headdresses and feathered dance skirts appeared in many of the ceremonies. Shaman insignia included a belt of human hair, with the ends hanging down behind, or sashes of otter skin; further decorations were of feathers, shells, and beads. At puberty, the girl's face, hands, forearms, and lower legs were painted red on the first day; on the fifth day she was draped with a blanket adorned with beads and dentalia, and wore a beaded halter and a basket cap. The Athapaskan girl sometimes wore a flicker wing feather in the nasal septum. At death, the corpse was washed and dressed in finery. Mourners cut the hair and put ashes and pitch on the heads and faces.

Garment Decoration

Dentalium shells were the most valued form of decoration, indicating wealth on the part of the wearer; the shells were not only used as ornament but were attached to garments. Feathers were also applied to clothing and were made into headdresses. The scalps of both the redheaded woodpecker and the pileated woodpecker were highly esteemed as articles of decoration. There was some painting done on leather tunics, but this did not involve crest designs. After the mid-nineteenth century a strong Plains influence appeared, as could be seen in the development of porcupine quillwork and beadwork. Weaving was present in the twined basketry caps, but in little else.

Face and Body Embellishment

Both sexes painted the center part in the hair red. For ceremonies they both decorated the face with red and white stripes. Warriors indicated war endeavors by the use of red and black stripes on the face. Men were tattooed only on one arm, a line for the purpose of measuring dentalium shells. Women were more extensively tattoed; they commonly had three vertical lines on the chin, as well as decorative tattoos on the arms and legs. Skull deformation was practiced among the Chinookans along the Columbia River and along the northern part of the Oregon coast, extending as far south as the Alsea and Siuslaw; there were also some groups that practiced this in the Willamette River Valley. The process included the use of a padded board or head presser over the infant's head in the cradle; this made for a broadened face as well as a sloping forehead. Only those of high rank could perform this head deformation; the practice was denied to those of slave status.

Masks

The only use of masks was as a disguise by a hunter wearing a deer head on his own head when approaching his prey.

Transitional Dress

Traditional clothing remained well into the nineteenth century, with the addition of traders' items, such as beads and cloth. But by mid-century the use of white garments was fairly general. About this time a Plains influence could be noticed, particularly in the adoption of porcupine quillwork and beadwork, which were used to embellish the garments of the well-to-do. Ceremonial costume continued well into the twentieth century, especially with feather headdresses; but with the Pan-Indian movement early in this century, the headdresses changed to the warbonnets of the Plains. Women continued to wear the basket cap well into the 1900s. Some commercial blankets were adopted in the late 1800s, especially plaid ones and those of the Pendleton Mills (after 1895), but they are seldom worn today.

Key Sources

Bakken, Lavola J. *Land of the Umpquas: Peaceful Indians of the West.* Grants Pass, OR, 1973.

Beckham, Stephen Dow. *The Indians of Western Oregon: This Land Was Theirs.* Coos Bay, OR: Arago Books, 1977.

Drucker, Philip. "Contributions to Alsea Ethnography." University of California *Publications in American Archaeology and Ethnology* 35(7): 81–101.

———. "The Tolowa and Their Southwest Oregon Kin." University of California *Publications in American Archaeology and Ethnology* 36(4): 221–299.

Gray, Dennis J. "The Takelma and Their Athapaskan Neighbors: A New Ethnographic Synthesis for the Upper Rogue River Area of Southwestern Oregon." University of Oregon *Anthropological Papers* 37.

Hall, Roberta L. *The Coquille Indians: Yesterday, Today and Tomorrow.* Lake Oswego, OR: Smith, Smith, and Smith Publishing, 1984.

Kendall, Daythal L. "Takelma." In *Handbook of North American Indians. Vol. 7: Northwest Coast.* Pp. 589–592. Washington: Smithsonian Institution.

Mackey, Harold. *The Kalapuyans: A Sourcebook on the Indians of the Willamette Valley.* Salem, OR, 1974.

Miller, Jay and William R. Seaburg. "Athapaskans of Southwestern Oregon." In *Handbook of North American Indians. Vol. 7: Northwest Coast.* Pp. 580–588. Washington: Smithsonian Institution.

Sauter, John and Bruce Johnson. *Tillamook Indians of the Oregon Coast.* Portland, OR: Binfords and Mort, 1974.

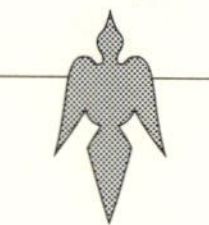

Seaburg, William and Jay Miller. "Tillamook." In *Handbook of North American Indians. Vol. 7: Northwest Coast.* Pp. 560–567. Washington: Smithsonian Institution.

Zenk, Henry B. "Alseans." In *Handbook of North American Indians. Vol. 7: Northwest Coast.* Pp. 568–571. Washington: Smithsonian Institution.

———. "Kalapuyans." In *Handbook of North American Indians. Vol. 7: Northwest Coast.* Pp. 547–553. Washington: Smithsonian Institution.

———. "Siuslawans and Coosans." In *Handbook of North American Indians. Vol. 7: Northwest Coast.* Pp. 572–579. Washington: Smithsonian Institution.

Puget Sound

Around Puget Sound and the Hood Canal there were many groups, many villages. The following peoples are listed by Ruby and Brown: Semiahmoo, Lummi, Nooksack, Samish, Swinomish, Skagit, Stillaguamish, Snohomish, Skykomish, Duwamish, Snoqualmie, Muckleshoot, Puyallup, Nisqually, Suquamish, Squaxin, Twana, and Chimakum. The Clallam of the Strait of Juan de Fuca are included here because of the similarity in customs and dress. Major languages are Lushootseed and Twana, both of the Salishan language family. The people lived along the rivers and the sound, a region of heavy rainfall and prodigious food resources; they fished for salmon and other fishes, hunted sea mammals on the coast and land mammals in the mountains, especially black-tailed deer and elk, and gathered berries and roots everywhere. They were a pale reflection of the dramatic cultures to the north of them. They followed the techniques of the Salish weavers and exhibited Plateau influences. Their first European contact was with Vancouver in 1792, with other trading ships soon following. Disintegration began in the 1840s with the arrival of missionaries and settlers. By the 1860s the acculturation was almost complete and by 1900 many of the tribelets or groups were extinct. Eells has been the most reliable and extensive source. Edward Curtis took the first photographs of the tattered remnants of these people.

Men's Basic Dress

Both sexes wore garments of cedar bark and occasionally buckskin, but the latter was not for everyday use because it was so unsuitable to the extremely wet climate. More of the buckskin was used for garments in the mountain areas. Men went naked in the summer or tied on an apron or breechclout of tanned leather or, in some areas, woven shredded cedar bark. In colder weather shirts of skin with long sleeves and underarm fringes were added, as well as skin leggings reaching from the thighs to where they were tied around the ankles. Where deerskin was unavailable, only robes were worn over the breechclouts of bark.

Women's Basic Dress

Women wore an apron or a knee-length skirt of shredded cedar bark, the strips of bark being strung on a cord and twined at the top. Some authorities record that a cedar-bark breechclout (apron?) was worn under the bark skirt. A cape of the same material was added when desired for warmth. For rougher work the women made skirts of cattails, and threw them away when the task was finished. Underhill mentions skirts of fringed wool, probably mountain-goat or "dog" hair. If their husbands hunted or if they lived upriver, the women wore buckskin wraparound skirts, tied around the waist and open at the side; some wore shirts or tunics and gartered knee-length leggings of buckskin.

Footwear

The Puget Sound people, especially those along the coast, went barefoot. Upriver or mountain people wore moccasins of elk skin or deerskin, simple affairs, one-piece with a seam up the front; a separate strip, often decorated with beads, was sewn over the seam. At times a flap was attached to form a cuff, which could be wrapped around the ankles in cold weather; for further warmth loose deer hair or fur lined the moccasins. Hunters in the mountains wore simple circular snowshoes with a loose thong webbing.

Outer Wear

Winter robes were of heavy bearskin or (most prized) sea-otter fur. Lighter weight mantles were of deerskin. A few rabbit skin robes were worn, made by cutting a pelt spirally into long strips that were dried and used

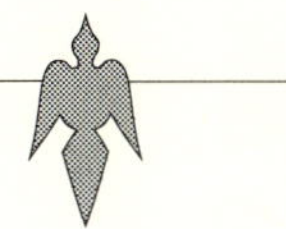

as weft in a simple cross weave. Bird skins were also cut in strips, dried, twisted, and used as weft for warm, light, but fragile robes. Other robes were of woven cedar bark or the pelts of small animals sewn together. Men occasionally wore rough ponchos of twined cattails. Many explorers and writers mention native garments of woven mountain-goat hair mixed with dog hair, which came from small dogs raised on islands (especially Tatoosh Island) in the Strait of Juan de Fuca; mixed with these fibers were duck down, fireweed, and other materials. Gustafson in her thoroughly researched work has suggested that these "dogs" were a breed of coyote. Robes made by the Salish weavers were a natural creamy white with occasional lines of color; they were either fastened with thongs at the neck and waist or were kept in place with blanket pins of wood or bone, often handsomely carved.

Hair Styles

Women never cut the hair, allowing it to hang loosely or braided into two or three plaits; some twined narrow strips of beaver fur or otter skin into the braids; others wrapped the braids with buckskin. Deer tallow was rubbed into the hair to make it smooth. Men also allowed the hair to grow long and let it hang loose, or braided it, or coiled it into a knot on the top of the head. Sometimes it was simply tied at the back with a buckskin thong. Curtis took a photograph of a young Twana boy with his hair loose except for a tiny braid at each side of the face. Some men wore a headband of tanned leather or fur to hold the hair in place. Hawk or eagle feathers were often tied into braids. Only a few sparse beards or mustaches were to be seen.

Headgear

Some women wore basketry hats that were high truncated cones with a flat top like those worn on the Plateau; others wore the shallow broad-brimmed type, more common among the Salish groups. Men went bareheaded, but in the winter both sexes wore caps of beaver, elk, or deer fur. The Lummi and the Skykomish men wore caps made of a young mountain-goat head with the ears and horns left intact; this was held in place with a chin strap.

Accessories

Most belts were of buckskin or of braided cedar bark; some wealthy men wore belts of sea-otter skin with the fur left on and lined with tanned leather. Garters were simple thongs or strips of deer or elk skin. Pouches were of leather also, with a drawstring at the top. Some flat bags were of twined or braided cedar bark.

Jewelry

Ear piercing was done at a special naming ceremony for the child. Square pieces of polished abalone and small rolls of native copper made popular earrings; the Lummi women wore distinctive earrings of a small, dangling metal cone. Aboriginal necklaces were of deer hooves, bird beaks, and animal teeth and claws. Dentalium shells were most favored ornaments, the cut and polished pieces appearing not only as earrings and necklaces but even formed into headbands and large breastplates. Bracelets were of carved mountain-goat horn or bone. Few, if any, labrets were worn. Only an occasional pierced nasal septum displayed a dentalium shell.

Armor

The peaceful peoples of Puget Sound wore no armor except for a tunic of doubled deer or elk skin. No helmets or shields were mentioned by authorities consulted.

Special Costumes

There were few manifestations of the dramatic ceremonialism of the northern tribes. Main events were the dances in quest of a personal guardian spirit, held during the winter. There were also secret societies, feasts and gift-giving, but not as extravagant as the potlatches of their northern neighbors. Some ceremonial headdresses were worn; most consisted of strands of mountain-goat wool or shredded cedar bark, human hair, and eagle feathers. A few spectators and participants wore Chilkat blankets.

Garment Decoration

Dentalium shells, feathers, and strips of otter fur were all popular forms of garment decoration. There was a little fringing on the buckskin clothing of the mountain peoples, and a small amount of beadwork. Cross weaves appeared in the rabbit- and bird-skin robes. Twining techniques were used in the making of the spruce-root basketry hats. Twill techniques were common in the making of the Salish robes or blankets. Besides the goat and dog hair indicated for the latter, milkweed fiber was often introduced. Salish women in the northern areas of Puget Sound used a spindle and whorl for spinning; to the south women spun fibers by rolling on the thigh. The loom consisted of two uprights with two roller bars, top and bottom, to form a continous warp.

Face and Body Embellishment

Painting was practiced, not only as protection for the face but as ornament, particularly for some of the secret-society dances, for which the face was painted in black streaks. Glittering powdered mica was often added to the paint. A rich vermilion paint was obtained by trade from lands east of the mountains. Many of the Puget Sound women were tattooed. Three vertical lines on the chin were displayed by some. More frequent were decorative tattoos on the lower arms and legs, with painted zigzag lines above and below the tattooed areas. Skull flattening was practiced around Puget Sound in general. The deformation was produced by the use of a padded board in the infant's cradle, which created a broadened face as well as a sloping forehead.

Transitional Dress

By 1860 the Indians of Puget Sound had almost all adopted European-style dress, except for some of the isolated mountain people. The men were wearing trousers, vests, hats, coats, cotton shirts, suspenders, and shoes and boots. Women wore long cotton dresses or cotton skirt/blouse combinations, with the addition of plaid or plain shawls and headscarves, tightly bound, of black or printed cotton. Braids were retained well into the twentieth century by both sexes. Ceremonial clothing was treasured and brought forth for special occasions. In the last few decades, there has been a revived interest in ceremonial dress and the reenactment of ancient traditional dances.

Key Sources

Curtis, Edward S. *The North American Indian.* Vol. 9. New York: Johnson Reprint Company, 1970.

Eells, Myron. *The Indians of Puget Sound: The Notebooks of Myron Eells.* George B. Castile, ed. Seattle: University of Washington Press, 1985.

———. "The Twana Indians of the Skokomish Reservation in Washington Territory." U.S. Geological and Geographical Survey of the Territories *Bulletin* 3(1): 57–114.

Emmons, Della G. *Leschi of the Nisquallies.* Minneapolis: Denison, 1965.

Gunther, Erna. "Klallam Ethnography." University of Washington *Publications in Anthropology* 1(5): 171–314. Seattle: University of Washington Press.

Haeberlin, Hermann K. and Erna Gunther. "The Indians of Puget Sound." University of Washington *Publications in Anthropology* 4(1): 1–83.

Heath, Joseph. *Memoirs of Nisqually.* Lucille McDonald, ed. Fairchild, WA: Ye Galleon Press, 1979.

Smith, Marian W. "The Coast Salish of Puget Sound." *American Anthropologist* 43(2): 197–211.

———. "The Puyallup/Nisqually." Columbia University *Contributions to Anthropology* 32.

Stern, Bernhard J. *The Lummi Indians of Northwest Washington.* New York: Columbia University Press, 1934.

Suttles, Wayne and Barbara Lane. "Southern Coast Salish." In *Handbook of North American Indians. Vol. 7: Northwest Coast.* Pp. 485–502. Washington: Smithsonian Institution.

Waterman, Thomas T. "Notes on the Ethnology of the Indians of Puget Sound." Museum of the American Indian *Indian Notes and Monographs. Miscellaneous Series* 9.

Quinault

The Quinault people lived along the Quinault River from the open shore of the Pacific to the foothills of the Olympic Mountains; with over 100 inches of rainfall a year, the area consisted of dense rain forest. They spoke Quinault, a branch of the Salishan language family, and belonged to a loose confederation of the Queet, the Hoh and the Quilleute. Their subsistence was based on the hunting of land and sea mammals, fishing, and gathering. Whaling was not so important as it was among the Makah to the north. Their first encounter with Europeans in 1775 was followed by many trading ships, and the Quinault were able to exchange their sea-otter furs and dried salmon for beads, blankets, and dentalium shells. After 1811 came the fur traders, followed by devastating epidemics in the 1830s and, by mid-century, missionaries and settlers. By 1890 their traditional culture was almost completely destroyed.

Men's Basic Dress

Men went naked in the summer; in the winter, despite the damp climate, which made the wearing of buckskin difficult, they wore a shirt of tanned deer or elk skin, sleeveless, seamed at the sides, and open down the front, where it was tied together with thongs. This hip-length garment was worn over a leather kilt to mid-thigh. For hunting in the mountains skin leggings and moccasins were added. These were undecorated.

Women's Basic Dress

In the summer the women wore a knee-length skirt of grass or shredded bark; this was made by taking the strands of shredded red-cedar bark or grass and weaving or sewing them into a belt that was tied at the back. Skirts were also made of long strands of cattail leaves looped over a belt of the same material and twined in place. A fringed skirt of deerskin may have been used, but that is not definitely established. The upper part of the body was left bare, except that a cape of shredded bark was sometimes added for warmth.

Footwear

Both sexes went barefoot throughout the year. However, men who went hunting in the mountains wore a crude type of moccasin made of the hock of the elk; the bend in the hock formed the heel, and the lower end was sewn together to make a toe. This "hock boot" was slit down the front to the instep, and several perforations made so it could be laced.

Outer Wear

Cloaks were made of sea-otter fur (the most cherished), deerskin, and the skins of small animals, such as marmot, weasel, and land otter, sewn with sinew to form robes; these robes were of various lengths from the waist to the ankles.

Some men wore a wildcat fur around the shoulders for warmth. Rabbit pelts were spirally cut into long strips that were twisted and dried and used as weft in making soft, warm robes. Bird skins, especially those of surf ducks, or scoters, were treated in the same way to make warm, luxuriant mantles. For the frequent rains, waterproof capes woven of cattail leaves, cedar-bark strands, or tule rushes were donned; these were thigh- or knee-length. They were conical or trapezoidal, with an opening made for the head; the neck opening and the lower edge were trimmed with fur or duck skin. The Quinault were said to have made wearing blankets from the wool of a small white dog kept for that purpose; these Salish blankets were woven on a "roller loom" with a continuous warp, creating a rectangular robe.

Hair Styles

Men wore the hair long and loose, tied with a thong in the back, or coiled in the back into a "club" that was wrapped with cord or cedar bark so it stuck out straight, a style termed "hair-in-a-bunch." Women also wore the hair long and loose or else formed it into two clubs or braids, worn forward over the shoulders. Baldness was unknown among these Indians until contact with whites and their hats. Eyebrows were plucked to a thin line and the men removed all facial hair.

Headgear

The Quinault basketry hats of twined spruce root were similar to those of neighboring groups; in fact, many were obtained in trade from them. A few men wore the Nootka "whaler's hat," with its tall, sloping brim, a knob on top, and whaling scenes painted on the brim. Both sexes wore the shallow-brimmed mushroom-shaped rain hat decorated with painted designs; attached to the inside of the hat was a twined skullcap with a braided edge to which chin ties could be attached. A third hat, which functioned as a sunshade, was similar to those of the Kwakiutl with its tall, sloping brim, made often of cedar bark in a checkerboard design. Nearly all these hats were decorated, either by woven-in figures such as birds, whales, and wolves or by painted designs in red, black, and white. Winter caps worn by the men consisted of the entire skin of small animals such as raccoon, mink, or land otter with the tail hanging down the back, and sometimes a visor attached. Both sexes throughout the year often wore a headband of bark, fur, or skin to keep the hair in place.

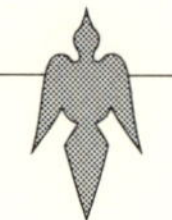

Accessories
Belts were made of plaited cedar bark or other grasses or of tanned leather. Pouches were also made of leather, often with a drawstring, to hold personal items such as fish hooks, painting material, or tobacco. Some bags were flat, woven of cedar bark in a twining technique, with a braided grass edging.

Jewelry
The Spaniards Heceta (also spelled Hezeta) and Bodega, who were the first European contacts (1775), reported that the Quinault women wore rings of native copper in the nasal septum, and wore many earrings. Dentalium shells, obtained from the Nootka of Vancouver Island, were worn as nose ornaments by the men and appeared in many necklaces, along with other shells such as abalone from the California coast. No labrets and few bracelets seem to have been worn. Later, the traders brought beads, which were added to the necklaces. They also brought metal, much coveted by the Quinault; one report told of a woman of high standing who wore a metal ax as a neck ornament.

Armor
When going into battle, the men wore long cloaks of tanned leather painted vividly with skulls representing their victims, symbols of their prowess. They also wore armor of tough elk skin or double layers of deerskin in the form of a sleeveless tunic or cuirass. A rod-and-slat armor of whalebone (baleen) or wood was occasionally worn in addition. Shields and helmets seem not to have been worn.

Special Costumes
Two types of ceremonies were observed: (1) gift-giving feasts, either local or intertribal, and (2) secret-society rituals in which the "Klokwalle" participants wore much shredded cedar bark and used mask disguises. During the dances the heads were sprinkled with duck, eagle, or goose down. The hair was cut as a symbol of mourning; the shorter the cut, the closer the wearer was to the deceased.

Garment Decoration
Little decoration was applied to garments. Painting, using hues of red, white, and black, could be seen on some hats and the warriors' cloaks. Weaving techniques consisted of twining (the spruce-root hats), cross weave (bird- and rabbit-skin robes, and cedar-bark rain hats), and some twilling (Salish "dog hair" blankets). Occasionally edges were trimmed with strips of fur or duck skin.

Face and Body Embellishment
Olson, in his excellent work on the Quinault, has given much information in this area. Both sexes painted the face, particularly for ceremonial occasions, with red being the most commonly used color, while warriors displayed black faces. A red ocher was found in the swamps; powdered charcoal mixed with seal or whale oil made a black paint, while white clay was also used in designs. Both sexes painted the part in the hair red. Men and women both bore tattooed designs on the chest, forearms, and lower legs. Skull deformation was considered a sign of good birth and was denied to orphans, slaves, and those of lowly birth. The process was similar to that used by the Chinook: a pad, filled with ashes or shredded cedar bark, was placed on the child's head in the cradle, the pressure tightened from time to time. This created a broadened face and a sloping forehead, considered great marks of beauty.

Masks
Masks are reported to have been worn for some of the secret-society dances, but they seem not to have endured in collections.

Transitional Dress
In the early nineteenth century the Quinault added buffalo robes to their traditional dress, acquired in trade from the tribes of the Lower Columbia River, who in turn got them from the Upper Columbia and the Plateau. By 1850, almost all traces of traditional dress had disappeared, except for occasional ceremonial attire.

Key Sources

Farrand, Livingston. "Traditions of the Quinault Indians." American Museum of Natural History *Memoirs* 4(3): 77–132.

Hadja, Yvonne. "Southwestern Coast Salish." In *Handbook of North American Indians. Vol. 7: Northwest Coast.* Pp. 503–517. Washington: Smithsonian Institution.

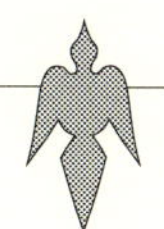

Olson, Ronald L. "The Quinault Indians." University of Washington *Publications in Anthropology* 6(1): 1–190. Seattle: University of Washington Press.

Willoughby, Charles C. "Indians of the Quinaielt Agency." Smithsonian Institution *Annual Reports,* 1889.

Tlingit

The northernmost groups of the Northwest Coast cultures were the Tlingit, the Haida, and the Tsimshian. The Tlingit lived along the southeast coast of Alaska, from Yakutat Bay to the Nass River. Inhabiting the rugged fjords and adjacent islands, they were seafarers and fishermen, making long sea voyages to trade copper, caribou skins obtained from the Athapaskans of the interior, sea-otter skins, and their famed Chilkat blankets for shell ornaments and slaves; as middlemen they supplied many of the coastal tribes with dentalium and abalone shells. Excellent entrepreneurs, they were wealthy people, exploiting to the full their abundant land and sea resources. Subsistence relied on roots and berries, salmon, sea mammals, shellfish, and land animals such as the mountain goat, black-tailed deer, and grizzly bear. They spoke a language remotely related to Eyak, which was of the Athapaskan linguistic family; their name in their language means "the people." The Eyak, neighbors to the north, were similar in customs and dress to the Tlingit. First European contact was with Chirikov, the Russian explorer, in 1741, followed by other Russian, British, and American traders. The Hudson's Bay Company, beginning in the 1830s, brought cloth, blankets, glass beads, dyed feathers, and mother-of-pearl buttons, all of which were added to Tlingit clothing and accessories. Despite frequent epidemics, the period of 1840 to 1867 was one of great prosperity for the Tlingit. But missionaries and Gold Rush miners and hangers-on devastated the native culture. Tomas de Suria, the artist with the Malaspina expedition of 1791, made many sketches of the Tlingit.

Men's Basic Dress

The men went naked in the summer or wore a skin breechclout. Having learned tailoring techniques from the Athapaskan tribes of the interior, for winter they wore skin trousers attached to moccasins, or some wore leggings of deer or caribou skin, fringed at the sides and bottoms, and decorated with several bands of porcupine quillwork and short fringes. A skin shirt with sleeves, fringed at the shoulders and the bottom edge, and often painted with heraldic animal designs, was additional attire. There were deer in the Tlingit area, but elk skin had to come in trade from the lower Columbia River and caribou from the interior. Some, especially chiefs, had shirts of sea-otter skins. From the early traders they acquired smocks, the type called "carter's smocks," which were often ornamented with ermine skins and eagle feathers.

Women's Basic Dress

In the summer women wore shredded cedar-bark skirts, with a cape added of the same material when

This Chilkat tunic, made in about 1910, is of mountain goat wool and cedar bark. Reserved for ceremonial use, its heraldic design echoes those of the five-sided blankets.

desired. They also wore, in cooler weather, one- or two-piece skirts of buckskin or a long-straight skin tunic belted at the waist.

Footwear

Usually the Tlingit, both men and women, went barefoot; even in the winter, they were able to walk in the snow without difficulty. But when traveling in the mountains, the men donned fur-lined moccasins, decorated with porcupine quills, later braid, ribbons, and cloth applique. For mountain trails, the simple snowshoes obtained from the Eyak, which had webbing only under the foot, sufficed, but those who traveled over the mountain passes into the interior wore the fine snowshoes made by the Athapaskans, sometimes adorned with woolen tassels. One Tlingit group, the Hoonah, attached spikes to their snowshoes to enable them to scramble after mountain goats.

Outer Wear

For daily wear in cool weather, men often wore a skin draped over one shoulder, while women wore capes of skin laced at the neck; these were undecorated. Larger robes were made of sea-otter furs (for chiefs), seals, and marmots, the skins neatly stitched together, sometimes with strips of swansdown sewn into the seams; bearskin robes for men were thigh length in front and longer in back. Some capes were of fur tied at the neck. Some wearing blankets were of soft twined cedar bark, frequently edged with fur. During the frequent rains, women wore capes of twined cedar bark, but the men relied on robes rather than capes.

Hair Styles

Women wore the hair parted in the center, shoulder length or longer, in braids or loose. Some, especially young girls, put the braid through a wooden ring at the nape of the neck, with the addition of two small braids, one at each side of the face. Another head ornament was made of rows of dentalium shells and beads, fastened over the braid in back, and at times extending almost to the ground. Men usually wore the hair loose to the shoulders and rubbed it well with bear grease, at times painting it red; some chiefs even added false hair to augment their own. Both sexes adorned the hair with feathers. Shamans, once they decided to become one, were forbidden to cut their hair or comb it, thereby presenting a wild, unkempt appearance.

Headgear

Twined spruce-root basketry hats were worn by Tlingits of both sexes. Some of these hats had designs woven in during the making, using dyed grasses and maidenhair-fern stems; a twilled self-pattern occasionally decorated the brim. Still others, for daily wear, had painted figures on the crown. These were shaped like those of the Kwakiutl—a high, sloping, wide brim with a flat crown. At times black and white beads outlined the edges of the brims and the crown. When "potlatch rings" were added to these hats, they became ceremonial wear. Some of the twined hats were more like shallow bowls in shape and had checkerboard weaving around the lower brim. Fur caps were worn in the winter, often using the entire head of an animal. A headdress was recorded in 1786 as consisting of a headband from which rose pointed "ears," one at each side, either real animal ears or simulated ones of fur or skin. Other headbands had a fringe all around, hanging over the eyes; it has been suggested that the fringe shaded the eyes from the glare of the sun or snow.

A nineteenth-century Tlingit Wolf Clan leader had this hat carved to represent the clan's power. Carved of yellow cedar and painted, the stylized wolf has shell eyes, copper lips and nostrils, and a fur tail. The six woven basketry rings may represent potlatches given by the owner.

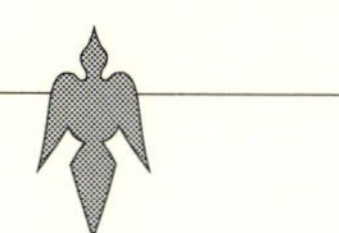

Accessories

Mittens for winter wear were of tanned leather trimmed with fur. Garters were of thongs or leather strips decorated with porcupine quills. Mountain-goat wool or shredded cedar bark was woven into belts, sashes, or backstraps, some with thongs on the ends for tying. At times, pieces of a Chilkat blanket were made into bags. Pouches for carrying personal items were also woven of wool or bark and adorned with quillwork. Some cases to hold ceremonial attire were made of a bear's intestines, cleaned, dried, slit into strips, and sewn together. Some men, particularly on ritual occasions, carried fans of eagle feathers.

Jewelry

Copper was the most common metal in use in early times for ornaments, which were often inlaid with abalone shell. Copper bracelets with the shell inlay and engraved with crest figures were highly popular; the same style was later used for silver bracelets crafted from American dollars. A few bracelets were carved of mountain-goat horn. Copper was also fashioned into anklets and into beads for necklaces and earrings. Iron, also acquired in trade from the interior tribes or from the traders, was used for beads and to make knives; Tlingit men customarily wore an iron knife in a leather sheath suspended at the neck. Charms might be made of carved ivory (from the Eskimos) or argillite (from the Haida), suspended on a neck thong or attached to clothing. Earlobes were pierced in several places for the insertion of ornaments of shell (especially abalone), shark teeth, animal claws, or, later, of silver and gold. Some men wore a ring in the pierced nasal septum. Labrets, circular pieces of wood or stone, such as serpentine, were worn only by women, and only by those of high status; the practice was obsolete by the 1850s.

Armor

Armor was of the wooden "rod-and-slat" type wrapped around the torso, with greaves of slats wrapped and tied around the lower leg. Atop the armor was a large wooden collar, with slits so that the wearer could see and breathe. Warriors also wore carved wooden helmets, visored and painted with a fierce scowling face (the ferocious face was a distinctive Tlingit characteristic); the helmet fitted closely over the eye area and the face was covered with a visor of bent wood, held in place by a loop of spruce root that the warrior clenched in his teeth. After armor was outmoded in the nineteenth century these helmets became clan hats for ceremonial use. Under the armor was worn a thick shirt of moose or elk skin, usually painted with the wearer's clan figure; this was worn without the armor when greater mobility was needed, or when the wearer was of minor social status.

Special Costumes

The wealth and artistic brilliance of the Tlingit were displayed in their rich ceremonial garb, which consisted of clan hats and headdresses, blankets, shirts and tunics, leggings, dance aprons, and the particular garb of the shamans. Basketry hats were finely woven of spruce root in the manner of everyday hats, but chiefs added at the top a number of basketry rings or cylinders, some banded with copper, each ring corresponding to a potlatch presented; these hats were often protected with an undecorated woven hat. Carved wooden hats (usually of red cedar) represented crest animals or figures such as a bear or a frog, often in a realistic manner; the eyes were sometimes inlaid with pieces of polished abalone shell and the teeth of opercula shells. These wooden hats were painted, using such colors as black, blue, and red, and some displayed the basketry "potlatch rings." Ermine skins or strands of human hair might erupt from the top. The major form of headdress was the "frontlet," a forehead mask of a carved and painted crest figure, with insets of teeth and eyes of abalone or copper, often with squarish pieces of abalone at the top and sides framing the face. Many ermine skins adorned the sides and were attached to a cloth or leather trailer down the back. Sea-lion whiskers stood upright around the top. The central face or figure was painted in red, blue-green, and black. The beautiful, magnificently woven Chilkat blanket was the core of Tlingit ceremonial garb, as it was with the Tsimshian, Haida, and Kwakiutl, and was widely traded all along the Northwest Coast. Forerunners of this blanket, as recorded by explorers such as Cook, were of various types—an undecorated cedar-bark blanket with a rounded lower edge, a bark blanket with decorative borders, and a blanket woven of bark and mountain-goat wool with figures painted on it; most of these early blankets had only geometric designs; some were edged with a fringe of black and yellow tassels. An early example had diving whales within rectangular "boxes." The true Chilkat blanket seems to have originated about 1825, possibly spurred on by the expansion of trade. It was named for a northern division of the Tlingit, who are said to have learned the techniques from the Tsimshian to the north of them. It was woven on a simple loom of two uprights and a cross beam from which the warp hung loosely; the twilled-twining technique was done with a warp of shredded cedar bark twisted with mountain-goat hair and the weft was of the goat hair alone. The woman worked from a pattern board painted by her husband, which was done in black and white and showed only a little over half of the design since it was bilaterally symmetrical; it was not necessary to show the colors for she followed traditional hue patterns. Colors were always (1) white, or the natural color of the goat hair; (2) black, dyed with mineral mud or a hemlock bark; (3) yellow, dyed with wolf moss; and (4) blue-green, from a dye made by steeping copper in urine. The weaver coiled the hanging warps into gut bags to keep them clean, for the weaving process took from six months to a year. The finished blanket was rectangular in shape with a rounded or a pointed lower edge, from which hung a long fringe, as much as 18 inches in length; the sides were also fringed. At the top were leather straps or loops through which the wearer could put his arms

Twined of mountain goat yarn and cedar bark fiber, this prized five-sided Chilkat blanket was collected on Douglas Island off Alaska's southwest coast in the late nineteenth century; the design is a highly stylized animal crest.

and thus hold the blanket in place. The design had three sections, incorporating highly stylized figures of animals, birds, and fish, with human-like faces. Because of the rounded forms, which are alien to weaving techniques, parts of the design were woven as separate panels, then sewed in place with sinew, the joining covered by a sort of false embroidery.

Toward the middle of the century, "button blankets" appeared, also reserved for ceremonial use. These were of stroud cloth or other heavy material such as Hudson's Bay blankets, usually dark blue, with a center applique of red felt or flannel delineating a crest figure; often a wide red border was added. The central design and border were outlined in white pearl buttons (earlier blankets used dentalia).

Ceremonial tunics or shirts, knee-length, were with or without sleeves. They were straight, unfitted, and with the wearer's clan crest on the front. Some were of painted hide, others in the Chilkat style, and still others in the button/applique form. They were embellished with strips of sea-otter fur at the side seams and around the cuffs and the neck, with shells, puffin beaks, ermine skins, quillwork, ribbons, teeth, and other objects. Some shirts displayed abstract foliate designs, showing eastern influence, occasionally mixed in with traditional crest designs. Leggings were in the Chilkat woven style (in fact, often they were pieces of old Chilkat blankets) or they were of tanned leather decorated with shells, beads, porcupine quillwork (also showing Athapaskan influence), or puffin beaks. Edgings were of fringes, often quill-wrapped, or strips of sea-otter fur. Dance aprons, worn by chiefs, shamans, or dancers, were like a Chilkat blanket in miniature, tied around the waist and extending to the knees, or worn as a cape; some were of painted skin with a long fringe. Ropes of twisted, shredded cedar bark were used as belts for dancing; a dance headband was made of twined cedar bark, dyed red. Dancers often wore collars or bibs with crest designs in the formline traditional style or in floral patterns. Shamans presented a wild, bizarre appearance with their uncut, tangled hair, painted faces, and headdresses of mountain-goat horns. They were usually bare chested, their lower bodies covered with dance aprons of painted hide or woven bark, decorated with shells, deer hooves, puffin beaks, and long fringes; in wild, gesticulating dances, with fringes whirling and beaks and hooves rattling and clacking, they awed the spectators. The down feathers of the eagle were a sacred part of the ritual as they floated in the air, released from the dancers' headdresses. A girl at puberty wore a large hood hung with tassels of dentalia to cover the eyes so she wouldn't look at the sky and bring on storms. Widows and mourners dressed in old clothes and cut or burned the hair off short.

Garment Decoration

There is almost a bewildering array of decorations found on Tlingit garments, the complexity probably due to their extensive trade network. Attached to garments were shell pendants, puffin beaks, ermine skins, strips of sea-otter fur, woolen tassels, and long fringes, often quill-wrapped. They used applique techniques, outlining figures with white buttons. They learned porcupine quillwork and beadwork, much of it in floral design style, from the eastern tribes. Employing the simplest of techniques, they used twining to produce their basketry hats, twilled-twining for the Chilkat blankets, and a simple cross weave for robes made of rabbit skin or bird skin. They painted their crest designs on their ceremonial garb; the most common colors of paint used were red, black, and green. In their art they stressed conventionalized forms, a horror of blank spaces, and the use of crest figures, particularly in ceremonial attire.

Face and Body Embellishment

Both sexes painted the face, usually in red and black, with rings around the eyes; the entire face was painted or only the lower or upper half. Black paint was made from charcoal and grease; red was cinnabar obtained in trade from California. Faces were painted as protection against cold, insects, or the glare of water when canoeing on the sea. Tattooing was practiced, but not as extensively as face painting. Women tattooed a few vertical lines on the chin; men sometimes had tattoos on the arms and breasts. Some men filed the teeth down to the gums with a piece of sandstone. Only the women wore labrets, made of wood, bone, or even ivory.

Masks

Shamans frequently wore portrait masks at rituals, carved of wood and painted in tones of red, black, and green; these were relatively realistic, with teeth of inlaid abalone or opercula shells, human hair, and, if a woman, a painted labret. Masks were not as widely used as by surrounding tribes because the Tlingit did not have secret societies. Some masks with mechanical contrivances may have come from the Kwakiutl.

Transitional Dress

Besides intertribal trade, the Tlingit early obtained European items from the traders, augmented by goods from the Hudson's Bay Company people after the 1830s. The Bay blankets became standards of value, acting as currency in the purchase of slaves, canoes, Chilkat blankets, and other items. Articles of European clothing were increasingly sought after, mixed with the Tlingit garments, until by 1885 practically all traces of aboriginal everyday dress had disappeared; however, traditional crest ornaments were still worn, and ceremonial attire was carefully treasured, brought out for the special occasions. Octopus bags, acquired from the interior tribes, became popular; called that because of the eight tabs at the bottom, in four pairs, they were beaded in exquisite floral designs. The Chilkat blankets continued to be created, although for a time they were less effective because of the introduction of commercial dyes and weaving shortcuts; but contemporary weavers have returned to traditional techniques and natural dyes. Cotton headscarves were commonly worn by the women early in this century. Also in the early 1900s a popular headdress was a stiff, wide, flat headband with hanging pendants of shells.

Key Sources

De Laguna, Frederica. "Tlingit." In *Handbook of North American Indians. Vol. 7: Northwest Coast.* Pp. 203–228. Washington: Smithsonian Institition.

———. "Under Mount Saint Elias: The History and Culture of the Yakutat Tlingit." 3 parts. Smithsonian *Contributions to Anthropology* 7.

Emmons, George T. "The Chilkat Blanket." American Museum of Natural History *Memoirs* 2.

———. "The Tlingit Indians." American Museum of Natural History *Memoirs* 70.

Henrikson, Steve. "Yeil Koowu: The Reemergence of Ravenstail Weaving on the Northwest Coast." *American Indian Art Magazine* 18(1): 58–67.

Jonaitis, Aldona. *Art of the Northern Tlingit.* Seattle: University of Washington Press, 1986.

Jones, Livingston F. *A Study of the Thlingits of Alaska.* New York: Fleming H. Revell, 1914. Reprinted 1970.

Kaiper, Dan and Nan Kaiper. *Tlingit: Their Art, Culture, and Legends.* Saanichten, British Columbia: Hancock House, 1978.

Kamenskii, Archimandrite Anatolii. *Tlingit Indians of Alaska.* Sergei Kan, transl. Fairbanks: University of Alaska Press, 1985.

Krause, Aurel. "The Tlingit Indians: Results of a Trip to the Northwest Coast of America and Bering Straits." Erna Gunther, transl. American Ethnological Society *Monographs* 26.

Rousso, Kathy. "Mother Robe Ends Journey." *Raven's Tail* 2(1). Juneau, AK: Ravenstail Weavers' Guild.

Samuel, Cheryl. *The Chilkat Dancing Blanket.* Seattle: Pacific Search Press, 1982.

———. *The Raven's Tail.* Vancouver: University of British Columbia Press, 1987.

Shotridge, Louis. "War Helmets and Clan Hats of the Tlingit Indians." University of Pennsylvania Museum *Journal* 10(1), 10(2): 43–48.

Tsimshian

The Tsimshian lived on the mainland between the Nass and Skeena rivers; their name means "people inside (or at) the Skeena River." They were much like the Tlingit and Haida in their material culture and rich ceremonialism, and in their class system of chiefs, commoners, and slaves. There were three divisions—the Tsimshian proper, the Niska, and the Gitksan; their language, Tsimshian, is unrelated to any other, so far as is known. Isolated in their heavily forested land and the precipitous slopes of the fjords, they depended for their subsistence on fishing (especially salmon and eulachon), the hunting of sea and land mammals, and gathering of roots and berries. First contact with Europeans was Caamano (1792), who left records of their culture. Fur traders followed, with the Hudson's Bay Company setting up a post in 1831. In 1857 William Duncan, an Anglican lay preacher, began missionary work leading in 1862 to the founding of Metlakatla, a "model Christian community." Other missionaries entered the field, seemingly succeeding in "civilizing" these people, but the resilient Tsimshian retained much of their traditional culture, with a thin veneer of white customs. Later in the century, canneries were established and a wage economy developed.

Men's Basic Dress

Men went naked in the summer or wore a skin breechclout. In cooler weather they donned skin clothing, consisting of a shirt and leggings, partially fitted, fastened with ties, and decorated in the Athapaskan fashion with fringes, paint, and porcupine quillwork. For traveling in brush, the men wore leggings of woven cedar bark.

Women's Basic Dress

Women wore an apron or skirt of shredded cedar bark or tanned leather in warm weather, adding when desired a poncho-like skin garment. Some, especially those living in the mountains, wore a somewhat fitted skin dress and knee-length leggings, with quillwork and fringes.

Footwear

Generally the Tsimshian went barefoot. Fine moccasins were of sealskin or bear hide, while lesser folk wrapped cedar-bark mats around the feet. Snowshoes, similar to the oval Athapaskan variety, were worn for winter travel and hunting.

Outer Wear

Blankets of woven yellow-cedar bark were worn, but the Tsimshian tended to rely on robes rather than bark garments for rainy weather; these were sometimes the complete hides of large animals such as deer, caribou, or moose, or small pelts such as marmots, raccoons, or the cherished sea otters (obtained from the Haida) sewn together. They also wove the famous Chilkat blanket of mountain-goat wool, but these were reserved for ceremonies.

Hair Styles

Both sexes wore the hair long; men left it loosely flowing or coiled it into a knot, while women usually wore a single braid down the back.

Headgear

Basketry hats of twined spruce root had wide, high, sloping brims and were typically unpainted, except

Tsimshian residents of the British Columbia coast wear ceremonial attire and display ceremonial items that include boxes, center, carved masks, and a painted drum, right. The children wear furs, and three men, center, wear Chilkat blankets and headdresses. Two women, seated right, wear button blankets and down in their hair.

for clan hats; however, the Tlingit women were not as adept in the craft, producing rather coarsely woven hats; their ceremonial clan hats were generally of Haida origin. Winter caps of fur were common in the mountains. A skin helmet is mentioned, which may or may not have been used as an adjunct to armor.

Accessories

Belts and packstraps were woven of shredded cedar bark or mountain-goat wool, or were of tanned leather; these were tied with thongs and were frequently ornamented with quillwork. Mittens for winter were like those of the interior—of tanned leather trimmed with fur and porcupine quillwork. Skin pouches were also trimmed with quillwork.

Jewelry

Both sexes had multiple perforations of the ear, the number based on rank, for the insertion of bone, shell, or copper ornaments; a piece of abalone shell dangling on a cord was a popular earring. A few men wore nose rings, but the custom was not common. Necklaces were made of dentalium shells from the south. Some charms were worn, made of polished bone and incised with bird or animal figures. Women wore elongated oval labrets made of stone (such as serpentine) or carved wood; temporary ones were of split cedar bark, inserted to save fine ones for special occasions. Labrets had disappeared by 1840.

Armor

Armor was fashioned from two or three layers of tough elk hide in a large, flat rectangle with an opening for the head; it was partially sewed together or tied on the sides.

Special Costumes

A ceremonious people, the Tsimshian had four societies, four dances, and many types of feasts or potlatches, at which guests assembled to witness (and validate) a house building, the naming of a child, a marriage, or a funeral. Their ritual attire was much like that of the Tlingit and Haida. They wore the "frontlet," a headdress carved of wood with a central image of a crest figure, ringed with pieces of abalone shell. Ermine skins were at the sides of the face and in rows across a long cloth trailer down the back. Above the headdress a circle of sea-lion or walrus whiskers stood erect. A distinctive Tsimshian feature was the addition of one or two rows of small carved faces around the large face; all faces had eyes and teeth of inlaid abalone shell. Wooden ceremonial crest hats were carved of wood, displaying the clan crest, and painted red, green, and black. Abalone inlays delineated teeth and eyes. Added to the top were "potlatch rings," each cylindrical basketry ring indicating a potlatch given by the wearer. Some leggings were made of cut-up pieces of Chilkat blankets. Others were of buckskin, adorned with bands of quillwork, puffin beaks, and strips of sea-otter fur. The Chilkat blanket was the core of the costume; woven of cedar bark and mountain-goat wool, it displayed the traditional, striking Northwest Coast designs of crest animals. Tsimshian blankets differed in having a straight edge instead of a curved one at the bottom and, often, braided tassels. These blankets were augmented, but not replaced, by the "button blankets," made of heavy cloth or trade blankets of dark blue with an appliqued design in the middle, outlined with white mother-of-pearl buttons; the central figure was often a depiction of the owner's guardian spirit. Unfitted tunics or shirts, with or without sleeves, were of painted hide, Chilkat-design weaving, or the button-applique style. Neck rings, in the early days of twisted iron, later of cedar bark, were of shredded strands wrapped around a central core, with added fringes of the bark. Dancing aprons, worn by shamans and dancers, were either miniature Chilkat blankets or were of deerskin embellished with deer claws, puffin beaks, rows of quillwork, and numerous other attachments. On his head the shaman wore a crown of grizzly-bear claws or mountain-goat horns on a leather base.

Garment Decoration

In their art the Tlingit used an abundance of human faces. Figures and faces were more significant as social rather than spiritual values, and were quite realistic. Weaving techniques consisted of plaiting, checkerboard, and twining. They made the Chilkat blanket, with some variations, and may have been the originators of it. From their Athapaskan neighbors over the mountains they learned porcupine quillwork and, later, beadwork in floral designs.

Face and Body Embellishment

Little if any face painting was practiced by the Tsimshian; tattooing, in the form of lineage crests, appeared only on the faces of wealthy women.

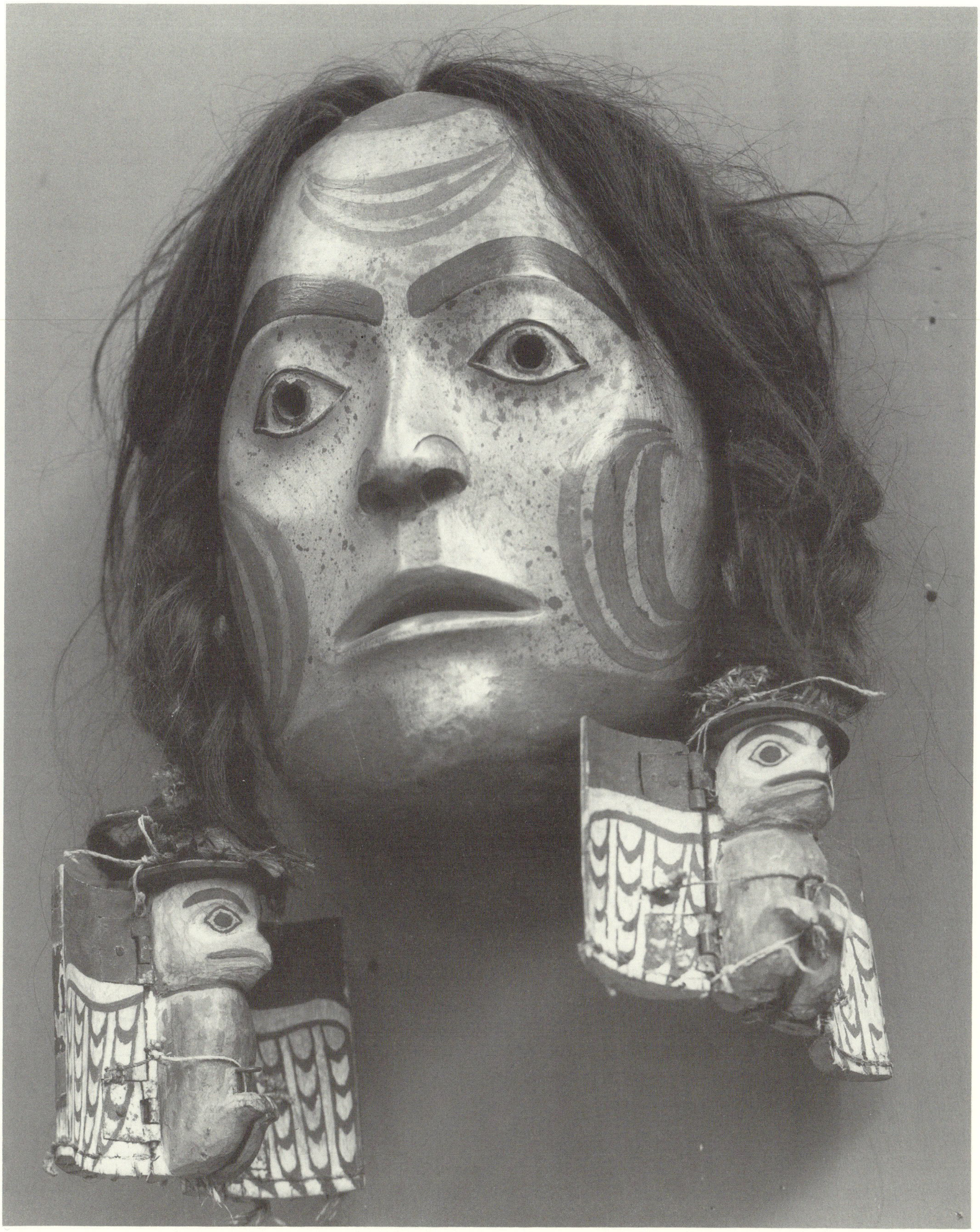

A wooden mask, carved to represent a young Tsimshian girl, is decorated with paint, hinged pendants, and braids of human hair. The mask, including the pendants, is 12 inches high and 8 inches wide.

Masks

Unlike the exaggerated excitement of the Kwakiutl masks, those of the Tsimshian had a lighter quality, were more realistic, and often were of human faces. Carved of wood and painted, they were somewhat flat and had no movable parts.

Transitional Dress

Because of the early appearance of explorers and traders, the Tsimshian early converted to European clothing, although it was often a strange, almost ludicrous combination of traditional and European garb. With the advent of the missionaries the transition was almost complete, and the men appeared in trousers, vests, coats, cotton shirts, and finally shoes. Women wore typical long dresses or blouse/skirt combinations, with cotton aprons. But the ceremonial costumes were retained and recent years have seen a stimulating revival of the Tsimshian arts of costume.

Key Sources

British Columbia Department of Education. *Tsimshian.* British Columbia Heritage Series 1. Our Native Peoples 6. Victoria, British Columbia: Don McDiarmid, Queen's Printer, 1952.

Garfield, Viola E. and Paul S. Wingert. *The Tsimshian Indians and Their Arts.* Seattle: University of Washington Press, 1966.

Halpin, Marjorie M. and Margaret Seguin. "Tsimshian Peoples: Southern Tsimshian, Coast Tsimshian, Nishga, and Gitskan." In *Handbook of North American Indians. Vol. 7: Northwest Coast.* Pp. 267–284. Washington: Smithsonian Institution.

Miller, Jay, and Carol M. Eastman, eds. *The Tsimshian and Their Neighbors of the North Pacific Coast.* Seattle: University of Washington Press, 1984.

Seguin, Margaret, ed. *The Tsimshian: Images of the Past, Views for the Present.* Vancouver: University of British Columbia Press, 1984.

Washington Coast

Along the Washington Coast in a narrow strip between the mountains and the sea lived numerous tribes with scores of dialects. The major groups, beginning on the Strait of Juan de Fuca, were: the Songish, Clallam, Makah, Ozette, Quileute, Hoh, Queets, Quinault, Humptulip, Wynooche, Satsop, Chehalis, Kwalhioqua, Chinook, and, along the north bank of the Columbia River, the Wahkiakum, Kathlamet, and Cowlitz peoples. (The Clallam are listed under Puget Sound, page 324; the Chinook and Quinault are treated in greater detail separately.) They were sea hunters for the most part; some, especially the Makah, were whalers. Fishing and gathering were also subsistence activities. Major languages were of the Shahaptian and Salishan linguistic families; despite the great diversity in dialects, there was a surprising similarity in their material cultures. First European contact for most of these tribes were the Spanish explorers Brunio Heceta and Bodega y Quadra (1775), who left fairly extensive records of lifeways. Other traders and trading posts followed; in the 1850s settlers began encroaching on the land, forcing the Indians into reservations by 1855. The rash of epidemics had decimated many of the tribes; further devastating effects were the attempts of the government to force these hunting, fishing, and gathering people to become farmers on land unsuitable to agriculture. Edward Curtis, early in this century, photographed and recorded much information on these groups.

Men's Basic Dress

The men wore little or nothing for every day; ponchos of twined cattails were added for wetter or cooler weather. Although occasionally skin ponchos were worn in winter, there was little use of skin garments because they were ineffective in the heavy rainfall of the coast.

Women's Basic Dress

Some of the women wore the skirt of strands of shredded cedar bark or cattails twined at the top and tied around the waist. To this was added a cape when desired, also of shredded cedar-bark strands twined at four- or five-inch intervals and tied at the neck.

Footwear

Most of these coast peoples went barefoot all year round; however, hunters in the mountains sometimes wore simple moccasins of leather or woven cedar bark wrapped around the feet.

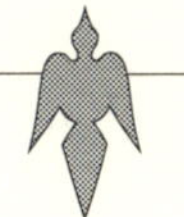

Outer Wear

Blankets were of woven cedar bark and sometimes of mountain-goat wool, which had to be obtained from the interior through trade. Some women along the northern coast wove blankets from the hair of a small "dog" kept for the purpose. (Gustafson, after careful research, suggests that they were rather a kind of coyote.) The hair was mixed with shredded cedar bark, and the blankets were usually white with occasional colored strands. Robes for chiefs were of luxurious sea-otter fur. Rabbit skin robes were made by some tribes, the pelts cut spirally into strips that were twisted, dried, and woven into warm robes.

Hair Styles

Both sexes allowed the hair to grow long. Men wore it loose or tied into a bunch at the back. Women wore the hair loose or in two braids or bunches, worn forward over the shoulders and often wrapped with skin. A headband of bark or skin kept the hair in place when desired. Men usually plucked the facial hair.

Headgear

The basketry hat, worn by both men and women, was woven of spruce root or, more commonly, shredded cedar bark in the shallow, domed shape common to the area. It was usually made with an inner hat attached at the brim, with a band inside at the crown to hold it snugly to the head. Typically these were undecorated and were beautiful in their simplicity. They were also efficent rain hats, further waterproofed by the application of boiled hemlock bark. Winter hats were of fur or bird skins.

Accessories

Belts were of tanned leather or braided cedar bark. Some bags or pouches were woven of the bark; a few were of deerskin, which were decorated with beadwork later in the nineteenth century.

Jewelry

Ear ornaments of shell, such as dentalia or abalone, or small rolls of copper were common. Necklaces were also of dentalia and abalone pendants, as well as other shells, beaver teeth, and bear claws. At first white contact both sexes wore nose rings of shell or copper, but the custom died out early in the nineteenth century. Later additions were the glass beads of the traders, most favored being the large blue ones.

Armor

Most warriors went into conflict naked or lightly dressed. A few, especially chiefs, might wear a cuirass of thick elk hide or slat armor made of wooden rods and slats or pieces of whalebone. Some mention is made of cedar shields among the Chehalis.

Special Costumes

Ceremonies were not as extensive as those of northern neighbors such as the Coast Salish and Kwakiutl, but there were a several ritual societies and some tribal and intertribal potlatches. The Quileute had a Black Face Society especially for warriors, at which were worn dancing skirts made of porcupine-wrapped thongs attached to a waistband of sea-otter skin; at the lower edge were deer-hoof tinklers. Some dancers wore head rings made of shredded cedar bark, extending in bunches at each side of the head. At puberty, a girl plucked her eyebrows to a thin line and braided the hair in two braids, weighted with stones at the end "to make them grow longer." Mourners cut the hair and painted the face with ocher.

Garment Decoration

Few weaving techniques were used except for the twining of hats and capes and some cross weaving for rabbit-skin robes. Garments were adorned with abalone pendants, dentalium shells, beaver teeth, deer hooves, and bear claws. Little painting was done on garments or accessories.

Face and Body Embellishment

Facial painting was practiced only during ceremonies, such as the Black Face Society of the Quileutes; the simple designs were done in black, red, and white. Both sexes tattooed the forearms and lower legs with lines of dots; only men were tattooed on the face. Infants of the wealthier classes had flattened heads, formed by pressing a board against the forehead of the baby in the cradle; slowly increasing pressure produced the desired effect of a sloping forehead and broad face. Paul Kane, the Canadian painter, has left us a painting of a Cowlitz woman showing the characteristic skull deformation.

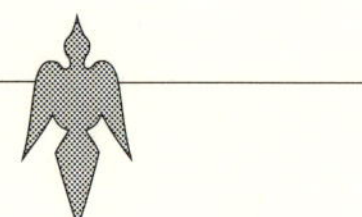

Masks

The only masks used were the wolf masks for the Klookwalli ceremony adapted from the Makah; these were really forehead masks that did not cover the face. They were carved from a solid piece of wood, and the lineaments of the wolf face were painted in red and black. Dances with these masks are still performed on the Washington coast today.

Transitional Dress

From 1800 to 1850 there was an increase in trade, and some of those of higher status were able to wear buffalo robes from the interior. By 1850 the traditional clothing was almost entirely replaced by European garb, the tribes of the coast effecting this transition more rapidly than those isolated in the mountains. By the end of the century buckskin clothing was used only on special occasions. A few ceremonial garments were kept and treasured, but many found their way into private and museum collections. There has been some attempt lately to return to traditional ways.

Key Sources

Curtis, Edward S. *The North American Indian.* Vol. 9. New York: Johnson Reprint Company, 1970.

Hajda, Yvonne. "Southwestern Coast Salish." In *Handbook of North American Indians. Vol. 7: Northwest Coast.* Pp. 503–517. Washington: Smithsonian Institution.

Krauss, Michael E. "Kwalhioqua and Clatskanie." In *Handbook of North American Indians. Vol. 7: Northwest Coast.* Pp. 530–532. Washington: Smithsonian Institution.

Pettitt, George A. "The Quileute of La Push, 1775–1945." University of California *Anthropological Records* 14(1).

Powell, James V. "Quileute." In *Handbook of North American Indians. Vol. 7: Northwest Coast.* Pp. 431–437. Washington: Smithsonian Institution.

Powell, James V. and Vickie Jensen. *Quileute: An Introduction to the Indians of La Push.* Seattle: University of Washington Press, 1976.

Chapter Nine

Costume of the Subarctic

Above, left: A Tahltan man wears a caribou skin shirt and glengarry-style fur hat.
Above: This Kutchin man's tunic has long points in front and back.
Left: The front of a Slavey-type moosehide tunic has an even hem and fringe. The yoke of the tunic (above, right) is fringed and has decorations on the shoulders and sleeves.

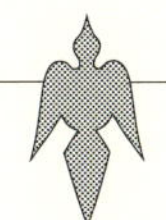

Subarctic

The Subarctic vastness fills Canada and the interior of Alaska with innumerable rivers, streams, lakes, and swamplands, truly a well-watered world, interspersed with coniferous forests, immense plains, enormous lakes like inland seas, and mountain peaks scraping the sky. There is the taiga of the north, the "land of little sticks," and the tundra, still farther north—windswept, rocky, and barren. It is a wilderness generally empty of human life but teeming with animal, fish, and bird life. It is a harsh land of long winters and short summers. The brief autumn and spring once virtually immobilized the native inhabitants, who depended on snowshoes and canoes for travel. Its northern boundary in general follows the tree line, the limit of the boreal forest, where the Eskimo world begins, with its ancient knowledge of adaptation to a treeless world of cold and ice.

Culturally, the region divided fairly readily into two parts. The inhabitants of the eastern Subarctic spoke Algonquian and were more influenced by the Woodland culture to the south than by the peoples to the west; theirs was a forest environment with little of the coastal element, for the Eskimo barred access to the sea in most places. The western Subarctic, from the Churchill River drainage and Hudson Bay to the interior of Alaska, was dominated by Athapaskan speakers, also called the Na-Dene people; the term *Athapaskan* came from a Cree word meaning "strangers." These western inhabitants were influenced by adjoining culture areas—the prairie Indians of central Canada took on many aspects of Plains life, those of British Columbia adopted some of the ways of the Northwest Coast peoples, and those of the north acquired a few Eskimo customs. In the east, moose and deer were basic to existence, in the central areas it was the buffalo and antelope, and in the north and west the caribou was dominant. Small bands

Peoples of the Subarctic

Ahtna
Algonquin
Bear Lake
Beaver
Beothuck, p. 349
Carrier, p. 351
Chilcotin
Chipewyan, p. 353
Dogrib
Eastern Cree, p. 355
Han
Hare
Ingalik, p. 357
Inland Tlingit
Kaska
Kolchan
Koyukon
Kutchin, p. 359
Métis, p. 363
Micmac, p. 364
Mississauga
Mistassini Cree
Montagnais/Naskapi, p. 367
Mountain
Nahani
Nipissing
Northern Ojibway
Rocky Cree, p. 376
Saulteaux
Sekani
Slavey, p. 369
Strongwood Cree, p. 376
Swampy Cree, p. 376
Tagish
Tahltan, p. 372
Tanaina, p. 374
Tanana
Tête de Boule Cree
Tsetsault
Tutchone
Western Cree, p. 376
Yellowknife

traveled in seasonal movements for food, dependent upon the fluctuation of the animal population, the availability of plant foods to be gathered, and the accessibility of fish. There is little information on primeval times in the Subarctic, but there seems to have been a long, slow continuity of culture. From about 9000 B.C. to the beginning of the Christian Era, "the people of the small knife" held sway; little has been found of them except for their tools of flint or other hard stones, and a few objects such as tubular beads of bone or stone, amulets shaped like beavers, and awls of bone, stone, and copper.

Contact with Europeans began with the explorations of Jacques Cartier in the east in 1535, but this contact had a profound effect, and the old material culture of the eastern Subarctic disappeared with astonishing rapidity. In 1650 the Hudson's Bay Company set up its first trading post "at the bottom of the bay" (Hudson Bay). There were many conflicts between the British and French fur traders, which continued until 1763 when New France was ceded to Great Britain. Then the Scottish traders, the "Montreal peddlers," established the Northwest Company, merging with the Hudson's Bay Company in 1821, creating a monopoly that continued to 1900.

Trapping for the fur traders led to settlements adjacent to the trading posts, with resultant diseases and alcoholism. Contact was rare in the west until Peter Pond entered the Mackenzie basin in 1778. By the middle of the nineteenth century missionaries and settlers had displaced the early trappers and traders. Next came treaties with the government and finally the reserves set aside for the Indians. These were usually established in the Indians' own territories, so there was not the difficulty of displacement and adjustment, as was experienced in the United States.

Concerning physical characteristics, these Indians were fairly uniform. Their hair was lank, black, and abundant, eyes were dark brown, and the skin was of various shades of coppery brown, depending upon exposure to the sun. Bodies were well proportioned but hands and feet were consistently smaller than those of the whites. Eastern Indians were of medium height, those of British Columbia tended to be short, and the men of the tribes north of the Plains were generally tall.

Since 1945 there has been an increase in government supervision, with added benefits in the areas of health and education. The native population has increased and subsistence has shifted to fishing instead of hunting, and to a wage economy with the whites. Native-clothing arts have continued, and have become a welcome source of income from tourists.

Subarctic Indians were painted by Paul Kane in the late 1840s and by Cornelius Krieghoff around 1850.

Regarding Subarctic clothing in general, because of the severe climate, skin and fur garments predominated; usually made of the hides of larger animals such as caribou, deer, elk, and occasionally moose, the hides were dehaired for summer wear. The garments were semitailored or fitted for greater warmth. The pelts of small animals were sewn together into robes. Clothing was decorated extensively with quillwork and beadwork. Clothing tended to be more elaborate from south to north.

General Dress

Men's Basic Dress

Aboriginally, men wore only a sleeveless shirt, poncho style, with the ends tucked between the legs and often laced together in lieu of a breechclout; some tribes seem not to have worn a breechclout until after European contact. When worn, the breechclout was of the fitted type with flaps in front and back. The basic garments for both sexes were essentially the same. A sleeved shirt, usually belted, was pointed at the bottom, front and rear, and often fringed; sleeves were frequently seamed in what we would term a "raglan" style. For winter wear, a trouser/moccasin was worn beneath the shirt; this was fastened with a drawstring around the waist. Frequently strips of quill or beadwork were attached below the knee area, around the ankles. Also, as protection aganst winter cold, two shirts were worn, the inner one with the fur turned inside, the outer one with the fur exposed; sometimes a woven rabbit-skin shirt was worn under the skin garment.

Women's Basic Dress

Women wore garments much like those of the men, but the leggings were generally shorter (knee-length) and the shirts were lengthened, some to mid-calf length, others even longer, particularly for winter wear; these usually lacked the pointed bottoms, typically cut straight across, and were sometimes longer in back. Dresses were adorned with strips of beadwork and fringes that were often beaded. The strap-and-sleeve dress was an early style found in the southern areas of the Subarctic. In some places pregnant women wore a strap of soft tanned caribou or moose skin to support the weight of the unborn child. Babies were either kept in a cradle or in a soft fur-lined skin bag, or were carried on the mother's back with the aid of a "baby belt."

Footwear

The prevailing type of moccasin in the Subarctic was a soft-sole one-piece style made of smoked moose hide, with a T-seam at the heel and a front seam to an insertion on the instep; this insertion, or vamp, was decorated with moose-hair embroidery in floral patterns or, later, beadwork. The vamp was edged with a piping of split bird quills or a coil of dyed horsehair. Leather cuffs were turned up and tied around the ankle with thongs. Later, the moccasins became what we would call "mukluks," worn by some of the northern tribes even before white contact; these were of caribou skin, often with the hair left on, and moose-skin soles that were crimped into the uppers. The tops, whether ankle-high or calf-high, were edged with beaver fur. Socks, pouches made in a foot form, were of caribou skin, twined rabbit skin, or knitted of grass or moose-hair yarn. Snowshoes were universally used throughout the Subarctic. They not only varied from tribe to tribe, especially in their embellishments, but even varied according to the type of snow encountered and the kind of activity involved. In general, the round "bearpaw" snowshoes were worn by women and children, or were made for temporary use. The eastern snowshoes tended to be broad, oval in shape, often with squarish toes; western snowshoes were typically longer, narrower, and had a right and a left. Some types were referred to as "swallowtail," others were "beavertail." The toes might be flat or upturned. A wooden frame (larch, willow, birch, or ash), bent into the desired shape, had toe and heel crossbars of wood or rawhide, and extra bars for strengthening. The foot netting was of twisted sinew or *babiche;* this *babiche* was made, preferably, of elk skin, although deer and caribou skin were also used. It was cut from the hide spirally in a long, thin cord. Great skill was required to cut the cord evenly, and because it was so well made by the Athapaskans, it was widely and eagerly sought as an item of trade. Some snowshoes were simply flat boards, cut in a rounded shape, and held to the foot with thongs. Hatt made a thorough study of snowshoes in 1915–1916.

A Yellowknife man and boy wear mittens, tanned leather shirts, leggings, and moccasins. The man drapes a caribou robe on his shoulders.

Outer Wear

The earliest outer garments were robes of buffalo, moose, or caribou hides, frequently painted with realistic scenes of conflict. Coats were more characteristic of the eastern Subarctic Indians, a fashion undoubtedly influenced by European men's garments, as can be seen by the front opening. The gored skirts of some of these coats, which were knee-length or longer, reflected the popular

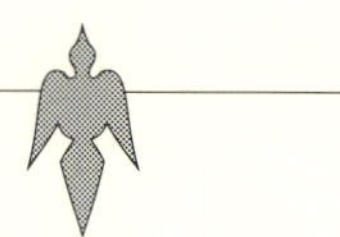

eighteenth-century skirted coat. These Subarctic coats were of skin (elk, moose, or deer) and were beautifully embroidered with moose hair, later silk thread. A second type of coat had straight sides, either made of cloth and finely embroidered, or made of blanket cloth in the *capote* style of the French *voyageur* garments. The *capote* featured a front opening; a long, pointed hood; and a long woven sash (the "Assomption" sash), which was wound several times about the waist and tied. A third type of wrap was the parka of the North, a hip-length shirt with an attached hood; this usually had a small front opening at the neck, and was slipped on over the head. Rabbit-skin robes were also worn, especially by women and children; the strips of rabbit fur were not woven in a cross-weave manner as was customary with tribes to the south, but were netted in a simple loop technique, similar to crocheting.

Hair Styles

Men wore the hair in a great variety of styles. In the northern prairies the roach was occasionally worn, usually accompanied by the scalplock in back. Some men braided the hair and colored it with red ocher. The women wore the hair loose, in two braids over the shoulders, or bound in a clump at the back, tied with a thong. Both sexes anointed the hair liberally with grease or oil.

Headgear

Winter hats were of rabbit skin or other furs. Sometimes separate hoods were worn, but generally hoods were attached to jackets or coats. Feather headdresses are mentioned briefly, but seem to have been confined to ceremonial costume. Occasionally one or two feathers were fastened in the hair, but they carried no particular significance.

Accessories

Arm and leg bands were skillfully woven of sinew interlaced with porcupine quills; since the trouser/moccasins were fastened to the belt, there was little need for garters, but decorative bands were often placed at the knees. Garters were worn when leggings were not attached to moccasins; these, too, were decorative bands of quillwork, beadwork, or embroidery. Mittens were necessary adjuncts to winter wear, either attached to the outer garment or on a cord strung through the sleeves so they would not be lost. They were of two types—a one-piece affair cut in a hand shape or a type with a sewn-in thumb; often of moose skin, mittens were embellished with embroidery or quillwork, and edged with beaver or other fur. Gloves were introduced by the whites, but they were not as warm as mittens, were more difficult to make, and could not be removed quickly. Carrying bags were of netted sinew or *babiche,* woven spruce roots, or the bladders, guts, and heads of animals; these were stitched with spruce root or sinew. The bags of netted *babiche* were adorned with quillwork, beadwork, and tassels of yarn. Later "octopus" bags came into fashion; these cloth bags had eight tabs at the bottom, ending in tassels, and were profusely embroidered or beaded in floral designs. Belts, typically of caribou skin, were also extensively decorated with quillwork or beadwork, commonly in diamond patterns. The Assomption sashes, finger-woven of yarn, were made by the eastern Indians beginning in the mid-eighteenth century and were widely traded. Every hunter wore a knife in a decorated sheath hanging on a thong at the neck. Children, at times continuing into adulthood, wore a bag containing the wearer's umbilical cord.

Jewelry

Beads for necklaces were of horn, soapstone, shell, and later of wampum from the Iroquois Indians. Buttons of pearl, brass, or shell were introduced in the nineteenth century; these were functional as well as ornamental. Some nose ornaments, such as pins or rings, were to be found among the western tribes, as were labrets. Native copper was fairly plentiful and was made into bracelets, earrings, and tinklers.

Armor

Armor was of doubled or tripled tough hide (moose, elk, or caribou); in some cases small pebbles fastened in place with pitch gave added protection. Western tribes also wore rod-and-slat armor.

Special Costumes

The Subarctic peoples had few special rituals, and their ceremonial costumes were generally an elaboration of everyday dress. Two rites were impotant to them. At puberty, a girl wore a menstrual hood of tanned leather, devised so others could not see her face; this

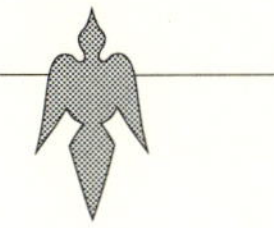

was often adorned with beadwork, quillwork, or fringes. As a sign of mourning, widows cut the hair, rubbed soot on the face, and wore special widow's ornaments around the neck.

Face and Body Embellishment

Face painting, rare in precontact days, commoner later, was more widely spread than tattooing, and was generally a male prerogative. Many vegetal and mineral sources were available, the most popular color being a bright red, probably obtained as vermilion from the traders. The face was frequently rubbed with grease for protection against sun glare, insects, and cold, and pigments were often added. Tattooing, especially by men, was more common in the west than the east, and was limited to a few lines on the cheeks. A few women of the western tribes had vertical lines tattooed on the chin.

Garment Decoration

The decoration of garments and accessories was done in the characteristic Indian style and with typical materials, such as paint, quills, fringes, and beads. Moose-hair embroidery on hide clothing looked much like quillwork with its geometric designs, until the floral forms, seemingly introduced by the French, took over. Much of this embroidery was actually of dyed horsehair, sold by the Hudson's Bay Company for that purpose; later, silk thread was commonly used. Quillwork, using porcupine or goose (or other bird) quills, was a difficult technique, either sewn by hand or done on a bow loom and applied to the tanned leather or cloth. Beadwork was predominantly of the floral type, typically done by couching, in which the beads were first strung on a sinew or thread, then caught down at short intervals with a second thread or sinew, a technique also called "overlay" or "spot stitch." Or a bow loom was used. Painting on hide featured figures of birds or animals as well as highly symbolic geometric designs.

Transitional Dress

Four hundred years of European contact in the eastern Subarctic (100 years in the west) have changed traditional ways radically, especially in the matter of clothing. Furs and skins have given way to woolen and cotton cloth. Characteristic shirts, trouser/moccasins, and jackets have been replaced by snowmobile suits with zippers, insulated boots, cloth trousers, and wool socks. The women have long been converted to cloth for dresses, and jeans instead of leggings. New materials such as silk thread, velvet, and satin ribbons have changed the nature of the clothing arts. Only moccasins, mittens, and mukluks are made in the old manner; they continue to be worn, but their sales are also an important source of family revenue.

Beothuck

In Newfoundland lived the mysterious Beothuck Indians. It is not known when or where they came from, and for a long time even their language was a puzzle, but it is now assumed it was Algonquian in origin. Their customs differed sharply from those of their neighbors, being more like those of the Dorset Eskimos. Cabot commented on the "redness" of the Beothucks. They are the original "red Indians" of British usage because they daubed their faces and bodies with red ocher, possibly to make themselves less conspicuous among their darker hued neighbors, perhaps as a form of tribal identity, or possibly simply as protection against mosquitos.

The French offered a bounty for Beothuck heads and the Micmac, with guns supplied by the French, hunted down the Beothuck relentlessly, driving the remnants of the tribe into the interior where subsistence was almost impossible. The last Beothuck, a woman named Shawnawdithit, died in 1829. Some of her people may have escaped across the strait to join the Montagnais of Labrador.

Men's Basic Dress

Summer wear for men was the breechclout of skin, augmented by a simple poncholike covering for protection from the sun and for added warmth. Leather leggings were also added for protection. These garments were of deer or caribou skin, displayed fringes as decorations, and were dyed red.

Women's Basic Dress

A drawing by Shawnawdithit shows a Beothuck woman wearing a skin skirt, mid-calf length, fringed at the bottom, and an overgarment, sort of a long, wide leather band with a deep fringe that extended well over the waist; it was tied on the right shoulder, passing under the left arm. Knee-length leggings completed the costume. Like Beothuck faces and bodies, these garments, too, were dyed with red ocher.

Footwear
Moccasins were of the one-piece Woodland type; one authority mentions a lacing, or it may have been thongs wrapped around an ankle cuff. Simply made snowshoes were worn by the hunters in the winter snows. Some socks were made of grass or fur, such as rabbit pelt.

Outer Wear
The most important item of clothing for both sexes was a cloak made of two caribou or deerskins sewn together, or it might be of otter, beaver, or other skins. Men wore the cloak off the right shoulder when hunting, to give greater freedom to the bow. Often the woman's robe had a hood added at the back for carrying an infant. At times separate sleeves were added. Some robes were fringed and had a large collar. Winter robes were worn with the fur inside, and the outer tanned surface was painted with red ocher mixed with grease or seal fat.

Hair Styles
Jacques Cartier (1534) said the Beothuck men wore the hair coiled into a knot on top, through which a wooden pin was inserted to hold it fast. Birds' feathers were often fastened into the coil. Women wore the hair loose as a rule. Both sexes painted the hair red.

Headgear
Fur or skin hats were worn in winter by the men. Women wore a hood, pointed at the back.

Accessories
Leather belts were used by the women to hold their robes or skirts in place. Men also wore belts to support leggings and breechclouts. Mittens of skin were necessary items in cold weather. A few pouches of skin carried equipment for sewing, or combs carved from antler bones.

Jewelry
Little is known about Beothuck ornaments. However, many bone pendants were found in ancient grave sites, delicately incised with geometric designs; they seem to have been pendants to be worn or to be attached to clothing.

Special Costumes
No mention is made of ceremonial dress, but it is known that the Beothucks had semiannual ceremonies at which certain initiates were painted with liberal quantities of red ocher.

Garment Decoration
Fringing and paint seem to have been the only means of decorating garments. No weaving techniques were recorded. They seem to have been too isolated to have adopted the beadwork of the whites.

Face and Body Embellishment
The Beothuck not only adorned their faces and bodies with red ocher mixed with grease, but also their hair, clothing, tools, corpses, and hunting equipment.

Transitional Dress
The Beothuck, forced to hide in the interior to avoid capture, were little influenced by the whites or by their neighbors, the Micmac; some who were captured and made slaves took on the dress of their captors. But the women clung to their red-dyed cloaks, wearing them over the European style clothing they had adopted.

Key Sources
Cormack, W. E. *Narrative of a Journey across the Island of Newfoundland in 1822.* F. A. Bruton, ed. London and New York: Longmans, Green, 1928.

Gatschet, Albert S. "The Beothuk Indians." American Philosophical Society *Proceedings* 22(120): 408–424; 23(123): 411–432; 28(132): 1–16.

Howley, James P. *The Beothucks or Red Indians: The Aboriginal Inhabitants of Newfoundland.* Toronto: Coles, 1980. Reprint of 1915 edition.

Lloyd, T. G. B. "On the 'Beothucs,' a Tribe of Red Indians, Supposed To Be Extinct, which Formerly Inhabited Newfoundland." *Journal of the Royal Anthropological Institute of Great Britain and Ireland* 4(1): 21–39.

Marshall, Ingebord. "A Study of Beothuk Decorated Bone Pieces." *Newfoundland Quarterly* 6(1): 17–25.
Reynolds, Barrie. "Beothuk." In *Handbook of North American Indians. Vol. 15: Northeast.* Pp. 101–108. Washington: Smithsonian Institution.
Rowe, Frederick W. *Extinction: The Beothuks of Newfoundland.* Toronto: McGraw-Hill Ryerson, 1977.
Speck, Frank G. "Beothuk and Micmac." Museum of the American Indian *Indian Notes and Monographs, Miscellaneous Series* 22.
Winter, Keith. *Shanaditti: The Last of the Beothuks.* North Vancouver, British Columbia: J. J. Douglas, 1975.

Carrier

The Carrier Indians, Athapaskan speakers and relatives of the Chilcotin, lived on the Upper Skeena and Fraser rivers. The name comes from a custom whereby a widow was required to carry on her back the ashes and bone fragments of her deceased husband for a mourning period of three years. Their name for themselves was Takulli—"people who go on the water." They hunted caribou, bears, beavers, marmots, rabbits, and moose, although there had been little hunting in the winter until they acquired snowshoes. Their main article of subsistence was the salmon, which furnished food as well as skins for clothing. They were much influenced by the Gitskans on the coast with whom they traded extensively despite the mountain barriers; from them they also acquired the potlatch custom and class ranking. First European contact was with Mackenzie in 1793. Thereafter the encroachment of whites—missionaries, miners, and settlers—eroded their culture.

Men's Basic Dress

Aboriginally, the men wore no breechclout, but wore leggings that left the genitals uncovered. Breechclouts of the Plains type were adopted in the early nineteenth century. In warm weather, the men frequently went naked. Thigh-length skin leggings, usually attached to moccasins, and a simple skin shirt laced at the shoulder were added when desired; most leggings were of moose or caribou skin, but some were made of salmon skin, which was neither as durable nor as soft as tanned leather. Tunics or shirts were cut straight across the bottom, unlike the pointed garments of their northern neighbors. Little decoration was applied except for short fringes.

Women's Basic Dress

Women wore a short kilt-type skirt to the knees of tanned leather (moose or caribou). Winter attire was of caribou skin—the usual Subarctic tunic and legging/moccasins. A skin apron is mentioned by some authorities, possibly worn under the tunic. The waist-tied upper garment was also made of the skins of smaller animals pieced together, sometimes of salmon skins. These were also cut straight across the bottom.

Footwear

Moccasins (also leggings) were rarely worn in the summer. In early times they were made of tanned elk or moose skins, untanned marmot skins, or salmon skins. These moccasins were the usual Athapaskan style—one-piece with a front seam from the toe to an inserted vamp, which was sometimes adorned with beadwork; edges were often pinked or scalloped. For winter, tall cuffs were added, which were then tied around the ankles with thongs. Grass was used for insulation in cold weather. The typical Athapaskan legging/moccasin garment was not worn much by these people. The Carriers were late in acquiring snowshoes; when they did, in the nineteenth century, they were the usual wooden frame with netted *babiche* in sections. The toes were often upturned with squared-off tips and rather long tails extended at the back. Women and children especially wore the bearpaw snowshoes.

Outer Wear

Robes were of the pelts of small animals pieced together, the most common animals being marmot, beaver, lynx, and muskrat. Rabbit-skin robes, woven of strips of rabbit fur, were worn by women and children. Women occasionally wore a short fur shoulder cape. One authority mentioned a man wearing a painted beaver robe.

Hair Styles

Women wore the hair loose or tied it in large loose knots over the ears, with braids gathered into the

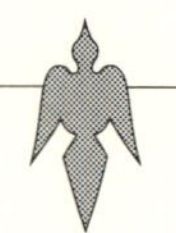

knots. Men wore the hair loose. Both sexes smeared the hair with fish oil.

Headgear

Winter caps were of marmot or rabbit fur. Otherwise, the Carrier went bareheaded.

Accessories

Some bags were made of salmon skins, when tanned leather was unavailable. Fire bags, carrying flint and tinder, were of skin with an "eared" top, a carrying cord, and tassels at the bottom. These were later beaded in floral designs. They were also used as shot pouches. Belts were of tanned leather or braided *babiche.* Skin mittens, with fur cuffs and beaded backs, were necessary for winter wear.

Jewelry

Bracelets were of wood, braided sinew, bone, horn, and copper. A few wore a dentalium ornament in the nasal septum. Stone or wooden labrets or lip plugs were displayed by the northern groups. Abalone shells were popular ear ornaments. Necklaces were of dentalium shells, copper tube beads, trader glass beads, and dyed, split, carved pieces of antler. The abalone, dentalia, and copper were all obtained in trade with the coastal Indians.

A drawing shows a Carrier wearing a wig which only men of high rank could wear at festal dances. The wig was made of ermine strips, dentalium shells, and strands of human hair.

Armor

Thick layers of moose hide made armor for the Carrier warriors. Oval shields were of wooden slats or of moose hide covered with tiny pebbles, fastened in place with pitch.

Special Costumes

Through trade with the coast the beautiful Chilkat blankets were acquired, treasured, and worn only by nobles for ceremonies that were adopted from the Gitksan and Tsimshian. Cedar-bark headbands and neck rings were also used for the rituals, which were similar to the potlatches of the coast but were not as extreme in the gift-giving. Some participants wore dance aprons embellished with thimble and deer-hoof tinklers. An unusual wig or headdress was worn only by those of high rank; it consisted of a netted cap with dentalium shells grouped in rows and long trains of twisted human hair. The top was decorated with bundles of sea-lion whiskers or strips of ermine fur. Shamans wore bear- or wolf-skin cloaks, necklaces of beaver teeth and grizzly bear claws, and a coronet of the same claws. During menstrual periods, adolescent girls wore a skin hood with long fringes to cover the face. Mourning was displayed with blackening of the face and a cutting of the hair.

Garment Decoration

Very little decoration appeared on early Carrier clothing except for fringes and, occasionally, the attaching of the claws and teeth of both caribou and beaver. The only weaving seems to have been the simple cross weave of rabbit-skin robes. Netting of snowshoes and braiding of sinew were the only other techniques used. Beadwork was a late addition, usually reserved for moccasin vamps or insets.

Face and Body Embellishment

This does not seem to have been important to the Carrier. Passing references are made to the smearing of the body with red ocher and some tattooing done with bone needles.

Masks

It is said that the shamans wore wooden face masks at the ceremonials.

Transitional Dress

The fur robes were replaced by Hudson's Bay Company blankets or by the *capotes,* the hooded jackets girdled with a woven sash, made from the blankets. Men wore fringed leather jackets, which were often purchased, then decorated with floral beadwork; instead of thin fringing, leather tabs appeared on sleeves and at the bottom of some jackets. Clothing was made of cotton cloth or blanket cloth, such as strouding. Printed cotton headscarves and neck scarves were commonly worn. Button blankets with appliques of family crests outlined in pearl buttons replaced the more expensive Chilkat blankets for ceremonials. Moccasins were made in a slip-on style, ankle-high, but still in the Athapaskan style of front seam and insert over the instep. Finally, mail-order clothing and shoes were worn by all the Carrier.

Key Sources

Goldman, Irving. "The Alkatcho Carrier of British Columbia." In *Acculturation in Seven Indian Tribes.* Ralph Linton, ed. Pp. 333–386. New York: Appleton.

Jenness, Diamond. "The Carrier Indians of the Bulkley River: Their Social and Religious Life." Bureau of American Ethnology *Anthropological Papers* 25, *Bulletin* 133.

Smith, Harlen F. "The Material Culture of the Carrier Indians." Canadian Ethnology Service Archives, MS 1192.2E2(B88-FS).

Tobey, Margaret L. "Carrier." In *Handbook of North American Indians. Vol. 6: Subarctic.* Pp. 413–432. Washington: Smithsonian Institution.

Chipewyan

The Chipewyan were the most numerous of the tribes in the area of the Great Lakes; their region was from Hudson Bay and the Churchill River drainage to the Great Slave Lake. The name was a Cree word for "people of the pointed skins," referring either to the men's pointed shirttails or to the manner in which they were said to have prepared beaver pelts. Besides the Chipewyan proper, there were the Yellowknives or Copper People, closely related to them in customs and costume; the Lakehead people north of Lake Athabasca; and the Athabascan band, which gave its name to the Athapaskan linguistic stock. The Chipewyan were not related to the Chippewa, who spoke Algonquian.

They lived on the edge of the barren grounds where the boreal forests give way to the tundra. Traveling in small family groups, they followed the migrations of the musk-ox, moose, and caribou. It was a hard life, especially for the women, who were perhaps the worst treated of any of the Athapaskan women; they were at the mercy of their husbands, and when food ran out, they were the first to go hungry. Winters were bitterly cold, summers short and plagued with clouds of mosquitos and black flies. Their culture was weak, with elements borrowed from the Cree; however, in their dress they adhered to Athapaskan garments and accessories.

There was contact with the fur traders when Fort Churchill was built on Hudson Bay in 1717; the tribe did not do much trapping because of the limited number of beavers in the area, but they acted as middlemen. The Cree, armed with guns purchased from the whites, pushed the Chipewyan westward. Smallpox almost destroyed them in 1781.

Men's Basic Dress

Men wore finely tanned skin clothes, usually of caribou, with the hair scraped off for summer wear but left on for winter garments, when the furred side was worn next to the skin. A breechclout with flaps at front and back was worn, often the only garment in summer; the flaps were sometimes worn outside the trousers. Skin trousers had a drawstring at the top or were tied to a belt; they were sometimes attached to moccasins, especially later. The shirt was mid-thigh in length and was belted singly or doubly; it was decorated on a yoke at the top and on the pointed bottom edges with fringes, ocher, quillwork (occasionally), and beadwork. Since it took 8 to 11 deer or caribou hides to make a complete outfit (shirt, trouser/leggings, moccasins, breechclout, robe, cap, and mittens), it took a good hunter to clothe himself and one or more wives to sew the garments.

Women's Basic Dress

Women wore a shirtlike garment similar to the men's, but it was longer, even to the ankles at times, and was belted at the waist; it was not pointed at the hemline, but it had the decorated yoke. Often it was made larger so a baby could be carried on the back next to the skin in the Eskimo fashion. Skin leggings were tied below the knees.

Footwear

Early moccasins were the typical Athapaskan type with an insert on the instep, which was plain for everyday usage but adorned with beadwork for dress; the "apron" or inset was usually bordered with a piping of horsehair wrapped with horsehair. These commonly had high ankle cuffs with thong ties.

Armed with a musket, a Chipewyan-Métis wears a smoked skin shirt decorated with fringes and red and black cloth epaulets. His leggings are fringed on the outer leg, and his moccasins have a black edged red cloth vamp. He has an Assomption sash around his waist in this 1862 watercolor.

Sometimes low moccasins were attached to leggings, but the legging/moccasins went out of style by the 1850s. Low moccasins alone were not worn until later in the nineteenth century. Caribou-skin boots with moose-skin soles were worn and the hair of moose or caribou was stuffed into the footwear for warmth, with additional pieces of leather for socks. Chipewyan snowshoes were made for right and left feet, with one straight side, an unusual shape. The frames of birch were steamed and bent into shape, and held in place with wooden crosspieces. Lacings were of *babiche* (thin strips of dehaired caribou skin) netted in a distinctive pattern. When traveling on fresh snow, a snowshoe with a rounder front was used, but when going on well-traveled trails, a small, slender shoe was substituted.

Outer Wear

Hooded and fur-trimmed parkas and robes of caribou were worn by both sexes; women and children wore the rabbit-skin garments woven of strips of rabbit fur cut spirally from the pelt; entire suits of rabbit-skin were made for children.

Hair Styles

Women wore the hair very long, a source of great pride; if a husband was jealous he cut her hair, a punishment much more severe than any bodily harm. Men wore the hair loose and flowing, or cut it in various styles. Unlike most American Indians, some men had bushy black beards, although most men plucked the facial hair.

Headgear

Headbands of fur or skin were popular. Some winter hats of fur were worn. Later in the nineteenth century appeared a "pill-box" style of hat, seemingly based on the Victorian "smoking cap": it was beaded or embroidered in a floral manner.

Accessories

Mittens of tanned moose or caribou skin were adorned with floral beadwork and were attached to a braided neck cord that passed through the sleeves; sometimes they were sewed directly to the sleeves. Pouches were made of *babiche* in an open-netting technique, bound at the top with a hide strip that was embellished with floral embroidery or beadwork;

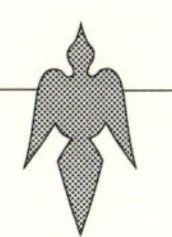

below this were several rows of wool-yarn tassels. Around the turn of the century tobacco pouches were popular, made of black velvet with a drawstring top and floral beadwork or embroidery on the front and back. Some bags were made from the skin of swan's feet or from a pelican's pouch. Belts were not only decorated with porcupine quills but also bird quills, the latter woven on a small loom, a weaving technique rarely found elsewhere except in northwestern Canada.

Jewelry
The Chipewyan seem not to have worn much jewelry; rather, they preferred to decorate their clothing with beads and dentalium shells, the latter considered extremely valuable and only available through trade.

Armor
The Chipewyan were said to have stripped down to breechclouts and moccasins for their attacks on Eskimos; also mentioned is the fact that when they went into battle they carried shields painted with symbols of their dreams or visions.

Special Costumes
The Chipewyan were involved in almost no ceremonialism and any special costuming was not considered. Widows cut off the hair and went into seclusion for a year.

Garment Decoration
The Chipewyan were not as practiced as the Slavey and other neighboring tribes in the decoration of garments, but they did engage in quillwork, fringing, and moose-hair embroidery. Since the acculturation process took place early, they developed an interest and skill in beadwork fairly early in the nineteenth century. There was almost no use of geometrical designs, but they focused on the floral patterns probably learned from the nuns in the mission schools. By the 1890s floral beadwork was widespread.

Face and Body Embellishment
Some tattooing was practised, but it was minor, mainly limited to straight lines on the cheeks and foreheads, said by Schoolcraft to have denoted the tribe or band to which the wearer belonged.

Masks
Ceremonial masks were not used by the Chipewyan, but they made a cap of the complete head of a caribou, wearing it as a sort of decoy when stalking their prey.

Transitional Dress
Although they were exposed earlier than most tribes to white contact because of their trading activities, little effect could be seen in their dress. They continued to wear the Athapaskan shirts and trouser/moccasins until late in the nineteenth century. Then there was a slow shift to white garments and shoes. Women wore cotton dresses and headscarves. Men adopted cloth neck scarves. But elaborately embroidered and beaded jackets and moccasins continued to be made, often for sale.

Key Sources

Birket-Smith, Kaj. "Contributions to Chipewyan Ethnology." *Report of the Fifth Thule Expedition, 1921–24* 6(3): 1–114.

Dempsey, Hugh. "The Chipewyan Indians." *Glenbow* 7(1).

Gillespie, Beryl C. "Yellowknife." In *Handbook of North American Indians. Vol. 6: Subarctic.* Pp. 285–290. Washington: Smithsonian Institution.

Smith, James G. E. "Chipewyan." In *Handbook of North American Indians. Vol. 6: Subarctic.* Pp. 271–284. Washington: Smithsonian Institution.

Eastern Cree

The Cree extended over a large area of Canada, from the eastern side of Hudson and James bays as far west as Alberta. They were generally divided into the Eastern Cree, the Western Cree, the Plains Cree (discussed in Chapter Three), and the Northern Ojibwa, their near kinsmen. The Eastern Cree may be divided further into the Eastern Main Cree, inhabiting the lowlands east of the bays; the Eastern Woods Cree of the boreal forests of Quebec, a group that included the Tête de Boule (Roundhead) Cree; the Eastern Swampy Cree; and the Moose Cree, the last two living near James Bay. All of these tribes spoke the Cree/Montagnais/Naskapi language, a division of Algonquian. They led a generally peaceful existence, except for raids by the Iroquois. Subsistence depended entirely on the products of their hunting, fishing and gathering. They did not practice any agriculture, living in a climate that would not support farming.

Men's Basic Dress

The Cree men wore a fitted skin breechclout with flaps and hip-length skin leggings, snugly fitted, fringed, and tasseled. Shirts were of dressed moose skin in the summer; for winter wear they were of beaver with the fur left on.

Women's Basic Dress

Women's calf-length dresses were of the strap-and-sleeve variety, having a flap about eight inches wide turned down at the top in front and back, and with detachable wrist-length sleeves that were sewed together below the elbow and were very large at the top; the dresses were held up by straps or thongs over the shoulders. For decoration, fringes and porcupine quillwork were common; frequently the lower part of the dress was painted, or a bottom edge stripe was sewn on. It was girded with a belt that was embellished with tassels and fastened behind. Knee-length leggings were gartered. When cloth, such as strouding, was acquired from the traders, garments were fashioned of that material but in the traditional style.

Footwear

Moccasins were of two types. One was of one piece of tanned leather with a front seam; the seam was often covered with a strip of quillwork. Embroidered, quilled, or beaded and fringed cuffs were frequently added. A second type was also made of one piece of skin but with an insert added over the instep, to which the toe skin was gathered. The vamps or inserts were often embroidered, quillworked, or beaded before they were added to the moccasin; these also had decorated cuffs. Tall moccasin cuffs for winter wear were folded around the lower legs and fastened with thongs. The snowshoe was most important to the Cree, for otherwise winter travel would have been impossible in the deep snows. Invented in the Old World, it spread widely across the North American regions. Beavertail snowshoes were used by the men when the snow was deep and powdery; the swallowtail was often used by both sexes when on the trail or when the snow was not too deep. Children generally wore the round bearpaw shoes. It was customary to decorate the snowshoes with colorful tassels, not only to delight the eye but to make them easier to find if lost in the snow. A Cree man used a balancing stick, held in both hands, when walking on snow; he also used a chest strap for pulling a toboggan.

Outer Wear

Aboriginally, fur robes were worn, with some use of rabbit-skin robes, woven in a netting technique rather than the usual cross weave. Some wore hooded parkas in the Eskimo style. Cree coats, worn by the men, were an artistic combination of white and Indian traditions, combining the style of the European coat with native tanned leather and using porcupine quillwork for decoration. In the middle 1700s smoked moose-hide coats featured the wide skirts of the European garments of the period; they had high collars, pinched waists, long sleeves, and, often, luxurious fringes. At times, trousers were made to match. Later coats were not as wide-skirted, but continued with the European front fastening and somewhat fitted style.

Hair Styles

Generally, both sexes wore the hair loose to the shoulders; however, some women tied the hair in back or fastened it in large "buns" over the ears. In this century, braids were adopted to some extent by both sexes.

Headgear

Caps of fur were winter wear. Women occasionally wore caps or peaked hoods of skin, tied at the neck and often decorated with moose-hair embroidery or quillwork; later they were made of wool with beadwork and ribbon adornment.

Accessories

Mittens of moose skin with quillwork or beadwork on the backs were often edged with fur. Garters were strips of quillwork or beadwork with thongs for tying. Bags made to carry shot were rounded at the bottom, square across the top, were fringed, and displayed

beadwork or embroidery in floral patterns. Powder was carried in carved antler horns. Drawstring bags were made of caribou fetus skins. Eastern Main Cree men had a special ceremonial cord of plaited caribou strips dyed red, with woolen tassels that hung from strands of seed beads; when wearing the cord while hunting geese, he had to catch a falling goose he had shot before it reached the ground, otherwise he could no longer wear the cord. Yarn tassels hung from leather belts.

Jewelry
Aside from a few necklaces of beads and/or shells worn by the women, the Cree did not wear much jewelry, but depended for adornment on their decorated garments.

Special Costumes
There was little concern with ritual or ceremony. Mourning was observed by a cutting of the hair, with much lamentation and some self-torture, such as the gashing of the arms or legs.

Garment Decoration
Cree women were highly skilled in porcupine quillwork achieved, in more contemporary times, on a bow loom; the designs were necessarily angular, and the results were used as strips to decorate garters and belts, and as panels on garments. Some authorities say designs were adopted from the birchbark biting patterns peculiar to the region. Finely sewn moose-hair embroidery was also expertly done; this was in the floral style, which led into the common use of beadwork. Painting on skin was another Cree craft; often repeat designs were made by stamping with small carved wooden stamps. Woolen tassels were frequent decorations.

Face and Body Embellishment
Like the neighboring Naskapi, but even more so, the Cree practiced tattooing, an unusual custom among the Algonquians; men were more extensively tattooed than the women, who limited their designs to a few lines on the face. There was some face painting with vermilion, white clay, and brown earth pigments.

Transitional Dress
With the early establishment of trading posts, particularly by the Hudson's Bay Company after 1670, the Eastern Cree acquired white goods, but used them in the traditional manner for costumes. Trade cloth replaced skin, beadwork was substituted for quillwork, and wool yarn was used for colorful tassels on garments. By 1900 the Cree had become accustomed to a wage economy and white goods, so that little remained of Cree dress. However, white garments such as jackets continued to be adorned with beadwork and tassels.

Key Sources

Burnham, Dorothy K. *To Please the Caribou: Painted Caribou-Skin Coats Worn by the Naskapi, Montagnais, and Cree Hunters of the Quebec-Labrador Peninsula.* Seattle: University of Washington Press, 1992.

Davidson, Daniel S. "Decorative Art of the Têtes de Boule of Quebec." *Indian Notes and Monographs* 10(9): 115–143.

———. "Notes on Tête de Boule Ethnology." *American Amthropologist* 30(1): 18–46.

McNulty, Gerard and Louis Gilbert. "Attikamet (Tête de Boule)." In *Handbook of North American Indians. Vol. 6: Subarctic.* Pp. 208–216. Washington: Smithsonian Institution.

Preston, Richard J. "East Main Cree." In *Handbook of North American Indians. Vol. 6: Subarctic.* Pp. 196–207. Washington: Smithsonian Institution.

Rogers, Edward S. *The Material Culture of the Mistassini.* National Museum of Canada Anthropological Series 80, Bulletin 218. Ottawa: National Museum of Canada.

Skinner, Alanson B. "Notes on the Eastern Cree and Northern Saulteaux." American Museum of Natural History *Anthropological Papers* 9(1).

Speck, Frank G. "Mistassini Notes." *Indian Notes* 7(4).

Ingalik

The Ingalik lived between the Yukon and Kuskokwim rivers of Alaska, an area rich in natural resources. With the neighboring Yupik (Southwestern Alaska) Eskimos, they intermarried, traded, used their language, and adopted some of their clothing styles. The name "Ingalik" seems to have come from

Russian traders who borrowed it from an Eskimo word meaning "having many nits (lice)," referring to the uncut hair styles of these people. They spoke the Ingalik dialect of Athapaskan. The Ingaliks traded many types of furs in exchange for sealskins, the hides of other sea mammals, squirrel skins, and dentalium shells. The annual life of seasonal migration was followed by small family groups—hunting, fishing, berry picking, and enduring hordes of insects in the summer. First major European contact, with the Russians in the 1830s, was vigorously resisted. The epidemics and the Gold Rush later in the century devastated the Ingalik culture. The major source for information on the Ingaliks is Cornelius Osgood, the anthropologist.

Men's Basic Dress

Men wore the characteristic Athapaskan shirt with the pointed hems front and back, usually of moose or caribou skin; a shoulder yoke was fringed and decorated with dentalia and quillwork. Typical of these northwestern Athapaskan shirts was a vertical line of decoration at the bottom of the pointed front. With the shirt they wore the trouser/moccasins combination with a drawstring at the top; these had strips of decoration down the front, around the knees, and just below the ankle. When fishing, men wore a lower garment of this type made of salmon or other fish skins.

Women's Basic Dress

The women's dress was almost identical to that of the men's shirt, but was longer, had a straight hem front and back, and lacked the vertical line of decoration at the front; in some areas a small fringed cape was worn instead of a shoulder yoke. They wore the footed trousers of caribou skin indoors, adding boots when they went outside.

Footwear

The trouser/moccasin combination was augmented by boots for outdoor activities. Men's boots of caribou skin were knee high; the soles were fashioned like mukluks, that is, the sole of dehaired skin was drawn up around the foot and gathered into the upper. The legs were of furred caribou skin. Women's boots were well above the knee in the front and sides, the back being lower for comfort. Boots were decorated with fur "mosaic," in the Eskimo manner—little pieces of fur of different colors sewn together into a patterned strip. Boots were also of salmon or other fish skins. Socks made of grass or inner caribou skin were worn by both sexes.

Outer Wear

Parkas, the hooded hip-length jackets, were of marten, summer-calf caribou, mountain-sheep, mink, hare, or muskrat skins. Typical decoration was of quillwork, fringes, and dentalia. Parkas for rainy weather were of seal or fish gut or of bird skins. Bears, although considered taboo by most of these Athapaskan tribes, were nevertheless made into robes by the Ingaliks.

Hair Styles

Little mention is made of Ingalik hair styles; one can only refer to the origin of their name and offer the suggestion that little was done with the hair.

Headgear

When parkas were not hooded, fur caps provided warmth in winter; these often showed a Russian influence with ear flaps to be pulled down in severe weather.

Accessories

Mittens of skin were adorned with quillwork, were heavily fringed, and were often edged with fur. The Russian Zagoskin in the 1830s collected gloves, but that seems to have been a temporary fashion. Pouches were made of leather, of fish skins, or of fur, and were frequently adorned with fur mosaic. Later bags, mostly for the tourist trade, featured limited beadwork. Belts were finger-woven of yarn, ending in fringes. Some pouches for carrying or storage were made of twined grass.

Jewelry

Little information can be found about jewelry. The use of labrets on masks would seem to indicate it was a custom in earlier days; male masks indicate labrets at both corners of the mouth. Because of their fondness for dentalia, ornaments may have been made of them.

Special Costumes

The Ingaliks had many ceremonies, most of them involving feasts and gift-giving, but they seem not to have involved special costumes, only the use of masks. At her menarche, a girl was isolated from her group for an entire year, wore a forehead band to which bear claws were attached, and donned the typical Athapaskan puberty hood of skin, which could be tied to cover her face from the gaze of others.

Garment Decoration

Beads were available early to the Ingaliks, but they seem to have been reserved for trading rather than beadwork. They were more influenced by their Eskimo neighbors, preferring to decorate their garments with fur, especially with the fur-mosaic technique in which small pieces of contrasting colors of fur were sewn together into patterns. The Eskimo garments of fur and gut that they copied did not lend themselves to quillwork or beadwork. Some overlay-stitch beadwork began to be produced in the late nineteenth century, but it seems to have been predominantly for the tourist trade rather than for wear. The only weaving appears to have been the making of the rabbit-skin robes in a looping technique rather than a cross weave.

Face and Body Embellishment

A few tattooed marks, particularly on the cheeks and chin, were limited to women.

Masks

Some Ingalik wooden masks have been preserved, considered unusual because masks are rare among the Athapaskans. Male masks show labrets at the sides of the mouth, while female masks often have a bead nose ornament and tattooed chin lines. Masks are very much in the Eskimo style.

Transitional Dress

By 1880 what little Athapaskan dress was worn was nearly lost between the influence of European-style dress and the tendency of the Ingaliks to adopt Eskimo clothing, especially for winter wear.

Key Sources

Hasley, Edward H. "The McGrath Ingalik." University of Alaska *Anthropological Papers* 9(2).

Osgood, Cornelius. *Ingalik Material Culture.* New Haven, CT: Human Relations Area Files Press, 1970. Reprint of 1940 edition.

Snow, Jeanne H. "Ingalik." In *Handbook of North American Indians. Vol. 6: Subarctic.* Pp. 602–617. Washington: Smithsonian Institution.

VanStone, James W. "Ingalik Contact Ecology: An Ethnohistory of the Lower Middle Yukon, 1790–1935." *Fieldiana: Anthropology* 71.

Kutchin

The Kutchins lived between the headwaters of the Yukon River and the lower Mackenzie River. Like the Hans, their neighbors, they were transitional between the Lake Athapaskans and those of the central Alaska region. The term "Kutchin" is equivalent to the word "dene" or "tinne," as used by most Athapaskans to designate themselves ("people"). The early French-Canadian *voyageurs* called them "Loucheux," meaning "squinty-eyed," a term that applies to the eastern Kutchins. They thought of themselves as "people of the deer," hunting especially the Barren Ground and woodland caribou. Their language, Kutchin, was a dialect of Athapaskan. They fought and traded with the Eskimos to the north and the Tlingit to the south, both of which groups influenced their dress. Earliest European contact was with Alexander Mackenzie in 1789. However, from the standpoint of costume, we are particularly indebted to Alexander Hunter Murray who traveled among the Kutchins in 1847–1848, leaving extensive notes and drawings detailing their precontact dress. With the influence of the Northwest Coast Indians through trade, they had a strong caste system featuring potlatches and similar ceremonies. A vital, independent people, they evidenced a love for excitement and exhibited a proud bearing.

Men's Basic Dress

Kutchin tailored clothing of finely tanned white caribou skin was of the Athapaskan type, heavily decorated with fringes, porcupine quillwork, *Elaeagnus* seeds, and dentalium shells. The man's shirt was short-waisted with long tails back and front ending in V-shapes; a shoulder yoke was edged with strips of dentalia or quillwork and skin or beaded fringes, as was the hem. The shirt was girded with a thong at the waist. A characteristic addition was the vertical line of decoration at the lower center front of the shirt. With this were worn trousers of caribou skin, held in place by a drawstring at the top; they featured a diamond-shaped gusset in the crotch and were attached to feet of moose skin. Footless trousers were worn with soft-soled moccasins. The trousers were embellished with porcupine quillwork, the most popular design being red and white squares in a strip. The strips were applied down the front of the trousers, around the knees, and at the ankles.

Women's Basic Dress

Women wore the same tunic as the men, but with some differences. It was cut straight across the front, above the knees, but with the long V-shaped dip in back. Generally it did not have the vertical decorative line in the front. It was girded with a thong at the waist and had the typical three–quarter-length sleeves. In the nineteenth century, a short cape, tied at the neck, was substituted for the yoke. Some women wore a shirt enlarged at the rear in order to carry an infant. The footed trousers, like the upper garment, were not as heavily ornamented with quillwork and dentalia as were the men's garments; however, women's garments were painted with red ocher along the seams. Both sexes wore winter garments with the fur left on and turned inside; over this might be worn garments with the fur outside.

Footwear

Moccasins, when worn with footless trousers, were the usual Athapaskan type—one-piece with a front center seam and a U-shaped insert over the instep; these moccasins either had a small cuff or a high cuff with ankle wraps of thong or hide strips. Edges were often scalloped or pinked. Later moccasins were more in the mukluk style of a seamless bottom unit gathered into an insert and a T-shaped seam at the heel. Snowshoes were highly important to the Kutchins living in timbered areas with fairly deep, close-packed snow. The long narrow frame was of willow or birch with a rounded, slightly upturned toe and a lacing of *babiche;* the snowshoes came in three sizes: (1) the largest, six to eight feet long, for moose hunting; (2) a trail snowshoe, averaging four or five feet; and (3) a small traveling shoe. They were made for right and left feet, and were often decorated with red wool tassels.

Outer Wear

A robe of caribou with the fur left on was worn in cold weather and was tied at the front with thongs. Rabbit-skin robes were worn by adults until 1840; after that, only small children or infants were dressed in the warm but fragile robes.

Hair Styles

Men wore the hair long, frequently gathered in a sort of ring at the nape of the neck; for special occasions it was well greased, painted with red ocher, covered with bird down, and often ornamented with inserted feathers. Women parted the hair in the center and brought part of it forward in two bundles that were fastened with a fur band or a string of shells; the back part was also gathered into a ring like those worn by the men. Both sexes wore a headband over the top of the head, tied at the back beneath the ring; these bands were embellished with quillwork or dentalium shells.

Headgear

Besides the headband mentioned above, the only other form of headgear was a caribou-skin hood for winter wear, with the fur inside, and decorated with fringes and quillwork or dentalia; the hood might be attached to the jacket or worn separately, and was tied on with thongs. Fur caps were also worn in winter.

Accessories

From the belt or around the neck hung a small skin bag that contained fire stones, charms, and other items. A knife sheath, usually worn around the neck, held the typical Kutchin volute or fork-handled knife; early knives were of copper. Mittens were attached to a neck cord in the Eskimo fashion, decorated with fringes and quillwork, and often painted with red ocher; they were longer than most Athapaskan mittens in order to cover the short sleeves of both sexes. Belts and garters were fringed and adorned with quillwork, dentalia, and *Elaeagnus* seeds. Game bags and smaller bags were of moose hide with a netting of *babiche* below. A shoulder strap of caribou skin, beaded and with tassels, and often called a "baby band," was used to support a baby carried in a blanket.

Jewelry

Women wore round nose ornaments of stone, wood, or shell; men had bone skewers or strings of shells

A Kutchin man at Fort Yukon in the Northwest Territories between 1877 and 1880 wears an Athapaskan tunic with long, fringed points front and back. The front point is decorated with a narrow vertical strip. His footed trousers, gartered at his knees, have beaded strips down their fronts, and he has a beaded or appliquéd bandolier bag around his neck.

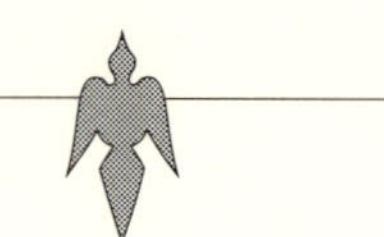

thrust through the nasal septum. Earrings, necklaces, and hair ornaments were usually of dentalium shells, so popular among the Kutchin.

Armor

Although war honors were mentioned by authorities consulted, armor was not. If worn, it would have been of layers of caribou hide laced together with thongs, a form characteristic of the Athapaskans.

Special Costumes

There were few ceremonies among the Kutchins —memorial potlatches and other feasts and dances in certain seasons; these did not involve special costumes, only the usual elaborate dress of these people. Mourning customs involved the cutting of the hair and the blackening of the face. A young girl at her first menstrual period was isolated from the group and made to wear a hood that covered the face so she could only see her feet; her gaze was deemed fearful, especially to hunters. The hood was edged with dried deer hooves that rattled as she moved and thus warned others of her approach.

Garment Decoration

Elaeagnus, oleaster, and other seeds were used for decoration in early times. Dentalium shells were the most common, almost the only, shells used by the Kutchins for garment decoration. Fringes, both of quill-wrapped skin and of strings of beads, were fastened to most articles of clothing. Quillwork (and some beadwork) in geometric designs was fairly common until the mid-nineteenth century, at which time there was a shift to the use of floral patterned beadwork. Garments, particularly along the seams, were painted with red ocher, probably hematite.

Face and Body Embellishment

Tattooing was considered a form of beautification for the women; it was created with soot and was typically applied in five radiating lines from the lips to the chin. Occasionally one vertical line adorned the forehead with four vertical lines on each side of the cheeks. Men were seldom tattooed except as an indication of war honors. Red ocher and black charcoal were used as facial paint, especially by the men.

Transitional Dress

As was true of the Athapaskan tribes throughout western Canada, the Kutchin culture changed due to the effects of epidemics, missionaries, gold miners, town life, and government involvement, but they retained some of their traditional dress blended with modern styles. During the early years of this century a pillbox-style "smoking hat," beaded and tasseled, was worn by the men. Women wore, and still wear, woolen shawls and cotton headscarves; they continue to use the "baby belt," embellished with loom-woven seed beads in floral patterns and silk tassels; this was slung over the shoulders to aid in carrying a baby. Men still hunt and fish, but with snowmobiles and outboard motors, and for dress they wear front-closing jackets heavily adorned with floral beadwork strips, fur, and tassels. Moccasins are worn and made today, generally for the tourist trade; they are round-toed slip-ons beaded all over, particularly with metal beads.

Key Sources

Cadzow, Donald A. "Old Loucheux Clothing." *Indian Notes* 2(4): 292–295.

Duncan, Kate C., *Northern Athapascan Art: A Beadwork Tradition.* Seattle: University of Washington Press, 1989.

———. "Yukon River Athapaskan Costume in the 1860s: Contributions of the Ethnographic Illustrations of William Dall." In *Faces, Voices and Dreams: A Celebration of the Sheldon Jackson Museum Centennial.* Seattle: University of Washington Press, 1987.

Duncan, Kate C. and Eunice Carney. *A Special Gift: The Kutchin Beadwork Tradition.* Seattle: University of Washington Press, 1988.

Leechman, Douglas. "The Vanta Kutchin." National Museum of Canada *Bulletin* 130, Anthropological Series 33.

McKennan, Robert A. *The Chandalar Kutchin.* Arctic Institute of North America *Technical Paper* 17. Montreal, 1965.

Murray, Alexander H. "Journal of the Yukon, 1847–1848." Canadian Archives Publications 4: 1–125. Ottawa, 1910.

Osgood, Cornelius. "Contributions to the Ethnography of the Kutchin." Yale University *Publications in Anthropology* 14: 1–189.

Slobodin, Richard. "Kutchin." In *Handbook of North American Indians. Vol. 6: Subarctic.* Pp. 514–532. Washington: Smithsonian Institution.

Thompson, Judy. *Preliminary Study of Traditional Kutchin Clothing in Museums.* Mercury Series, Ethnology Service Paper 1. Ottawa, Canada: National Museum of Man, 1972.

———. *Pride of the Indian Wardrobe: Northern Athapaskan Footwear.* Published for the Bata Shoe Museum. Toronto: University of Toronto Press, 1990.

Métis

The Métis were "mixed-bloods." The Southern Métis were the offspring of the French *coureurs de bois* and Ojibway or Cree women; they were typically Catholic and lived in and around the Red River Valley. The Northern Métis, in the vicinity of the Saskatchewan River, were the offspring of Scottish and English traders and Athapaskan women and usually followed the Anglican religion. The Métis, workers in the fur trade and transport systems as interpreters, guides, and intermediaries, were bilingual; the men, especially, traveled widely. Socially marginal, they have been the object of some bigotry in Canada.

It is difficult to approach the subject of Métis costume in the same manner as that of other tribes since, by definition, they are postcontact and have thus worn transitional dress, having adopted the garb of the fur traders and others in the field. However, there are some indications to be given, especially for the eighteenth and nineteenth centuries.

Men's Basic Dress

The men wore colorful cloth garments. Especially popular were the long coats, similar to those of the Cree, with native and European elements combined. They had a front opening and were heavily fringed—at the bottom, at the shoulders, at the lapels, and above a pleat at the lower back; decorations were of porcupine quillwork, moose-hair embroidery, and beadwork, much of it in the double-curve motif. Around the waist was worn the "Assomption" or "arrow-point" sash. With these coats, the men wore "half-leggings," leather rectangles, cloth-lined, which were rolled around the lower leg and gartered at the knee; they served to protect the expensive cloth trousers from rough use. Vests, of European cut but heavily beaded in the floral style, were commonly worn.

Women's Basic Dress

The women wore the dress of the tribes among which they lived—Cree, Northern Ojibway, or Athapaskan.

The back of this tanned leather Métis or Plains Cree man's frock coat, modeled after white attire of the mid-nineteenth century, has quill embroidery and fringe at the shoulders, hem, and back pleat.

Footwear
The moccasin was the typical one of the Subarctic—a front seam to a U-shaped insert that was decorated with floral beadwork, quillwork, or embroidery. High cuffs were fastened with thongs in the winter.

Outer Wear
The Métis coat has been mentioned above. They also wore the *capote,* the coat with a front opening made from a Hudson's Bay Company blanket, girded several times about the waist with the long, fringed Assomption sash.

Hair Styles
Men wore the styles of the Europeans they served. The women adopted the styles of the tribes in which they lived.

Headgear
The fur hat of beaver or other fur was a common item for the men. A "medicine hat," said to have great power, was made of goose-feather quills and adorned with other feathers.

Accessories
The finger-woven Assomption sash was long, often 60 inches, with the addition of a long fringe. Mittens were made extra large to allow for inner mittens; they were embellished with silk embroidery, ribbonwork, or beadwork. At times they had perforated leather tabs at the sides. The Métis carried many bags made of moose or deer hide, typically adorned with beadwork. Some pouches were three-sided, a form based on the animal scrotum from which bags had originally been made. Some carried the cloth "octopus" bag, with its eight tabs and fringe at the bottom, and its elaborate floral embroidery.

Garment Decoration
Embroidery was worked with moose hair, later with silk floss or cotton thread, introduced in the 1850s. Beadwork and ribbonwork were more common than quillwork; motifs, such as five-pointed stars, narrow leaves, and three-part plant forms, were outlined in linear beading. The only form of weaving seems to have been the finger-weaving of the sashes with their arrow-point, chevron, and other diagonal designs. Some coats were decorated with geometric designs, the repeats stamped with carved wooden stamps.

Key Sources
Barbeau, Charles M. "Assomption Sash." National Museum of Canada *Bulletin* 93, Anthropological Series 24.

Brasser, Ted. "Métis Artisans." *Beaver* Outfit 306(2): 52–59.

Burger, Joanne Overvold and Allan Clovis, eds. *A Portrayal of Our Métis Heritage.* Yellowknife, Northwest Territories: Métis Association of the Northwest Territories, 1976.

Giraud, Marcel. *The Métis in the Canadian West.* 2 vols. Edmonton: University of Alberta Press, 1987.

Harrison, Julia. *Métis: People between Two Worlds.* Calgary, Alberta: Glenbow-Alberta Institute, 1985.

Lussier, Antoine S. and D. Bruce Sealey. *The Other Natives: The Métis.* 3 vols. Winnipeg: Manitoba Métis Federation Press, 1978.

Slobodin, Richard. *Métis of the Mackenzie District.* Ottawa, Ontario: Saint Paul University, Canadian Research Centre for Anthropology, 1966.

———. "Subarctic Métis." In *Handbook of North American Indians. Vol. 6: Subarctic.* Pp. 361–371. Washington: Smithsonian Institution.

Thompson, Judy. "Turn-of-the-Century Métis Decorative Art from the Frederick Bell Collection." *American Indian Art Magazine,* Autumn 1983.

Micmac

The Micmacs, inhabitants of the Gaspe Peninsula, the Maritime Provinces, and Newfoundland (after they exterminated the Beothucks), were the northernmost speakers of the eastern Algonquian language. They were a migratory people, hunting moose, caribou, and porcupine in the winters, and spending the summers along the coast. They were marginal to the Woodland tribes, but in their costume they were closest to the interior Quebec tribes. Their first European contact may have been with the Norsemen around A.D. 1000. In 1497

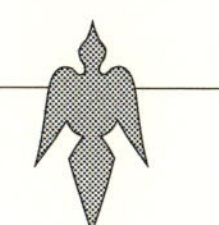

Sebastian Cabot visited them and took three of the tribe back to England. But there was little real contact until the Jesuit fathers appeared in the early seventeenth century. The origin of the name is unknown; some say it meant "allies." There were many intermarriages with the French and they were allies of the French during the seventeenth and eighteenth centuries. In appearance they were well proportioned and had fair skin, dark eyes, and black, occasionally auburn, hair.

Men's Basic Dress

Men wore little in the summer except for moccasins and a tanned-leather breechclout with flaps in front and back. For cooler weather they added a "jacket," which seems to have been a poncholike covering; this was made of the belly, shoulders, and forelegs of a moose, the legs forming detachable sleeves that could be added for warmth when needed. It was fastened with wooden pins. Leggings of deer or moose skin were the footless stirrup type; they were split down the front and instep and fastened in place with thongs wrapped around the legs. The thongs were of *babiche,* a word from the Algonquian used by the Canadian French that may have come from the Micmac word "ababich" meaning "cord." Winter leggings were of beaver skin.

Women's Basic Dress

Women, also, wore an apron or a wraparound skirt of skin and a poncholike jacket such as the men wore, but it was longer and was girded with two belts, one above the stomach, one below. They seem to have worn a side-seam dress in some cases. Skin leggings, also split down the front, were knee-high and were fastened with thongs.

Footwear

Moccasins were made of a folded piece of skin sewed at both ends; they had holes along each side near the top for the insertion of a drawstring to ensure a better fit; the top at the front was doubled back and finely gathered. At one time the Micmacs used the skin of young seals for moccasins, a very durable material; the custom may have been copied from their Eskimo neighbors. Later moccasins had embroidered/beaded designs on an instep insert. Muskrat, rabbit, or woodchuck skins were used for socks. Snowshoes, probably adopted from the Europeans, had square toes. Long ones were used for traveling on light snow; smaller, lighter ones were used for crusty snow formed after a freezing rain.

Outer Wear

Aboriginally, cloaks of skin were hung around the neck and tied with two thongs, often with the right arm exposed; in winter, sleeves of beaver skin were attached, tied at the back. Rain gear consisted of a piece of birchbark with a hole cut for the head; it was difficult to wear in the forest, but satisfactory in the clearing or in a canoe. One of the most famous items of Micmac clothing was the "chief's coat," worn for ceremonial or festive occasions. Although made of European materials in the foreign style, it was nevertheless a distinctive tribal garment. It had the front opening and set-in sleeves of the Prince Albert coat, but with added bands of embroidery, usually featuring the double-curve motif on the upper sleeves, the cuffs, down the front, around the hem, and often a horizontal band at the top of the back. These coats of black or dark-blue stroud cloth were girded at the waist with a brightly colored sash, at the back of which hung a moose-skin tobacco pouch. At times a large silver brooch held the coat at the neck.

Hair Styles

Lescarbot (1606) reported that both sexes wore the hair loose over the shoulders, but that the men often tied the hair at the crown of the head with a thong, letting it fall at the back like a ponytail. The French said at that time that the absence of beards and the long hair worn by both sexes made it difficult for them to distinguish male from female. By 1675 the hair was ornamented with short strings of beads or wampum. Later, both sexes wore the hair long, braided, doubled or even redoubled, and fastened into two bunches that fell forward over the shoulders, a style that continued throughout the nineteenth century; the bunches were often tied with eel skin. After 1911 men did not wear this hair style.

Headgear

At the time of European contact, the Micmacs did not wear head coverings, but they quickly adopted caps made of skin, bark, or fur, which differed

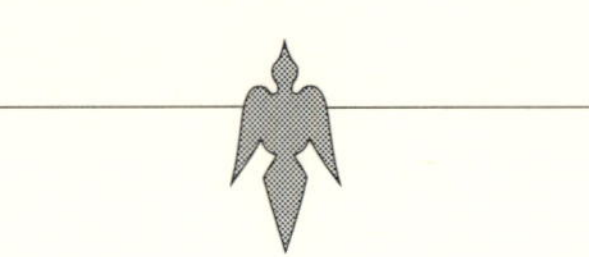

according to sex and rank. Later the women wore the high peaked hood of dark-blue or black strouding, which was beautifully beaded and embroidered in designs featuring the double-curve scrolls. Men's hats or hoods were not as high, were of skin, were pointed in front, and had a flap that could be tied down for protection against sun or cold or tied over the top of the head like some of our modern winter caps. Sharply pointed hats of birchbark were also worn, with a bunch of feathers as ornament. Simply made cones of birchbark frequently sufficed as temporary rainhats.

Accessories

Bags and pouches carried important personal items; these were in the form of drawstring pouches or flat wallets, with some use of quillwork decoration. By the nineteenth century these items, at first of leather, later of stroud cloth, were adorned with beautiful beadwork or embroidery. Early belts were of thongs or leather straps; later they were sashes, finger-woven of red, blue, and white yarn in chevron, arrow, or diagonal designs. Mittens, also adorned with embroidery or beadwork, were often edged with fur. In the nineteenth century beaded collars were worn by many of the women.

Jewelry

Ornaments were few and simple, the women wearing more than the men; strings of black beads, brightly colored shells, bells dangling from the ears, and carved pendants of wood were characteristic adornments. Some bracelets were embellished with porcupine quillwork designs.

Garment Decoration

The Micmacs were divided into clans, each with its own symbol, which was painted on their garments or worked into designs with quills, beads, or moose-hair embroidery to be applied to garments or accessories. The Micmacs had few equals in their use of these crafts for clothing decoration. They used complex patterns and elegant, curvilinear designs composed of a variety of forms—circles, diamonds, points, broken chevrons, and, most common, the double curve. Designs were also painted on skin garments. Ribbonwork was adopted in the nineteenth century, particularly for use on women's clothing. A popular accessory, the woven sash, had beads inserted to outline the design. Weaving seems to have been confined to the finger-weaving of the sashes. Some knitting of socks and mittens was done with moose-hair spun into strands.

Face and Body Embellishment

Some tattooing seems to have been practiced aboriginally, especially with the clan symbols. Face painting was reserved for special occasions such as battle (red) and mourning (black).

Masks

The only masks were those made of the head of a deer or moose with antlers, worn by the hunters in order to decoy their game.

Transitional Dress

By the early nineteenth century the women were wearing short gowns or petticoats of cloth; later they followed the white styles in the wearing of dresses. Both sexes substituted blankets for fur cloaks. Women wore headscarves of cotton cloth. By the end of the century the men were wearing European-style clothing, reserving their chief coats for formal or ceremonial occasions. In this century purchased clothing has taken over; the traditional Micmac garb is no longer worn.

Key Sources

Bock, Philip K. "Micmac." In *Handbook of North American Indians. Vol. 15: Northeast.* Pp. 109–122. Washington: Smithsonian Institution.

———. "The Micmac Indians of Restigouche: History and Contemporary Description." National Museum of Canada *Bulletin* 213, Anthropological Series 77.

Maillard, Pierre. *An Account of the Customs and Manners of the Mikmakis and Maricheets Savage Nations, Now Dependent on the Government of Cape-Breton.* London: Printed for S. Hooper and A. Morley, 1758.

Mechling, William H. "The Malecite Indians with Notes on the Micmacs 1916." *Anthropologica* 7: 1–160, 8: 161–274.

Sayres, William C., ed. *Sammy Louis: The Life History of a Young Micmac.* New Haven, CT: Compass, 1956.

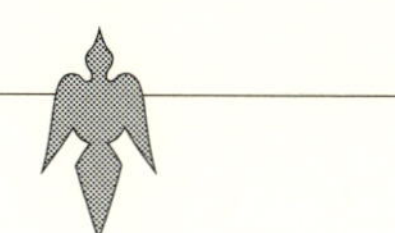

Speck, Frank G. "Beothuk and Micmac." *Indian Notes and Monographs* Miscellaneous Series 22.

Wallis, Wilson D., and Ruth S. Wallis. *The Micmac Indians of Eastern Canada.* Minneapolis: University of Minnesota Press, 1955.

Montagnais/Naskapi

The Montagnais and Naskapis are usually treated as one tribe, for their customs and costumes were, and are, almost identical. The Montagnais (French for "mountaineer") lived in the south, the Naskapis ("rude uncivilized people") in the north of the rugged country of Quebec and Labrador. They both spoke a dialect of Algonquian, commonly referred to as Montagnais/Naskapi/Cree. Although they were one of the first of the Indian tribes to come in close contact with Europeans, they remained in a primitive state longer than any other Canadian tribes. These people engaged in no agriculture and did a little gathering, but were predominantly fishermen and hunters, with Barren Ground caribou and moose as the mainstay of their existence; they also hunted small game and waterfowl. They fought intermittently with their enemies, the Eskimos, along the Labrador coast and with the Iroquois to the south and west. The usual devastating diseases and a diminishing supply of game have led to impoverishment and resultant difficulties.

Men's Basic Dress

From Champlain's map of New France (1613) we find some evidence of the aboriginal dress of these people. Men wore a short "kilt" (possibly an Iroquois influence) with a bare torso. Breechclouts were also worn; these were of skin, preferably of caribou hide, later of blue strouding. Leggings, high up in the front, were attached to the belt and were footless with straps under the feet to hold them in place. Often there was a fringe along the stitched edge with beads or small ornaments attached. Some of the leggings were dyed red; other legging adornment consisted of decorative bands at the knees and ankles. Winter leggings were of fur. The Montagnais/Naskapis wore leggings long after other Indians had adopted trousers. Shirts were of caribou skin with the fur inside for cold weather. They were fitted garments, a necessity in the cold climate, and had set-in two-piece sleeves, collars, and gussets where needed; they were frequently adorned with bead pendants and charms to assure success in hunting.

Women's Basic Dress

An aboriginal style for women was the strap-and-sleeve dress, a slip of skin held up by straps at the shoulders; the sleeves, very large at the top, covered the chest and shoulders. A wide belt girded the waist. Knee-length leggings were gartered at the knees, fringed at the outer edges, and had decorative bands at the bottoms.

Footwear

Moccasins were of the soft-sole type, rather high, almost a boot; these featured an insert or vamp over the instep, which was often painted or otherwise embellished in floral designs. The high cuffs were tied about the ankles with thongs. Sealskin was used to make watertight soles for use in wet weather. In extreme cold, several pairs of moccasins might be worn one over the other for warmth. The abundance of snow in the area necessitated well-made snowshoes, and the Montagnais/Naskapis were skilled in their design and construction. The bearpaw, the swallowtail, the elbow, and the beavertail shapes were all used, some having upturned toes. Skis were unknown in North America, but the Indians of that region, when they lacked *babiche,* made snowshoes of thin, flat pieces of wood with four eyelets through which thongs were threaded to lash the shoes in place. These were not skis, for they did not glide but had to be lifted like snowshoes. The pointed snowshoe was adopted after 1900.

Outer Wear

Robes were of bearskin, moose hide, or beaver skins with a front opening tied with thongs, and with detachable sleeves, which were so large at the top they almost came together when fastened in place. Both robes and sleeves were ornamented with broad decorative stripes. In cold weather the robe was pulled up tighter and belted, often with a flap pulled up to serve as a pocket. Lighter weight skin robes were worn casually over the shoulders and tied at the neck. In the northern part of the area the Eskimo style of parka was worn, made of caribou skin with a hood, and with the hair left on and the skin turned inward. Beautiful, soft, white tanned leather was used to make the famous coats of the Montagnais/Naskapis. Early coats seem to have displayed a flared skirt, like the eighteenth-century gentleman's coat; later styles reflect the straight-cut Prince Albert coat of the nineteenth century. The coats were decorated with bands of linear designs, featuring particularly the double-curve motif; these decorations were achieved through the use of stamps carved of wood, bone, or antler and applied with ink (usually red and blue) to the bands. These coats, which were worn well into the twentieth century, were thought to bring good luck to a hunter for a year, which meant that a new one had to be made each year. At times they were fitted with an attached hood. Women's coats were similar in construction and adornment but below the knees in length. Some rabbit-skin robes were made to be worn by women and children.

Hair Styles

Aboriginally, both sexes wore the hair long and loose. In the nineteenth century women liked to wind their long hair on flat pieces of wood of a modified hourglass shape to form large "spools" below the ears. Men occasionally wore sparse beards and mustaches.

Headgear

Both men and women generally went bareheaded. As winter head coverings they had hats or hoods of caribou skin with the hair turned inward; some hoods were made of the entire head of a caribou with the ears left protruding. Headbands of fur or hide were frequently worn. With European contact, cloth hats were worn, the most common being of red and dark-blue or black cloth, six panels sewn together in alternating colors; later the women attached these to a sort of beret and pulled the top forward so the center point was at the front. Some men wore a short visored cap with a wide headband, both decorated in the typical linear style.

Accessories

Bags and pouches were generally of caribou skin, embellished in the Montagnais/Naskapi style with quillwork, beadwork, moose-hair embroidery, or stamping; some skin purses were rolled and tied. Belts were of tanned leather, also often adorned. Caribou-hide mittens featuring moose-hair embroidery were necessary winter wear.

Jewelry

Some men wore hoops in the ears. A few necklaces were made of shells and beads, but for the most part jewelry was not commonly worn.

Armor

Some authorities say warriors may have carried moose-hide shields and adopted the wooden-slat armor of the Iroquois, but in fighting with their enemies, the Eskimos, they dispensed with shield and armor.

Special Costumes

Religion was a personal affair among the Montagnais/Naskapis, so there was almost no communal ritual, except the gathering together for feasts. Puberty rites were observed for a girl at her first menses; she was required to wear a hood or a veil decorated with quills and a fringe to hide the face from the sight of others, and gloves because she was not permitted to touch her body with her hands. There were few mourning customs, for the aged were often simply abandoned through necessity.

Garment Decoration

Elaborate painted decorations appeared on Montagnais/Naskapi garments. Characteristic parallel lines were achieved with a multipronged tool, which could also vary the width of the lines. Paints used were red and yellow ocher plus trade-acquired vermilion and indigo. The double curve was the most common motif. These painted decorations were replaced by quillwork, beadwork, and moose-hair embroidery, the latter some of the finest produced anywhere. Ribbonwork, too, was created, frequently appearing on moccasin vamps. Trade beads were used in conjunction with porcupine quills before supplanting them; the beads were threaded on warps by means of a bow loom and the strips applied to garments or accessories. Some "couching" beadwork was done in bold floral designs.

Face and Body Embellishment

Rather than using a needle and sinew, tattooed designs were created by rubbing pigments into a

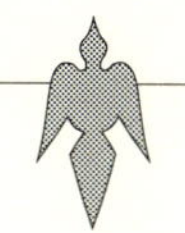

series of cuts made in the skin with a piece of flint. Faces and bodies were smeared with seal oil as a protection against insects. Some men wore a streak of red paint down the forehead and nose.

Masks

Some ceremonial masks were made of caribou hide, often with the hair of the animal still retained on the mask.

Transitional Dress

Living in the fastnesses of interior Quebec, the Montagnais/Naskapis were slow to change completely to European garb. However, they did shift to cloth for some of their garments. Men wore cloth coats, knee breeches, and a type of "gaiter." Stockings were simply rolls of cloth secured around the legs. Women wore cloth dresses and coats and cotton neckscarves, but retained their distinctive hats for some time. The caribou-skin garments were brought out for festive and ceremonial occasions.

Key Sources

Burnham, Dorothy K. *To Please the Caribou: Painted Caribou-Skin Coats Worn by the Naskapi, Montagnais, and Cree Hunters of the Quebec-Labrador Peninsula.* Seattle: University of Washington Press, 1992.

Douglas, Frederic H. "A Naskapi Painted Skin Shirt." *Material Culture Notes.* Denver: Denver Art Museum, 1969.

Hind, Henry Y. *Explorations in the Interior of the Labrador Peninsula, the Country of the Montagnais and Nasquapee Indians.* 2 vols. London: Longman, Green, 1863.

Levesque, Carole. *La Culture materielle des Indiens du Quebec: Une etude de raquettes, mocassins, et toboggans.* Mercury Series, Ethnology Service Paper 33. Ottawa: National Museum of Man.

Rogers, Edward S. and Eleanor Leacock. "Montagnais-Naskapi." In *Handbook of North American Indians. Vol. 6: Subarctic.* Pp. 169–189. Washington: Smithsonian Institution.

Speck, Frank G. *Naskapi: The Savage Hunters of the Labrador Peninsula.* Norman: University of Oklahoma Press, 1935.

Webber, Alika Podolinsky. "Ceremonial Robes of the Montagnais/Naskapi." *American Indian Art Magazine,* Winter 1983.

Slavey

The Slavey Indians lived between Lake Athabaska and Great Slave Lake and along the Mackenzie River. The name may possibly have been a mispronunciation of the Beaver name for them —"Tsade," which means "timid people," or it may have come from the Cree, who called them "captive slaves" and drove them out of the Lake Athabaska area. Their name for themselves was "Etchaottine." A peaceful, inoffensive people, they were seldom attacked by other tribes because they were believed to have great skill in witchcraft. Unlike the majority of northern Athapaskans, the Slavey were kind to women and the elderly. Although the Slavey were extremely mobile, they clung to the coniferous boreal forest, reluctant to hunt on the Barren Grounds where the caribou were; rather, they depended on moose for subsistence. Their first European contact was with Mackenzie in 1789. Fur traders came and posts were established in their territory, but the Slaves were able to get along comfortably without trade goods.

Men's Basic Dress

The Slavey made fairly extensive use of moose hide for their typical Athapaskan garments—the pointed tunics or shirts and the footed leggings; a skin trouser was also worn with separate moccasins. A breechclout of moose skin was worn; one authority said that in place of a breechclout, the men wore a "tassel" of leather. Their garments were more heavily bordered with fringes than their neighbors, and featured more quillwork (porcupine and goose quills) and moose-hair embroidery.

Women's Basic Dress

In early times women wore a long moose-hide skirt with an overgarment tied in front with thongs. Later they wore the Athapaskan tunic with long leggings, possibly trousers with a drawstring at the top. In the mid-nineteenth century they were wearing an "applique tunic," a straight-cut moose-hide garment with a deep fringe at the bottom, set-in sleeves, and a square or round cape collar. The tunics and collars were ornamented with bands of applique with white beaded edges.

Footwear

Moccasins were of tanned moose or caribou skin with the wraparound ankle flaps, the usual Athapaskan one-piece style with the front seam ending at a vamp over the instep; the vamp displayed fine moose-hair embroidery. Moccasins of this century were constructed with a larger toe area gathered into a longer vamp, many of them a slip-on style with no cuffs or with fur cuffs; these featured floral beading or quillwork on the insert. Snowshoes were also the customary Athapaskan types—a narrow shoe for breaking and following trails and a wider, longer shoe for tracking large game animals. The lacing was *babiche* and the frame was of spruce wood stained red-brown; some toes were pointed, others were rounded, upturned, and were wrapped with *babiche* and colorful porcupine quills.

Outer Wear

Rabbit pelts were cut into strips, woven in a netting technique, and were used for robes for women and children and for moss bags for carrying babies. Moose hide, with the hair left on, made warm robes for winter wear; lighter robes were of skin with the hair removed.

Hair Styles

Both sexes either wore the hair long, or long in the back and cropped short in front of the ears. Men usually plucked the facial hairs.

Headgear

Headbands, worn by both sexes, were strips of tanned leather handsomely decorated with porcupine quills, animal claws, and ermine skins. Fur hats were necessary winter wear. After trade cloth became available, women wore hoods with colored cloth bands sewn on, and a tassel at the point. In the late nineteenth century a "smoking cap" was popular—a round pillbox hat, usually of black velvet, and featuring decorations.

Accessories

Belts and garters were bands of tanned leather embellished with quillwork and edged with fringes. Larger straps were adorned in like manner and were used to carry babies like a tumpline. Armlets were similarly made. Mittens of caribou skin had quillwork or moose-hair embroidery on the backs and on the cuffs; a neck cord kept them from getting lost. Men wore a decorated knife sheath around the neck on a cord, making the knife readily available. Bags and pouches displaying quillwork or embroidery were useful for carrying shot, fire-making equipment, paints, or sewing materials. The "octopus" bag with its eight tabs at the bottom

The front of a Slavey-type moosehide tunic with a stand-up collar shows an appliqued yoke and epaulets, and fringes characteristic of the nineteenth century.

was a popular item. Some hunting bags were of netted *babiche* with colorful tassels and a decorated band at the top.

Jewelry
Bracelets, like garters, were leather straps featuring geometric quillwork designs. Men often displayed necklets of polished caribou antler. Some men passed a bone or a goose quill through the nasal septum. Necklaces were made of polished pieces of wood, horn, or bone.

The back of a Slavey-type moosehide tunic showing fringe and decorations on the sleeves.

Armor
Warriors wore cuirasses of willow twigs and protected themselves further with wooden shields. Their war headdresses were adorned with bear's claws or ringed with feathers.

Special Costumes
There were few elaborate ceremonies among the Slavey. At puberty, a girl was isolated and required to wear a hood or veil over her head so others could not gaze at her. Mourning feasts were held, and occasionally mourners cut their hair to show sorrow.

Garment Decoration
The Slavey women were skilled at quillwork, using both bird and porcupine quills; work was done on a traditional bow loom with sinew as warp and warp spacers made of bark. A wooden shuttle carried the weft thread, also of sinew, over and under the warp threads to secure the quills. The finished band was mounted on a strip of caribou skin or applied to a garment. The women also did exquisite moose-hair embroidery, keeping to the use of moose hair even to present times; some flower or berry designs were made with bundles of moosehair, bending the ends and trimming them into little tufts. They used a netting technique for the rabbit-skin robes. Although traders' beads were available to them early, they preferred to use their traditional materials, at times using beads to outline designs; but elaborate floral beadwork was not typical of this tribe.

Face and Body Embellishment
Men were often tattooed with a black or blue double line on each cheek from the chin to the nose.

Transitional Dress
By 1900 both men and women had given up most of their traditional dress, except for moccasins and mittens. Women wore cloth skirts, blouses, and dresses, adding a plaid shawl for warmth, worn over the head. Men wore the purchased white garments—trousers, vests, coats, and cotton shirts; occasionally they appeared on special occasions in the decorated and fur, edged jackets so popular in the mid-twentieth century.

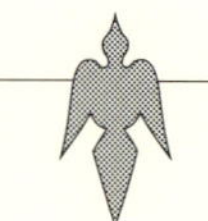

Key Sources

Asch, Michael I. "Slavey." In *Handbook of North American Indians. Vol. 6: Subarctic.* Pp. 338–349. Washington: Smithsonian Institution.

Dempsey, Hugh. "The Slavey Indians." *Glenbow* 7(4). Calgary: Alberta: Glenbow-Alberta Institute.

Honigmann, John. "Ethnography and Acculturation of the Fort Nelson Slave." Yale University *Publications in Anthropology* 33.

Mason, J. Alden. "Notes on the Indians of the Great Slave Lake Area." Yale University *Publications in Anthropology* 34: 1–46.

Tahltan

The Tahltan lived on the Stikine River and its tributaries in northwestern British Columbia. Although neighbors of the Sekani, they were closer to the Carrier in their customs and clothing. The name is said to have come from a low flat at the mouth of the Tahltan River; they were also called "Kunana," meaning "northern." The Tahltan language was in the Kaska branch of Athapaskan. They traded extensively with the Tlingit on the coast, offering them furs, hides, snowshoes, clothing, and fancy bags in exchange for slaves, salmon, eulachon oil, dentalium and abalone shells, copper, and some ceremonial clothing, passing them on to the Kaska and other interior tribes. They also acquired many Tlingit customs. Important natural resources to the Tahltan were moose, caribou, and mountain goats and sheep, along with smaller animals such as marten, beaver, mink, and muskrat. First contact with Europeans was in 1799.

Men's Basic Dress

The early upper garment for men was a simple shirt laced at the shoulders; later the Athapaskan tunic was worn but, unlike those of northern tribes, it was cut straight across the bottom and displayed little decoration except for short fringes or punctuated tabs and a limited amount of quillwork. With this tunic or shirt, men wore footed trousers or thigh-high leggings of moose, elk, or caribou hide, the leggings worn in the summer with separate moccasins. The footed trousers had a gusset in the crotch and a larger inset at the center back; decoration consisted of a beaded strip down the front of each leg and smaller strips around the ankles and below the knees. Aboriginally, breechclouts were not worn; they were adopted in the early nineteenth century.

Women's Basic Dress

In summer women wore a knee-length kilt of caribou skin. With this, when desired, was worn a piece of skin tied at the neck in the form of a cape, and short leggings of skin. By the time of contact they were wearing the Athapaskan tunic, but it, too, was cut straight across the bottom and was decorated with the characteristic punctuated tabs in place of fringes and some strips of quillwork.

Footwear

The Tahltan wore the typical Athapaskan moccasin with the center front seam going up to a vamp or insert over the instep; winter moccasins had ankle-wraps of thongs. The vamps were not generally decorated except for a small skin piping around the inset. Early in the twentieth century, the basic construction was of a larger sole gathered into a longer vamp, in the mukluk fashion. Some later moccasins also featured a square-cut toe with a horizontal seam. Snowshoes were not acquired until late in the eighteenth century; then they were either bearpaw in shape, or else had small squared-off tips at the toes and rather long tails.

Outer Wear

Lightweight robes were of caribou with the skin removed. Winter cloaks were made of the pelts of small animals such as beaver, ground squirrel, or marmot sewn together and lined with skin; these often featured a leather band edged with beading applied at the top of the cloak, with thongs for tying at the neck.

Hair Styles

With limited information about the Tahltans in precontact times, little is known about aboriginal hair styles; probably both sexes simply wore it loose. Soon after contact both sexes adopted the white styles of wearing the hair.

Headgear

Generally the Tahltan went bareheaded. Fur hats were worn with a feather or two as decoration.

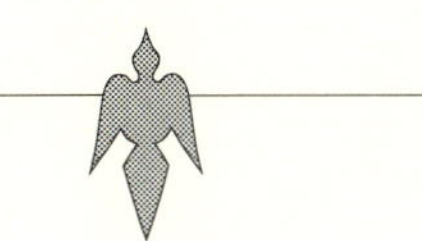

A Tahltan man wears a glengarry-style fur hat with feather; a caribou skin shirt with fringe wider than that of Plains Indians at the hem, sleeves, and shoulder; and a beaded knife sheath hangs at his neck.

Accessories
Many bags were carried to contain necessary personal articles. A collection from Emmons shows a man's work bag and contents, including paint bag, a knife, awl for sewing, whetstone, *babiche* for sewing and lashing, and other items. "Fire bags" of caribou or moose skin, worn over one shoulder or around the neck, originally carried ammunition or equipment for making fire; later they were worn only for ceremonial occasions. Knife sheaths—narrow, pointed pouches to contain a knife—were decorated and worn around the neck. Garters, armbands, and belts were straps of leather, sometimes embellished with quillwork or, later, beadwork. Mittens of caribou skin were winter items, occasionally decorated with fringe or punctuated tabs. Some containers carrying castoreum (substance from a beaver's gland smeared on snares and traps) hung from the belt. Collars of tanned caribou skin with beaded decoration were worn by young girls before marriage.

Jewelry
Necklaces and hair ornaments were worn, especially during the period between a girl's first menstrual period and her marriage; these included dentalium shells, stone pendants, traders' beads, and yarn tufts or tassels. The Tahltans did not adopt the labrets of the coastal and some interior tribes.

Armor
For armor the men wore tunics or cuirasses of thick, tough mountain-goat skin and helmets of the same material.

Special Costumes
Ceremonies were Tlingit in origin, rather than Athapaskan; in fact, the garments worn were usually also Tlingit in origin, such as the occasional Chilkat blanket and the button blankets. Dance shirts for the men differed, however; hip-length, they displayed appliqued and beaded patches on the chest or over the front opening, as epaulettes or a beaded yoke, and as cuffs.

Motifs and techniques were Tahltan, not Tlingit. At puberty, a girl wore a willow framework on the head covered with fringe to hide her face from the sight of others, especially hunters. A widow blackened her face as a sign of mourning and for four years wore a special necklace of a caribou-skin strap holding a large stone pendant.

Garment Decoration
The Tahltan did no moose-hair embroidery and little porcupine quillwork. Fringes were wide tabs rather than thin cords and were sometimes punctuated with holes at the ends. Couched beading was preferred to bead weaving, most commonly done on a ground of red flannel. Motifs were either geometrical or highly abstracted floral designs. Strips of beadwork were frequently attached to garments.

Face and Body Embellishment
Tattooing was done by puncturing the skin, tapping a bone awl with a light mallet, and rubbing pigment into the holes. It was not extensively practiced.

Transitional Dress
Traditional Tahltan clothing gradually gave way to European garments, although the footed leggings continued to be worn until the end of the century. Moccasins are worn up to the present time.

Key Sources
Duncan, Kate C. "Tahltan." In *Northern Athapaskan Art: A Beadwork Tradition.* Pp. 158–173. Seattle: University of Washington Press, 1989.

Emmons, George T. "The Tahltan Indians." University of Pennsylvania Museum *Anthropological Publications* 4(1).

MacLachlan, Bruce B. "Tahltan." In *Handbook of North American Indians. Vol. 6: Subarctic.* Pp. 458–468. Washington: Smithsonian Institution.

Teit, James. "Field Notes on the Tahltan and Kaska Indians, 1912–1915." *Anthropologica* 3: 40–171.

Tanaina
The Tanaina, living in the mountains along Cook Inlet and inland, were the only northern Athapaskans living on or near the sea coast; it was an area rich in land and sea resources. They shared many cultural traditions with the neighboring Eyak and Tlingit, particularly the emphases on rank and feasting. They spoke Tanaina, a subdivision of the Athapaskan

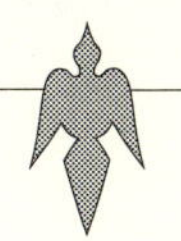

linguistic stock, and their name is a self-designation in their tongue. Their subsistence was dominated by salmon, although hunting was also important, particularly for Pacific harbor seals and beluga whales in the Inlet, and for moose, caribou, bear, mountain goats, and Dall sheep in the interior. European contact was early; by 1778 James Cook had met the Tanaina and in 1791 the Russians entered Cook Inlet. The Russians, especially Zagoskin, gathered extensive material on the customs and clothing of these people, and many items were collected for Russian museums. Although the Tanaina had many conflicts with the Eskimos to their west, they were a part of a huge trade network in southern Alaska in the eighteenth century, actively exchanging native copper, furs, skins, sea-mammal products, porcupine quills, and slaves for Russian, English, and Indian trade goods, especially dentalium shells and glass beads.

Men's Basic Dress

Men wore a knee-length shirt or tunic of tanned caribou skin (or sometimes moose or mountain-goat skin) with the hair removed. Richard Conn, in his *Robes of White Shell and Sunrise,* gives a pattern for one of these shirts and comments on its uniqueness among American Indians; it was made from one piece of skin, cut and folded so that the sleeves had double seams, and the front and back ended in the characteristic Athapaskan points. Decoration was of quillwork and fringes, threaded with silverberries *(Elaeagnus)*, around the collar or yoke area and at the hem, with red ocher outlining the seams. At the bottom of the center front and center back was a vertical line of thongs and beads. Some tunics were trimmed with otter fur at neck and wrists. With the shirt men wore the footed trousers (like leggings but with gussets in the crotch area), which displayed bands of quilling down the front and around the ankles, often with cords tied around knees and ankles for a snug fit. Heavier footless trousers and moccasin or boot combinations were winter wear; the fur was retained for warmer garments.

Women's Basic Dress

Women's dresses were also of tanned skin, usually of caribou, but sometimes of moose or mountain-goat skin, longer than the men's tunics, without the points at the bottom, but generally with the same decoration. At times the fringes were wide tabs instead of cords. They also wore the footed trousers with heavier trouser-and-moccasin combinations in the winter.

Footwear

Moccasins were the Athapaskan one-piece type with the center front seam to a vamp or insert. Large cuffs, which were wrapped around the ankle with ties, and a tongue were added. Knee boots of caribou or sheep-skin had soles of brown-bear or beluga hide. Waterproof boots were of salmon skin. The snowshoe was acquired by the Tanainas in the 1850s; the frame was generally of birch wood with *babiche* or lacings of bear or moose rawhide. It was at times adorned with tufts of fur.

Outer Wear

The Tanaina women trapped ground squirrels and marmots, making warm robes or parkas of the pelts; these were worn over the shoulders and tied at the neck. Some waterproof parkas were made of whale membrane. Salmon skins were shaped into rain capes.

Hair Styles

Women wore the hair loose or in two braids. Men sometimes wore one long braid down the back covered with grease and bird down, or they gathered the hair in the back into a knot, or let it hang loose. Men also inserted feathers in the hair for special occasions.

Headgear

Men wore hoods of tanned leather, either attached to the tunic or hanging freely; these were decorated with quilled (later beaded) bands, hanging thongs, a wide fringe at the bottom, and occasionally fur edging. Some men wore quilled or beaded headbands. Fur caps were necessary winter wear.

Accessories

Mittens of white caribou skin, constructed with an extra piece for the thumb, were adorned with porcupine quills and *Elaeagnus* seeds. For winter wear for both sexes, mittens were made with the fur left on the hide for warmth; the mittens were connected by a long cord wrapped with quills. Gloves, constructed in the European style, were worn by the men for rowing boats; embellishment consisted of quilled bands at the cuffs and fur edgings. Every man wore a knife sheath around the neck containing his ever-ready knife; the front (sometimes the back as well) was decorated with quilled bands. Belts were adorned with quill embroidery and dentalium shells. Fire bags of hide, containing fire-making equipment, were decorated with dentalium shells.

Jewelry
Bracelets were straps of leather displaying fine quillworked designs. Men prided themselves on their necklaces of bear claws and dentalium shells. The ears and nasal septums of both sexes were pierced for the insertion of shell pendants, feathers, or wooden skewers. Labrets of stone, wood, or bone were inserted in the lower lip.

Special Costumes
Although the Tanainas adopted the Tlingit focus on rank and potlatch-giving, they did not seem to have acquired the Northwest Coast ceremonial dress, possibly because of the pervasive influence of the Russian Orthodox Church. Shamans, however, were important in their religion in curing rites, wearing costumes of individual preference. The only other special costume was the hood worn by a girl while in seclusion during her menses; it covered her face so others could not see it.

Garment Decoration
The Tanaina women worked predominantly with porcupine quills, sometimes bird quills, with the inevitable geometric designs. Although they were exposed early to beads, and sometimes used the large pony beads, they never developed seed beadwork as did the other Northern Athapaskans. Fringes were common decorations on garments and accessories, either of cords wrapped with quills or of tabs. *Elaeagnus* seeds and tufts of fur were also used to adorn articles of clothing. Skin garments were painted with red and brown pigments, especially the outlining of seams.

Face and Body Embellishment
On ceremonial occasions, faces were painted in stripes or designs with red ocher and black lead; these were sometimes clan designations. Wealthy women had lines tattooed on the lips and chins, and also on the hands.

Masks
During the curing rites, shamans wore carved wooden masks.

Transitional Dress
Missionization by Russian Orthodox priests, epidemics, the fur trade, the Gold Rush, and the growth of commercial salmon canneries all contributed to the slow breakdown of the Tanaina traditional culture. With the entry of American traders after 1867 with fabrics, ready-made garments, and shoes, transitional dress was firmly established; by the end of the century, there was no more Tanaina costume.

Key Sources
Osgood, Cornelius. "The Ethnology of the Tanaina." Yale University *Publications in Anthropology* 16.

Townsend, Joan B. "Tanaina." In *Handbook of North American Indians. Vol. 6: Subarctic.* Pp. 623–640. Washington: Smithsonian Institution.

Varjola, Pirjo. "Alaskan Athapaskans." In *The Etholen Collection: The Ethnographic Alaskan Collection of Adolf Etholen and His Contemporaries in the National Museum of Finland.* Pp. 110–130. Helsinki: National Board of Antiquities, 1990.

Western Cree
The Western Cree consisted of two main divisions: (1) the Western Main Cree or Swampy Cree, living on the lowlands along James and Hudson bays, and (2) the Western Woods Cree, who inhabited the area from the bays into Alberta, and who included the Rocky Cree, the Western Swampy Cree, and the Strongwood or Bois Fort Cree. They spoke various dialects of the Cree language, which belonged to the Algonquian linguistic family. Earlier the Cree were called the Christenaux or Knistenaux (with many variant spellings). They were hunters of moose, woodland caribou, hare, other small game, and waterfowl, with some fishing and some gathering of berries and wild rice. First European contact seems to

have been Alexander Mackenzie in the 1790s. Peter Rindisbacher did sketches and paintings of the Cree in 1821, and Paul Kane was also in the area in 1846.

Men's Basic Dress

Men wore a skin breechcloth, called an *assian,* with flaps before and behind. Hip-length leggings of tanned leather were snugly fitted and gartered at the knees, and had quillwork and fringes down the sides. A skin shirt or tunic was knee-length. These traditional garments were made of tanned moose, elk, or caribou hide, and were undecorated or featured some porcupine quillwork and fringes; later, as traders' beads appeared, floral beadwork was applied.

Women's Basic Dress

Early women's dress consisted of a wraparound skirt and a poncholike upper garment. At the time of contact they seem to have been wearing a strap-and-sleeve dress, fastened over the shoulder with cords or straps, and a flap turned down at the top; large detachable sleeves, seamed from elbows to cuffs, were added as desired. Calf-length, the dress was ornamented with fringe and quillwork. A tasseled belt at the waist was fastened behind. Short leggings, gartered, completed the costume. According to some informants, a breechclout may have been worn at the time of menstruation or in the winter.

Footwear

Moccasins were made from one or two pieces of moose or caribou hide in the characteristic Athapaskan style with the front seam to a vamp or insert, which was decorated with quillwork or beading. At times a beaded cuff was added that was made to stand up and display the beading. Some moccasins were without the front seam, but had the sole gathered into the vamp, called the "puckered-toe" style. Socks of hare skin or caribou skin had the fur or hair retained inside for warmth. In the nineteenth century the traders introduced Eskimo-made sealskin boots, much more efficient for wear in the marshes. Snowshoe frames were often of birch or tamarack with lacings of *babiche.* They were of two types, an elongated oval shape and a pointed shape; they were much longer than the eastern snowshoes—seven or eight feet in length.

Outer Wear

Rabbit-skin robes, made from strips cut spirally from the rabbit pelt, were made in a looped netting technique, and were worn particularly by women and children. Robes were also made of moose or caribou hide with the hair left on for warmth; some were made of the pelts of small animals sewn together. With the coming of the trading posts, the *capote* was a popular outer garment, made of the Hudson's Bay Company blanket with attached hood and girded with a fringed Assomption sash wound several times about the waist. The company blankets were also worn for winter wear. In the early to mid-nineteenth century the Cree men wore a "frock coat," European in cut but made of native materials and adorned with quillwork and quill-wrapped fringes.

Hair Styles

Both sexes wore the hair in braids or hanging loosely to the shoulders. Sometimes the women wore it tied in a clump at the back or coiled over the ears. Men generally plucked the facial hair and women plucked the eyebrows.

Headgear

Some men wore a small peaked hat adorned with feathers. Winter caps were of fur, or the head of a small animal with the tail hanging behind as ornament; these were often fastened under the chin. Some women in the eastern part of the area wore the elaborately decorated hoods of the Eastern Cree. Men at times wore headdresses made of the feathers of swans, eagles, or other birds.

Accessories

Mittens were of hare or beaver skin for winter wear, or of tanned leather ornamented with fringe and quillwork, later floral beading and yarn tassels. Garters also featured decorative elements such as tassels and quillwork. Some pouches were flat and decorated in the same manner. The "octopus" bag, with its eight tabs at the bottom and its elaborate floral patterns, was popular in the nineteenth century. Belts were of tanned leather, well decorated; or the Assomption sash, acquired in trade, was worn. Cree men in the north wore carved wooden snow goggles to guard against the glare of snow and ice.

Jewelry

The nasal septum was pierced and a bead inserted, a custom that persisted even into postcontact times. Both sexes pierced the ears for the use of earplugs or earrings of various types. Necklaces were of beads and shells. After contact the women enjoyed the metal jewelry of the traders, such as bracelets and rings.

Armor

The Cree were in frequent conflict with their Athapaskan neighbors until stopped by the Chipewyans. There is little evidence for the use of armor. A painting by Paul Kane (1846) depicts a Cree warrior wearing a horned war cap embellished with ermine skins.

Special Costumes

The Western Cree seldom engaged in rituals or ceremonies, except for feasting and some curing rites, none of which involved special costumes. At puberty, a girl was isolated, wore her hair disheveled, and donned a cap or hood with a fringe to cover her face.

Garment Decoration

Aboriginally, geometric porcupine quillwork was the usual form of decoration with the addition of some fringes, often quill-wrapped. Beadwork, at first geometric, later floral, took over in this respect; the double curve was a common motif. Commercial yarns led to the frequent use of tassels. Feathers and the claws and horns of various animals were also used as adornment. The only weaving done was the use of the looped-netting technique for the making of rabbit-skin robes.

Face and Body Embellishment

Both sexes painted the face, the men more than the women; they used native blue, white, and brown ochers, charcoal, and, from the traders, vermilion. Tattoos decorated the face and hands, created by drawing a needle beneath the skin colored with charcoal. Women generally had three vertical lines tattooed on the chin. Some men were tattooed on the body, the technique used being that of punctuation with needles set in a wooden frame; charcoal was then rubbed into the holes.

Transitional Dress

By the early eighteenth century the English and French had begun establishing their forts and posts, and throughout the century traditional dress continued. However, the end of the century brought commercial cloth and glass beads, gladly acquired by the Cree women. Throughout the next century, garments shifted to the white styles and finally to purchased clothing. Robes gave way to blankets, skin tunics to cotton shirts and *capotes,* leggings to trousers. The women adopted plaid or striped shawls and cotton headscarves. Gloves were preferred to mittens, especially with the heavily beaded or embroidered gauntlet cuffs. One traditional garment that remained in popularity was the tanned leather jacket for the men with its floral embroidery, deep fringes, and beadwork.

Key Sources

Honigmann, John J. "The Attawapiskat Swampy Cree: An Ethnographic Reconstruction." University of Alaska *Anthropological Papers* 5(1): 23–82.

———. "West Main Cree." In *Handbook of North American Indians. Vol. 6: Subarctic.* Pp. 217–230. Washington: Smithsonian Institution.

Mason, Leonard. "The Swampy Cree: A Study in Acculturation." National Museums of Canada *Anthropology Papers* 13.

Smith, James G. E. "Western Woods Cree." In *Handbook of North American Indians. Vol. 6: Subarctic.* Pp. 256–270. Washington: Smithsonian Institution.

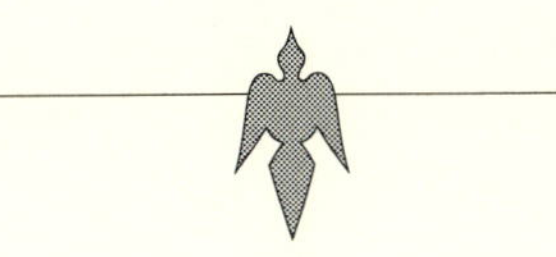

Chapter Ten

Costume of the Arctic

Above: Aniak Eskimo mukluks from the 1930s made of caribou, wolverine, and sealskin.

Above: In summer, a light shawl replaces a Caribou Eskimo woman's winter outer parka.
Below, right: Greenland Eskimo women used European glass beads to decorate collars.
Below, left: The Aleut made lightweight windproof and waterproof parkas,*kamleika,* of animal intestines.

Arctic

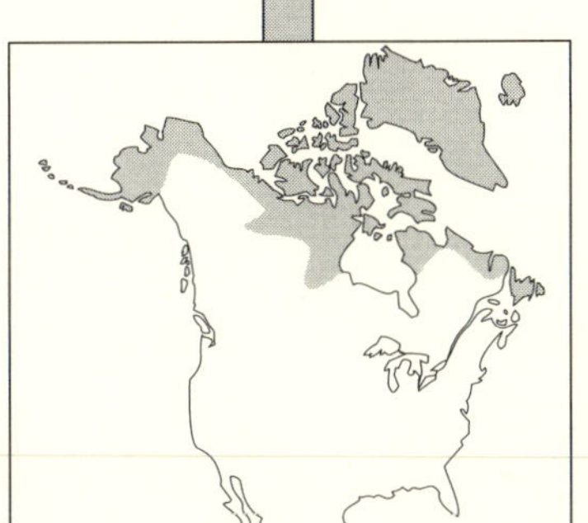

The Arctic is a cold and forbidding wilderness, a land of ice and snow, of long, dark winters and brief, bright summers. That the Eskimo have not only survived but flourished in this harsh environment is a tribute to the amazing ingenuity of their culture, their patience and skill in hunting, and, surely, their saving grace of humor. They are primarily a maritime people, their subsistence based on the hunting of sea mammals along the coast, with occasional forays inland for caribou, moose, and beaver. Their dependence on animals has led to a highly animistic religion.

It is inappropriate to refer to the Eskimo as "tribes." They are one people, but organized in socially and politically autonomous groups stretching 6,000 miles from the western Aleutian Islands to eastern Greenland. Despite their vast territory, they share a language and culture. The Eskimo-Aleut language is spoken across the Arctic, with three main subdivisions: Aleut, Yupik, and Inuit-Inupiaq. Their tools, their religion, their occupations, and their clothing were and are much the same.

The name *Eskimo* may be derived from an Algonquian word meaning "eaters of raw meat." Their name for themselves is *Inuit,* meaning "people" in their own language; the terms are often used interchangeably, but *Eskimo* will be used here because of its widespread popular usage and because it is the dominant term in most anthropological sources.

The term *Arctic (artikos,* Greek for "Great Bear") has many definitions, leading to various boundaries; for our purposes it will be considered the region north of the tree line because of the ramifications for culture and clothing.

The Eskimo were the first of the native inhabitants of North America to experience contact with Europeans—the Norsemen in A.D. 1000—but

Above: This Eskimo man from Nunivak, an island off Alaska's southwestern coast, wears a forehead mask representing a bird with a fish in its beak.

Peoples of the Arctic

Aleuts, p. 386
Asiatic and St. Lawrence Island Eskimo, p. 390
Baffinland Eskimo, p. 393
Bering Strait Eskimo, p. 395
Caribou Eskimo, p. 398
Copper Eskimo, p. 401
Greenland Eskimo, p. 404
Iglulik Eskimo, p. 407
Kotzebue Sound Eskimo, p. 408
Labrador Eskimo, p. 410
Mackenzie Delta Eskimo, p. 412
Netsilik Eskimo, p. 414
North Alaska Eskimo, p. 415
Pacific Eskimo, p. 418
Polar Eskimo, p. 421
Quebec Inuit, p. 422
Southwest Alaska and Nuivak Island Eskimo, p. 424

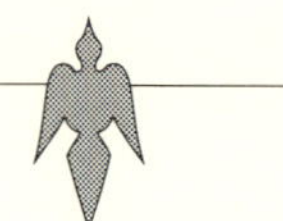

one group, the Copper Eskimo, were not contacted by Europeans until 1910. Vitus Bering, the Russian explorer, was the first European to encounter native Alaskans; he arrived in 1741, followed by other explorers and fur traders, the latter cruelly exploiting the Aleut in the drive for sea-otter furs. Traders, whalers, missionaries, and government officials all had profound effects on Arctic cultures.

The Russians recorded much valuable information on the Eskimo, especially in the accounts of explorers and government officials. The paintings of Mikhail Tikhanov (1817–1819), Pavel Mikhailov in the 1820s, and Voznesenski in the 1840s are particularly useful for costume studies. The earliest painting of an Eskimo (a Labrador man), however, was made in 1567, and was followed by the works of John White (1570s), John Webber (a member of Cook's Third Expedition in 1778), Louis Choris (1816–1817), and many others. Innumerable photographers recorded Eskimo lifeways from the mid-nineteenth century, the most famous being Edward S. Curtis.

Traditional Eskimo clothing was, of necessity, very carefully fitted; it was a matter of life and death that garments protect against the extreme climate. The Eskimo seamstress was skilled at cutting the skins in many pieces, using darts and gussets for a snug fit, and sewing the seams precisely. The garments demanded daily attention, not only the initial sewing, but the softening and drying needed, as well as the constant repair. An eyed needle of bone (polar bear bone was preferred because of its hardness) was threaded with sinew of caribou, beluga, or narwhal (the last especially sought for its great length). The precious needles were kept in needlecases of delicately incised bone or ivory. Thimbles of bone or leather and sharp-pointed bone awls helped force the sinew through the tough hide. In the summer, garments were worn with the fur toward the body; in the winter, garments were added that had the fur turned outward. These double layers afforded greater insulation because of the air pocket warmed by body heat. Pliability was also important in clothing, for the hunter needed to move readily in the severe cold. Snow beaters, which were used to remove snow from garments before going indoors, were important accessories, helping to keep clothing from deteriorating in the humid atmosphere inside. Besides all of these concerns, Eskimo women stitched items carefully to placate the spirit of the animal upon which subsistence depended, and they also took the time to decorate garments artistically.

General Dress

Men's Basic Dress

Men and women dressed much alike, with a few differences dictated by their activities. It is difficult to differentiate between basic and outer wear, because it was almost all outer wear. A tunic or shirt of sealskin, with the fur turned inside, was the usual summer wear, along with sealskin trousers, which were tied below the knees with a drawstring and tucked into boots. Sealskin was preferred for summer wear because it was more waterproof; caribou hide was soft and light for winter wear, and warmer because the hollow hairs trapped the body heat. Furs of land animals were the warmest, but difficult to come by. When indoors, both sexes stripped, and seem to have worn some kind of an undergarment made of caribou calfskin, much like what we would call a "brief," but there is little information on this subject.

Women's Basic Dress

Women wore a lighter weight tunic or shirt in the summer, usually of sealskin, and larger at the top (whether or not a hood was attached) so a baby could be carried by the mother, and so it could be brought to the front for nursing. A sling of thongs or a hide strap was used to help distribute the weight of the infant. Women wore trousers, but these were generally footed, to be worn under boots or slippers.

Footwear

In the central Arctic, slippers were worn in summer instead of boots; otherwise, boots were year-round wear. They were knee-high for men, higher in front for women, with uppers of sealskin, especially that of the spotted seal, and soles of the skin of the *ugruk,* or bearded seal (tough as walrus hide but lighter). They were generally made in the "mukluk" style; that is, the sole was cut large, with the edges crimped and sewed into a vamp. Ornamentation consisted of bands and geometric pieces of fur in different colors, forming pleasing patterns. Dried grass or moss was stuffed into the soles to absorb moisture. In some

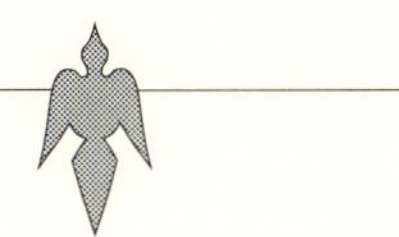

cases, bone or ivory "hobnails" were attached on the bottom for walking on ice. In many areas of the Arctic, especially Alaska, socks or stockings were made of woven grass. There was little snow in the arid North, and in many places the strong winds swept the ground bare, so snowshoes were not as imperative as in the Subarctic; those made were of small, roundish frames with coarse webbing.

Outer Wear

The "parka" (a Russian term), called *anorak* in the central Arctic and Greenland, was the major garment of the Eskimo; it was put on over the head, was generally hooded, and had tails in front and back of varying lengths, longer in back for sitting on ice. It was usually of caribou hide (for winter) or sealskin (summer). The length was to the hips or the knees, depending on the locality. A large ruff of wolverine or wolf hair around the face helped shed the ice crystals formed from breathing. The parka featured designs made with pieces of fur; a common motif was the "walrus tusks," two curving elongated triangles at the neck, usually of white caribou-fur applique. These tusk motifs were to be found on parkas all across the Arctic, varying somewhat in shape but almost always present. Parkas of the skins of birds such as puffins, cormorants, or other waterfowl were worn only by men; they were highly treasured and handsomely decorated. Waterproof parkas sewn from strips of seal or walrus intestines—cleaned, dried, and aired in the cold to make them white—were closely fitted at the neck and wrists and tied to the rim of the kayak opening. These were stitched together as horizontal or vertical bands, and had tassels and other embellishments in the seams. Parkas for both sexes were also fashioned from the skins of smaller animals such as ground squirrels and rabbits.

Hair Styles

Women allowed the hair to grow full length and either braided it or piled it on top of the head and fastened it with a bone pin; it was necessary to wear the hair close to the head because of the parka hood (or to have a high hood because of the topknot). Men usually cut the hair short; in some localities it was cut square across the forehead, the rest left long enough to cover the ears. The tonsure was worn by some men.

Headgear

Because of the hoods on the parkas, no caps were worn in the Arctic, except for an occasional fur hat. In summer, the hood was often removed. A baby generally wore a little cap when riding in its mother's hood in cold weather. Eyeshades or visors were worn by hunters in kayaks to reduce glare.

Accessories

Snow goggles were mandatory; made of wood or ivory, they prevented snow blindness, or the glare on the sea or ice; the insides were often blackened with charcoal to further reduce glare. Early goggles had small holes for the eyes, but slits were found to be more efficient for later wear. Mittens (with finger stalls) were necessary, not only for warmth but also to protect the hands from rope burns when landing sea mammals. Most mittens were of caribou hide, but some were of woven grass (often used as inner mittens), of bear paws, or of caribou leg skins. Gloves were unknown aboriginally. Toggles, carved of ivory or bone, were used as buttons for fastening garments. Belts girded parkas and held up trousers; they were not only functional, but represented a symbolic line of demarkation of the soul. Men's belts frequently had an animal's tail suspended in the rear, or amulets or charms attached to the belt.

Jewelry

Eskimos were too enveloped in fur clothing to wear much jewelry. Labrets, however, could be displayed on the face. These were of carved wood, stone, bone, or ivory; men's labrets were small round plugs, one at each side of the mouth, typically surmounted with a large blue bead or carved to represent faces. The woman's labret was fastened into the lower lip, in some places elaborately designed with beaded clusters added. Later labrets were of trade beads, nephrite, or jade as well as the aboriginal materials. A few nose rings were displayed, but these went out of favor after contact. An ivory ear pendant would occasionally be seen. The Eskimo, especially the men, put great faith in amulets to propitiate the spirit world and thereby bring success in hunting. These small objects were intricately carved of stone, bone, or ivory; walrus ivory was most treasured because of its rich luster, but it was difficult to work because of its hard marbled core and outer layer of enamel. A few necklaces were worn consisting of beads of shell, carved ivory or bone, or amber from Norton Sound.

Armor

What little armor was worn (chiefly in western Alaska) was created from plates of walrus ivory stitched together with sinew.

Special Costumes

Although shamanism was central to Eskimo religion, and the shaman was an essential performer in curing rites and dances, the shaman costumes were highly individualistic in character; often they wore gut-skin parkas and headdresses of variegated fur with a loon bill at the top. The leader of a whaling crew traditionally wore the skin of a raven, with the beak pointing downward toward the whales being pursued.

Garment Decoration

No weaving was done by the Eskimo, except for the making of socks or stockings of grass. No porcupine quills were used in decorations, but quillwork in some areas was created with split quills of feathers. The application of differently colored bands of fur to garments was the most common form of adornment. The throat gussets ("walrus tusks") of white fur were a part of these designs. After 1920, "fur mosaic," a designed patchwork of fur pieces, was developed extensively and skillfully. Bird down, feathers, and later yarn tassels were used as trim in seams of parkas, particularly the gut-skin garments. Greatly esteemed white ermine tails were suspended on clothing, as were bear teeth, bear claws, and amulets. Eskimo decoration on clothing tended to emphasize the body joints, such as shoulders, waists, and knees, since they were considered the locations of the soul of the wearer.

Face and Body Embellishment

Face painting was rare among the Eskimo. However, tattooing was widespread, displayed by both sexes. Men tended to tattoo only short bars on the face. In the western Arctic, whaling men kept tally of their successes by means of bars on the cheeks. Women were more extensively tattooed, with designs on chin, cheeks, brow, arms, and sometimes breasts. It was said that only the souls of brave hunters and women with large, beautiful tattoos were admitted to the afterworld. By the late nineteenth century, tattooing had almost disappeared in the Arctic.

Masks

Masks, generally carved of wood, were used in ceremonies, both religious and secular, varying significantly in style from one area to another. A unique custom in southwestern Alaska was the use of tiny finger masks, one for each finger, contributing to the visual rhythms of the dance.

Transitional Dress

The Russians, explorers, whalers, and fur traders brought new concepts and materials for clothing to the Eskimo, who adopted some but made them peculiarly their own by adapting European styles into garments of native materials. By the end of the nineteenth century, however, many traditional garments were replaced with textile clothing, especially for summer wear. With the diminishing of the caribou herds and sea mammals, and the rise of a wage-labor economy, the Eskimo hunter had little time for hunting and little success. Today, men wear snowmobile suits, down jackets, cloth trousers, and rubber boots. The women wear mail-order dresses, jackets, and pants. The development of tourism has kept some of the clothing arts alive and has meant the revival of others, a great help in the struggle for survival in the Arctic.

Aleut

The Aleut lived on the bare, treeless islands of the Aleutians, windswept and visited by violent storms, heavy fogs, and frequent rains. Over 100 islands, large and small, stretch a thousand miles from the Alaska Peninsula westward into the Pacific Ocean. It is an unstable zone, visited by earthquakes, erupting volcanoes, and hot springs, and there is little vegetation except for grasses and flowers, but the islands are rich in sea mammals. The name *Aleut* is of uncertain origin; it may have been given to them by the Russians, possibly from the Chukchi or Koryak languages. Their culture was much like that of their Eskimo neighbors, but they also adopted a system of rank from the Tlingit: chiefs and those of high status, commoners, and slaves (purchased or obtained in warfare). Vitus Bering arrived at the

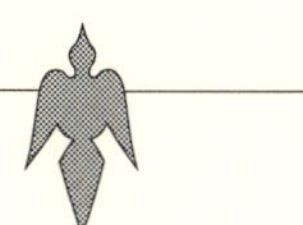

islands in 1741, followed by Russian fur traders excited by the riches to be obtained from sea-otter furs. There ensued a shameful exploitation of the Aleut; the men were captured and forced to hunt the sea otters under brutal conditions; many Aleuts were wantonly killed, and those that escaped were cut down by the devastating diseases of the foreigners. However, before they destroyed the culture, the Russians recorded in words and pictures much information on Aleutian lifeways; even today the Russian influence is felt among the few Aleuts remaining in the many Russian names and their devotion to the Russian Orthodox religion.

Men's Basic Dress

At the time of Russian contact, the Aleut men were wearing a belted gown or tunic with short or long sleeves of bird skins (tufted puffins, murres, or cormorants, the last the most preferred); these were knee-length or ankle-length, and were decorated with bands of soft sea-lion esophagus skin painted red and black. Tassels of red cloth were used as adornment as cloth became available. These reversible bird-skin parkas or gowns were eminently suited to the climate, for in rainy weather the waterproof feathers were outside, and in cold but dry weather, the feathers turned inward kept the body warm. These parkas were cut square across the bottom. Aboriginally, trousers of sea-lion throat skin were said to have been worn.

Women's Basic Dress

Women wore the long tunic or gown, ankle-length, and cut straight across the bottom. There was no hood (babies were carried in cradles), but on some parkas there was a front opening to enable the mother to nurse the baby. The upright collar was decorated. Sleeves were long or short. The parkas were made of sea-otter or fur-seal skins, not of bird skins, for that was the male prerogative; however, the women later wore parkas of bird skins when the Russians refused to let any Aleuts wear sea-otter skins, which were reserved strictly for trade. The accomplished needlewomen used sewing needles of ivory or the leg bones of sea gulls; these were not eyed, but had a notch at the larger end to carry the thread. Long thongs or leather straps were used as decoration on the parkas.

Footwear

The Aleut went barefoot almost exclusively. However, the eastern Aleut, near the Alaska Peninsula, occasionally wore a boot made of dark leather on the sole and lower part, and light leather on the upper section, with a border of fur and tufts of red yarn as trim. Some slippers were made from the very thin membrane of an animal's kidney, which retained its original shape with a few tucks added for fit. Occasional mention is made of boots in a sack-like shape made of the esophagus or throat skin of a sea lion with soles of thick sealskin; these were lined with dried grass and were decorated with dots and lines of red paint. With their skill in basketry, the women made socks of dune grass in a two-strand twining technique.

Outer Wear

The beautiful bird-skin parkas of the Aleut were eagerly sought as trade items and as gifts for Russian officials. They were of black and white horned puffin skins, as a rule, sewn together into a long parka with an upstanding collar and no hood; the bird skins, worn outside in case of rain, were turned inward in cold weather. Embellishments were bands of caribou skin painted a brownish red; appliques of the esophagus of a sea lion, also painted reddish; sea-otter fur trim at cuffs and hem; and fringes, feathers, and tassels (earlier of fur, later of red cloth or yarn) with tufted-puffin beaks attached. At the throat, there was typically a squarish yoke with three vertical bands on it; it is not known whether these represented walrus tusks. Before the coming of the Russians, some parkas were made of white fox or other fur, but this was forbidden after contact. The *kamleika* was the waterproof parka worn by the Aleut in his kayak. It was made from the intestines of a seal, sea lion, walrus, or whale, sometimes from the soft skin of the sea lion's esophagus; the guts were cleaned, dried, slit into long strips, and sewn together, horizontally or vertically, into garments. They were hooded, with a drawstring to hold the hood snugly to the face and drawstrings at the wrists as well; the hunter would lash himself into the cockpit (built to fit his body), so he was completely protected against wind and rain and heavy seas. These *kamleikas* were worn over the bird-skin parkas, not only to protect the expensive garments, but for warmth as well. They were embellished with tiny fringing in the seams of cormorant feathers and human hair, with painted esophagus skin, and with short tufts of red and green woolen yarn. *Kamleikas* in the early nineteenth century were made in the Russian fashion, with a stiff upright collar and no hood; the neck area, cuffs, and hem were decorated in applique work, fringing, and embroidery. By mid-century, gut-skin capes were being fashioned in the style of a Russian officer's cape. These featured the same type of decoration as the *kamleikas,* and were chiefly made to be given as gifts to visiting dignitaries by the Russians.

Hair Styles

Captain Cook said that the Aleut men wore the hair loose in back and short in front. The women let their hair grow long, then bundled it up in the back. Some had bangs in front. Some men had sparse beards and mustaches.

Headgear

The bentwood hunting hats of the Aleut men may not have been aboriginal. Certainly they were more common after contact; the steel knives the Russians brought made the necessary chiseling of the wood into thin sheets much easier. The sheets of wood, usually spruce, were steamed or soaked in hot water, bent so that the sides came together at the back, to be sewed with sinew, forming a seam that was covered with a carved ivory piece as a brace. The hat was painted, typically with concentric stripes, then adorned with sea-lion or walrus whiskers that were strung with beads and feathers. Wing-like or bird-like pieces of carved ivory were fastened at the sides, and carved amulets decorated the front. It was held on the head with a tie string threaded through holes at the sides. It was worn with pride by hunters of high status; lesser men wore the bentwood hunting visors. The latter were made like the hunting hats, but of three pieces stitched together with sinew, the crown thus being left open. It was also painted, had a brace at the back, ivory carvings at the sides, amulets at the front, and sea-lion whiskers or feathers as adornment. The Aleut also made hats of gut skin in the style of the seamen's caps of the early nineteenth century, with various designs on top such as concentric circles or pie-shaped wedges. Using wild rye grass, the women wove close, spherical hats in a two-strand twining technique; these were decorated with false embroidery and small tufts of yarn. They may have been made for the Europeans rather than for their own wearing.

Accessories

Besides the hunting hats and visors, the Aleut men wore goggles carved of wood or ivory to further reduce the sun's glare. The women, skillful basket weavers, made envelope-type containers of dune grass in a two-strand twining technique; bags or pouches were also made of the sea lion's esophagus skin or of gut strips, decorated with caribou-hair embroidery, strips of fur, tiny woolen fringes in the seams, and/or gut-on-gut applique. These flat pouches or wallets were often carried around the neck on a cord. The Unalaska Aleut were said to have worn a belt against the naked body with mysterious knots and markings as protection against sudden death. Some mittens were of twined dune grass. The Aleut men wore special gloves for dancing, made of sealskin adorned with puffin beaks, which rattled with the action of the dancer.

Jewelry

Labrets of ivory, jet, limestone, or wood were worn by men and women in the eastern Aleutians, but only by women in the west. Nasal septums of both sexes were pierced, with the men usually wearing a bone or ivory pin, the women a cluster of beads. The pierced ears displayed bead ornaments or feather quills. Bracelets and anklets were of strips of black sealskin or other fur. Captain Cook said some Aleuts fixed beads in the upper lip under the nostril. Many carved-ivory animal effigies were worn as charms, attached to garments or accessories.

Armor

Armor of cedar rods lashed together with sinew was commonly worn by the Aleut warrior, further fortified with a painted wooden shield constructed of two boards fastened together, with knobs on the back for attaching a handle. It is said that battle helmets and special battle *kamleikas* were donned for war, but no examples have survived.

Special Costumes

For ceremonies, the Aleut wore their finest parkas and *kamleikas,* beautifully decorated. Ritual hats were

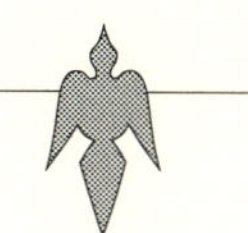

worn by the chiefs—high crowned in a mitre shape of sealskin or bird skins embellished with colored designs made of painted gut or esophagus membrane strips, white caribou-hair embroidery, and red and green woolen fringes in the seams. Besides the hats, ritual wear included masks, forehead fillets, and special belts of seal fur or bird skins, beautifully decorated. Dancing shawls of gut were worn by some. At the time of death mourners cut the hair short; old men gave their close relatives a lock of hair, a piece of a garment worn, or a part of a battle weapon, urging them to carry the item at all times as a defense against misfortune.

Garment Decoration

The only weaving done by the Aleut women was the two-strand twining of dune grass or sea grass, embellished with false embroidery or tufts of woolen yarn. Other decorations on garments and accessories were the use of gut strips, esophagus membranes, feathers, sea-lion whiskers, and caribou-hair embroidery; seams were accented with fringes of wool (red and green) and human hair. Incised ivory amulets were attached as pendants in many places. The bird skins of the men's parkas were painted reddish brown to create various patterns. The hunting hats and visors were also painted, especially with concentric arcs or other geometric figures; other motifs used as decoration were crosshatch, zigzags, diagonals, and circles. A special technique was application of colored gut on gut in various patterns.

Face and Body Embellishment

No face or body painting was practiced by the Aleut, but tattooing of the face and hands, using a moistened thread covered with soot, was fairly common. Designs were simple, typically confined to a few lines.

Masks

At the winter feasts when ancestors were celebrated, portrait masks were worn for dancing; these carved wooden masks were quite naturalistic in their representation of spirits and ancestors. Masks for dancing to the success of whalers tended to be anthropomorphic and zoomorphic in their features.

Transitional Dress

From the mid-eighteenth century to 1867, when the United States purchased Alaska, the Aleutians were dominated by the Russians. Louis Choris, in his 1816 paintings, was already showing the effects of this occupation, the women especially adopting Europeanized clothing. The gut capes and caps were in the Russian style, but the *kamleikas* continued to be made in the traditional fashion, even to the present. The acquisition of colored yarns increased opportunities for decoration; embroidery changed from caribou hair to trade silks and floss. With the constant translocation of the few Aleuts remaining, they adopted the garb of the peoples with whom they settled and little of Aleut costume was worn.

Key Sources

Black, Lydia T. *Atka: An Ethnohistory of the Western Aleutians.* Kingston, Ontario: Limestone, 1984.

Black, Lydia T. and R. G. Liapunova. "Aleut: Islanders of the North Pacific." In *Crossroads of Continents: Cultures of Siberia and Alaska.* Pp. 52–57. Washington: Smithsonian Institution, 1988.

Collins, Henry B., Jr., Austin H. Clark, and Egbert H. Walker. *The Aleutian Islands: Their People and Natural History.* War Background Studies 21. Washington: Smithsonian Institution.

Dumond, Don E. *The Eskimos and Aleuts.* London: Thames and Hudson, 1977.

Ivanov, S. V. "Aleut Hunting Headgear and Its Ornamentation." *Proceedings of the 23rd International Congress of Americanists* 477–504.

Jochelson, Vladimir. *History, Ethnology and Anthropology of the Aleuts.* Carnegie Institution of Washington Publication 432. Washington, 1933.

Lantis, Margaret. "Aleut." In *Handbook of North American Indians. Vol. 5: Arctic.* Pp. 161–184. Washington: Smithsonian Institution.

Laughlin, William S. *Aleuts: Survivors of the Bering Land Bridge.* New York: Holt, Rinehart, & Winston, 1980.

Liapunova, Roza G. "The Aleut." In *The Etholen Collection: The Ethnographic Alaskan Collection of Adolf Etholen and His Contemporaries in the National Museum of Finland.* Pp. 136–215. Pirjo Varjola, ed. Helsinki: National Board of Antiquities, 1990.

Ray, Dorothy Jean. *Aleut and Eskimo Art.* Seattle: University of Washington Press, 1981.

Asiatic and St. Lawrence Island Eskimo

The Asiatic Eskimo live on the very eastern tip of the Chukchi Peninsula of Siberia and on St. Lawrence Island. Speaking a dialect of the Yupik language, they were not Chukchis but Eskimo, sharing a maritime culture with an emphasis on whaling and the hunting of sea mammals, and with a limited focus on reindeer for subsistence. First contact on the Chukchi side was with Cossacks in the seventeenth century; Vitus Bering reached St. Lawrence Island in 1728. There was extensive contact between the two groups until 1948, when the Cold War divided them; today they are again closely associated. Essentially they are a part of the Northern Alaska culture.

Men's Basic Dress

Men wore a hoodless shirt of reindeer skin, belted at the waist and with an unusually large collar; snugly fitted underpants of hair-seal or reindeer skin were tucked into boots. For summer wear the shirt had the fur turned inside; the winter shirt had the fur exposed. When inside their sleeping room, both sexes stripped to what we would term a "brief" of skin, decorated with tassels or fringe; some men, particularly wrestlers, wore an apron of skin.

Mukluks made in the 1930s have caribou soles, patterns of caribou, wolverine, and sealskin, and woven wool tassels.

Women's Basic Dress

Women wore fur underpants, over which was worn a *khonba,* a hoodless combination suit with pants and top all in one; these had long, large sleeves, which were too cumbersome to be efficient. Infants and toddlers wore a similar combination suit, with a flap at the crotch for changing the moss of the diapers.

Footwear

Lightweight boots were for summer wear, heavier furred boots for winter. The uppers were usually of mottled brown and white reindeer skin, obtained in trade from the Chukchis until the St. Lawrence Islanders had their own herds; the heavy, thick sole was of the hide of the bearded seal, crimped at the heel and toe to the upper. Ankle ties on the calf-high men's boots gave support; the knee-high women's boots had ties wrapped around the calves. A drawstring was at the top of both types of boots. Decoration consisted of bands of cut-out designs of bleached sealskin and reindeer-hair embroidery. Inside the boots were deerskin stockings. For hunting on ice, carved ivory cleats were strapped to the bottom of the boots for traction. Simple snowshoes were worn occasionally.

Outer Wear

Parkas, with the fur exposed, were knee-length, hoodless, and were worn belted by the men, unbelted by the women. The woman's parka had a decorated bib-shaped piece applied at the neck. Large collars were typical. Parkas of the skins of guillemots or other birds were worn, but by the end of the nineteenth century they were replaced by reindeer parkas. Straight-sided, hooded gut-skin parkas covered other garments for protection against wind and rain; these were made in the usual fashion, with strips of cleaned, dried, and split intestines sewed together in horizontal or vertical bands and adorned with crested auklet feathers and fur. Some hunters wore gut-skin pants with a drawstring at the top.

Hair Styles

Women let the hair grow long, usually braided on the sides. Men favored the tonsure, the top shaved with a fringe of hair around the head; some men cut the hair, leaving a long lock on top. A few men shaved the head entirely.

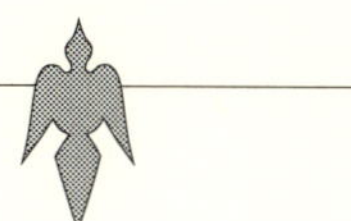

Headgear

Despite the severe climate, parkas were not hooded. Toddlers sometimes wore a fur hood adorned with beads. Occasionally a man with a shaved head would wear a thong headband with a few beads hanging from it. The leader of a whaling party demonstrated his status by the wearing of a visor.

Accessories

Mittens of tanned sealskin had bands of reindeer-hair embroidery around the thumb and at the bottom. For protection from evil spirits, amulets were attached to clothing and accessories; the Asiatic Eskimos believed that swallows protected the sea hunters, and amulets of swallows often hung from the belt, as well as bead clusters, charms, and knives. Belts were frequently embellished with hair embroidery. Purses in an envelope style were made of skin embroidered with reindeer hair and decorated with beads; they were generally worn on the belt. Wrist guards, carved of ivory and embellished with delicately incised designs, protected the wrists from the snap of the bowstring. Goggles of carved wood or ivory were necessary for the sea hunters to guard the eyes from the glare on the water.

Jewelry

Clusters of beads, trade beads or those of bone or shell, were worn as long earrings by the women, or as necklaces by both sexes; sometimes strands of beads were braided into the woman's hair. Men at times wore a few beads dangling from the pierced ears. Bone nose pins were also a form of jewelry for the men; women occasionally wore nose rings. Both sexes

Called a *kamleika* by Aleuts, this hooded windproof and waterproof parka consists of cleaned and dried strips of seal or walrus intestines split and sewn with sinew. Seam decorations include cormorant and auklet feathers.

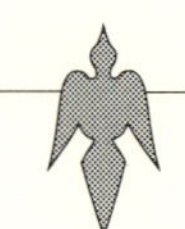

wore labrets, the men with the plug at each side of the mouth, the women with single labrets and sometimes with beaded ornaments at each side of the mouth. An early explorer called them "tooth people" because of the large labrets worn by the men.

Armor

Warfare was common among the Asiatic Eskimo, the Chukchis and other peninsula peoples, and the Bering Strait Eskimo. Early armor consisted of pieces of bone plate fastened together with sinew. Later armor was of hoops of doubled sealskin, increasing in size from the top down; because of the manner in which they were put together, they could be raised and tied around the waist, leaving the warrior free for running. A large, cumbersome wooden shield covered with sealskin was carried by means of wrist straps; after shooting an arrow, the warrior could turn his back, thus protecting himself from retaliation. Some shin guards, actually made of mammoth ivory, offered further protection.

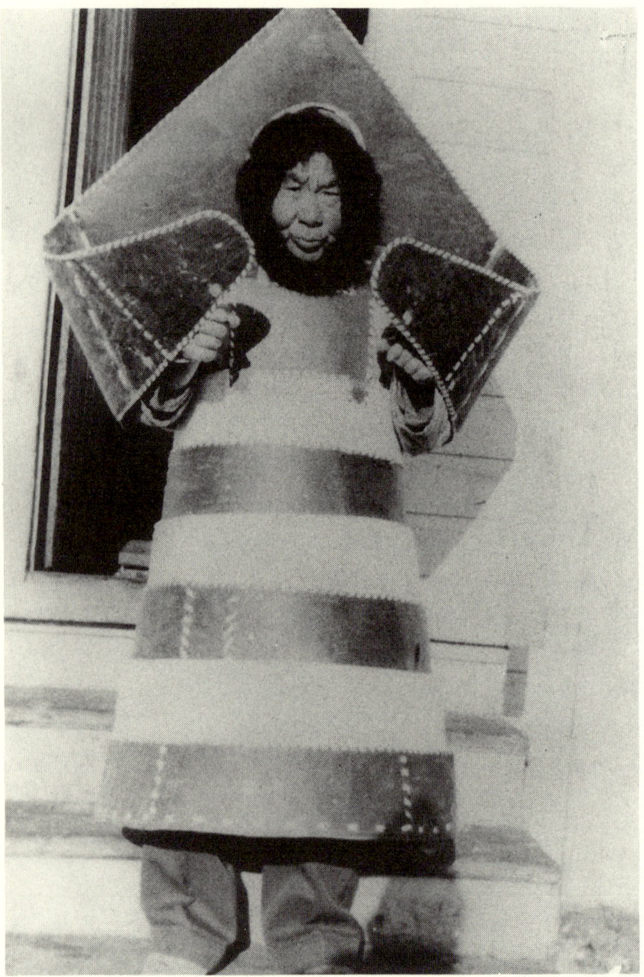

An Asiatic Eskimo models sealskin and wood armor. The lower portion is telescoped so that the wearer can pull it up around his waist while running.

Special Costumes

Ceremonies were concerned with the sea mammals, either in pleading with them for success in the hunt or thanking them for past accomplishments. Shamans were powerful, compelling respect for their curing rites; they had no special costume, but pendants, tassels, and a tobacco pouch indicated status. Some shamans were women. Persons who were ill would sometimes change their clothes entirely, hoping to confuse malevolent spirits into thinking the person was someone else. When a whale hunt was successful, the captain's wife wore a special costume, which included a headband of white reindeer hair.

Garment Decoration

Embroidery involved reindeer hair, rather than caribou; it was done in simple abstract designs. Tassels and fringe, at first of skin, later of yarn, were popular forms of decoration as were auklet feathers, strips of fur, bands of bleached sealskin, and attached carved charms or amulets. Colorful glass trade beads, especially the large blue Chinese beads, were attached to garments and accessories, but beadwork was not generally developed.

Face and Body Embellishment

Faces were painted with stripes of red ocher or graphite to indicate atonement or to placate evil spirits. Tattooing seems to have been more common among the women, with vertical lines on chin and cheeks; some tattooing may have had ritual significance.

Masks

Painted wooden masks were representations of human faces, with black eyebrows and beard and with wrinkles carved into the forehead. Nose pins and labrets were further additions.

Transitional Dress

Because of their relative isolation, these Eskimo continued with their traditional dress into the twentieth century. The men adopted such articles of European-style dress as trousers and jackets, but found that the traditional parkas were much more effective; however, they did add hoods. The gut-skin parka is worn today, the best protection against wind and rain. Many of the women and girls wear the *kupsuck,* the "Eskimo dress" of colorful printed cotton, lined with a heavier cloth such as duffel, with a flounce on the bottom, and with long sleeves. Boots and mittens in the old style have been retained.

Key Sources

Ackerman, Robert E. *The Eskimo People of Savoonga.* Phoenix, AZ: Indian Tribal Series, 1976.

Bogoras, Waldemar. *The Eskimo of Siberia.* New York: AMS Press, 1975.

Hughes, Charles C. "Asiatic Eskimo: Introduction." In *Handbook of North American Indians. Vol. 5: Arctic.* Pp. 243–246. Washington: Smithsonian Institution.

———. "Saint Lawrence Island Eskimo." In *Handbook of North American Indians. Vol. 5: Arctic.* Pp. 262–277. Washington: Smithsonian Institution.

———. "Siberian Eskimo." In *Handbook of North American Indians. Vol. 5: Arctic.* Pp. 247–261. Washington: Smithsonian Institution.

Moore, Riley D. "Social Life of the Eskimo of St. Lawrence Island." *American Anthropologist* 25(3): 339–375.

Baffinland Eskimo

The Eskimo of southern Baffin Island called themselves "Nunatsiaqmiut," or "people of the beautiful land." And yet it was, and is, a land of violent storms; tremendous tides; a long, dark, cold winter; and a brief summer of lasting daylight. Like the Eskimo throughout the Arctic they adjusted to the climate, made use of all the sea and land mammals available to them, endured periods of famine, and found comfort and laughter in their familial and communal living. They were a coastal people, hunting the ringed seal, walrus, narwhal, beluga whale, and polar bear; in autumn they journeyed inland for caribou, and winter found them trapping for foxes. First European contact was with Martin Frobisher in 1576, who took some of them to England; John White did watercolors of those visitors, the earliest surviving pictures of Eskimos. William Baffin visited these Eskimos in 1616, followed by the whalers, traders, missionaries, and finally government officials with their services. Peter Pitseolak, an Eskimo photographer, did some fine photos in the 1940s of Baffinlanders in traditional dress. The Baffin Islanders spoke a dialect of Inuit-Inupiaq.

Men's Basic Dress

Men wore a hooded inner parka of caribou or sealskin, or a combination of the two, loosely constructed to allow for evaporation of perspiration. This was slightly rounded or straight across the bottom in front with a long flap in the back (which disappeared in the nineteenth century). There were

A sixteenth-century Baffin Island Eskimo wears a hooded sealskin parka with a long tail, and trousers tucked into high boots.

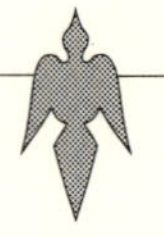

patches of skin at the inner elbows. Pants of the same material had patches at the inner crotch and were tucked into the knee-high boots. Some pants of polar-bear fur were ankle length, worn over the boots.

Women's Basic Dress

Women's inner parkas were also of seal or caribou skin or a combination of the two. They had an unusually large hood for carrying an infant; thongs or braided cords formed a harness at the front to aid in distributing the weight of the baby. A short flap in front, either rounded or squared in shape, and a long flap in back were forms that continued well into the twentieth century. The picture by John White (1577) shows patches on the inner sleeves, both upper and lower arms, and the "walrus tusk" inserts of white fur at the neck. These inner parkas later featured beaded edgings and other designs on the front flaps. Pants of the same material were tucked into the knee-high boots. Brief undergarments of skin were worn by the women, possibly also by the men. In this century hoods were formed with a yoke over the shoulder decorated with bands of fringe in alternating hues.

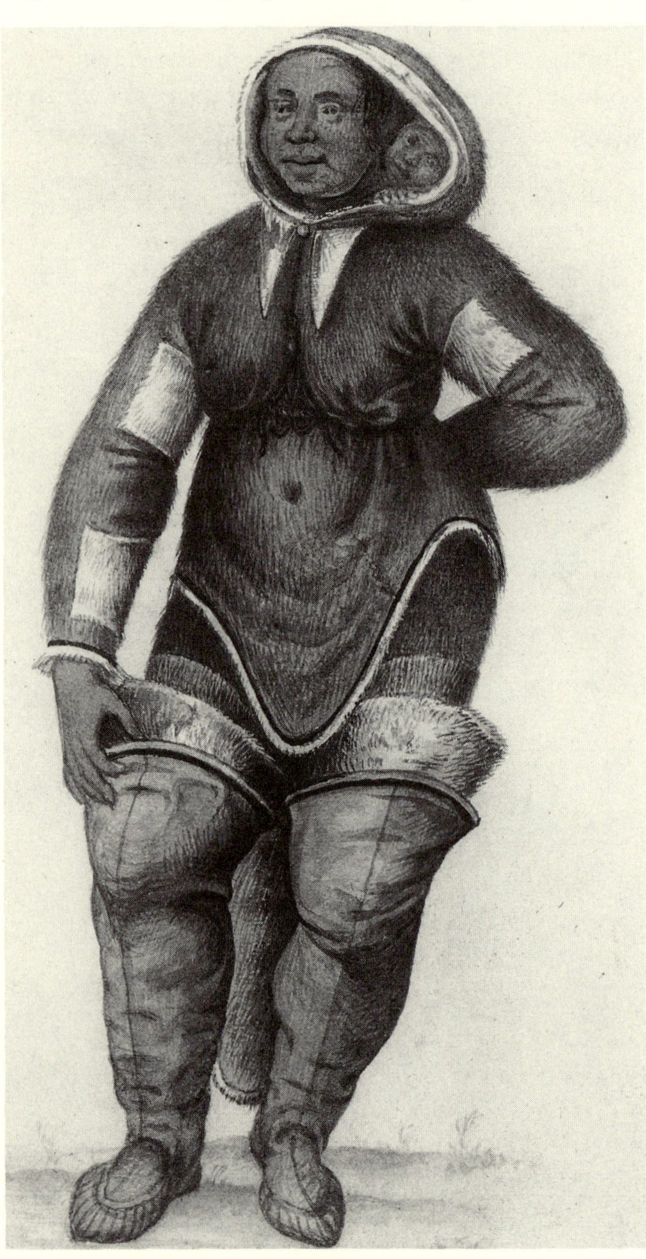

A Baffin Island woman keeps her child tucked into the roomy hood and shoulders of her parka. She wears high boots and her parka has a long tail. Patches of contrasting fur decorate her parka. The pattern at her neck is called walrus tusk. Painted by Englishman John White in 1557.

Footwear

Boots of sealskin, with its superior waterproof feature, were for summer wear; winter boots were of the warmer caribou skin, but with sealskin soles. Men's boots were to the knee or higher and were fastened with thongs below the knee; women's were higher, flaring at the top. The mukluk style was used, with the larger sole crimped into a vamp area. Boots sometimes had a decorative white band down the front. Inner stockings of skin and stuffing of grass helped keep the feet warm. Overboots of sheepskin were worn over the winter boots, fastened with ankle ties.

Outer Wear

Outer winter parkas had the fur side out. Women's parkas had a pointed hood (rounded in the Davis Strait area), the tails or flaps squared off at the front corners. The walrus-tusk motifs were applied at the neck. Men's winter parkas were either straight all around the hem, or had a slit up the front. Parkas for both sexes were decorated with broad bands of white and dark fur at the cuffs, all around the lower edges, and on the front edges of the hoods. Hoods were trimmed with wolverine fur when possible in order to reduce the problem of ice crystals formed from breathing. Gut-skin parkas were worn over the winter parkas when the men were hunting in the kayaks; these often had dog fur sewed in the sleeves to reduce noise that would alert the prey.

Hair Styles

Women parted the hair in the center and fixed it in two braids, sometimes tying the braids together

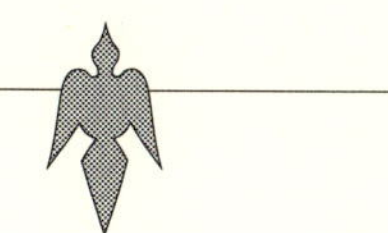

at the back. Men wore the hair short, sometimes with bangs in the front. Some men had mustaches.

Headgear
Since the parkas were hooded, almost no caps were worn; occasionally an infant in the hood had a fur, later wool, cap on its head.

Accessories
Goggles carved of wood with a visor and narrow eye slits were tied around the head to protect the wearer from glare on snow, ice, or water. Some men wore a skin "wind mask" when hunting during rough weather. Bags of fish skin or caribou skin were used to contain necessities, perhaps sewing supplies, such as needles in an ivory needlecase and sinew thread, or other equipment. Mittens were of fur or caribou skin.

Jewelry
Jewelry was rarely worn, confined to an occasional necklace of carved bone or shell beads. Amulets, representing the individual's relationship to the spirit world and usually carved in animal forms, were attached to garments and accessories. Labrets were not worn by these people.

Special Costumes
Although the shaman was an important personage, involved in curing rites and the arrangements of feasts and other ceremonies, there were no special costumes for the shaman, nor for dancers at the feasts.

Garment Decoration
Although garments and accessories were skillfully made, there was little ornamentation in the clothing of the Baffinland Eskimo. The major form of decoration was the use of bands of white and dark fur as edging on garments. In this century beading has been applied to garments, especially the women's parkas; fringes have also been used as decoration, but in a limited amount. One illustration shows a woman's parka adorned with silver spoons down the front. Although netting techniques were known, they were used in making bird nets, not for costumes. The Baffin Islanders did not weave.

Face and Body Embellishment
Although tattooing and face and body painting may have been practiced, neither was mentioned by authorities consulted.

Transitional Dress
Traditional skin garments were worn at least until the 1940s. Before that time, however, some men and women had changed to the wearing of parkas made of "duffel," a wool material sold by the Hudson's Bay Company. These were white and had the typical bands (dark) at hems and edges. By the 1960s some women were wearing cotton skirts over their pants and under the parkas. Men adopted the fur caps, down jackets, dark pants, and rubber boots available at the trading posts. But many were reluctant to give up their sealskin boots, so suitable to the Baffinland climate.

Key Sources

Bilbey, Julian W. *Among Unknown Eskimo: An Account of Twelve Years Intimate Relations with the Primitive Eskimos of Ice-bound Baffin Land, with a Description of Their Ways of Living, Hunting Customs and Beliefs.* London: Seeley Service, 1923.

Boas, Franz. "The Eskimo of Baffin Land and Hudson Bay." American Museum of Natural History *Bulletin* 15.

Hantzsch, Bernard A. *My Life among the Eskimos: Baffinland Journeys in the Years 1909 to 1911.* Leslie H. Neatby, ed. and transl. Saskatoon: University of Saskatchewan, 1977.

Kemp, William B. "Baffinland Eskimo." In *Handbook of North American Indians. Vol. 5: Arctic.* Pp. 463–475. Washington: Smithsonian Institution.

Pitseolak, Peter and Dorothy Eber. *People from Our Side: A Life Story with Photographs by Peter Pitseolak and Oral Biography by Dorothy Eber.* Edmonton, Alberta: Hurtig, 1975.

Bering Strait Eskimo
The Eskimo living along the Bering Strait from the Yukon Delta north to Cape Espenburg on the Seward Peninsula were both coastal and interior peoples. Along the coast they hunted for sea mammals (except

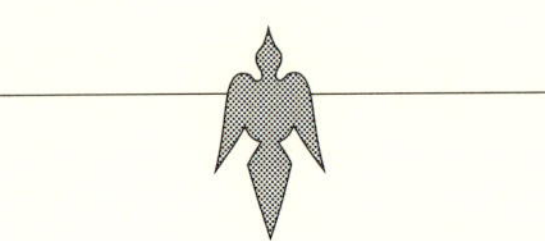

the large whales) and in the forests of the interior they hunted caribou, grizzly bears, and small animals, and fished. The people had a great respect for the animals on which their livelihood depended, apologizing to them for the necessity of killing them; this respect was also shown in their masks, amulets, and ceremonies. The southern groups spoke Yupik; those in the north were Inupiaq speakers. First contact with Europeans was with Russian Cossacks and Chukchis in 1711. Russians came in the early nineteenth century for furs, but trading was peaceful; the Eskimo were not brutally treated as the Aleut had been. Zagoskin in his journals of the 1840s gave much information on their lifeways, as did the anthropologist Edward Nelson, who lived among them from 1877 to 1881.

Men's Basic Dress

The inner parka, often hooded and belted, was worn in the summer, the fur being turned inward; these were cut straight at the sides and around the bottom. Decoration consisted of sea-otter fur (when available) at the neck and wrists, white caribou-fur insets ("walrus tusks") at the neck, and light and dark fur bands at the wrists and upper arms. Sometimes a large collar or yoke was a part of the parka. Knee-length pants, of strong sealskin or the pale-brown hair of a caribou leg, had a yoke piece at the top and a tanned-leather fringe across the back; caribou fur edged the bottom of each leg.

Women's Basic Dress

Women dressed much like the men, but their parkas had deep, curving hems in front and back; a large collar or yoke was typical, as were the walrus-tusk insets of white caribou fur at the neck, and the bands of light and dark fur edging the wrists and hem. A belt adorned with caribou teeth was a popular item. The hoods were not generally large, except those for carrying infants. Women either wore knee-length pants like the men, which were worn with boots, or in some places footed trousers, which were worn with sealskin slippers in the summer. A harness of braided cords helped keep the infant securely in the hood.

Footwear

Boots were of various types and materials. Land boot uppers were of seal, caribou, or reindeer skin, and the soles were of the tough skin of the *ugruk,* or bearded seal, crimped and sewn into the uppers; these varied from ankle-high to hipboots. Waterproof boots were made of dehaired sealskin. Insoles of caribou skin and dried grass or moss were used for insulation. Boots were decorated with strips of colored skin, dyed dog hair, wolverine fur, and long tassels. Sometimes squares of bearskin were tied about the feet to keep them warm on ice. Small, oval-shaped snowshoes with a short tail and coarse webbing were worn, particularly by the Eskimo of the interior.

Outer Wear

Parkas for winter wear for both sexes were made with the fur turned inward, being worn over the inner parkas, the air trapped between the two, affording insulation. The parkas, hooded or hoodless, were made of furs such as ground squirrel, mink, wolf, wolverine, or the brown and white mottled reindeer fur. Men's parkas were straight around the bottom; the women's were slit on the sides with deeply curving edges front and back, the front flap smaller than the back. They featured the large fur collars, the walrus-tusk insets of white caribou fur, and trimming of strips of hide and fur at wrists, around the edges, and on the upper arms or shoulders. *Kamleikas,* the parkas or shirts made of sea-mammal intestines, were worn over the fur parkas for protection against rain and wind. Some neck-high body suits of gut skin kept the men dry when setting salmon nets in deep water. Highly valued were the bird-skin parkas made by women only for their own wear; the finest were of cormorant throat skin.

Hair Styles

Some men displayed the tonsured hair style; others cut it straight across the brow, with the rest of the hair fairly short. Women braided the hair, sometimes wearing the braids looped up or fastened together in back; the braids were occasionally wrapped with strips of fur or cloth.

Headgear

Since parkas were hooded, especially in winter, few caps were worn, although mention is made of men wearing a bird-skin cap (but nothing else) in the sweat bath, and Nelson recorded a headdress made of a whole Arctic fox, with the head of the fox resting on

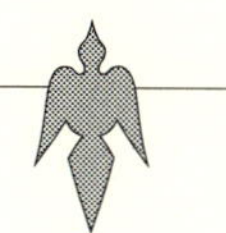

the wearer's head and the body and tail hanging down the back. Sea hunters in Norton Sound wore a bentwood hunting hat similar to those of the Aleut, except that the wood was unpainted and at the back of the hat there was a flourish of feathers. One hat has an ivory ornament depicting the smiling-husband and frowning-wife spirit faces. Louis Choris, in one of his paintings, shows a man wearing a headband of beads.

Accessories

The women kept their sewing supplies—needles, awls, and crimpers for boot soles—in a "housewife" or work bag of caribou skin. Bags for other purposes were made of skin or gut. A special woman's belt was of rawhide with two or three rows of caribou incisors, the sign of a successful hunter; these were fastened with skin loops and ivory toggles at the end. Mittens of seal or walrus gut were useful when hunting in the kayak; these were sometimes kept together with a cord or harness. Men used a respirator, constructed of grass or wood twigs, to cover the mouth while taking a sweat bath, to avoid injuring the throat with the steam. Wrist guards of bone or ivory protected the wrist from the snap of the bowstring.

Jewelry

Earrings, pendants, hair ornaments, and amulets were carved of ivory, characteristically in the form of a human face. The amulets were used by men, particularly, attached to their belts and garments to ensure success in hunting; these often had large blue and white Chinese beads on them. Women wore a central labret below the lower lip, frequently quite elaborate with strings of beads attached. Men displayed a labret at each corner of the mouth; these were of carved ivory incised with human "spirit faces," a smiling face (the husband) and a frowning face (the wife). Buttons for fastening garments also featured faces.

Armor

Vital organs were afforded protection by the use of armor constructed of slats of wood, bone, or ivory lashed together with tough sinew; walrus-hide straps over the shoulders held the armor in place. Some armor had the back heightened to protect the neck.

Special Costumes

Winter was the time for ceremonials, for feasts and dancing; ceremonies were gift-giving festivals, memorial rituals for the dead, and masked dances. Men wore dance mittens made of sealskin and adorned with rattling puffin beaks and feathers. Women wore dancing headbands of ermine fur with a heavy beaded fringe that obscured the vision, implying a transformation to a spiritual vision. Men, too, wore headbands for dancing, especially the leaders of whaling crews; to these were attached large blue and white beads and many amulets of spiritual significance. Men also wore armlets of fur, special pants, and masks for dancing. At menstruation, girls were isolated, wore mittens with no thumbs, and hoods to avoid the gaze of others.

Garment Decoration

Frequently used motifs were the nucleated circle (dot within a circle) and the smiling face (male) and frowning face (female). The walrus-tusk insets appeared at the neck of the parkas of both sexes. Bands of dark and light skin or fur were typical edgings. Sea-otter or other furs were used as trim at collars and wrists. The large blue and white Chinese beads were popular, attached to charms, labrets, garments, and accessories. No weaving or embroidery seems to have been done by these Eskimo.

Face and Body Embellishment

Women displayed tattoo marks on the face—lines on the chin, a line down the nose, and designs on the cheeks; at times they had tattoos on the upper body. Tattooing was done at the time of puberty on the wrists of boys and girls, the former to celebrate the first kill, the latter to indicate the arrival of the first menstruation. Little face or body painting was practiced, although the men and boys were sometimes spotted with paint as they paraded from house to house during ceremonies. Neutrality during conflict was indicated by blackening the face.

Masks

Masks were regularly used in dancing and special ceremonies. There were two major forms: (1) the *tunghak* or transformational masks representing combinations of the spirits of animals, birds such as ravens, and persons and (2) the *inua* or spirit masks of various creatures. The *tunghaks* were sometimes enormous masks, suspended from the roof, to be danced behind. Some masks were hooped, representing the cosmos, and also reflecting the prevailing circle-and-dot motif. Characteristically, openings were made for the eyes, the mouth, and a circle on the forehead; the nose was often twisted, human hair was attached to fall over the eyes, and a cylindrical hair ornament was frequently added. In the southern part of the area, the Yupik women danced with finger masks.

Transitional Dress

Traditional dress was worn by the Bering Strait Eskimo until well into the twentieth century. Then the women began to wear the typical "Eskimo dress" or *kupsuck* of printed cotton cloth, often lined, with long sleeves and a large flounce at the bottom edged with braid. For winter wear, a fur collar or hood would be worn; during the summer, wool headscarves or lined cloth hoods were popular. The cotton dress was worn with fur pants to the knees and knee-high boots. Men continued to wear the hooded parkas (today they are often zippered), but have substituted heavy cloth trousers and wool socks. Nowadays, in summer, usual attire is jeans, plaid shirts, and rubber boots. Walrus-tusk inserts are no longer to be seen.

Key Sources

Fienup-Riordan, Ann. "Eye of the Dance: Spiritual Life of the Bering Sea Eskimo." In *Crossroads of Continents: Cultures of Siberia and Alaska.* Pp. 256–270. Washington: Smithsonian Institution, 1988.

Fitzhugh, William W. and Susan A. Kaplan. *Inua: Spirit World of the Bering Sea Eskimo.* Washington: Smithsonian Institution, 1982.

Nelson, Edward W. "The Eskimo about Bering Strait." Bureau of American Ethnology *Annual Reports* 18(1).

Ray, Dorothy Jean. "Bering Strait Eskimo." In *Handbook of North American Indians. Vol. 5: Arctic.* Pp. 285–302. Washington: Smithsonian Institution.

———. *Eskimo Masks: Art and Ceremony.* Seattle: University of Washington Press, 1967.

———. *The Eskimo of Bering Strait: 1650–1898.* Seattle: University of Washington Press, 1975.

Caribou Eskimo

The Padlermiut were the "people of the yellow thickets," but the whites called them and their neighboring groups the Caribou Eskimo, for their economy was based on the hunting of the Barren Ground caribou. They lived on the tundra on the west side of Hudson Bay from the Manitoba boundary north to Cape Fullerton and inland about 300 miles. They were Inuit-Inupiaq speakers. During the summer they hunted sea mammals along the coast, traveling inland for the rest of the year for caribou and musk-oxen. There was hostility with the Indians of the interior, but also much trade. They met some of the European voyagers in the seventeenth century, but the first real contact was the establishment by the Hudson's Bay Company of the post that later became Churchill. Nineteenth-century whalers, missionaries, miners, and traders eroded their culture. Today they have adopted a wage economy with heavy subsidization by the Canadian government.

Men's Basic Dress

Men wore a hooded parka in summer of caribou fur, with the hair inside; some were waist length in front with a long tail in back, others had slits at the sides

A detail of an 1832 watercolor by John Halkett shows a Caribou Eskimo with fishing and hunting gear. He wears mukluk-style boots and a hooded parka with a long tail flap.

with deep flaps in front and back, and still others were cut straight all around and were knee length. A long fringe at the bottom anchored the parka so it was not lifted in the wind. Some of these inner parkas were beaded around the edges and at the rim of the hood, a skill learned from the Indians of the interior; the only other decoration consisted of bands of white skin as edging. With these were worn pants of skin to the knees, tucked into knee-high boots. From a watercolor by John Halkett (1832), we can see pictured a Caribou Eskimo with his parka, short in front, with a long tail in back, and trimmed with wide bands of white fur. Some costumes had pants and moccasins or boots all in one piece.

Women's Basic Dress

The inner parka, worn in the summer, was of caribou skin with the hair inside; it had an unusually large hood for carrying a baby, and a harness of cords to help distribute the weight of the infant and keep it securely in place. Young girls had small hoods on their parkas, which increased in size as they matured. This parka was a fitted garment requiring a complicated pattern of small pieces and demanding superb tailoring on the part of the seamstress. The curved tail in front was smaller than the one in back; the back flap often had loops so it could be folded up and fastened to be out of the way. The parka was embellished with elaborately beaded panels in front, bands of white fur, thin strips of white skin, fringe, and tassels; the enormous shoulder pieces were decorated with further beadwork and beaded fringes. The pants worn with the parka also had the hair inside for summer wear, extended to below the knees, and had a very large pouch, which functioned as a pocket, at the outer side of each knee.

Footwear

Boots of caribou leather and fur were in the characteristic mukluk style, with the large sole of tough sealskin crimped and sewn into a leather vamp; the uppers of fur often had a white fur edging and a drawstring for a snug fit. Women's boots were sometimes ankle-high, with long pants or footed trousers tucked in. Moccasins of the typical Subarctic Indian pattern with its front seam to the vamp and a heel seam were for summer wear. Stockings of skin were worn under the boots.

Outer Wear

Winter parkas for both sexes were of caribou skin with the fur turned outward. The man's parka was cut straight across the bottom in front with a knee-length flap in the back; it was decorated with a fringe at the bottom and a wide band of white fur above the fringe and at the wrists. The woman's winter parka, like the summer one, had very large shoulders, a harness with an ornamented toggle for carrying a baby, a small scooped-shape fringed flap in front and a long flap in back, also fringed. Contrasting bands of fur adorned the bottom and cuffs. Remnants of the "walrus tusk" motif could be seen in the two vertical, rectangular bands at the neck. With these parkas, pants of caribou skin were worn with the hair outward; the woman's pants had the large pockets at the knees.

Hair Styles

Men wore the hair short, occasionally cut square across the forehead; some men had mustaches. Women braided the hair, sometimes tying the braids together in back, at times wrapping them with skin or red cloth. The Caribou women, along with the Netsilik and Iglulik, utilized "hair sticks": these were long, polished wooden rods, the length of the braids, which were attached to the rods by wrappings of beaded bands or alternating strips of light and dark fur.

Headgear

Since parkas were hooded, no caps were worn by the Caribou Eskimo. In this century, women have worn a brow band made of brass, preferably, or other metal obtained from the traders; some were hammered out of old telescopes. The band was adorned with long strands of glass beads.

Accessories

Carved wooden goggles were tied around the head with thongs or a beaded band. Mittens had the fur inside and had a decorative border of bands of light and dark fur. A few pouches of caribou skin were made to carry necessary items such as needles, awls, and sinew for sewing.

Jewelry

Jewelry was minimal, consisting generally of strands of glass beads that were attached to the brass brow bands or worn as necklaces. Protective charms and amulets were worn, especially by children.

Special Costumes

There was little ceremonialism among the Caribou Eskimo. Shamans occupied a significant position in society because of their curing rites and rituals to ensure hunting success; while curing the sick, the shaman wore red cloth bindings on his parka.

Garment Decoration

Early decoration was limited to the application of bands of white fur or skin on the brown caribou fur or leather with the addition of skin fringes. In the late nineteenth century the techniques of beadwork were learned from the Indians to the south, leading to the use of beaded bands and elaborately beaded panels as garment decoration. Some authorities feel that the resultant effect was not as fine artistically as their use of the native materials.

Face and Body Embellishment

A few women exhibited facial tattooing, generally thin vertical lines on the chin.

Transitional Dress

Traditional dress was retained well into the present century, but cloth was so much easier to obtain and use than tanned hides that it was gladly purchased and made into cotton summer dresses, often lined and sometimes hooded, to wear over the skin pants. Woolen shawls took the place of some women's parkas. Other parkas were made of duffel, the heavy material sold by the posts; these had zippers up the front, but added a

A Caribou woman wears a brass brow band and her hair wound around sticks and wrapped with strips of white hide. In winter she wears this inner parka under an outer parka, and in summer she wears a shawl instead. Elaborate beadwork, including a version of the walrus-tusk pattern at her neck, and fringes decorate the front and over-sized shoulders of this late 1920s parka.

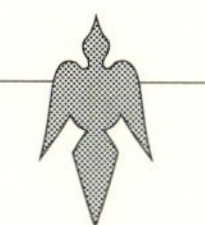

hood trimmed with fur and embroidered borders. However, traditional boots, mittens, and parkas are still worn today by many of the Caribou Eskimo.

Key Sources

Birket-Smith, Kaj. "The Caribou Eskimo: Material and Social Life and Their Cultural Position." W. E. Calvert, transl. In *Report of the 5th Thule Expedition, 1921–1924* 15(1). Copenhagen, 1929.

Clark, Brenda L. *The Development of Caribou Eskimo Culture.* Mercury Series, Archaeological Survey Paper 59. Ottawa: National Museum of Man, 1977.

Gabus, Jean. *Vie et coutumes des Esquimaux caribous.* Paris: Payot, 1944.

Harper, Francis. "Caribou Eskimos of the Upper Kazan River, Keewatin." University of Kansas Museum of Natural History *Miscellaneous Publications* 36.

VanStone, James W. and Wendell H. Oswalt. *The Caribou Eskimos of Eskimo Point.* NCRC-59-2. Ottawa: Department of Northern Affairs and National Resources, Northern Coordination and Research Centre.

Copper Eskimo

The Copper Eskimo live in a land of tundra and ice in north-central Canada around Coronation Gulf, between the Coppermine and Perry rivers. The name refers to the deposits of copper in the area, from which the aboriginal people made tools. They spoke a dialect of the Inuit-Inupiaq language. Their clothing was almost exclusively made of the skins of caribou, which they hunted in August when the skins were at their best. Fall and winter were the times for sewing, when 40 or 50 women would gather to work on clothing. These Eskimo were the last to be contacted by whites. In 1853 they found an abandoned whaling ship in the gulf, from which they salvaged everything possible, including treasured metal, wood (little driftwood came to the area), leather, and woolen cloth. In 1906 they were visited briefly by whalers. In 1910 Vilhjalmur Stefansson came and in 1914 the Canadian Arctic Expedition arrived under the leadership of Diamond Jenness; these contacts not only furnished valuable information on the Copper Eskimo, but also began the transition into a wage economy dependent upon trade goods. Also in the early twentieth century, there was an influx of Eskimos from the west, bringing in new ideas about clothing and clothing styles. By the 1960s almost all vestiges of aboriginal culture had vanished.

Men's Basic Dress

For summer wear, the caribou-skin inner parka with the fur turned inside was the basic garment; it generally had a small, close-fitting, pointed hood, was cut straight across the waist in front, and had a long flap in the back for sitting on the ice. Some had short sleeves with undersleeves. There was little if any decoration on these inner parkas. Worn with this inner parka was a pair of pants that were quite roomy, knee-length, and with white bands for decoration.

Women's Basic Dress

Women's inner parkas, like those of the men, were of caribou skin with the hair turned inward, were typically cut square across the waist, and had a long narrow flap at the back. But the shoulder pieces were grossly exaggerated and the hood was bag-like, especially large for those women carrying an infant. Some parkas had a small narrow V flap hanging from

A Copper Eskimo man jigs for fish at Barnard Harbour northwest of Coronation Gulf. He wears goggles with eye slits to reduce snow glare. His waist-length outer parka has a long tail in back; both the parka and outer pants are of sealskin. Photographed between 1914 and 1916.

the waist at center front. Inner trousers, some with a triangular inset at the crotch, were worn, and over them were large, bulky pants, like leggings, suspended from the waist at the sides; these were usually ankle-length, worn with heavy moccasins. Decoration, as with that of the men's garments, was minimal.

Footwear

Knee-high summer boots were of waterproof sealskin. Winter boots were of caribou skin, adorned with white bands and widely spaced fringing. Women's boots were large and roomy, with straps at the top for attaching to a belt. Slippers of sealskin, with a front seam, had a drawstring round the top; they were worn with two sets of fur stockings in winter.

Outer Wear

The outer parkas had the fur turned outward, otherwise they were much the same as the basic inner parkas. Men's were cut square across the waist (as were the women's), had a long flap at the rear and a close-fitting pointed hood, and were worn with rather full trousers to the knees. The women's outer parkas had the exaggerated shoulders, large rounded hood, and a narrow flap in the back. Decoration for parkas of both sexes consisted of a few sparse fringes and broad and narrow bands of white caribou fur or skin, forming a nice contrast with the brown fur. The "walrus tusks" were different from the curved, elongated triangles of the western Eskimo; the characteristic Copper inserts were large white triangles, broad across the shoulders, tapering in a curve to a narrow width at the waist. Women's winter trousers, with the fur turned outward, were the basic leggings attached at the waist with straps. Men hunting sea mammals in their kayaks wore jackets of sealskin.

A rear view of a Copper man, left, and woman, right, shows details of their dance costumes, which have contrasting bands of fur. Both parkas have long tails to make sitting on ice and snow more comfortable.

Hair Styles

The hair was worn simply. Women wore it in two long braids. Men cut it short, and many practiced the odd special custom of shaving the forehead. Some men had a small mustache.

Headgear

Since hooded parkas were sufficient, no caps were worn except for ceremonies.

Accessories

Accessories were few. Mittens of caribou fur, edged with white bands, were long because of the shortness of some sleeves; mittens of polar-bear fur were particularly treasured because they shed ice quickly. Goggles of carved wood or ivory helped reduce snow blindness. Belts were of leather or braided sinew.

Jewelry

Jewelry was almost nonexistent. A few amulets or charms carved of ivory were attached to clothing to propitiate the spirits of the sea and the land.

Special Costumes

These were not a ceremonious people. Few rituals were observed, but gatherings featured dancing, at which one's best clothes were worn; at the back of the parkas, strips of red-dyed skin and ermine pelts were

A Copper Eskimo woman sews clothing for the Canadian Arctic expedition in 1915. She wears a hooded parka with the walrus-tusk motiff at the neck. Her outer pants, made of sealskin with the hair worn on the inside, fasten at her waist. The stripes of her inner pants show, at left.

hung. A special dancing cap of loon skin and caribou fur was worn by both sexes; beaks of loons and ermine pelts were attached.

Garment Decoration

Decoration consisted almost entirely of wide and narrow bands of white fur or skin at the edges of the parkas, around the sleeves, and around the pant legs. The characteristic Copper Eskimo walrus-tusk insert was found on the parkas of both sexes. Fringing, when it appeared on trousers and parkas, was of skin and rather straggly.

Face and Body Embellishment

Women displayed tattoos on the chin (a few vertical lines), cheeks, nose, brow, arms, and hands. Usually these were thin lines with some geometric designs.

Transitional Dress

By the 1960s little of fur clothing was worn, except for the lining and ruffs of parka hoods; some jackets still retained the walrus tusks. Women sewed socks of duffel (a heavy cloth) and cotton dresses on their portable sewing machines. These dresses were of printed cloth (polka dots a favorite), were often lined, and had a wide flounce at the bottom, edged with braid. Cloth headscarves and knit wool caps were sometimes used in place of the fur-lined hoods. The carved-ivory goggles were now abandoned in favor of commercial sunglasses.

Key Sources

Boas, Franz. *The Central Eskimo.* Lincoln: University of Nebraska Press, 1964.

Damas, David. "Copper Eskimo." In *Handbook of North American Indians. Vol. 5: Arctic.* Pp. 397–414. Washington: Smithsonian Institution.

———. "The Copper Eskimo." In *Hunters and Gatherers Today.* Pp. 3–50. New York: Holt, Rinehart & Winston, 1972.

Jenness, Diamond. *The Life of the Copper Eskimos.* Report of the Canadian Arctic Expedition, 1913–1918. Vol. 12(A). Ottawa: King's Printer, 1922.

———. *Material Culture of the Copper Eskimos.* Report of the Canadian Arctic Expedition, 1913–1918. Vol. 16. Ottawa, 1946.

Momatink, Yva and John Eastcott. "Still Eskimo—Still Free: The Inuit of Umingmaktok." *National Geographic* 152 (5): 624–647.

Greenland Eskimo

The Eskimo of Greenland, Inuit-Inupiaq or Eastern Eskimo speakers, seem to have migrated from the west by way of northern Greenland; it is not known when they made the journey, but by A.D. 1000 they had traveled down the cold, inhospitable east coast or the warmer west coast to southern Greenland, where they may have encountered the Norsemen. Eventually some settled on the west coast as far north as Melville Bay. The Norse colonies had collapsed by the fifteenth century; whether the Eskimo had a part in that collapse is not known. Occasional traders in the next century brought beads, clothes, and other items. In the early eighteenth century Danish colonization began with the arrival of Lutheran and Moravian missionaries on the south and west coasts; because of the severe cold and the forbidding ice pack, East Greenland remained unknown until the 1880s. The Greenland coast is an area of extensive resources; sea mammals, including whales, abound, as well as fish and huge flocks of migratory birds. Today the Eskimo are involved in commercial fishing and a wage economy dependent on oil and traders' goods.

Men's Basic Dress

At the time of European contact, men's parkas or jackets were knee-length with a small flap in center front and center back; later these were shortened to hip-length and were either cut straight across the bottom or curved to a short dip in front. These hooded parkas *(anoraks)* were of sealskin with the fur turned inward for summer wear and had a large collar; under European influence, jackets of the eighteenth century often had a front closure. Trousers were short (above the knees), later longer, with the boot height adjusted accordingly; a stripe of contrasting color adorned the sides. Indoors, very short underpants of skin, called *naasit,* were worn by both sexes.

Women's Basic Dress

At the time of contact a long inner coat or jacket *(anorak)* was above the knees in length and had the fur turned inward; usually of sealskin, it had a large, open collar, a very high decorated hood, was broad at the shoulders, and had larger flaps than the men's jackets. Cuffs and collars were often of black dog fur. Later jackets were hip-length, curved to a dip in front, and had a long, narrow flap in back. A harness, fastened to a large button or toggle in front, kept an infant in the hood secure, and helped distribute the weight. Sealskin trousers came to below the knees, embellished with front thigh panels made of many bits of varicolored leather in a fur "mosaic." In warm weather the women wore very short pants, leaving the thighs bare to the above-knee boots. Decoration consisted of colored leather insets in the seams around the arms and at the bottom of the jacket, a designed insert at the neck, and vertical stripes or panels on the pants. Women, too, wore the short underpants *(naasits)* indoors.

Footwear

Summer sealskin boots for women had the fur turned inside; they had black soles and two types of uppers: (1) Some boots *(kamiks)* had white uppers with a broad decorative band just below the knees embellished with either floral or geometric designs, and a wide band of lace above this, either commercial or hand-crocheted lace, placed effectively against the black fur tops. (2) Other *kamiks* were of painted skin, usually red, sometimes blue, with a black and white band at the front separating into a V at the top, above which were broad bands of black and white fur. These fancifully adorned boots were worn by most women everyday; only a few wore plain boots. Men's boots were simpler and shorter, calf-high or knee-high, with only a band of contrasting fur at the top. Stockings of skin, later of wool, encased the legs and feet under the boots. A few simple slippers or moccasins were for summer wear. When seal hunting, men often tied squares of hairy skin under their boots to deaden the sound when approaching their prey.

Outer Wear

The outer jackets or *anoraks* were of warm caribou fur, with the fur outside, exhibiting the same characteristics as the inner garments—the same flaps, hoods, and contrasting bands of color for decoration; some displayed the "walrus tusk" motif. A few bird-skin anoraks were created, as well as gut skin jackets for hunting in the kayak; these were laced tightly into the wooden ring surrounding the opening of the kayak; wrists and the hood were also laced tightly to keep the kayaker dry. Body suits of sealskin were worn by the whalers; they had parka, mittens, and boots, all attached, with a large hole at the top for entering into the garment. Women at times wore a wide fur or cloth waistband over their winter *anoraks.*

Hair Styles

Men generally cut the hair short; in fact, it was sometimes cut round like a bowl. Women had a unique hair style: they pulled the hair up tight to the crown, bound it around with a strap of leather (later ribbon or a beaded band), and let the rest remain coiled on top; beaded ornaments were often worn at the front. This topknot has gone out of style in the twentieth century, to be replaced by braids or a short cut. Many men sported mustaches; some had beards.

Headgear

Both sexes wore hooded parkas (the woman's hood fashioned to contain the topknot), so no caps were worn.

Accessories

Mittens of polar-bear fur were popular; mittens of sealskin had two thumbs in order for the mitten to be

With the arrival of European glass beads in Greenland in the late nineteenth century, Eskimo women began to make collars such as this one from the 1920s. The geometric designs on a netted base were individual creations that are now proudly worn as ethnic symbols.

turned when the palm got wet. Gloves of depilated skin could be tied snugly at the wrists for use in the kayak. Various bags or pouches of tanned skin carried necessary articles, such as fire-making or sewing equipment; these were decorated with colored skin in the "mosaic" manner. Snow goggles, to reduce the glare of the sun on sea and snow, were carved of driftwood or ivory. Women, beginning in the late nineteenth century, have worn magnificent beaded collars; made of glass beads on a netted base, they featured geometric designs, each one individually devised by the wearer herself. They are still worn today at celebrations as a symbol of ethnicity.

Jewelry

Before contact, necklaces made of beads of soapstone, amber, carved ivory, and antler were worn. Later, particularly in East Greenland rather than West Greenland, a few women wore dangling ear ornaments and chokers and elaborate necklaces of beads. Some carved charms or amulets were worn as pendants attached to garments. Children sometimes had charms attached by cords to the front and back of the body to guard the child from harm.

Special Costumes

These people had few rituals. At the time of death the corpse was dressed in the finest clothes in preparation for burial, while mourners dressed in an unkempt, dirty condition to show their grief.

Garment Decoration

Greenland is one of the few Eskimo areas where skins were dyed for decorative purposes; in other places the natural colors of the skins were used to form designs. Red, the most common dye, was made from a concoction of driftwood bark, but early traders brought dyes, such as vermilion. These colored leathers were put together into mosaic designs or as bands of contrasting colors on garments. Bands of black and white furs offered effective accents. No weaving was done by the women, except for the netting technique that produced the bases for the colorful beaded collars. There was early exposure to beads from the traders, but beadwork seems not to have been worked until the late nineteenth century. Some crocheting of lace was done, but most lace was of commercial origin.

Face and Body Embellishment

Only women, and not all women, were tattooed; geometric figures of lines and points or dots were used on face, breasts, arms, and legs. Tattooing was done at puberty, using a bone needle and sinew rubbed with soot.

Masks

A few carved wooden masks have survived from precontact days; these were said to have been used by dancers, possibly shamans, during curing and other rites.

Transitional Dress

From 1900 to the present, the trend has been toward European clothes, but much of Greenlandic costume remains, especially for celebrations. With the development of commercial fishing and a money economy, it has been more advantageous for the Eskimo to sell the furs acquired from hunting and buy ready-made clothing, or at least make some garments from cloth. Men still wear sealskin outfits when hunting, but the *anorak* for summer is of white cotton. The women occasionally wear their distinctive native costumes, a matter of ethnic pride, with the colorful lace- and embroidery-embellished boots, the sealskin pants, and the brilliantly beaded collars. For everyday wear, they don cotton dresses and an *anorak* without a hood; some wear the traditional sealskin boots.

Key Sources

Birket-Smith, Kaj. "Ethnology of the Egedesminde District, with Aspects of the General Culture of West Greenland." *Meddelelser om Gronland* 66.

———. "The Greenlanders of the Present Day." In *Greenland.* Vol. 2. Pp. 1–207. M. Vahl et al., eds. London: Oxford University Press, 1928.

Gad, Finn. *The History of Greenland.* 3 vols. Montreal: McGill-Queen's University Press, 1971–1982.

Holm, Gustav F. "Ethnological Sketch of the Angmagsalik Eskimo." *Meddelelser om Gronland* 39.

Ostermann, Hother B. S. "Knud Rasmussen's Posthumous Notes on the Life and Doings of the East Greenlanders in Olden Times." *Meddelelser om Gronland* 109(1).

Porsild, Morton P. "Studies on the Material Culture of the Eskimo of West Greenland." *Meddelelser om Gronland* 51(5).

Thalbitzer, William. "The Ammalssalik Eskimo: Contributions to the Ethnology of the East Greenland Natives." *Meddelelser om Gronland* 39, 40, 53.

Iglulik Eskimo

The Iglulik Eskimo inhabited Melville Peninsula and the northwestern part of Baffin Island. Inuit-Inupiaq speakers, they were renowned walrus hunters. They also hunted other sea mammals, including whales and polar bears, and in the fall they went into the interior for caribou. The abundant migratory waterfowl were also important for subsistence. First European contacts were with Scottish whalers in 1819, who caused disastrous epidemics. American whalers came in the 1860s. In this century there have been the three major elements of Canadian development: the RCMP or "Mounties," the missionaries (in this case Anglican and Catholic), and the Hudson's Bay Company posts.

Men's Basic Dress

The Iglulik man's inner caribou parka (the *anorak)* had a peaked hood (at times it was hoodless), and long flaps in front and back (shorter in front), curved up to the sides. In some areas, such as Pond Inlet, the front of the parka was slit at the bottom, somewhat in the manner of a European coat. Trousers of caribou skin, with the hair turned inward like the inner parka, were cut square across the bottom, ending below the knee. Both parka and trousers were decorated with bands of white skin or fur; some had a fringe below the white band of the parka.

Women's Basic Dress

The woman's inner parka had long, narrow, curved flaps, front and back, almost to the heels in back, sometimes fringed. The hood *(amaut)* was enormous for carrying an infant; a harness, with toggles at the armholes, helped distribute the weight and kept the baby secure. The armholes were large to accommodate the nursing of the baby. The pants were calf-length or lower to meet the boots, with a large pouch at each lower leg, said to function as a pocket. These inner garments, with the hair turned inward, were of caribou or sealskin (the latter waterproof); were banded with white fur at the bottom edges, the cuffs, and around the *amaut;* and were worn alone in the summer.

Footwear

Boots were of sealskin, with soles of tough bearded-seal skin. Summer boots, particularly, had to be sewn carefully so they were watertight. Winter boots were of caribou, much warmer. Stockings were of caribou skin or duck skin.

Outer Wear

The winter *anoraks* for both sexes were of caribou skin with the hair turned outward, the men's cut square across the bottom at the knees, the women's longer. A mother's outer parka had an enormous hood for carrying an infant. The white bands and occasional fringes were the sole decorations on the parkas.

Hair Styles

Men generally wore the hair cut quite short; many of them had mustaches, a few had sparse beards. Women wore the hair in braids, sometimes tied at the back. "Hair sticks" were popular—polished wooden rods around which the hair was twined, then wrapped with strips of colored leather or, later, cloth. Sometimes the hair was simply gathered at the sides and looped, coiled, or knotted with thongs.

Headgear

Hoods were sufficient, so no caps or other types of headgear were worn.

Accessories

The major accessory was the pair of snow goggles, so critical for reducing the glare of the sun on ice and water. These had narrow slits for the eyes and were of carved ivory or wood, both scarce materials with the Igluliks; they were tied around the head with thongs. Some pouches for carrying necessities were of sealskin, undecorated. Mittens were of sealskin, especially in the summer, and of caribou fur in the winter. Parkas were unbelted and trousers carefully fitted, so belts seem not to have been important.

Jewelry
Little jewelry was worn. Carved hair ornaments of ivory decorated with dots, or sometimes later of beads, were almost the only type of adornment favored by the Igluliks. Some charms or amulets of carved ivory were sewn to garments to guarantee immunity from the acts of evil spirits.

Special Costumes
Women, after acquiring beads and other items from the traders, wore a special parka for ceremonies; this inner parka of caribou skin had elaborate decorations of beadwork, many rows of fringes, metal danglers, and bands of colored skin. The shoulders were exaggerated, almost like epaulettes. There were two panels in front, which may have been related to the walrus motif. The large hoods also displayed ornate beadwork. The shaman wore a special belt and a garment he himself designed, based on his own visions; one particular shaman pictured wore a parka of caribou fur in a mosaic of brown and white patterns, with hands shown to ward off evil spirits. However, most shamans wore only the special belt with their regular attire.

Garment Decoration
The major form of decoration was the use of bands of white fur on parkas and trousers, and occasional strips of colored skin. Some ivory ornaments displayed the dot or dot-and-circle motif. Some fringing was used. With the acquisition of beads, the women decorated their special parkas with simple geometric designs or scallops. Otherwise, no beadwork was done.

Face and Body Embellishment
Tattooing was confined to women, and was performed on a girl at the time of puberty; designs were plain lines and geometrics, placed on the face and other parts of the body.

Transitional Dress
Some women continued to wear *anoraks* with flaps on the front and back; others wore the parka cut straight around the bottom. These were of white cloth from the late nineteenth century on, but the large hood was retained, as well as the harness with toggles. The parkas were worn with cloth skirts, trousers, and boots, and featured decorative colored bands at the edges. Men in this century began to wear cloth trousers and white hooded parkas edged with colored bands, often with fur edges on the hoods. Some wear rubber boots when hunting sea mammals; for winter the caribou boots continue to be worn by many. Today, most of the Iglulik clothing is purchased at the post or through mail order.

Key Sources

Lyon, George F. *The Private Journal of Captain G. F. Lyon of H.M.S. Hecla, during the Recent Voyage of Discovery under Captain Parry.* London: John Murray, 1824.

Mary-Rousseliere, Guy. "Iglulik." In *Handbook of North American Indians. Vol. 5: Arctic.* Pp. 431–446. Washington: Smithsonian Institution.

Mathiassen, Therkel. "Material Culture of the Iglulik Eskimos." *Report of the Fifth Thule Expedition 1921–1924* 6(1). Copenhagen, Denmark: Gyldendanske Boghandel.

Parry, William E. *Journal of a Second Voyage for the Discovery of a North-West Passage from the Atlantic to the Pacific. Performed in the Years 1821-22-23, in His Majesty's Ships Fury and Hecla.* London: John Murray, 1824.

Rasmussen, Knud. "Intellectual Culture of the Iglulik Eskimos." *Report of the Fifth Thule Expedition 1921–1924* 7(1).

Kotzebue Sound Eskimo
The Kotzebue Eskimo lived around the sound of that name, from Cape Espenberg on the Seward Peninsula north to Cape Thompson and inland. They had a rich material culture based on abundant resources—whales and other sea mammals along the coast, caribou and small game in the interior, fish in the many rivers, plentiful waterfowl, and bountiful roots and berries. They were Inuit-Inupiaq speakers. Kotzebue entered the area in 1816, followed by many European ships. By 1850 the Kotzebue Sound Eskimo had begun a sharp decline in population and culture with the introduction of alcohol, diseases, and guns. Late in the century missionization came to the area; the caribou, which had decreased greatly in numbers, began to return; and the government had

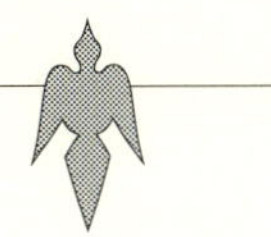

inaugurated its program of establishing reindeer herds. The Kotzebue people came back in numbers and strength. One of the significant events of the region was the Sheshalik Fair held each summer, to which Eskimos (and Indians) came from all over Alaska to trade and visit—the largest concentration of Eskimos anywhere. Louis Choris, the artist with Kotzebue's expedition, did many paintings and sketches of these Kotzebue Sound Eskimo.

Men's Basic Dress

The hip-length inner parka for summer wear was of caribou skin with the hair turned inward; the attached hood was rounded and the bottom of the parka was straight. Decorative bands of white fur trimmed the edges, while the walrus-tusk motif and coat-like bands in the front completed the embellishment. Pants of caribou skin, again with the hair turned inward, were worn with this parka; these had a drawstring at the top and came to just below the knees. The members of Kotzebue's crew were amazed to see these Eskimo going barefoot and at times wearing only pants in 50-degree weather.

Women's Basic Dress

The inner parka for a woman was of ground squirrel or caribou skin, with the hair inside; it came to below the knees, with large U-shaped flaps front and back and deep slits at the sides. The pointed hood, edged with wolf or wolverine fur, was very full in order to carry an infant; the torso area was also large to enable the mother to bring the baby around to the front for nursing. Sometimes the sleeves were extra large at the top (possibly an oversleeve). The pants and socks of caribou or reindeer skin were together, like the footed trousers of the Athapaskans, held up by means of a drawstring. The top of the parka was decorated with two vertical bands of white fur or skin, coupled with the walrus-tusk motifs; below the breast the two bands angled off to the sides, giving a coat-like effect. Decorative borders of black and white fur or skin edged the bottom of the parka.

Footwear

Boots for both sexes were of caribou or reindeer skin with the fur turned inward for summer, outward for winter; the soles of tough sealskin were crimped at the toe and heel to the uppers. A drawstring at the top and thongs around the ankles helped keep the boots in place. Duck down or moss was used to keep the feet warm and dry. Women at times wore slippers or moccasins of leather in the summer. Snowshoes were necessary to get about in the deep snows of the interior.

Outer Wear

The long knee-length winter parkas of both sexes were of caribou hair with the fur outward. The men's parka was cut straight across; the women's featured the huge hood and the U-shaped flaps front and back, although later, in this century, their parkas had straight bottom edges also. Both sexes displayed the walrus tusks or the coat-like bands in front. A distinctive feature was the band of black and white geometric figures around the bottom with a fur band below it, a characteristic of the parkas of northern and northwestern Alaska. Pants were of caribou or reindeer fur; women sometimes wore pants with broad, alternating black and white vertical bands.

Hair Styles

Men cut the hair straight across the forehead, allowing the back to grow; a few wore the tonsure. Some had beards and mustaches. Women parted the hair in the center and braided it into two braids that were sometimes tied together at the back, or even bound around the head.

Accessories

Heavy fur mittens were winter wear; gloves, too, had the fur inside. Both were decorated with strips of fur, especially wolverine, and usually had a neck cord attached to keep them from getting lost. Goggles, to avoid snow blindness, were typically in two pieces, one for each eye, with thongs or beaded strings across the nose part. They had slits for the eyes and were tied around the head. Men wore a heavy belt around the winter parka with a wolverine tail or ermine pelt hanging in the back. Some women wore the leather belt adorned with rows of caribou incisors, characteristic of northwestern Alaska.

Jewelry

Men wore strings of beads around the head and circular labrets, one at each side of the mouth; these were of ivory, jade, steatite, or other stones, later of

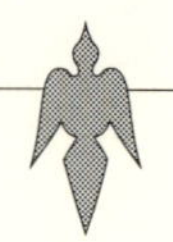

blue glass. The size of the labrets established the wearer's prestige; the largest represented the leader of a whaling crew. Women wore clusters of beads as earrings, and a few wore a bead in the pierced nasal septum. Some wore bracelets of iron or copper, probably obtained in trade from the Chukchis. Carved amulets of ivory were attached to the garments of both sexes to assure success in hunting and avoidance of misfortune.

Armor

Armor, when worn, was of plates of bone or ivory fastened together with sinew; at times the top was of tough hide rather than the plates.

Special Costumes

The Kotzebue Eskimo were not a ceremonious people; they had no special attire except that they wore their best clothing for festivals and dancing.

Garment Decoration

Most decoration consisted of bands of skin or fur, with black and white being a typical combination. The only designs were the simple geometric figures of the bottom band of the winter parkas, and a few dots or dots and circles in incised ivory amulets. The walrus tusks and the coat-like bands on the parkas of both sexes were distinctive.

Face and Body Embellishment

Women were tattooed with a few vertical lines on the chin.

Transitional Dress

Men in this century have worn trousers of cloth and cloth parkas, fur-lined and hooded, often with zippers. Women have adopted the *kupsuck* or Eskimo dress (some authorities call it a calico-covered parka) of printed cotton with a deep flounce at the bottom and a hood; it was frequently edged with wolverine fur and often lined. They wear slacks and traditional boots with this outfit and wool headscarves if they do not have hoods. Most of the clothes for both sexes are purchased.

Key Sources

Burch, Ernest S., Jr. "Kotzebue Sound Eskimo." In *Handbook of North American Indians. Vol. 5: Arctic.* Pp. 303–319. Washington: Smithsonian Institution.

Giddings, James L., Jr. "The Arctic Woodland Culture of the Kobuk River." University of Pennsylvania *University Museum Monograph* 8.

———. "Forest Eskimos: An Ethnographic Sketch of the Kobuk River People in the 1880s." University of Pennsylvania *Museum Bulletin* 20(2): 1–55.

Kotzebue, Otto von. "A Voyage of Discovery into the South Sea and Bering's Straits." *Bibliotheca Australiana* 17–19. New York: Da Capo Press, 1967.

Nelson, Edward W. "The Eskimo about Bering Strait." Bureau of American Ethnology *Annual Reports* 18: 3–518. Reprint edition.

Ray, Dorothy Jean. "Arts and Crafts in the Kotzebue Basin." *Alaska Geographic* 8(3): 154–168.

VanStone, James W. "An Early Nineteenth Century Artist in Alaska: Louis Choris and the First Kotzebue Expedition." *Pacific Northwest Quarterly* 51(4): 145–158.

———. "The Bruce Collection of Eskimo Material Culture from Kotzebue Sound, Alaska." *Fieldiana: Anthropology* n.s. 1.

Labrador Eskimo

The Eskimo of Labrador lived from the north shore of the Gulf of St. Lawrence along the coast to the tip of the Labrador Peninsula. They spoke a dialect of Inuit-Inupiaq called Labrador-Inuit. A maritime people, they hunted whales (Greenland and belugas), walruses, and seals; in the fall they hunted caribou in the interior. The sea waters were rich in codfish; migratory waterfowl also added greatly to their subsistence pattern. It is not known when these Eskimo were first contacted by the Europeans; it may have been by the early cod fishermen. There is a woodcut of a Labrador woman and child, kidnapped by French sailors and taken to Europe in 1566. A painting by John Russell (1767) of another Labrador woman and child is further evidence of contact. But the Eskimo seemed to avoid the Europeans. French and British colonization troubled them little, but a slow growth of dependence on traders' goods began. They also developed a wage economy based on commercial codfishing. They had kinship ties with the Quebec Inuit, but had little contact with the neighboring Montagnais and Naskapis.

Men's Basic Dress

The inner parka, or *anorak,* hair turned inside, had a small rounded hood or else a fur collar. It was hip-length and earlier had a long tail at the back, but this had disappeared by the mid-eighteenth century; some parkas had a slit in the center front. Worn with the parka was a pair of caribou or sealskin pants, also hair inward, that were knee-length and fit rather snugly; patches of fur were applied between the upper legs and on the insides of the elbows. The decoration of broad and narrow bands of white fur or skin was similar to that of the Baffinland Eskimo to the north.

Women's Basic Dress

The woman's *anorak* had a small flap in front covering the crotch and a long flap in back. Made of sealskin or caribou in the summer, the hair was turned inward, and it had an enormous hood for carrying an infant; a harness of cords kept the weight of the infant adjusted. After the Moravian missionaries came, women decorated their parkas with ribbons—blue for married women, pink for unmarried girls, and white for widows. Other decoration was similar to the Baffinland parkas with their bands of fur or skin. Worn with the parkas were footed trousers of skin (girls favored moleskin); sometimes for summer wear knee-length pants were worn with separate stockings. A child's combination suit had a front opening with a flap that tied over to one side.

Footwear

Boots for both sexes were of sealskin with front seams. Earlier the women's hip boots were extremely wide at the top; one painting shows a child being carried in the boot instead of in the hood, the boots probably fastened to a belt at the waist. By 1900 the women's boots fitted the leg like the men's. Most boots were the mukluk type with the large sealskin sole crimped into the edges of a vamp on the instep. Some moccasins of the Subarctic type were worn with the front seam and vamp or U-shaped insert. After the mid-nineteenth century, snowshoes were worn by the men for hunting; these were of the swallowtail design, similar to those of the Montagnais/Naskapis.

Outer Wear

Outer parkas were like the inner ones, but with the fur outward; they were generally of caribou or seal, but dog and bearskins were also used. Again, the decoration was like those of the Baffinland Eskimo—the broad and narrow bands of white fur or skin edging the bottom and hoods. In addition, there were special garments of depilated sealskin for the men to wear when hunting sea mammals. A combination suit, which entirely covered the body except for the face, was used when flensing whales in deep water; another form for the same purpose was that of wading pants, which covered the body to the chest. Jackets of cleaned and split seal intestines sewn in strips kept the kayak hunters dry, for they were fastened to the wooden rim of the kayak with a drawstring.

Hair Styles

Men wore the hair short, sometimes cut square across the forehead. Women wore the hair parted in the center and coiled at the sides into knots. Some wore the topknot of the Greenland Eskimo women.

Headgear

Caps were not worn, the hoods of the parkas being sufficient. Many women wore decorative headbands.

Accessories

Sealskin mittens were sometimes decorated with fur strips on the cuffs. Pouches and bags of sealskin carried necessary items such as tobacco or sewing equipment. Some pouches were made of loon skin adorned with beads and yarn tassels. Snow goggles to reduce the threat of snow blindness were of carved ivory or wood.

Jewelry

The most intriguing jewelry items were the long (to below the breast) ear ornaments made of clusters of beads in bands of different hues. Other than that, no mention of jewelry is made by sources consulted.

Special Costumes

Rituals among the Labrador Eskimo were not elaborate. Shamanism was central to their lives, consisting of curing rites and foretelling the future, but no special costumes were involved.

Garment Decoration

The influence of the Baffinland Eskimo can be seen in the decorative bands on parkas; walrus tusk motifs were occasionally to be seen. Beadwork was encouraged by the Moravian missionaries in the nineteenth century, but it was not as elaborate in style as that of the neighboring Subarctic groups, seldom going beyond simple geometric designs.

Face and Body Embellishment

Women were tattooed, with several vertical lines on the chin and horizontal lines across the cheeks and forehead.

Masks

Masks made of fur or sealskin were used in a ritual at Epiphany (6 January), in which masked performers went from door to door.

Transitional Dress

Under the influence of the Moravian missionaries, women wore long, full cotton skirts, to the ankles, under their parkas, which were white and retained the decorative bands. Early in this century men had converted to cloth garments, but for a long time clothing of both commercial and traditional garments was mixed together. Women adopted wool headscarves and plaid shawls, still to be seen today.

Key Sources

Cartwright, George. *A Journal of Transactions and Events during a Residence of Nearly Sixteen Years on the Coast of Labrador: Containing Many Interesting Particulars, Both of the Country and Its Inhabitants Not Hitherto Known.* 3 vols. Newark, England: Allin and Ridge, 1792.

Grenfell, Wilfred et al. *Labrador: The Country and the People.* New York: Macmillan, 1922.

Hawkes, Ernest W. "The Labrador Eskimo." Geological Survey *Memoir* 91, Anthropological Series 14. Ottawa: Canada Department of Mines.

Hutton, Samuel K. *Among the Eskimos of Labrador: A Record of Five Years' Close Intercourse with the Eskimo Tribes of Labrador.* London, England: Seeley Service.

Kleiven, Helge. *The Eskimos of Northeast Labrador: A History of Eskimo-White Relations, 1771–1955.* Oslo: Norsk Polarinstitutt Skrifter, 1969.

Speck, Frank G. "Labrador Eskimo Mask and Clown." *The General Magazine and Historical Chronicle* 37(2): 159–172.

Tanner, Vaino. *Outlines of the Geography, Life and Customs of Newfoundland-Labrador. Based upon Observations Made during "the Finland-Labrador Expedition" in 1939 and upon Information Available in the Literature and Cartography.* 2 vols. New York: Macmillan, 1947.

Taylor, J. Garth. "Historical Ethnography of the Labrador Coast." In *Handbook of North American Indians. Vol. 5: Arctic.* Pp. 508–521. Washington: Smithsonian Institution.

Mackenzie Delta Eskimo

Along the multiple channels of the Mackenzie River delta lived the Eskimo of that name; they are more precisely called Tchiglet, a word referring to the labrets worn by the men at the corners of the mouth. They spoke two dialects of Inuit-Inupiaq; one was similar to the North Slope dialect spoken by the Alaskans to the west, the other a Coast Dialect much like the speech of the Copper Eskimo to the east. They had a rich subsistence based on whales and other sea mammals; the caribou, musk-ox, and occasional moose they hunted in the interior; and an abundance of fish and berries. Despite some hostility, they traded with the Indians to the south and west. They enjoyed an elaborate social life. In the late nineteenth century, American whaling ships came, and there was an influx of Alaskan Eskimo and whites; by 1920 the basic Tchiglet culture had disappeared.

Men's Basic Dress

The hooded inner parka of caribou skin had the hair turned inward for summer; it was hip-length with no flaps, was belted, and had the cuffs, hem, upper arms, and hood trimmed with fur. Pants, also of caribou skin, were calf-length with a decorative band and fur edging the bottom; in the days before contact, the pants had a diagonal section on each leg from the inner thigh to the hip, which may have constituted a form of legging.

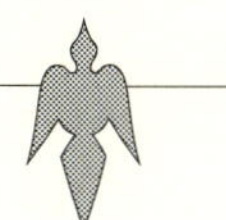

Women's Basic Dress

The woman's parka, also of caribou skin with the hair turned inward for summer, had a large hood, which was where an infant was carried, and flaps in the front and rear. Edges were trimmed with strips of mountain-sheep skin or other fur. At the bottom of the parka was sometimes an angled line with the point upward. The trousers, also of caribou, were footed. Children wore a combination suit from the hood to the toes; the animal's ears were retained on the hood as a sort of charm.

Footwear

The knee-high boots for both sexes had caribou-skin uppers with soles of beluga whale or bearded-seal skin, the soles being crimped into the uppers around an insert. Stockings were made of muskrat pelts or other fur.

Outer Wear

The outer garments, usually of caribou skin, were like the inner ones, but with the hair turned outward, the space between the parkas forming an effective air pocket of insulation. The woman's parka retained the flaps and the large hood, which was trimmed with wolverine fur, but over the footed trousers she wore a type of "culotte," pants cut off at the knee. Some waterproof garments of sealskin or fish skin were worn, but not commonly.

Hair Styles

Men cut the hair short, often square across the forehead; some men favored the tonsure and many had beards and/or mustaches. Women wore two braids, sometimes with part of the hair coiled into a double-bun chignon on top.

Headgear

Since all the parkas were hooded, no caps or other headgear were worn by these Eskimo.

Accessories

Eyeshades, to protect against snow blindness, were often made of a strip of sealskin with eye slits; these were sometimes adorned with glass beads from the traders. Snow visors were also used. Mittens were of sealskin or caribou skin with the hair inside. Bags and pouches were of caribou skin or wolverine fur, decorated with glass beads (red and blue the most popular colors), and often suspended at the neck with a thong. Men's belts were frequently embellished with a whole animal pelt suspended at the front. Containers of wolverine fur decorated with beads, clipped hair, and fur carried such items as tobacco and fire-making equipment.

Jewelry

The men's labrets, of ivory or polished steatite, showed status by size; when beads became available, they were adorned with large blue beads. Necklaces of polished steatite or glass beads were treasured by the women. Both sexes pierced the earlobes and nasal septums, into which pendants of glass beads or incised ivory were inserted

Special Costumes

Men wore a special parka for dancing that had brown and white fur borders, and beads and tufts of hair sewn on. The hood was cone shaped, the walrus tusk motifs were present, and a flap hung at the back. Many talismans, in the form of carved ivory or wood pendants or animal pelts, were attached to garments to propitiate evil spirits.

Garment Decoration

The major form of decoration was the use of brown and white strips of fur or skin on the edges of parkas and boots. Tufts of hair were attached to some garments. Beadwork was minimal; occasional beads were applied, but not in a formal fashion. The walrus-tusk motif was frequently used on parkas.

Face and Body Embellishment

At puberty boys and girls had the ears and nasal septums pierced for ornaments; boys had holes at the mouth edges pierced for labrets and also had the lower incisors filed to gum level. Men had lines across the cheeks to indicate the wearer had committed homicide; small crosses or "flukes" on the cheeks or shoulders kept tally of the number of whales taken. Women had several vertical lines on the chin; some had little marks indicating the success of the husband at whaling.

Transitional Dress

There was such a short transitional period that it is difficult to separate Mackenzie Delta wear from that of the Alaskan Eskimo who came into the area. Both sexes wore European-style clothing as it became available. Women adopted the Eskimo dress—a calico-covered dress of duffel (a kind of coarse woolen cloth) with a fur-lined hood, and a flounce at the bottom edged with braid. The aboriginal Mackenzie Delta culture had virtually disappeared by 1920.

Key Sources

Ostermann, Hother B. S., ed. "The Mackenzie Eskimos after Knud Rasmussen's Posthumous Notes." In *Report of the Fifth Thule Expedition, 1921–1924* 10(2): 5–164. Copenhagen, Denmark.

Petitot, Emile. *Les Amerindiens du nord-ouest Canadien au 19e siecle selon Emile Petitot. Vol. 1: Les Esquimaux Tchiglit.* Donat Savoie, ed. Mackenzie Delta Research Report 9. Ottawa: Department of Indian Affairs and Northern Development, Northern Science Research Group.

Smith, Derek G. "Mackenzie Delta Eskimo." In *Handbook of North American Indians. Vol. 5: Arctic.* Pp. 347–358. Washington: Smithsonian Institution.

Netsilik Eskimo

The Netsilik, "people of the ringed seal," lived in northern Canada between Queen Maud Gulf and the Gulf of Boothia and north to the Boothia Peninsula. Inuit-Inupiaq speakers, they were expert seal hunters; they went out on the ice for sea mammals in the winter and spring. Fall found them in the interior after caribou, and the women spent the winter making the necessary clothing of seal and caribou skin. An aggressive, hostile people, they were often in conflict with their Eskimo and Indian neighbors. Whalers came at the end of the nineteenth century, followed by the usual trading posts, the "Mounties," and the missionaries. The decrease in numbers of caribou found them turning more and more to traders' cloth as a substitute for skin.

Men's Basic Dress

The inner parka of caribou skin, hair inward, had a small flap in back, sometimes pointed, and a round or pointed hood; it was bordered with fringes and had a long tassel or tail in the front. With this, trousers were worn, also of caribou skin, which went to below the knees or to the ankles.

Women's Basic Dress

The woman's inner parka had a small flap in front and a larger, longer one in back; a large hood, for those mothers who had babies, could contain the infant, and was held in place with a harness of thongs, which went under the breast to the back and was fastened with a toggle. As trade goods became available, parkas were decorated with such things as beaded fringes and articles of metal, such as spoon bowls. Worn with the parkas were ankle-length trousers, also of caribou, with the hair turned inward; some of these trousers were footed.

Footwear

Summer boots for both sexes were of waterproof sealskin; winter boots were of caribou fur, which was warmer. These were calf-high with the pants tucked into them or worn outside. Both types had soles of tough *ugruk* or bearded-seal skin with a seam up the front. A low moccasin or slipper was worn of the Subarctic style with a front seam and the sole sewed into an insert over the instep; these were worn by both sexes with the long or footed trousers. A watercolor by John Ross, about 1830, shows a Netsilik woman wearing boots that are widened considerably at the top with what looks like additions that are fastened to the belt at the top, in the manner of the outer leggings of the Copper Eskimo women.

Outer Wear

The *kuliktok* or outer coat was of caribou, fur outward, and for the men (sometimes the women) was below the knee or calf-length, while some had flaps front and back edged with fringe. It was hooded with the large hood for the women with babies. Trousers of caribou fur were generally ankle-length, occasionally decorated with broad bands of white fur encircling the lower legs. When hunting in the kayak, men wore short jackets that could be laced into the wooden frame of the cockpit; they were also fastened snugly around the wrists and face to protect the kayaker in heavy seas.

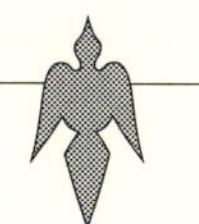

Hair Styles
Men wore the hair short, often cut square across the forehead; many had mustaches and sparse beards. Women wore the hair loose or in two braids; some coiled it into a topknot. Some would braid the hair around tapered, polished wooden rods, called "hair sticks," then bind the hair with wrappings of light and dark skin alternating, a hair style found frequently among the Eskimo women of central Canada. A few, especially little girls, wore the hair in knots at each side bound with sinew.

Headgear
Since all parkas for both winter and summer were hooded, no type of headgear was worn.

Accessories
Accessories were few. Snow goggles were of carved ivory or wood, tied at the back of the head with thongs, with slits for the eyes to guard against snow blindness. Mittens of caribou skin with the fur inward kept the hands warm in winter; mittens of sealskin kept them dry in the summer. Straps of leather were used as belts, particularly around the longer parkas. Pouches or bags to carry necessities, such as tobacco, fire-making, and sewing equipment, were of caribou or fish skin.

Jewelry
Little jewelry was worn. A few charms or amulets of carved wood or ivory were attached to garments.

Special Costumes
These were not a ceremonious people. Few rituals were followed, but the shaman held an important position in Netsilik society until the coming of the missionaries; he wore a special belt consisting of a strap of leather with carved antler objects suspended from it, a fringed breast ornament, and a brow band of caribou skin with a few loops of beads at the front.

Garment Decoration
The Netsilik clothing was largely undecorated, limited to a few bands of white fur or colored skin edging some garments. Although the Netsiliks were exposed to the glass beads of the traders, they did not develop beadwork and few beads were attached to garments. Occasional buttons or toggles of ivory were incised with dots or a dot-and-circle motif.

Face and Body Embellishment
Women were tattooed in order to gain admittance to the afterworld; designs consisted of lines or simple geometric figures on the chin or cheeks, the hands, and the legs.

Transitional Dress
With the decrease in numbers of caribou, the cloth or garments of the traders replaced the parkas of caribou fur. Both sexes wore the white parkas similar to those of the Baffinland Eskimo, with their edgings of colored bands—the men's hip-length and cut straight on the bottom, the women's with flaps front and back. A few women adopted the "Eskimo dress" of calico-covered duffel with the fur-lined hood and the deep flounce at the bottom. Wool knit caps and woolen headscarves are popular today, along with mail-order garments and clothing bought at the trading post. Most continue to wear the traditional boots, but many have converted to store-bought shoes and boots.

Key Sources

Balikci, Asen. *The Netsilik Eskimo.* Garden City, NY: Natural History Press, 1970.

———. "Netsilik." In *Handbook of North American Indians. Vol. 5: Arctic.* Pp. 415–430. Washington: Smithsonian Institution.

De Poncins, Gontran. *Kabloona.* New York: Reynal & Hitchcock, 1941.

Maxwell, James A., ed. "The Arctic: Dwellers in an Icy World." In *America's Fascinating Indian Heritage.* Pp. 354–391. Pleasantville, NY: Reader's Digest Association, 1978.

Rasmussen, Knud. "The Netsilik Eskimos: Social Life and Spiritual Culture." *Report of the Fifth Thule Expedition, 1921–1924* 8(1–2).

Taylor, J. Garth, ed. *Netsilik Eskimo Material Culture: The Roald Amundsen Collection from King William Island.* Oslo: Universittetsforlaget, 1974.

North Alaska Eskimo
The North Alaska Eskimo lived from Point Hope to the Canadian border; there were two groups: (1) the Tagiugmiut or "people of the sea," who lived along

the coast and were mainly hunters of whales and other sea mammals, and (2) the Nunamiut or "people of the land," who were caribou hunters of the interior. Both groups spoke dialects of Inupiaq. Whaling ships came to the area around 1850, leading to the decline of the whales, and by 1920 whaling was ended, at least commercially. A few North Alaskans continued the hunts, with special status conferred upon the *umialik,* or owner of the boat. The interior was not explored until the late nineteenth century, and was abandoned after 1920, although some have returned to places like Anaktuvuk Pass with the development of the North Slope oil resources.

Men's Basic Dress

The inner parka for summer was typically of caribou skin with the fur turned inward; some were of sealskin, ground-squirrel skin, muskrat, mountain-sheep skin, or, for special occasions, brown and white ermine pelts, all depending on availability. These parkas were hip-length, square across the front, with a slightly rounded flap in the back. Decorative bands of black and white fur, clipped hair, or red-dyed skin adorned the upper arms and the bottom edge. Many parkas displayed the white inserts symbolic of walrus tusks at the neck. The hood was edged with wolf or wolverine fur. Trousers or leggings, also with the fur turned inward, were worn with these parkas. Men embarking on a whale hunt must wear new clothes, to appease the *inua* of the whale.

Women's Basic Dress

The inner parkas for summer were of seal, ground-squirrel, or muskrat skins, with the fur side in. They had large, rounded flaps both front and back with smaller, narrower flaps over the large flaps. They not only featured the walrus-tusk inserts but also the strips of fur delineating the coat-like effect, from the shoulders to the waist and angling to the sides; bands of fur were around the upper arms. The rounded hood was lined with wolf or wolverine fur. Women did not, as a rule, have the extended hood for carrying a baby, although it may have been added for young mothers. Footed trousers were the usual wear with these parkas.

Footwear

Knee-high boots were of waterproof sealskin (for summer) or warm caribou skin (for winter). Soles were of the tough skin of the *ugruk,* or bearded seal, crimped into the U-shaped vamp. Duck down or moss was stuffed into the boots to keep the feet warm and dry. Drawstrings at the tops and ankle ties kept the boots in place. These were decorated with bands of contrasting fur (horizontal or vertical) or bands of black and white fur in a mosaic pattern. Some boots were of mottled brown and white reindeer fur. When cloth was available from the traders, red felt was a popular trim. Snowshoes were used only in the forest areas of the interior, usually acquired in trade from the Athapaskans; they were the long, narrow, pointed type.

Outer Wear

The outer parkas were much like the inner parkas, except the fur was turned outward, and they were often longer (knee-length). Women, especially, wore the "sunburst," the huge ruff of wolverine fur around the face. The decorative bands of black and white mosaic fur edged the bottoms of the parkas; the women's parkas had bands around the upper arms, around the U-shaped flaps front and back (or around the bottom when cut straight), and the coat-like effect in the front. The walrus tusks of white fur were often applied. Pants of caribou fur, turned outward, were typically knee-length and were adorned with hanging strips of fur and a broad band at the bottom. Sea-mammal intestines were cleaned, dried, and slit into strips to be sewed into jackets for the whale hunters on the coast; a complete bodysuit of gut had a large head opening so it could be stepped into, had a drawstring around the face, and was embellished with tufts of hair along the arms. In the interior the rain gear was of the skins of salmon or other large fish. Warm, light parkas were also made of the skins of such birds as cormorants, dovekies, geese, and ducks.

Hair Styles

Women wore the hair with a center part and loose or in braids. Men generally kept the hair short with a square cut across the forehead.

Headgear

No caps were worn since the parkas were hooded. Some men had a band of leather or beads around the forehead. The brow band of the *umialik,* or leader of the whaling crew, was hung with beads and the teeth of mountain sheep, as an indication of his importance.

Accessories

Mittens of caribou or sealskin were frequently decorated with bands of contrasting fur. The important snow goggles, worn to protect the eyes against snow blindness, were more often of carved wood than of ivory, since the former was less apt to freeze against the wearer's face; these were tied around the head with a thong and were often carved to represent guardian spirits. Belts girded the winter parkas to keep icy drafts from the upper body; most were straps of leather, to which were attached various amulets, and at the back hung an animal tail, typically that of a wolverine. Sometimes these were elaborate, such as one shown decorated with black and white ptarmigan quills in a checkerboard pattern. Some women wore belts enhanced with two or three rows of caribou incisor teeth. Bags and pouches for carrying necessities were of tanned caribou or sealskin.

Jewelry

Little jewelry was worn by these Eskimo, except for the labrets of the men, usually inserted in pairs at the corners of the mouth. Made of soapstone, bone, slate, or ivory, these lip plugs were of graduated sizes, the smallest inserted by young boys at puberty, the largest worn by the leader of the whaling boat. Often incised with animal spirit figures, they were also adorned with the treasured, large blue glass beads of the traders. Amulets, frequently in the shape of a whale, were attached to garments to ensure success in hunting. Some bracelets, straps of leather with ties, enhanced with the large blue beads and fur, were used by the men to secure the parkas tightly at the wrists. The *umialik* often wore an ivory chest piece or gorget.

Armor

Armor, which was rarely worn, was made of overlapping slats of bone or ivory laced together with sinew, the upper part at times like a sleeveless jacket of tough hide.

Special Costumes

There were few special costumes except in connection with the all-important whaling. The leader had to see to it that the crew members wore new clothes for the occasion; he himself, over his new clothes, wore a shoulder wrap of the skin of a raven with the beak downward, pointing to the whale. If the expedition was successful, the leader's wife, dressed in new finery, greeted them upon their return. For the Messenger Feast (a variation of the Northwest Coast potlatch), a special cap was worn, made of the beak and skin of the yellow-billed loon. A shaman had charms representing the *inuas,* or spirits of animals.

Garment Decoration

The major form of decoration on clothing and accessories was the fur "mosaic," bands of black and white fur in geometric patterns. Pelts and tails of small animals and charms carved of ivory or wood were also added as ornament. Although bird quillwork was known, it does not seem to have been a significant type of decoration.

Face and Body Embellishment

Women generally had thin vertical lines tattooed on the chin. The leader of a whaling crew sometimes kept tally of successful hunts with tattoos on the cheeks.

Masks

Aboriginal masks were carved of wood, typically portrait masks worn by the leader (and owner) of the whaling boat as he went from house to house inviting everyone to a whale feast. With the decline of whaling, mask-making also declined; during the 1960s the craft was revived for the tourist trade, and it became an important source of income for Anaktuvuk. These masks were made of caribou skin, again in a portrait manner, with a fur ruff and carved labrets.

Transitional Dress

The transitional period, from the 1880s into the 1920s, saw the growth of commercial goods and garments worn by the Eskimo of northern Alaska. Men wore cloth pants, jeans, T-shirts, and such. Women adopted the *kupsuck,* the overdress made of duffel with a printed-cotton cover and a large flounce edged with braid at the bottom; many continued to wear the huge sunburst of wolverine fur around the face. Traditional boots were worn by both sexes, but the men shifted to rubber boots for the occasional whaling trips.

Key Sources

Bockstoce, John R. *Eskimos of Northwest Alaska in the Early Nineteenth Century: Based on the Beechey and Belcher Collections and Records Compiled during the Voyage of H.M.S.* Blossom *to Northwest Alaska in 1826 and 1827.* Pitt Rivers Museum Monograph Series 1. Cambridge, England: Oxford University Press, 1977.

Burch, Ernest S., Jr. *The Traditional Eskimo Hunters of Point Hope, Alaska: 1800–1875.* Barrow, AK: North Slope Borough, 1981.

Chance, Norman A. *The Eskimos of North Alaska.* New York: Holt, Rinehart & Winston, 1966.

Hall, Edwin S. "Interior North Alaska Eskimo." In *Handbook of North American Indians. Vol. 5: Arctic.* Pp. 338–346. Washington: Smithsonian Institution.

Ingstad, Helge M. *Nunamiut: Among Alaska's Inland Eskimos.* F. H. Lyon, transl. London: Allen and Unwin, 1954.

Murdoch, John. "Ethnological Results of the Point Barrow Expedition." Bureau of American Ethnology *Annual Reports* 9: 19–441.

Rausch, Robert. "Notes on the Nunamiut Eskimo and Mammals of the Anaktuvuk Pass Region, Brooks Range, Alaska." *Arctic* 4(3): 147–195.

Ray, Dorothy Jean. *Eskimo Art: Tradition and Innovation in North Alaska.* Seattle: University of Washington Press, 1977.

Ray, Patrick H. *Ethnographic Sketch of the Natives of Point Barrow, Alaska.* Report of the International Polar Expedition to Point Barrow. Washington: Government Printing Office, 1885.

Spencer, Robert F. "North Alaska Coast Eskimo." In *Handbook of North American Indians. Vol. 5: Arctic.* Pp. 320–337. Washington: Smithsonian Institution.

VanStone, James W. "The Bruce Collection of Eskimo Material Culture from Port Clarence, Alaska." *Fieldiana: Anthropology* n.s. 1.

Pacific Eskimo

The Pacific Eskimo consisted mainly of (1) the Koniags of Kodiak Island and the southern part of the Alaska Peninsula up to Cook Inlet, (2) the Chugach Eskimo living from the end of the Kenai Peninsula all around Prince William Sound, and (3) a small group, the Kenais, inhabiting the southern end of the peninsula of that name. Theirs was a littoral and maritime existence, dependent upon the sea mammals—whales, sea lions, seals, and sea otters; land animals were of little significance. Salmon were caught in the rivers, and the vegetation, more abundant than in most Eskimo areas, also added to the subsistence pattern. They spoke the Pacific-Yupik dialect of the Eskimo language. Their culture was typically Eskimo, but there were influences from the Tlingit of the Northwest Coast. The Russians came in 1783 and, as they did to the Aleut, forced the Pacific Eskimo to hunt sea otters, to the neglect of their normal hunting and fishing. This, coupled with the devastating diseases introduced by the Russians and others, brought on the decline and almost total destruction of these natives. John Webber, the artist with Captain Cook in 1778, did some fine watercolors of these people, as did Mikhail Tikhanov in 1818.

Men's Basic Dress

Both sexes wore long, hoodless tunics, almost to the ankle, with a stand-up collar and with long, tight sleeves that were not set in but were a part of the shoulder yoke; these sleeves were nonfunctional, for the arms were kept inside for warmth and thrust out through slits at the sides for working. Originally, only the men wore a bird-skin tunic of horned-puffin or razorbill-puffin skins, which was made of the white feathers of the breast surrounded by the black back feathers. Men of high status wore a tunic of auk skin enhanced with auk beaks and trade cloth. Some tunics were of caribou skin with the tails of small animals attached. In the 1820s a Russian artist painted a Koniag man wearing a cormorant tunic trimmed with strips of fur. These tunics were worn without undergarments, except that pants were worn in severe weather; these were of caribou leg skin adorned with skin tassels, some ending in puffin beaks.

Women's Basic Dress

Women also wore the long, hoodless tunics with the narrow, nonfunctional sleeves. The most treasured tunics were of the beautiful iridescent pelagic-cormorant throat skins, sewn into horizontal strips, the seams piped with ermine. These were further decorated with an upstanding collar of red cloth, fringes of sea-lion esophagus membrane painted a reddish brown, and tassels of red and green wool. Some tunics (seldom worn by the men) were of caribou calfskin (from the interior) with a stand-up collar, a large V-shaped yoke with a medallion of fur mosaic, and fringes just below the waistline of tufts of rabbit fur and razorbill-puffin beaks. Another type of woman's tunic (occasionally worn by the men) was of ground-squirrel skins with a yoke of marmot skins (obtained in trade from the Tanainas), the paws and tails left on as adornment.

Footwear

Footwear was practically nonexistent before the arrival of the Russians. A few boots were worn in cold weather; these were in the mukluk style with the large sole of sealskin crimped into a U-shaped vamp. They were knee-high and adorned with white and brown fur and tassels.

Outer Wear

At times a warmer tunic was worn over an inner tunic, but usually there was but the one tunic. However, in rainy weather *kamleikas* (a Siberian Russian term) were donned; these hooded garments were of seal or sea-lion intestines and were cleaned, dried, and cut into long strips sewn together either horizontally or vertically, often decorated with hair, skin, and feather tassels. Some *kamleikas* reached the ankle, others were hip-length jackets that could be attached to the wooden rim of the cockpit of a kayak. With drawstrings around the face and wrists, protection from rain and heavy seas was ensured. Some men wore a combination suit of a bearskin, with the skin of the head providing a hood. Before the Russians came, some sea-otter cloaks were worn by men of rank.

Hair Styles

Little was done with the hair. Before contact, some men had gathered the back hair into a bunch, but later they simply left it loose. Women had bangs across the forehead, sometimes gathering the front hair into a knot on top. For special occasions the hair was greased, painted with red ocher, and further enhanced with eagle or duck down.

Headgear

The Pacific Eskimo had several elaborate types of headgear. Men wore the bentwood conical hunting visors with the open crown, adorned with sea-lion whiskers, blue and white glass beads, and small, carved ivory or bone seals or other charms to guarantee success in hunting. More common were the basketry hats of twined spruce root, similar to those of the Tlingit, but also with characteristic Chugach or Koniag features. These were painted at the top of the brim, but with figures quite different from the formline art of the Tlingit; the entire hat usually had a wash of blue-green paint. Some had crest designs of the Tlingit added. Typical of these Eskimo hats was the addition of black and white glass beads and dentalium shells, the band (often of baleen) inside the crown to hold it in place, and an embroidered, beaded ribbon to pass under the chin. Some of these basketry hats had the "potlatch rings" on top. Hats were sometimes protected with a cover of a truncated cone made of thin membrane, in eight sections, with fringes added, and a casing under the brim with a drawstring to hold the cover snugly in place. Some women wore a pillbox-shaped hat of muskrat fur with the caribou-skin tunic. Some hats were of bird skin (swan or cormorant) decorated with fringes of gound-squirrel pelts and tassels of red and white wool yarn. Some were of decorative bands with feathers erupting from the top. Still others were of various types of fur, also with a decorative headband. Seal hunters wore wooden helmets carved to represent a seal's head; these decoy helmets were used to steal up on their prey. By 1850 many of the men were wearing peaked caps with visors, reflecting the style worn by Russian officers.

Accessories

Accessories were few among the Pacific Eskimo. Gloves, mittens, and belts were almost unknown. A few bags or pouches were made, including the kit that Eskimos called a "housewife," which contained a woman's sewing equipment. Some bags were made of salmon skin, some of caribou skin.

Jewelry

Both sexes pierced the nasal septum, from which hung bead clusters, or through which a bone pin, often incised, was thrust. Earrings and necklaces of beads made of ivory, bone, jet, shell, and amber were worn by both men and women. A few pendants of abalone shell, rarely worn by the Eskimo, were attached to garments. Most of the men's labrets, worn at each corner of the mouth in pairs, were carved of wood, a few of ivory; some were of jet (coal) with a red-ocher inlay.

Armor
Armor reflected Tlingit influence (with whom the Chugach were frequently at war); it consisted of a cuirass of wooden slats across the front and back, laced together with sinew, and rods under the arms fastened in a similar manner; a small area on the chest was painted. Under this armor a hide tunic was worn.

Special Costumes
Ceremonial life was complex, with festival cycles and whaling rituals, but few special costumes were worn. A shaman had no particular attire, but his face was painted and he wore feathers on the head; sometimes he performed dances naked. Spectacular headdresses enhanced the women dancers on certain festive occasions; these were heavily beaded, the beads strung on sinew in horizontal rows, with a beaded flap down the back and a beaded fringe across the forehead, obstructing the dancer's view, which was a spiritual requirement of the dance. Some marriage headdresses were of ermine pelts and cormorant skins, also rich in beadwork and red wool tassels. At the time of death mourners cropped their hair, blackened their faces, and retired into seclusion.

Garment Decoration
No weaving was done by these Eskimo except for the twining of the spruce-root hats. Beadwork was simple, consisting mainly of strung beads forming horizontal patterns. Garments were made of fur (ermine, caribou, ground-squirrel, and other small animal skins), bird skins (cormorant, auk, puffin), and sea-mammal skins, esophagus, and intestines. Red cloth was used for collars, cuffs, and tassels. Some skin was dyed reddish brown. Designs were geometric. The vertical bands on the center yoke may have been representative of the walrus-tusk motif. Red and black were the most favored colors of the Pacific Eskimo.

Face and Body Embellishment
Girls had vertical lines tattooed on the chins at puberty. In addition, women were tattooed on the backs, cheeks, and breasts. Male homosexuals, who wore female costumes and did women's work, were also tattooed on the chin. Heads had some occipital flattening; this may not have been intentional, but simply caused by the use of wooden cradle boards.

Masks
The Pacific Eskimo made several types of carved wooden masks. One unique mask had a very high forehead with narrow slits for the eyes and holes for the nostrils; this may have represented one of the pointed-head evil spirits. Other masks were similar to those of the Bering Sea Eskimo, with the hoops and feathers representing stars and the heavens, circular appendages, and painted spots.

Transitional Dress
By 1850 most of traditional dress had disappeared, except that the bird-skin and ground-squirrel parkas, as well as the *kamleikas* of gut skin, were retained, for no European garments were as satisfactory in the damp, raw climate of the north Pacific Ocean. But indoors people wore cloth shirts, pants, and dresses. During the rest of the century, European-style garments were made of native materials. In this century the Pacific Eskimo have kept little of their traditional garments and accessories.

Key Sources
Birket-Smith, Kaj. "The Chugach Eskimo." *Nationalmuseets Skrifter Etnografisk Raekke* 6.

———. "Early Collections from the Pacific Eskimo: Ethnographical Studies." *Nationalmuseets Skrifter Etnografisk Raekke* 1: 121–163.

Black, Lydia, ed. and transl. "The Konyag (The Inhabitants of the Island of Koniak) by Iosaf [Bolotov] (1794–1799) and by Gideon (1804–1807)." *Arctic Anthropology* 14(2): 79–108.

Bushnell, David I., Jr. "Drawings by John Webber of Natives of the Northwest Coast of America, 1778." Smithsonian Institution *Miscellaneous Collections* 80(10).

Clark, Donald W. "Pacific Eskimo: Historical Ethnography." In *Handbook of North American Indians. Vol. 5: Arctic.* Pp. 185–197. Washington: Smithsonian Institution.

Heizer, Robert. "Notes on Koniag Material Culture." University of Alaska *Anthropological Papers* 1(1).

Holm, Bill. "Art and Culture Change at the Tlingit-Eskimo Border." In *Crossroads of Continents: Cultures of Siberia and Alaska.* Pp. 281–293. By William W. Fitzhugh and Aron Crowell. Washington: Smithsonian Institution, 1988.

Hrdlicka, Ales. *The Anthropology of Kodiak Island.* Philadelphia: Wistar Institute of Anatomy and Biology, 1945.

Varjola, Pirjo."The Pacific Eskimos." In *The Etholen Collection: The Ethnographic Alaskan Collection of Adolf Etholen and His Contemporaries in the National Museum of Finland.* Pp. 219–258. Helsinki: National Board of Antiquities, 1990.

Polar Eskimo

The Polar Eskimo, the northernmost inhabitants of the world, called themselves "Inuit," meaning "great and beautiful human beings," and when they were discovered by John Ross in 1819, they believed themselves to be the only people in the world. Living exclusively on animal food, they hunted the polar bear, musk-ox, arctic fox, and arctic hare on land, and the narwhal, whale, walrus, and the bearded and ringed seals of the sea. Speakers of Inuit-Inupiaq (Eastern Eskimo), they were isolated for centuries, although they may possibly have met the Norsemen. In 1861 Igluliks from Baffin Island of central Canada migrated to the north and east and joined the Polar Eskimo, bringing with them the use of the kayak, the igloo, and bows and arrows; the Igluliks in turn learned about the Eskimo sled. Admiral Peary based his polar expedition (1891–1909) among these people, some of whom went with him to the North Pole. In 1910 Knud Rasmussen, with the help of Peter Freuchen, established a trading post at Thule, beginning the shift to a trade economy dependent upon European tools, food, and some clothing. Arthur Kroeber, Rasmussen, and Freuchen have all written extensively on the Polar Eskimo.

Men's Basic Dress

Inner parkas *(anoraks)* were generally made of bird skins—auk, murre, or dovekie; these were snugly fitted and had the feather side in. Some summer parkas were of sealskin. If the weather was "warm" (40 or 50 degrees), the men went with the torso bare. According to a lithograph of 1818, men's parkas had a front closure, were edged with fur, and came to a point front and back, but this was not typical. Trousers were characteristically of polar-bear skin; one bearskin would make three pairs of the pants. They were knee-length with a drawstring at the top and were worn in all seasons. Poor men had to make do with pants of dog skin. Under the pants were worn "briefs" of dehaired sealskin.

Women's Basic Dress

Women also wore a close-fitting *anorak* of bird skins or of sealskin with the feathers or fur turned inward; these were crotch-length and were worn with short trousers of blue and white fox skins. At the front of the parka there was a small, narrow, pointed flap. Under the trousers a woman wore very short underpants of depilated sealskin, her only garment in the warmth of the igloo. On the day after a baby was born, the mother made new clothing for herself and threw away the old garments. For sewing, women used eyed needles of bone (later of steel) with the long sinew thread of the narwhal.

Footwear

Both sexes wore boots *(kamiks)* of dehaired sealskin, the men's being knee-high and the women's covering the thighs; the soles were of tough bearded-seal skin. At times, in bitter-cold weather, men wrapped a strip of polar-bear fur or fox skins around the tops of the boots; an insole of dried grass helped keep the feet warm and dry. Stockings of the arctic hare or caribou skin often had an edging of polar-bear fur at the top.

Outer Wear

The hooded outer parkas or *anoraks* were of fox skins, blue fox skins for the parka itself and white fox skins for the hood; blue foxtails framed the face. Sealskins with the fur side out were also made into winter *anoraks;* the fox furs were warmer, yet also fragile, requiring frequent mending. A mother carrying a baby wore the *amaut,* a parka with a large hood in

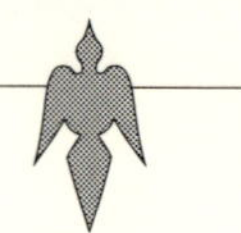

which the baby was carried naked; in addition, the woman wore a separate hood for herself. A harness of thongs helped adjust the the weight of the infant.

Hair Styles

Little was done with the hair. The men wore it hanging to the shoulders; the women also allowed it to grow and hang loose. A few women cut it off in bangs at the forehead. At the time of contact the women were wearing the topknot of the southern Greenland women, but by 1900 they were wearing the hair in a small bun in the back, kept in place by a string or thong.

Headgear

Since the *anoraks* were hooded, no caps were needed; after contact, European hats and caps were adopted. A few men and women wore a headband to hold the hair in place.

Accessories

Both sexes wore sealskin mittens, which were generally unadorned. Snow goggles, carved from antler or wood, helped reduce the glare of the sun on ice or snow. Few, if any, pouches or bags were worn, although large containers were necessary for traveling on sleds in the winter. Women kept their needles in needlecases of carved ivory.

Jewelry

Occasionally, carved ivory pendants were strung on a thong for a necklace, but jewelry was uncommon among the Polar Eskimo. Charms and amulets, tiny pendants in animal shapes, were attached to the garments of the hunters to propitiate the spirits of the animals hunted and make them acquiesce in their capture.

Special Costumes

No special costumes were worn by these people, but a mourning custom was that for a five-day period a widow sat, never standing or lying down, with the pants of her husband upon her head.

Garment Decoration

Most garments were unadorned, except for the attachment of tails of foxes and other animals. Sometimes a decorative effect was achieved by piecing furs of various textures and shades together to create a pattern. Rarely, fringes were added to garments.

Face and Body Embellishment

Some of the Iglulik women who came in 1861 had their faces tattooed, but the idea seems not to have been adopted by the Polar Eskimo women.

Transitional Dress

Men and boys continue to wear the polar-bear pants, and both sexes usually wear the traditional boots. However, men now wear sweatshirts, wool caps or visor caps, and cotton *anoraks* of European manufacture. Women in the 1920s began to wear the Eskimo dress of calico-covered duffel with its hood and large flounce at the bottom. Today they wear European-style upper garments with the hip-high boots. Cotton has replaced grass as lining for boots.

Key Sources

Ekblaw, Walter E. "The Material Response of the Polar Eskimo to Their Far Arctic Environment." *Annals of the Association of American Geographers* 17: 147–198; 18: 1–24.

Freuchen, Peter. *Arctic Adventure: My Life in the Frozen North.* New York: Farrar and Rinehart, 1935.

———. *Book of the Eskimos.* Dagmar Freuchen, ed. Cleveland, OH: World Publishing, 1961.

Gilberg, Rolf. "Polar Eskimo." In *Handbook of North American Indians. Vol. 5: Arctic.* Pp. 577–594. Washington: Smithsonian Institution.

Holtved, Erik. "Contributions to Polar Eskimo Ethnography." *Meddelelser om Gronland* 182(2).

Kroeber, Alfred L. "The Eskimo of Smith Sound." American Museum of Natural History *Bulletin* 12(21): 265–397.

Malaurie, Jean N. *The Last Kings of Thule: A Year among the Polar Eskimos of Greenland.* Gwendolyn Freeman, transl. New York: Crowell, 1956.

VanStone, James W. "The First Peary Collection of Polar Eskimo Material Culture." *Fieldiana: Anthropology* 60: 3–123.

Quebec Inuit

The Quebec Inuit (the term *Eskimo* is not used in Quebec) lived along the south shore of the Hudson

Strait, on the east coast of Hudson Bay, and on adjacent islands. Inuit-Inupiaq speakers, they hunted caribou (a major source of skins for clothing), fished, snared waterfowl, and gathered roots and berries. Fearful of the Cree, Montagnais, and Naskapis of the interior, they kept to the seacoast. They were visited by sixteenth century ships searching for the Northwest Passage, but these contacts had little effect on their culture; however, they were able to acquire European items from the many ships that were wrecked in the Strait. In the mid-nineteenth century, acculturation began with the establishment of a Hudson's Bay Company post, the arrival of Moravian missionaries, and the presence of the RCMP ("Mounties"). *Nanook of the North,* filmed by Robert Flaherty in 1922 among these Inuits, was the last depiction of their traditional lifeways; by 1960 almost all traces of the Quebec Inuit culture had disappeared, except in isolated areas.

Men's Basic Dress

The hooded inner parkas of the men were usually of the skin of the caribou, hunted in late summer when the skins were at their best; along the coast these inner parkas were often of the skin of the ringed seal. They were hip-length, square across the bottom, sometimes curved in the back, had rounded hoods, had the fur turned inward, and were largely undecorated. Bird-skin garments, made of eider ducks, were generally worn only by older people and children. On the Belcher Islands, where caribou were few, parkas were of bird skins—male ducks for men's parkas, female ducks for women's. The white feathers of the male duck's back were used for a panel at the back of a man's hood, signifying his hunting prowess. Worn with the parkas were skin pants to below the knees; on some of the offshore islands, pants were of polar-bear skin.

Women's Basic Dress

Women's inner parkas *(amautiks)* were of caribou or eider-duck skins; they had huge, rounded hoods for carrying babies, a smallish rounded or pointed flap in the front, and a longer, rounded flap in the back. Some were of fox or hare skins, which were especially used for women and children; soft fawnskin or unborn caribou skins were reserved for infants. The edges were trimmed with white fur strips, narrow on the coast, broader in the southern areas; some parkas were embellished with conical carved-ivory pendants. Trade goods also appeared as decoration—glass beads, tin or lead pendants, or the bowls of pewter spoons. A harness of thongs with a toggle helped support the weight of an infant. Worn with the parkas were trousers of caribou skin, fur inward, or, for the elders, of birdskin, feathers inward. The women seamstresses used bone or ivory needles, thimbles, and fresh sinew for thread taken from caribou or beluga whales; if that was not available, they cut the esophagus skin of a sea gull into thin strips.

Footwear

Knee-high boots had uppers of ringed sealskin and the soles of *ugruk,* or bearded seal; they were trimmed with fur strips, placed vertically for men, horizontally for women. Thigh boots of dehaired sealskin were worn along the coast of Hudson Bay. Special textured soles were worn over some boots to get traction on the ice; these were corrugated by looping narrow strips of leather to the soles. Stockings were of eider-duck skins with bits of fur as reinforcement.

Outer Wear

The outer parkas were similar to the inner ones, but with the fur or feathers turned outward. Some garments of ringed seal were worn for rainy days; fish skins or eider-duck skins were made into parkas for the young people. Hooded waterproof parkas and pants for the sea hunters were of vertical strips of seal gut, cut square across the bottom in front, rounded in back.

Hair Styles

Both sexes wore the hair long, but women often braided it or rolled it at the sides into knots before the ears, sometimes sticking sewing equipment into the rolls.

Headgear

Until trade goods appeared, the Quebec Inuit wore no hats or caps. Men at times wore a brow band to keep the hair in place.

Accessories

Carved wooden goggles, tied around the head, protected the eyes from snow blindness. Mittens were of caribou skin with the fur turned inward; some mittens were of polar-bear skin. Belts were leather straps tied with thongs.

Jewelry

Few ornaments were worn by these people. Necklaces were made of animal teeth, small, carved-ivory beads, or beads of steatite. Carved ivory or wood amulets were attached to garments to propitiate evil spirits and ensure successful hunting.

Special Costumes

No special costumes were worn, but for festive occasions garments were elaborately decorated.

Garment Decoration

The most common form of decoration was the use of caribou fur strips, the white of the ventral area contrasting nicely with the brown of the dorsal area. Although glass beads were available from the traders and trading posts fairly early, little was done in the line of beadwork except for some beaded fringes. The walrus-tusk motif seems not to have been used by these Quebec Inuit.

Face and Body Embellishment

Tattooing was practiced mainly on women after puberty, simple designs appearing on chins, cheeks, arms, and breasts. Men displayed a nasal or shoulder tattoo indicating they had killed a white man or a bowhead whale. Tattooing had virtually disappeared by the end of the nineteenth century.

Transitional Dress

Men, especially, converted early to the cloth garments available at the trading posts; the white parkas of heavy cloth with the colored stripes at the bottom were, and are, great favorites with them. By the 1920s the caribou-skin garments were a thing of the past. The wool cap with a tassel is still the "trademark" of the Quebec Inuit men. Women purchased dresses of cotton or heavier cloth and plaid tartan shawls as daily wear. However, the traditional boots continue to be worn by both sexes in many places.

Key Sources

D'Anglure, Bernard Saladin. "Inuit of Quebec." In *Handbook of North American Indians. Vol. 5: Arctic.* Pp. 476–507. Washington: Smithsonian Institution.

Oakes, Jill and Paula Gustafson. "Coats of Eider from the Ungava Inuit of the Belcher Islands." *American Indian Art Magazine,* Winter 1991: 68–72.

Turner, Lucien M. "Ethnology of the Ungava District, Hudson Bay Territory." Bureau of American Ethnology *Annual Reports* 11: 159–350.

Southwest Alaska and Nunivak Island Eskimo

The Southwest Alaska Eskimo inhabited the area from the delta of the Yukon River south to the Alaska Peninsula; Nunivak Island Eskimo are considered a part of this group. They spoke a dialect of the Central Alaskan Yupik language. The region is watery, with many rivers, lakes, and deltas. The climate is cold, damp, and foggy. Subsistence was based on the hunting of caribou as well as a large assortment of smaller animals such as otter, mink, marmot, and ground squirrel. Some fishing, especially for salmon, was done. Sea mammals included seals, walruses, and beluga whales. The Russians came in the early nineteenth century, forcing the men into sea-otter hunting, as they had done with the Aleut; this had little effect on the traditional culture but almost destroyed the people because of the lack of seasonal hunting for food. American whaling ships after 1850 brought diseases, guns, and alcohol, also devastating to the Southwest Eskimo. In this century the American government has attempted to establish reindeer herds and later musk-ox herds, but the success of both projects has been questionable. Edward Curtis photographed some of these Eskimo, especially those of Nunivak Island.

Men's Basic Dress

Men wore inner hooded parkas of caribou skin, fur inward, or of bird skin, feathers inward. These were quite long, to the knees or below, sometimes having to be hitched up with a belt for work; they were cut straight across the bottom and were generally undecorated. Worn below the parka were knee-length trousers, also of caribou or bird skin (some authorities say ankle-length, but this may have referred to winter trousers).

Women's Basic Dress

Women's inner parkas were of caribou, reindeer, or sealskin, with the hair turned in, and were shorter than those of the men. They had rounded flaps, front and rear, although by 1900 the parkas were generally flat across the bottom. A young mother wore a parka with a large hood, in which she carried her baby; a harness of thongs helped keep the infant secure. Parka cuffs were often of seal fur. Under the parka women wore knee-length pants held in place by a belt. From the Kuskokwim Delta north, some women wore footed trousers. Some women wore fish-skin pants in the summer.

Footwear

Boots for both sexes were knee-high and made of the brown fur of caribou leg skin, although other furs, such as reindeer, beaver, and sealskin were used; soles were of bearded-seal skin or walrus skin, crimped or pleated into the uppers in the mukluk style. Sometimes a band of fur edged the top, unless the pants had fur trim. These boots often had leather straps at the top to tie them to a belt under the parka at the waist; ankle ties were used on some boots. Women who wore footed trousers had a boot that was only ankle-high. Boots were trimmed with fringes or tassels of caribou fur, later of red yarn. Men's boots, for wear when hunting in the kayak,

Anthropologist E.W. Nelson photographed this couple at a Kuskokwim River settlement in the late nineteenth century. They wear long, loose-fitting outer parkas most likely of ground squirrel, beaver, and perhaps muskrat.

A young woman of Nunivak Island off Alaska's southwest coast wears chin and nose ornaments. The stitching of her *kamleika,* or waterproof parka, shows clearly, as do the decorations on the hood.

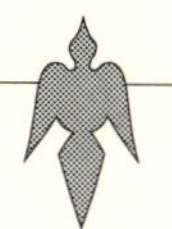

were of sealskin well saturated with oil to make them waterprooof. Socks were of grass woven in a twining technique, the soles tighter than the tops.

Outer Wear

Hooded outer garments of fur had the fur turned outward for warmth; they were somewhat loosely made, the space between inner and outer parkas giving added insulation. Ground-squirrel skins were the most popular fur for both sexes, beaver or muskrat often being used for women's parkas. The yoke at the top sometimes had walrus-tusk inserts applied; other decoration consisted of tassels of caribou fur and rectangular patches embellished with applique and embroidery. Women's parkas had the large hood for a baby or the huge "sunburst" ruff of wolverine fur so typical of Alaskan women's attire; another later Alaskan feature was the addition of a band of black and white fur sewn into geometric designs and applied around the straight bottom edge. Some women's parkas in this century have been elaborately decorated, both back and front, with bands of white sealskin on the dark fur background. On Nunivak Island, parkas were usually of the skins of birds such as cormorant, murre, and eider duck, with the beaks, feet, and feathers added as ornament. Men wore pants of fur that reached from hips to ankles; women's fur pants were knee-length or were footed. *Kamleikas,* the garments made of strips of seal gut or membrane sewn together, were worn over the parkas to protect them in rainy weather. The men's *kamleikas* were hip-length, hooded, with drawstrings at the wrists, face, and hips, the latter made to fit into the wooden rim of the kayak's cockpit; they were decorated with tassels of fur or flax dyed blue. Women's *kamleikas* were longer, with the rounded flaps front and back; they were more ornate, with many tassels, gut fringing inserted in the seams, and some gut strips painted reddish brown.

Hair Styles

Little was done with the hair. Men cropped it short and some had beards and/or mustaches. Women parted it in the center and either braided it or let it hang loose.

Headgear

Men wore the bentwood hunting hats or visors; these were frequently painted white and blue with carved ivory decorations. Both sexes wore hood-like headdresses of fur or hair, including caribou, sea otter, ermine, ground squirrel, and others. These were tied under the chin and had many tassels of fur strung with blue and white beads or red yarn tassels. Some men wore hats of white fox skin or caps of fur with ear flaps. Women wore rain hats made from seal intestines.

Accessories

Mittens of ground-squirrel or caribou skin had the fur inside. Some mittens were woven of twined grass; they were used as liners for outer mittens of fish skin. Carved wooden goggles protected the eyes from snow blindness. Women's outer belts were of rawhide with rows of caribou incisor teeth; they were fastened with loops at the end and carved ivory toggles or large blue beads.

Jewelry

Labrets of wood, bone, or ivory were worn by the men at the corners of the mouth. Nose rings were displayed by men and women. The people of Nunivak Island wore particularly elaborate ornaments, long, dangling ear pendants of beaded fringe and similar dangling pendants for labrets for both sexes. Many charms and amulets carved of ivory were hung on thongs or attached to garments; these were worn to propitiate the *inua,* or spirit, of the animal being hunted. Some necklaces featured rare dentalium shells with beads, typically large blue and white glass beads. Belt ornaments and fasteners were also of carved ivory.

Armor

Armor was made of plates of bone or ivory, laced together with sinew in a vest-like arrangement with straps over the shoulders.

Special Costumes

Major festivals involved dancing and feasting, much like the potlatches of the Northwest Coast. Some women and girls wore caps with button decorations and beaded pendants. Some women dancers wore ermine-skin dance fillets that hung over the forehead, obstructing their view; this had significance referring to spiritual vision. Some men dancers wore a forehead mask or hoop of a bird with carved wings carrying a

A Nunivak wears a forehead mask of a bird with a fish in its beak.

fish in its mouth; men dancers typically wore gauntlets of sealskin with many puffin beaks attached, serving as rattles.

Garment Decoration

Most decoration involved the arrangement of fur strips of various colors in pleasing patterns; black and white furs were worked into geometric designs on borders. Tassels of fur or red yarn were further adornments. Incised ivory ornaments used motifs such as concentric circles, dot and circle (both representing a spiritual worldview), and short or long parallel lines.

Face and Body Embellishment

Tattooing was minimal, being confined mostly to a few vertical lines on the women's chins.

Masks

Dancers at the winter feasts wore carved wooden masks meant to represent friendly or hostile spirits, many with distorted semihuman faces. Some were transformation masks, shifting during the dance into a representation of a different spirit. Some masks had hoops and feathers exemplifying the cosmos. Finger masks were a unique form with these people; made of wood and long caribou hairs, they were worn by the women dancers on all the fingers, fluttering and waving with the dance rhythms.

Transitional Dress

By 1890 store cloth was available to the women of Southwest Alaska; with it they made the characteristic *kupsuck* dress of bright printed cotton with a deep flounce at the bottom, sometimes lined with heavier cloth, or else of one thickness worn over a fur parka. These were sometimes hooded, the hood edged with a huge ruff of wolverine fur; lacking that, a wolverine-fur collar trimmed the dress. Some women wore cotton or woolen headscarves, even with the hood. Some women wore a hooded fur parka with a long cloth skirt underneath. Men have adopted commercially made garments, although many still wear fur parkas in the winter, if available. But little hunting is done because, like most Eskimo, they have converted to a wage/money economy. A few wear the traditional fur boots, but rubber boots are more common.

Key Sources

Lantis, Margaret. "Nunivak Eskimo." In *Handbook of North American Indians. Vol. 5: Arctic.* Pp. 209–223. Washington: Smithsonian Institution.

———. "The Social Culture of the Nunivak Eskimo." American Philosophical Society *Transactions* 35(3): 153–323.

Mason, Lynn D. "Hard Times along the Kuskokwim." *Natural History* 84(7): 66–73.

VanStone, James W. *Eskimos of the Nushagak River: An Ethnographic History.* Seattle: University of Washington Press, 1967.

———. "Mainland Southwest Alaska Eskimo." In *Handbook of North American Indians. Vol. 5: Arctic.* Pp. 224–242. Washington: Smithsonian Institution.

Varjola, Pirjo. "The Bering Sea and North Eskimo." In *The Etholen Collection: The Ethnographic Alaskan Collection of Adolf Etholen and His Contemporaries in the National Museum of Finland.* Pp. 220–322. Helsinki: National Board of Antiquities, 1990.

Appendix One

Clothing Arts of the American Indians

He stands against the sky, the wind gently ruffling the sweeping feathers of his warbonnet, the sun catching the glint of the beaded designs and the soft brown of his buckskin garments. We recognize him instantly. He is an American Indian. His costume is unique—no other in the world like it.

This is, of course, a stereotype, yet one would never mistake an American Indian in full dress for any other ethnic personality. The uniqueness of American Indian costume arises from the materials used, the methods of making the garments and accessories, and the manner in which they are worn. Materials, methods, and manner of dress are all conditioned by the environment in which the clothing is made and worn, an environment peculiar to each cultural region—the climate and soil, flora and fauna.

The non-Indian looks at true Indian garments and is astounded at the infinite patience required for their making. Hides were painstakingly tanned and sewn together with a simple bone awl and a length of deer sinew. Many hours were spent attaching elk teeth to a dress yoke, or in spinning buffalo hair into fibers to be finger-woven into a belt.

When considering these clothing arts, it is important to understand that there was much shifting of ideas and materials. There were extensive trade networks. Far from the ocean, dentalium shells were widely used for decorative purposes. Copper, the only metal used to any great extent before European contact, was traded widely from its sources in

Wisconsin and Michigan. Not only materials, but ideas and techniques of sewing and decoration passed from tribe to tribe, changing character as they moved across cultural boundaries.

With the coming of the Europeans, the native peoples adopted new ideas of ornamentation and added European garments to their own. New materials appeared, such as tin and silver, and steel needles quickly began to replace bone awls. Cloth made an immediate impact, replacing deerskin that is so time-consuming in preparation. Glass beads and ribbons were used to create adornment in uniquely Indian designs. Even the shapes of garments finally changed, influenced by European fashions.

Following is an overview of clothing arts organized by sources of materials: terrestrial animals; birds; water animals; plants; and rocks, minerals, and earth. A final section describes the use of European materials, such as cloth, obtained in trade.

Terrestrial Animals

Furs

Animals, large and small, were sought by the Indians for their furs. Furs were mostly used on the hide. As preparation for use, the inside was carefully scraped clean with a fleshing tool; then the brains of the animal were mixed with oil into a paste that was rubbed into the skin, and the fur was ready for use. Furs were primary necessities for existence in the frozen North, and they were needed for winter across most of the continent, even in the Southwest for cold nights in desert areas. Furs were also supremely important because of their spiritual and decorative significance in ceremonial occasions.

The main use for furs was as robes; these consisted of the entire skin of larger animals, such as deer, elk, moose, and bear, while the skins of smaller animals, such as squirrels, marmots, otters, and rabbits, were sewn together. Robes were worn over the shoulders and fastened with a thong or thongs at the neck and chest, or they were worn over one shoulder leaving the other arm bare and were cinched with a belt at the waist. Women frequently wore waist-length robes or capelets. Robes also served as bedding.

Some groups, particularly in the Northwest, removed the entire pelt of a smaller animal in one piece, turned it wrong side out, scraped it clean, applied the brain paste, then turned it right side out again; these pelts were sewn together with sinew, creating a warm robe with fur both on the inside and on the outside.

Rabbits were common almost everywhere on the continent and the rabbit-skin robe was perhaps the most common Indian garment, aside from those made of deerskin. The rabbit pelt was first cleaned on the inside, a difficult task because of its fragility; it was then cut in a spiral to make a long strip about one-half inch wide. After these strips were dried, they were twisted around a fiber of some sort, such as yucca, tule grass, or cedar bark. The next step was the weaving, which was done on a "half-loom" (an upper bar and side bars with no lower bar); this was usually a frame that could be leaned against a tree or a wall. The warp was either strips of fur-covered cord or the cord itself; the weft was fur-covered cord. The weaving was a simple "cross weave" (over and under) or a "checkerboard" weave (two strands over, two strands under); occasionally, using two strips at a time, a cross-over was made between each warp. Forty skins were needed for a child's robe, perhaps a hundred for an adult robe. Most of these robes were worn by women and children, unless hunting for larger animals was very difficult. There are few of these rabbit-skin robes in museums today, not only because of their fragility, but because at the beginning of this century they were discarded in favor of wool blankets, which were easier to keep free of moths and other pests.

Furs made up other garments and accessories, such as leggings, breechclouts (occasionally), footwear, anklets, bracelets, headbands, caps, capes, and belts. Moccasins were often lined with fur. Raccoon or skunk tails were sometimes worn trailing behind at the heels of their moccasins. "Hock boots" were constructed from the lower legs of larger animals, the fur carefully removed in one piece and drawn together with sinew at the bottom to form a tallish boot. The Chipewyan of the Subarctic and the Central and Eastern Eskimo frequently tied pieces of fur over the sole of a regular boot, which gave added traction on ice and also made it possible for a hunter to tread silently across the ice to the breathing hole of a seal. Plateau chiefs liked to wear a wolf's head as a cap or to carry a wolf pelt over the arm. Winter caps of fur were widely used, worn by both sexes and children. In the central Plains the most treasured headwear was the otter-skin turban, which consisted of a band of fur around the head with the tail extending horizontally, the whole decorated with porcupine quillwork. Some kilts were made of furs, especially in the Southwest and California. A deer pelt will lose its hair with dampness, so deerskins with the hair were satisfactory in dry climates, especially the far North, but elsewhere deer hides had to be tanned. Eskimo parkas were made of fox, ground squirrel, and wolverine fur; the latter, a delicate fur, was especially useful for edging hoods because the hairs did not become frosted with the wearer's breath in the icy cold. Polar bear trousers were a familiar feature of the costume of the Eastern and Greenland Eskimo. Variegated furs were used throughout the North, often pieced together to create simple geometric designs for edgings and other applications, a technique called "fur mosaic."

Tanning

The laborious process of tanning was used to make animal hides thin and flexible for clothing. Many hides were tanned in this way—deer, caribou, beaver, buffalo, seal, and even white beluga whale skin. The first step was to wash the blood and dirt off the hide. Next, in order to remove the hair easily, the hide was either buried in moist earth for several days, or steamed over a very slow fire, or soaked for some time in warm water. It was then either staked out horizontally six inches to a foot above the ground or fastened to a wooden frame that could be leaned against a tree or a wall; the hair was then removed with a dull knife. After being left to dry in the sun for a few days, the hide was turned over and the inner side "fleshed" with a sharp knife or a "flesher," which was made of the foot or leg bone of a large animal, and which had minute notches along one side forming a dentate edge. With this tool the flesh and fat were removed.

The next step was termed "braining"; the inner surface of the hide was rubbed with a mixture of the decomposed brains of the animal, which had been made into a paste with oil. Other substances used were liver, marrow, or wood ashes. After the paste was carefully rubbed in by hand, the hide was again dried in the sun, taken off the frame, saturated with water, and rolled up to be left overnight. In the morning the water was squeezed out of the hide, which was then pounded and stretched to make it soft and pliable. The hide was further softened by working it back and forth through rawhide loops attached to a tree or pole.

Some skins were browned by smoking them over a smoldering wood fire; this not only colored the skins but also kept them pliable and soft even when dampened with snow or rain. Various types of wood used for the smoking turned the hides different colors; old white cedar gave a dark tan skin; new white cedar, corn cobs, or buffalo chips made a yellow hue; and oak or willow made the hide turn dark brown. To clean the hide, moist clay of a suitable color was rubbed in and brushed off when dry. Fine white clay was then applied to close the pores and smooth the surface. Hides were often stored with sweet grass to keep them fresh smelling.

To make rawhide, the Indians used only the first few steps—the hide was cleaned, the hair scraped off, if desired, and the skin was then allowed to dry to a hard rigid leather. Rawhide was difficult to work; it was also difficult to wear, especially in wet weather, for it hardened into an uncomfortable shape. A primary source for rawhide was the buffalo, but elk, deer, seal, sea lion, white beluga whale, and other skins were also used. It was made into thongs for tying garments and footgear; the heavy sections became shields, tunics for armor, soles for moccasins, belts, and sandals (the last with the fur side up).

Use of Tanned Hides

The tanned hides had many uses in the various culture areas, depending especially on availability. The Eskimo and Subarctic peoples preferred caribou skin because of its light weight and insulating properties; caribou calfskins provided fine underclothing and boot liners. Sealskin, with its waterproof qualities, was made into summer boots, wading pants that reached the chest, and mittens (with two thumbs in case one got wet). The skin of the *ugruk,* the giant bearded seal, was sought for its toughness and formed into boot soles. Many Subarctic Indians used moose hide as their primary source for clothing, while elk skin was preferred for the beautifully tailored coats of eastern Canada. *Babiche* was a specialty of the western

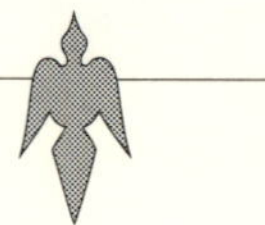

Subarctic tribes; the babiche thongs were carefully cut from elk hide, usually in a spiral beginning at the center of the skin. The most common use was in the making of lacings for snowshoes and for nets. It was in great demand and was widely traded.

Tanned leather was used almost everywhere for moccasins, breechclouts, shirts, leggings, and dresses. In California, the women's double aprons were sometimes entirely of tanned deerhide, or were a combination of deerskin in back and fiber fringes in front. Deerskin, available almost everywhere except in the far North, was indispensable for clothing. If tanned carefully and smoked to a pliable softness, it was equal to cloth in quality and superior to cloth in durability. Women's stockings might be made of doeskin, but hides from fawns were the finest of all. The hide of the buffalo was too heavy and stiff to use for clothing (except for men's robes); however, the size and texture of the skin of a two-year-old female was suitable for garments, as were the skins of calves and unborn calves, the latter prized for children's and infant's wear. Old, smoke-softened tipi covers of buffalo hide were recycled into moccasins, leggings, shirts, dresses, and such. Buffalo rawhide made virtually indestructible shields and durable moccasin soles.

Construction and Sewing of Skin Garments

Because sewing was difficult and tedious, garments were usually of simple construction, following as much as possible the shape of the skin being worked; in fact, construction was a compromise between the shape of the skin available and the shape of the human body. Early garments were one-piece, poncho-like affairs held in place with ties or thongs or lacings; or pinned with splinters of hard wood, bone, or antler; or latched with "toggles" of bone, ivory, or antler. There were no side seams. As construction became more complicated, such as the two- and three-piece dresses, it was necessary to cut the skin with a knife, often a sharp tool of flint or obsidian. The "strap-and-sleeve" dress was held in place by straps over the shoulders, and the sleeves were separate, tied in place when the weather turned colder; there were no underarm seams, the sleeves being fastened together only at the wrists. Sleeves in the two-piece or two-skin dress were often cut as part of the dress. In the nineteenth century the set-in sleeve made its appearance.

In the North careful fitting of garments was required, for snugness was a matter of survival in bitter cold weather. This meant sewing together many small pieces of fur or skin, using darts, gussets, and gores to shape the garment and achieve a close fit. The Eskimo garb of sealskin required daily attention; the skin was fragile, but it was light and warm and worth the involved labor.

The basic tool was the awl, sharp-pointed, two to six inches long, made of a fish bone, a sharpened splinter of hardwood, a polished and pointed piece of ivory, or, rarely, a thin fragment of copper. Needles, prized possessions, some as fine as needles of today, had eyes drilled in the ends and were made of materials similar to the above; these were kept in needlecases of ivory, wood, or rawhide. Making holes in the hide with an awl, the seamstress pushed the end of the sinew through the holes or used a threaded needle.

Generally the thread used was sinew, which came from the large tendon lying along each side of the backbone of the deer, elk, moose, or caribou. It was stripped out and dried. When needed, it was pounded into softness, then shredded into the desired thickness. Often the seamstress softened it for use by chewing. Other fibers were used as well: plant fibers, such as agave, tule, nettle, and mescal; or sea gull esophagus, dried and cut into thin strips. Southwestern Indians used yucca spines as needles with attached fibers as thread. The Eskimo found sealskin sinew excellent, for it swelled slightly when wet, making the seams waterproof.

The most common stitch used in sewing was the running stitch, making either an inside or an outside seam. Some seams were overcast. The whipstitch was used when the two edges were simply butted together. The strongest seam was the overlay (what we refer to as a "flatfell" seam), with the two edges of the material overlapping. In some cases, as with moccasins, one edge was puckered to ease into a straight edge.

Decoration of Tanned Hide

Leather for garments was decorated in many ways. Not only was it dyed and painted, but it was also fringed, pinked, and perforated. As articles of clothing were cut out of a skin, fragments were left along the edges; instead of being cut off, they were fringed. Either a garment was fringed in this way or a separate piece of skin was fringed and sewn onto the garment. Fringes appeared on the bottoms of shirts, dresses, and leggings, down the sides, across the shoulders—anywhere the decoration and resultant movement could be enjoyed. Fringes were long on the Plains, but the Indians of the Eastern Woodland kept fringes short to avoid entanglement in the underbrush. The California front apron of buckskin featured fringing on the lower half, producing not only ventilation but also greater movement. Beads, seeds, shells, and nuts were tied into the buckskin or fiber fringes in various patterns. On the southern Plains, fringes were extremely long, very thin, and typically gathered into bunches. In that area also, long heel fringes trailed behind, supposedly to erase footprints. A form of fringing was the use of thongs, usually in pairs, tied onto a dress or shirt in rows as decorative patterns of movement.

Pinking, usually found on dresses, shirts, leggings, and moccasins, featured edges that were scalloped or saw-toothed. This type of adornment was especially popular on the Columbia Plateau and on the southern Plains. Some Plains moccasins had pinked cuffs.

Perforations consisted of small holes punched into the leather, typically in a random pattern. Perforated garments were to be found among the Chippewa and other tribes of the Upper Great Lakes before 1830; later, they were found mostly on the garments of the Crow, Blackfeet, Flathead, and Nez Perce. The older Plateau shirts were very short, barely waist-length, often covered with perforations. There are divergent explanations for this form of decoration; some have suggested that it was done as a magical protection against arrows, while others have declared it to be a practical form of ventilation.

Garments were also decorated with embroidery, most frequently done with moose hair, which could take delicate hues in dyeing. Some "false embroidery" was at times a part of the coiling process or other weaving techniques, in which colored strands of fiber were wrapped around weft threads.

Use of Other Animal Parts

A recurring theme throughout any study of American Indian clothing is the practical use of everything possible in the environment. For example, George Catlin, while painting Indians in the 1830s, told about the many ways the buffalo was used: the hide was used for robes, blankets, and tipis. Ladles and spoons were made from the horns. The brains were used for dressing skins. Sinews were used as thread for sewing and to make thongs and bowstrings. The feet were boiled to produce glue. The hair was spun into fiber for various uses. Even the tail was used as a flywhisk.

Heads of many animals were used in their entirety, either for winter caps or for ceremonial headdresses. At times the heads were worn as a disguise so the hunter could approach within arrow range of his prey. Deer hooves were made into pendants and necklaces and produced clicking sounds when worn. Dewclaws (the false hooves of deer and other ungulates) were added as decoration, particularly on Plains dresses. Grizzly-bear claws were greatly prized; usually they were strung on a thong into a necklace. Much of their value was due to the difficulty in attacking and killing the dangerous bear. The claws of other bears, as well as the claws of other animals, also were used as ornamentation.

The teeth of many animals became decorative elements. Elk teeth were often the most desirable, especially the two incisors; in some cultures this may have been due to the observation that the incisors alone remained after the rest of an elk carcass had crumbled into dust; furthermore, they would last longer than the life of a man, so they became a symbol of longevity. Sioux and Crow dresses were characteristically heavily embellished with rows of elk teeth, sometimes as many as three hundred appearing on the yoke of a single dress. These teeth were not generally used by men unless they were made into a necklace.

Animal horns were commonly used in headdresses, often the entire head being used, but at times the horns were attached to a skin or fur cap made from the hide of another animal. Deer antlers, used in the same manner, were also popular; bracelets were frequently carved from horns or antlers. Mountain-goat horns were not only used for headdresses in the Northwest but were also split and steamed into shape to create bracelets, armlets, ankle bands, and hair ornaments.

Horsehair was fastened into bundles, wrapped with porcupine quills, and used to decorate shirts, dresses, leggings, and other garments. Crow men, who generally wore their hair very long, added horsehair to lengthen their locks still further. The hair of the white-tailed deer was dyed red (usually), mixed with porcupine guard hairs, and formed into a fringe, which was worn on the top of the head like a cockscomb; termed a "roach," this was worn as a headdress in the Southeast, the Northeast, and the eastern Plains areas. The hairs were held upstanding by means of a "roach spreader," which was attached in turn to the scalplock at the back of the head. The roach is a distinctive feature of many of today's Indian dancers, but since they lack the scalplock, they tie the roach under the chin for security during dances. Moose hair found its greatest use in embroidery, done especially by the women of the Northeast and, later, the Subarctic. The white hairs from the dewlap, mane, and rump of the animal, about five inches long, were chosen because of their length and pliancy; also, the texture of the hairs meant they could take delicate hues in dyeing.

Porcupine Quill Decoration

The use of porcupine quills in decoration is a technique peculiar to the North American Indians. An ancient craft, it probably existed long before Columbus. The earliest recorded piece of quillwork, on the toe piece of a pair of moccasins, came from Promontory Point in Utah. Early work of this kind was found mainly in the northern Plains among the Cree, Cheyenne, Arapaho, and Sioux. Unlike tanning, which required great strength, quillwork demanded outstanding dexterity, delicacy, and patience.

The quill of the porcupine is a round, hollow tube about five inches long, white for the most part of its length, with a small barbed tip. The average porcupine has about 30,000 such quills. On removal from the animal (a fairly easy task), they were sorted into four sizes; the largest and coarsest quills came from the tail, the next largest from the back, the thinnest and most delicate from the neck, and the finest from the belly. Sorted quills were kept in waterproof pouches, sometimes made of buffalo bladder, or in rawhide boxes.

The quills could be dyed in beautiful, gentle hues with vegetable dyes; more garish colors came after about 1880 with the appearance of aniline dyes. The natural white also appeared in designs. Before dyeing, the quills were washed to remove natural oils.

Softening, the next step, was done by holding the quills in the mouth to moisten them. The quiller might have as many as six in the mouth at one time, holding them until needed. For use, they were flattened, either by drawing the quill through the teeth, or by using the fingernails, or by rubbing them with a "flattener" of bone.

Quilling was based on four different techniques: wrapping, braiding or plaiting, sewing, and weaving. In wrapping, the quills were folded around a single thread of sinew, which was then sewn to skin or cloth; this type of quilling was used especially in the Northeast where embroidery had a linear quality to it. Alternatively, the quills were wrapped across two threads or sinews, either in a horizontal or a diagonal manner.

The second technique, braiding, was more elaborate; it was done by using single quills, weaving back and forth between two threads, or it was worked with two quills, usually of contrasting colors, in a braiding style. This technique created a wider band with a diamond design.

Sewing involved attaching the quills through buckskin or cloth by drawing sinew through the material in a running stitch and wrapping the quills around the loops formed. The simplest technique was the spotstitch described above. The backstitch (similar to our present embroidery backstitch) and the loop stitch (like a buttonhole stitch) created firmer work. Two, three, and even four quills might have been used at one time to work back and forth between lines of stitches for more complicated designs.

Weaving was a technique found especially among the Canadian Cree and Ojibwa, creating the finest of all quillwork. Sinew warps were stretched tightly, a weft sinew was loosely woven in, then the quills were woven in as alternate wefts; they were then pushed tightly together hiding the sinew wefts, the loops having the appearance of small, cylindrical beads. This form of quillwork was particularly used for making belts.

Weaving with Animal Hair or Wool

Many animals produced hair or wool that could be used in weaving. Mountain-goat hair and mountain-sheep wool offered fine fibers for weaving, particularly in the Northwest. Mountain goats ranged along the

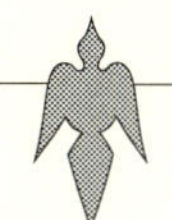

Pacific coastal ranges from Washington to Alaska, and into the interior in British Columbia and parts of the Rocky Mountains. The soft underhair of the goat was used with a minimum of the coarse outer hair; it was collected by nonviolent means—gathered from bushes and nests where it clung when the goats shed their winter coats. Two major forms of weaving used goat hair as fiber: the Chilkat blankets (the Chilkat being a division of the Tlingit of southeastern Alaska) and the blankets woven by the Coast Salish of Washington and British Columbia.

The famous Chilkat blankets used warps of shredded cedar bark twisted (spun) with mountain-goat hair; the wefts were of the goat hair alone. The hair of the mountain sheep, or bighorn, was used to a lesser extent; these sheep ranged throughout the Rockies from Canada to Mexico. Dall sheep, serving the same purpose, were found in northern Alaska and in the Yukon. Chilkat blankets were not made on true looms; the warps were hung from a horizontal bar that was placed at the top of two forked poles set into the ground. These "looms" of black alder or maple were often finely carved and, because of their simplicity, were easily portable. The goat hair was not spun in the usual way (with a spindle), but the woman would take a piece of the fiber and roll and twist it on her thigh until it was the right thickness.

The warps were fastened to the loom to hang straight down, and the warp ends were gathered into small bundles that were kept in bags made of animal bladders, so that the strings remained free and untangled. The weaving was done in a "twilled-twining" technique, that is, two wefts at a time were used with each row splitting the warps of the previous row.

The blankets were rectangular in shape except that the bottom was either curved or ended in a shallow "V." The sides were fringed and a long, luxuriant fringe fell from the bottom. The blankets were not all woven in one piece but in separate panels, which were then joined with sinew or wool-and-bark cord as the weaving progressed. The joining was concealed with a form of false embroidery, which was also used to cover the edges of the different color elements. Chilkat blankets were always done in four colors: the natural white or cream of the wool; black, which was made from mud rich in iron or sulphur, or from hemlock bark boiled with urine; yellow, which came from wolf moss; and a bluish-green made by soaking copper in urine. The designs were unilaterally symmetrical, characterized by the use of rectangles with rounded edges and an avoidance of empty space. Design content was totemic, based on a clan crest or animal, highly conventionalized in form.

Coast Salish weavers differed from their Chilkat neighbors to the north in that they added to the red cedar bark and goat-hair fibers from two plants: Indian hemp and stinging nettle. If there was a shortage of any of these fibers, a "filler" was spun into the yarn, made from the fluff of fireweed, milkweed, cattail, or other plants. Several observers and explorers have mentioned the use of dog hair as one of the fibers commonly used; however, Paula Gustafson, in her work on Salish weaving, examined many Salish blankets but found none with dog hair as a component. One blanket in the Smithsonian Institution's collections was found to contain fibers closely resembling coyote hair. So there the matter rests. Another difference between Salish and Chilkat weaving was that the Salish women used a spindle on which to wind the spun yarn, or "roving," after it had been rolled on the thigh. It was not a "drop" spindle, but was held pointing upward and the yarn was drawn down as the spindle was turned. The spindle whorls were carved in beautiful symbolic designs.

The most common dyes used by the Salish were green, black, red-brown, orange-brown, and yellow. Red from cochineal and blue from indigo seem to have been obtained in the protohistoric period by trade with Mexican Indians who had procured the dyes from the Spanish.

The Salish loom was not a "true" loom, for it lacked the heddle and shed rod to control the raising and lowering of the warp threads. Correctly called a "fixed warp frame," it consisted of two flat, upright bars with rectangular slots in the upper and lower ends; these slots functioned to keep the two crossbars in place with the use of wedges for tightening. With a continuous warp thread, the Salish women were able to make tubular weaving; at the end of the task, the warp threads were removed from the crossbars, cut across, and a rectangular piece emerged, with a fringe at each end.

Two weaving techniques were used—twilling and twining. In the former, the weft crosses the warp

threads over-two, under-two, with a shift in each row to different warp threads. In twining, the weft threads are each crossed alternately over one (or two) warp threads. Plaids and bars were typical of early Salish blankets.

Birds

Whole Birds

Whole birds were often displayed as headdresses or simply attached to garments as decoration. Chief Red Bird was so called because of the stuffed red bird he wore on his shoulder. The Comanche chief Quanah Parker has been described as wearing a brightly colored bird in each ear as earrings. In the Condor Dance of California, the entire bird was used as part of the costume, with the wings tied to the dancer's arms and the condor's head covering the dancer's head.

Bird Skins

Whole bird skins were sewn onto buckskin to create headdresses, aprons, skirts, ceremonial robes, and other garments. Large birds, such as loons, wild geese, eagles, crows, and others, were skinned and made into robes and other garments. This is an ancient art, for robes of this type have been discovered in Nevada and dated to 4,500 years ago. Mallard skins, particularly the colorful iridescent heads, were formed into "matchcoats" in the Southeast; they were especially cherished because of the difficulty involved in their making. The Eskimo appreciated the warmth and lightness of parkas made of the skins of the crested auklet, the white-bodied puffin (a fairly tough skin), the double-crested cormorant (a light and warm but fragile skin), and the guillemot. Their whalers, particularly the crew leaders, wore the skin of a raven on the shoulders, the beak pointing downward as if to a whale. The Eskimo made dance caps of loonskin and stockings of eider-duck skins. The Miwok of California used pelican skins, removed in one piece, as dance costumes. The Hupa and other tribes of northern California were noted for their spectacular Red-Headed Woodpecker Dance, wearing headdresses made from the scalps of the pileated woodpecker or sapsucker; the scalps were carefully attached to a strip of buckskin, which was then tied across the forehead with the ends left to flap to the rhythms of the dance.

Bird skins were also used to make robes in the manner of the rabbit-skin robe. The bird skin was laid out flat, and a spiral was made starting from the center; as it was cut, the skin curled into a feathered strip. These strips were then woven in a simple cross weave. Robes like this were found especially among the Indians of the Northwest and the Arctic, where rabbit was not widely available.

Feathers

Feather mantles were worn on ceremonial occasions; the individual feathers were either inserted into a fine netting (the usual technique) or were tied into cords and used as warps. It is suggested by many that these feather cloaks were influenced by the Mexican cultures; the early Zuni, the Natchez of the Southeast, and the Indians of the southern Plains all wore garments of this type; although due to the difficulties in making them, the robes were usually reserved for chiefs or others of high authority. Early southern Plains mantles were sometimes made of parrot or macaw feathers, indicative of early trade with Mexico. Of course eagle feathers were used to make the most treasured robes, but many local birds were also made into cloaks—ravens, hawks, buzzards, magpies, and, in the Southeast, flamingos.

Both species of North American eagles were sought for feathers: the bald eagle and the golden eagle or "calumet," so called because of the use of its feathers as decorations on calumet pipes. The bald eagle ranged across the continent, while the golden eagle's range was from the eastern side of the Rockies to the Pacific Ocean. Golden-eagle feathers were often preferred, especially the tail feathers of the immature bird, those that we think of as "eagle feathers"—white with a black tip. The tail feathers were most prized, then the wing feathers, and after those the short brown feathers of the body. The birds could not be domesticated, but they were sometimes captured and held in captivity until needed. As one means of capture, a pit was made and covered with branches, leaves, and suitable bait; the trapper stayed hidden in the pit until the eagle came down for the bait; and the man reached through the branches and seized the bird, not an easy matter, for eagles are powerful birds.

The Plains Indians, particularly, accumulated and wore great quantities of feathers—in the hair, tied to their garments, fastened to horn headdresses, attached to the fringes of their leggings and, of course, in their warbonnets. The latter were of two types: the "halo" bonnet and the "stand-up" bonnet.

The halo warbonnet, with its sweeping arc of feathers and the long trail of feathers behind, has become a stereotypical trademark of North American Indians. Opinions differ, but it is generally thought to have originated with the Western or Teton Sioux. It was constructed on a skullcap base of tanned leather with a long strip of buckskin hanging behind. The eagle feathers were attached in a great circle and down the "trail" in back. Through each feather ran a thong that held the feathers in place. Across the forehead was a heavily beaded band. Ermine pelts were added at the sides of the forehead band. A thong under the chin held the headdress in place during windy weather or when riding horseback.

The stand-up bonnet was a favorite with the Blackfeet and adjacent tribes. This was a stiff circlet of eagle feathers standing erect from a beaded or quilled headband, with ermine strips hanging at the sides. There was no tail or trail of feathers. Woodland Indians of the Northeast and Southeast also wore the stand-up headdresses, but these were not usually of eagle feathers; rather, they were made with feathers of cranes, herons, turkeys, hawks, or other birds. This form seems to have reached its peak among the Natchez of Mississippi.

The Coast Salish men of the Northwest wore a cap of feathers attached to a small skullcap, and on the top was a single owl or eagle feather set into a swivel in such a way that it moved with every movement of the head. Oddly, across the continent, the Iroquois Indians wore a similar hat or cap with the rotating feather on the top.

An intriguing piece of headgear was the "Big Head" of the central California tribes. This consisted of slender rods of dogwood emanating from a foundation cap of woven tule grass; each wooden rod was tipped with a quill section from the tail feather of an eagle. The effect was that of a gigantic pincushion.

Feathers in the hair were a common ornament, the feathers being either inserted into the scalplock at the back of the head, in hair nets (California), or in a bun of hair worn by men at the nape of the neck, the hair style of the Kutchin and neighboring tribes of the Subarctic. Some men bound feathers to wooden hairpins, which helped affix them firmly to the scalp.

Fans were made of turkey feathers or eagle feathers from the tail or wing; swan wings were also used as fans.

Eagle and crow feathers formed the "crow" or feather bustle worn by Indian dancers of the past and of today. Worn at the back and resting on the buttocks, it was held in place by a leather belt. It could be fashioned from a rawhide frame covered with the entire head of an eagle; from the frame, two buckskin pendants hung down the wearer's legs. Projecting from the frame were two stiff upright shafts of feathers tipped with red horsehair. Many other decorations appeared on the bustle—loose feathers, fur, or entire bird skins. Because of the manner of construction, the feathers swayed gently with the dance rhythms.

Use of Other Bird Parts

Swansdown, eagle down and eider down lent spiritual significance to many occasions. The down was stuck to greased hair for ceremonial dances on the Plains. In the Northwest it was placed in a special headdress so that during the dance the down was released to float through the air and settle on the spectators. California Indians placed the down of a white owl or osprey in the hair nets they wore. Down was also twisted into fibers used for weaving.

Bird beaks and claws were strung on thongs for necklaces or simply attached to a garment as ornamentation. The Tsimshian of the Pacific coast sewed bird beaks into the seams of their leggings as rattling accompaniments to dancers' movements.

Bird bones were cherished for beads, the most common use, especially the leg bones of pelicans, herons, and other waterfowl. Since the bones were thin-walled, the tubular shape made for easy stringing. There were other uses for bird bone. An eye could be drilled into a sharpened bone making a fine needle. Ear tubes were popular with many tribes, as well as bird bones thrust through the septum. The Pomo of California made exquisitely engraved hairpins of bones or quills.

Eskimo women, if they lacked sinew for thread, used the esophagus of a sea gull, dried and cut into thin strips. Guillemot tendons were sometimes used in this manner.

The use of bird quills for embroidery to replace porcupine quills was more common than the literature might indicate. The split quills took dyes better than porcupine quills and were handled in much the same way.

The Eskimo occasionally made handsome belts of ptarmigan quills, using the black tail quills and white wing quills woven into a checkerboard pattern.

Materials from Ocean, Lake, and Stream

Sea Mammals

Seals were of extreme importance to the Eskimo way of life. Their fur, warmer than wool and light in weight, was used during the summer months for clothing. Men wore tight sealskin underpants. For wading, they wore pants of depilated sealskin, which came up to the chest; neck-high suits were useful when setting salmon nets in deep water. The Labrador Eskimo had a special suit of sealskin that covered the entire body, which was worn when flensing whales in comparatively deep water; these were also worn by the Greenland Eskimo and were donned by means of a large circular hole at the front of the neck. A combination suit of sealskin, with parka, mittens, trousers, and boots all attached, was worn by men in Alaska as well as by children all across the Arctic; it was generally tied with thongs at the front.

Captain James Cook observed that women wore sealskin much more than men, who often wore bird garments. The parka so commonly worn was a hooded coat of sealskin; a large hood was used in some areas for carrying an infant. Children were frequently clothed in the skin of the baby seal.

An important item of clothing was the rainproof parka made of the intestines of the seal. The intestines were cleaned, dried in the sun to bleach, which made them translucent, and split open. The next step was to cut them into strips of sufficient length for a jacket; these strips were sewn together with sinew, usually vertically and without seams on the outside. The parkas were particularly adapted to kayaking, for they were fastened around the cockpit with a drawstring so no water could get into the kayak. Drawstrings around the face and at the wrists also waterproofed the kayaker.

Boots were made out of sealskin, which proved to be as durable as rawhide. The hide of the giant bearded seal, the *ugruk,* was used for the tough soles; harp-seal fur was often used for the instep and ring-seal fur for the uppers.

Whales furnished tough skin that was invaluable in areas where rawhide was unobtainable. The skin, particularly that of the beluga whale, was used as soles for boots throughout the Arctic and was a significant item of trade with Subarctic peoples. The sinew of the beluga was used to stitch sealskin so that the seams were waterproof and almost invisible. Some frontlet headdresses of the Northwest Coast were made of baleen; this substance was also used by the Eskimo and others to make rod-and-slat armor. The Haida women made belts of whale sinew, which were worn ceremonially while their husbands were at sea whaling.

The intestines of whales and other sea mammals besides seals were used to make waterproof parkas. Wearing these parkas with the addition of a belt of sea-lion fur, and tied into the rim of the kayak, the Eskimo had no fear of being swamped in ocean swells.

Sea-lion or walrus whiskers were sought by the Indians of the Northwest to be used as decoration on their frontlet headdresses. The Eskimo and especially the Aleut affixed the whiskers to their wooden hunting visors. The teeth of the sea lion or otter were used for decorative purposes as well. Along the Pacific coast these teeth often appeared as nose and ear pendants, in necklaces, and on forehead bands. The young Chumash men of California wore leather belts thickly set with sea-lion teeth.

The ivory of the walrus tusk was a valuable trade item among the Eskimo and groups to the south. These tusks, with their hard marble core and outer layer of enamel, were the preferred sources of ivory. Working the hard substance was difficult, but it retained its beautiful lustre. Before being carved, it was soaked in urine to soften it, then scored with a sharp stone (later a metal knife) until a small chip could be broken off. Made into charms and amulets,

ivory insured success in hunting and other affairs of life. It was fashioned into many household articles: fine needles, needlecases, and buttons and toggles to fasten garments. Snow goggles of ivory helped prevent blindness caused by the sun glare on water, ice, and snow. Rectangular pieces of ivory with carved points were attached to boot soles with leather straps to give traction when walking on ice or snow crust. Plate armor of ivory slats was held together with straps and sinew. Small ivory beads and pendants, intricately carved, enhanced garments.

Ivory labrets were worn among the peoples of the northern Pacific coast and the western Arctic; these were small "plugs" or buttons that were inserted through a perforation in the lower lip. Sometimes two labrets were worn, one at each corner of the mouth. In the Northwest labrets were worn only by women, but farther north the practice was also found among men. Small pins were inserted through the flesh in childhood, being changed for larger pins or labrets through the years. Labrets were also of stone and wood, but ivory was deemed most valuable and was prized as a symbol of wealth.

Fish

Fish were a major item of food for the Indians, but they were also useful in the making of clothing and cherished as ornaments. In the north, the skins of such fish as salmon and halibut made waterproof parkas; the bladders were also used for this purpose. Moccasins were made of sturgeon skins, and waterproof boots were fashioned of salmon skin in the Subarctic. The Kolchan Indians of the Mackenzie Delta wore capes of salmon skin as raingear.

Elsewhere, fish furnished items of ornament. Fish vertebrae were strung into necklaces; even the Ute of the arid Great Basin managed to make necklaces of this type. Tribes in the Southeast acquired shark's teeth and barracuda jaws from Florida to be made into necklaces. The Tlingit of the Northwest also used shark's teeth as decoration, especially for earrings. The Calusa Indians of Florida inserted a small, oblong fish bladder into a slit in the ear. The Chumash of California treasured a "swordfish headdress" for ceremonies, the "sword" of the fish standing out from the forehead.

Shells

Shells were widely used in North America as ornaments and also functioned in some places as money. A display of shells might thus have been a display of wealth, a custom that at times reached astonishing lengths, with men or women wearing several pounds of shells on their persons. Shells were formed into the most common type of beads, for they were fairly easy to produce, often just by grinding off the tips of some species. Easily transported, they were an important item of trade.

Some shells, particularly large ones, had two holes drilled at the top so they could hang as pendants on the chest (often called "gorgets"). Thick cylindrical beads were created from the columella or central axis of a spiral univalve, by cutting it in sections. Shells were drilled by using a pointed stone hand drill or a wooden rod with water and grains of sand.

The abalone shell *(Haliotis rufescens* and other genera), with its shimmering, mother-of-pearl inner surface, was traded from the West Coast as far as the Plains. The best specimens were found along the central California coast; thinner, less colorful types were obtained on the Queen Charlotte Islands off the coast of southeastern Alaska. Abalone shells were cut into many shapes, commonly into squares and rectangles. In the Pacific Northwest abalone shell was frequently found as inlay on masks and headdresses. The basic shape of the shell often inspired the carver, who worked it into totem characters, such as ravens and whales. Nose rings or nose pins were fashioned of abalone. Abalone was also used on the fringes of fiber skirts in California.

The olivella shell *(Olivella biplicata, Olivella porphyria,* and others), was used almost entirely for ornamentation. A beautifully shaped, smooth, polished shell, it ranges in color from lavender to a deep purple. Sometimes the tip was ground off to create a free-form ornament; at other times, beads were ground and drilled from the wall and columella of the shell.

Dentalia are small marine mollusks, usually one to two inches long, having a curved, tapering shell open at both ends. The shell is extremely hard and milk-white. Dentalia were found off the western shore of Vancouver Island, on the shores of the Queen Charlotte Islands, and along the coast to

Sitka, Alaska. To collect them the Nootka used a special pronged device on the end of a long pole, which was thrust into the depths to retrieve the delicate shells.

Because dentalia were used widely as a medium of exchange, they were measured on a fixed ratio; forty shells were standard for one fathom or six feet. They were matched for size and strung end to end (wide to wide and narrow to narrow, so they would not telescope into each other). These were so precisely valued, particularly among groups in northwestern California, that the men had tattoos of measured length on their left arms in order to check the value of each shell. Dentalia were traded as far north as the Alaska plateau area, to the Yukon region, east to the Plains, and, rarely, to the Southwest; the shells seldom reached the lands east of the Mississippi River. Dentalia that were too small to use as money were made into necklaces, earrings, nose pins, pendants, and ornaments on belts; they were often gathered into clusters to attach to fine robes and dresses. Other shells were valued as ornaments and money. In central California, where dentalia were unavailable, the coin of the realm was the shell disk bead. Cowrie shells were found on both coasts and were usually made into necklaces; as decoration on women's garments they were applied in much the same manner as elk teeth. The large pink or queen conch shell *(Strombus gigas)* occurred off the coast of Florida and was greatly valued for its size and color.

Wampum has been perhaps the most famous of the shell beads used by the Indians as currency. In fact, among many whites it became the standard word for money. Two varieties of shells provided sources for beads in the East. White wampum came from the columella of the knobbed and channeled whelk *(Busycon* spp.) and from a variety of other shells. Purple wampum, much more valuable than the white, was made from the quahog *(Venus mercenaria* and other genera). The disk-shaped beads, about one-third of an inch long and one-fourth of an inch in diameter, were painstakingly ground from the shell, perforated with flint drills, and rounded by rolling the strings of beads over sandstone. After the Europeans came, metal tools were used, but before that the Indians of Long Island and coastal Connecticut and Rhode Island were famous as wampum makers, trading the beads up and down the coast and into the interior; however, wampum was rarely found west of the Mississippi River. Wampum was made into spectacular belts, worn by messengers as a form of identification and as an indication of promises or guarantees between tribes at intertribal councils. It was also a mnemonic device enabling messengers or representatives to remember treaty terms. Finally, and most important, it was a medium of currency, its value in the seventeenth century reckoned by the guilders of Nieu Amsterdam.

As an example of conspicuous consumption, wampum appeared in rows on women's dresses, the hair was bound with wampum, caps were solidly decorated with the beads, and bracelets, necklaces, and belts were embellished with wampum. Huron women wore strings of it slung about the hips. Forehead bands of wampum were popular in some areas. Men also wore necklaces of wampum and pierced the ears to dangle clusters of the beads from several slits. An early depiction of wampum is that of Ninigret, a Niantic sachem, wearing a checkerboard headband, earrings, and a necklace of wampum. The Cherokee wore collars of wampum. Virginia Indians had different names for the two varieties; the purple, which was also considered most valuable by them, was called "wampum peak," and the white was termed "roanoke" and was said to be made from cockleshells.

The hairpipe breastplate, so typical of late–nineteenth-century Plains garb, was made of shell or bone. The shell used was the *Strombus gigas,* a large shell found predominantly off the coast of Florida. A part of the large lip was broken off, and a hole drilled through the center, first from one end, then the other until the holes met. It was rubbed on stones until it achieved a long cylindrical shape, five or six inches long, large at the middle, thin at the ends. Finally, it was polished with sand and water. The hairpipes were held together with thongs in a "window blind" shape of two sections with about eleven rows on each side; often an abalone pendant was attached. A thong at the top secured the breastplate around the neck, and a bottom thong was tied about the waist.

These long tubular shells were anciently worn, a necklace of eight hairpipes having been found at an archaeological site and dated as early as 4,000 years ago. With the arrival of European settlers, a firm in New Jersey began to make the hairpipes with shells

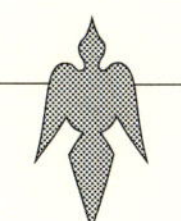

used as ballast in ships from the West Indies, a profitable venture. It was not until after 1850 that the breastplate as we know it was developed; it was an accessory rather than armor, as was thought by some, for it would scarcely stop an arrow, let alone a bullet, but protection came from the power inherent in the shells. Hairpipes used as ornaments were hung from the hair at the sides of the forehead, made into necklaces, and occasionally hung from the earlobes. Some of these tubular beads were made of deer leg bones. Today they are often fashioned of plastic.

Gorgets, also called breastplates, were sometimes formed of large shells from six to eight inches in diameter; they were made from both fresh and saltwater clams, especially scallop shells and Venus clams. The convex surface was frequently intricately carved, the most common subject being the human face. Pearls were found in the Southeast, in river mussels and Atlantic coast bivalves, the latter being the most esteemed. Cofitachequi was a famous pearl center, said to have chests of pearls. Men of that area, particularly those of Virginia, liked to hang many clusters of pearls from the earlobes. Burial customs in the Southeast favored multiple ropes of pearls wrapped around the body of the deceased.

Plants

Grasses

Almost every plant was useful in some way, but many were of particular value in weaving and the making of Indian garments, and these plants will be discussed in greater detail: yucca, Indian hemp, nettle, milkweed, cotton, cattails, tule and other rushes, mescal, bear grass, sagebrush, cornhusks, and grasses.

Yucca was the standard desert material in the Southwest and up into the Rockies. It was used anciently; some of the oldest articles of Indian clothing extant are yucca sandals found in Fort Rock Cave in Oregon and believed to be some 9,000 years old. Many of the sandals in the Southwest were done in a simple technique (over one, under one) with both warp and weft elements made up of bundles of yucca fibers. In California yucca sandals were worn only in rough terrain, otherwise the Indians of the area went barefoot. The Basketmakers of the Southwest made square-toed sandals of woven cords and twined yucca. The early Navajo boiled strips of yucca, then pounded the mass with a stone; these fibers were then twisted and braided with other grasses to make sandals. Many of the California and Southwest tribes made yucca-string aprons. Yucca was also used as a fiber in weaving rabbit-skin robes.

Indian hemp *(Apocynum cannabinum)* is found all over the United States and into Canada. The long, strong fibers of the stems were used in the Southwest for making sandals. It had been used for twine and cord as well as for weaving. The fibers were treated in the common manner: retted, or allowed to soak in water until the soft tissues rotted, beaten to separate the fibers, then rinsed and combed clean. In the Southeast, Indian hemp was often used as an alternative to mulberry bark.

Nettle (the scientific name *Urtica* coming from *uro,* "I burn"), despite its stinging qualities, seems to have been used all across North America except Alaska and the Far North. The long white threads of considerable strength were used in making fine cloth as well as twined or braided into rope and cord. The Woodland Indians made storage bags and sashes of it. In the Southeast it was also used as a substitute for the more commonly used mulberry bark.

Milkweed *(Asclepias)* is also found generally throughout the continent except in the Far North. Its most frequent use was in California, where it was made into the skirts and aprons of that region. Called "weepah" by the Basin Indians, it was twisted into a strong twine. In general it was made into cordage—strings, nets, cords, and such.

Cotton was grown in the Southwest in precolumbian times. It may have come from Mexico or lands even farther south. It was used long before the arrival of Europeans; there is evidence of its use among the Anasazi before 700. This domestic cotton *(Gossypium)* was grown and used widely after that time, especially among the Pueblo Indians. The seeds were picked out by hand, a laborious process, then the cotton was worked into condition for spinning by whipping it with switches on beds of sand. Cotton dresses, shawls, and blankets were made by the Puebloans, who continued to weave with cotton until the Spanish brought sheep in 1629.

Tule is a form of rush belonging to the *Juncus* genera of grasses. Cattails, with their familiar tufts at the top, are a also form of rush. Tule was abundant in California, especially in the central area of the San Joaquin Valley. Not only was it made into the apron/skirts of the women but also into leggings and moccasins for the men and capes for both sexes to wear in inclement weather. It was braided and twined.

Mescal or agave, is found in southern California and portions of the arid Great Basin. The fine fibers were made into sandals for rough travel, sometimes with soles one-half inch thick or more. The fibers were soaked in mud to soften them, then made into twisted bundles, which were woven back and forth over a looped cord, thus forming the thick sole pads.

Bear grass *(Xerophyllum tenax)* is found in the mountain meadows, on the dry slopes, and in the open forests of the West. The eastern form, called "turkey beard," is found in pine barrens and mountain woods. The white fibers were used as decorative overlay in the making of basketry hats. Some California skirts were made of fringes wrapped with the lustrous bear-grass fibers. Shaman's ornaments were sometimes made of the braided fibers.

Sagebrush *(Artemisia)* is found abundantly in the high deserts of the Great Basin as well as elsewhere in the West. The Ute and the Paiute used it for dresses of twined bark, for stockings, and for winter boots. In some areas sagebrush was a sacred plant; for the Sun Dance of the Plains Indians, it was formed into wreaths for the head, and rings of sage were held in the hands or tied to the wrists.

Only the Iroquois and Delaware are said to have used cornhusk as a fiber aboriginally; of this material they made temporary footwear. In the nineteenth century it came into more general use as a fiber, particularly for the exquisitely woven bags and pouches of the Plateau.

Maidenhair fern *(Adiantum)* was occasionally used on the Plains as a substitute for porcupine quills. It appeared as imbrication or overlay in the basketry hats of the Plateau, its blackness effectively bringing out the patterns of the designs. Also, giant fern stems were dyed red with alder bark for use in those designs.

In California, iris leaf fibers were used in the making of hair nets; the firm silky fibers were extracted by means of an artificial thumbnail of mussel shell. Of a creamy color, it was used naturally or dyed yellow.

Silk grass was found in the Columbia River region and also in the Southeast. Hodge says it was a form of yucca; it may have been something else in the former area. Lewis and Clark journals mention that it was made into fringe skirts, the fibers being twisted or braided and knotted at the ends. In the Southeast it was said to be made into thread "stronger than hemp." The Creek and Chickasaw were said by the Spanish to make thread of silk grass "as good as the best thread from Portugal."

Sweetgrass, a fragrant grass that retains its aroma a remarkably long time, is found generally throughout the United States. It was used by the Indians to keep garments sweet-smelling in storage as well as made into belts and ornaments, giving a pleasant scent to the wearer.

Spanish moss *(Tillandsia)* was found only in the Southeast, where it was made into grass skirts worn by girls in the Carolinas, Louisiana, and surrounding areas. Other mosses found generally on the continent were used to stuff moccasins and boots for winter warmth.

The wild cucumber was made into necklaces that were worn by the Luiseño of California for girls' puberty rites.

Basketry hats were found on the Northwest Coast as far as the Aleut of Alaska, on the Plateau, the Basin, and in California. They took various shapes; those with brims were usually rainhats, those without were frequently used with tumplines to ease the strain of carrying heavy burdens. The hats were also used as protection from the sun and to keep pitch out of the hair when gathering piñon nuts. All were decorated with designs, either as a part of the weaving process (shifting to various techniques), as a form of imbrication or overlay, or as a painted design. Fibers were most comonly dyed in three colors—white or cream (often by the use of bear grass), black (from maidenhair ferns), and red (dyed with alder bark), The hats were tied under the chin with a cord; some had an inner band or skullcap that fitted snugly to the head.

In the Northwest, spruce root was the most common material for the hat itself. On the Plateau, where hats tended to be taller, Indian hemp formed the foundation; in more recent times, the base was often of cornhusk fibers with the designs worked in commercial yarns. The Gosiutes of the Basin used cottonwood, willow or spruceberry wood for the foundation. The Californians used many fibers for their hats—tule, of course, also hazel shoots and conifer roots; oddly, the Pomos, makers of world-famous baskets, did not wear basketry hats. Northern California basket hats were typically woven in a twining technique, while the southern hats were done usually in a coiling manner; in central California, coiling and twining appeared together. The northern hat was worn habitually, the southern hat was used mostly for carrying a burden.

Dyes

Everywhere the Indians gathered plants to make dyes. The process was fundamentally the same everywhere and with all plants. Roots and strips of bark were crushed. These and other parts of the plants were soaked in water for some time, then boiled in water heated by hot stones or in a pot over a fire pit; the boiling time varied according to the tint desired and the ability of the fiber to make a strong dye. The fiber was usually, but not always, dyed before spinning. Porcupine quills were held in the dye bath briefly; too long exposure caused the core to soak out. The material was placed in the dye bath and carefully stirred to make sure all areas were evenly dyed; sometimes fibers were placed in two or more dye baths to create different hues.

Mordants were used to "set" the dyes, not only to give more clarity to the color but also to make it colorfast. The most common mordant was urine, heated with hot stones so the fibers could be boiled. Salt was also used, as were raw alum, ashes, iron, and copper.

Ikat, a resist dyeing of yarn, was found in the Southwest; in this technique a continuous length of yarn or fiber is coiled and the sections of the coil placed in different dye baths, a process that produces unusual distinctive designs when the yarn is woven. It is not known if this is a traditional form; it seems to be either Mexican in origin or, more likely, Guatemalan, where *ikat* has been a standard technique for some time.

Following are some of the most frequently used plants for each color:

Black: Black dyes were made using hemlock bark boiled in salt water; the barks of maple, black walnut, white maple, elm, and birch trees; nuts such as black walnut, hickory, and butternut; some tree roots; iron-rich muck or mud found in swamps; and some leaves such as wild grape or fox grape.

Green: Green was difficult for aboriginal Indians to obtain; it was only when they were able to obtain verdigris, a basic carbonate of copper (usually from the traders), that they had a good green. However, some green dyes could be made from yucca leaves, Russian thistle, moosewood, princess pine bark, and the bark of the birch tree.

Blue: Blue, generally a fugitive hue, was also not obtainable as a dye aboriginally; indigo, which was only grown in the Southeast, was not the type that gave a good blue color. One source mentioned the blue bark of the beech tree with hardwood ashes added as a mordant. The Indians of the Northwest created a fairly bright blue-green dye by immersing copper in urine. Also, iron (usually meteoric) and hemlock bark boiled in urine made a blue of sorts.

Brown: Like black, most sources for brown dye were to be found in tree bark—maple, hemlock, mountain mahogany (reddish-brown), dogwood, balsam, and oak. Hazelnuts, black walnuts, and hickory nuts were likely sources. Further mention has been made of wild grapes, Mormon tea, one-seeded juniper, red-stemmed dock, and some forms of lichen.

Purple: This hue was also difficult to achieve. Some tints were made using wild plums, chokecherries, pokeberries, and other berries.

Red: Alder bark was the most common source for red dye, but other barks were used, such as red cedar, white birch, sassafras, and tamarack. Roots were more effective—bloodroot (called "red puccoon" in the Southeast), snakeberry root, madder root, mountain mahogany, and roots of bulrushes. Buffalo berries, squawberries, sumac fruit, bedstraw, prickly pears, chokecherries, and wild plums were all red dye sources. The Indians of the Southwest, after the coming of the traders, unraveled *bayeta,* a red baize cloth, and used the yarn as was, or steeped it with other dyes to strengthen the red. Vermilion, a strong red, was made from cinnabar, a crystalline mercuric sulphide, obtainable from California, but used more for a paint than a dye. The traders brought in cochineal, a strong red produced from an insect found in Mexico and other places.

Orange: Most orange dyes were merely a lighter shade of brown. They could be obtained from alder and hemlock bark, madder root, Navajo tea, and from lichens (probably wolf moss).

Yellow: The petals of many flowers gave fine yellow hues: coneflowers, sunflowers, single-flowered *Actinea* (a greenish-yellow), cliff rose, goldenrod, and dahlias. Onion skins made a fine clear yellow. Roots were useful as well: Oregon grape, sourdock, hoary puccoon, dock, and sorrel roots. Scrub-oak galls produced a golden tone. Also used were many lichens and mosses (tree moss, yellow moss, and wolf moss).

Weaving

Although some animal hairs, such as mountain-goat and buffalo, were used as fibers, the bulk of Indian weaving was done with vegetable fibers. It should be explained that the aboriginal Indians did not know weaving on what is referred to as a "true" loom, that is, a loom using a heddle by means of which alternate warp threads can be raised, forming an opening or "shed" through which the weft threads on a shuttle can be passed. Nevertheless, several forms of finger weaving were employed and simple loom weaving was characteristic of some tribes. Finger weaving can be categorized as looping, coiling, and plaiting or braiding. But first the fiber had to be prepared by spinning. The fibers were cleaned, straightened, and twisted into yarn. Some fibers, particularly coarse ones, were rolled along the leg or thigh, but cotton and wool hair were twisted on a spindle—a wooden rod with a whorl or platter-like disk of wood, stone, or pottery at one end to act as a flywheel. The yarn was often respun to make it hard and smooth.

Looping was done by taking a long single strand and making a series of loops over a long needle or a stick, then passing back over itself to hang loops on the first row of loops; the third row repeats the process, with other rows continuing the looping as long as desired. Netting was made by twisting or knotting the loops as they were being formed. The thread could be wound on a bobbin or shuttle for greater efficiency. Loose elastic bags for carrying articles, as well as hair nets, were made by this technique in California. Netted sashes were made in the East. Knitting and crocheting, forms of netting and looping, were not done by the Indians until after European contact.

Coiling was used in the making of basketry hats in central California (with twining) and in southern California. In this technique the fibers were formed into a thin bundle that was coiled into a spiral for the top of the hat, each row being fastened with lashing stitches to a previous row. The coiling continued across the top and down the sides.

Twining approached weaving; warps were hung from a horizontal bar placed across two uprights, and at times a lower bar was used to stretch the warp threads for firmness. Pairs of weft threads were crossed in and out of the warps (one over, one under) to form a tight, slightly ribbed surface. The famous Chilkat blankets of the Northwest Coast were twined. Twilling was similar, the weft threads being floated over two or more warps, each pair of threads being moved one strand to the right or left, to create a diagonal pattern.

The belt loom was of this type; warps were looped or tied to a bar that was fastened to a tree or wall, the other ends of the warps being tied or looped over a bar attached to the weaver's waist. The weaver could move back and forth to tighten or loosen the tension. Belt looms were thought to have been brought from Mexico around A.D. 100. They were used by the Puebloans and the Navajo to weave sashes for women's dresses, as well as hair ties and garters for ceremonial attire.

Three-bar looms had a frame of two posts at the sides and a bar across the top, leaving the warps to hang free. The next step was the four-bar loom, a four-sided frame, properly called a "fixed warp" loom, which was leaned against a tree or a wall. Salish women wove their blankets on this type of frame using a continuous warp thread. The true loom, with heddle and sheds, was first brought in by the Spanish to the Southwest; at the same time, the Spanish brought in sheep, whose wool would replace cotton.

Wood

Cedar bark (both red and white cedar) was used extensively in the Northwest; it was lightweight and water resistant. Garments were woven of shredded cedar bark: tunics, cloaks, skirts, and raingear such as rainhats and ponchos. Shredded cedar bark was fashioned into plaited head rings. The shredded inner bark of the spruce tree was used for basketry hats, but more important to hat-making was the spruce root; farther south in California the long thin roots of the Joshua tree served the same purpose. Basswood and elm bark were popular in the Northeast for making carrying bags. Birchbark was important in that area not only for making canoes but also for raingear—conical caps and poncho-like garments.

A significant use for wood was for armor. Some armor was made into tunics consisting of two or more layers of hide. But most armor was of the rod-and-slat variety; this was constructed of straight, smooth, round rods fastened together with cords or sinew into a kind of corselet. Slats instead of rods were used under the arms for more comfort and maneuverability. Armor of hide was used almost exclusively on the Plains; otherwise the stick armor appeared everywhere, even in the Far North where the Eskimo were almost entirely dependent on driftwood. This armor was seldom functional; it could stop an occasional arrow, but its psychological effect was significant—it was supposed to strike terror in the heart of a foe. It also indicated rank, for its use was reserved for chiefs and noted warriors, and it may have appeared with symbols of former accomplishments.

Helmets were important articles of attire in warfare. They were typically of carved wood, and most helmets rested on a high wooden collar that in turn rested on the shoulders. Some helmets had a large wooden visor with eyeholes. Wooden masks were a part of battlegear in some locations, especially the Northwest; these masks were commonly carved with ferocious features to frighten the enemy. Some warriors carried wooden shields, large carved pieces of wood that were sometimes coated on the outside with pitch and pebbles for further protection. Thigh guards and greaves for the lower legs were also of wooden rods.

Snowshoes were a necessity in mountain areas and all across the northern regions; without them there could be no hunting in the winter. Snowshoes were generally one of three shapes: round (or bearpaw), oval, or tailed. The first two were the simplest to make, often being no more than a round or oval frame of bent wood with a simple webbing of twigs, lengths of vines, sinew, or babiche thongs; these were worn by the women and children of most tribes.

The long, tailed snowshoes, sometimes reaching a length of eight feet, were found in the Subarctic particularly; they were technically so finely made that some even had rights and lefts. The best wood for the frame was ash, although everywhere it depended on the wood available. The Eskimo, who lived beyond the treeline, had only driftwood for their snowshoes; failing that, they occasionally used ivory. The wood was first soaked in water or steamed, and bent into shape and fastened until it dried. The sinew or babiche webbing was often fashioned into intricate designs. Loops were made to hold the front of the foot and the heel in place. In some areas snowshoes were made of wooden slats or flat pieces of wood.

The Eskimo and other peoples carved wooden goggles to protect themselves from snow blindness; if they had no driftwood, they used ivory, but wood was less apt to freeze to the face than ivory. The Chugach, the Aleut, and other northern tribes made sunshade hats of thin wood, steamed, bent, and painted, some elaborately so.

Hair sticks were a popular item with many tribes—small straight sticks, peeled, polished, and often ornamented with carved or painted designs. Among the Plains Indians, these ornaments fastened into the hair often indicated battle prowess. The Netsilik and neighboring Eskimo peoples used hair sticks to lengthen and stiffen the hair. Hair sticks were also used to fasten headdresses securely.

Many ornaments were carved of wood. Early Indians of the Great Lakes decorated these articles with thin sheets of copper.

Finally, wood was important for skin ornamentation, for the charcoal from partly burned wood was used as a base for tattooing. The process was performed, frequently in a ceremonial manner, by running an awl or needle beneath the skin and drawing through this a thread rubbed with charcoal that had been mixed with grease, forming a line; a series of dots was made by puncturing the skin and rubbing in charcoal. Other pigments were used, but charcoal was by far the most common material for this purpose. Sharp bones, splinters of wood, thorns, or spines from cacti functioned as needles in some areas. Tattooing was common to the vast majority of tribes of North America and was often a part of the puberty rites of both sexes.

Although tattooing was mainly a form of decoration, in some areas it also indicated tribal identity or showed the caste or class of the wearer. Some tribes of the Southwest believed that unless a person was tattooed, it was impossible to enter the land of the dead. Usually the face was tattooed with parallel vertical lines (often three) on the chin, lines on the cheek from the nose to the jawbone, and some lines on the forehead. For the most part, lines or dots were the common form, although some tribes featured more elaborate designs; only in rare instances, such as the coastal tribes of central California, were animal or human representations created. Among the many materialistic tribes of northern California, the men typically had lines tattooed along one arm in order to measure dentalium shells, their standard form of currency. Tattooing was minimal on the Plains, possibly because painting was so much more popular.

Rocks, Minerals, and Earth

Rocks and Minerals

Pebbles and rocks, particularly those of lively color or intriguing shape, were picked up, worked, and cherished—made into earrings, pendants, necklaces, whatever the stones suggested.

Flint is nearly pure silica and very hard. Sometimes it was formed into "tinklers" to be hung in the fringes of garments to create rhythmic tinkling sounds during the dance. Shamans of the Northwest Coast sometimes used flint pieces in their costumes to strike off blue sparks.

California and neighboring states yielded many stones of gem quality—topaz, opal, agate, jasper, and turquoise, the last of highest importance to the Navajo and Pueblo Indians. Shaped chunks of quartz crystals were valued as ornaments. Jade, found farther north, particularly in British Columbia, was cherished for its hardness and translucent beauty; it was made into labrets by northern peoples. Nephrite, a less valuable form of jade, was also made into ornaments. A few rare diamonds were found in the East.

Argillite, a black slate, was a product of British Columbia and especially the Haida country (Queen Charlotte Islands); it was comparatively soft while being carved, but hardened on further exposure to air. The Haida did superb carvings of argillite. Tlingit shamans wore amulets of argillite to concentrate their powers on a patient during a curing rite.

Obsidian, a hard volcanic rock resembling glass, occurred in California, the Great Basin, and the Plateau. Both red and black types were widely traded for use as bangles or tinklers.

Soapstone, a variety of talc, was also easily worked, and was found throughout the North and the Eastern Woodlands, as well as California.

Magnesite, a magnesium carbonate, was called "kolkol" by the Pomo of central California; they had large deposits of it on their land and were the major traders. A white chalk-like substance, it was roasted in ashes to assume a delicate salmon color. It was typically ground into cylinders, which were drilled and formed into beads and pendants.

Slate, a cleavable rock, appeared in many colors: gray, black, red, and bluish-gray; it was made into beads, gorgets, and pendants.

The mineral asphaltum, or pitch, was valuable in attaching shells and other objects to wood or stone to form adornments. It also was smeared on the soles of sandals to strengthen them and to provide traction on rough ground.

Mica, with its shimmering surface and thin plates, was easily worked and was an important trade item for the Southeastern tribes. The best quality came from North Carolina. Most popular were gorgets of mica with finely carved silhouettes and bas-relief representations.

Catlinite, a red indurated clay, was named for George Catlin, famed painter of Indians in the nineteenth century. It was also called "pipestone" and was found in a large quarry in southwestern Minnesota. Its major use was for the making of pipes, but ornaments were also created from it. Like argillite, it was easily carved and hardened on exposure to air.

Copper was the only metal found by the Indians in abundance in North America, appearing on the ground in nuggets and chunks. The shores of Isle

Royale in Lake Superior were the best source of the metal, although it was found as far south as northern Illinois as "float" copper carried there by the glacial action. Copper deposits were also in the northern Subarctic in the Copper River, White River, and Coppermine River areas. It was used particularly by the Copper Eskimo, but it was also traded throughout the North. A huge trade network in copper flourished for centuries, although it did not seem to carry as far as California or the Southwest.

The material was hammered into thin sheets by means of alternate hammering and heating; North American Indians did not practice smelting. When the copper was thin enough, it was cut into shape by means of sharp tools of flint, then ground and polished, and designs or figures were incised with a hard pointed object.

Many articles were created of copper. Hammered very thin it was tightly rolled to form beads, earrings, nose ornaments, and other articles. Larger rolls of the metal were pounded into "C" shapes for bracelets and anklets. Beaten plaques were made into larger earrings, gorgets, and headbands (in the Northeast), and they appeared as part of the frontlet headdresses of the Northwest.

Iron ore (hematite) was either found in deposits or on the ground; some of the latter may have been meteoric iron. Of various colors, such as gray, brown, or red, it was used mainly for tools, occurring only sporadically as ornamentation.

Paints

Paints were used both as application to garments and to the human body. Sources of paint were not as widespread as dye sources because a substance was required that could be ground into powder.

Red ochers were the most common and popular sources of paint. They occurred in hematite, in earth ochers, and in cinnabar. The last, a mercuric oxide, was composed of brilliant red crystals and was much prized, but it is thought that the diseased bones found in some grave sites may have been caused by the mercury, known to be poisonous.

Yellow ochers yielded a dull yellow or yellow-brown. Yellow clay came from the banks of the Yellowstone River. Buffalo gallstones also provided yellow. White paint came from a diatomaceous clay or from burnt clamshells. Blue clay, often a copper-impregnated earth, provided that color. Black was made from ground-up charcoal, graphite, manganese, or lignite; powdered lignite provided a gray as well as a shiny black. Green could be made from copper sulphite or from green algae scum. Orange was another earth ocher. Brown came from walnut juice mixed with earth to form a paste. Commercial paints were not available until the traders brought them in during the 1770s.

The pigment was first ground in a stone mortar, then mixed with some substance to form a paste—salmon roe or other fish eggs, elk fat, oil, or beargrease. A watery sizing was made of boiled buffalo hooves, hide scrapings, or beavertails. This sizing was either mixed with the paint or spread on the surface before or after painting, producing a hard glossy surface that was as durable as many modern paints. Each color was kept in a separate bag. During the process, the paint was contained in tortoiseshell paint cups

The paint was generally applied with the fingers, although some tools were used. Brushes were of porous bones, bristles, or vegetable fibers fastened to wood or bone handles. Buffalo-tail brushes served for larger areas. Single lines or multiple lines were made with a paint stick. In some areas the paint was applied by means of stamps carved of bone or antler.

Various objects were painted. Skin garments, especially on the Plains, were often elaborately painted—robes, leggings, shirts, and dresses. The garment or hide was dampened and stretched on a frame for better control of the paint, and the object was kept moist during the process. Basketry hats of the West were painted not only for decorative reasons but also as a form of waterproofing and as a display of wealth. Of course the Plains tipis were painted, to be recycled later into garments when they were old and softened.

Face and body painting occurred among many tribes, most commonly being achieved with red ocher. Faces were painted black in time of war and as a symbol of mourning. Hair was often rubbed with paint and oil to make it colorful and glistening. The central part of the hair was frequently painted red as a sign of joy and celebration. The Nootka and others liked to throw sparkling sand (bits of mica) on top of face paint for ceremonial occasions. The Beothuks of Newfoundland were called the "Red Paint People,"

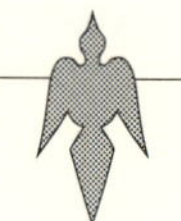

because they used it for face and body painting, in the hair, on their clothing, and on objects buried with the dead. The Eskimo did not resort to face or body painting, although neighboring Aleut sometimes did.

European Contributions to Indian Clothing Arts

Cloth

A major contribution was that of cloth. Cotton cloth, in calico prints, gingham, or plain, was made into dresses, at first cut in the Indian style, later similar to the fashions of European women. Steel needles and scissors were further boons. Scraps of cloth made colorful applique designs. Some of the most famous applications of this technique were in the "button blankets" of the Northwest, consisting of totemic designs appliqued on blankets and outlined in white pearl buttons obtained from the traders. The Seminole women of Florida made unique garments—full skirts and blouses for the women, long, full-sleeved shirts for the men—which featured patchwork designs, possibly adapted from the pieced quilts of the white women. They were the first to acquire sewing machines, a treasure that later appeared on the reservations. Cotton sewing thread, embroidery thread, and wool yarns added further to the clothing arts. Commercial dyes came in after 1870—garish aniline dyes that lacked the delicacy of the vegetable dyes.

Robes of fur and hide were eschewed in favor of blanket cloth made by the whites. A preferred fabric was stroud cloth, a cheap felted cloth used as "blotting" material in the woolen mills of England; this came in red, blue, and occasionally green, the blue by far the most popular. Stroud cloth had white selvages that were often worked into the design of a robe, perhaps with a white stripe down the center. Breechcloths were frequently made of strouding.

Ribbon applique, introduced by the French about 1750 to the Indians of the Northeast, was first made from silk ribbon. Later, broadcloth ribbon, cheaper and more readily available, was substituted. Cut ribbonwork featured simple designs, floral or geometric, cut simultaneously in ribbons of two colors; the mirror images were sewn together, or sewn separately on a ribbon of a contrasting color; the strips were used to decorate the edges of primarily women's garments, but men's apparel, such as breechcloths, leggings, and moccasins, were also trimmed in this manner. Applique ribbonwork sometimes involved the use of elaborate floral designs, cut out and sewn to panels of contrasting color. The Great Lakes and Prairie tribes were most famous for their ribbonwork, particularly the Osage women.

Weaving

Knitting and crocheting, forms of finger weaving done with commercial needles and hooks, were introduced into the Southwest in the nineteenth century. These techniques were especially used in the making of stockings.

The introduction of the "true" loom by the Spanish led in the Southwest to the development of a weaving culture that reached great heights in weaving artistry. This treadle loom was brought in by Spanish settlers about 1639; sheep had been brought in about ten years earlier. Cotton had been used by the Pueblo Indians for centuries and continued to be in use for some time, but wool took over to become the dominant fiber. Blankets and dresses were the main products of these looms. Wool yarn was used to create the embroideries on Southwest wool dresses, or mantas.

Beads

Beads were, and still are, one of the most important contributions of the Europeans to the Indian clothing arts. Columbus brought the first beads in 1492, and the Spanish ships brought them to the Pacific coast in 1772. At first the beads were often used as substitutes for porcupine quillwork, so difficult to work, and the designs followed traditional patterns. Later, beading took on its own characteristics. The large "pony" beads, so called because they were brought by the traders on ponies, came to the Plains about 1800; the tiny "seed" beads appeared about 1840. During the late nineteenth century, beading became more and more elaborate, even flamboyant, until some garments featured surfaces entirely covered with beads. Glass beads provided flexibility in creating designs, whether elegantly floral or rigidly geometric or a combination of the two.

There were four major techniques in the beading process: weaving, spotstitch, lazy-stitch, and netting.

Weaving was done with the warp threads stretched on a bow loom or a belt loom; the beads, on a thread, were threaded through and fastened to the warps in various patterns, usually of an angular sort.

Spotstitch beading was created by laying threaded beads in a design and catching them down at frequent intervals with a second needle and thread. This resulted in designs of a linear or floral nature.

The lazy-stitch technique also involved threaded beads caught down by a second needle and thread, but the beads were in short rows fastened at the ends. This was a fast method for filling in background areas, resulting in a pattern of ridges in parallel rows.

Netting was done in the usual manner—looping coils on to a preceding row of looped coils—but the beads were secured in the knots or in place of knots. The Mojave of California wore magnificent collars of beaded netting.

Metal

Brass, tin, and silver formed tinklers to be sewn onto women's dresses. Brass was also hammered into thin sheets and fashioned into ornaments much like the early ones of copper.

By 1800 silver was formed into admirable brooches by the Iroquois. By them, it was introduced to the metalworkers of the Plains, who in turn taught its use to the Southwestern artisans. By the turn of the century it appeared among the Northwest Coast people in the forms of fine bracelets and pins.

At first the silver was obtained from coins; later, ingots were made available to the craftsmen. The silver was handled in various ways; it was hammered into sheets and then in forms to create convex or concave surfaces, it was stamped with designs, it was engraved with an awl, or it was melted and cast into molds. Silver has been a valuable contribution to the economy of the Southwest and Northwest tribes.

Gold has never been widely used among Indian metalworkers, except in the case of a few modern craftsmen.

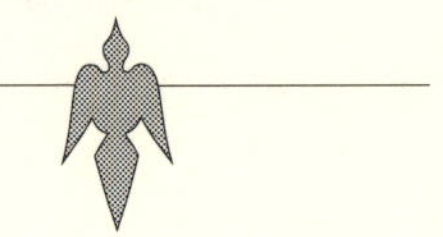

Moccasins

three-piece with rawhide sole

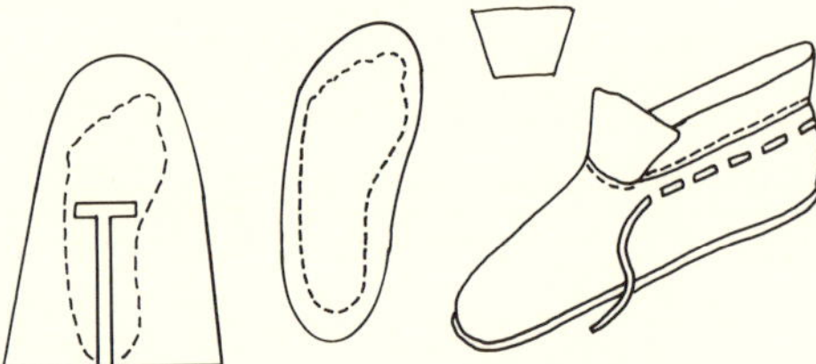

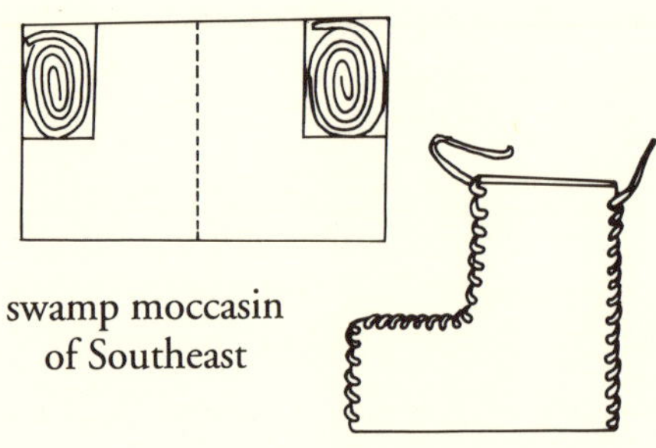

swamp moccasin of Southeast

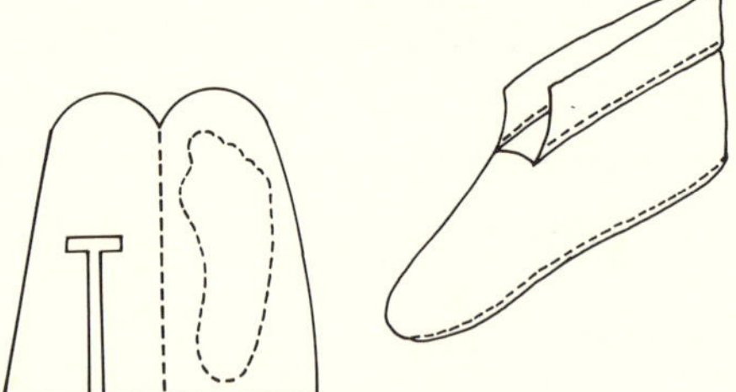

one-piece with added cuff

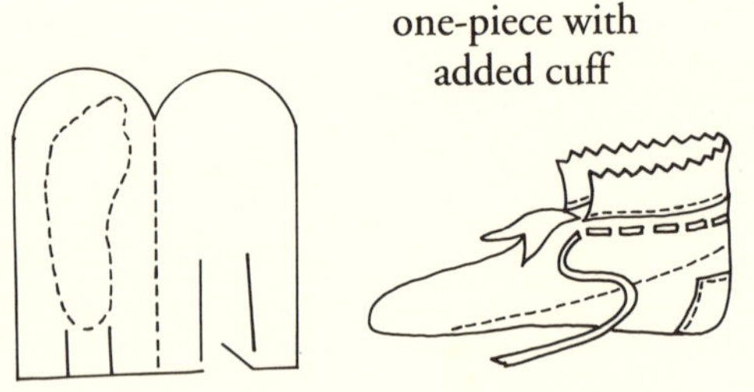

one-piece with added cuff

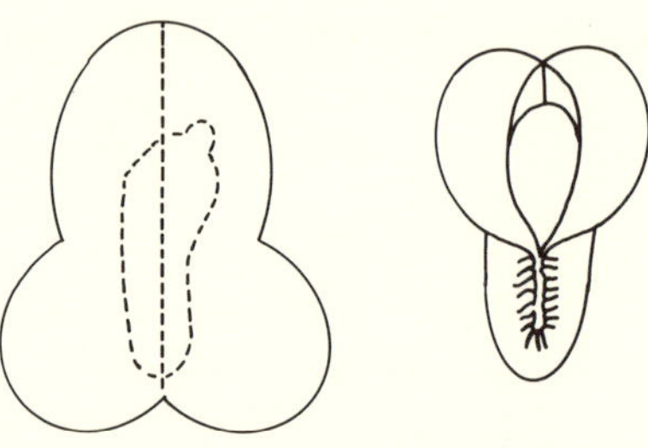

one-piece with front seam

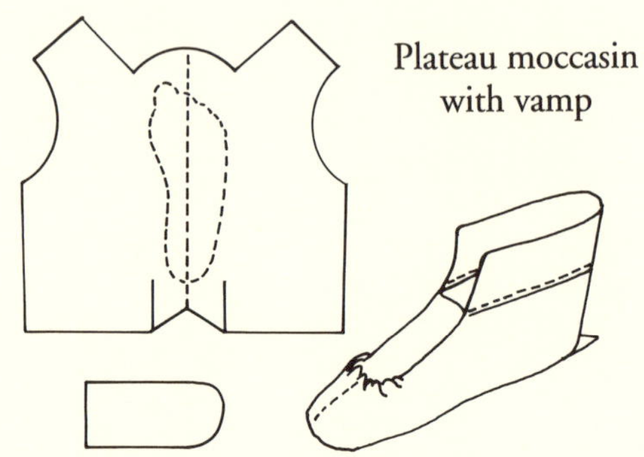

Plateau moccasin with vamp

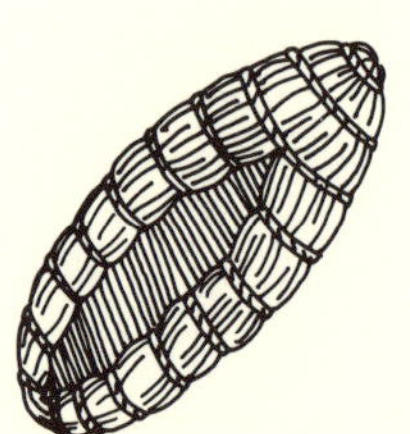

twined tule moccasin of California

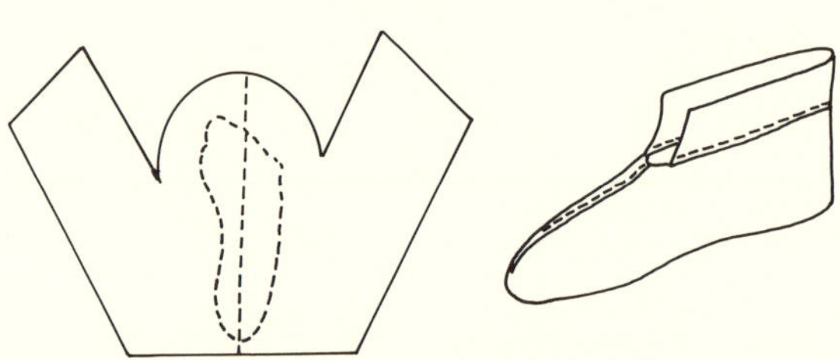

one-piece with front seam and added cuff

Leggings

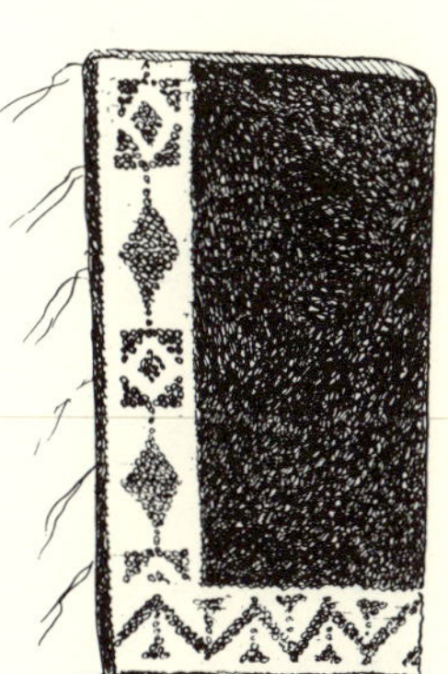

beaded cloth women's leggings

Plains hide leggings

women's cloth leggings with ribbonwork

Men's Plateau cloth leggings

Athapaskan footed trousers

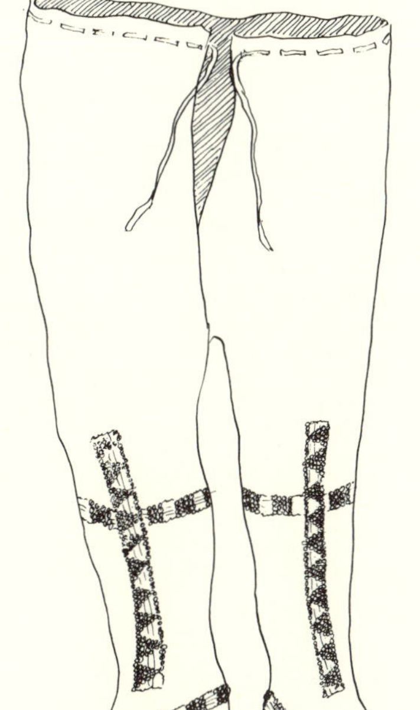

Chilkat leggings with puffin beaks

modern powwow Dancers' leggings of angora fur

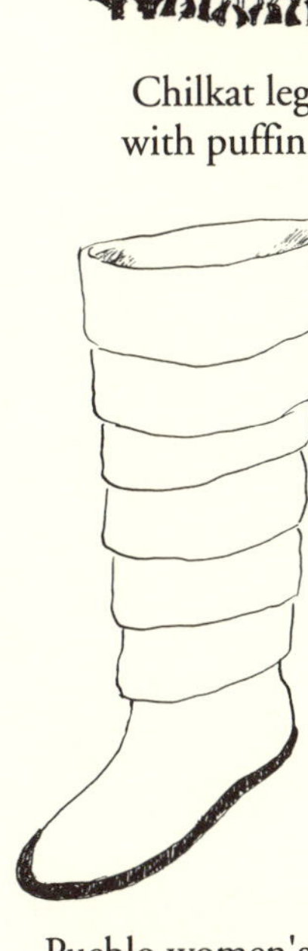

Pueblo women's wrapped leggings

Dresses

wraparound hide skirt with hide poncho

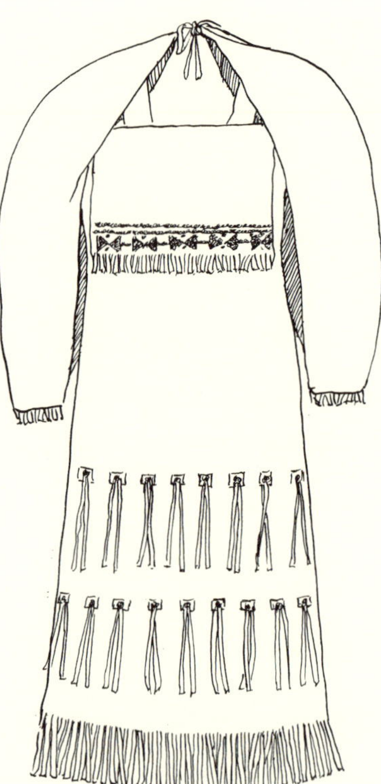
strap-and-sleeve dress

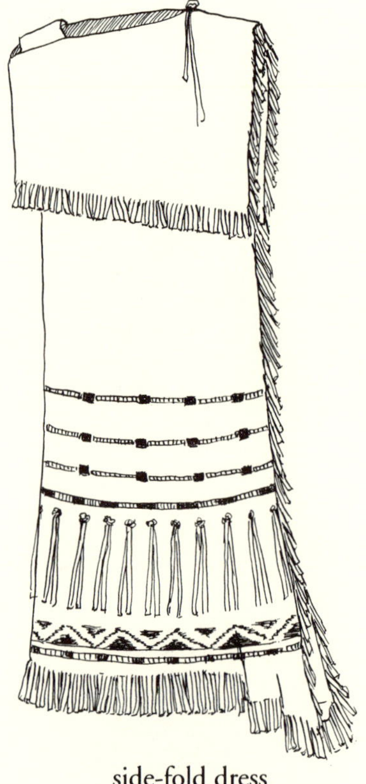
side-fold dress

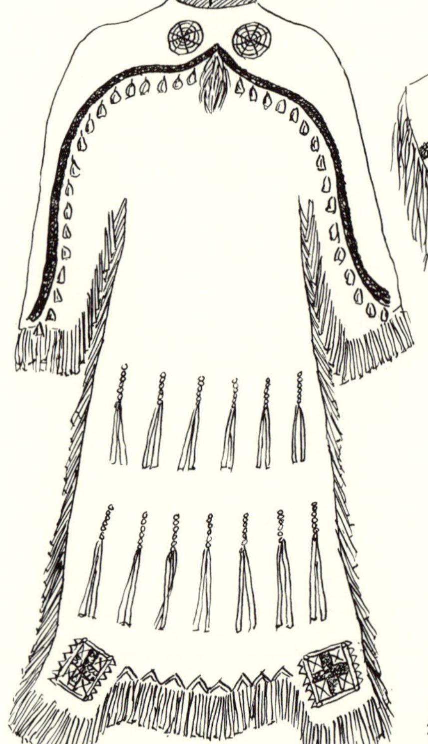
two-skin or deertail dress

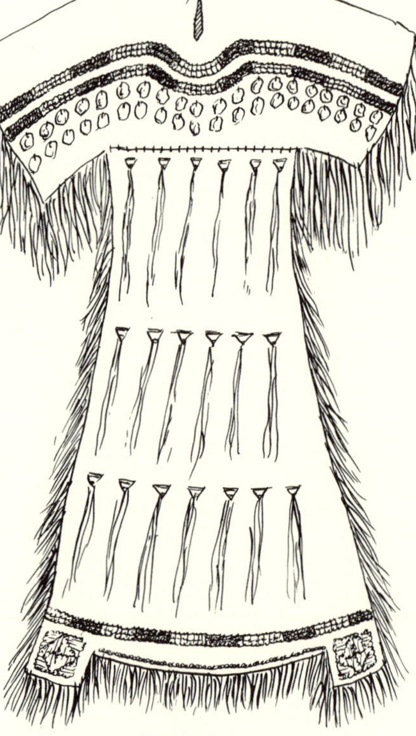
three-skin dress

Plateau dress of cloth

Skirts

fiber skirt

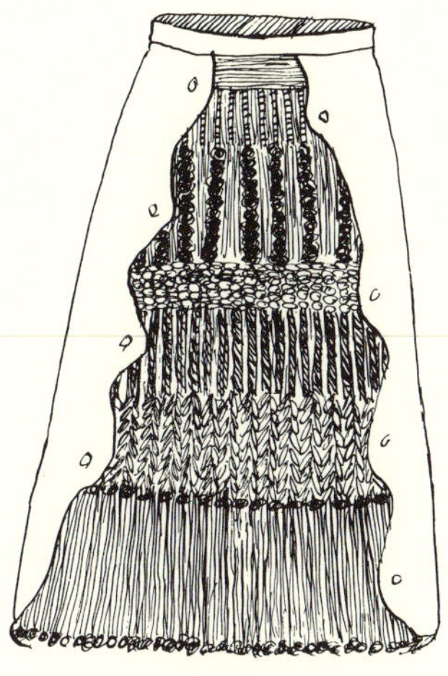
California double apron

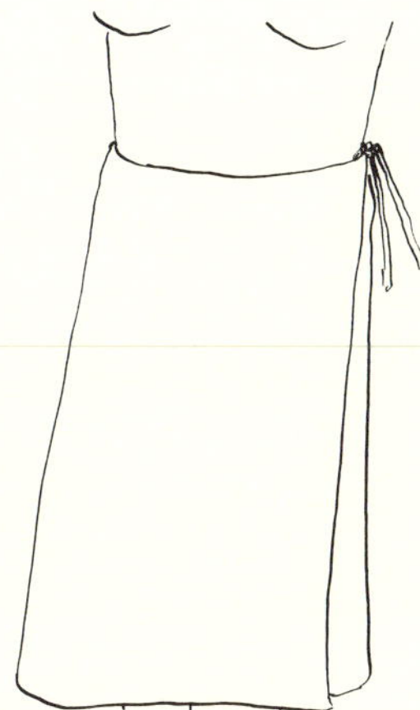
hide wraparound skirt

Hupa dance skirt

Powhatan draped apron

hide fringed apron

ribbonwork skirt

Seminole patchwork skirt

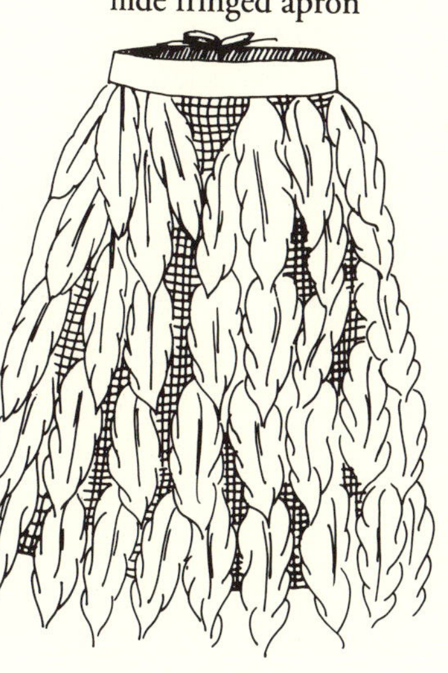
Shaman's skirt
swan feathers on net

Breechclouts

fitted with girdle

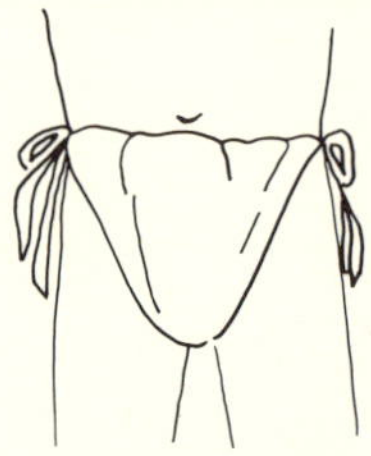

fitted breechclout

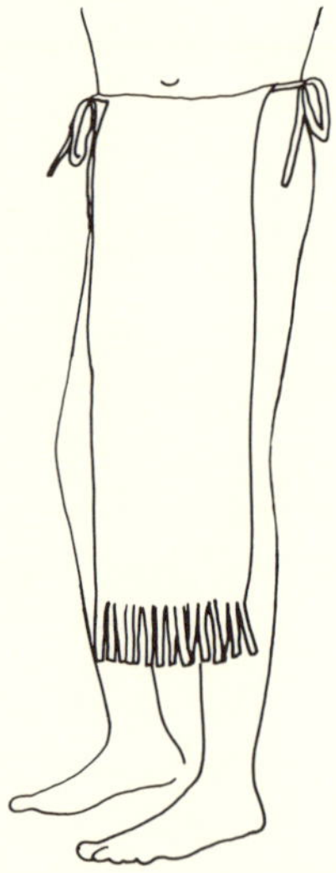

fitted breechclout with flaps

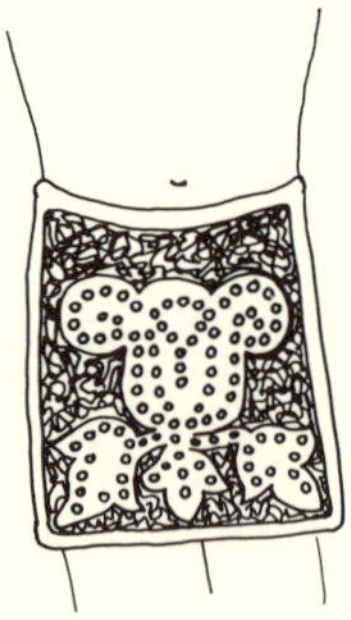

beaded cloth
breechcloth

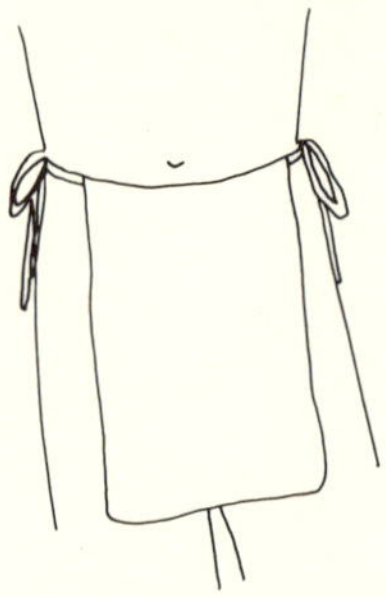

small apron

cloth double apron
with ribbonwork

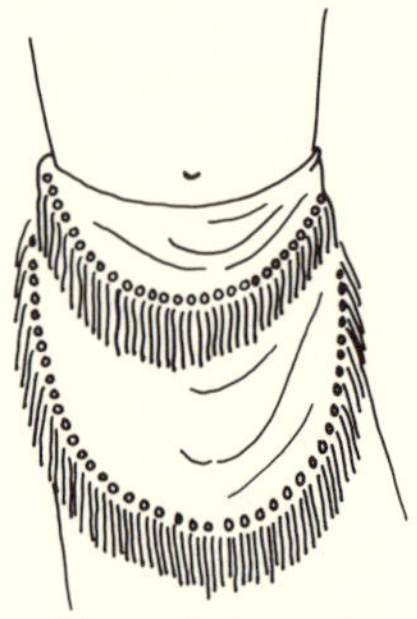

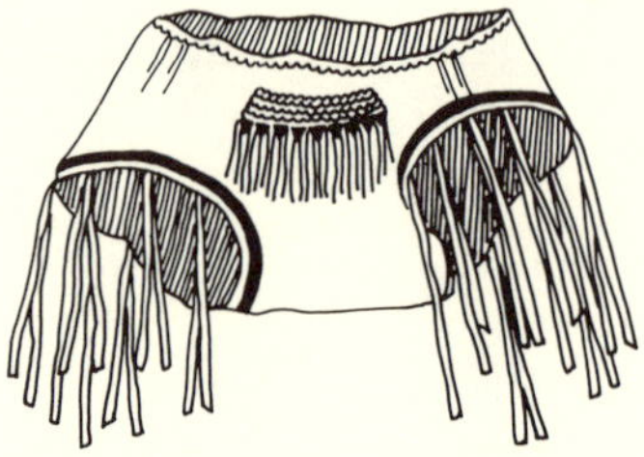

Eskimo brief

Pueblo kilt
as worn

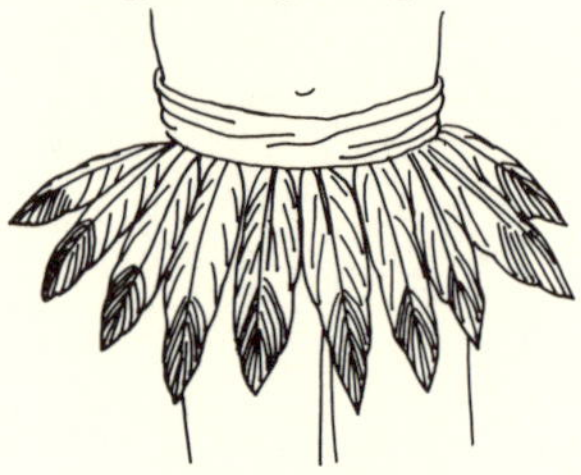

fringed draped apron

fringed Breechclout
with feathers

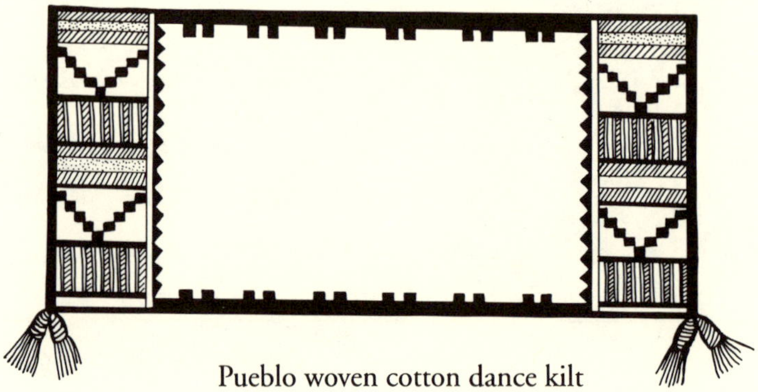

Pueblo woven cotton dance kilt

Shirts and Tunics

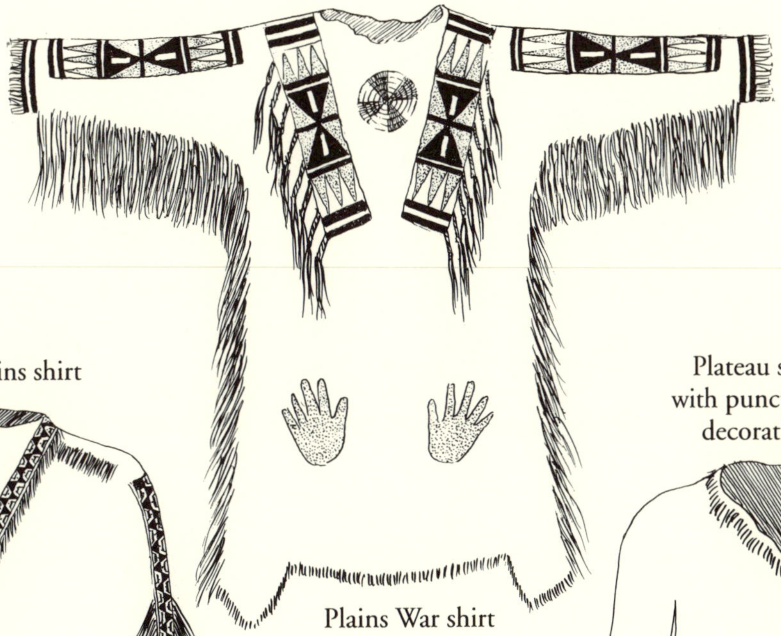

Plains War shirt

Southern Plains shirt

Plateau shirt with punctuated decoration

Chilkat woven tunic of Northwest Coast

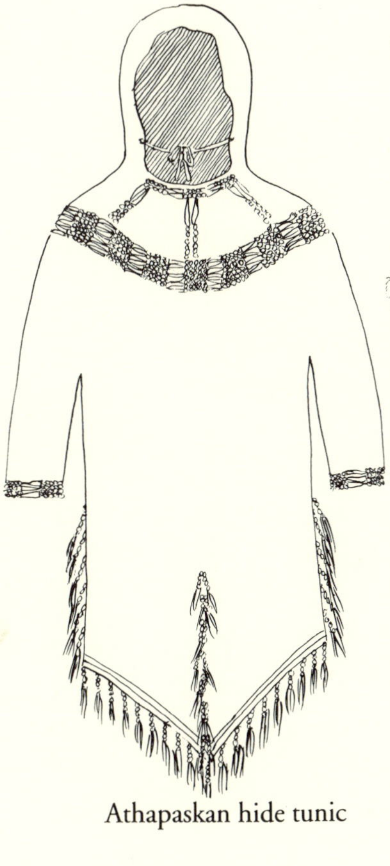

Athapaskan hide tunic

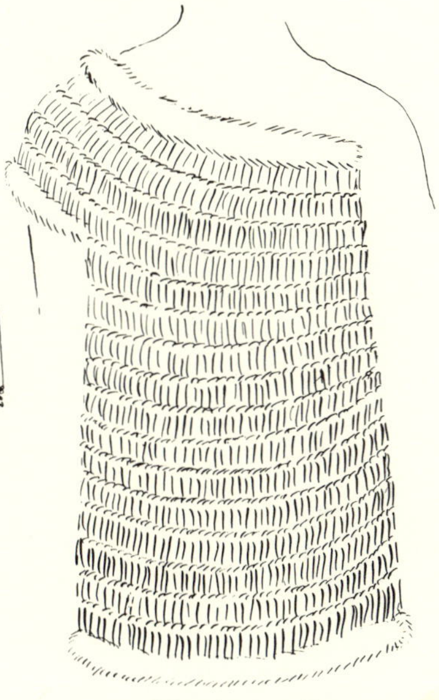

Northwest Coast tunic of shredded cedar bark

Headgear

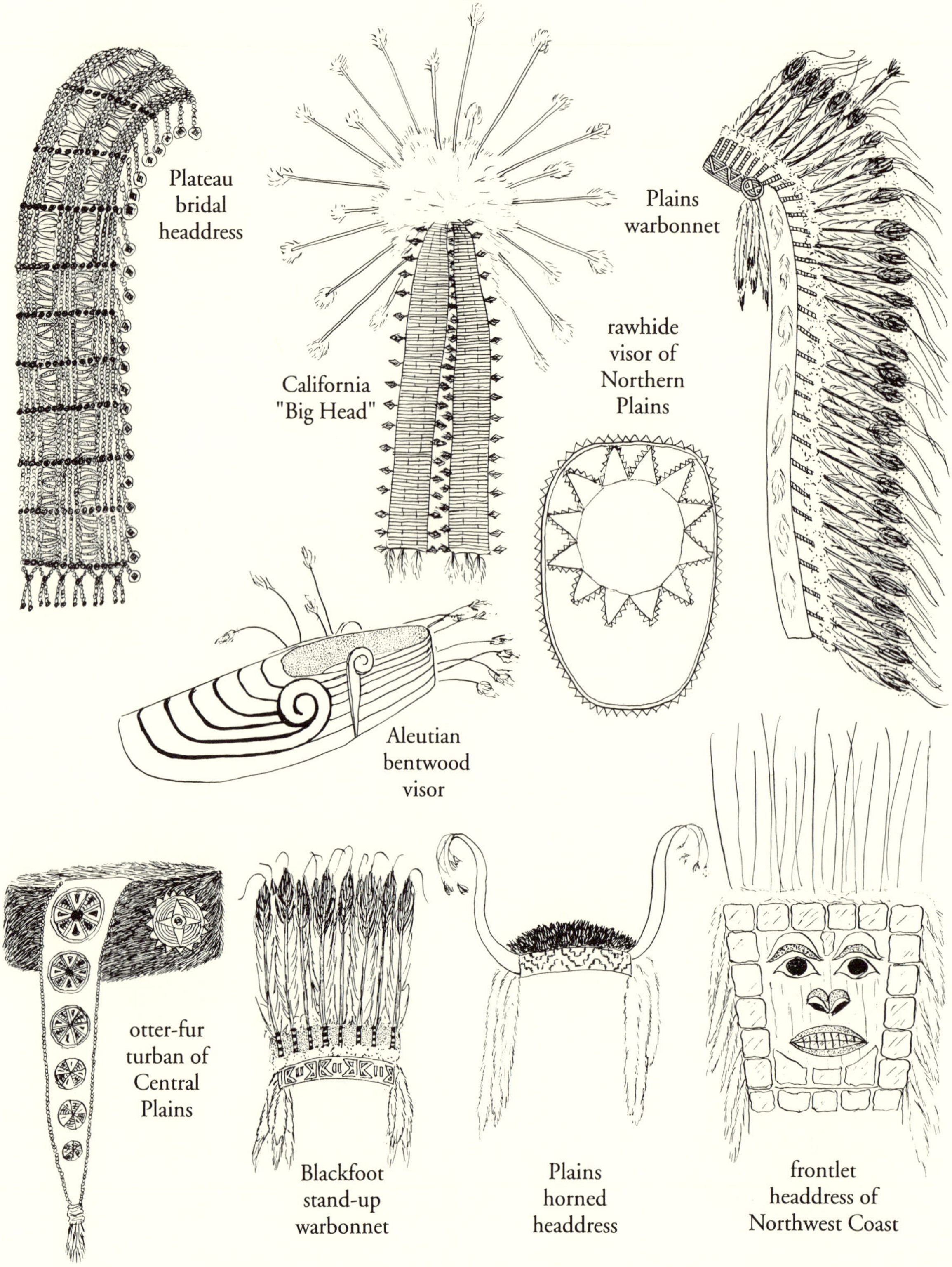

Plateau bridal headdress

California "Big Head"

Plains warbonnet

rawhide visor of Northern Plains

Aleutian bentwood visor

otter-fur turban of Central Plains

Blackfoot stand-up warbonnet

Plains horned headdress

frontlet headdress of Northwest Coast

Appendix Two

Glossary

Algonkin Split Skirt: An early hide skirt with overlapping edges, forming a slit on the side, worn especially on the northern Plains.

Amulet: An ornament, gem, or a package containing a relic; the amulet was worn as a charm or as a preservative against evil.

Anklet: An ornament embracing the ankle.

Anorak: Another name for the parka, especially in eastern Canada and Greenland. The *anorak* was made of hide or, later, of cloth.

Apron: A piece of material, generally of fiber or buckskin, worn by women, hanging from the waist in front. California women frequently wore a double apron, with a second apron in back.

Armband: Also "armlet." A strip fastened around the upper arm, often of fur, frequently with attached skins of small animals. Later armbands were often of metal, especially silver.

Armor: Clothing worn as protection in battle. Garments consisted of a corselet covering the chest, thigh guards, greaves, and a helmet. "Rod-and-slat" armor was of rods and flat pieces of wood or bone, which were laced together with thongs. Armor was also made in the form of a tunic of one or more layers of elk or moose hide.

Assomption Sash: A long sash woven by the Indians of the eastern Subarctic and widely traded. Of various dyed fibers and featuring arrow and chevron designs, it was also called an "arrow point sash." It was usually worn with a *capote.*

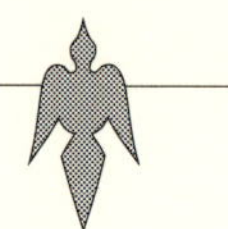

Babiche: Thongs or cords of elk skin or caribou skin, preferably the former. Used especially in netting for snowshoes and in making netted bags.

Baby Harness: A strap of leather or braided thongs around the back of an Eskimo woman's parka, fastened in front with a toggle, to help carry and distribute the weight of a baby in the hood. In the Subarctic a wide embroidered strap, called a "baby belt," was used for the same purpose.

Bag: A sack or pouch used for holding articles in lieu of pockets. Most were hung from the belt or on a thong around the neck.

Bandolier Bag: A rectangular bag worn at the side and suspended by means of a wide strap over the shoulder. These bags, commonly worn by men, were often decorated with quillwork, beadwork, or embroidery. Some authorities believe they may have been adapted from seventeenth-century military bags.

Basket Cap: A close-fitting cap woven of grass, root, or other fibers, worn by the women of the Plateau, Northwest Coast, and California. Also called a "basket hat."

Belt: A strip of tanned leather, rawhide, cloth, or other material encircling the waist. A belt could hold an article of clothing in place, could support weapons, or could have bags or pouches suspended from it. It was commonly tied with thongs. After European contact, metal buckles were often used.

Big Head: A headdress worn by the Indians of central California consisting of a pincushion-like device with slender rods exploding in all directions, the ends tipped with feathers or flowers, such as California poppies. Fastened at the back were two long bands decorated with flicker quills.

Blanket: Heavy material or fabric used as a robe or as a bed covering, sometimes both. As clothing, it was often called a "wearing blanket."

Blanket Strip: A beaded or quilled strip, often embellished with rosettes, over the center seam of a robe of hide or stroud cloth.

Body or Combination Suit: An Eskimo garment covering the entire body except for the face and hands, usually of fur for infants and young children; body suits of gut skin were used by men when working in water.

Boot: A covering for the foot and leg rising to above the ankle, sometimes to the hips. Boots were usually of leather with heavier soles and were sometimes laced for a snug fit.

Bracelet: An ornamental band worn about the wrist made of strips of finger-woven fibers, fur, leather, or metal.

Braiding: Also called plaiting. A finger-weaving technique using three or more strands crossing over each other.

Breastplate: A plate covering the breast composed of hairpipe beads in ornamental patterns. Worn more as decorative apparel than for protection.

Breechcloth: A garment to cover the lower body, especially the male genitals. It was rarely worn by a woman except occasionally by very young girls. Although the term is commonly used interchangeably with *breechclout,* it is used here to refer to coverings made of cloth, especially stroud cloth.

Breechclout: A piece of material, such as buckskin, used to cover the male genitals, esteemed as a symbol of masculinity. Depending on the style, it varied in length from one to five feet long and was about twelve inches wide. Breechclouts were often fashioned of various grasses or other fibers.

Bridal Cap: A headdress or cap elaborately adorned with beads and shells, worn by brides, especially in the Northwest and in the Plateau area.

Brooch: A small, round ornamental object attached to a garment. Usually of silver, most brooches were made after European contact.

Bustle, Framework: A decorative framework, typically a large rosette of feathers, worn on the back below the waist, commonly by male dancers. Also called a "crow."

Button Blanket: A ceremonial blanket/robe of the Northwest Coast area made of heavy fabric, such as a trade blanket, on which was appliquéd a red cloth family crest pattern, which was then outlined with white pearl buttons.

Camp Dress: A cotton dress worn by Apache women of the Southwest featuring a long full skirt and a full overblouse of the same material, typically with a square yoke.

Cap: A brimless head covering, sometimes with a visor in front; it was occasionally made of the entire pelt of a small animal with the tail hanging down the back.

Cape: A sleeveless garment hanging from neck to waist or neck to feet. Capes were made of a large, flat piece of material, often circular in shape, of buckskin, strips of animal intestines, cloth, cedar bark or other fibers.

Capote: A coat of heavy blanket cloth with a front opening and usually a peaked, attached hood. A long sash was often wound several times around the waist, with the tasseled ends hanging in front. Characteristic garment of the French *voyageurs* of the Subarctic. Typically made of a Hudson's Bay Company blanket.

Chief's Coat: A coat of military origin bestowed by government officials and others on chiefs of the northern Plains and other areas.

Chilkat Blanket: A blanket made by the Chilkat Tlingit of the Northwest Coast. Warps were of mountain-goat wool with a core of cedar bark. Rectangular in shape with a wide fringe at the bottom, the blankets were widely used for ceremonial occasions and were an important item of trade.

Choker: A short necklace worn closely around the neck, often of several rows of beads, especially dentalium shells, or a padded roll.

Chongo: A hair style, worn by both sexes, in which the hair was coiled at the nape of the neck and wound with a thong or a strip of cloth; common in the Southwest, especially among the Navajo.

Cloak: Also called a mantle. A loose outer garment, square, circular, or rectangular in shape, suspended from the neck down, similar to a cape but usually longer. Not sewn but draped or pinned about the body.

Clubbed Hair: A hair style in which the hair was gathered into a large clump at the nape of the neck, at the sides, on the crown of the head, or over the forehead; these arrangements were often secured with wooden pins.

Coat: An outer garment for the upper part of the body commonly worn by men. A front opening in the coat was usually indicative of European influence.

Coiling: A technique used in weaving in which single fibers or bundles of fibers are attached to the preceding role by sewing.

Collar: A piece of material encircling the neck and, at times, the shoulders; some collars were nearly as large as capes.

Concha Belt: A leather belt to which were affixed large silver medallions; worn especially in the Southwest.

Crocheting: A finger-weaving technique using a crochet hook and yarn or other fibers to create continuous loops. Crocheting was not used by American Indians until the late nineteenth century.

Cross Belt: A strap, generally heavily embellished with beadwork, worn over one shoulder, often ending in a bandolier bag.

Cross Weave: A simple weave in a checkerboard pattern of over-one, under-one, reversing to under-one, over-one in the next row.

Deertail Dress: A dress worn on the northern Plains made of deerskin, on which the deertail was retained on the yoke as ornament.

Dewclaw: The false hoof of deer and other ungulates, often used as ornament on garments.

Dewlap: Loose skin hanging from the throat of an animal, the hairs of which, particularly those of moose and caribou, were frequently used in embroidery.

Dress: A garment for women, knee-length or longer. Early dresses included four major types: strap-and-sleeve, side-fold, two-skin, and three-skin.

Duffel: A heavy blanket cloth, often used in the Arctic to line dresses and to make mittens, parkas, and other articles of clothing.

Ear Ornaments: Many varied articles were used for ear ornamentation. Earrings were round hoops or

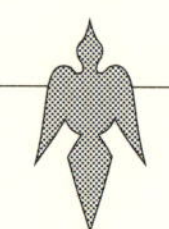

dangling strings of beads or shells such as dentalia and abalone. Earspools and earplugs were popular in some areas. Often the ear would be pierced in several places to increase the number of earrings worn. At times, a large slit was made in the earlobe, which was then wrapped with wire.

Exploit Robe: A robe worn by the men of the northern Plains in which the tanned leather surface was painted with representations of the wearer's exploits in battle.

Fan: A broad, flat article with a handle, to be moved gently to and fro, either for cooling purposes or for display. Some fans consisted of feathers, such as those of the eagle, owl, turkey, and goose, strung together. Some were flat wooden disks, which may have been richly decorated.

Feather Mantles: Cloaks or mantles made of colorful feathers fastened into a fiber netting. Costly and time-consuming in their making, they were saved for important personages and special occasions. Found generally in the southern areas, they were considered by some authorities to represent a Mexican influence.

Finger Masks: Caps, typically with faces, worn on the fingers during a dance, especially by women in southwestern Alaska.

Finger Weaving: Weaving without a loom, which involved the techniques of looping, netting, braiding, and twining. Belts, sashes, tumplines, and some blankets, such as Chilkat and Salish blankets, were made by finger weaving.

Firebag: A pouch of clamshells, or of leather lined with clamshells, used to carry burning coals. Also used to refer to a pouch, often decorated, containing fire-making equipment.

Forelock: A hair style of the northern Plains and the Plateau in which one lock of hair hung down over the nose, cut off straight at the bottom.

Friendship Bag: A rectangular pouch of fiber richly embroidered, worn by the women of the Plateau area.

Frontlet Headdress: A wooden headdress carved in the form of a face, worn by the Indians of the Northwest Coast. Reserved for ceremonial use, it featured inlaid pieces of abalone shell, a crown of upstanding sea-lion whiskers, and strips of ermine.

Fur Mosaic: A form of decoration made by Eskimo women in which small pieces of fur of different hues were applied to strips in geometric patterns; used as edging on dresses and parkas.

Garter: A leather strap, woven strip, or band of fur fastened around the knee to support a legging or stocking, often embellished with shells, feathers, tinklers, or other ornaments.

Gauntlets: Gloves worn in the northern areas with large cuffs often heavily decorated with beadwork or embroidery.

Ghost Dance Garments: Shirts, leggings, or dresses worn during the Ghost Dance movement that swept the country in the late nineteenth century. Made of cotton cloth and painted with celestial symbols, the garments were said by some to protect the wearer from bullets.

Goggles: A "screen" for covering the eyes with a narrow slit to see through. These were typically of ivory, wood, or fur and usually tied with a thong around the head. They protected the eyes against blindness caused by glare on water, ice, or snow.

Gorget: Typically a large shell, such as a conch, with two holes drilled at the top so it could be strung with a thong or ribbon and hung around the neck. Often called "pectorals," gorgets were also made of wood, slate, bone, ivory, and later metal.

Grizzly Bear–Claw Necklace: A necklace of the claws strung on a thong with beads between and often with a strip of otter fur added. Because of the difficulty in killing the huge beasts, the necklace represented great courage.

Gut Parka: A hooded, waterproof jacket made of strips of the intestines of such sea mammals as seal, sea lion, walrus, and whale.

Hair Net: A net made of iris fibers, worn by the men of central California to keep their long hair enclosed and to secure headdresses and ornaments.

Hair Plate: An ornament consisting of a leather strap to which were affixed decorative silver medallions.

The strap hung from the back of the head to the waist or below.

Hair Rolls: A hair style favored by the Yuma men of California. The hair was formed into many long rolls to which clay was applied for added stiffness. At times the rolls were coiled on the top of the head into a huge turban.

Hairbow: Also "hairtie." A bow-shaped ornament, usually beaded, worn by men at each side of the forehead, by women on the hair clubbed in the back. Larger ones were called hair binders.

Hairpin: A large pin of wood, bone, or ivory used to fasten a large coil of hair. These were frequently incised with designs.

Hairpipe Beads: Beads, two to five inches long, usually made from the shell of the *Strombus gigas.* The beads were used mostly to make breastplates, but were also made into necklaces and ornaments.

Hairstick: A wooden stick, often decorated and with feathers attached, fastened into the hair. In the central Arctic, Eskimo women used sticks to stiffen their braids, the whole then wrapped with cloth or skin strips.

Halo Headdress: The warbonnet of the northern Plains men featuring a wide circlet of feathers, often with a trail of feathers in the back. This headdress was widely adopted by Indian men in the twentieth century for ceremonies and for events staged for tourists.

Hat: A head covering consisting of a brim and a crown, although the spruce-root hats of the Northwest Coast had the brim and crown together. Materials used included fur, wood, and a variety of fibers.

Headband: A strip of material used to encircle the head made of fur, bark, leather, woven fiber or yarn, or a cotton cloth scarf folded into a strip. Occasionally feathers were attached to the headbands. These bands were sometimes used as tumplines.

Headdress: A decorative covering for the head, often quite elaborate and usually worn by a man. Some well-known headdresses were the "halo" warbonnet of the Plains, the "stand-up" headdress of the Blackfeet and other tribes, the horn headdress featuring buffalo horns, the "frontlets" of the Northwest Coast, the "Big Head" headdress of California, and the dance headdresses of the Southwest.

Heddle: A rod used during the weaving process to pull certain warp threads up or forward in order to slide a shuttle through.

Helmet: Head covering worn either for warfare or as a decoy when hunting. Usually made of wood, sometimes of hide, the war helmet was generally painted, sometimes with a ferocious face.

Hockboot: A foot covering made from the tarsal joint of a moose, elk, or other large animal. The skin was removed in one piece, left in its original shape, and the bottom sewn to form a boot.

Hood: A soft covering for the head, separate or attached to a parka or *capote,* either rounded in back or pointed.

Horn Headdress: A headdress reserved for warriors of the highest status among the northern Plains tribes. It was formed of a skullcap base of buffalo hide with the hair left on the outside and the tail appended; then the horns were attached, one on each side. Other items were added for decoration, such as feathers, ermine strips, and shells.

Housewife: A small buckskin pouch or bag used to hold a woman's sewing equipment, such as awls, needles, and sinew.

Hudson's Bay Blanket: A blanket made by the Hudson's Bay Company of Canada and widely distributed throughout the colder regions. It was usually white with wide, contrasting stripes of color at either end, and it exhibited small black stripes at one side to indicate the number of beaver pelts a particular blanket required in trade.

Ikat: A technique used in weaving in which the yarn is coiled and dipped in various dyes to produce a soft, variegated effect.

Imbrication: A method of creating designs when using the coiling technique by wrapping various colored strips of fiber about the coils as they are being stitched down.

Indian Hat: A tall, black hat with flat brim and with a flat or rounded crown on top. It was widely adopted during the nineteenth and early twentieth centuries.

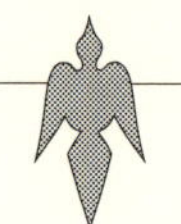

Indian Princess Dress: A long dress of buckskin with beadwork decoration and many long fringes. As an article of attire worn by young Indian girls at modern powwows, it is typically worn with a beaded headband and one or two upstanding feathers.

Kamik: A tall boot, decorated with embroidery or variegated leather pieces, worn by Greenland Eskimo women.

Kamleika: A waterproof parka or long cape made of strips of sea mammal intestines sewn together, worn by the Eskimo and Aleut of southern Alaska.

Khomba: A body suit of fur worn by Asiatic Eskimo women and children.

Kilt: A short garment wrapped around the hips, made of woven and embroidered cotton, and worn by the dancers of the Southwest, particularly the Puebloans.

Knife Sheath: A container for a knife, often beaded, which was worn around the neck on a thong, especially by men in the Subarctic area.

Knitting: A finger-weaving technique involving the use of two long needles and yarn or other fiber to create a continuous series of loops. Knitting was not adopted by Indian women until late in the nineteenth century.

Kupsuck: An Eskimo dress made of cotton, often lined with duffel, featuring a full dress falling from a yoke with a wide flounce at the bottom, and often trimmed with braid. Lined *kupsucks* generally had an attached hood edged with wolverine fur.

Labret: A piece of wood, bone, ivory, or stone worn in a perforation of the lower lip. Most labrets were circular or rectangular.

Leggings: Coverings for the legs, one for each leg. Men's leggings were tied with thongs to a thong or belt at the waist and were ankle-length, occasionally gartered at the knees. Women's leggings were from the knees to the ankles and were always knee-gartered. In some areas, leggings connected with the moccasins. Leggings were commonly of buckskin, but some were of tule rushes or other fibers; after European contact they were frequently made of blue stroud cloth.

Loom: A construction for weaving. Simple looms involved only uprights and crosspieces. More complex looms, introduced by the Spanish, had heddles and sometimes foot treadles.

Loop Necklace: An ornament worn in the Plateau and northern Plains areas, consisting of several strings of beads of diminishing lengths fastened to side pieces.

Manta: The woolen dress of the Pueblo women, embellished with embroidery and fastened on the right shoulder, leaving the left shoulder bare.

Mask: A covering for the face made of carved wood, cornhusks, leather, or other material, often decorated. Masks were significant elements in dances and other ceremonies.

Matchcoat: A cloak or mantle of skin, short or long, usually tied on the shoulder and often girdled. This term, used by the English in referring to a garment worn by the Southeastern Indians, has caused confusion because the garment is not a coat, having no set-in sleeves and no front opening.

Medallion: A decorated disk, commonly of silver, often attached to garments or worn in the hair. Some medallions were attached to leather straps and worn as belts or as hair ornaments.

Medicine Bag: A small pouch containing small items of sacred significance to the wearer, worn especially on the Plains.

Medicine Hat: A headdress worn by a shaman or medicine man.

Mirror Board: A small wooden frame with a set-in mirror, attached to a garment for decoration. Used especially in the central and northern Plains.

Mitten: A covering for the hand of leather or fur, having one or two thumb stalls.

Moccasin: A foot covering, usually of buckskin, sometimes with a hard sole of rawhide and at times with attached cuffs, often elaborately decorated with quillwork or beadwork.

Mojave Collar: A large netted collar, worn by the Mojave women of California, in which were placed blue and white beads in intricate designs.

Mukluk: A soft-soled boot of reindeer, elk, or similar hide, worn by the Subarctic Indians and the Eskimo. It had a large sole puckered into a vamp.

Naasit: A brief undergarment of tanned leather worn by both sexes in Greenland.

Nah-leen: A bead-on-leather hair ornament, typically in a bow shape, worn by girls in the Southwest.

Navajo Blanket: A wool blanket woven by Navajo women, and characterized by stripes, diamonds, and zigzag patterns. Woven on a true loom—one that can form a "shed" for the shuttle to pass through.

Navel Amulet: A beaded charm made of buckskin containing the umbilical cord of the wearer. Often in the shape of a turtle or lizard, both symbols of longevity, and sometimes worn throughout life.

Neck Ring: A large ring, generally of shredded cedar bark, sometimes of iron or copper, worn around the neck by men in the Northwest Coast area for ceremonial occasions. Also called a "potlatch ring."

Necklace: An ornament worn around the neck consisting of strings of beads, shells, teeth, bones, or other materials.

Neckscarf: A cotton "bandana" or square of cloth tied around the neck or the head. Worn especially in the southern Plains or the Southwest after European contact.

Netting: A finger-weaving technique, generally done with a shuttle, in which the fibers were looped in continuous rows. Netted articles were girdles, belts, collars, dance kilts, and mantles.

Nose Ornaments: Many North American Indians pierced the nasal septum in order to wear such ornaments as rings, bone pins, wooden skewers, dentalia, or other types of shells.

Octopus Bag: A pouch or bag, usually of cloth, that was embellished with floral embroidery. Named for the eight tabs at the bottom of the bag, it was made particularly in the Subarctic and was widely traded.

Otter-Fur Bag: A bag made of a complete otter (sometimes beaver) pelt, the feet and tail decorated with beadwork; an important adjunct to the ceremonies of the Midewiwin Society of the Upper Great Lakes and prairie tribes.

Otter-Fur Turban: A wide headband of a folded otter skin with the tail left hanging or arranged to stand out horizontally at the side. Worn especially in the central Plains, these turbans were further decorated with beaded rosettes, ribbons, feathers, or such.

Parka: An outer, shirt-like garment, usually with attached hood, of skin, fur, birdskin, sea mammal intestines, or cloth, worn in the northern areas. Native terms for *parka* include *anorak, amaat, amaut,* and *amautik.*

Peace Medal: A decorated silver disk given by the government to a chief or other person of distinction. It was usually hung around the neck by means of a ribbon or thong.

Pendant: An ornament hung from the nose, ears, or other parts of the body or attached to garments. Materials included shell, stone, wood, bone, and metal.

Pendleton Blanket: A woolen blanket made by the Pendleton Mills of Oregon, which featured Indian designs. These blankets were extremely popular throughout the West in the very late nineteenth and early twentieth centuries.

Peyote Fan: A fan of eagle or hawk feathers used as a part of the peyote ritual of the Native American Church.

Plaiting: A finger-weaving technique involving the process of passing three or more fibers over and under each other. Also termed "braiding."

Plateau Dress: A cloth garment worn by the women of the Plateau featuring short squarish sleeves with an undersleeve or underblouse.

Pompadour: A hair style in which the hair is made to stand erect above the forehead, popular in the northern Plains.

Poncho: A flat piece of material, commonly buckskin, with a slit or hole cut in the center for a head opening. Worn as a type of shirt or cloak.

Pony Beads: Large glass beads, so called because they were brought in by the traders on ponies.

Protective Belt: A "chastity" belt, worn by women of the central and northern Plains, made of strips of cloth or tanned leather wrapped around the thighs and through the crotch. It was considered inviolable by the men of those tribes, especially the Cheyennes.

Punctuation: A technique of punching holes in leather in a decorative or random manner. Used especially among groups of the Columbia Plateau.

Quillwork: A decorative technique using dyed porcupine or bird quills to create distinctive patterns.

Quill-Wrapped Fringe: The product of wrapping porcupine or bird quills around the inner end of fringes, found especially among the Crow, Nez Perce, and other northern Plains tribes.

Rabbit-Skin Robe: A robe or mantle made of strips of rabbit skin woven together loosely in a straight cross weave.

Raingear: Protective outer garments worn in rainy areas. These were in the form of cloaks or capes and hats and were of birchbark, birdskins, sea mammal intestines, and woven cedar bark or other fibers.

Ribbonwork: A sewing process in which silk or broadcloth ribbons obtained in trade were cut in various patterns and sewn to garments, usually dresses or skirts, sometimes moccasins and vests. The technique was especially popular among the prairie tribes, the Osage women being the finest of ribbonworkers.

Ring: A decorative band worn on the finger, usually of carved wood, bone, shell, or copper. Few were worn before European contact; after that they were ordinarily of silver.

Roach: A manner of wearing the hair in which the head was shaved except for a "cockscomb" or crest in the middle. Later roaches were sometimes made artificially of deer hair, porcupine guard hair, moose mane, or skunk hair, often painted red. Roaches were fastened to a scalplock and the hairs separated by means of a "roach spreader." Modern male dancers wear a roach, but it is tied under the chin because they lack a scalplock.

Robe: A mantle or flowing outer garment of fur, such as buffalo, bear, or caribou, or of smaller animal pelts sewn together. These were fastened with thongs at the neck and were often belted. Worn for warmth, they were also important items of ceremonial dress.

Rosette: A beaded medallion worn on the chest and back or as part of a blanket strip.

Sandal: A foot covering consisting of a sole of rawhide or woven fibers attached to the foot by means of thongs or straps. Sandals were rarely worn outside of the extreme southern areas of California or the Southwest.

Sash: A long band of material, finger-woven in diamond, zigzag, or similar geometric patterns. These were worn around the waist or over the shoulders.

Third Scalplock: A third braid (or a single braid) hanging from the crown of the head. It was sometimes seized in battle and cut off with the attached skin for a "scalp."

Scatter Beading: Beads sewn on in a random pattern, generally to fill in a background, often used on moccasin vamps.

Seed Beads: Tiny beads of many hues replacing the large pony beads of the early nineteenth century.

Seminole Collar: A large collar, often wrist-length, made in the characteristic Seminole patchwork style.

Shawl: A square or oblong piece of skin or cloth, frequently fringed, used as a loose covering for the shoulders. A shawl was often draped under one arm and fastened on the opposite shoulder, or was held with the hand in front.

Shield: A round, oval or rectangular plate or frame of rawhide or wood held by a warrior for protection in battle. Some shields were very large, covering most of the body; others were smaller, to cover the torso. Shields were often decorated with painted designs, feathers, strips of fur, shells, or other ornaments set in pitch.

Shield Cover: A light cover of deerskin, or of canvas or other cloth, for a shield, often decorated. Covers were often removed prior to conflict to expose the spiritual power of the shield itself.

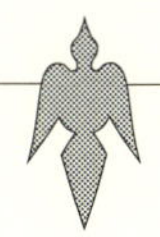

Shirt: A garment for the upper part of the body worn by men and generally made of buckskin. Early shirts were one-piece affairs like a poncho with sleeves formed by tying thongs or sewing sleeve seams; later shirts had set-in sleeves. Shirts were thigh-length or knee-length on the Plains, waist-length on the Plateau. Decoration consisted of short or long fringes (some of twisted cords), quillwork, beadwork, locks of hair, medallions, and such. In the nineteenth century cotton shirts became popular, some featuring the "Lord Byron" collar.

Shoulder Bag: A bag worn at the side, held in place by a strap over the shoulder, both strap and bag generally heavily beaded or embroidered.

Shuttle: A small wooden stick on which wool or other fiber was wrapped; it was used for ease in weaving by passing it through the warp threads.

Side-Fold Dress: An early buckskin dress worn on the northern Plains and in the Northeast. It was made of a large piece of skin, folded over and fastened at the side, with a fold-over yoke and shoulder straps.

Sinew: Tendons stripped from along the backbone of caribou, deer, or moose, used as thread in sewing.

Skirt: A woman's garment, from the waist to the knees or below, of buckskin or other leather, strands of fiber, or woven fibers. When the whites introduced cloth, skirts were long and full, often with flounces at the bottom in imitation of the women's dresses of the period.

Skull Deformation: A process of applying pressure to the skull of a child with pads, boards, or bandages in order to produce a slanting forehead. It was widely practiced in the Northwest and in the Plateau area, as well as among some tribes of the Southeast.

Snowshoe: Footwear made of a bent ash frame crisscrossed with webbing, which enabled the wearer to travel across deep snow. A few were crudely made of flat, round pieces of wood. Some were flat, some had upturned front edges. Snowshoes were made in different shapes and lengths: "bearpaw" snowshoes were round, and were typically worn by women and children, while "swallowtail" snowshoes had a lengthened back piece and were worn by men.

Socks: Leg and foot coverings made of woven sheep wool, fur, soft skin, or woven grasses, worn for warmth inside boots.

Spindle: A long stick on which fibers are wound after being spun.

Spindle Whorl: A flat, round disk attached to one end of a spindle to function as a flywheel, made of wood, steatite, whale bone, or other materials, often beautifully carved.

Squash Blossom (Hopi): A hair style worn by Hopi maidens in which the hair at each side is wound onto a large whorl. Sometimes called the "butterfly" style.

Squash Blossom (Navajo): A necklace of cast silver beads and items in a squash-blossom shape, made by Navajo craftsmen and widely traded. Many featured inlaid pieces of turquoise and, sometimes, coral.

Squaw Dress: A brightly colored cotton dress worn especially in the Southwest. The skirt was full with flounces and had decorative bands; the blouse part usually had full sleeves.

Stand-Up Warbonnet: The warbonnet of the Blackfeet and neighboring tribes consisting of a band encircling the head to which are attached erect feathers.

Strap-and-Sleeve Dress: A deerskin dress, belted, and held in place with shoulder straps, separate sleeves being tied on when desired or needed.

Strike-a-Light Bag: A pouch in which were carried materials for starting a fire, such as flint and tinder.

Stroud Cloth: Also "strouding." A heavy woolen cloth made in Stroudwater, England, usually scarlet red or dark navy blue, sometimes green. Originally it was a "blotter cloth," a cheap cloth used to soak up excess dyes used in making finer material. It was primarily traded to America for the Indian trade. It was also used as a light blanket.

Sunburst Bustle: A large circle of feathers, generally worn at the back of a dancer's costume.

Sunburst Hood: A hood, often attached to a parka, with a large ruff of wolverine fur to frame the face, commonly worn by Alaska Eskimo women.

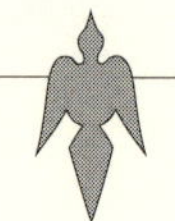

Swamp Moccasin: A calf-high moccasin or boot of buckskin worn in the Southeast.

Tablita: Also *tableta.* A headdress worn by women Pueblo dancers consisting of a large cutout of painted wood.

Tack Belt: A leather belt ornamented with brass tacks or studs in decorative patterns.

Tanning: A process used in making deerskin and other hides soft and flexible for wear.

Taparabo: A kilt worn by the Mission Indians of California.

Tattooing: Skin decoration made by puncturing the skin or drawing a thread beneath the skin, and rubbing in charcoal, soot, or other pigment. It was employed not only for beautification but often as a means of tribal identification.

Thimble: Finger cap used by seamstresses to force an awl through heavy skin. Later thimbles, brought by the traders, were attached to dresses to function as tinklers.

Tinkler: Small cone, about an inch long, made of native copper, later of tin, sewed to a garment for the pleasing sound effects occurring with the movements of the wearer.

Tobacco Bag: Small buckskin pouch used to carry smoking equipment, such as small pipes and tobacco, commonly attached to the belt.

Toggle: A small carved item of wood, typically with pointed ends, used with a loop to fasten garments.

Tonsure: A hair style in which the top of the head is shaved and a short fringe of hair is left around the head; sometimes used by the Eskimo men of western and northern Alaska.

Trailer: One or two long strips of cloth or deerskin hanging down the back of a warbonnet, to which feathers were attached.

Trousers: An outer garment, usually of buckskin, covering both legs and extending from the waist to the ankles, worn by both men and women in the Subarctic and Arctic. They were held in place by means of a drawstring at the top and often had attached feet.

Tumpline: A headband to which was attached a large net or sack, used to ease the strain of carrying heavy burdens.

Tunghak: A transformational mask, revealing a second spirit or character beneath the first, used especially in southwestern Alaska.

Tunic: A garment worn by men or women, knee-length or longer, without sleeves or with very short sleeves. It was of skin, cloth, or cedar bark.

Turban: A nineteenth-century headdress of wrapped cloth, worn especially in the Southeast, similar to the wrapped turbans of the Europeans of the period. Often feathers were attached as well as various ornaments.

Twilling: A form of weaving in which the weft threads pass over a different group of warps in each row.

Twining: A weaving technique in which two weft threads are crossed over between each pair of warp threads.

Ugruk: The large bearded seal whose tough hide was commonly used for boot and mukluk soles by the Eskimo.

Umiliak: The leader of an Eskimo whaling crew, generally owner of the boat as well, a man of great importance.

Vamp: The oval or "U"-shaped insert on a moccasin above the instep, typically heavily ornamented with quillwork or beadwork.

Vest: A sleeveless garment worn by men covering the chest. The front opening showed European influence. The early Indian vest was not fitted, but rather was characterized by straight sides. By the late nineteenth century these vests were often completely covered with beadwork. Beaded vests are worn today at Indian powwows.

Visor: A headband with a projecting piece to shade the eyes from the sun. It was made of rawhide on the Plateau and the northern Plains and of bent wood among the Aleut.

Walrus Tusk Motif: Two white inserts in the shape of walrus tusks at the top of Eskimo parkas, found all across the Arctic.

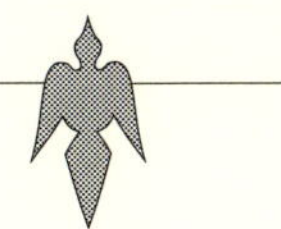

Wampum: Small cylindrical beads made by drilling holes in pieces of clamshell. Wampum beads were purple and white, the former considered more valuable. The beads became a type of currency in the Northeast, as well as a form of decoration throughout the East.

Wampum Belt: A belt made of wampum in symbolic patterns. These belts, made and worn especially in the Northeast, were used to identify messengers and ambassadors, to record tribal histories, as gifts to important personages, and as ceremonial pledges to confirm treaties.

War Shirt: A buckskin shirt of the northern Plains. Decoration often consisted of wide bands of porcupine quillwork or beadwork extending over the shoulders, sometimes with similar bands down the sleeves. At the neck was a rosette or square or rectangle of quillwork or beadwork. When trimmed with scalplocks or ermine skins, the war shirt was considered to have great power and was supposed to be worn only by warriors who had distinguished themselves in battle. Also called a "scalp shirt."

Warbonnet: The large feathered headdress of the Plains Indians, especially the western Sioux, later adopted by Indians throughout the country. There were three major types: the halo headdress, the stand-up headdress, and the horned headdress.

Warp: The vertical strands forming the base for weaving.

Weft: The horizontal strands passing through and intertwining with the warp threads to form patterns in weaving.

Wristguard: A wide band of leather snugly fitting the wrist. It was worn to protect the wrist from the snap of the bowstring.

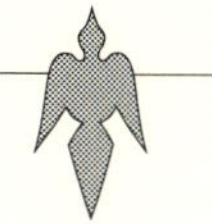

Bibliography

General Works on American Indian Costume

Austin, Robert. "Fingerweaving." *Powwow Trails* 6(7).

Brafford, C. J. and Laine Thom, comps. *Dancing Colors: Paths of Native American Women.* San Francisco: Chronicle Books, 1990.

Bushnell, D. I. "The Various Uses of Buffalo Hair by the North American Indians." *American Anthropologist* 11(3): 401–425.

Carr, L. "Dress and Ornaments of Certain American Indians." *Proceedings of the American Antiquarian Society.* New series 11: 381–454.

Conn, Richard. "Braided Sashes." *American Indian Tradition* 9(1).

———. "A Classification of Aboriginal North American Clothing." Master's thesis, University of Washington, 1955.

———. *Robes of White Shell and Sunrise.* Denver: Denver Art Museum, 1975.

Conn, Richard and Frederic H. Douglas. "Indian Women's Clothing: Fashion and Function." Denver Art Museum *Indian Leaflet Series* 1951 109.

Dall, William H. "On Masks, Labrets and Certain Aboriginal Customs, with an Inquiry into the Bearing of Their Geographical Distribution." Bureau of American Ethnology *Annual Reports* 3 (1884): 67–203.

Davidson, D. S. "Snowshoes." *Memoirs of the American Philosophical Society* 6. Philadelphia, PA.

Douglas, Frederic H. "Hide Sewing and Bead Sewing Techniques." Denver Art Museum *Indian Leaflet Series* 1930 2.

———. "Porcupine Quillwork." Denver Art Museum *Indian Leaflet Series* 1967 103.

Driver, Harold E. "Puberty Rites in Western North America." *Anthropological Review* 6: 21–90. Berkeley: University of California.

Ewers, John Canfield. "Blackfeet Crafts." *Indian Handcrafts* 9.

Fecteau, Susan. *Primitive Indian Dresses: Leather Dress Styles and Decoration.* Cheyenne, WY: Frontier Printing, 1979.

Feder, Norman. "Bottom Tab Leggings." *American Indian Tradition* 8(4).

———. "Elk Antler Roach Spreaders." *Material Culture Monograph* 1. Denver: Denver Art Museum, 1970.

———. "Head and Tail Fans." *Powwow Trails* 1965.

———. "Otter Fur Turbans." *American Indian Tradition* 1961 7(3).

———. "Quill and Horsehair Feather Ornaments." *American Indian Hobbyist* 1960 6(9, 10).

———. "Ribbon Applique." *American Indian Hobbyist* 1956 3(2).

———. "The Side Fold Dress." *American Indian Art Magazine* (Winter 1984): 48–55, 75, 77.

Feder, Norman and Milford G. Chandler. "Grizzly Claw Necklaces." *American Indian Tradition* 1961 8(1).

Fenstermaker, G. B. *Susquehanna Iroquois Colored Trade Bead Chart, 1575–1753.* Lancaster, PA: Fenstermaker, 1974.

Hatt, Gudmund. "Moccasins and Their Relation to Arctic Footwear." American Anthropological Association *Memoirs* 1916 3: 149–250.

Hofsinde, Robert. *Indian Costumes.* New York: Morrow, 1968.

Holmes, William H. "Prehistoric Textile Art of the Eastern United States." Bureau of American Ethnology *Annual Reports* 13 1891–1892 (1896): 9–46.

Horse Capture, George P. *Native American Ribbonwork: The Visual Characteristics.* Cody, WY: Buffalo Bill Historical Center, 1980.

Hough, Walter. "Primitive American Armor." United States National Museum *Reports* 1893: 626–651.

Howard, James H. "Firecloud's Omaha or Grass Dance Costume." *American Indian Crafts and Culture* 1972 6(2): 2–9.

———. "The Roach Headdress." *American Indian Hobbyist* 1960 6(7, 8).

Hungry Wolf, Adolf. *Traditional Dress Issue: Knowledge and Methods of Old-Time Clothing.* Fort Macleod, Alberta: Good Medicine Books, 1971.

Hunt, W. Ben. *The Complete How-To Book of Indian Crafts.* New York: Collier Books, 1973.

———. *The Golden Book of Indian Crafts and Lore.* New York: Simon & Schuster, 1960.

Hunt, W. Ben and J. F. Buckshears. *American Indian Beadwork.* New York: Collier, 1951.

Jacobson, Oscar B. *North American Indian Costumes.* Nice, France: Szwedzicki, 1952.

Jester, Margo. "Peace Medals." *American Indian Tradition* 1961 7(5).

Johnson, Michael G. "North American Moccasin Construction." *Whispering Wind* 1978 11(4).

———. "A Note on Indian Coats and Jackets." *Powwow Trails* 1969 5(8).

Karklins, Karlis and Roderick Sprague. "Glass Trade Beads in North America: An Annotated Bibliography." *Historical Archaeology* 1972 6: 87–101.

King, Arden R. "Aboriginal Skin Dressing in Western North America." Ph.D. dissertation. Berkeley: University of California, 1947.

Kinietz, Vernon. "Notes on the Roached Headdress of Animal Hair among the North American Indians." Michigan Academy of Science, Arts and Letters *Papers* 1940 26(1).

Koch, Ronald P. *Dress Clothing of the Plains Indians.* Norman: University of Oklahoma Press, 1977.

Kracinski, David A. "Unusual Beadwork Techniques," *American Indian Tradition* 1963 9.

Krieger, Herbert W. "American Indian Costumes in the United States National Museum." Smithsonian Institution *Annual Reports* 1928 (1929).

LaQuay, E. "Beadwork." *Powwow Trails* 1964 1(6).

Loeb, Barbara. "Mirror Bags and Bandoleer Bags: A Comparison." *American Indian Art Magazine* (Winter 1980) 6(1): 46–53, 88.

Lyford, Carrie A. *Quill and Beadwork of the Western Sioux.* Lawrence, KS: United States Indian Service, 1940.

Marriott, Alice. "Ribbon Applique Work of North American Indians, Part 1." Oklahoma Anthropological Society *Bulletin* (March 1958) 6.

Mason, Bernard S. *The Book of Indian Crafts and Costumes.* New York: Barnes, 1946.

Mason, Otis T. "Aboriginal Skin Dressing." United States National Museum *Reports* 1889 (1891): 553–589.

Minor, Marz and Nono Minor. *The American Indian Craft Book.* Lincoln, NE: University of Nebraska Press, 1972.

Orchard, William C. *Beads and Beadwork of the American Indian.* New York: Museum of the American Indian, Heye Foundation, 1929, 1975.

———. *The Technique of Porcupine Quill Decorations among the Indians of North America.* New York: Museum of the American Indian, Heye Foundation, 1916, 1971.

Parker, Arthur C. *The Indian How Book.* New York: Dover, 1975. Reprint of 1927 edition.

Penney, David W. "Floral Decoration and Culture Change: An Historical Interpretation of Motivation." *American Indian Culture and Research Journal* 1991 15(1): 53–77.

Peyer, Arthur. *Indianer Nordamerikas, 1760–1860.* Deutschen Ledermuseum-Deutsches Schuhmuseum, Offenbach, Germany, 1968.

Pohrt, Richard A. "Plains Indian Moccasins with Decorated Soles." *American Indian Art Magazine* 1977 2(3): 32–39, 74.

Powell, Louis H. "A Study of Indian Bead Work of the North Central Plains." St. Paul Science Museum *Indian Leaflets* 1953 5–7.

Rudofsky, Bernard. *Are Clothes Modern?* New York: Museum of Modern Art, 1944.

———. *The Unfashionable Human Body.* Garden City, NY: Doubleday, 1974.

Salomon, Julian H. *Book of Indian Crafts and Indian Lore.* New York: Harper, 1928.

Schneider, Richard C. *Crafts of the North American Indians: A Craftsman's Manual.* New York: Van Nostrand & Reinhold, 1972.

Seton, Julia M. *American Indian Arts: A Way of Life.* New York: Ronald, 1962.

Sinclair, A. T. "Tattooing of the North American Indians." *American Anthropologist* 1909 11: 362–400.

Taylor, Colin. "Early Plains Quill Techniques in European Museum Collections." *Plains Anthropologist* 1962 7: 58–69.

Thom, Laine, comp. *Becoming Brave: The Path to Native American Manhood.* San Francisco: Chronicle Books, 1992.

Turner, Geoffrey. *Hair Embroidery in Siberia and North America.* Oxford, England: Pitt-Rivers Museum, Oxford University, 1955.

Van der Sleen, W. G. N. *A Handbook on Beads.* York, PA: Liberty Cap, 1967.

Webber, Alika Podolinsky. *North American Indian and Eskimo Footwear: A Typology and Glossary.* Toronto: The Bata Shoe Foundation, 1989.

White, George M. *Craft Manual of North American Indian Footwear.* Ronan, MT: George M. White, 1969.

Wissler, Clark. *Indian Beadwork: A Help for Students of Design.* New York: American Museum of Natural History, 1946.

———. "Indian Costumes in the United States." *Guide Leaflet* 1931 63: 1–32. New York: American Museum of Natural History.

———. "The Material Culture of North American Indians." *American Anthropologist* 1914 16.

General Works on American Indian Art

Appleton, Leroy H. *Indian Art of the Americas.* New York: Scribner's, 1950.

Archuleta, Margaret, ed. *Shared Visions.* Exhibit catalog. Phoenix: Heard Museum, 1991.

Boas, Franz. *Primitive Art.* New York: Dover, 1955. Reprint of 1927 edition.

Brace, Martha A. and Nancy J. Parezo. "Arizona State Museum." *American Indian Art Magazine* (Winter, 1984) 10(1): 24–31.

Coe, Ralph T. *Lost and Found Traditions: Native American Indian Art, 1965–1985.* Seattle: University of Washington Press, 1986.

———. *Sacred Circles: Two Thousand Years of North American Indian Art.* London: Arts Council of Great Britain, 1977.

Collins, Henry B. *The Far North: 2000 Years of American Eskimo and Indian Art.* Bloomington: Indiana University Press, 1977.

Conn, Richard. *Native American Art in the Denver Art Museum.* Denver: Denver Art Museum, 1979.

———. *A Persistent Vision: Art of the Reservation Period.* Denver: Denver Art Museum, 1986.

Covarrubias, Miguel. *The Eagle, the Serpent and the Jaguar: Indian Art of the Americas.* New York: Knopf, 1954.

Dawdy, Doris Ostrander. "Annotated Bibliography of American Indian Painting." Museum of the American Indian, Heye Foundation, *Contributions* 1968 21(2).

Dockstader, Frederick. *Indian Art of the Americas: The Arts and Crafts of the North American Indian.* Greenwich, CT: New York Graphic Society, 1966.

Douglas, Frederic H. and Rene d'Harnoncourt. *Indian Art of the United States.* New York: Museum of Modern Art, 1941.

Dunn, Dorothy. *American Indian Painting of the Southwest and Plains Areas.* Albuquerque: University of New Mexico Press, 1968.

Dutton, Bertha P. *Sun Father's Way.* Albuquerque: University of New Mexico Press, 1963.

Eaton, Linda B. "The Heart of the Region: The Anthropology Collections of the Museum of Northern Arizona." *American Indian Art Magazine* (Summer 1991) 16(3): 46–53.

Ewing, Douglas. *Pleasing the Spirits: A Catalogue of a Collection of American Indian Art.* New York: Ghylen, 1982.

Fane, Diana, Ira Jacknis, and Lisa Breen. *Objects of Myth and Memory: American Indian Art at the Brooklyn Museum.* Brooklyn, NY: Brooklyn Museum and Seattle: University of Washington Press.

Feder, Norman. *American Indian Art.* New York: Abrams, 1965, 1969.

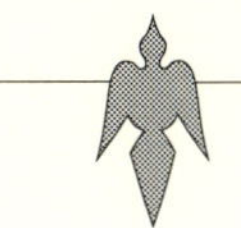

———. "American Indian Art before 1850." Denver Art Museum *Quarterly* (Summer 1965).

———. "The Malaspina Collection." *American Indian Art Magazine* 1977 2(3): 40–51, 80.

———. *Two Hundred Years of North American Indian Art.* New York: Whitney Museum of American Art, 1971.

Feest, Christian F. *Native Arts of North America.* Oxford, England: Oxford University Press, 1980.

Fraser, Douglas. *Primitive Art.* Garden City, NY: Doubleday, 1962.

Furst, Peter T. and Julia L. Furst. *North American Indian Art.* New York: Rizzoli International, 1982.

Haberland, Wolfgang. *The Art of North America.* New York: Crown, 1964.

Highwater, Jamake. *Song from the Earth: American Indian Painting.* Boston: New York Graphic Society, 1976.

Hunt, W. Ben. *Indian Silversmithing.* Milwaukee: Bruce Publishing, 1960.

Isaac, Barbara, ed. *The Hall of the North American Indian: Change and Continuity.* Cambridge, MA: Peabody Museum Press, 1990.

Mathews, Zena Pearlstone and Aldona Jonaitis, ed. *Native North American Art History.* Palo Alto, CA: Peek, 1982.

Maurer, Evan M. *The Native Heritage: A Survey of North American Indian Art.* Chicago: Chicago Art Institute, 1977.

Rabineau, Phyllis. "North American Anthropology at the Field Museum of Natural History." *American Indian Art Magazine* 1981 6(4): 30–37, 79.

Ritzenthaler, Robert E. *Masks of the North American Indians.* Milwaukee: Milwaukee Public Museum, 1964.

Roosevelt, Anna Curtenius and James G. E. Smith, ed. *The Ancestors: Native Artisans of the Americas.* New York: Museum of the American Indian, Heye Foundation, 1979.

Siebert, Erna and Werner Forman. *North American Indian Art.* London: Hamlyn, 1967.

Sloan, John and Oliver LaFarge. *Introduction to American Indian Art.* New York: Exposition of Indian Tribal Arts Council, 1930.

Snodgrass, Jeanne O. *American Indian Painters: A Biographical Directory.* New York: Museum of the American Indian, Heye Foundation, 1968.

Thompson, Judy. *The North American Collection: A Catalogue.* Berne, Switzerland: Berne Historical Museum, 1977.

Walters, Anna Lee. *The Spirit of Native America: Beauty and Mysticism in American Indian Art.* San Francisco: Chronicle Books, 1989.

Wardwell, Allen. *Objects of Bright Pride from the American Museum of Natural History, New York.* New York: Center for Inter-American Relations and the American Federation of Artists, 1978.

Wode, Edwin L., Carol Haralson, and Rennard Strickland. *As in a Vision: Masterworks of American Indian Art.* Norman: University of Oklahoma Press and Philbrook Art Center, Elizabeth Batter Cole Collection, 1983.

Wooley, David. *Eye of the Angel: Selections from the Derby Collection.* Northampton, MA: White Star, 1990.

Artists and Photographers

Anderson, John Alvin. "Frontier Photographer." *Nebraska History* 1970 51(4): 469–480.

Andrews, Ralph W. *Curtis' Western Indians.* Seattle: Superior, 1962.

———. *Photographers of the Frontier West.* New York: Bonanza Books, 1965.

Bighart, Robert and Clarence Woodcock. "The Rinehart Photographs: A Portfolio." *Montana* (October 1979) 29(4): 14–25.

Blomkvist, E. E. "A Russian Scientific Expedition to California and Alaska, 1839–1849: The Drawings of I. G. Voznesenskii." Basil Dmytryshyn and E. A. P. Crownhart-Vaughan, trans. *Oregon Historical Quarterly* 1972 73(2): 101–170.

Bolton, Theodore. *Early American Portrait Draughtsmen in Crayons.* New York, 1923.

Britain, J. W. *Kalispell, Montana Indian Portraits.* Washington: Library of Congress, 1902.

Broder, Patricia Janice. *Shadows on the Grass: The Indian World of Ben Wittick.* Savage, MD: Rowman & Littlefield, 1990.

Brown, Mark H. and W. R. Felton. *The Frontier Years: L. A. Hoffman, Photographer of the Plains.* New York: Bramhall House, 1955.

Bushnell, David I., Jr. "Drawings by John Webber of Natives of the Northwest Coast of America, 1778." Smithsonian Institution *Miscellaneous Collections* 1910 80(10).

———. "Drawings of A. de Batz in Louisiana, 1732–1735." Smithsonian Institution *Miscellaneous Collections* 1927 80(5).

Catlin, George. *Letters and Notes on the Manners, Customs and Conditions of the North American Indians.* 2 vols. New York: Dover. Reprint of 1844 edition.

Choris, Louis. *San Francisco 100 Years Ago.* San Francisco: A. M. Robertson, 1913.

Coke, Van Deren. *Photography in New Mexico from the Daguerrotype to the Present.* Albuquerque: University of New Mexico Press, 1979.

Current, Karen and William Current. *Photography and the Old West.* New York: Abrams, 1978.

Curtis, Edward S. *The North American Indian.* 20 vols. Cambridge: University Press and Norwood, MA: Plimpton (vols. 6–20), 1907–1930.

Davis, Barbara. *Edward S. Curtis: The Life and Times of a Shadow Catcher.* San Francisco: Chronicle Books, 1985.

Donnelly, Joseph P., ed. *Wilderness Kingdom, Indian Life in the Rocky Mountains, 1840–1847: The Journals and Paintings of Nicholas J. Point, S.J.* Chicago, 1967.

Donaldson, Thomas. "The George Catlin Indian Gallery in the United States National Museum." Smithsonian Institution *Annual Reports* 1885 (1887).

Ewers, John C. *Artists of the Old West.* Garden City, NY: Doubleday, 1965, 1973.

Farber, Joseph C. and Michael Dorris. *Native Americans 500 Years After.* New York: 1975.

Fleming, Paula Richardson and Judith Luskey. *The North American Indians in Early Photographs.* New York: Dorset, 1986.

Fowler, Don D. *In a Sacred Manner We Live: Photographs of the North American Indian by Edward S. Curtis.* New York: Weathervane Books, 1972.

Grant, Bob. "Lee Morehouse, Early Photographer Leaves 10,000 Plates." *Pioneer Trails* (April 1979) 3(3): 3–5.

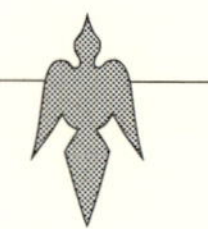

Graybill, Florence Curtis and Victor Beosen. *Edward Sheriff Curtis: Visions of a Vanishing Race.* New York: Crowell, 1976.

"Gustavus Sohon's Portraits of Flathead and Pend d'Oreille Indians, 1854." Smithsonian Institution *Miscellaneous Collections* 1948 110: 1–66.

Harper, J. Russell. *Paul Kane's Frontier.* Austin: University of Texas Press, 1971.

Harriot, Thomas. *A Briefe and True Report of the New Found Land of Virginia: The Complete 1590 Theodor de Bry Edition.* New York: Dover, 1972.

Hassrick, Royal B. *The George Catlin Book of American Indians.* New York: Promontory, 1987.

Henry, John F. *Early Maritime Artists of the Pacific Nothwest Coast, 1741–1841.* Seattle: University of Washington Press, 1984.

Hewitt, John N. B. and Myrtis Jarrell, eds. *Journal of Rudolf Friedrich Kurz: The Life and Work of This Swiss Artist.* Lincoln: University of Nebraska Press, 1970.

Holm, Bill and George I. Quimby. *Edward S. Curtis in the Land of the War Canoes: A Pioneer Cinematographer in the Pacific Northwest.* Seattle: University of Washington Press, 1980.

Honour, Hugh. *The New Golden Land: European Images of America from the Discoveries to the Present Time.* New York: Pantheon, 1975.

Horan, James D. *North American Indian Portraits: The McKenney-Hall Portrait Gallery of American Indians.* New York: Crown, 1975

Hulton, Paul H. and David B. Quinn. *The American Drawings of John White, 1577–1590.* 2 vols. Chapel Hill: University of North Carolina Press, 1964.

Hunt, David C., Marsha V. Gallagher, and William J. Orr. *Karl Bodmer's America.* Omaha: Joslyn Art Museum and University of Nebraska Press, 1984.

Hurt, Wesley R. and William E. Lass. *Frontier Photographer: Stanley J. Morrow's Dakota Years.* Lincoln: University of Nebraska Press and University of South Dakota, 1956.

Jackson, William H. *Descriptive Catalogue of Photographs of North American Indians by W. H. Jackson.* Columbus, OH: Weatherford, 1978. Reprint of 1877 edition.

———. *Picture Maker of the Old West.* New York: Scribner's, 1947.

Johnson, Patricia Cardon. "The Indian Photographs of Roland Reed." *American West* 1978 15(3): 44–57.

Josephy, Alvin M., Jr. *The Artist Was a Young Man: The Life Story of Peter Rindisbacher.* Fort Worth, TX, 1970.

Kane, Paul. *Wanderings of an Artist among the Indians of North America from Canada to Vancouver's Island and Oregon, Through the Hudson's Bay Company's Territory and Back Again.* Toronto: Raddison Society of Canada, 1925. Reprint of 1859 edition.

Lewis, James Otto. *The American Indian Portfolio.* Kent, OH: Volair, 1980.

Lockwood, Luke Vincent. "The St. Memin Indian Portraits." *New York Historical Society Quarterly* 1928 12(1): 3–26.

Lorant, Stefan, ed. *The New World: The First Pictures of America Made by John White and Jacques Le Moyne and Engraved by Theodor de Bry.* New York: Duell, Sloan, Pearce, 1946.

Lyman, Christopher M. *The Vanishing Race and Other Illusions: Photography of Indians by Edward S. Curtis.* Washington: Smithsonian Institution and Pantheon, 1982.

Mahood, Ruth, ed. *Photographer of the Southwest: Adam Clark Vroman, 1856–1916.* Los Angeles: Ward Ritchie, 1961.

Maximilian, Alexander Philip, Prinz von Wied-Neuwied. *Travels in the Interior of North America, 1832–1834.* In Reuben G. Thwaites, *Early Western Travels,* vol. 25. Cleveland, OH: Arthur H. Clark, 1906.

McCracken, Harold. *The Charles M. Russell Book.* New York: Doubleday, 1957.

———. *Frederic Remington, Artist of the Old West.* Philadelphia, 1947.

———. *George Catlin and the Old Frontier.* New York: Bonanza Books, 1959.

———. *Portrait of the Old West.* New York: McGraw-Hill, 1952.

McDermott, John F. *Seth Eastman, Pictorial Historian of the Indian.* Norman: University of Oklahoma Press, 1961.

McKenney, Thomas L. and James Hall. *The Indian Tribes of North America.* 3 vols. Edited by Frederick Webb Hodge and David I. Bushnell. Edinburgh, Scotland, 1933–1934.

McLuhan, T. C. *Portraits from North American Indian Life.* New York: Promontory, 1972.

Miller, Alfred Jacob. *The West of Alfred Jacob Miller (1837) from the Notes and Watrercolors in the Walters Art Gallery; With an Account of the Artist by Marvin C. Ross.* Norman: University of Oklahoma Press, 1951, 1968.

Mitchell, Lynn Marie. "George E. Trager: Frontier Photographer at Wounded Knee." *History of Photography.* (October–December 1989): 303–309.

Mollhausen, Baron Balduin. *Diary of a Journey from the Mississippi to the Coasts of the Pacific with a United States Government Expedition.* Mrs. Percy Sinnett, trans. London: Longman, Brown, Green, Longman, and Roberts, 1858.

Monroe, Robert. "Frank LaRoche: Washington's 'Other' Indian Photographer." *Northwest Photography* 1981.

Nolan, Edward W. "Summer at the Lakes: An Album of Frank Palmer's Photographs." *Idaho Yesterdays* (Summer 1990): 16–20.

Packard, Gar and Maggy Packard. *Southwest in 1880 with Ben Wittick, Pioneer Photographer of Indian and Frontier Life.* Santa Fe, NM: Packard Productions, 1970.

Peckham, Howard H., ed. *The Journals and Indian Paintings of George Winter, 1837–1839.* Indianapolis: Indiana Historical Society, 1948.

Poesch, Jessie. *Titian Ramsey Peale (1799–1895).* Philadelphia, 1961.

Quimby, George I. *Indians of the Western Frontier: Paintings of George Catlin.* Chicago: Chicago Natural History Museum, 1958.

Quinn, D. B., ed. *The American Drawings of John White, 1577–1590, with Drawings of European and Oriental Subjects.* Chapel Hill: University of North Carolina Press, 1964.

Rich, W. C., Jr. "American Indian Life Preserved in Portraits (Roland Reed)." *Minneapolis Journal* (Sunday, 20 January 1935).

Rinehart, Frank A. *Frank A. Rinehart's Prints of North American Indians.* Omaha, NE: Frank A. Rinehart, 1900.

Roe, JoAnn. *Frank Matsura: Frontier Photographer.* Seattle: University of Washington Press, 1981.

Ruby, Jay, ed. "Photographs of the Piegan by Roland Reed." *Studies in Visual Communication* (Winter 1981) 7(1): 48–62.

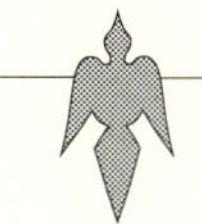

Russell, Charles M. *Good Medicine: Memories of the Real West.* Garden City, NY: Garden City Publishing, 1930.

Scherer, Joanna Cohan and Jean Burton. *Indians: The Great Photographs that Reveal North American Indian Life 1847–1927 from the Unique Collection of the Smithsonian Institution.* New York: Crown, 1973.

Schmitt, Martin F. and Dee Brown. *Fighting Indians of the West.* New York: Scribner's, 1948.

Schoolcraft, Henry. *Information Respecting the History, Condition and Prospects of the Indian Tribes of the United States.* 5 vols. Philadelphia: Lippincott, Grambo, 1884.

Sellers, Charles Coleman. *Mr. Peale's Museum: Charles Willson Peale and the First Popular Museum of Natural Science and Art.* New York: Norton, 1980.

Shur, L. A. and R. A. Pierce. "Artists in Russian America: Mikhail Tikhanov (1818)." *Alaska Journal* 1976 6(1): 40–49.

Sutton, Royal. *The Face of Courage: Indian Photographs of Frank A. Rinehart.* Fort Collins, CO: Old Army, 1972.

Taft, Robert. *Artists and Illustrators of the Old West, 1850–1900.* New York: Scribner's, 1953.

Thomas, David and Karin Ronnefeldt, eds. *People of the First Man: Life among the Plains Indians in Their Final Days of Glory.* Watercolors by Karl Bodmer. New York: Promontory, 1982.

Truettner, William. *The Natural Man Observed: A Study of Catlin's Indian Gallery.* Washington: Smithsonian Institution, 1979.

Tyler, Ron. *Alfred Jacob Miller: Artist on the Oregon Trail.* Fort Worth: Amon Carter Museum, 1982.

Van Stone, James W. "An Early Nineteenth Century Artist in Alaska: Louis Choris and the First Kotzebue Expedition." *Pacific Northwest Quarterly* 1960 51(4): 145–148.

Van Valkenberg, Richard. "Ben Wittick: Pioneer Photographer of the Southwest." *Arizona Highways* 1942 18(8): 36–39.

Viola, Herman J. *The Indian Legacy of Charles Bird King.* Washington: Smithsonian Institution, 1976.

Wagner, Henry R., ed. and trans. *Journal of Tomas de Suria of His Voyage with Malaspina to the Northwest Coast of America in 1791.* Glendale, CA: Arthur H. Clark, 1936.

Webb, William and Robert A. Weinstein. *Dwellers at the Source: Southwestern Indian Photographs from the A. C. Vroman Collection in the Natural History Museum of Los Angeles County.* New York: Grossman, 1973.

Southeast

Adair, James. *The History of the American Indians.* New York: Johnson, 1968. Reprint of 1777 edition.

Beverley, Robert. *The History and Present State of Virginia.* Louis B. Wright, ed. Chapel Hill: University of North Carolina Press, 1947. Reprint of 1705 edition.

Burt, Jesse and Robert B. Ferguson. *Indians of the Southeast: Then and Now.* Nashville: Abingdon, 1973.

Bushnell, David I. "Villages of the Algonquian, Siouan, and Caddoan Tribes West of the Mississippi." Bureau of American Ethnology *Bulletin* 77 (1922).

Foreman, Grant. *The Five Civilized Tribes.* Norman: University of Oklahoma Press, 1934.

Fundaburk, Emma Lila. *Southeastern Indians: Life Portraits.* Luverne, AL: Emma Lila Fundaburk, 1958.

———. *Sun Circles and Human Hands: The Southeastern Indians/Art and Industries.* Luverne, AL: Emma Lila Fundaburk, 1957.

Harriot, Thomas. *A Briefe and True Report of the New Found Land of Virginia: The Complete 1590 Theodor de Bry Edition.* New York: Dover, 1972.

Holmes, William H. "Prehistoric Textiles of Eastern United States." Bureau of American Ethnology *Annual Reports* 13 (1891–1892): 9–46.

Hudson, Charles. *The Southeastern Indians.* Knoxville: University of Tennessee Press, 1976.

Medford, Claude, Jr. "Native Clothing of the Southeastern Indian People." *Indian America* 1975 9(1): 42–47.

Southwell, Sir Robert. "The Method the Indians of Virginia and Carolina Use to Dress Buck and Doeskins." *Philosophical Transactions* 1691 17: 532–533.

Stirling, Matthew W. "Indians of the Southeastern United States." *National Geographic* December 1948: 53–74.

Swanton, John R. "Aboriginal Culture of the Southeast." Bureau of American Ethnology *Annual Reports* 42 (1928).

———. *Indians of the Southeastern United States.* New York: Scholarly Publications, 1969. Reprint of 1946 edition.

———. "Tribes of the Lower Mississippi Valley and Adjacent Coast of the Gulf of Mexico." Bureau of American Ethnology *Bulletin* 43 (1911).

Van Doren, Mark, ed. *Travels of William Bartram.* New York: Dover, 1955. Reprint of 1928 edition.

Northeast

Barratt, Joseph. *The Indians of New England and the Northeastern Provinces.* Middletown, CT, 1851.

Bartram, John. *Observations on the Inhabitants, Climate, Soil, Rivers, Productions, Animals, and Other Matters Worthy of Notice, Made by Mr. John Bartram in His Travels from Pennsylvania to Onondago, Oswego and the Lake Ontario, in Canada.* London: Printed for J. Whiston and B. White, 1751.

Beckwith, Hiram W. *The Illinois and Indiana Indians.* New York: Arno Press, 1975.

Blair, Emma. *The Indian Tribes of the Upper Mississippi Valley and Region of the Great Lakes.* 2 vols. Cleveland: Arthur H. Clark, 1911.

Douglas, John M. *The Indians in Wisconsin's History.* Milwaukee: Milwaukee Public Museum, 1954.

Flint Institute of Arts. *Art of the Great Lakes Indians.* Flint, MI: Institute of Arts, 1973.

Gillette, Charles E. *Wampum Beads and Belts.* Albany: New York State Museum, 1970.

Glubak, Shirley. *Art of the Woodland Indians.* New York: Macmillan, 1976.

Grand Rapids Public Museum. *Beads and Their Use by Upper Great Lakes Indians.* Grand Rapids, MI: Grand Rapids Public Museum, 1977.

Gringhuis, Dirk. *Indian Costume at Mackinac: Seventeenth and Eighteenth Centuries.* Mackinac Island, MI: Mackinac Island State Park Commission, 1972.

Hartman, Sheryl. *Indian Clothing of the Great Lakes: 1740–1840.* Ogden, UT: Eagle's View, 1988.

Hyde, George E. *Indians of the Woodlands.* Norman: University of Oklahoma Press, 1962.

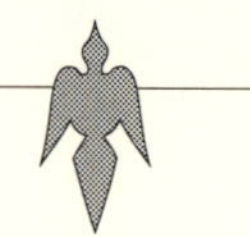

Katonah Gallery. *Many Trails: Indians of the Lower Hudson Valley.* Katonah: Katonah Gallery, 1983.

King, Jonathan C. H. *Thunderbird and Lightning: Indian Life in Northeastern North America, 1600–1900.* London: British Museum, 1982.

———. "Woodland Artifacts from the Studio of Benjamin West, 1738–1820." *American Indian Art Magazine* (Winter 1991) 17(1): 35–47.

———. "Woodlands Art as Depicted by Sarah Stone in the Collection of Sir Ashton Lever." *American Indian Art Magazine* (Spring 1993) 18(2): 32–45.

Kinietz, W. Vernon. "The Indian Tribes of the Western Great Lakes, 1615–1760." University of Michigan Museum of Anthropology *Occasional Contributions* 10 (1940).

Lanford, Benson E. "Great Lakes Woven Beadwork." *American Indian Art Magazine* 1986 11(3): 62–67, 75.

Lessard, F. Dennis. "Great Lakes Indian 'Loom' Beadwork." *American Indian Art Magazine* 1986 11(3): 54–61, 69.

Lewis, James Otto. *The American Indian Portfolio.* Kent, OH: Volair, 1980.

Lurie, Nancy Oestreich. *Wisconsin Indians.* Madison, WI: Wisconsin State Historical Society, 1980.

Penney, David W., ed. *Art of the Great Lakes Indians.* Detroit: Wayne State University Press, 1989.

Quimby, George I. *Indian Life in the Upper Great Lakes: 11,000 B.C. to A.D. 1800.* Chicago: University of Chicago Press, 1960.

Ritzenthaler, Robert E. and Pat Ritzenthaler. *The Woodland Indians of the Western Great Lakes.* Garden City, NY: Natural History, 1970.

Speck, Frank G. "The Double Curve Motif in Northeastern Algonquian Art." Geological Survey of Canada *Memoirs* 42 (1914).

Stirling, Matthew W. "America's First Settlers, the Indians." *National Geographic* (November 1937).

Trigger, Bruce G., ed. *Handbook of North American Indians. Vol. 15: Northeast.* Washington: Smithsonian Institution, 1978.

Wallace, Paul A. W. *Indians in Pennsylvania.* Harrisburg: Pennsylvania Historical and Museum Commission, 1961.

Whiteford, Andrew H. "Fiber Bags of the Great Lakes Indians." *American Indian Art Magazine* 1977 2(3): 52–64, 85.

———. "The Origins of Great Lakes Beaded Bandolier Bags." *American Indian Art Magazine* 1986 11(3): 32–43.

Wilbur, C. Keith. *The New England Indians.* Chester, CT: Globe Pequot, 1978.

Willoughby, C. C. "Dress and Ornament of the New England Indians." *American Anthropologist* 1905 7: 499–508.

———. "Textile Fabrics of the New England Indians." *American Anthropologist* 1905 7: 85–93.

Wooley, David, ed. *On the Border: Native American Weaving Traditions of the Great Lakes and Prairies.* Moorhead, MN: Plains Art Museum, 1990.

Plains

Beilman, Vern. "Porcupine Headdress of the Plains Indian." *American Indian Crafts and Culture* 1973 7(3).

Biddle, Nicholas. *The Journals of the Lewis and Clark Expedition.* 2 vols. New York: Heritage, 1962.

Conn, Richard. *Circles of the World: Traditional Art of the Plains Indians.* Denver: Denver Art Museum, 1982.

———. "Northern Plains Bustles." *American Indian Tradition* 1960 7(1).

Cotterill, R. S. *The Southern Indians.* Norman: University of Oklahoma Press, 1954.

Curtis, Edward S. *The North American Indians.* Vols. 3–6, 16, 17, 19. New York: Johnson Reprint, 1970.

Denig, Edwin Thompson. *Five Indian Tribes of the Upper Missouri: Sioux, Arikaras, Assiniboines, Crees, Crows.* Norman: University of Oklahoma Press, 1961.

———. "Indian Tribes of the Upper Missouri." Bureau of American Ethnology *Annual Reports* 46 1928–1929 (1930): 375–626.

Douglas, Frederic H. "Plains Beads and Beadwork Designs." Denver Art Museum *Indian Leaflet Series* 1936 73–74.

———. "Plains Indian Clothing." Denver Art Museum *Indian Leaflet Series* 1931 24.

Ellison, Rosemary. *Southern Plains Indian Painting.* Anadarko: Oklahoma Indian Arts and Crafts Cooperative and United States Department of the Interior, 1972.

Engel, Lorenz. *Among the Plains Indians.* Minneapolis: Lerner, 1981.

Evans, Dennis. "Southern Plains Women's Boots." *American Indian Tradition* 1962 8(5).

Ewers, John C. "A Century of Plains Indian Art Studies." *American Indian Art Magazine* (Autumn 1992) 17(4): 36–47.

———. "Hair Pipes in Plains Indian Adornment: A Study in Indian and White Ingenuity." Bureau of American Ethnology *Bulletin* 164 (1957): 29–85.

———. *Indian Life on the Upper Missouri.* Norman: University of Oklahoma Press, 1968.

———. *Plains Indian Painting: A Description of an Aboriginal American Art.* Palo Alto, CA: Stanford University Press, 1939.

Farabee, W. C. "Dress among the Plains Indian Women." *University of Pennsylvania Museum Journal* 1921 8.

Feder, Norman. *Art of the Eastern Plains Indians: The Nathan Sturgis Jarvis Collection.* Brooklyn, NY: Brooklyn Museum, 1964.

———. "Plains Hair and Roach Ornaments." *American Indian Hobbyist* 1958 4(9, 10).

———. "Plains Indian Metalworking with Emphasis on Hair Plates." *American Indian Tradition* 1962 8(2): 55–76; 8(3): 93–110.

———. "Plains Pictographic Painting and Quilled Rosettes: A Clue to Tribal Identification." *American Indian Art Magazine* (Spring 1980) 5(2): 54–62.

Gallagher, O. R. and L. H. Powell. "Time Perspective in Plains Beaded Art." *American Anthropologist.* New series 1953 55.

Hail, Barbara. *Hau, Kola! The Plains Indian Collection of the Haffenreffer Museum of Anthropology.* Providence: Brown University Press, 1980.

Harrington, M. R. "Indians of the Plains." Southwest Museum *Museum Leaflet* 1942 15.

Hartmann, Horst. *Die Plains und Prarieindianer Nordamerikas.* Berlin: Veroffentlichungen des Museums für Volkerkunde, 1976.

Holm, Bill. "Plains Indian Cloth Dresses." *American Indian Hobbyist* 1958 4.

Howard, James H. "Northern Plains Grass Dance Costume." *American Indian Tradition* 1960 7(1).

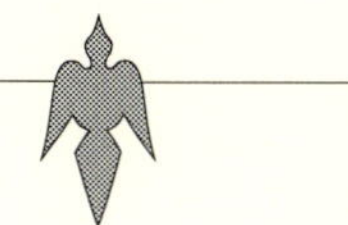

Hyde, George E. *Indians of the High Plains from the Prehistoric Period to the Coming of the Europeans.* Civilization of the American Indian Series 54. Norman: University of Oklahoma Press.

Koch, Ronald P. *Dress Clothing of the Plains Indians.* Norman: University of Oklahoma Press.

Kurz, Rudolph Friederich. "Journal of Rudolph Friederich Kurz: An Account of His Experiences among Fur Traders and American Indians on the Mississippi and Missouri Rivers during the Years 1846–1852." Bureau of American Ethnology *Bulletin* 115 (1937).

Lessard, F. Dennis. "Plains Pictographic Art: A Source of Ethnographic Information." *American Indian Art Magazine* (Spring 1992) 17(2): 62–69, 90.

Lowie, Robert D. *Indians of the Plains.* Garden City, NY: Museum of Natural History Press, 1963.

Mails, Thomas. *Dog Soldiers, Bear Men and Buffalo Women.* Englewood Cliffs, NJ: Prentice-Hall, 1973.

———. *Mystic Warriors of the Plains.* Garden City, NY: Doubleday, 1971.

Markoe, Glenn E. *Vestiges of a Proud Nation: The Ogden B. Reed Northern Plains Collection.* Burlington, VT: Robert Hull Fleming Museum, 1986.

Martin, Evelyn M. "Analysis of Indian Ceremonial Costumes of Central Oklahoma." Master's thesis, University of Southern California, 1942.

Maurer, Evan M., ed. *Visions of the People: A Pictorial History of Plains Indian Life.* Catalog of an exhibition at the Minneapolis Institute of Arts, 11 October 1992–3 January 1993. Seattle: University of Washington Press, 1992.

Newcombe, William W. *The Indians of Texas from Prehistoric to Modern Times.* Austin: University of Texas Press, 1980. Reprint of 1961 edition.

Penny, David W. *Art of the American Frontier: The Chandler-Pohrt Collection.* Seattle: University of Washington Press, 1992.

Petersen, Karen Daniels. *Plains Indian Art from Fort Marion.* Norman: University of Oklahoma Press, 1971.

Pohrt, Richard A. "The Identification of Northern Plains Indian Beadwork." *American Indian Art Magazine* 1989 15(1): 72–79.

———. "Plains Indian Moccasins with Decorated Soles." *American Indian Art Magazine* (Summer 1977) 2(3): 32–40.

Powell, Louis H. "A Study of Indian Beadwork of the North Central Plains." St. Paul Science Museum *Indian Leaflets* 1953 5–7.

Powers, William K. *Indians of the Northern Plains.* New York: Capricorn Books, 1969.

———. *Indians of the Southern Plains.* New York: Putnam's, 1971.

Schneider, Mary Jane. "Plains Indian Clothing: Stylistic Persistence and Change." Oklahoma Anthropological Society *Bulletin* 1968 17: 1–55.

Schulenberg, Raymond F. "Indians of North Dakota." *North Dakota History* 23(3–4).

Spriggs, Lynn E. "The Chandler-Pohrt Collection: Art of the American Indian Frontier." *American Indian Art Magazine* (Spring 1993): 64–73.

Stirling, Matthew W. "Indians of Our Western Plains." *National Geographic* (July 1944): 73–108.

Taylor, Colin. *The Warriors of the Plains.* New York: Arco, 1975.

Thorp, Rowena W. "The Dress of the Plains Indian Women and Children." Master's thesis, Southern Methodist University, 1935.

Tyrell, Joseph Burr. *David Thompson's Narrative of His Explorations in Western America, 1784–1812.* Toronto: Champlain Society, 1916.

Wissler, Clark. "Costumes of the Plains Indians." American Museum of Natural History *Anthropological Papers* 1915 17(2).

———. "Distribution of Moccasin Decorations among the Plains Tribes." American Museum of Natural History *Anthropological Papers* 1927 29(1).

———. "North American Indians of the Plains." American Museum of Natural History *Handbook Series* 1920 1.

———. "Structural Basis to the Decoration of Costumes among the Plains Indians." American Museum of Natural History *Anthropological Papers* 1916 17(3)(1916).

Wright, Muriel. *A Guide to the Indian Tribes of Oklahoma.* Norman: University of Oklahoma Press, 1951.

Southwest

Atkinson, Mary Jourdan. *Indians of the Southwest.* San Antonio, TX: Naylor, 1963.

Bahti, Tom. *Southwestern Indian Tribes.* Flagstaff, AZ: KC Publications, 1968.

Bandelier, Adolph F. *The Delight Makers.* New York: Dodd, Mead, 1918.

Bird, Allison. *Heart of the Dragonfly: The Historical Development of the Cross Necklaces of the Pueblo and Navajo People.* Albuquerque: Avanyu, 1992.

Cirillo, Dexter. *Southwestern Indian Jewelry.* New York: Abbeville, 1992.

Collier, John. *On the Gleaming Way.* Denver: Sage Books, 1949.

———. *Patterns and Ceremonials of the Indians of the Southwest.* New York: Dutton, 1949.

Curtis, Edward S. *The North American Indian.* Vols. 1, 2, 12, 16, and 17. New York: Johnson Reprint, 1970.

———. "Vanishing Indian Types: The Tribes of the Southwest." *Scribner's Magazine* (May 1906).

Dale, Edward Everett. *Indians of the Southwest.* Norman: University of Oklahoma Press, 1950.

Dienes, Andre de. "Costumes of the Southwest Indians." *Natural History* 1947 56: 360–367.

Dutton, Bertha P. *Indians of the Southwest.* Santa Fe, NM: Association on Indian Affairs, 1965.

———. *American Indians of the Southwest.* Albuquerque: University of New Mexico Press, 1983.

———. *Indians of the American Southwest.* Englewood Cliffs, NJ: Prentice-Hall, 1975.

Frank, Larry. *Indian Silver Jewelry of the Southwest, 1868–1930.* West Chester, PA: Schiffer, 1990.

Goddard, Pliny Earle. *Indians of the Southwest.* Handbook Series. New York: American Museum of Natural History, 1931.

Hewett, Edgar L. *Ancient Life in the American Southwest.* Indianapolis: Bobbs-Merrill, 1930.

Holstein, Philip M. and Donnelley Erdman. *Enduring Visions: 1,000 Years of Southwestern Indian Art.* New York: Publishing Center for Cultural Resources, 1979.

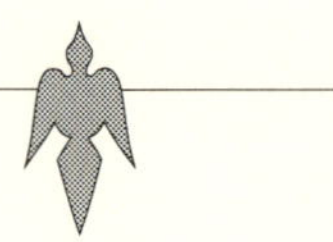

Houlihan, Patrick, Jerold L. Collings, Sarah Nestor, and Jonathan Batkin. *Harmony by Hand: Art of the Southwest Indians.* San Francisco: Chronicle Books, 1987.

Kent, Kate Peck. "The Cultivation and Weaving of Cotton in the Prehistoric Southwestern United States." American Philosophical Society *Transactions* New series 1957 47(3).

———. *Prehistoric Textiles of the Southwest.* Albuquerque: University of New Mexico Press, 1983.

Lange, Charles H. and Carroll L. Ridey. *The Southwestern Journals of Adolph F. Bandelier, 1880–1882.* Albuquerque: University of New Mexico Press and Santa Fe, NM: Museum of New Mexico Press, 1966.

Mera, Harry Percival. *The Alfred I. Barton Collection of Southwestern Textiles.* Santa Fe, NM: San Vicente Foundation, 1978. Reprint of 1949 edition.

———. *Indian Silverwork in the Southwest.* Globe, AZ: King, 1959.

Monthan, Guy and Doris Monthan. *Art and Indian Individualists.* Flagstaff, AZ: Northland, 1975.

Nestor, Sarah, ed. *Spanish Textile Traditions of New Mexico and Colorado.* Santa Fe, NM: Museum of New Mexico Press, 1979.

Ortiz, Alfonso, ed. *Handbook of North American Indians. Vol. 9: Southwest.* Washington: Smithsonian Institution, 1979.

———. *Handbook of North American Indians. Vol. 10: Southwest.* Washington: Smithsonian Institution, 1983.

Pike, Donald G. *Anasazi: Ancient People of the Rock.* New York: Crown, 1977.

Rodee, Marian E. *Southwestern Weaving.* Albuquerque: University of New Mexico Press, 1977.

Sides, Dorothy Smith. *Decorative Art of the Southwestern Indians.* New York: Dover, 1961. Reprint of 1936 edition.

Smith, Mrs. White Mountain. *Indian Tribes of the Southwest.* Palo Alto, CA: Stanford University Press, 1933.

Spier, Leslie. *Yuman Tribes of the Gila River.* Chicago: University of Chicago, 1933.

Stirling, Matthew. "Indian Tribes of Pueblo Land." *National Geographic* 1940 78(5): 549–596.

Tanner, Clara Lee. *Southwest Indian Craft Arts.* Tucson: University of Arizona Press, 1968.

———. *Southwest Indian Painting.* Tucson: University of Arizona Press, 1973.

Tanner, Clara Lee and Joe Ben Wheat. *Ray Manley's Portraits and Turquoise of the Southwest Indians.* Tucson: Ray Manley Photography, 1975.

Weaver, Thomas, ed. *Indians of Arizona: A Contemporary Perspective.* Tucson: University of Arizona Press, 1958.

Webb, William and Robert A. Weinstein. *Dwellers at the Source: The Southwestern Indian Photographs from the A. C. Vroman Collection in the Natural History Museum of Los Angeles County.* New York: Grossman, 1973.

Great Basin

Cline, Gloria G. *Exploring the Great Basin.* Norman: University of Oklahoma Press, 1963.

D'Azevedo, Warren L., ed. *Handbook of North American Indians: Vol. 11: Great Basin.* Washington: Smithsonian Institution, 1986.

Forbes, Jack. *Native Americans of California and Nevada.* Happy Camp, CA: Naturegraph, 1989.

Fowler, Catherine S. *Great Basin Anthropology: A Bibliography.* Desert Research Institute Social Sciences and Humanities Publication 5. Reno: University of Nevada, 1970.

Madsen, David B. and James F. O'Connell, eds. "Man and Environment in the Great Basin." Society for American Archaeology *Papers* 1982 2.

Steward, Julian H. "Native Cultures of the Intermontane (Great Basin) Area." Smithsonian Institution *Miscellaneous Collections* 1940 100: 445–502.

Stewart, Omer C. *Indians of the Great Basin: A Critical Bibliography.* Bibliographical Series of the Newberry Library Center for the History of the American Indian. Bloomington: University of Indiana Press, 1982.

Plateau

Boller, Henry A. *Among the Indians: Eight Years in the Far West, 1858–66, Embracing Sketches of Montana and Salt Lake.* Philadelphia: T. Ellwood Zell, 1867.

Chittenden, Hiram M. and Alfred T. Richardson, eds. *Life, Letters, and Travels of Father Pierre-Jean de Smet.* 4 vols. New York: F. P. Harper, 1905.

Coues, Elliott, ed. *New Light on the Early History of the Greater Northwest. The Manuscript Journals of Alexander Henry and David Thompson, 1799–1814.* 3 vols. New York, 1897.

Curtis, Edward S. *The North American Indian.* Vols. 7, 8. New York: Johnson Reprint, 1970.

Feder, Norman and Clyde Feltz. "Modern Plateau Dance Costume." *American Indian Hobbyist* 1957 3(9, 10).

Loeb, Barbara. "Crow and Plateau Beadwork in Black and White: A Study Using Old Photographs." In *Crow Indian Art.* Pierre, SD: Chandler Institute, 1989.

Ray, Verne F. "Culture Element Distributions, 22: Plateau." University of California *Anthropological Records* 1942 8: 99–262.

Ruby, Robert H. and John A. Brown. *Indians of the Pacific Northwest: A History.* Norman: University of Oklahoma Press, 1981.

Swanson, Earl H., Jr. "The Emergence of Plateau Culture." Idaho State University Museum *Occasional Papers* 1968 22.

United States Department of the Interior. *Contemporary Indian Artists: Montana, Wyoming, Idaho.* Washington, 1972.

Walker, Deward E., Jr. *American Indians of Idaho. Vol. 1: Aboriginal Cultures.* Anthropological Monographs 2. Moscow: University of Idaho, 1973.

California

Abella, Ramon and Jean Saenz de Lucio. ["Reply to the Interrogatorio of 1812, Mission San Francisco."] In *San Francisco or Mission Dolores* by Zephyrin Engelhardt, pp. 147–153. Chicago: Franciscan Herald, 1924.

Aginsky, Burt W. "Culture Element Distributions, 24: Central Sierra." University of California *Anthropological Records* 1943 8(4): 393–468.

Bancroft, Hubert H. *The History of California.* 7 vols. San Francisco: History Company, 1886–1890.

———. *The Native Races of the Pacific States of North America.* 5 vols. New York: Appleton, 1874–1876.

Baumhoff, Martin A. "California Athabascan Groups." University of California *Anthropological Records* 1958 16(5): 157–238.

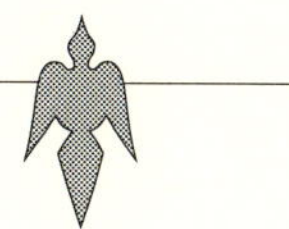

Blackburn, Thomas C. and D. Travis Hudson. *Time's Flotsam: Overseas Collections of California Indian Material Culture.* Menlo Park, CA: Ballena Press and Santa Barbara, CA: Santa Barbara Museum of Natural History, 1990.

Bolton, Herbert E., ed. *Historical Memoirs of Fray Francisco Palou, O.F.M.* 4 vols. Berkeley, CA: University of California Press, 1976.

Brown, Vinson. *Native Americans of the Pacific Coast: Peoples of the Sea Wind.* Happy Camp, CA: Naturegraph, 1977.

Browne, J. Ross. *The Indians of California.* San Francisco: Colt, 1944.

Curtis, Edward S. *The North American Indian.* Vols. 13–15. New York: Johnson Reprint, 1970.

Cutter, Donald C. *California in 1792: A Spanish Naval Visit.* Norman: University of Oklahoma Press, 1992.

Driver, Harold E. "Culture Element Distributions, 10: Northwest California." University of California *Anthropological Records* 1939 1(6): 297–433.

———. "Culture Element Distributions, 5: Southern California." University of California *Anthropological Records* 1937 1(1): 1–52.

———. "Culture Element Distributions, 6: Southern Sierra Nevada." University of California *Anthropological Records* 1937 6(2): 53–154.

Faber, Gail and Michael Lasagna Alamo. *Whispers from the First Californians: A Story of California's First People.* Magpie Publications.

Forbes, Jack D. *Native Americans of California and Nevada.* Healdsburg, CA: Naturegraph, 1989.

Harrington, John P. "Culture Element Distributions, 19: Central California Coast." University of California *Anthropological Records* 1942 7(1): 1–46.

Heizer, Robert F., ed. *Handbook of North American Indians. Vol. 8: California.* Washington: Smithsonian Institution, 1978.

Heizer, Robert E. and Albert B. Elsasser. *The Natural World of the California Indians.* Berkeley: University of California Press, 1980.

Heizer, R. E. and M. A. Whipple, eds. *The California Indians: A Source Book.* Berkeley: University of California Press, 1971.

Jackson, Helen M. (Hunt). *A Century of Dishonor: A Sketch of the United States Government's Dealings with Some of the Indian Tribes.* New York: Harper, 1881.

Johnson, Paul C., ed. *The California Missions: A Pictorial History.* Menlo Park, CA: Lane, 1981.

Keyworth, C. L. *California Indians.* New York: Facts on File, 1991.

Klimek, Stanislaw. "Culture Element Distributions, 1: The Structure of California Indian Culture." University of California *Publications in American Archaeology and Ethnology* 1935 37(1): 1–70.

Kroeber, Alfred L. "Elements of Culture in Native California." University of California *Publications in American Archaeology and Ethnology* 1922 13(8): 259–328.

———. *Handbook of the Indians of California.* Berkeley: California Book Company, 1970. Reprint of 1925 edition.

Kroeber, Theodora. *Ishi in Two Worlds.* Berkeley: University of California Press, 1976.

Kroeber, Theodora and Robert Fleming Heizer. *Almost Ancestors: The First Californians.* New York: Sierra Club, 1968.

Lowie Museum of Anthropology. *An Exhibition of the Robert H. Lowie Museum of Anthropology. 2 January–17 October 1968.* Berkeley: University of California Printing Department, 1968.

Margolin, Malcolm. *The Ohlone Way: Indian Life in the San Francisco-Monterey Bay Area.* Berkeley: Heyday Books, 1978.

Merriam, C. Hart. "Ethnographic Notes on California Indian Tribes." 3 parts. University of California *Archaeological Survey Reports* 1966–1967 68.

———. *Studies of California Indians.* Berkeley: University of California Press, 1955.

Powers, Stephen. "The Northern California Indians." University of California Archaeological Research Facility *Contributions* 1975 25.

———. *Tribes of California.* New York: Dover, 1976. Reprint of 1877 edition.

Rawls, James J. *Indians of California: The Changing Image.* Norman: University of Oklahoma Press.

Sherwin, J. "Face and Body Painting Practices among California Indians." University of California Archaeological Survey *Reports* 1963 68: 81–140.

Society of Friends. *Indians of California: Past and Present.* San Francisco: American Friends Service Committee, 1957.

Wilson, Benjamin D. *The Indians of Southern California in 1852.* San Marino, CA: Huntington Library, 1952.

Voegelin, Erminie Wheeler. "Culture Element Distributions, 20: Northeast California." University of California *Anthropological Records* 1942 7(2): 47–252.

Northwest Coast

Andrews, Ralph Warren. *The Art Work of Seattle and Washington.* Seattle, 1907.

Backlin-Landman, Hedy, ed. *Art of the Northwest Coast.* Catalog of an exhibition 22 January–2 March 1969. Princeton, NJ: Princeton University Art Museum, 1969.

Bancroft, Hubert H. *The Native Races of the Pacific States of North America.* 5 vols. New York: Appleton, 1874–1876.

Bancroft-Hunt, Norman and Werner Forman. *People of the Totem: The Indians of the Pacific Northwest.* New York: Putnam's, 1979.

Beaglehole, John G., ed. *The Journals of Captain James Cook on His Voyages of Discovery. Vol. 3: The Voyage of the Resolution and Discovery, 1776–1780.* Cambridge, England: Cambridge University Press for Hakluyt Society, 1967.

Beckham, Stephen Dow. *The Indians of Western Oregon: This Land Was Theirs.* Coos Bay, OR: Arago Books, 1977.

Beyer, Don E. *The Totem Pole Indians of the Northwest.* New York: Franklin Watts, 1989.

Biddle, Nicholas, ed. *The Journals of the Expedition under the Command of Capts. Lewis and Clark.* 2 vols. New York: Heritage, 1962.

Black, Martha. "Display and Captures: Some Historic Photographs from the Northwest Coast." *American Indian Art Magazine* (Winter 1992) 18(1): 68–75.

Blackman, Margaret B. "Contemporary Northwest Coast Art for Ceremonial Use." *American Indian Art Magazine* (Summer 1985) 10(3): 24–35.

Boas, Franz. "Facial Paintings of the Indians of Northern British Columbia." American Museum of Natural History *Memoirs* 2 (1898).

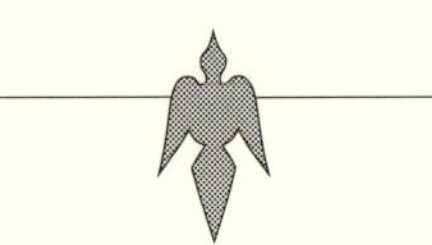

———. "The Use of Masks and Head Ornaments on the Northwest Coast of America." *Internationale Archiv fur Ethnographie* 1890 3(7): 7–15.

Brown, Vinson. *Native Americans of the Pacific Coast: Peoples of the Sea Wind.* Happy Camp, CA: Naturegraph, 1985.

Bruggmann, Maximilien and Peter Gerber. *Indians of the Northwest.* New York: Facts on File, 1987.

Bushnell, David I. "Drawings by George Gibbs in the Far Northwest, 1849–1851." Smithsonian Institution *Miscellaneous Collections* 1938 97(8).

Carlson, Roy L., ed. *Indian Art Traditions of the Northwest Coast.* Burnaby, British Columbia: Simon Fraser University, 1976.

Cressman, L. S. *The Sandal and the Cave: The Indians of Oregon.* Portland, OR: Beaver Books, 1962.

Curtis, Edward S. *The North American Indian.* Vols. 7–11. New York: Johnson Reprint, 1970.

Davis, Robert T. *Native Arts of the Pacific Northwest.* Palo Alto, CA: Stanford University Press, 1949.

Deloria, Vine, Jr. *Indians of the Pacific Northwest.* New York: Doubleday, 1977.

Diomedi, Alexander. *Sketches of Indian Life in the Pacific Northwest.* Fairfield, WA: Ye Galleon, 1986. Reprint of 1894 edition.

Drucker, Philip. "Culture Element Distributions, 26: Northwest Coast." University of California *Anthropological Records* 1950 9(3): 157–294.

———. *Cultures of the North Pacific Coast.* San Francisco: Chandler, 1965.

———. *Indians of the Northwest Coast.* Garden City, NY: Natural History Press, 1963. Reprint of 1955 edition.

Duff, Wilson, Bill Holm, and Bill Reid. *Arts of the Raven: Masterworks by the Northwest Coast Indian.* Vancouver: Vancouver Art Gallery, Seattle: University of Washington Press, 1967.

Garfield, Viola. *Native Americans of the Pacific Northwest.* Seattle: Viola Garfield Collection, University of Washington Libraries, 1949. Microfilm.

Garrod, Stan. *Indians of the Northwest Coast.* Don Mills, Ontario: Fitzhenry and Whiteside, 1981.

Goddard, Pliny E. *Indians of the Northwest Coast.* New York: American Museum Press, 1945.

Grumet, Robert S. *Native Americans of the Northwest Coast: A Critical Bibliography.* Published for the Newberry Library. Bloomington: Indiana University Press, 1979.

Gunther, Erna. *Art in the Life of the Northwest Coast Indians; With a Catalog of the Rasmussen Collection of Northwest Indian Art at the Portland Art Museum.* Portland, OR: Portland Art Museum, 1966.

———. *Indian Life on the Northwest Coast of North America As Seen by the Early Explorers and Fur Traders during the Last Decades of the Eighteenth Century.* Chicago: University of Chicago Press, 1972.

———. *Indians of the Northwest Coast.* Catalog of an exhibition at the Taylor Museum of the Colorado Springs Fine Arts Center and Seattle Art Museum. Seattle, 1951.

———. *Northwest Coast Indian Art.* Catalog of an exhibition at the Seattle World's Fair Fine Arts Pavilion, 21 April–21 October 1962. Seattle: Century 21 Exposition, 1962.

Haberland, Wolfgang. "Thunderbird and Killer Whale." *American Indian Art Magazine* (Spring 1980) 5(2): 36–38, 80.

Hannon, Nan and Richard K. Olmo. *Living with the Land: The Indians of Southern Oregon.* Medford: Southern Oregon Historical Society, 1990.

Harner, Michael J. and Albert B. Elsasser. *Art of the Northwest Coast.* Berkeley: University of California Press, 1965.

Hawthorn, Audrey. *Art of the Kwakiutl Indians and Other Northwest Coast Tribes.* Seattle: University of Washington Press, 1967.

———. *People of the Potlatch: Native Arts and Culture of the Pacific Northwest Coast.* Vancouver: Vancouver Art Gallery and University of British Columbia, 1956.

Hays, H. R. *Children of the Raven.* New York: McGraw-Hill, 1975.

Holm, Bill. *The Box of Daylight: Northwest Coast Indian Art.* Catalog of an exhibition at the Seattle Art Museum, 15 September 1983–8 January 1984. Seattle: University of Washington Press and Seattle Art Museum, 1984.

———. *Crooked Beak of Heaven: Masks and Other Ceremonial Art in the Pacific Northwest.* Seattle: University of Washington Press, 1965.

———. *Northwest Coast Indian Art: An Analysis of Form.* Seattle: University of Washington Press, 1965.

———. *Spirit and Ancestor: A Century of Northwest Coast Indian Art at the Burke Museum.* Seattle: Burke Museum and University of Washington Press, 1987.

———. "A Wooling Mantle Neatly Wrought: The Early Historic Record of Northwest Coast Pattern-Twined Textiles, 1744–1850." *American Indian Art Magazine* 1982 8(1): 34–47.

Holm, Bill and William Reid. *Form and Freedom: A Dialogue on Northwest Coast Indian Art.* Houston: Rice University Institute for the Arts, 1975.

Holmberg, Heinrich Johan. *Holmberg's Ethnographic Sketches.* Marvin W. Falk, ed., Fritz Jaensch, trans. Fairbanks: University of Alaska Press, 1985.

Hunt, Norman Bancroft. *People of the Totem.* New York: Putnam's, 1979.

Inverarity, Robert Bruce. *Art of the Northwest Coast Indians.* Berkeley and Los Angeles: University of California Press, 1950.

Jonaitis, Aldona. *From the Land of the Totem Poles: The Northwest Coast Indian Art Collection of the American Museum of Natural History.* New York: American Museum of Natural History, 1988.

Keddie, Grant R. "The Use and Distribution of Labrets on the North Pacific Rim." *Syesis* 1981 14: 59–80.

Kew, Della and P. E., Goddard. *Indian Art and Culture of the Northwest Coast.* North Vancouver, British Columbia: Hancock House, 1974.

King, J. C. H. *Portrait Masks from the Northwest Coast of North America.* London: Thames and Hudson, 1979.

Kirk, Ruth. *Tradition and Change on the Northwest Coast.* Seattle: University of Washington Press, 1986.

———. *Wisdom of the Elders: Native Traditions on the Northwest Coast.* Vancouver: Royal British Columbia Museum, 1988.

Levi-Strauss, Claude. *The Way of the Masks.* Sylvia Modelski, trans. Seattle: University of Washington Press, 1982.

Lewis, Albert. "Tribes of the Columbia Valley and Coast of Oregon and Washington." American Anthropological Association *Memoirs* 1906 1.

Lyons, Grant. *Pacific Coast Indians of North America.* New York: Messner, 1983.

MacCullum, Spencer. *Art of the Northwest Coast.* Catalog of an exhibition 22 January–2 March 1969 at the Art Museum, Princeton University. Princeton, NJ: Princeton Printing Company, 1969.

Macnair, Peter L., et al. *The Legacy: Tradition and Innovation in Northwest Coast Indian Art.* Seattle: University of Washington Press, 1984.

McFeat, Tom, ed. *Indians of the North Pacific Coast.* Seattle: University of Washington Press, 1966.

Malin, Edward. *A World of Faces: Masks of the Northwest Coast Indians.* Portland, OR: Timber Press, 1986.

Newman, Barnett. *Northwest Coast Indian Painting.* New York: Betty Parsons Gallery, 1946.

Rogers, Edward S. *Indians of the North Pacific Coast.* Toronto: Royal Ontario Museum, 1970.

Ruby, Robert H. and John A. Brown. *A Guide to the Indian Tribes of the Pacific Northwest.* Norman: University of Oklahoma Press, 1986.

———. *Indians of the Pacific Northwest: A History.* Norman: University of Oklahoma Press, 1981.

Stewart, Hilary. *Cedar: Tree of Life to the Northwest Coast Indians.* Vancouver: Douglas & McIntyre, 1984.

———. *Indian Artifacts of the Northwest Coast.* Vancouver: Hancock House Publishers, 1973.

———. *Looking at Indian Art of the Northwest Coast.* Seattle: University of Washington Press, 1979.

Suttles, Wayne, vol. ed. *Handbook of North American Indians. Vol. 7: Northwest Coast.* Washington: Smithsonian Institution, 1990.

Stirling, Matthew W. "Indians of Our North Pacific Coast." *National Geographic* (January 1945).

Swanton, John R. "Publications of the Jesup North Pacific Expedition 5." American Museum of Natural History *Memoirs* 1905 8(1): 1–300.

Thwaites, Reuben G., ed. *Original Journals of the Lewis and Clark Expedition 1804–1806.* New York: Antiquarian Press, 1959.

Underhill, Ruth. *Indians of the Pacific Northwest.* Riverside, CA: Sherman Institute, 1983. Reprint of 1945 edition.

University of British Columbia, Museum of Anthropology. *Indian Masterpieces from the Walter and Marianne Koerner Collection.* Vancouver: University of British Columbia Press, 1975.

Wardwell, Allen. "Some Discoveries in Northwest Coast Indian Art." *American Indian Art Magazine* 1993 18(2): 46–55.

———. *Yakutat South: Indian Art of the Northwest Coast.* Chicago: Art Institute of Chicago, 1964.

White, Sid and S. E. Solberg, eds. *People of Washington.* Pullman: Washington State University Press, 1989.

Wright, Robin. *A Time of Gathering: Native Heritage in Washington State.* Seattle: Burke Museum and University of Washington Press, 1991.

Wyatt, Victoria. *Images from the Inside Passage.* Seattle: University of Washington Press, 1989.

Subarctic

Ashwell, Reg. *Indian Tribes of the Northwest.* Seattle: Hancock House, 1977.

Bailey, Alfred G. *The Conflict of European and Eastern Algonkian Cultures, 1504–1700: A Study in Canadian Civilization.* Toronto: University of Toronto Press, 1962.

Barbeau, Charles M. "Assomption Sash." National Museum of Canada *Anthropological Series* 24 *Bulletin* 93.

Barbeau, Marius. *Indian Days in the Canadian Rockies.* Illustrated by W. Langdon Kihn. Toronto: Macmillan, 1924.

Bifelt, Selina M. "Athabaskan Clothing before European Contact." Unpublished manuscript, Fairbanks, AK. Listed in *Alaska Native Arts and Crafts.* Anchorage: Alaska Geographic, 1983.

Biggar, Henry P., ed. *The Works of Samuel de Champlain.* 6 vols. Toronto: University of Toronto Press, 1971.

Brasser, Ted. *Bo'jou, Neejee! Profiles of Canadian Indian Art.* Ottawa: National Museum of Man, 1976.

Bryce, George. *The Remarkable History of the Hudson's Bay Company.* Franklin, 1968. Reprint of 1904 edition.

Burpee, Lawrence J. *Journals and Letters of Pierre Gaultier de la Verendrye and His Sons.* Toronto: Champlain Society, 1927.

Champlain, Samuel de. *Voyages of Samuel de Champlain, 1604–1618.* W. L. Grant, ed. New York: Scribner's, 1907.

Clark, Annette M. *The Athapaskans: Strangers of the North.* Ottawa: National Museum of Man, 1974.

Condon, Richard D., ed. *Arctic Anthropology* 1991 28(1).

Crowe, Keith J. *A History of the Original Peoples of Northern Canada.* Montreal: McGill-Queen's University Press, 1974.

Davidson, Daniel S. "Snowshoes." American Philosophical Society *Memoirs* 1937 6: 1–207.

Dickason, Olive Patricia. *Indian Arts in Canada.* Ottawa: Department of Indian Affairs and Northern Development, 1972.

Duncan, Kate C. *Northern Athapaskan Art: A Beadwork Tradition.* Seattle: University of Washington Press, 1989.

Feder, Norman. "The Jasper Grant Collection." *American Indian Art Magazine* (Summer 1985) 10(3): 46–51.

Glenbow Museum. *The Spirit Sings: Artistic Traditions of Canada's First People, A Catalog of the Exhibition.* Calgary, Alberta: Glenbow-Alberta Institute and McClelland & Stewart, 1987.

Hail, Barbara A. and Kate C. Duncan. *Out of the North: The Subarctic Collection of the Haffenreffer Museum of Anthropology.* Bristol, RI: Brown University Press, 1989.

Hatt, Gudmund. "Arctic Skin Clothing in Eurasia and America: An Ethnographic Study." *Arctic Anthropology* 1969 2(2).

———. "Moccasins and Their Relation to Arctic Footwear." American Anthropological Association *Memoirs* 1916 3: 151–250.

Helm, June, ed. *Handbook of North American Indians. Vol. 6: Subarctic.* Washington: Smithsonian Institution, 1981.

———. *The Indians of the Subarctic: A Critical Bibliography.* Bibliographical Series of the Newberry Library Center for the History of the American Indian. Bloomington: Indiana University Press, 1976.

Hodge, Frederick W., ed. *Handbook of the Indians of Canada.* Ottawa: King's Printer, 1913.

Holm, Bill. "Making a Blanket 'Capote.'" *American Indian Hobbyist* 1956 3(1).

Jenness, Diamond. *The Indians of Canada.* Toronto: University of Toronto Press, 1977. Reprint of 1932 edition.

Johnson, Michael G. "Indian Beadwork from the Canadian Plains." *Powwow Trails* 1969 5(10).

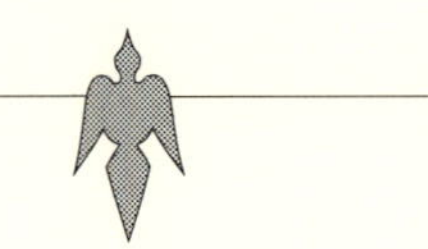

Kane, Paul. *Paul Kane's Frontier including Wanderings of an Artist among the Indians of North America.* J. Russell Harper, ed. Toronto: University of Toronto Press, 1971.

Langdon, John E. *Canadian Silversmiths: 1700–1900.* Toronto: Stinehour, 1966.

Lotz, James R. "Pelts to Parkas." *The Beaver* (Autumn 1962) 293: 16–19.

Mackenzie, Alexander. *Voyages from Montreal on the River St. Lawrence through the Continent of North America to the Frozen and Pacific Oceans in the Years 1789–1793.* Readex Microprint, 1966.

McClellan, Catherine. *Part of the Land, Part of the Water.* Vancouver: Douglas & McIntyre, 1987.

McLean. *Native Tribes of Canada.* Toronto: Coles, 1980. Reprint of 1896 edition.

McMillan, Alan D. *Native Peoples and Cultures of Canada: An Anthropological Overview.* Vancouver: Douglas & McIntyre, 1988.

Morris, James L. *The Indians of Ontario.* Toronto: Ontario Department of Lands and Forests, 1943.

Murray, Alexander Hunter. "Journal of the Yukon, 1847–1848." L. J. Burpee, ed. Ottawa: Government Printing Bureau.

Musée de l'Homme. *Masterpieces of Indian and Eskimo Art from Canada.* Paris: Société des Amis du Musée de l'Homme, 1969.

Orr, R. B. "Snowshoes." Ministry of Education *Annual Archaeological Report* 1920: 19–37. Toronto.

Osborne, Carolyn M., Kristyn Appleby, and Pat Kershner. "A Technical Analysis of Three Forms of Sub-Arctic Snowshoes." *Arctic Anthropology* 1977 14(2): 41–78.

Patterson, Nancy-Lou. *Canadian Native Art: Arts and Crafts of the Canadian Indians and Eskimos.* Don Mills, Ontario: Macmillan, 1973.

Phillips, Ruth. *Patterns of Power: The Jasper Grant Collection and Great Lakes Indian Art of the Early Nineteenth Century.* Kleinburg, Ontario: McMichael Canadian Collection, 1984.

Reid, Dennis and Joan Vastokas. *From the Four Quarters: Native and European Art in Ontario, 5000 BC to 1867 AD.* Toronto: Art Gallery of Ontario, 1984.

Sheppe, Walter, ed. *First Man West: Alexander Mackenzie's Journal of His Voyage to the Pacific Coast of Canada in 1793.* Berkeley: University of California Press, 1952.

Speck, Frank G. "Eastern Algonkian Block-Stamp Decoration: A New World Original or an Acculturated Art." Archaeological Society of New Jersey *Research Series* 1947 1.

Steinbright, Jan. *Athabaskan Art of Alaska.* Fairbanks: Institute of Alaska Native Arts, 1983.

Symington, Fraser. *The Canadian Indians.* Toronto: McClelland & Stewart, 1969.

———. *Pride of the Indian Wardrobe: Northern Athapaskan Footwear.* Toronto: University of Toronto Press, 1990.

Thwaites, Reuben G., ed. *The Jesuit Relations and Allied Documents: Travels and Explorations of the Jesuit Missionaries in New France, 1610–1791.* 73 vols. Cleveland: Burrows, 1896–1901.

Van Stone, James W. "Athapaskan Clothing and Related Objects in the Collection of the Field Museum of Natural History." *Fieldiana Anthropology.* New series 4.

Arctic

Andrews, Clarence L. *The Story of Alaska.* Caldwell, ID: Caxton, 1953.

Ayre, Robert. *Eskimo Graphic Art.* Ottawa: Canadian Arctic Producers, 1967.

Bancroft, Hubert H. *History of Alaska 1730–1885.* San Francisco: History Book Company.

Birket-Smith, Kaj. *The Eskimos.* W. E. Calvert, trans. London: Methuen, 1936.

———. "Ethnological Collection from the Northwest Passage." *Report of the Fifth Thule Expedition, 1921–1924.* 1945 6: 218–288.

Brody, Hugh. *Living Arctic: Hunters of the Canadian North.*Vancouver: Douglas & McIntyre, 1987.

Burch, Ernest S. *The Eskimos.* Norman: University of Oklahoma Press, 1988.

Burland, Cottie A. *Eskimo Art.* London: Hamlyn, 1973.

Collins, Henry B., Frederica De Laguna, Edmund Carpenter, and Peter Stone. *The Far North: 2,000 Years of American Eskimo and Indian Art, 1973.* Washington: National Gallery of Art, 1973.

Corey, Peter L., ed. *Faces, Voices, and Dreams: A Celebration of the Centennial of the Sheldon Jackson Museum.* Seattle: Division of Alaska State Museums and Friends of the Alaska State Museum, 1987.

Crowe, Keith J. *A History of the Original Peoples of Northern Canada.* Montreal: Arctic Institute of North America and McGill-Queen's University Press, 1974.

Curtis, Edward S. *The North American Indian.* Vol. 20. New York: Johnson Reprint, 1970.

Damas, David, ed. *Handbook of North American Indians. Vol. 5: Arctic.* Washington: Smithsonian Institution, 1984.

Driscoll, Bernadette. *The Inuit Amautik: I Like My Hood To Be Full.* Winnipeg: Winnipeg Art Gallery, 1980.

———. "The Inuit Parka." Master's thesis, Carleton University, 1983.

Dumond, Don E. *The Eskimos and Aleuts.* London: Thames and Hudson, 1977.

Fair, Susan W., ed. "Alaska Native Arts and Crafts." *Alaska Geographic* 1985 12(3).

Fitzhugh, William and Aron Crowell. *Crossroads of Continents: Cultures of Siberia and Alaska.* Washington: Smithsonian Institution, 1988.

Flaherty, Robert. *Robert Flaherty, Photographer and Film-Maker: The Inuit 1910–1922.* Catalog of exhibition organized by the Vancouver Art Gallery. Vancouver: Vancouver Art Gallery, 1979.

Frost, Orcutt William, ed. *Cross-Cultural Arts in Alaska.* Anchorage: Alaska Methodist University Press, 1970.

Graburn, Nelson H. H. *Eskimos of Northern Canada.* 20 vols. New Haven, CT: Human Relations Area Files, 1972.

Griffiths, Helen M. "Arctic Handknitted: One Hundred Percent Qiviut." *Handweaver and Craftsman* 1971 22(1): 6–8, 38.

Gunther, Erna. *Sheldon Jackson Museum.* Sitka, AK: Sheldon Jackson Museum, 1976.

Hall, Judy. "Geologists, Whalers, and Anthropologists: The Building of a Museum Collection of Inuit Clothing." *American Indian Art Magazine* 16(4): 38–47, 86.

Hatt, Gudmund. "Arctic Skin Clothing in Eurasia and America: An Ethnographic Study." *Arctic Anthropology* 1969 2(2).

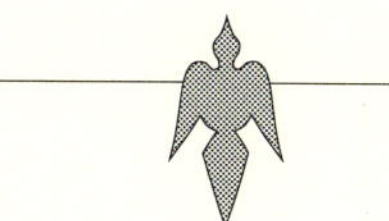

———. "Moccasins and Their Relation to Arctic Footwear." American Anthropological Association *Memoirs* 1916 3: 151–250.

Hawkes, Ernest W. "The Dance Festivals of the Alaskan Eskimos." University of Pennsylvania Museum *Anthropological Publications* 1914 6(2).

Herbert, Wally. *Hunters of the Polar North: The Eskimos.* Amsterdam: Elsevier, 1981.

Hoffman, Walter James. "The Graphic Art of the Eskimos." United States National Museum *Reports* 1895 (1897): 739–968.

Hulley, Clarence C. *Alaska: Past and Present.* Portland, OR: Binfords and Mort, 1970.

Kaplan, Susan A. and Kristin J. Barsness. *Raven's Journey: The World of Alaska's Native People.* Philadelphia: University of Pennsylvania Museum, 1986.

Kotzebue, Otto von. *A Voyage of Discovery into the South Seas and Bering's Straits.* New York: Da Capo. Reprint of 1821 edition.

Lantis, Margaret. "Alaskan Eskimo Ceremonialism." American Ethnological Society *Monographs* 1947 11.

———. "Mme. Eskimo Proves Herself an Artist." *Natural History* 1950 59(2): 68–71.

Lipton, Barbara, ed. *Survival: Life and Art of the Alaskan Eskimo.* Dobbs Ferry, NY: Morgan and Morgan, 1977.

Lopez, Barry. *Arctic Dreams.* New York: Scribner's, 1986.

Lot-Falck, Eveline. "Les Masques Eskimo et Aleoutes de la Collection Pinart." *Journal de la Société des Américanistes.* New series 1957 46: 5–43.

McKeevor, Thomas. *A Voyage to Hudson's Bay During the Summer of 1812: A Description of the Esquimeaux and North American Indians; Their Manners, Customs, Dress, Language, etc.* London: Phillips, 1819.

Michael, Henry M., ed. *Anthropology of the North: Translations from Russian Sources.* 9 vols. Arctic Institute of North America. Toronto: University of Toronto Press, 1961–1974.

Morgan, Lael, ed. "Alaska's Native People." *Alaska Geographic* 1979 6(3). Anchorage: Alaska Geographic Society.

Musée de l'Homme. *Masterpieces of Indian and Eskimo Art from Canada.* Paris: Société des Amis du Musée de l'Homme, 1969.

Oakes, Jill. *Inuit Annuraangit/Our Clothes: A Traveling Exhibition of Inuit Clothing.* Edmonton, Alberta: Thumb Prints, 1987.

Oswalt, Wendell H. *Alaskan Eskimos.* New York: Chandler, 1967.

Oswalt, Wendell H., ed. *Modern Alaskan Native Material Culture.* Fairbanks: University of Alaska Museum, 1972.

Patterson, Nancy-Lou. *Canadian Native Art: Arts and Crafts of the Canadian Indians and Eskimos.* Don Mills, Ontario: Collier Macmillan, 1973.

Phebus, George. *Alaskan Eskimo Life in the 1890s, As Sketched by Native Artists.* Washington: Smithsonian Institution, 1972.

Ray, Dorothy Jean. *Aleut and Eskimo Art: Tradition and Innovation in North Alaska.* Seattle: University of Washington Press, 1977.

———. *Artists of the Tundra and the Sea.* Seattle: University of Washington Press, 1961. Revised edition, 1980.

———. *Eskimo Masks: Art and Ceremony.* Photographs by Alfred A. Blaker. Seattle: University of Washington Press, 1967.

———. "Graphic Arts of the Alaskan Eskimo." *Native American Arts* 2. Washington: Indian Arts and Crafts Board, 1969.

Rich, Edwin E. *The History of the Hudson's Bay Company, 1670–1870.* 2 vols. London: Hudson's Bay Record Society, 1958–1959.

Soderberg, Bertil. "Jungle Rattles of Puffin Beaks." *Ethnos* 1969 1(4): 58–68.

Stellar, Georg Wilhelm. *Journal of a Voyage with Bering, 1741–1742.* Palo Alto, CA: Stanford University Press, 1988.

Stefansson, Vilhjalmur. *My Life with the Eskimo.* New York: Macmillan, 1913.

Varjola, Pirjo. *The Etholen Collection: The Ethnographic Alaskan Collection of Adolf Etholen and His Contemporaries in the National Museum of Finland.* Helsinki: National Board of Antiquities, 1990.

Weyer, Edward M., Jr. *The Eskimos: Their Environment and Folkways.* New Haven, CT: Yale University Press, 1932.

Illustration Credits

Cover: *Péhriska-Rúhpa, Moennitarri Warrior in the Costume of the Dog Danse.* After Karl Bodmer; Joslyn Art Museum, Omaha, Nebraska. Gift of the Enron Art Foundation.

Contents Page

vii Denver Art Museum 1980.352.

Introduction

xi Denver Art Museum 1959.191.

Chapter One – Costume of the Southeast

2 [Creek man] National Anthropological Archives 43,796, Smithsonian Institution.

4 [Cherokee chief] Painting by George Catlin (1836); Gilcrease Institute of American History and Art, Tulsa 0226.1571.

4 [Seminole family] Denver Art Museum.

4 [Mantle] Ashmolean Museum M1234, Oxford, England.

5 [Shoulder bag] Denver Art Museum 1971.406.

12 Painting by George Catlin (1836); Gilcrease Institute of American History and Art, Tulsa 0226.1571.

13 Denver Art Museum 1971.406.

14 After a painting by Sir Joshua Reynolds; National Anthropological Archives 1063-H-1, Smithsonian Institution.

17 After George Catlin (1834); Smithsonian Institution.

22 From an engraving by Theodor de Bry after a drawing by John White; National Anthropological Archives 57,522, Smithsonian Institution.

23 From an engraving by Theodor de Bry after a drawing by John White; National Anthropological Archives 57,527, Smithsonian Institution.

24 From an engraving by Theodor de Bry after a drawing by John White; National Anthropological Archives 57,527, Smithsonian Institution.

25 Ashmolean Museum M1234, Oxford, England.

29 Denver Museum of Natural History 79-231.

31 [Seminole family] Denver Art Museum.

Chapter Two – Costume of the Northeast

38 [Sauk] *Keokuk (The Watchful Fox), Chief of the Tribe* by George Catlin (1835); National Museum of American Art 1985.66.1, Washington, D.C./Art Resource, New York.

40 [Potawatomi shirt] Denver Art Museum 1966.237.E

40 [Potawatomi blouse] Denver Art Museum 1950.118.

40 [Potawatomi women] Denver Art Museum 1701.

40 [Potawatomi boy] Chicago Historical Society ICHi-13896.

41 [Delaware bag] Denver Art Museum 1955.199.

43 Photograph by De Lancey Gill; National Anthropological Archives 723-C, Smithsonian Institution.

50 Denver Art Museum 1955.199.

54 Peabody Museum 40-39-10/19328, Harvard University.

57 American Museum of Natural History 13561, New York.

67 Denver Art Museum 1966.237.E

68 Denver Art Museum 1950.118.

69 [Potawatomi women] Denver Art Museum 1701.

70 Chicago Historical Society ICHi-13896.

71 Photograph by Alexander Gardner; National Anthropological Archives 692, Smithsonian Institution.

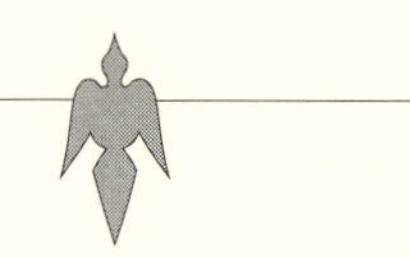

72 From a painting by George Catlin (1835). National Museum of American Art 1985.66.5, Washington, D.C./Art Resource, New York.
73 [roach] Detroit Institute of Arts 81.94.
73 [roach spreader] Detroit Institute of Arts 18-351.

Chapter Three – Costume of the Plains

80 *Máhchsi-Karéhde, Mandan Man.* Karl Bodmer; Joslyn Art Museum, Omaha. Gift of the Enron Art Foundation.
82 [Oto] Photograph by William Dinwiddie; National Anthropological Archives 3828-A, Smithsonian Institution.
82 [Sarci] Notman Photographic Archives MP14(196), McCord Museum of Canadian History, Montreal.
82 [amulet] Photograph by Jens Gunelson; private collection.
82 [robe] Denver Art Museum 1948.144.
83 [Assiniboine] Photograph by William Henry Jackson 19501; Colorado Historical Society.
89 Photograph by Frank A. Rinehart; Southwest Museum N-22994, Los Angeles.
90 Photograph by John K. Hillers; National Anthropological Archives 70-B, Smithsonian Institution.
98 Photograph by Frank A. Rinehart (1898); Southwest Museum 18688, Los Angeles.
100 National Anthropological Archives 55,477, Smithsonian Institution.
101 Denver Art Museum 1948.93.
102 Stanley J. Morrow Collection N190; W. H. Over State Museum, Vermillion, South Dakota.
105 Denver Art Museum.
107 Denver Art Museum 886.
108 Denver Art Museum 2139.
110 Peabody Museum 10/85928, Harvard University.
114 Photograph by De Lancey Gill; National Anthropological Archives 3906 B, Smithsonian Institution.
117 National Anthropological Archives 1433-B-2, Smithsonian Institution.
120 *Dance of the Mandan Women.* After Karl Bodmer; Joslyn Art Museum, Omaha. Gift of the Enron Art Foundation.
121 *Four Bears, Second Chief, in Full Dress.* By George Catlin (1832); National Museum of American Art 1985.66.128, Washington, D.C./Art Resource, New York.
122 *Bison-Dance of the Mandan Indians.* After Karl Bodmer; Joslyn Art Museum, Omaha. Gift of the Enron Art Foundation.
129 National Anthropological Archives 55500, Smithsonian Institution.
130 Denver Art Museum.
134 Photograph by R. E. Roye; Denver Art Museum 1990.
136 Photograph by J. H. Bratley, BR61-297; Denver Museum of Natural History.
137 *Dacota Woman and Assiniboin Girl.* After Karl Bodmer; Joslyn Art Museum, Omaha. Gift of the Enron Art Foundation.
138 Denver Art Museum 292.
139 Photograph by J. H. Bratley, BR61-177; Denver Museum of Natural History.

Chapter Four – Costume of the Southwest

144 [Navajo] Photograph by Ben Wittick; Museum of New Mexico 15713, Santa Fe.
146 [Zuni women] Photograph by Ben Wittick; Museum of New Mexico 16454, Santa Fe.
146 [Jemez shirt] Denver Art Museum 1939.329.
146–147 [Apaches] Rose Collection 857, Western History Collections, University of Oklahoma Library, Norman.
149 Photograph by Ben Wittick; Museum of New Mexico 15978, Santa Fe.
150 Photograph by Matilda Coxe Stevenson; National Anthropological Archives 2185 A, Smithsonian Institution.
152 From a photograph by Burton Frasher, Sr.; Frasher Fotos, Pomona, CA.
155 Photograph by Lawrence Reynolds; Southwest Museum CT 131, Los Angeles.
160 Photograph by Adam C. Vorman; Southwest Museum N-20381, Los Angeles.
161 Photograph by Adam C. Vorman; Southwest Museum N-35608, Los Angeles.

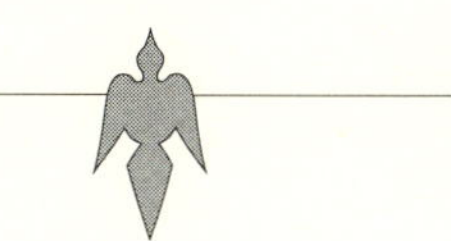

164 Photograph by Orloff Westmann; National Anthropological Archives 2568, Smithsonian Institution.
165 Photograph by Marie Van Vuren; Denver Museum of Natural History 81-066.
171 Photograph by Larry Reynolds; Southwest Museum CT 130, Los Angeles.
172 Denver Museum of Natural History 0093-227.
173 Photograph by Thordis Simonsen (1981); Denver Museum of Natural History 0091-651.
178 Denver Art Museum 1959.191.
179 National Anthropological Archives 2145, Smithsonian Institution.
180 Watercolor by Pablita Velarde (1953); Denver Art Museum 1954.260.
183 Museum of New Mexico 72694, Santa Fe.

Chapter Five – Costume of the Great Basin

186 [Ute] National Anthropological Archives 46,785 D, Smithsonian Institution.
188 [Shoshone] National Anthropological Archives 31,378 F, Smithsonian Institution.
188 [robe] Denver Art Museum 1947.268.
188 [Paiute] Photograph by Mark R. Harrington; Southwest Museum PO4879, Los Angeles.
189 [doll] Peabody Museum 05-53-10/65715, Harvard University.
194 National Anthropological Archives 31,378 F, Smithsonian Institution.
196 Denver Art Museum 1947.268.
198 National Anthropological Archives 1607, Smithsonian Institution.
199 Photograph by Mark R. Harrington; Southwest Museum PO4879, Los Angeles.
201 Photograph by Timothy H. Sullivan; National Anthropological Archives 46,785, Smithsonian Institution.
202 Peabody Museum 05-53-10/65715, Harvard University.
203 Photograph by Stephen Olop; Denver Museum of Natural History OL78-001.

Chapter Six – Costume of the Plateau

206 [Flathead] Photograph by J. K. Hillers (1884); National Anthropological Archives 2999 A, Smithsonian Institution.
208 [Yakima women] National Anthropological Archives 2880 C 9, Smithsonian Institution.
208 [Kutenai man] Canadian Museum of Civilization 41202, Hull, Quebec.
208 [Nez Perce hat] Denver Art Museum 1966.426.
209 [Nez Perce shirt] Denver Art Museum 1956.204.
211 National Anthropological Archives 2900 B, Smithsonian Institution.
212 Bruce Wynn Collection, University of Colorado Museum, Boulder.
214 Photograph by Lee Moorhouse; National Anthropological Archives 3073 B 83, Smithsonian Institution.
215 Photograph by Lee Moorhouse; National Anthropological Archives 3073-19, Smithsonian Institution.
221 Canadian Museum of Civilization 27059, Hull, Quebec.
222 Canadian Museum of Civilization 20830, Hull, Quebec.
224 Canadian Museum of Civilization 41202, Hull, Quebec.
226 Photograph by A. Z. Shindler; National Anthropological Archives 2923 A, Smithsonian Institution.
227 Photograph by Rodman Wanamaker; American Museum of Natural History 317281, New York.
228 Denver Art Museum 1966.426.
229 Denver Art Museum 1956.204.
232 Photograph by Lee Moorhouse; National Anthropological Archives 2899 B 2, Smithsonian Institution.
234 Photograph by Edward S. Curtis; *The North American Indian,* Vol. VII: *Nez Perces, Wallawalla, Umatilla, Cayuse, Chinookan Tribes,* plate 281. Edward S. Curtis. Norwood, MA.: Plimpton Press, 1911.
236 Photograph by De Lancey Gill; National Anthropological Archives 2870 A, Smithsonian Institution.
237 National Anthropological Archives 2880 C 9, Smithsonian Institution.
238 Denver Art Museum 1964.156.

Chapter Seven – Costume of California

240 [Klamath] Denver Art Museum 33.
242 [Tolowa] Photograph by A. W. Erickson; Denver Art Museum.
242 [Chumash skirt] Southwest Museum N.19307, Los Angeles.
242 [Hupa man] Photograph by A. W. Ericson; Denver Art Museum.
242–243 [Hupa dancers] Photograph by P. E. Goddard; Peabody Museum, Harvard University N28549.
245 Peabody Museum, Harvard University 08-4-10/73364.
250 Southwest Museum N.19307, Los Angeles.
252 From a watercolor by Louis Choris (1816); Bancroft Library, University of California, Berkeley.
254 Photograph by A. W. Ericson; Denver Art Museum.
255 Photograph by A. W. Erickson; Denver Art Museum.
256 Photograph by A. W. Ericson; Field Museum of Natural History A22847, Chicago.
262 Sketch by Captain W. Smyth, R.N., *California: A History of Upper and Lower California* by Alexander Forbes (1839); Bancroft Library, University of California, Berkeley.
263 From a watercolor by Louis Choris; Bancroft Library, University of California, Berkeley.
267 From a watercolor by Louis Choris (1816); Bancroft Library, University of California, Berkeley.
269 Photograph by Ben Wittick; Museum of New Mexico 15956.
270 Photograph by William Henry Jackson 6464; Colorado Historical Society.
271 Denver Art Museum 1948.127.
273 National Anthropological Archives T11799, Smithsonian Institution.
281 Detail of a watercolor by Louis Choris; Bancroft Library, University of California, Berkeley.
284 Photograph by Ben Wittick; Museum of New Mexico 15921, Santa Fe.
287 Denver Art Museum 1944.40.
288 Denver Art Museum 1944.50.

Chapter Eight – Costume of the Northwest Coast

290 [Kwakiutl] Photograph by Edward S. Curtis; *The North American Indian,* Vol. 10: *Kwakiutl,* plate 329. Edward S. Curtis. Norwood, MA: Plimpton Press, 1915.
292 [Haida dancers] National Anthropological Archives 72-509, Smithsonian Institution.
292 [Kwakiutl dancer] From a photograph by Edward S. Curtis. *The North American Indian,* Vol. 10: *Kwakiutl,* plate 336. Edward S. Curtis. Norwood, MA: Plimpton Press, 1915.
292 [blanket] Denver Art Museum 1953.216.
293 [mask] American Museum of Natural History 331711, New York.
296 Photograph by Vincent I. Soboleff 54; Denver Art Museum.
298 Denver Art Museum 1996.
299 Photograph by G. T. Emmons; Royal British Columbia Provincial Museum PN 1781, Victoria.
302 Photograph by E. Hattorff; Glenbow Archives NA-860-1, Calgary. Alberta.
303 Photograph by E. Hattorff; Glenbow Archives, Calgary NA-250-8, Calgary, Alberta.
304 American Museum of Natural History 331711, New York.
311 Photograph by Larry Reynolds. Southwest Museum CT.45/749.G.100, Los Angeles.
314 Denver Art Museum 1948.229.
315 Portland Art Museum 48.3.410, Oregon.
318 Royal British Columbia Museum PN 4712, Victoria.
319 Denver Art Museum 1952.607.
329 Denver Art Museum 1935.191.
330 Denver Art Museum 1938.369.
332 Denver Art Museum 1926.26.
335 Royal British Columbia Museum PN 4330, Victoria.
337 Portland Art Museum 46.14, Oregon.

Chapter Nine – Costume of the Subarctic

342 [Tahltan] Photograph by G. T. Emmons; The University Museum, University of Pennsylvania G8-12736.

344 [Tahltan man] Canadian Museum of Civilization 33099, Hull, Quebec.
344 [Kutchin man] Photograph by Edward W. Nelson; National Anthropological Archives 6362, Smithsonian Institution.
344 [tunic, front] Canadian Museum of Civilization 73-11298, Hull, Quebec.
345 [tunic, back] Canadian Museum of Civilization 73-11299, Hull, Quebec.
347 From a lithograph by Robert Hood in *Narrative of a Journey to the Shores of the Polar Sea in the Years 1819, 20, 21, and 22* by Sir John Franklin. London: John Murray, 1823 (reprinted Hurtig. Edmonton, Alberta, 1969).
352 Detail of a drawing by Adrien G. Morice. "Notes Archaeological, Industrial and Sociological on the Western Dénés with an Ethnographical Sketch of the Same" by A. G. Morice in *Transactions of the Canadian Institute,* Vol. 4 (1892-93), page 176, Toronto, 1895.
354 Watercolor by Émile Petitot (1862).
361 Photograph by Edward W. Nelson; National Anthropological Archives 6362, Smithsonian Institution.
363 Denver Art Museum 1937.323.
370 Canadian Museum of Civilization 73-11298, Hull, Quebec.
371 Canadian Museum of Civilization 73-11299, Hull, Quebec.
373 Canadian Museum of Civilization 33099, Hull, Quebec.

Chapter Ten – Costume of the Arctic

380 [Copper Eskimo] Photograph by Sir Hubert Wilkins (1916); Canadian Museum of Civilization 51234, Hull, Quebec.
382 [mukluks] Denver Art Museum 1949.270.
382 [Caribou woman] Photograph by Thierry Mallet; Hudson's Bay Company Archives 1987/363-E-140/58 (N9043), Provincial Archives of Manitoba, Winnipeg.
382 [collar] Denver Art Museum 1946.84.
382 [Aleut parka] Denver Art Museum 1949.191.
383 [Nunivak man] Photograph by Edward S. Curtis, *The North American Indian,* Vol. 20: *Nunivak, King Island, Little Diomede Island, Cape Prince of Wales, Kotzebue,* facing page 82. Edward S. Curtis. Norwood, MA: Plimpton Press, 1930.
390 Denver Art Museum 1949.270.
391 Denver Art Museum 1949.191.
392 Potosky Collection, Denver Art Museum 108-19-E.
393 Watercolor by John White (1577); British Library PS 234062, London.
394 Watercolor by John White (1577); British Library PS 205220, London.
398 Detail of a watercolor by John Halkett (1832); Hudson's Bay Company Archives 1987/363-E-130/161 (N8118), Provincial Archives of Manitoba, Winnipeg.
400 Photograph by Thierry Mallet; Hudson's Bay Company Archives 1987/363-E-140/58 (N9043), Provincial Archives of Manitoba, Winnipeg.
401 Photograph by George H. Wilkins; Canadian Museum of Civilization 50927, Hull, Quebec.
402 Photograph by Sir Hubert Wilkins; Canadian Museum of Civilization 51235, Hull, Quebec.
403 Photograph by George H. Wilkins; Canadian Museum of Civilization 51571, Hull, Quebec.
405 Denver Art Museum 1946.84.
425 Photograph by E.W. Nelson; National Anthropological Archives 6914, Smithsonian Institution.
426 Photograph by Edward S. Curtis, *The North American Indian,* Vol. 20: *Nunivak, King Island, Little Diomede Island, Cape Prince of Wales,* plate 693. Edward S. Curtis. Norwood, MA: Plimpton Press, 1930.
428 Photograph by Edward S. Curtis, *The North American Indian,* Vol. 20: *Nunivak, King Island, Little Diomede Island, Cape Prince of Wales, Kotzebue,* facing page 82. Edward S. Curtis. Norwood, MA: Plimpton Press, 1930.

Appendix One

431 [Sioux boy] From a photograph by J. H. Bratley, BR61-285; Denver Museum of Natural History.

452–458 All other drawings in Appendix One by the author.

Appendix Two

461 Denver Art Museum 1970.423.

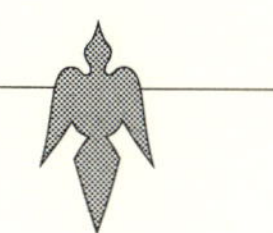

Index

Page numbers in **bold** indicate illustrations.

Abalone ornamentation
- Californian, 246, 248, 250, 252, 255, 259–260, 266, 272, 277, 282, 285, 286, 287
- Eskimo, 420
- Great Basin, 196, 204
- Northwest Coast, 297, 304, 312, 319, 325, 336
- Plains, 98, 110, 123
- Plateau, 220, 222, 225, 229, 231, 235, 238
- Southwestern, 151, 152, 157
- Subarctic, 352

Abenaki
- confederacy of, 65
- Eastern, 42, 65
- Western, 45–46

Achumawi, 274–276
Acoma, 151–153, **152,** 177
Acorn Dance, 248, 253, 260, 283
Affalati, 321
Agate, 262
Akichita Society, 138
Alabama, 6, 8–9, 18
Albino bison, **120,** 123
Albino deerskins, 255–256, **256,** 288, **288**
Aleut, 321, 384, 386–389
Alsea, 323
Amautiks, 421–422, 423
Amber, 30
Ammonites, 90
Amulets and charms
- Eskimo, 385, 391, 395, 397, 400, 402, 406, 408, 410, 417, 422, 424, 427
- umbilical cord, 93, 95, 102–103, 109, 118, 139, 322, 348

Anasazi, 147, 150, 177, 182
Anoraks, 385, 404–407, 411, 421. *See also* Parkas
Antelope garments, 92
Antler horn purse, 248, 255, 287, 322
Apache, 148, 153–156, 169
- boots, **155**
- Chiricahua, 153, 156–158
- Jicarilla, 153, 164–167, **164, 165,** 200
- Kiowa, 116, 153
- Lipan, 153
- Mescalero, 153, 167–169
- Western, 153

Apocynum. See Indian hemp garments
Applegate River, 321
Aprons. *See* Breechclouts; Kilts; Skirts and dresses
Arapaho, 88–91, **89, 90,** 99, 132
Arctic Indians, 383–386
- Aleut, 384, 386–389
- *See also* Eskimo; *specific tribes and groups (list on page 383)*

Argillite, 310, 311, 312, 331
Arikara, 91–93, 128
Arkansas Band (Osage), 126
Armbands, **194**
- Californian, 285
- Great Basin, **194,** 195
- Northeastern, 56
- Northwest Coast, 297
- Plains, 102
- Plateau, 213, 231, 233, 238

Armor
- Aleut, 388
- basketry, 151
- Californian, 246, 248, 255, 258, 260, 273, **273,** 275, 277, 288
- Eskimo, 386, 392, **392,** 397, 410, 417, 420, 427
- Great Basin, 197
- Navajo, 173–174
- Northeastern, 45, 48, 55, 57, 61, 63
- Northwest Coast, 299, 306, 309, 311, 315, 319, 322, 328, 331, 336, 339
- Plains, 86, 90, 93, 95, 98, 110, 115, 119, 142
- Plateau, 213, 222, 229
- Puebloan, 166, 179
- rod-and-slat, 48, 255, 258, 299, 306, 311, 319, 328, 331, 348, 420
- Southeastern, 7, 19, 21, 27, 35
- Southwestern, 151, 173–174
- Subarctic, 348, 352, 371, 374
- whalebone, 328, 339

Asiatic Eskimo, 390–393
Asphaltum, 249, 250, 253, 266
Assagunticook, 65
Assiniboine, 93–96, 131, **137**
Assomption sash, 63, 348, **354,** 363, 364, 377
Atakapa, 141
Athabascan band, 353
Athapaskan, 247–248, 293, 295, 300, 301, 330, 336, 345, 353
- half-breeds (Métis), 363
- Hupa, 247, 253–257
- Subarctic Athapaskan-speaking tribes, 345, 351–355, 358–363, 369–376

Atsina, 88, 96
Atsugewi, 274–276
Awls, 384

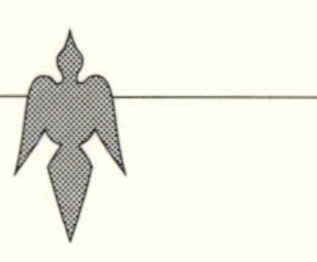

Babiche, 347, 348, 351, 354, 360, 367, 370, 375, 377
Baby band, 360, 362, 370
Badger-skin boots, 192
Badger society, 113
Baffin Island Eskimo, 393–395, **393, 394,** 412
 Igluglik, 407, 421
Bags and pouches
 Aleut, 388
 animal pelt pouches, 273
 Apache, 168
 babiche, 354
 birdskin, 355
 bobcat-skin, 77
 Californian, 246, 249, 252, 255, 258, 259, 264, 266, 268, 272, 275, 277, 279, 280, 287
 caribou fetus, 357
 Cherokee, **13**
 Delaware, **50**
 Eskimo, 395, 397, 406, 411, 413, 415, 417, 419
 friendship bags, 60, 212–213, **212, 215, 227,** 229, **237**
 Great Basin, 192, 195, 199, 203
 "housewife," 419
 netted, 272
 Northeastern, 44, 46, 48, 50, 52, 54, 55, 56, 59, 60, 61, 65, 66, 68, 74, 75, 77
 Northwest Coast, 297, 302, 306, 308–309, 311, 314, 319, 322, 325, 328, 331, 334, 336, 339
 octopus, 229, 334, 348, 364, 370, 377
 otter, 125, 126
 palmetto, 30
 Plains, 90, 92, 95, 97, 102, 109, 112, 115, 118, 125, 126, 127, 130, 133, 138–139
 Plateau, 212–213, **212,** 215, **215,** 219–220, 222, 225, **227,** 229, 231, 233, **237,** 238
 Puebloan, 179
 salmon-skin, 352, 419
 Southeastern, 7, 9, 13, 15, 17, 18, 19, 21, 24, 27, 30, 36
 Southwestern, 149, 160, 173, 179
 Subarctic, 348, 350, 352, 354–355, 356–357, 358, 360, 364, 366, 368, 370, 374, 376
 wolverine, 413
Bandana scarves, 106, 268, 285
Bannock, 190, 191, 193
Bark garments and blankets
 Californian, 262, 272, 275, 286
 Great Basin, 190, 191, 195, 199
 Northwest Coast, 295, 301, 302, 304, 306, 307, 310, 313, 317, 318, 322, 324, 325, 330, 331, 335, 338
 Plateau, 212, 223
 production of, 295
 Southeastern, 6, 11, 19, 36
Barracuda Dance, 250
Basketmaker peoples, 150, 189
 sandals, **178**
Basketry hats
 Californian, 246–249, 252, 254, **255,** 256, 258, 259, 262, 275, 277, 279, 280, 287, **287,** 288
 Eskimo, 419
 Great Basin, 190, 192, 195, **198,** 199, 203
 Northwest Coast, 312, 331
 Plateau, 212, 215, **215,** 217, 222, 223, 225, **227,** 229, 231, 233, 236
 Southwestern, 150
Basketry "potlatch" rings, **311,** 315, 319, 330, **330,** 331, 336, 419
Battle dress. *See* Armor; Ceremonial costumes; Shields
Batz, A. de, 16, 20–21
Beaded collars, **405,** 406
Beads and beadwork, 17
 Apache, 155, 169
 bow loom, 349
 Californian, 270, 271, **271,** 273, 275, 277
 "chief," 306
 drilling, **179**
 Eskimo, 392, 395, 400, 408, 412, 413, 420
 glass bead production, 93, 123
 Great Basin, 191, 192, 197, 204
 Mojave collar, **271**
 Northeastern, 44, 45, 48–49, 53, 55, 61, 63, 65, 67, 68, 70, 74
 Northwest Coast, 300, 306
 Plains, 86, 87, 90, 93, 98, 99, 106, 110, 119, 126, 127, 131, 133, 140
 Plateau, 213, 217–218, 220, 225, 229, 231, 238
 Puebloan, 167
 scatter beading, 228
 Southeastern, 7, 17, 19, 30, 32, 35, 36
 Southwestern, 151, 152–153
 Subarctic, 348, 349, 355, 357, 359, 366, 368, 374, 378
Bean Dance, 161
Bear Dance, 135, 140, 166
Bear intestine, 331
Bear paw mittens, 385
Bear paws motif, **129**
Bear Society, 126
Bear teeth, 275
Beard. *See* Facial hair
Bear-fur moccasins, 280
Bear-hide armor, 275
Bearpaw-style snowshoes, 47, 62, 64, 76, 347, 351, 356, 367, 372
Bear skin
 mittens of, 402, 405
 moccasins of, 15, 27, 335
 parkas of, 419
 trousers of, 394, 421, 423
 See also Bear-skin robes and blankets
Bear-claw ornamentation
 Californian, 253, 275, 281
 Great Basin, 195–196, 204
 Northeastern, 52, 53, 56, 74, 77
 Northwest Coast, 319, 336
 Plains, 86, 92, 95, 98, 109, 113, **114,** 115, 123, 125, 130, 131, 133, 139
 Plateau, 218, 238
 Pueblo, **150**
 Southwestern, 157
 Subarctic, 376
Bear-skin robes and blankets
 Californian, 279
 ceremonial costume, 131

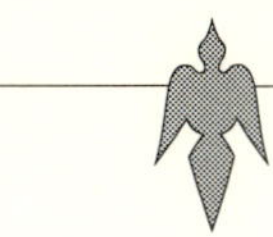

Great Basin, 203
Northeastern, 44, 49, 54, 56, 68, 73, 75, 77
Northwest Coast, 295, 313, 318, 324, 330
Southeastern, 15
Subarctic, 352, 358, 367
Beaver Indians, 369
Beaver skin
breechclout of, 66
hats of, 309
headband of, 266
leggings of, 365
parka of, 427
robes of, 44, 46, 49, 54, 56, 59, 62, 64, 68, 73, 112, 132, 351, 367, 372
shirt of, 356
sleeves of, 365
Beaver teeth, 319
Beavertail–style snowshoes, 347, 356, 367
Bella Bella, 301, 313
Bella Coola, 294, 301–305, **302, 303**
mask, **304**
Bells, 125, 127
Belt loom, 173, 179
Belts
Apache, 168
"baby band," 360, 362, 370
Californian, 246, 248, 251, 258, 266, 275, 277, 280, 282, 285
chastity, 101, 137
deer hoof, 251
Eskimo, 385, 391, 397, 402, 413, 417, 424, 427
floated warp, 179
Great Basin, 190, 192, 195, 203
human hair, 277, 279
Northeastern, 46, 48, 50, 55, 63, 65, 68, 75
Northwest Coast, 297, 306, 309, 311, 314, 322, 325, 328, 336, 339
Plains, 86, 95, 102, 106, 109, 118, 127, 142
Plateau, 213, 220, 222, 225, 229, 231, 233
Puebloan, 166
snakeskin, 7, 50
Southeastern, 7, 10, 11, 15, 17–18, 19, 21, 22, 24, 30–32, 36
Southwestern, 151, 154, 159, 166, 173
Subarctic, 348, 350, 352, 360, 368, 370, 377
Beothuck, 349–350
Bering Strait Eskimo, 392, 395–398
Big Cypress Indians, 28
Big Dog Society, 110
Big Head Dance, 266, 277
Big Head headdress, 273, 283
"Bil" dress, 170
Birchbark hats, 366
Birchbark rain cape, 66
Bird's head robes, 23, 27, 33
bird skin
bags of, 355
headgear of, 20, 322, 396, 417, 419
mantles and robes of, 244, 266, 280, 281, 286, 289
pants of, 423, 424
parkas of, 385, 387, 389, 390, 396, 405, 416, 421, 423, 424, 427
sleeves of, 387
tunic of, 416, 418
Black Bear Dance, 248
Black bonnet, 85
Black Face society, 339
Blackfeet Sioux, 135
Blackfoot, 96–99, **98,** 131, 212, 213, 219
Blankets, aboriginal
bark, 295, 302, 306, 307, 310, 313, 317, 318, 322, 325, 330, 331, 335, 338, 374
Californian, 284
chief, **171**
Chilkat, 297, **298,** 299, 301, **302,** 309, 310, 311, 316, 325, 331–333, **332,** 334, 336, 352, 374
"dog" (or coyote), 306, 308, 325, 327, 328, 338
goat wool
Plateau, 224
Puebloan, 183
rabbit fur, 221
Salish, 221, 223, **224,** 297, 307–309, 316, 325, 328
Southwestern, 150, 166, 175
Southwestern (Navajo), 106, 163, 166, 171, **171,** 183
See also Robes and capes
Blankets, non-native
button blanket, **296,** 300, 301, 309, 312, 315, 316, 333, 336, 353
Hudson's Bay blankets, 48, 55, 60, 63, 65, 87, 93, 97, 99, 103, 111, 132, 140, 224, 226, 301, 304, 305, 308, 309, 316, 333, 334, 353
Pendleton blankets, 99, 103, 111, 140, 163, 166, 168, 171, 178, 192, 195, 197, 203, 213, 217, 224, 231, 323
blanket coats. *See Capotes*
blanket dress *(manta),* **149,** 151–152, **152,** 158–159, 163, 177–178, 182
Blood (Kainah), 96
Blouses
Apache, 157
Northeastern, 78
Blue Jay Dance, 220
Boar tusk, 106
Boas, Franz, 301, 313
Bobcat-skin medicine pouch, 77
Bodmer, Karl, 52, 84, 88, 92, 94, 96, 110, 119, 120, 124, 126, 135, 223, 225
Bois Brules, 135
Bois Fort Cree, 376
Boots
Aleut, 387
animal leg (hock boot), 44, 46, 56, 190, 327
Apache, **155,** 156
Cheyenne, **101**
child carrier, 411
cleats or hobnails, 385, 390
cowboy, 119
Eskimo, 384–385, 390, 394–396, 399, 402, 405, 407, 409, 411, 413, 414, 416, 419, 421, 423, 425, 427
Eskimo (16th century), **393, 394**
fur mosaic, 358
Great Basin, 190, 202
kamiks, 405
mukluks, 347, 358, 360, 384, **390,** 411, 419, 425

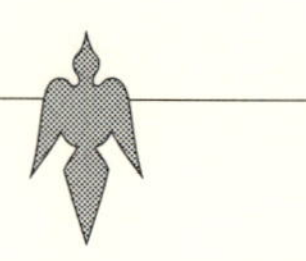

Plains, 118
Puebloan, **152, 183**
salmon-skin, 351, 358, 375
sealskin, 384–385, 390, 394–396, 399, 402, 405, 407, 409, 411, 413, 414, 416, 419, 421, 423, 425, 427
Southwestern, 152, 154, 157
Subarctic, 347, 358, 375
See also Leggings; Moccasins
Border and hourglass motif, 105
Bow loom, 349, 357, 371
Box and border, 61, 115, 137
Bracelets
Aleut, 388
Californian, 248, 285
Eskimo, 417
Northeastern, 61
Northwest Coast, 297, 302, 309, 314, 319, 325, 331
Plains, 103
Plateau, 218
Puebloan, 166
Southeastern, 7, 27
Subarctic, 352, 366, 371, 376
See also Jewelry
Brass ornamentation, 220, 229, 301, 314
browband, 399, **400**
rings, 102
Breastplates
Apache, 168
Plains, 86
Plateau, 220
Puebloan, 179
reed, 273
Southeastern, 7, 19
See also Armor; Gorgets; Hair pipe breastplates
Breechcloths
Apache, **164**
assian, 377
Californian, 258, 271, 284
Great Basin, 200
Kickapoo, **43**
Northeastern, 74
Plateau, 214, 221, 230, 233, 235
Southeastern, 6, 8, 16, 18, 26, 34
Southwestern, 148, 169, 175
Southwestern (Apache), 154, 156, **164**
Southwestern (Puebloan), 151, 158, 162, 177, 182
stroud, 111
Subarctic Cree, 377
See also Breechclouts
Breechclouts
bark fiber, 190, 191, 198, 200, 233
beaver, 66
Californian, 244, 249, 257, 261, 268, 282
Californian (Athapaskan speakers), 247, 253–254
Californian (Hokan speakers), 272, 274, 279, 284
Californian (Penutian speakers), 251, 259, 265, 277, 280
Cheyenne, **100**
colored, as status marker, 21
draped, 23, 27
female, 9, 27, 84, 104
fitted, 6, 16, 18, 35, 42, 54, 62, 64, 72, 84, 100, 114, 116, 120, 126, 132, 151, 356
Great Basin, 190, 191, 193, **194,** 198, 200
Northeastern, 42, 45, 47, 49, 54, 56, 59, 61, 62, 64, 66, 67, 72, 75, 76
Northwest Coast, 310, 321, 324, 329, 335
palmetto, 28
Plains, 84, 88, 92, 94, 96, 100, 104, 107, 112, 114, 116, 119–120, 124, 126, 128, 131–132, 135
Plateau, 210, 214, 224, **232,** 233
Plateau (Salishan-speaking), 216, 219, 220–221, 230, 235
Plateau (Shahaptian speakers), 214, 216, 226, 235
rabbit fur, 272
raccoon, 72
Southeastern, 6, 8, 9, 10, 12, 15, 16, 18, 21, 23, 27, 28, 33, 35
Southwestern, 148, 169–170, 175
Southwestern (Apache), 156, 165, 167
Southwestern (Puebloan), 151, 158, 162, 177, 182
Subarctic, 346, 349
Subarctic (Algonquian speakers), 349, 356, 365, 367, 377
Subarctic (Athapaskan speakers), 351, 353, 369
three-piece, 76
See also Breechcloths
Bridal headdress, 233, **234,** 238, **238,** 420
Brocading, 161–162, 179, 181
Broken Bows, 135
Brown paints and pigments, 308
Bry, Theodor de, 265
Buffalo bull's tails, 103
Buffalo Cult, 113
Buffalo Dance, 163, 184
Buffalo hair bags, 77
Buffalo hair weaving, 61
Buffalo head headdresses, 123
Buffalo hide shields, 196–197
Buffalo horn headdress
Plains, 86, 98, 102, 103, 106, 109, 113, 115, **122,** 123, 132, 138
Plateau, **214,** 219
Puebloan, 163
Buffalo Horn society, 98
Buffalo robes and blankets
Great Basin, 190, 195, 203
Northeastern, 47, 52, 56, 59, 68, 73, 75, 77
Northwest Coast, 328, 340
Plains, 85, 88, 92, 94, 97, 101, 105, 109, 112, 115, 118, 122, 125, 130, 132, 137
Plateau, 210, 215, 219, 224, 230, 236
Shoshone, **196**
Southeastern, 6, 9, 12, 15, 21
Southwestern, 152, 159, 163, 166, 168, 170, 183
Teton Sioux, **137**
white buffalo, 101, **120,** 123
Buffalo Society, 91, 123
Bull Dance, 163, 164
Bull society, 97
Bull-nose moccasins, 54
Burial customs
Californian, 271, 276, 278
Eskimo, 406

Northwest Coast, 312, 322
Plateau, 220, 222, 231
Puebloan, 164, 181
Southwestern, 153
Burnt Woods, 135
Busk festival, 20
Button blankets, **296,** 300, 301, 309, 312, 315, 316, 333, 336, 353, 374
Buttons, 348, 385, 397, 415

Cabeza de Vaca, 141
Caddo, 9–10
California condor. *See* Condor
Californian Indians, 148, 243–247, 253, 267, 278, 283, 285
Athapaskan speakers, 247–248, 253–257
Chumash, 249–251
Hokan speakers, 261–265, 272–276, 278–279, 283–285
Klamath and Modoc, 257–258
Mission Indians, 249, 261–265
Mojave, 265–271
Penutian speakers, 251–253, 259–260, 265–267, 276–278, 280–281
Yuki, 282–283
Yurok, 286–289
See also specific tribes and groups (list on page 243)
Calusa, 10–11, 28
Camas Dance, 220
Camp dress (Apache style), 154, 157, 175, 184, 176, 184
Cane of office, 152, 163, 179, 183, 184
Cannibal Dance, 315
Capes. *See* Robes and capes
Capotes, 65, 87, 96, 97, 111, 132, 219, 228, 348, 353, 364, 377
Cardero, Jose, 251, 317
Caribbean peoples, 10
Caribou Eskimo, 398–401, **398, 400**
Caribou fetus bag, 357
Caribou-head hood, 368
Carney, Peter, 305
Carrier Indians, 301, 351–353, 372
wig, **352**
Carter's smocks, 329
Catawba, 6, 33
Catfish-style snowshoes, 59, 76
Cathlamet, 305
Cathlapotle, 305
Catlin, George, 16, 17, 18, 47, 52, 58, 60, 67, 75, 76, 83, 88, 92, 94, 96, 100, 104, 107, 109, 111, 114, 116, 119, 120, **121,** 124, 126, 127, 128, 131, 135, 137, 138, 223, 226
Catlinite, 151
Cato, 247
Cattail poncho, 338
Cayuga, 55
Cayuse, 213–216, **214, 215**
Cedar-bark garments, production of, 295. *See also* Bark garments and blankets
Ceremonial costumes
Aleut, 388–389
Apache, 155, 156, 157–158, 168–169
Californian, 246, 248, 250–251, **250,** 253, 255, 260, 263, 266, 270–271, 273, 275–279, 281, 283, 285, **287,** 288, **288,**
Eskimo, 386, 392, 397, 400, 408, 411–412, 413, 415, 417, 420, 427–429
female use of male attire, 197
Great Basin, 192, 197, **199**
Northeastern, 48, 56, 63, 66, 67
Northwest Coast, 299–300, **302, 303,** 304, 309, 311, 315, 319, 322, 325, 328, 331, **335,** 336, 339–340
Plains, 86–87, 90–91, 93, 95, 97, 98, 103, 110, 113, 115, 119, 123, 125–126, 130, 131, 138, 140
Plateau, 220
Southeastern, 7, 16, 17, 19–20
Southwestern, 148, 153, 162, 176
Southwestern (Navajo), 174
Southwestern (Pueblo), **150,** 160–161, 163–164, 166, 181, 184
Subarctic, 348–349, 350, 352, 358–359, 362, 368, 374, 376
See also Burial customs; Dance costumes; Masks; Mourning customs; Shamans and medicine men
Chastacosta, 321
Chastity belt, 101, 137
Chehalis, 338, 339
Chelamela, 321
Chelan, 230
Chemehuevi, 148, 198
Cheraw, 33
Cherokee, 6, 11–15, **14**
beaded bag, **13**
turban, **12**
Chesapeake, 22
Chetco, 321
Cheyenne, 88, 99–103, **100, 101, 102,** 204
Chickahominy, 22
Chickasaw, 15–16
Chief beads, 306
Chief blankets, **171**
Chief Joseph, 226
Chief's coat, 85, 113
Chilcotin, 301, 351
Children's clothing
breechclouts, 84, 104
buffalo robe, 92
Comanche, **105**
Crow girl's dress, **108**
Eskimo infant headgear, 385, 391, 395
face paint, 167
footgear, 125, 168
headgear, 159
Potawatomi, **70**
Powhatan, **24**
Puebloan, **180**
tiny pink bow on penis, 141
See also Rabbit-skin robes
Chilkat, 300, **302**
Chilkat blanket, 297, **298,** 299, 301, 309–311, 316, 325, **329,** 331–333, **332,** 336, 352, 374
loom for, 332
post-contact manufacture of, 334
Tsimshian originators of, 336
Chilluckittequaw, 305
Chilula, 247
Chilwitz, 321

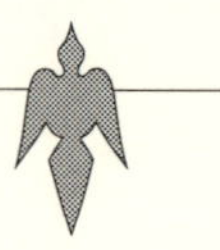

Chimakum, 324
Chinese coins, **234**, 238, **238**, 248, 254, 309, 312
Chinook, 235, 305–307, 323, 338
Chipewyan, 131, 353–355, **354**, 378
Chippewa, 47–49, 51, 62, 64, 67, 70, 219
Chiracahua Apache, 153, 156–158
Chitimacha, 6
Choctaw, 6, **17**
Chokers. *See* Necklaces
Chongo, 152, 159, 163, 171, **172**, 173, 179
Choris, Louis, 251, 264, 265, **267**, 384, 389, 397, 409
Chugach Eskimo, 418–420
Chukchi, 392, 410
Chulamni, **281**
Chumash, 249–251, **250**
Chunkey, 16, 17
Cibecue Apache, 153
Civet-skin apron, 255
Clackamuse, 305, 321
Clallam, 324, 338
Clamshell ornamentation
  Californian, 250, 252, 253, 266, 268, 272, 274, 276, 277, 281
  Northeastern, 44
  Plains, 86, 92
  Plateau, 220, 233
Clan headgear, 312, **330**
Classic Salish blanket, 308
Clatsop, 305, 321, 322
Clover Dance, 248
Clowns, 161, 166, 181, 184
Clowwewalla, 305
Coalhuitecans, 141
Coast Salish, 220, 294, 300, 307–310
  blanket. *See* Salish blanket
Coats
  birdskin, 266
  blanket *(capotes),* 65, 87, 96, 97, 111, 132, 219, 228, 348, 353, 364, 377
  chief's, 113, 365
  matchcoats, 6, 9, 12, 23, 27, 33
  Métis, **363**
  Montagnais/Naskapi, 368
  moose foreparts, 365
  Subarctic, 347–348, 356, 363, 364, 365, 368, 378
  See also Robes and capes; Transitional dress
Cocopa, 267, 283
Cofitachiqui, 18
Collars
  Eskimo, **405**, 406
  Mojave style, 268, **270**, **271**
  Northeastern, 74
  wolf-skin, 125
Collier, John, 148
Colonial Salish blanket, **224**, 308
Colorado River Indians
  Mojave, 148, 198, 246, 267–271, **269**, **270**
  Yuma, 148, 198, 267, 283–285, **284**
Columbia River Indians, 148, 216–218, 267, 338
  Chinook, 305–307
  Sanpoil–Nespelem, 216, 230–231
  Yakima, 216, 235–239
Colville, 230
Comanche, 104–106, 116, 153
  children's clothing, **105**
Comb, **318**
Coming-of-Age Dance, 253
Comox, 307
Conchas, 103, 118, 125, 155, 166, 173, 179, 203
Condor, 251, 255, 263, 266, 283, 286, 288
Condor cult, 251
Condor Dance, 283
Conoy, 49, 50
Contemporary clothing. *See* Transitional dress
Coos, 321, 322
Coosa, 18
Copper Eskimo, 401–404, **401**, **403**, 412
  dance costumes, **402**
copper knives, 360
copper ornamentation
  Northeastern, 44, 48, 50, 59, 65, 68, 70, 75, 77
  Northwest Coast, 297, 302, 304, 306, 311, 314, 315, 319, 325, 328, 331, 339
  pigment, 308, 316
  Plains, 103, 123, 142
  Plateau, 229
  shields, 299
  Southeastern, 7, 9, 13, 24, 27, 30, 33
  Subarctic, 348, 352
Copper People, 353
Coquille, 321
Coral, 151, 152
Cordage fringes, 11
Corn Dance, 153, 163
Cornhusk bag, 212–213, 215, **215**, **227**, 229
Cornhusk mask, **57**
Cornhusk moccasin, 49, 56
Costanoan, 251–253, **252**, 281
Coton, 264
Cottonwood bark, 175
Coushatta, 6
Cow Creek Indians, 28
Cowasuck, 45
Cowboy boots, 119
Cowichan, 307
Cowlitz, 338, 339
Cowrie shells, 93, 95, 101, 120, 137, 140, 238
Coyote (or "dog") blankets, 279, 306, 308, 325, 327, 328, 338
Coyote Dance, 260
Cradle board
  Californian, 267
  Eskimo, 420
  Great Basin, **203**, 204
  Southwestern, 151, 162, 174
Crawling Around Man Dance, 53
Cree, 131, 353, 369, 423
  Eastern, 355–357, 377
  half-breeds (Métis), 363
  Plains, 131–133, 355
  Western, 355, 376–378
Creek, 6, 18–20, 35

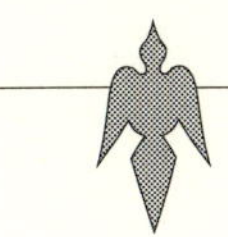

Confederacy, 8
    Seminole, 28
Crochet, 256
Crow bows, 109
Crow Indians, 98, 103, 107–111, **107**, **110**, 219, 226
    girl's dress, **108**
Crow Owners Society, 140
Crow stitch, 110
Crowns, 16
Curing rites
    Eskimo, 400, 411
    Plateau, 220
    Southwestern, 162, 174
    Subarctic, 376
Curling iron, 109
Curtis, Edward S., 84, 100, 107, 153, 158, 175, 177, 210, 223, 226, 247, 305, 307, 313, 315, 324, 384, 424
Cushing, Frank Hamilton, 10, 11
Czechoslovakian shawls, 159, 178, 183

Dakota Sioux, 111–113, 133
Dance costumes
    Apache, 155, 156, 158, 168–169
    Californian, 246, 248, 250–341, **250**, **252**, 253, 255, **255**, **256**, 260, 263, 266, 267, 273, 275, 277, 279, 281, 283, 288
    Eskimo, 397, 402, **402**, 413, 420, 429
    Great Basin, 197
    Mandan, **122**
    Northeastern, 66
    Northwest Coast, 299, 300, 304, 306, 309, 312, 322, 328, 333
    Plains, 86, 90–91, 95, 98, 103, 110, 119, 126, 135, 140
    Plateau, 220
    Puebloan, 161, 163, 164, 166, 184
    Southeastern, 17
    Southwestern, 153, 176
    Subarctic, 352
Dance mittens, 397
De Batz, A., 16, 20–21
De Bry, Theodore, 27, 265
De Saint Memin, Balthazar Fevret, 126
De Suria, Tomas, 251, 317, 329
Deer Dance, 184, 322
Deer head mask, 67, 323, 366
Deer hoof belt, 251
Deer hoof necklace, 275
Deer hoof rattle, 362
Deer leg shirt, 124, 128
Deer tail dress
    Great Basin, 202
    Plains, 96, 107, 120, 132, 135
    Plateau, 214, 219, 228, 233, 235
Deerskin Dance, 288
Delaware, 49–51
    pouch, **50**
Dentalium shell ornamentation
    Californian, 248, 252, 253, **254**, 255, 258, 275
    Eskimo, 427
    Northwest Coast, 297, 302, 306, 309, 314, 317, 319, 322, 323, 325, 328, 336, 339
    Plains, 115, 123, 139
    Plateau, 220, 222, 231
    Subarctic, 352, 355, 376
Diamonds, 13
Diegueño, 261, 264
Digger Indians, 189
Dog company (Ute), 204
Dog Dancers, 110
Dog hair (or coyote) blankets, 306, 308, 325, 327, 328, 338
Dog Men Society, 103
Dog Society, 98
Dolls, **202**
    kachina, 160–161, 181
Dorset Eskimo, 349
Drilling technique, **179**
Duffel, 400, 414
Duwamish, 324

Eagle-claw necklace, 281
Eagle Dance, 17, 263
Eagle feather fans, 92, 95, 97, 109, 113, 115, 118, 123, 139, 166, 222, 225, 331
Eagle-head headdress, 138
Eagle-skin mantle, 59, 287
Ear ornamentation
    Aleut, 388
    Californian, 246, 248, 250, 252–253, 255, 262, 266, 268, 273, 275, 277, 279, 281, 285, 287
    Eskimo, 385, 391, 397, 410, 411, 413, 419, **426**, 427
    Great Basin, 191, 192, 196, 199, 204
    Northeastern, 50, 52, 57, 59, 63, 66, **72**, 74–77
    Northwest Coast, 302, 306, 309, 311, 322, 325, 328, 331, 339
    Plains, 86, 90, 103, 106, 109–110, 115, 123, 125, 127, 130, 133, **134**
    Plateau, 222, **227**, 231
    Puebloan, 166, 179
    Southeastern, 7, 10, 19, 21, 24, 27, 30, 32, 33, 35, 37
    Southwestern, 151, 157, 173
    Subarctic, 362, 368, 376, 378
Eastern Abenaki, 42
Eastern Apache, 153
Eastern Cree, 355–357, 377
Eastern Shoshone, 193
Eastman, Seth, 111
Elbow-style snowshoes, 367
elk moccasins, 15
elk robes, 73, 195, 203, 215
elk teeth, **89**, 95, 101, 108, 109, 110, 120, 137, 193, 195
elk-hide armor. *See* Armor
elk-hock boot, 56
elk-horn purse, 248, 255, 287
elk-skin headgear, 229, 279
Embroidery. *See* Moose-hair embroidery
Ericson, 247, 254
Erie, 54
Ermine skins, 98, 195, **298**, 331, 336
Ermine tails, 105, 110, 123, 130, 182, 238, 386
Eskimo, 359, 367, 383–386
    Asiatic (Siberian), 390–393
    Baffin Island, 393–395, **393**, **394**, 407, 412, 421

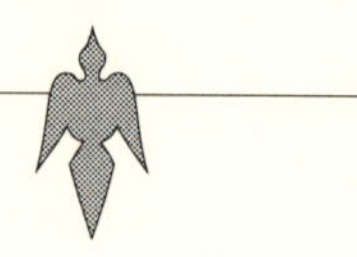

Bering Strait, 392, 395–398
Caribou, 398–401, **398, 400**
Chugach, 418
Copper, 384, 401–404, **401, 402, 403,** 412
Dorset, 349
Greenland, 404–406, **405**
Iglulik, 407–408, 421, 422
kayaking garments, 385, 387, 394, 402, 405, 411, 414, 425, 427
Koniag, 418–420
Kotzebue Sound, 408–410
Labrador, 410–412
Mackenzie Delta, 412–414
Netsilik, 414–415
North Alaska (Tagiugmiut and Nunamiut), 415–417
Nunivak Island, 424–429, **426, 428**
Pacific, 418–420
Polar, 421–422
Quebec Inuit, 411
Southwest Alaska, 424–429, **425, 426**
St. Lawrence Island, 390–393
Yupik, 357
See also specific tribes and groups (list on page 383)
Esopus, 49
European styles. *See* Transitional dress
Eyak, 329, 330, 374
Eye protection
shades or visors, 90, 92, 97, 102, 109, 132, 159, 258, 275, 312, 327, 385
snow goggles, 195, 377, 385, 388, 391, 395, 399, **401,** 402, 406, 407, 409, 411, 413, 415, 417, 422, 423, 427

Face and body painting
Apache, 155, 169
Californian, 246, 251, 253, 256, 258, 260, 263, 267, 271, 274, 275, 278, 279, 283, 285
children, 167
Eskimo, 392, 397, 420
Great Basin, 192, 197, 199, 204
Northeastern, 45, 48, 51, 53, 55, 57, 60, 61, 63, 65, 70, 74, 76, 77
Northwest Coast, 300, 306, 309, 312, 316, 320, 323, 326, 328, 333, 339
Plains, 87, 91, 93, 95, 99, 103, 106, 110, 113, 115–116, 119, **122,** 123–124, 126, 127, 131, 133, 140, 142
Plateau, 213, 216, 220, 223, 225, 230, 231, 235, **237,** 238
prostitutes, 20
Southeastern, 8, 9, 10, 11, 16, 17, 18, 20, 26, 28, 33, 36
Southwestern, 153, 162, 176
Southwestern (Puebloan), 164, 167, 181
Subarctic, 349, 350, 352, 357, 362, 366, 369, 376, 378
Facial hair
Arctic, 388, 395, 399, 402, 405, **405,** 407, 409, 413, 415, 427
Californian, 249, 252, 254, 259, 266, 268, 277, 279, 280
Great Basin, 203
Northwest Coast, 297, 306, 308, 314, 318, 322, 325, 327, 338
Plains Indians, 105, 122, 130, 142
Plateau, 231
Southeastern, 21, 24
Southwestern, 154
Subarctic, 354, 368, 370, 377
Fans
Northeastern, 48, 74, 75
Northwest Coast, 319, 331
Plains, 86, 90, 92, 95, 97, 102, 109, 113, 115, 118, 123, 130, **130,** 139
Plateau, 222, 225
Puebloan, 166
Southeastern, 17, 21, 34, 36
Feather capes and robes
Californian, 251, 252, 259, 260, 266, 273, 283
Great Basin, 190
Northeastern, 49, 51, 56
Northwest Coast, 307
Southeastern, 6–7, 9, 12, 17, 19, 21, 23, 27, 28, 33, 36
Southwestern, 150, 163
Feather Dance, 248, 283
Feather fans. *See* Fans
Feather headdresses
"Big Head," 273, 283
Californian, **245,** 246, **252,** 255, 256, 260, 262, 266, 275, 277, 281, 288, **288**
Great Basin, 195, 199, 203
halo-style, 85
Northeastern, 44, 48, 54, 56, 59, 64–67, 74
Northwest Coast, 322, 323
Plains, 85, 97, 105–106, 109, **121,** 122–123, 125, 130, **130,** 138, 140
Plateau, 212, 222, 225, 228, 236
Southeastern, 7, 13, 15, 17, 19, 21, 24, 30, 34, 36
Southwestern, 150, 166
Subarctic, 348, 364, 371, 377
See also Warbonnets
Feather skirts or kilts, **199,** 253, 263
Feathered circle, 85
Fernandiños, 261
Finger masks, 302, 386, 398, 429
First Fruits Dance, 266
First Grass Dance, 253
First Salmon Dance, 306
First Salmon Feast, 322
Fish bladder, 35
Fish skin
bags of, 352, 419
boots and moccasins of, 351, 358, 375
garments of, 351, 358, 375, 416, 423, 425
mittens of, 427
Five Nations, 55
Fixed warp frame, 308
Flaherty, Robert, 423
Flathead, 210
Floated warp belts, 179
Flower Dance, 260
Flute Dance, 161
Fly brush, 125
Fool Dance, 95
Forest Potawatomi, 67
Fort Marion, Florida, 100
Fossil ornamentation, 90
Fox, Nancy, 162

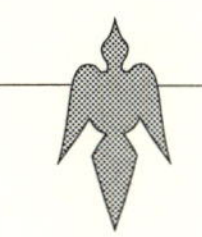

Fox Indians, 51–53, 70
chiefs of, **71**
Fox skin
capes of, 277
headdress of, 44, 396–397, 427
parka of, 387, 421, 423
Foxtail, 47
Fremont culture, 289
Fremont moccasin, 190
Friendship bags, 60, 212–213, **212**, **215**, 229, **237**
Frontlet headdress, 304, 312, 315, 331, 336
Fur mosaic, 358, 359, 386, 422, 429

Gabrieliño, 261
Gallice, 321
Games, 16, 17
Gan Dancers, 155, 156, 158, 168–169
Gardner, Alexander, 84, 88
Garnet, 262
Garters
Northeastern, 42, 44, 46, 48, 50, 56, 59, 65, 66, 74
Northwest Coast, 325, 331
Plains, 102, 106, 109, 115, 125, 126, 133
Plateau, 231, 233, 238
Seminole, **29**
Southeastern, 10, 15, 17, 18, 19, 21, 22, 24, 30, 36
Southwestern, 159
Subarctic, 348, 356, 360, 370, 371, 377
Gauntlets
Eskimo, 429
Great Basin, 197
Plains, 99
Plateau, 213, 225
Ghost Dance, 119, 260, 277, 279, 281, 283
Gibbs, George, 286
Gitksan, 334, 351, 352
Glengarry-style hat, 58, **373**
Gloves
Aleut, 388
Californian, 275
Eskimo, 406, 409
Subarctic, 348, 375–376, 378
See also Gauntlets; Mittens
Goat wool robes and blankets, 221, 223, 306, 308, 310, 325, 332, 335, 338
Goggles, 195, 377, 385, 388, 391, 395, 399, **401**, 402, 406, 407, 409, 411, 413, 415, 417, 422, 423, 427
Gold ornamentation
Northwest Coast, 301, 302, 312
Southeastern, 30, 34
Gorgets
abalone, 260
Californian, 246, 260
ivory, 417
Northeastern, 48, 57, 61, 63, 65, 68, 77
Plains, 86, 115, 123, 127, 133, 139
Puebloan, 166, 183
Southeastern, 7, 9, 11, 16, 19, 30, 35
Gosiute, 193
Gourd stitch, 119
Government medals. *See* Peace medals

Grand Pawnee, 128
Grass Dance, 95, 98, 126, 197
Great Basin Indians, 189–204
See also specific tribes and groups (list on page 189)
Great Osage, 126
Green Corn Dance, 20, 283
Greenland Eskimo, 404–406, **405**
Grinnell, George Bird, 100
Grizzly-bear claw, 52, 53, 74, 77, 86, 92, 95, 98, 113, 115, 123, 125, 133, 139, 336. *See also* Bear-claw ornamentation
Grizzly-bear skin, ceremonial costume, 131
Gros Ventre of the Prairies, 88, 96
Gros Ventre of the River, 107
Gutskin cases, 331
Gutskin garments, 318, 385, 387–390, **391**, 394, 396, 405, 411, 416, 419, 423, 427
recent styles, 393
shaman's parka, 386
Gutskin hats, 388, 427

Haida, 294, 310–312, **311**, 329, 331, 335
Hair bow, 86, 123
Hair cutting techniques, 36, 90, 92, 125. *See also* Hair styles
Hair nets, 254, 259, 260, 266, 267, 273, 275, 277, 278, 282, 283, 289
Hair plates, 88, 106, 139, **201**, 203
Hair sticks, **161**, 399, 407, 415
Hair styles
Aleut, 388
Californian, 246, 249, 257, 262, 268, 282, 286
Californian (Athapaskan speakers), 247, 254
Californian (Hokan speakers), 272, 275, 279, 284
Californian (Penutian speakers), 252, 259, 266, 277, 280
Carrier wig, 352, **352**
cedar-bark headband, 308
for children, 275
chongo, 152, 159, 163, 171, **172**, 173, 179
clan distinctions, 115
curling, 119
Eskimo, 385, 390, 394–395, 396, 399, 402, 405, 407, 409, 411, 413, 415, 416, 419, 421, 423, 427
Great Basin, 190, 192, **194**, 195, 198, 203
lengthening with human or animal hair, 94, 109, 118, 122, 137, 215, 311, 330
Navajo, 171, **172**, 173
Northeastern, 44, 46, 47–48, 50, 52, 54, 56, 59, 61, 62–63, 64, 66, 68, 73–74, 75, 77
Northwest Coast, 297, 302, 306, 308, 311, 314, **318**, 328, 322, 325, 327, 330, 335, 338
Plains, 85, 88–90, 91, 92, 94–95, 97, 102, 103, 105, 109, 112, 115, 118, 122, 125, 127, 130, 132, 137
Plateau, 212, 224–225, **232**, 233, **236**
Plateau (Salishan-speaking), 217, 219, 221–222, 231, 236
Plateau (Shahaptian-speaking), 215, 217, 228, 236
Powhatan, **22**
Sauk, **73**
shamans, 7, 333
Southeastern, 7, 9, 10, 11, 12–14, 15, 17, 19, 21, 24, 27, 28, 30, 32, 33, 34, 36
Southwestern, 150, 171, 173, 175–176
Southwestern (Apache), 154, 157, 166, 168

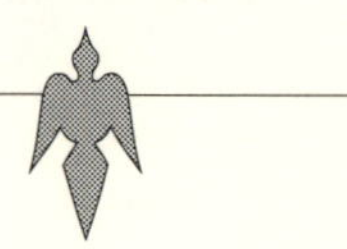

Southwestern (Puebloan), 152, 159, **160, 161,** 163, 179, 183
spiked, 248
squash blossom, 159, **160, 161**
Subarctic, 348
Subarctic (Algonquian speakers), 350, 356, 365, 368, 377
Subarctic (Athapaskan speakers), 351–352, 354, 358, 360, 370, 372, 375
tonsure, 19, 21, 385, 390, 396, 409, 413
war, 7, 34, 48, 63, 68, 77, 142, 248, 260, 285
See also Mourning customs; Roach; Transitional dress

Hair tie, 10, 154, 157, 166
Hairpins, 246, 250, 252, 272, 273
Hairpipe breastplates
Apache, 168
Great Basin, 195, 203
Plains, **90,** 95, **100,** 102, 106, 119, 139, 140
Plateau, 220, 238
Puebloan, 166

Hairpipe ornamentation
Apache, 157
Great Basin, 203
Northeastern, 59
Plains, 86, 93, 118, 123, 133, **139**
Puebloans, 183
Southwestern, 155

Haisla, 313
Halchidoma, 267, 283
Halkett, John, **398,** 399
Halo headdress, 85. *See also* Feather headdresses; Warbonnets
Hamatsa Society Dance, 315
Hand symbolism, 135, 137
Hanis Coos, 321
Hans, 359
Harriot, Thomas, 27
Head deformation. *See* Skull deformation
Headgear
albino bison fur, **120**
animal disguise (for hunting), 44, 46, 67, 132, 169, 355, 419
Arctic, 385, 388, 391, 396–397, 405, 416, 419, 427
badger-fur cap, 95
bark, 11
bear-claw, 77
beaver-skin, 309
bentwood hunting hat, 388, 397, 419, 427
birchbark hat, 46, 66, 366
birdskin cap, 20, 322, 396, 417, 419
buffalo head, 123
Californian, **245,** 246, 249, 258, 262, 282, 287
Californian (Athapaskan speakers), 247–248, 254
Californian (Hokan speakers), 275, 279, 284–285
Californian (Penutian speakers), 252, 259, 266, 277, 280
Cherokee turban, **12**
child's, **70,** 159
clan, **311,** 312, **330**
cornhusk, 229
eagle-head, 138
Eskimo, 417, 420
for Eskimo babies, 385, 391, 395
for Fox, Sauk, and Ioway chiefs, **71**
frontlet headdress, 304, 312, 315, 331, 336
Glengarry-style bonnet, 58, **373**
gold, 11
Great Basin, 190, 192, 195, 199
gut-skin, 388, 427
hair nets, 254, 259, 260, 266, 267, 273, 275, 277, 278, 282, 283, 289
hooded, 66, 67
human hair, 309
Medicine Hat, 103
Métis medicine hat, 364
Mexican-style, 154, 166, 203
moose-hump, 46
mountain-goat head, 325
mushroom-shaped hat, 308, 327
Navajo, 173
netting, 15
Northeastern, 44, 46, 48, 50, 52, 54, 56, 59, 61, 63, 64–65, 66, 68, **71,** 74
Northwest Coast, **296,** 297, **298,** 302, 306, 308, 311, 314, 315, 318–319, 322, 325, 327, 330, **330,** 331, 335–336, 338
otter-fur turban, **43,** 52, 59, 68, 74, 86, **114,** 115, 118, 125, 127, 130, 168
palm-leaf, 11, 30, 34
pillbox style, 354, 370, 362, 419
Plains, 85–86, 90, 92, 95, 97, 102, 105–106, 109, 112–115, **114,** 118, **121,** 122–123, 125, 127, 130, 132, 138
Plateau, 212, **214, 215,** 225, **228,** 233
Plateau (Salishan speakers), 217, 219, 222, 231, 236
Plateau (Shahaptian speakers), 215, 217, 228–229, 236
potlatch rings, **311,** 315, 319, 330, **330,** 331, 336, 419
rabbit-skin hat, 348, 352
sharpheads, 309
silver, 9, 61
smoking hat, 362
snakeskin, 24, 50
Southeastern, 7, 9, 10, 13, 15, 17, 19, 21, 24, 27, 28, 30, **31,** 32, 34, 36
Southwestern, 150, 173, 176
Southwestern (Apache), 154, 157, 166, 168
Southwestern (Puebloan), 152, 159, 160, 163, 179, 183
stuffed animal, 34
Subarctic, 348, 350, 364, 362, **373**
Subarctic (Algonquian speakers), 350, 356, 365–366, 368, 377
Subarctic (Athapaskan speakers), 352, 354, 358, 360, 370, 372, **373,** 375
sun visors, 212, 258, 275, 327, 385, 389, 413
tall "Indian hat," 86, 99, 197, 203, 218
threads, 15
war cap, 155, 168, 173
wedding attire, 233, **238**
Western-style hat, 154, 166
whaler's hat, 306, 318, **319,** 320, 327
wolf's head cap, 228
wolf-skin cap, 95
See also Basketry hats; Feather headdresses; Horned headdresses; Turbans; Warbonnets

Heiltsuk, 313
Helmets
Aleut, 388
Nez Perce, 229

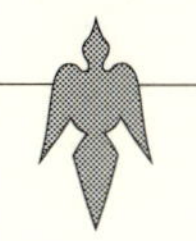

Northwest Coast, 299, 304, 306, 312, 322, 331, 336
seal decoy, 419
Subarctic, 374
Hesselius Gustav, 49
Hidatsa, 107, 110, 119
Hillers, John K., 84, 198
Hiqua, 297
Hock boot, 44, 46, 56, 190, 327
Hoh, 326, 338
Hohokam culture, 147
Hoods, 66, 67, 348, 350, 356, 375. *See also* Headgear; Parkas
Hoofprint designs, 94
Hoonah, 330
Hopi, 158–162, **160, 161,** 177, 183
Horned headdresses
Apache, 168
Northeastern, 48, 52, 67, 73, 77
Northwest Coast, 333, 336
Plains, 86, 95, 97, 102, 103, 106, 109, 113, 115, 122–123, 132, 138
Plateau, 219
Southwestern, 157
Subarctic Cree, 378
Horse paint, 216
Horsehair embroidery, 349
Horses society, 119
Horseshoe symbolism, 135
Horse trappings, **214**
Houma, 6
Hourglass motif, 97
Houser, Allan, 156
Housewife bag, 419
Huchnom, 282
Hudson's Bay blankets, 48, 55, 60, 63, 65, 87, 93, 97, 99, 103, 111, 132, 140, 224, 226, 301, 304, 305, 308, 309, 316, 333, 334, 353
Human hair
belts of, 277, 279
cordage of, 150
garments of, 149
hats of, 309
Human scalp tippet, 217
Humptulip, 338
Hunkpapa, 135
Hupa, 247, 253–257, **254,** 286
Huron, 53–55
Lorette, 54
moccasins, **54**

Iglulik Eskimo, 407–408, 421
Illinois confederacy, 60
Indian gold, 273
Indian hemp garments, 49, 149, 221, 230, 248
Ingalik, 357–359
Interior Salish, 220–223, **221, 222,** 224
Inua, 397–398
Inuit, 383
Polar, 421–422
Quebec, 411, 422–424
See also Eskimo
Iowa chief, 71
Ioway, **114,** 114–116
Ipais, 261
Iron implement for tattooing, 26
Iron ornamentation
Eskimo, 410
Northwest Coast, 297, 311, 314, 331, 336
Ironwood armor, 306
Iroquois, 42, 55–58, 225, 356, 367
masks, **57**
Northern (Huron), 53–55
Plateau, 235
Ishi, 278–279
Ivory, 331, 385, 397, 408, 410, 413, 422
armor, 386, 392, 410
chestpiece, 417
cleats, 390
mammoth, 392

Jackson, William Henry, 84
Jaclah, 173
Jasper, 262
Jemez, 162–164
Jewelry
Aleut, 388
Blackfoot, **98**
buffalo bull's tails, 103
Californian, 246, 248, 250, 252, 255, 258, 259–260, 262–263, 266, 268–269, 272–273, 275, 279, 281, 282, 285, 287
Eskimo, 385, 391, 395, 397, 399–400, 406, 408, 409–410, 411, 413, 417, 419–420, 422, 424, **426**
Great Basin, 191, 192, 195–196, 199, 203–204
lip ornamentation (labrets), 348
Northeastern, 44, 46, 52, 54, 56–57, 59, 61, 63, 65, 66, 68, 74, 75–76
Northwest Coast, 297, 301, 302, 306, 309, 311, 314, 319, 322, 325, 328, 331, 336, 339
Plains, 86, 90, 92–93, 95, 98, 102–103, 106, 109–110, 113, 115, 118–119, 123, 125, 130, 133, 139, 142
Plateau, 213, 215–216, 217–218, 220, 222, 225, 229, 231, 233–235, 238
semi-precious stones, 262
Southeastern, 7, 9, 13, 16, 17, 19, 21, 24, 30, 33, 35, 36
Southwestern, 151, 176
Southwestern (Apache), 155
Southwestern (Navajo), 173
Southwestern (Puebloan), 152–153, 160, 163, 166, 179, 183
Subarctic, 348, 350, 352, 355, 357, 358, 360, 362, 366, 368, 371, 374, 376
See also Ear ornamentation; Necklaces; Nose ornamentation; *specific types and materials*
Jew's harp pendant, **269,** 270
Jicarilla Apache, 153, 164–167, **164, 165,** 200
Joseph, Chief, 226
Joshua tree, 198
Juaneño, 261
Jumano, 141, 142
Jumping Dance, 255, 288, **288**
Juniper bark garments, 190

Kabotie, Fred, 158
Kachina, 160–161, 181
Kahoki, 60
Kaibab Paiute, 197
Kaigani, 310
Kainah, 96
Kalapooia, 321
Kamiks, 405
Kamleika, 387–388, 389, **391**, 396, 419, **426**, 427.
    See also Gutskin garments; Parkas
Kane, Paul, 59, 67, 84, 94, 216, 305, 307, 308, 309, 339, 346, 377, 378
Kansas, 124, 126
Karankawa, 141
Karok, 286
Kasehta, 18
Kaska, 372
Kaskaskia, 60
Kathlamet, 338
Kayaking garments, 385, 387, 394, 402, 405, 411, 414, 425, 427
Kent, Kate Peck, 162
Key Marco, 10, 11
Khonba, 390
Kickapoo, **43**
Kicked-in-the-Bellies Crow, 107
Kidney membrane slipper, 387
Kilts
    Californian, 244, 249, 253, **254**, 259, 264, 274, 277, 279
    feathered, 263
    Northeastern, 56
    Southwestern, 148, 158, 161, 166
    Southwestern (Pueblo), **150**, 151, 177, 181
    Subarctic, 367, 372
    Yakima, 235
King, Charles Bird, 8, 12, 18, 47, 52, 74, 75, 76, 114, 116, 124, 128, 130
Kiowa, 104, 116–119, **117**
Kiowa Apache, 116, 153
Kishquaki, 52
Kit Fox Society, 98, 103, 110, 115, 123, 140
Kitunahan speakers, 223
Klamath, 257–258, 276
Klatskanie, 321
Klickitat, 231
Klokwalle, 328
Klookwalli ceremony, 340
Knife sheaths
    Northeastern, 50, 59, 61
    Northwest Coast, 331
    Plains, 86, 95, **102**, 113, 123, 133, 139
    Subarctic, 348, 360, 370, **373**, 374, 376
Kodiak Island, 418
Koniag, 418–420
Konkow Maidu, 259, 260
Koshares, 161, 181
Kotzebue Sound Eskimo, 408–410
Krieghoff, Cornelius, 346
Kristenaux, 131
Kroeber, A., 278
Krok, **245**
Kuchin, 359–362
Kuksu, 260, 266, 267, 277, 278, 279
Kuliktot, 414
Kupsuck, 393, 398, 410, 415, 417, 429
Kurz, Rudolph Friederich, 84, 94, 107, 114, 132
Kusiut, 304
Kutchin, **361**
Kutenai, 209, 210, 212, 223–225, **224**
Kwakiutl, 294, 300, 301, 309, 313–316, 331
    mask, **314**, **315**
    Northwest Coast, 304
Kwalhioqua, 338

Labrador Eskimo, 410–412
Labrets, 348
    Aleut, 388
    Eskimo, 385, 392, 397, 409–410, 412, 413, 417, 420, **426**, 427
    Northwest Coast, 297, 299, 304, 311, 315, 319, 331, 336
    Plains, 142
    Southeastern, 7, 11
    Subarctic, 348, 352, 358, 359
Lace, 406
Laguna, **149**, 151, 177
Lake Athapaskans, 359
Lake Indians, 220
Lakehead people, 353
Lakota (Teton) Sioux, 15, 111, 133–140
Larocque, Francois, 107
Lassik, 247
Latham, Edward, 210
Le Moyne, Jacques, 34
Leggings
    beaver, 365
    buffalo-hair, 15
    Californian, 244, 254, 257, 259, 272, 274, 279, 286
    Great Basin, 190, 191, 193, 198, 200–201, **201**
    human hairlocks, 128, 135, 149
    Kickapoo, **43**
    Northeastern, 42, 45–46, 47, 49, 52, 54, 56, 59, 61, 62, 64, 66, 67, 72, 75, 76
    Northwest Coast, 295, 317, 321, 327, 329, 333, 335
    Plains, 84, 88, 92, 94, 95, 96, 100, 104, 107, 112, 114, 116, **117**, 120, 124, 126, 128, 132, 135
    Plateau, 210, 224, **232**, **236**
    Plateau (Salishan speakers), 216, 219, 221, 230
    Plateau (Shahaptian-speaking), 214, 216, 226
    salmon-skin, 351, 358
    Seminole, **29**
    skunk-skin, 135
    Southeastern, 6, 8, 9, 10, 12, 18, 21, 23, 32, 33, 35
    Southwestern, 148–149, 170, 175
    Southwestern (Apache), 154, **155**, 157, 165, 167
    Southwestern (Puebloan), 151, 158, 159, 163, 177, 182
    strouding, 111
    Subarctic, 346–347, 349, 351, 354, 356, 363, 365, 367, 369, 372, 377
    "whole deerskin" pattern, 92
    wolf-skin, 132
Lewis, James Otto, 47, 52, 60, 67, 75, 76, 135
Lillooet, 220, 221, 223

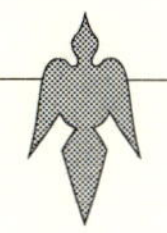

Lip ornamentation (labrets), 348
Lipan Apache, 153
Little Osage, 126
Llanero, 164
Lone Chief, **129**
Looking-glass boards, 123, 127, 130
Looms
  for beadwork, 349
  for beltmaking, 173, 179
  Californian, 264
  Chilkat blanket weaving, 332
  fixed warp frame loom, 308
  Navajo, **172**
  Northwest Coast, 295, 308, 320
  Pueblo, 179
  for quillwork, 356, 371
  rabbit-skin robe making, 192, 285
  Southeastern, 13
  Southwestern, 148, 159
  Subarctic, 349, 355, 371
Lorette Huron, 54
Loup Pawnee, 128
Lower Kutenai, 223–225
Lowie, Robert, 107
Lowlands People (Plains Cree), 131
Luckiamute, 321
Luiseño, 261
Lumbee, 6
Lummi, 324, 325

MacCauley, Clay, 30
Mackenzie Delta Eskimo, 412–414
Magnesite, 266, 272–273, 276, 277, 279, 282
Mah-to-to-pa, 120, **121,** 123
Maiden shawls, 181
Maidenhair fern, 87, 255, 256, 277, 286
Maidu, 259–260, 279
Makah, 317–320, 338, 340
Malecite, 65
Maltese Cross motif, 91
Mammoth ivory, 392
Mandan, 119–123, **120, 121, 122**
Mangas, 264
Mantas, 151–152, **152,** 158–159 163, 177–178, **180,** 181, 182
Maple bark, 286
Maricopa, 174, 175
Marmot robes, 313, 330
Mary's River, 321
Mascouten, 60, 67
Masks
  Aleut, 389
  animal head, 169, 253, 283, 323, 366
  Apache, 156, 158, 169
  cornhusk, 57
  Eskimo, 386, 395, 397–398, 406, 412, 417, 420, 427–429, **428**
  finger, 386, 398, 429
  Iroquois, **57**
  Northeastern, 53, 57, 66, 67
  Northwest Coast, 300–301, 304, 309, **314,** 315, **315,** 316, 320, 323, 328, 333, **335, 337,** 338, 340
  Plains, 95
  Southeastern, 8, 11, 14
  Southwestern, 162, 174
  Southwestern (Puebloan), 164, 181, 184
  Subarctic, 352, 355, 358–359, 366, 369, 376
  transformation, 301, 312, 315, 316, 320, 397–398, 429
  wind, 395
  wolf, 309, 340
Matachine Dance, 163
matchcoats
  Northeastern, 49
  Southeastern, 6, 9, 12, 23, 27, 33
Mattole, 247, 248
Maurer, 228
Mdewakanton, 111
Medals. *See* Peace medals
Medicine bags. *See* Bags
Medicine hat, 222, 309
Medicine man. *See* Ceremonial costumes; Shamans and medicine men
Medicine Mask Dance, 309
Memin, Balthazar Fevret de Saint, 126
Menomini, 58–60
Menstruation customs
  Californian, 253
  Eskimo, 397
  Southwestern, 157
  Subarctic, 348–349, 352, 359, 362, 368, 374, 376
Merrow, S. J., 92
Mescal fiber sandals, 268
Mescalero Apache, 153, 167–169
Messenger Feast, 417
Métis, **354,** 363–364
  coat, **363**
Mexican influences, 6, 154, 156, 264
Miami, 60–61
Michigami, 60
Micmac, 65, 349, 364–366
  persecution of Beothuck, 349, 350
Midewiwin, 48, 52, 63, 77
Mikhailov, Pavel, 384
Mikosuki, 6, 28
Milkweed-fiber garments, 27, 251, 260, 326
Miller, Alfred James, 107, 135, **138**
Miluk Coos, 321
Minneconjous, 135
Mirrors, 123, 127, 130, 216
Mission Indians of California, 261–265, **262, 263**
Mississquoi, 45
Mittens
  Aleut, 388
  bear-paw, 385
  dance costume, 397
  Eskimo, 385, 391, 395, 397, 399, 402, 405–406, 407, 409, 411, 413, 415, 417, 422, 423–424, 427
  fish-skin, 427
  Northeastern, 48
  Northwest Coast, 309, 331
  Plains, 95, 97, 133
  Plateau, 222, 225
  polar-bear, 402, 405

sealskin, 405–406
Subarctic, **345,** 348, 350, 352, 354, 356, 358, 360, 364, 366, 368, 370, 374, 375, 377
Miwok, 251, 265–267, **267**
Moccasins
animal-hock, 190, 327
bear-fur, 15, 27, 280, 335
buckskin, 12
bullnose, 54
Californian, 244, 257, 262, 286
Californian (Athapaskan speakers), 247, 254
Californian (Hokan speakers), 272, 275, 279
Californian (Penutian speakers), 259, 265, 280
caribou, 302
Cheyenne, **100**
children's, 125, 157, 168
cornhusk, 49, 56
of dewclaws, 190
elk-skin, 15
Eskimo, 399, 409, 411, 414
Fremont, 190
Great Basin, 190, 192, 195, 198, 202
Huron, **54**
Métis, 364
marmot, 351
mescal-fiber, 268
moose, 302
mukluks, 347, 358, 360
Navajo, 170
Northeastern, 42–44, 46, 47, 49, 52, 54, 56, 59, 61, 62, 64, 66, 67, 72–73, 75, 76
Northwest Coast, 295, 302, 305, 307, 310, 317, 321, 324, 327, 330, 335, 338
partridge, 62
Plains, 84–85, 88, 92, 94, 97, 101, 104–105, 109, 112, 114, 118, 120, 122, 125, 127, 128, 130, 132, 137
Plateau, 210, 224, 233
Plateau (Salishan-speaking), 217, 219, 221, 230, 236
Plateau (Shahaptian-speaking), 214–215, 217, 228, 236
pointed, 112, 132
puckered toe, 30, 42, 47, 54, 62, 64, 66, 92, 112, 377
salmon-skin, 351, 358
sealskin, 335, 365, 367, 377
Seminole, **29**
Southeastern, 6, 9, 10, 12, 17, 19, 21, 23, 27, 30, 33, 34, 35
Southwestern, 149, 170
Southwestern (Apache), 154, 157, 165–166, 168
Southwestern (Puebloan), 159, 163, 178, 182–183
stocking, 21, 27, 62
Subarctic, 347, 350, 364
Subarctic (Algonquian speakers), 350, 356, 365, 367, 377
Subarctic (Athapaskan speakers), 351, 354, 360, 370, 372, 375
swamp, 6, 9, 10, 12, 23, 33, 36
tailed, 195
three-piece, 42–44, 46
two-piece, 56, 62
See also Boots; Transitional dress
Modoc, 257–258, 276
Mogollon, 148
Mohawk, 55
Mohawk hairstyle. *See* Roach
Mojave, 148, 198, 246, 267–271, **269, 270**
Mojave collar, 268, **270, 271**
Moki-stripe, 159
Molala, 321
Moleskin pants, 411
Mollhausen, H. B., 268
Mono, 191
Montagnais, 349, 356, 367–369, 411, 423
Moorhouse, Lee, 210
Moose Cree, 355
Moose moccasins and boots, 46, 302
Moose-hair embroidery
Métis ("half-breed"), 363, 364
Northeastern, 46, 54, **54,** 56, 59, 60, 63, 66, 68, 77
Subarctic, 349, 357, 363, 364, 366, 368, 371
Moose-head mask, 366
Moose hide
armor of, 95, 352
robes of, 46, 66
shields of, 304
shirt of, 356
Morning Star ceremony, 130, 131
Mosaics, 151
fur mosaic, 358, 359, 386, 422, 429
Moss garments, 19, 23, **24,** 27, 28, 33, 34, 141
Mountain Crow, 107
Mountain–goat skin armor, 374
Mountain–goat skin skirt, 94
Mountain Maidu, 259, 260
Mountain-lion skin, 160, 173
Mourning customs
Californian, 246, 248, 253, 255–256, 258, 260, 263, 266, **270,** 273, 275, 281, 283, 285
Eskimo, 406, 420, 422
Great Basin, 195, 197, 204
Northeastern, 45, 48, 52–53
Northwest Coast, 312, 315, 319, 322, 328, 333, 339
Plains, 87, 91, 98, 110, 113, 115, 119, 138, 140
Plateau, 223, 231
Puebloan, 164
Southeastern, 7
Southwestern, 164, 176
Subarctic, 349, 352, 355, 357, 362, 366, 371, 374
Mourning Dance, 253
Mouse-skin robes, 190
Muckleshoot, 324
Mud, as body covering, 251
Mudheads, 161, 181
Mukluks, 347, 358, 360, 384, **390,** 411, 419, 425
Mulberry bark, 6, 7, 16, 18–19, 33, 35–36
Multnomah, 305
Munsee, 49
Murray, Alexander, 359
Mushroom-shaped hat, 308, 327
Muskogee, 28
Muskrat fur, 19
Musquakie, 52
Mustaches. *See* Facial hair

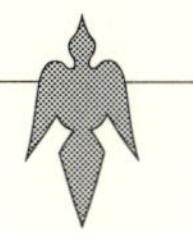

Naasit, 404
Na-Dene, 345
Nah-leen, 157
Nanook of the North, 423
Nanticoke, 49
Naskapi, 356, 357, 367–369, 411, 423
Natchez, 20–22
Navajo, 148, 151, 153, 158, 160, 169–174, **172, 173,** 183, 268
Navajo blankets, 106, 163, 166, 171, **171,** 183
Neagle, John, 128
Necklaces
  Arapaho, **89**
  Blackfoot, **98**
  Californian, 248, 252, 253, 255, 259–260, 266, 273, 279, 282, 285
  deer-hoof, 275
  Eskimo, 406, 413, 419–420, 424
  Great Basin, 191, 195–196, 199, 203
  mirror, 216
  mourning, 260
  Northeastern, 46, 54, 56, 59, 61, 66, 74, 75, 77
  Northwest Coast, 297, 302, 306, 309, 314, 319, 322, 325, 336, 339
  Plains, 95, 98, **98,** 103, 109–110, 113, 118, 123, 125, 127, 130, 133, **139**
  Plateau, 216, 222, 225, **227,** 229, 231, 233, **234, 236,** 238
  Southeastern, 7, 9, 19, 21, 24, 27, 35, 36, 37
  Southwestern, 153, 157, 173, 176
  Southwestern (Pueblo), **150,** 160, 166, 179, 183
  Subarctic, 352, 368, 371, 374, 378
  toenail, 314
  turtle bone, 118
  See also Bear-claw ornamentation
Needles, 384, 387, 422
Nelson, Edward, 396, **425**
Nespelem, 216, 230–231
Netsilik Eskimo, 414–415
Netting, 248
  bags, 272
  Californian, 248, 273
  hair nets, 254, 259, 260, 266, 267, 273, 275, 277, 278, 282, 283, 289
  human hair leggings, 149
  rabbit-skin robes, 356, 370, 371, 378
Nettle fiber garments, 59, 62, 64, 68, 72, 126, 221
Neutral Indians, 54
Newfoundland, 41, 349–350
Nez Perce, 210, 225–230, **226–229**
  Cayuse culture and, 213
Nicollet, Jean, 47, 58, 76
Night Way, 174
Nipple ornaments, 142
Nisenan, 259
Niskas, 334
Nisqually, 324
Nomlaki, 276
Noisemakers. *See* Tinklers
Nongatl, 247
Nooksack, 324
Nootka, 294, 300, 313, 317–320, **318,** 328
North Alaska Eskimo (Tagiugmiut and Nunamiut), 415–417
Northeast Maidu, 259
Northeastern Indians, 41–45, 75
  Abenaki, 45–46
  Algonquian speakers, 47–53, 58–76
  Iroquois speakers, 53–58
  Siouan speakers, 76–78
  See also specific groups and tribes (list on page 41)
Northern Molala, 321
Northern Ojibwa, 355
Northern Paiute, 190, 191–192
Northern Shoshone, 193
Northern Valley Yokuts, **281**
Northwest Coast Indians, 293–301
  Chinook speakers, 305–307
  Haida, 310–312
  Oregon, 321–323
  Quinault, 326–328
  Salishan speakers, 301–305, 307–310, 324–326, 338–340
  Tlingit, 329–334
  Tsimshian, 334–338
  Wakashan speakers, 312–320
  Washington Coast, 338–340
  See also specific tribes and groups (list on page 293)
Nose flattening, 267
Nose ornamentation
  Aleut, 388
  Californian, 246, 248, 250, 252–253, 260, 263, 266, 268, 273, 275, 277, 279, 281, 282, 285
  Eskimo, 385, 391, 392, 410, 413, 419, 427
  Great Basin, 196, 204
  Nez Perce, 225
  Northeastern, 48, 50, 52, 63, 65, 66, 75
  Northwest Coast, 297, 302, 306, 309, 311, 314, 319, 322, 328, 331, 336, 339
  Plains, 86, 103, 106, 127
  Plateau, 218, 222, 229, 235
  Southeastern, 9, 10, 13, 16, 19
  Southwestern, 151
  Subarctic, 348, 352, 360, 362, 371, 376, 378
Nunamiut, 416–417
Nunivak Island Eskimo, 424–429, **426**
  forehead mask, **428**

Obsidian, 191, 247, 248, 253, 288
Octopus bags, 229, 334, 348, 364, 370, 377
Oglala, 135
Ohlone, 251
Ojibwa, 47, 62, 355
  half-breeds (Métis), 363
  Okanagon, 220, 221
Old Pecos Bull Dance, 163
Olivella, 152
Olleros, 164
Omaha, 124–126
Omaha Dance, 126, 140
Oneida, 55
Onondaga, 55
Opal, 263
Opossum hair, 33
Oregon, Native Americans of, 294, 305, 321–323
  See also specific tribes and groups (list on page 293)

Organized Salish blankets, 308
Osage, 116, 124, 126–128
Oshkosh, 52
Ottawa, 47, 64–65, 67
Otter-fur turbans
Apache, 168
Kickapoo, **43**
Northeastern, 52, 59, 68, 74, **71**
Plains, 86, **114**, 115, 118, 125, 127, 130
Otter skin or fur
armor, 90
bags, 77, 125, 126
collar, 226
headdress, 44
pouch, 77
robes, 217, 252, 322, 327
turbans, **43**, 52, 59, 68, **71**, 74, 86, **114**, 115, 118, 125, 127, 130, 168
See also Sea otter skin
Ozette, 294, 308, 317, 320, 338

Pacific Eskimo, 418–420
Pacific Northwest. *See* Northwest Coast Indians
Padlermiut, 398
Paiute, **198**, **199**, 233, 267, 268
Kabib, 197
Northern, 190, 191–192
Southern, 197–200
Palmetto garments, 11, 28
Palm-leaf headgear, 11, 30, 34
Palouse, **211**
Pamlico, 26
Pamunkey, 22
Panamint, 191
Panther robes, 11, 13
Pants
Aleut, 387
birdskin, 423, 424
Californian, 264
Eskimo, 384, 394, 396, 399, 401, 402, **403**, 407, 409, 411, 412, 414, 421, 423, 424, 427
fish-skin, 425
moleskin, 411
polar-bear, 394, 421, 422, 423
sealskin, 384, 387, 396, 405
Southwestern, 170
Subarctic, 353, 356, 358, 360, 369, 372, 375
Papago, 148, 174
Parkas, 385, 387–388, 390, 393–405, 407, 409, 411–416, 419, 421–427
Baffin Island (16th century), **393**, **394**
ceremonial, 386, 408
amaat, 421–422
amautiks, 423
birdskin, 385, 387, 389, 390, 396, 405, 416, 421, 423, 424, 427
ceremonial attire, 388–389
children's, 413
Copper Eskimo, **401**, **402**, **403**
duffel, 400
fish-skin, 416, 423
recent styles, 393, 395, 424
kamleika (seal-gut), 385, 387–388, 389, 390, **391**, 393, 394, 396, 405, 411, 416, 419, 423, **426**, 427
kuliktot, 414
Southwestern Alaska, **425**
Subarctic, 348
Subarctic (Algonquian speakers), 356, 367
Subarctic (Athapaskan speakers), 354, 358, 375
wolverine ruff, 385, 394, 416, 427
Parker, Quanah, 106
Passamaquoddy, 65
Patwin, 277
Pawnee, 128–131, **129**, **130**
Arikara, 91–93
Peace medal, 30, 45, 86, 99, **114**, 116, 128, 168, 204
Pearls, 7, 9, 10, 19, 21, 24, 27, 30, 35
Pecunnie, 96
Pelican pouch, 355
Pelican-skin coat, 266
Pendants
Californian, 282
Eskimo, 397, 422
Northeastern, 46, 68
Plains, 93, 133
Plateau, 220
Puebloans, 179
Southwestern, 151
Subarctic, 350
See also Necklaces
Pennacook, 45
Penobscot, 45, 65–67
Pentlatch, 307
Peoria, 60
Petalesharo, 130
Petun, 54
Peyote religion, 106
Peyote stitch, 119
Piankeshaw, 60
Picuris pueblo, 182
Piegan, 96
Pigwacket, 65
Pima, 148, 174–176
Pioneer dresses, 192
Pipestone, 151
Pit River Indians, 274
Pitseolak, Peter, 393
Plains Cree, 131–133, 355
Plains Indians, 83–88
Algonquian speakers, 88–91, 96–103, 131–133
Caddoan speakers, 91–93, 128–131
Great Basin styles and, 189, 193
Kiowa, 116–119
Plateau culture and, 210
Puebloan styles and, 182, 183
Shoshonean speakers, 104–106
Siouan speakers, 93–96, 107–116, 119–128, 133–140
Texas, 141–142
See also specific tribes and groups (list on page 83)
Plateau Indians, 209–213
Chinook speakers, 231–239
Columbia River, 216–218

Kutenai, 223–225
Salishan speakers, 216, 218–223, 230–231, 235–239
Shahaptian speakers, 213–218, 225–230, 235–239
See also specific tribes and groups (list on page 209)
Pocahontas, 26
Point, Nicholas, 210
Polar Eskimo, 421–422
Polar-bear mittens, 402, 405
Polar-bear pants, 394, 421, 422, 423
Polecat moccasin cover, 195
Pollywog snowshoes, 66
Pomeioc, 26
Pomo, 272–274, **273**
Ponca, 124, 126
Ponchos
Apache, 157
cattail, 338
Mission Indians, 264
Navajo, 268
Northeastern, 42, 47, 59
Northwest Coast, 338
Plains, 92, 112, 116, 127
Plateau, 230
Pueblo, 162
Southeastern, 12, 15
Southwestern, 148
Pony beads, 87, 217
Porcupine quillwork. *See* Quillwork
Potawatomi, 47, 64, 67–70
ribbon applique, **69**
shirt, **67**
Potlatch, 299, 304, 309, 311, 313, 336, 339, 351, 359, 362
Potlatch rings, **311**, 315, 319, 330, **330**, 331, 336, 419
Potomac, 22
Pouches. *See* Bags and pouches
Powell, John Wesley, 198
Powhatan, 22–26, **22**, **23**
Powhatan's Mantle, 23, **25**
Prairie Potawatomi, 67
Prostitutes, 20
Puberty customs
Apache, 155, 156, 157–158, 168–169
Californian, 255, 260, 263, 275, 278, 279, 281, 283, 285
Eskimo, 397, 408, 413, 420
Northwest Coast, 312, 319, 322, 333, 339
Puebloan, 166–167
Southwestern, 176
Subarctic, 348, 359, 368, 371, 374, 378
Puberty Dance, 255
Puccoon root, 33
Pueblo peoples, 147, 148, 177–181, **180**
Acoma, 151–153
hairstyles, **160**, **161**
Hopi, 158–162
Jemez, 162–164
Navajo and, 169, 170
Taos, 182–184
Zia, **150**
Zuni, 153
Puffin-skin tunic, 416
Puget Sound Indians, 294, 324–326
Puma-skin cap, 160
Puyallup, 324

Quapaw, 124, 126, 127
Quartz, 262
Quebec Inuit, 422–424
Quechan, 283–285
Queet, 326, 338
Quileute, 326, 338, 339
Quiller's Societies, 101, 103
Quillwork
buffalo robes, 101
Californian, 258, 275, 277, 278
Cherokee, 12, 13
Delaware pouch, **50**
Eskimo, 386
Great Basin, 197
looms for, 355, 357, 371
Northeastern, 46, 48, 53, 56, 59, 60, 61, 63, 65, 66, 68, 74, 77
Northwest Coast, 297, 300, 323
Plains, 87, 91, 103, 107, 110, 112, 113, 126, 130–133
Plateau, 213, 214, 216, 218, 220, 224
Southeastern, 19, 22
Southwestern (Navajo), 174
Subarctic, 348, 349, 355, 357, 359, 362, 366, 368, 371, 376, 378
Quinault, 326–328, 338

Rabbit-fur glove, 275
Rabbit-skin robes
Californian, 244, 247, 248, 252, 259, 262, 265, 268, 272, 277, 278, 279, 280, 282, 284, 285
Great Basin, 190, 192, 195, 198, 203
loom for, 285
netting technique, 356, 370, 371, 378
Northeastern, 44, 56, 59, 62, 64, 68
Northwest Coast, 305, 324–325, 327, 338
Plains, 105, 125, 132
Plateau, 210, 219, 221, 224, 228, 230, 236
Southeastern, 27
Southwestern, 150, 152, 159, 163, 170–171, 175, 178, 183
Subarctic, 348, 351, 352, 354, 356, 359, 360, 368, 370, 371, 377, 378
Rabbit-skin shirt, 346
Rabbit-skin socks, 192
Raccoon breechclout, 72
Raccoon robes, 97
Rainmaking dances, 176
Rancheria peoples, 148, 174–176, 283
Rappahannock, 22
Rattlesnake Dance, 281
Raven skin, 386, 417
Real Dogs, 119
Redwood bark, 272
Reed breastplates, 273
Reindeer-hair embroidery, 392
Reiss, Winold, 96, 99
Republican band (Pawnee), 128
Respirators, 397
Reynolds, Joshua, 14

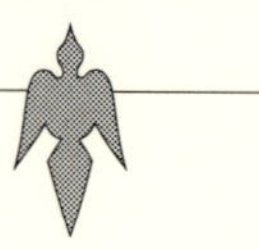

Ribbonwork
  Northeastern, 45, 53, 60, 61, 70, **72**, 74, 75, 76
  Plains, 113, 116, 126, 127, 133, 140
  Potawatomi, **69**, 70
  Subarctic, 366
Rindisbacher, Peter, 76, 94, 377
Rinehart, Frank A., 84
Rings
  Northwest Coast, 302
  Plains, 103
  Southeastern, 9, 36
  Southwestern, 153
River Crow, 107
River People (Plains Cree), 131
Roach
  artificial, 44, 52, 59, 68, 73
  Northeastern, 44, 52, 54, 56, 59, 61, 64, 68, 73, **73**, 77
  Plains, 85, 92, 102, 112, 115, 125, 127, 130
  Plateau, **232**
  Powhatan, **22**
  Southeastern, 7, 9, 12–14, 15, 17, 19, 24, 27, 30, 32, 36
Roach spreader, 7, 44, 52, **73**, 77, 92, 103, 125, 130
Roanoke, 26
Robes and capes
  antelope, 92
  bark capes or blankets, 6, 19, 36, 190, 195, 212, 262, 272, 275, 295, 302, 306, 307, 310, 313, 317, 318, 322, 325, 330, 331, 335, 338
  bearskin, 15, 44, 49, 54, 56, 68, 73, 75, 77, 131, 203, 279, 295, 313, 318, 324, 330, 352, 358, 367,
  beaver, 44, 46, 49, 54, 56, 59, 62, 64, 68, 73, 112, 132, 351, 367, 372
  bird's head, 23, 27, 33
  birdskin, 190, 244, 266, 280, 281, 286
  blanket (aboriginal production), 150, 166, 171, 175, 183
  blanket coats *(capotes),* 87, 96, 97, 132, 219, 228, 348, 353, 364, 377
  buffalo. *See* buffalo robes and blankets
  Californian, 244, 257, 262, 268, 282, 286
  Californian (Athapaskan speakers), 247, 254
  Californian (Hokan speakers), 272, 275, 279, 284
  Californian (Penutian speakers), 259, 265, 277, 280
  caribou, 311
  chief's coat, 85
  children's, 217
  Czechoslovakian shawls, 159, 178, 183
  "dog" hair (or coyote), 306, 308, 325, 327, 328, 338
  duck scalp, 257
  elk-skin, 73, 88, 109, 195, 203, 215
  ermine, 195
  fox-skin, 236, 277
  front-tied, 88, 126
  Great Basin, 190, 192, 195, **196**, 198, 203
  marmot, 313, 330
  matchcoats, 6, 9, 12, 23, 27, 33, 49
  moosehide, 46, 66
  mountain–goat hair, 306, 308, 310, 325, 335, 338
  mouse-skin, 190
  Navajo, 171
  Northeastern, 44, 46, 47, 49, 52, 53, 54, 56, 59, 61, 62, 64, 66, 68, 73, 75, 77
  Northwest Coast, 295–297, 302, 305–306, 307–308, 310–311, 313–314, 317–318, 322, 324–325, 327, 328, 330, 338, 340
  otter, 217, 252, 322, 327
  palmetto, 28
  panther, 11, 13
  Plains, 85, 88, 92, 94, 97, 101, 105, 109, 112, 115, 118, **120**, 122, 125, 127, 130, 132, 137, **137**
  Plateau, 210, 212, 224, 233
  Plateau (Salishan-speaking), 217, 219, 221, 224, 236
  Plateau (Shahaptian-speaking), 215, 217, 228, 231, 236
  Powhatan's Mantle, 23, **25**
  quilling, 101
  raccoon-skin, 97
  sea otter, 249, 252, 262, 295, 302, 305, 310, 313, 318, 324, 327, 330, 335, 338
  seal gut, 318
  sealskin, 295, 330
  serape, 154, 171, 175
  Southeastern, 6–7, 9, 11, 12, 15, 17, 19, 21, 23, 27, 28, 33, 34, 36
  Southwestern, 150, 171, 175
  Southwestern (Apache), 154, 157, 166, 168
  Southwestern (Puebloan), 152, 159, 163, 178, 183
  squirrel, 53, 54, 59, 62, 64, 68, 217, 233
  status designation, 137
  Subarctic, **345**, 347–348
  Subarctic (Algonquian speakers), 350, 356, 367–368, 377
  Subarctic (Athapaskan speakers), 351, 354, 360, 370, 372, 375
  weasel-skin, 322
  whale-skin, 375
  wildcat, 327
  wolf, 73, 123, 233
  See also Blankets, aboriginal; Blankets, non-native; Coats; Feather capes and robes; Rabbit-skin robes
Rocky Cree, 376
Rod-and-slat armor, 48, 255, 258, 299, 306, 311, 319, 328, 331, 348, 420
Rogue River Indians, 321
Romans, Bernard, 15
Ross, John, 414
Roundhead Cree, 355
Russell, John, 410
Russian influences, 386, 388, 389

Saclan Miwok, **267**
Sacred Bear Cult, 113
Sacred Medicine Pipe, 97
Sage ornamentation, 140
Sagebrush garments, 190–193, 195, 198, 202, 221, 223, 257
St. Lawrence Island Eskimo, 390–393
Salish
  Coastal, 220, 294, 300, 307–310
  Interior, 220–223, **221**, **222**, 224
  Puget Sound Indians, 324–326
Salish blankets, 297, 307–308, 309, 316, 325, 328
Salmon skin
  bags of, 352, 419
  boots and moccasins of, 351, 358, 375
  garments of, 351, 358, 375, 416

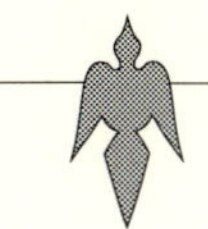

Samish, 324
San Carlos Apache, 153
San Felipe Pueblo, **179**
San Nicoleño, 261
Sandals
  Apache, 168
  bark, 249
  Basketmaker, **178**
  Californian, 244, 249, 262, 264, 268, 277, 280
  Great Basin, 190, 192, 198, 202
  Joshua tree, 198
  Plateau, 221
  Pueblo, 159, 178
  Southwestern, 149, 151, 170, 175
Sanpoil, 216, 230–231
Sans Arcs, 135
Santa Fe blankets, 103
Santee Sioux, 111–113, 133, 135
Santiam, 321
Saponi, 33
Sarci, 96
Sashes
  Assomption sash, 63, 348, **354,** 363, 364, 377
  Northeastern, 44, 48, 50, 52, 53, 55, 56, 59, 63, 65, 74, 75
  Plains, 110, 119, 130
  Puebloan, 179, 181
  rain sash, 11
  Seminole, **29**
  Southeastern, 6, 15, 17, 18, 19, 22, 29, 36
  Southwestern, 149, 152, 161, 179, 181
Satsop, 338
Sauk, 47, 51–53, 70–74
  chief, **71**
Scalp cape, 217
Scalp Dance, 197
Scarification, 142
Scatter beading, 228
Scouts (Pawnee), 131
Sea-lion teeth, 255, **256,** 288
Sea-lion whiskers, **298,** 304, 312, 315, 331, 336, 352
Sea-otter skin
  belt of, 325
  parkas of, 419
  robes of, 249, 262, 272, 282, 295, 302, 305, 310, 313, 318, 324, 327, 330, 335, 338
Seal decoy helmet, 419
Seal-intestine garments, 318, 385, 386–389, **391,** 393, 394, 396, 405, 411, 416, 419, 423, 427
Sealskin
  armor of, 392, **392**
  boots of, 384–385, 390, 394–396, 399, 402, 405, 407, 409, 411, 413, 414, 416, 419, 421, 423, 425, 427
  gauntlets of, 429
  mittens of, 405–406, 407, 411, 417, 422
  moccasins of, 335
  pants of, 384, 387, 396, 405
  robes of, 295, 330
Seaweed Dance, 250
Sechelt, 307
Secotan, 26–28
Secret societies. *See* Societies
Sekani, 372
Semiahmoo, 324
Seminole, 6, 28–32, **29, 31**
Semi-precious stones, 262
Seneca, 55
Serranos, 261, 262
Sewing machines, 170
Seymour, Samuel, 128
Shamans and medicine men
  Californian, 251, 259, 287
  Eskimo, 386, 392, 395, 400, 408, 411, 415, 417, 420
  Navajo, 174
  Northwest Coast, 300, 312, 315, 319, 322, 330, 333, 336
  Plains, 87, 98, 124, 131
  Southeastern, 7, 16, 24, 27
  Subarctic, 352, 376
  See also Ceremonial costumes
Sharphead hats, 309
Shasta, 274–276
Shawnawdithit, 349
Sheaths
  Northeastern, 50, 59, 61
  Northwest Coast, 331
  Plains, 86, **102,** 113, 123, 133, 139
  Subarctic, 348, 360, 370, **373,** 374, 376
Shells. *See* Abalone ornamentation; Clamshell ornamentation; Dentalium shell ornamentation; Gorgets; Wampum
Sheshalik Fair, 409
Shields
  Aleut, 388
  Apache, 155, 157, 168
  Californian, 248, 270
  copper, 299
  Eskimo, 392
  Great Basin, 191, 196–197, 204
  Northeastern, 48, 55, 57, 61, 65
  Northwest Coast, 299, 304, 306, 339
  Plains, 86, 93, 95, 98, 103, 106, 110, 113, 119, 123, 131, 139
  Plateau, 220, 222, 229
  Southeastern, 19, 27
  Southwestern, 176
  Southwestern (Pueblo), 160, 163, 166, 181
  Subarctic, 352, 355, 368, 371
Shin guards, 392
Shirts and tunics
  Aleut, 387
  Apache, 154, **164,** 167
  beaver-skin, 356
  birdskin, 416, 418
  Californian, 264, **270**
  deer-leg style, 124, 128
  Eskimo, 384, 390, 416, 418
  Great Basin, 200
  moose-skin, 356
  Northeastern, 52, 59, 61, 62, 76, 78
  Northwest Coast, **299,** 307, 333
  Plains, 84, 88, 92, 94, 96, 100, 104, 107, **107, 110,** 112, 113, 114, 116, **117,** 120, 124, 126, 128, 131, 132, **134,** 135
  Plateau, **211,** 219, 221, 224, **224,** 226, 229, 233

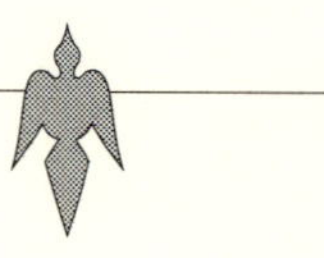

Potawatomi, **67**
Pueblo, 162–163, 177
rabbit-skin, 346
sealskin, 384, 387
Seminole, 30
Southwestern, 148, 155, 170
subarctic, 346, 353, 358, 359–360, **361**, 367, 369, **370**, **371**, 372, **373**, 375, 377
Shoshone, 191, 193–197, **194**, **196**, 218, 233
Northern (Comanche), 104–106
Western, 116
Shuswap, 220, 221
Siberian Eskimo, 390–393
side-fold dress
Plains, 84, 96, 100, 120, 132, 135, **137**
Plateau, 210, 219, 235
Siksika, 96
Siletz, 321
Silk embroidery, 13
Silver
conchas, 118, 125
Great Basin, 196, 197, 203
headbands, 61
Navajo, 173
Northeastern, 45, 48, 60, 61, 65, 70, 74, 75, 76, 78
Northwest Coast, 301, 302, 312, 314
Plains, 86, 99, 103, 106, 118, 125, 128, 139
Southeastern, 30, 32, 34, 36
Southwestern, 153, 173
Southwestern (Pueblo), 160, 166, 179, 183
Simcoe, Mrs. J., 60
Sinkyone, 247
Siouan, 33–34
Sioux, 131, **134**, **136**, **138**, **139**, 196, 226
Assiniboine, 93
Chippewa and, 47
Dakota (Santee), 111–113, 133, 135
Teton (Lakota), 15, 111, 133–140
Yanktonai, 93, 133
Sisaok, 304
Sisseton, 111
Siuslaw, 321, 323
Six Nations, 55
Skagit, 324
Skidi Pawnee, 128
Skilloot, 305
Skirts and dresses
Algonkin split skirt, 84
antelope, 92
Apache ceremonial, **165**
Apache camp dress, 154, 157, 175, 176, 184
Arapaho, **89**
bark-fiber, 190, 191–192, 193, 198, 202, 272, 286
birdskin, 191
bison-hair, 16
breechclouts, 27
bustle, 284
Californian, 244, 249, **250**, 253, 257, 261, 264, 268, **270**, 282, 286, **287**
Californian (Athapaskan speakers), 247, 254
Californian (Hokan speakers), 272, 274–275, 279, 284
Californian (Penutian speakers), 251–252, 259, 265, 277, 280
children's (Crow), **108**
cotton pioneer, 165
cotton underdress, 152, 178
deer-tail dress, 96, 107, 120, 132, 135, 202, 214, 219, 228, 233, 235
duffel, 414
Eskimo *(kupsuck)*, 393, 398, 410, 414, 415, 417, 429
feathered, 253, 284
Great Basin, 190, 191–192, 193, 195, 198, **198**, 202
Indian-hemp, 49, 230
manta, **149**, 151–152, **152**, 158–159, 163, 177–178, **180**, 181, 182
moss, 23, 27, 28, 33, 34, 141
Mother Hubbard, 168
of mountain-goat skin, 94
Navajo, 170, **173**
nettle underskirts, 59, 62, 64, 72
Northeastern, 42, 46, 47, 49, 52, 54, 56, 59, 61, 62, 64, 66, 72, **72**, 74, 75, 76, 78
Northwest Coast, 295, 302, 305, 307, 310, 313, 317, 321, 324, 327, 329–330, 335, 338
pioneer dresses, 192
Plains, 84, 88, 92, 94, 96–97, 100, 104, 107–109, 112, 114, 116, 118, 120, 124, 126, 128, 132, 135–137, **136**
Plateau, 210, **212**, 224, 233
Plateau (Salishan-speaking), 216–217, 219, 221, 230, 235–236
Plateau (Shahaptian-speaking), 214, 216–217, 228, 235–236
rabbit, 198
Seminole, 31–32, **31**
side-fold dress, 84, 96, 100, 120, 132, 135, **137**, 210, 219, 235
Southeastern, 6, 8, 9, 12, 15, 16, 18–19, 21, 27, 28, 33, 34, 35, 149, **149**, 170, 175, 176
Southwestern (Apache), 154, 156–157, 165, *165*, 168
Southwestern (Puebloan), 151–152, **152**, 158–159, 163, 177–178, **180**, 181, 182, 184
strap-and-sleeve dress, 42, 47, 54, 59, 62, 64, 66, 76, 84, 92, 96, 100, 112, 132, 135
Subarctic, 347, 363–364
Subarctic (Algonquian speakers), 349–350, 356, 365, 367, 377
Subarctic (Athapaskan speakers), 351, 353–354, 358, 360, 369–370, 372, 375
three-skin dress, 84, 88, 96–97, 100, 104, 112, 116, 124, 126, 137, 154
two-skin dress, 84, 88, 92, 94, 96, 100, 107, 112, 120, 126, 132, 165, 192, 202
See also Sleeves; Transitional dress
Skull deformation
Californian, 258, 267, 275
Eskimo, 420
Flathead Indians, 218
Northwest Coast, 300, 304, 306, 309, 320, 323, 326, 328, 339
Plains, 127–128, 142
Plateau, 213, 216, 218, 235
Southeastern, 8, 9, 16, 18, 22, 33
Southwestern, 151, 162, 174
"sugar loaf," 300, 304, 316

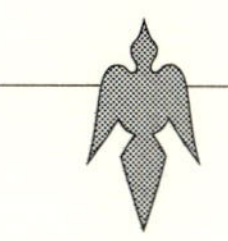

Skunk
ankle band of, 77
leggings of, 135
moccasin ornamentation of, 137
tail of, 105
Skykomish, 324, 325
Slate ornamentation, 46, 48, 55, 63, 65
argillite, 310, 311, 312, 331
Slavey (Slave Indians), 369–371
tunic, **370, 371**
Sleeves
beaver, 365
birdskin, 387
Eskimo, 387, 418
nonfunctional, 418
Northeastern, 42, 45, 47, 54, 62, 64
Northwestern, 365
Plains, 84, 112, 131, 135
Slippers
Arctic, 384, 387, 402, 409
cornhusk (Iroquois), 56
Smocks, 329
Smoking hat, 362
Snake Dance, 161
Snake Indians, 104, 116, 193
Snakeskin
belts of, 7, 50
headband of, 50
headdress of, 24, 50
mask of, 14
Snohomish, 324
Snoqualmie, 324
Snow beaters, 384
Snow goggles, 195, 377, 385, 388, 391, 395, 399, **401**, 402, 406, 407, 409, 411, 413, 415, 417, 422, 423, 427
Snow visors, 413
Snowshoes
Apache, 166
babiche, 347, 351, 354, 360, 367, 370, 375, 377
bear-paw, 47, 62, 64, 76, 347, 351, 356, 367, 372
beavertail, 347, 356, 367
Californian, 244, 257, 259, 275, 277, 284, 286
catfish, 59, 76
elbow, 367
Eskimo, 390, 409, 411, 416
Great Basin, 190, 195, 202
Northeastern, 44, 47, 49, 54, 59, 62, 64, 66, 72, 76
Northwest Coast, 295, 302, 307, 317, 321, 324, 330, 335
Plains, 88, 92, 101, 112, 114, 132, 137
Plateau, 217, 221, 228, 230, 233, 236
pollywog, 66
spiked, 330
Subarctic, 347
Subarctic (Algonquian speakers), 350, 356, 365, 367, 377
Subarctic (Athapaskan speakers), 347, 351, 352, 354, 360, 370, 372, 375
swallowtail, 347, 356, 367, 411
Soapstone. *See* Steatite
Societies
Great Basin, 204
Northeastern, 48, 52, 63, 77
Northwest Coast, 325, 328, 336, 339
Plains, 93, 95, 97, 98, 101, 103, 110, 113, 115, 119, 123, 125–126, 138, 140
Socks. *See* Stockings
Sohon, Gustavus, 213, 215, 218, 226
Sokoki, 45
Soldier society, 95
Songish, 338
Southeastern Indians, 5–8
Algonquian speakers, 22–28
Caddoan, 9–10
Cherokee, 11–15
Muskhogean speakers, 8–9, 10–11, 15–22, 34–35
Seminole, 28–32
Siouan speakers, 33–34
Yuchi, 35–37
See also specific tribes and groups (list on page 5)
Southeastern Ojibwa, 62–63
Southern Maidu, 259
Southern Molala, 321
Southern Paiute, 197–200
Southwest Salish, 307
Southwestern Indians, 147–151
Apache, 153–158, 164–169
Athapaskan speakers, 153–158, 164–174
Pima, 174–176
Puebloan, 151–153, 158–164, 177–184
rancheria peoples, 175–176
Shoshonean speakers, 158–162
See also specific tribes and groups (list on page 147)
Southwestern Alaskan Eskimo, 424–429, **425**
Spanish moss. *See* Moss garments
Spindles, 308, 326
Spinning, 308, 326
Spokane, **212,** 216
Squash-blossom necklace, 173, 179
Squaxin, 324
Squirrel-fur parka, 427
Squirrel-skin robes, 53, 54, 59, 62, 64, 68
Stanley, John Mix, 14, 84
Steatite, 246, 250, 260, 262, 413
Steward, Julian H., 198
Stillaguamish, 324
Stockings
Aleut, 387
Eskimo, 385, 399, 405, 407, 413, 421, 427
Great Basin, 192, 198
Plateau, 221
Pueblo, 177
Southwestern, 149
Subarctic, 347, 350, 358, 365, 377
Stoney Indians, 94
Strap-and-sleeve dress
Northeastern, 42, 47, 54, 59, 62, 64, 66, 76
Plains, 84, 92, 96, 100, 112, 132, 135
Plateau, 210, 217, 219, 235
Strongwood Cree, 376
Stroud cloth, 8, 45, 58, 87, 101, 110–111, 119, 124, 140
Subarctic Indians, 107, 345–349
Algonquian speakers, 345, 349–350, 355–357, 364–369, 376–378

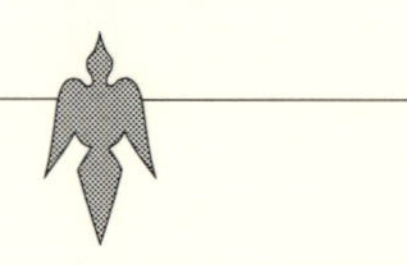

Athapaskan speakers, 345, 351–355, 357–363, 369–376
Métis ("halfbreed"), 363–364
See also specific tribes and groups (list on page 345)
Sugar-loaf skull deformation, 300, 304, 316
Sumptuary laws, 21, 295
Sun Dance, 86, 90–91, 95, 98, 103, 140, 197
Sun visors, 90, 92, 97, 102, 109, 132, 159, 212
Sunburst design, 92, 115, 137
Suquamish, 324
Suria, Tomas de, 251, 317, 329
Swallowtail-style snowshoes, 347, 356, 367, 411
Swamp moccasins, 6, 9, 10, 12, 23, 33, 35
Swampy Cree, 131
Swinomish, 324
Swordfish Dance, 250
Sxwayxwey dancers, 309

Tablita, 152, 180
Tagiugmiut, 415–417
Tahltan, 372–374, **373**
Takelma, 321
Takulli, 351
Tall Ones Society, 140
Tanaina, 374–376
Taos, 182–184
boots, **183**
Tappage Pawnee, 128
Tatooche, 319
Tattooing
Aleut, 389
Californian, 246, 248, 253, 255, 256, 258, 260, 263, 267, **267, 269,** 271, 273–274, 275, 278, 279, 281, **281,** 283, **284,** 285, 289
Eskimo, 386, 392, 397, 400, 404, 406, 408, 410, 412, 413, 417, 420, 424, 429
Great Basin, 192, 197, 200, 204
of homosexuals, 420
iron-searing method of, 26
measuring marks, 253, 323
Northeastern, 51, 57, 61, 63, 65, 76
Northwest Coast, 300, 306, 309, 312, 320, 323, 326, 328, 339, 333, 336
Plains, 95, 106, 110, 116, 119, 124, 126, 127, 131, 133, 140, 142
Plateau, 218, 223, 225
Southeastern, 8, 9, 10, 13–15, **14,** 16, 20, 21, 22, 26, 27–28, 30, 34, 35
Southwestern, 176
Subarctic, 349, 352, 355, 357, 359, 362, 366, 368–369, 371, 374, 376, 378
Tchiglet, 412–414
Teit, James, 220
Tekesta, 11
Teninos, 216
Tête de Boule Cree, 355
Teton (Lakota) Sioux, 111, **136, 138, 139**
Texas, 6, 141–142
Thanksgiving Dance, 283
Thimbles, 384
Thompson Indians, 220, 222, 223
Three Fires confederation, 64, 67
Three-skin dress
Great Basin, 195, 202
Plains, 84, 88, 96–97, 100, 104, 105, 112, 116, 124, 126, 137
Plateau, 219, 220
Thunder Society, 125
Tikhanov, Mikhail, 384, 418
Tilenan, Wilhelm von, 251
Tillamook, 321
Tilma, 170
Timucua, 34–35
Tinklers
Californian, **255**
Great Basin, 197
Northeastern, 48, 63
Northwest Coast, 319
Plains, 88, 103, 106, 111, 113, 116, 140
Plateau, 220
Subarctic, 352
Tippet, 217
Tlingit, 294, 295, **296, 298, 299,** 315, 329–334, 359, 372, 374, 386, 418, 420
clan hat, **330**
Tobacco Indians, 54
Tohono, 174
Tolowa, 247, **255**
Tomahawks, 57
Tonkawa, 141
Tonsure, 19, 21, 385, 390, 396, 409, 413
Tonto Apache, 153
Tooth blackening, 22
Tooth filing, 333
Topaz, 262
Tortoise, 11, 55, 118
Transitional dress
Aleut, 389
Californian, 248, 251, 253, 256–257, 258, 260, 264, 267, 271, 275, 278, 279, 281, 283, 285, 289
Eskimo, 386, 392, 395, 400, 404, 406, 408, 410, 412–415, 417, 424, 429
Great Basin, 192, 197, 200, **203,** 204
Northeastern, 45, 46, 48, 51, 53, 55, 58, 60, 61, 63, 65, 70, 74, 77–78
Northwest Coast, 301, 304, 306–307, 309, 316, 320, 323, 326, 328, 334, 338
Plains, 87–88, 91, 93, 95–96, 103, 106, 110–111, 116, 119, 124, 126, 133, 142
Plateau, 213, 216, 218, 220, 223, 225, 230, 231, 235, 238
Puebloan, 181, 184
Southeastern, 8, 9, 10, 13–15, 16, 18, 20, 26, 28, 30–32, 34–36
Subarctic, 349, 353, 355, 357, 359, 362, 369, 371, 376, 378
Transformation masks
Eskimo, 397–398, 429
Northwest Coast, 301, 312, **314,** 315, **315,** 316, 320
Trousers. *See* Pants
True loom, 148, 264
Trumbull, 18
Tsimshian, 294, 299, 315, 329, 331–332, 334–338, 352
ceremonial costumes, **335**
mask, **337**

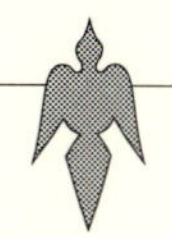

Tualatin, 321
Tulareños, 280
Tule garments, 191, 218, 257, 272, 275, 279, 288
Tumpline, 44, 56, 152, 159, 192
Tunghak, 397–398
Tunics. *See* Shirts and tunics
Turbans
  Californian, 284–285
  child's, **70**
  Northeastern, 61, **71**
  Plains, 115
  Southeastern, 30, 31–32, **31**
  transitional styles, 36, 126
  See also Otter-fur turbans
Turquoise ornamentation
  Californian, 270
  drilling, **179**
  Great Basin, 191
  Southwestern, 151, 160, 163, 173, 176, 179
Turtle, 11, 55, 118
Tuscarora, 33, 55
Tutelo, 33
Tututni, 321
Twana, 324
Two Kettles, 135
Two-skin dress
  Californian, 244, 254
  Great Basin, 192, 202
  Plains, 84, 88, 92, 94, 96, 100, 107, 112, 120, 126, 132
  Plateau, 210, 214, 217, 219, 228, 233, 235

Ucheans, 35–37
Uintah, 200
Umatilla, 213, 216
Umbilical-cord amulet, 93, 95, 102–103, 109, 118, 139, 322, 348
Umpqua, 321
Unalaska Aleut, 388
Uncompahgre, 200
Undergarments
  chastity belts, 101, 137
  Eskimo, 384, 390, 404, 405, 421
  Plains, 101, 137
  Pueblo, 178
  Southwestern, 152, 178
United Southeastern Tribes (USET), 6
Upper Kutenai, 223–225
Upper Nez Perce, 226
USET, 6
Ute, 104, 167, 182, 183, 190, 191, 198, 200–204, **201, 203**

Velarde, Pablita, **180**
Velveteen garments, 170, 177
Verelst, 18
Vests, 154, 363
Visors, 212, 258, 275, 327, 385, 389, 413
Voznesenski, 384
Vroman, A. C., 158, 175, 177

Wabin, Joseph, 60, 75
Wahkiakum, 338
Wahpekute, 111
Wahpeton, 111
Waiakida, 115
Wailaki, 247, 248, 283
Walapai, 268
Walker River Northern Paiute, 192
Walla Walla, 213, 216
Walrus
  armor of, 397
  ivory from, 385, 386
  tusk motif of, **394,** 397, 400, 402, **403,** 404, 405, 409, 410, 412, 413, 416
  whiskers from, 336
Wampum
  Northeastern, 44, 50, 56
  Plains, 115
  Southeastern, 19, 24, 26
  Subarctic, 348
Wampum belts, 56
Wanapums, 216
Wappo, 282
War cap, 168, 173
War clubs, 57
War Dance, **252,** 283
War shirts
  Apache, 157
  Plains, 100, 113, 120, 124, 126, 135
  Plateau, **222**
  Southwestern, 167
Warbonnets
  Apache, 154, 166
  Great Basin, 195, 203
  Plains, 85, 92, 97, 102, 109, 123, 125, 138
  Plateau, 102, **121,** 212, **214,** 215, 222, **222,** 228, 236
  women's use of, 197
Warm Springs Indians, 216
Wasco, 209, 216, 217, 231–235, **232,** 238, 305
Washington Coast Indians, 294, 305, 338–340
  Quinault, 326–328, 338
Washo, 191
Waterman, T., 278
Wayan, 77
Wea, 60
Weasel
  robes, 322
  headdress, 24
  tail-hair ornaments, 225
Webber, John, 317, 320, 384, 418
Wedding attire, 161, 233, 238, 420
Wenatchi, 216
Wengler, Johann Baptist, 47, 76
West, Benjamin, 49
Western Abenaki, 45–46
Western Apache, 153
Western Cree, 355, 376–378
Western Shoshone, 195
Whalebone armor, 328, 339
Whaler's hat, 306, 318, **319,** 320, 327
Whale-fin ornamentation, 50
Whale-skin robes, 375
Whilkut, 247

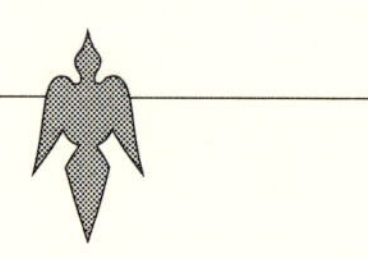

White, John, 16, 26, 384, **393, 394**
White buffalo, 101
White Buffalo Cow Society, **120,** 123
White Deerskin Dance, 255, **256**
White Mountain Apache, 153
White paint and pigments, 251, 253, 260, 306, 316
White River Ute, 200
Wicasas, 135
Wigs, 352, **352**
Wildcat caps, 160
Wildcat robes, 19, 327
Wildschut, William, 107
Willow bark, 175
Wind mask, 395
Winnebago, 76–78, 114
Winnepesaukee, 45
Winooski, 45
Winter, George, 60, 67
Winter Dances, 299, 300
Wintun, 272, 276–278
Wintu, 276
Wishram, 209, 231–235, **234,** 238, 305
Wittick, Ben, 158, 167, 175, 177, 268
Wolf skin
- cap of, 228
- cloak of, 352
- collar of, 125
- fur headband of, 255, 288
- leggings of, 132
- masks of, 309, 340
- neckpiece of, 204
- robe of, 73, 123

Wolf Clan, **330**
Wolf Dance, 197
Wolf ritual, 319
Wolf-tail moccasin, 94
Wolverine fur bags, 413
Wolverine ruff, 385, 394, 409, 416, 417, 427, 429
Women's dress. See Skirts and dresses
Woodchuck-skin bags, 66
Woodland Cree, 131
Woodpecker scalps, 247, 248, 253–255, 260, 266, 274, 276, 277, 279, 287, 288, 289, 323
Wristguards, 27, 166, 173, 174, 179, 391, 397
Wyandot, 53
Wynooche, 338

Yahi, 278–279
Yakima, 213, 216, 231, 235–239, **236, 237**
Yamel, 321
Yana, 278–279
Yanktonai Sioux, 93, 133
Yaquina, 321
Yeibichai, 174
Yellowknife, **347,** 353
Yokut, 280–281, **281**
Yoncalla, 321
Yucca-fiber garments, 149, 150, 159, 166
Yuchi, 35–37
Yuki, 282–283
Yuma, 148, 198, 267, 283–285, **284**
Yupik, 357, 398
Yurok, 286–289, **287, 288**

Zia, **150**
Zuni, 153, 160, 177